Japan
a country study

Federal Research Division
Library of Congress
Edited by
Ronald E. Dolan and
Robert L. Worden
Research Completed
September 1990

On the cover: The sun rises over the islands of Japan.

Fifth Edition, First Printing, 1992.

Library of Congress Cataloging-in-Publication Data

Japan : a country study / Federal Research Division, Library of
   Congress ; edited by Ronald E. Dolan and Robert L. Worden.
        p.   cm. — (Area handbook series, ISSN 1057-5294) (DA
pam ; 550-30)
      "Supersedes the 1983 ed."—Pref.
      Includes bibliographical references (pp. 511-571) and index.
      ISBN 0-8444-0731-3
      1. Japan.   I. Dolan, Ronald E., 1939-   . II. Worden,
   Robert L., 1945-   . III. Series. IV. Series: DA pam ; 550-30.
   DS806.J223   1991   91-29874
   952—dc20   CIP

Headquarters, Department of the Army
DA Pam 550-30

For sale by the Superintendent of Documents, U.S. Government Printing Office
Washington, D.C. 20402

Foreword

This volume is one in a continuing series of books prepared by the Federal Research Division of the Library of Congress under the Country Studies—Area Handbook Program sponsored by the Department of the Army. The last page of this book lists the other published studies.

Most books in the series deal with a particular foreign country, describing and analyzing its political, economic, social, and national security systems and institutions, and examining the interrelationships of those systems and the ways they are shaped by cultural factors. Each study is written by a multidisciplinary team of social scientists. The authors seek to provide a basic understanding of the observed society, striving for a dynamic rather than a static portrayal. Particular attention is devoted to the people who make up the society, their origins, dominant beliefs and values, their common interests and the issues on which they are divided, the nature and extent of their involvement with national institutions, and their attitudes toward each other and toward their social system and political order.

The books represent the analysis of the authors and should not be construed as an expression of an official United States government position, policy, or decision. The authors have sought to adhere to accepted standards of scholarly objectivity. Corrections, additions, and suggestions for changes from readers will be welcomed for use in future editions.

Louis R. Mortimer
Chief
Federal Research Division
Library of Congress
Washington, D.C. 20540

Acknowledgments

The authors wish to acknowledge their use and adaptation of information from various chapters in the 1983 edition of *Japan: A Country Study*, edited by Frederica M. Bunge. The authors are also indebted to a number of individuals and organizations who gave their time and special knowledge of Japanese affairs to provide research data and perspective. Among those who gave generous and timely help were Warren M. Tsuneishi, Chief of the Asian Division, Library of Congress, who commented on the completed manuscript. Also instrumental in providing timely and useful data were Shojo Honda and other staff members of the Japanese Section of the Asian Division.

Others who provided insight and research materials to the authors were Haruyuki Furukawa of the Japanese National Diet staff and Col. Isao Mukunoki of the Japanese Embassy in Washington. Yoriyoshi Naito of the *Asahi Shimbun* and Rikuo Sato of the Mainichi Newspapers, both in Washington, were extremely helpful in providing photographs for use in the book.

Various members of the staff of the Federal Research Division of the Library of Congress assisted in the preparation of the book. Timothy Merrill reviewed the maps and geographical references in the book. David P. Cabitto prepared the artwork for the cover illustration and coordinated the production of all maps and figures. Alberta J. King provided research and word processing assistance for sections of the book and contributed to the final proofreading. Janie L. Gilchrist provided word processing assistance on parts of the book, and Barbara Edgerton and Izella Watson performed final word processing for the completed manuscript. Sandra W. Meditz made helpful suggestions during her review of all parts of the book and coordinated work with Ralph K. Benesch, who oversees the Country Studies—Area Handbook program for the Department of the Army. Marilyn L. Majeska managed editing and production of the book, with assistance from Andrea T. Merrill and Martha E. Hopkins.

Other Library of Congress staff who assisted with the preparation of the book were Ewen Allison and Carol Winfree, both of the Congressional Research Service, who provided research assistance and word processing support, respectively, for the chapter on foreign relations. Malinda B. Neale of the Library of Congress Composing Unit prepared camera-ready copy, under the direction of Peggy F. Pixley.

The authors also want to thank other individuals who contributed to the preparation of the manuscript: Marcie D. Rinka of John Carroll University for word processing support for the chapter on society and environment; Greenhorne and O'Mara for preparation of the map drafts; Reiko I. Seekins and Marti Ittner, who designed the illustrations on the title pages of chapters one and chapters two through eight, respectively; and Wayne Horne for his graphics support. Additionally, special thanks go to Ann H. Covalt, who edited the manuscript; Catherine Schwartzstein, who performed the final prepublication editorial review; and Joan C. Cook, who prepared the index.

Finally, the authors are especially grateful to those individuals and organizations who donated photographs and artwork for the illustrations used in the book, many of which are original work not previously published. They are acknowledged in the illustration captions.

Contents

Chapter 5. International Economic Relations 253
Edward J. Lincoln

Chapter 6. The Political System 303

Appendix. Tables

Bibliography

Glossary

Index

List of Figures

Preface

This edition supersedes the fourth edition of *Japan: A Country Study,* published in 1983. It provides updated information on one of the most economically powerful nations in the world in a period of significant economic change. Although much of what was reported in 1983 has remained the same in regard to traditional behavior and organizational dynamics, world events have continued to shape Japanese domestic and international policies. Improved relations with virtually all countries of the Asia-Pacific region, democracy movements in Eastern Europe, the general improvement in East-West relations, volatile changes in the Middle East, economic uncertainty throughout the world, competition for international markets, high-technology developments, and the whole panoply of Japanese relations with its major business and security partner, the United States, have all affected Japan as it moves toward a new century.

The aim of the authors of the new edition of *Japan: A Country Study* has been to analyze Japanese society with respect to its ancient traditions and postwar transformation. Both its long historical and societal evolution and its emergence in the second half of the twentieth century as a major actor on the international political and economic scene are considered in depth.

The Hepburn system of romanization is used for Japanese personal names, which generally appear in standard order, with the family name first. In cases of certain well-known historical figures, such as Tokugawa Ieyasu (Ieyasu), or members of famous families, such as the Fujiwara, the individual is referred to by given name. The spelling of place names follows usage of the United States Board on Geographic Names. The pinyin system of romanization is used for most Chinese names and terms. Measurements are given in the metric system; a conversion table is provided to assist readers unfamiliar with metric measurements (see table 1, Appendix).

Users of this book are encouraged to consult the chapter bibliographies at the end of the book. Selected specialized bibliographies have been listed in the Bibliography for those wishing to do further reading and research. Additionally, users may wish to use other bibliographies, such as the Japan Foundation's *Catalogue of Books in English on Japan, 1945-81* (Tokyo, 1986) and *An Introductory Bibliography for Japanese Studies* (4 vols., Tokyo, 1975-82), which covers Japanese-language materials; the Association for Asian Studies' *Bibliography of Asian Studies* (Ann Arbor, annual) and Frank Joseph

Shulman's *Japan* (World Bibliography Series, 103; Santa Barbara, California: ABC–CLIO, 1989), both of which include entries in English, Japanese, and other languages; and the Kokusai Bunka Shinkokai's *K.B.S. Bibliography of Standard Reference Books for Japanese Studies* (Tokyo, semiannual editions), a comprehensive listing of Japanese-language materials. Other useful bibliographies of Japanese-language sources are John W. Hall's *Japanese History: A Guide to Japanese Reference and Research Materials* (1954) and Naomi Fukuda's *Japanese History: A Guide to Survey Histories* (1984-86), both of which were published by the Center for Japanese Studies at the University of Michigan.

Table A. Chronology of Major Historical Periods

Dates	Period *
ca. 10,000–300 B.C.	Jōmon
ca. 300-B.C.–A.D. 300	Yayoi
ca. A.D. 300–710	Kofun (also called Yamato)
A.D. 710–94	Nara
A.D. 794–1185	Heian
1185–1333	Kamakura
1333–36	Kemmu Restoration
1336–1573	Muromachi (also called Ashikaga)
1573–1600	Azuchi-Momoyama
1600–1867	Edo (also called Tokugawa)
1868–1912	Meiji (Mutsuhito)
1912–26	Taishō (Yoshihito)
1926–89	Shōwa (Hirohito)
1989–	Heisei (Akihito)

* The last four periods are identified by reign titles; the name of the emperor is given in parentheses. Reign titles are used only after the death of the emperor.

Country Profile

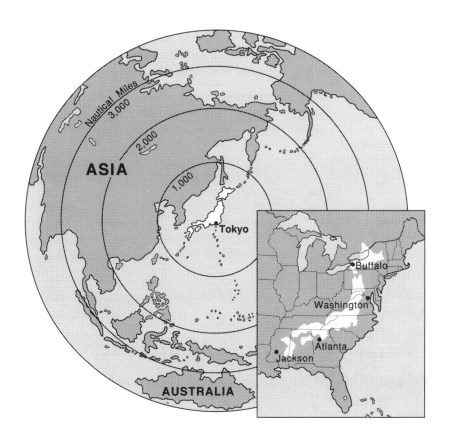

Country

Formal Name: Japan (Nihon Koku or Nippon Koku, literally, Source of the Sun Country or Land of the Rising Sun).

Short Form: Japan.

Term for Citizens: Japanese.

Capital: Tokyo

Geography

Size: Total 377,835 square kilometers, land area 374,744 square kilometers.

Topography: Mountainous islands with numerous dormant and active volcanos. Four main islands (Hokkaidō, Honshū, Shikoku, and Kyūshū) and numerous smaller islands to north and south, all prone to earthquakes. Highest point Mount Fuji (3,776 meters). Numerous, rapidly flowing rivers largely unnavigable but provide water for irrigation and hydroelectric-power generation.

Climate: Generally rainy, high humidity. Diverse climatic range: warm summers, long, cold winters in north; hot humid summers, short winters in center; long, hot, humid summers, mild winters in southwest.

Society

Population: 124,225,000 in July 1990; in 1988 about 77 percent in urban areas. High population density—324 persons per square kilometer for total area, 1,523 persons per square kilometer for habitable land, more than 50 percent of population lives on 2 percent of land.

Ethnic Groups: 99.2 percent Japanese, 0.8 percent other, mostly Korean, some Chinese. Ainu and *burakumin* comprise native Japanese minority groups.

Language: Japanese. Emphasis on English as second language.

Religion: Most (84 percent) observe both Shinto and Buddhist rites, 16 percent other religions, including 0.7 percent Christian.

Health: In 1988 life expectancy 81.3 for women, 75.5 for men, mortality rate 6 per 1,000. Health-care system in late 1980s included 8,700 general hospitals, 1,000 mental hospitals, and 1,000 comprehensive hospitals with total capacity 1.5 million beds, plus 79,000 outpatient clinics and 48,000 dental clinics. More than 190,000 physicians, nearly 67,000 dentists, and 333,000 nurses, primarily in urban areas.

Education: Compulsory, free nine-year education (elementary—grades one through six; lower-secondary—grades seven through nine) followed by public and private upper-secondary schools—attended by about 94 percent of all lower-secondary school graduates (grades ten through twelve); supplemented by preschool and after-school education. In 1988, 490 universities of which 357 were private, formed the top echelon of the 7,430 institutions of post-secondary education. Supervised by Ministry of Education, Science, and Culture. Literacy rate 99 percent in 1990.

Economy

Gross National Product (GNP): US$2.9 trillion in 1989. Per capita GNP (US$23,616), first among major industrial nations in 1989.

Gross Domestic Product (GDP): ¥343.2 trillion in 1987 (for value of the yen— ¥—see Glossary).

Resources: Coal reserves in north and southwest; otherwise minerals negligible. Most resources, including almost all non-renewable energy sources, imported.

Industry: 32.6 percent of GDP in 1987. Basic industries: automobile manufacturing, consumer electronics; nonferrous metals, petrochemicals, pharmaceuticals, bioindustry, aerospace, textiles, and processed foods also important; older heavy industries— mining, steel, and shipbuilding—in decline but still important worldwide; high-technology industries prevalent (for example, semiconductors, computers, optical fibers, optoelectronics, video discs, facsimile and copy machines, industrial robots).

Services: 56.6 percent of GDP in 1987. Wholesale and retail trade dominant; advertising, data processing, publishing, tourism, leisure industries, entertainment grew rapidly in 1980s.

Agriculture: 2.8 percent of GDP in 1987. Intense cultivation of diminishing arable land, already in short supply. Rice grown on most farmland, intercropping common. Heavy use of fertilizers, mechanization, experimental high-yield crops. Wood abundant— about 70 percent of country covered with forests; large lumber industry. World's largest fishing nation; seafood essential to food industry.

Exports: Approximately US$265 billion in 1988. Major partners United States, Federal Republic of Germany, Republic of Korea, Taiwan.

Imports: Approximately US$187 billion in 1988. Major partners United States, Republic of Korea, Australia, China, Indonesia, Taiwan.

Balance of Payments: Large and growing positive trade balance since early 1980s. Exports represented 59 percent, imports 41 percent of total annual trade in 1988.

Transportation and Communications

Maritime: Primarily on coastal seas. Inland Sea (Seto Naikai) serves major industrial areas of central Japan.

Railroads: In late 1980s, about 18,800 kilometers of routes run by Japan Railways Group; another 3,400 kilometers operated by private companies; and small, new companies financed with private and local government funds. Electric-powered Shinkansen 'bullet' trains operate at speeds up to 240 kilometers per hour on special track. Key bridges and tunnels carrying trains and automotive transportation link four major islands.

Subways: Major cities served by full metro systems, Tokyo largest. Supplemented by light rail in suburbs.

Roads: In 1987 some 1,098,900 kilometers of road, 65 percent paved. Extensive expressway and highway network.

Ports: Largest at Yokohama, Nagoya, and Kōbe; other major facilities at Chiba, Hakodate, Kitakyūshū, Kushiro, Ōsaka, Tokyo, and Yokkaichi.

Airports: International facilities at Tokyo (Narita and Haneda), Ōsaka, Nagoya, Nagasaki, Fukuoka, Kagoshima, and Naha. Japan Airlines and All Nippon Airways major world carriers. Both, along with Japan Air System and South-West Air Lines, also serve domestic routes.

Telecommunications: World-class radio and television systems available to virtually all citizens, those living in remote and mountainous areas via satellite. There were 64 million telephones in use in 1989.

Government and Politics

Government: Constitutional monarchy with emperor symbol of state. Parliamentary form of government, elected bicameral legislature (Diet: House of Councillors—upper house, House of Representatives—lower house), majority party president serves as prime minister. General elections every four years or upon dissolution of lower house, triennially for half of upper house.

Administrative Divisions: Country has forty-seven administrative divisions: forty-three rural prefectures (*ken*), two urban prefectures (*fu*—Kyōto and Ōsaka), one metropolitan district (*to*—Tokyo), and one district (*dō*—Hokkaidō). Large cities (*shi*) divided into wards (*ku*), then into precincts (*machi* or *chō*) or subdistricts (*shichō*) and counties (*gun*).

Justice: Civil law system heavily influenced by British and American law. Independent judiciary with Supreme Court, high courts, district courts, and family courts in late 1980s.

Politics: Liberal Democratic Party (LDP) majority party, with numerous factions, since 1955; other major parties: Japan Socialist Party (held majority in House of Councillors in 1990), Democratic Socialist Party, Kōmeitō (Clean Government Party).

Foreign Affairs: A major aid donor to developing countries. Maintains diplomatic relations with virtually all countries of world. Closely aligned since World War II with United States policies but neutral and independent stand on some issues. Member of Asian Development Bank, Colombo Plan for Cooperative Economic and Social Development in Asia and the Pacific, International Whaling Commission, Organisation for Economic Co-operation and Development, and the United Nations and its affiliated agencies, and a number of other internaitonal organizations.

National Security

Armed Forces: Article 9 of Constitution precludes existence of offensive military forces. Self-Defense Forces numbered about 247,000 in 1989: Ground Self-Defense Force 156,200, Maritime Self-Defense Force 44,400, and Air Self-Defense Force 46,400. Reserves 48,000.

Military Units: Five armies, five maritime districts, three air defense forces. Main bases in Hokkaidō, eastern Honshū, central and western Honshū and Shikoku, and Kyūshū.

Equipment: Ground forces: medium tanks, reconnaissance vehicles, armored personnel carriers, towed and self-propelled howitzers, mortars, single rocket and multiple rocket launchers, air-defense guns, surface-to-surface missiles, antitank missiles, fixed-wing aircraft, attack helicopters, and transport helicopters. Maritime forces: submarines, guided missile destroyers, frigates with helicopters, frigates, patrol and coastal combatants, mine warfare ships, amphibious ships, auxiliaries, fixed-wing aircraft, and helicopters. Air forces: ground attack aircraft, fighters, reconnaissance aircraft, airborne early-warning aircraft, transport aircraft, surface-to-air missiles, air-to-air missiles, and air-defense control and warning units.

Military Budget: Approximately US$2.8 billion in FY 1990. Efforts made for political reasons to keep direct defense expenses at around 1 percent of GNP.

Foreign Military Treaties: Treaty of Mutual Cooperation and Security with United States (1960); can be revoked on one-year's notice by either party, updated by minutes periodically.

Police Forces: Independent municipal and local police forces; National Rural Police at prefectural level; all under supervision of National Police Agency in 1990.

Introduction

JAPAN IN 1990 WAS a modern, thriving democracy, yet it retained a long and esteemed imperial tradition. The Japanese took great pride in being "unique," yet much of Japanese civilization was composed of selective borrowings, from the Chinese written language in the sixth century to United States semiconductors in the latter half of the twentieth century. Although Japan lacked almost all raw materials, it was a highly urbanized and industrialized economic power supplying vast export markets. Yet farming interests still exerted a strong influence on the ruling Liberal Democratic Party (LDP) and its trade policies. Japan was a rich country, ranking first among major industrial nations in per capita gross national product (GNP—see Glossary), but many of its people were crowded into inadequate housing lacking such basic amenities as indoor plumbing. Although the *bushidō* (way of the warrior) legacy of the feudal era still exerted a definite influence on modern society, the ultranationalism that it had spawned was repudiated and the military machine that earlier in the twentieth century had conquered much of the Asia-Pacific region had been replaced by streamlined Self-Defense Forces, well trained but underequipped and barely able to defend the home islands.

Japan consists of the four main islands of Hokkaidō, Honshū, Shikoku, and Kyūshū, along with a plethora of smaller islands, and is separated from the Asian mainland by the Sea of Japan and bordered on the east by the Pacific Ocean (see fig. 1). Nearly 75 percent of the country's land surface is covered by mountains, and the climate, although generally humid, ranges from cool in the north to subtropical in the south. Historically, when Japan was a predominantly agricultural country, its varied climate made for regional diversity in economy and culture, and its insular geography and rugged terrain helped it limit and control foreign access. Since World War II, however, as Japanese society has become overwhelmingly urban, industrial, and internationalized, climatic and geographical effects have become much less significant.

The origins of Japanese civilization are buried in legend, with the country's first written records dating from the sixth to the eighth centuries A.D., after Japan had adopted the Chinese writing system. Early in the sixth century, Chinese Buddhism was introduced to Japan by way of Korea, and with it came many Chinese governmental and fiscal practices. A society of individual military rulers, each responsible for his own area, evolved into an imperial system codified in the Taihō-ryōritsu (Great Treasure Code) of 701. Imperial control was gradually spread throughout the main island of Honshū and eventually to all of Japan by military conquest. The leaders of these conquests were rewarded with large landholdings. By the tenth century, these military leaders had evolved into a warrior class—the *bushi* or samurai—that supplanted the central authority of the emperor; and Japanese society evolved into a feudal economy with the large landholdings of the samurai supported by local peasants, artisans, and merchants. Beginning in the seventeenth century, the Tokugawa shoguns, like earlier military rulers under the same title, asserted control over a newly reunified Japan. They also closed the country to outside influences and developed the national premodern economy.

When Japan was reopened in the middle of the nineteenth century, the traditional political, military, and economic systems were no match for powerful foreign intruders, and the shogun's government failed. It was replaced by a new oligarchy of strong regional leaders who brought about the Meiji Restoration—the ostensible restoration of imperial power—in 1868. The Meiji rulers carried out wholesale radical reforms. The government hired thousands of foreigners to teach modern science, mathematics, and foreign languages and sent a multitude of students and envoys to Europe and North America to learn the lessons that had bypassed them during the years of exclusion. They returned to combine foreign ideology and modern methods with Japanese traditions, devising a governmental and economic system that was totally new yet uniquely Japanese. The government also built factories and shipyards to help private businesses get started. These businesses developed rapidly into large conglomerates, some of which dominated the world of business in the early 1990s. Transportation and industry were modernized; the military was reorganized and equipped with up-to-date weapons; and under the 1889 constitution, Japan took the first steps toward representative government.

For the remainder of the nineteenth century and into the twentieth century, the economy grew at a moderate rate although it remained heavily dependent on agriculture. After the development of a strong economic and industrial base at home, successful wars annexing Taiwan and Korea, and the growth of spheres of influence over a large part of the Chinese mainland, Japan began to exert its influence throughout the Asia-Pacific region. In the late 1920s, industry outstripped agriculture, and in the 1930s industry, little affected by the Great Depression plaguing the rest of the industrialized world, continued to grow. Using the strong Japanese economy to support their imperialistic designs, ultranationalist military officers succeeded in stifling the young democracy and took control of the government in the name of the emperor. With their power unchecked, the militarist government led the nation into a series of military conflicts that culminated in the almost total destruction of the nation during World War II.

World War II destroyed nearly half of Japan's industry. Japan's economy was completely disrupted, and the country was forced to rely on United States assistance and imports of essential food and raw material. Large-scale procurements by United States armed forces during the Korean War (1950–53) revived Japanese industry, and the country invested heavily in replacing the destroyed factories with modern, well-equipped factories. By the mid-1950s, modern plants staffed by a well-educated, disciplined work force had brought the Japanese economy back to pre-World War II levels. For the remainder of the 1950s, however, Japan endured chronic trade deficits. Unhampered by large military expenditures, the Japanese economy continued to grow at a rapid pace into the next decade. Japanese trade relations improved dramatically during the 1960s, attaining a favorable balance, and Japanese industry felt confident enough to compete in the international market in such heavy industrial products as automobiles, ships, and machine tools.

The Ministry of International Trade and Industry (MITI), formed in 1949, played a major role in the 1950s and 1960s in formulating and implementing Japan's international trade policy, assisting the development of domestic industry and protecting it from foreign competition. MITI's authority gradually decreased as private industry and other ministries took more responsibility on themselves. By the late 1980s, MITI's control over international trade policy was greatly reduced. The Japan External Trade Organization (JETRO) was established by MITI in 1958 to promote Japan's external trade. Over the years JETRO's role diversified; it went from promoting exports to fostering all aspects of Japan's trade relations and enhancing understanding with trading partners.

In the immediate postwar period, the operations of Japanese financial institutions were severely restricted. In the 1970s, controls began to loosen, and these institutions rapidly expanded their international activities. By the late 1980s, they were major international players, opening branches abroad to foster foreign investments and making Tokyo a world financial center. During the late 1980s, Japan became the world's largest creditor nation and was home to some of the world's largest banking and financial institutions. Japanese securities firms played a major role in international finances and were members of major world stock exchanges. In 1988 the Tokyo Securities and Stock Exchange became the world's largest, while the Ōsaka Stock Exchange ranked third behind Tokyo and the New York Stock Exchange. Beginning in 1986, the Tokyo exchange permitted foreign brokerage firms to be members. Japan also played an increasing role in international economic organizations and agreements, especially the Asian Development Bank and the General Agreement on Tariffs and Trade. Japan has a strong private enterprise economy, although public corporations played a very important role in the early postwar period. By the 1980s, however, their role was considerably decreased, and some of the largest were privatized. The thriving private enterprise sector was dominated by large corporations with affiliated smaller firms. Labor-management relations were generally harmonious, and labor productivity was high.

In the late 1980s, Japan squeezed nearly 124 million people into less than 400,000 square kilometers of land, much of which was uninhabitable. But population growth, rapid in the last half of the nineteenth century and the first half of the twentieth century, had slowed drastically by the 1980s. This low fertility rate, combined with high life expectancy, was making Japan a rapidly aging society, placing an increasing burden on the shrinking working-age population.

Women traditionally had occupied an inferior position in Japanese society. Even though they were given the right to vote in 1946 and were accorded equal rights under the 1947 Constitution and the Civil Code of 1948, their general status did not significantly improve. As Japan faced a shrinking work force in the 1980s and 1990s, however, increasing numbers of women were brought into the labor market, resulting in improved educational, political, and economic opportunities. Nevertheless, women's status still remained far short of that for men.

Japan promoted exports by developing world-class industries and providing incentives for firms to export. In the postwar period, export incentives mainly took the form of tax relief and government assistance to build export industries along with heavy import barriers. As Japanese industry regained its strength in the 1960s, the government gradually liberalized its trade policy, and tax incentives were eliminated. In the 1970s, a strong rise in the value of the yen (for value of the yen—see Glossary) under the new system of floating exchange rates and the oil price shocks of 1973 and 1979 brought large trade deficits. The situation spurred Japan to reduce its dependence on unreliable foreign petroleum by conservation and diversification of sources and to sharply increase its exports to offset the high costs of raw materials. In the 1980s, with the dramatic drop in the cost of raw materials, Japan developed a large trade surplus. Export policy shifted to export restraints on certain products that were causing the greatest tensions with trading partners, and Japan greatly increased its foreign investment. This trend continued through the 1980s. Japan continued to be the target of complaints from trading partners, however, especially for nontariff barriers such as standards, testing procedures, and restrictive distribution practices.

In the 1980s, manufactured imports still made up a share of the gross national product far below that of other developed countries, and in 1989 Japan was named an unfair trading partner by the United States government. Although certain Japanese industries, such as automobile manufacturing, were heavily export oriented, Japan exported a lower percentage of its GNP than most major industrialized nations. During the 1960s and 1970s, import growth kept up with exports, but in the 1980s, import growth fell off drastically, leading to large trade surpluses. The United States was the largest single destination of Japanese exports (34 percent in 1988) as well as its largest single source of imports (22.4 percent). Japan's major international industries in the late 1980s were motor vehicles, consumer electronics, computers, semiconductors and other electronic components, and iron and steel. The rapid increase in the value of the yen in the late 1980s made Japanese exports less price competitive and imports more price competitive, but it was unclear in 1990 what effect the increased value of the yen would have on the balance of trade in the long term.

Japan has traditionally run a deficit in services: transportation, insurance, travel expenditures, royalties, licensing fees, and income from investment. In the early 1980s, however, this deficit was somewhat offset by the rapid growth of Japanese foreign investment. In the late 1980s, increased travel expenses again produced a marked increase in the services deficit despite a rapid growth in foreign investments. Although most barriers to foreign investment were removed in the 1980s, Japan's heavy investment in other countries remained a major cause of tension with those countries.

Japan's foreign aid program, begun in the 1960s as World War II reparations to other Asian countries, grew rapidly during the 1980s. In the late 1980s, Japanese assistance consisted of bilateral grants and loans as well as support to multilateral aid organizations.

Japan, one of the world's most literate nations, places great value on education. It provides children with compulsory free education from first grade through ninth grade. A high percentage of children also attends preschools and continues through into upper-secondary and higher education. Educational standards are high, and Japanese students consistently finish at or near the top in international academic tests. Teachers are held in great esteem by Japanese society and are charged with imparting sound moral values to their students along with academic information. Any antisocial behavior on or off campus is considered to reflect on the teacher. Entrance to higher education is by examination and is extremely competitive, causing great stress to students trying to get into the "right" school. Education rarely ends with graduation from the formal school system. Japan also has extensive, well-utilized adult education.

The Japanese have shown widespread interest in their traditional culture: the tea ritual, calligraphy, flower arranging, and Nō, Kabuki, and *bunraku* (puppet) theater, as well as classical works of art. At the same time, educated Japanese are expected to have a good understanding of classical Western music and art, and modern Western music, drama, and art have been imported and adapted to develop distinctive new Japanese forms. In addition, extensive print and broadcast media provide information and entertainment.

The Japanese do not consider themselves a religious people. Their world view, however, is guided by a basic philosophy deeply rooted in ancient Shinto beliefs on human origins and relations with the spirit world, modified by later adaptations of Confucian ideas on societal relationships and order and Buddhist concepts of karmic causation and an afterlife. Japanese are very conscious of their position in society and the various roles that they are expected to play throughout their lives. They put a high premium on social harmony and will go to great pains to avoid bringing disgrace on their families and other groups with which they are associated by disrupting that harmony. For this reason, more than any other, in 1990 the overall crime rate remained quite low in comparison with other major industrialized nations, and Japanese cities were among the safest in the world.

The 1947 Constitution, with its stipulation of a symbolic role for the emperor, guarantees of civil and human rights, and renunciation of war, remained the operative basis for Japanese government in 1990. By pragmatic collaboration with big business, small business, agriculture, and professional groups, the LDP has dominated Japanese politics since it was formed as a coalition of smaller conservative groups in 1955. Although LDP fortunes have risen and ebbed over the years since its establishment, no opposition party has been able to oust it from power. On occasions, such as the Lockheed bribery scandal in the mid-1970s and the Recruit influence-peddling scandal of 1988–89, LDP dominance appeared to be in danger. In the upper house (House of Councillors) elections of July

1989, the LDP actually became the minority party behind the Japan Socialist Party and a coalition of smaller opposition groups. But voters have continued to give the LDP control of the more powerful lower house (House of Representatives). This fact results as much from the opposition's inability to present a viable alternative as from popular support for the LDP. The voters have preferred to chastise the LDP for its mistakes rather than to oust the party.

In the postwar period, Japan concentrated on rebuilding its economy, attempted to cultivate friendly ties with all nations, and relied on the United States for military security. By the 1970s, this foreign policy began to be called into question as Japan came into its own as a world economic power. In the 1980s, Japan became a leading industrial nation, the world's largest creditor nation and largest donor of foreign aid, and a major actor in international financial institutions such as the World Bank (see Glossary) and the International Monetary Fund (see Glossary). As it entered the 1990s, people at home and abroad expected Japan to play a diplomatic role proportionate to its economic power and its role in foreign assistance, trade, and investment. But popular sentiment in Japan and its Asian neighbors continued strongly to oppose Japan's assuming the military role expected of a world power.

Because of their tragic experience with a military-controlled government before and during World War II, the Japanese people readily accepted the military restrictions written into the 1947 Constitution at the insistence of occupation forces and, even in 1990, generally interpreted Article 9 of the Constitution as forbidding the Japanese Self-Defense Forces from being deployed outside of the country or possessing nuclear weapons. Japan still depended on the 1960 Treaty of Mutual Cooperation and Security with the United States, which mandated the United States to come to its aid in the event of a large-scale invasion and allowed for United States provision of a nuclear umbrella. There is little popular sentiment for change in this arrangement.

As Japan moved toward the twenty-first century, it was faced with a series of dilemmas. How could it continue to grow as a world economic leader without assuming a greater political role? And, how could it be considered a political leader when it could not even provide for the security of its own territory without foreign assistance? Its trading partners complained that Japan enjoyed an unfair advantage. Yet when Japanese firms invested in their economies, they raised the specter of Japanese domination. Each international crisis found Western powers calling on Japan to "contribute its fair share" to the peacekeeping forces. At the same time, the Japanese people and their Asian neighbors, remembering the terrible lessons of World War II, demanded that there be no foreign projection of Japanese military power. With less than ten years until the next century, Japan had yet to come to grips with these questions. The answers seemed far off.

January 22, 1991

*   *   *

As the manuscript for this book was being completed, the Japanese economy continued to grow at a healthy rate. After a weak 2.6 percent annualized growth in GNP in the fourth quarter of 1990, the GNP jumped to an 11.2 percent annualized growth in the first quarter of 1991. But the fact that more than half of this increase came from exports seemed to indicate that overall growth for 1991 would slow considerably from the first quarter figure.

Japan's tardiness in providing promised support to the United States-led coalition forces opposing the Iraqi occupation of Kuwait exacerbated already tense Japanese-United States trade relations. In March 1991, Japan's legislature, the National Diet, finally approved the US$13 billion promised several months earlier, relieving some of the tension in Japanese-United States relations. With the attention of Congress and the American public diverted to other areas of the world, Japanese and United States government officials were able to quietly negotiate a trade agreement on semiconductors and an agreement to open Japanese construction projects to United States companies. Japan's refusal to open up its rice market to foreign suppliers remained a serious problem for agricultural trade.

Although the Kaifu administration in November 1990 was unsuccessful in getting Diet authorization for the Self-Defense Forces to participate in peacekeeping operations, in early February 1991 the Japanese government dispatched military transport aircraft to evacuate refugees from the Persian Gulf war from Jordan and Syria to Egypt at the request of the United Nations International Organization for Migration. After the war, Japan sent a small flotilla of four Maritime Self-Defense Force minesweepers and two support ships to the Gulf to clear Iraqi mines. In the summer of 1991, the Kaifu administration drafted a new proposal setting aside a force of 1,000 troops and 50 cease-fire monitors to be available for United Nations peacekeeping operations. The proposal appeared to have substantial public support.

On July 18, 1991, after several months of difficult negotiations, Prime Minister Kaifu Toshiki signed a joint statement with the

Dutch prime minister, Ruud Lubbers, head of the European Community Council, and the European Commission president, Jacques Delors, pledging closer Japanese-European Community consultations on foreign relations, scientific and technological cooperation, assistance to developing countries, and efforts to reduce trade conflicts. Japanese foreign ministry officials hoped that this agreement would help to broaden Japanese-European Community political links and raise them above the narrow confines of trade disputes.

The much heralded visit to Japan of Soviet president and general secretary of the Communist Party of the Soviet Union Mikhail Gorbachev occurred in April 1991. Although Gorbachev and Kaifu signed several low-level agreements on environmental protection, nuclear energy, and cultural exchanges, they made no progress in resolving the main obstacle to Japanese-Soviet relations, the Soviet Union's continued occupation of Shikotan, Etorofu, Kunashiri, and the Habomai Islands north of Hokkaidō. In September 1991, Gorbachev resigned as general secretary of the communist party and his government was in transition, causing further uncertainties about that government's relations with Japan and other nations.

In the early 1990s, the Japanese government was making a concerted effort to enhance its diplomatic stature, especially in Asia. Kaifu's much publicized spring 1991 tour of five Southeast Asian nations—Malaysia, Brunei, Thailand, Singapore, and the Philippines—culminated in a May 3 major foreign policy address in Singapore, in which he called for a new partnership with the Association of Southeast Asian Nations (ASEAN) and pledged that Japan would go beyond the purely economic sphere to seek an "appropriate role in the political sphere as a nation of peace." As evidence of this new role, Japan took an active part in promoting negotiations to resolve the Cambodian conflict.

In Northeast Asia, Japan conducted lengthy negotiations with the Democratic People's Republic of Korea (North Korea) aimed at establishing diplomatic relations with P'yŏngyang while maintaining its relations with Seoul. The Japanese government also revived Sino-Japanese exchanges and offered support to Mongolia's political and economic restructuring. In January 1991, Japan began normalization talks with P'yŏngyang with a formal apology for its 1910–45 colonial rule of the Korean Peninsula. The negotiations were aided by Tokyo's support of a proposal for simultaneous entry to the United Nations by North Korea and the Republic of Korea (South Korea); the issues of international inspection of North Korean nuclear facilities and the nature and amount of Japanese economic assistance, however, proved more difficult to negotiate.

Japan took the lead in restoring trade and economic agreements with China, suspended following Beijing's June 1989 Tiananmen Incident. Japan-China trade, which began to recover in September 1990, increased rapidly in 1991. In March 1991, the Japan Export-Import Bank resumed loans to China, and in April Japan announced its support for restoration of Asian Development Bank loans to China. A series of unilateral and multilateral loans followed.

Frequent meetings between high-level Japanese and Chinese government officials also took place in 1991. In March Japanese foreign ministry officials met in Tokyo with Chinese foreign ministry officials to discuss a wide range of bilateral and international issues; in May former prime ministers Nakasone Yasuhiro and Takeshita Noboru, in Beijing to attend the opening of a Japan-China youth center, met with leading Chinese officials; and in June the Chinese minster of foreign affairs, Qian Qichen, visited Tokyo. The culmination of government-to-government exchanges came with Prime Minister Kaifu's August 1991 visit to Beijing, the first by a leader of a major industrialized nation since the Tiananmen Incident. During the visit, Kaifu discussed a full range of bilateral and international issues with Chinese leaders and offered substantial economic assistance. Kaifu also visited Ulaanbaatar and offered Japanese encouragement and financial support to Mongolia's efforts to reorganize its government and economy.

The political fortunes of leading Japanese political figures changed in 1991. Doi Takako, who in late 1989 and early 1990 had been considered a possible candidate for prime minister on the strength of her Japan Socialist Party's victory in the July 1989 House of Councilors election, resigned her post in late July 1991 following the party's crushing defeat in local elections. And, in October Prime Minster Kaifu, despite his high rating with the Japanese public, announced that he would not run for another term as president of the LDP when he failed to attain Diet passage of a political reform bill and lost the support of powerful LDP factions. Miyazawa Kiichi, a strong political figure whose career dates from World War II and the United States occupation, was elected president of the LDP on October 27, 1991, and prime minister on November 5. On December 7, Prime Minister Miyazawa indicated that Japan felt 'deep responsibility' for the suffering that it inflicted in World War II, but believed that it had atoned for its conduct by its contribution to peace and prosperity since the war. It remained to be seen, however, what general policy changes the Miyazawa administration would bring to Japan and its relations with the rest of the world.

December 9, 1991   Ronald E. Dolan

Chapter 1. Historical Setting

The ideograph wa, *translated as "harmony," considered a basic Japanese social value; written by Reiko I. Seekins*

"NOTHING SIMILAR MAY be found in foreign lands," wrote Kitabatake Chikafusa when he described Japan in his fourteenth-century *Jinnō shōtō ki* (Chronicle of the Direct Descent of the Divine Sovereigns). Although Japan's culture developed late in Asian terms and was much influenced by China and later the West, its history, like its art and literature, is special among world civilizations. As some scholars have argued, these outside influences may have "corrupted" Japanese traditions, yet once absorbed they also enriched and strengthened the nation, forming part of a vibrant and unique culture.

Early in Japan's history, society was controlled by a ruling elite of powerful clans. The most powerful emerged as a kingly line and later as the imperial family in Yamato (modern Nara Prefecture or possibly in northern Kyūshū) in the third century A.D., claiming descent from the gods who created Japan. An imperial court and government, shaped by Chinese political and social institutions, were established. Often powerful court families effected a hereditary regency, having established control over the emperor. The highly developed culture attained between the eighth and the twelfth centuries was followed by a long period of anarchy and civil war, and a feudal society developed in which military overlords ran the government on behalf of the emperor, his court, and the regent. Although the Yamato (see Glossary) court continued control of the throne, in practice a succession of dynastic military regimes ruled the now-decentralized country. In the late sixteenth century, Japan began a process of reunification followed by a period of great stability and peace, in which contact with the outside world was limited and tightly controlled by the government.

Confronted by the West—inopportunely during the economically troubled late eighteenth and early nineteenth centuries—Japan emerged gradually as a modern, industrial power, exhibiting some democratic institutions by the end of World War I. Beginning in the mid-nineteenth century, phenomenal social upheaval, accompanied by political, military, and economic successes, led to an overabundance of nationalist pride and extremist solutions, and to even faster modernization. Representative government was finally replaced by increasingly authoritarian regimes, which propelled Japan into World War II. After the cataclysm of nuclear war, Japan rebuilt itself based on a new and earnest desire for peaceful development, becoming an economic superpower in the second half of the twentieth century.

Early Developments

Ancient Cultures

The literature of Shinto (Way of the Gods; see Religious and Philsophical Traditons, ch. 2) employs much mythology to describe the supposed historical origins of Japan. According to the creation story found in the *Kojiki* (Record of Ancient Matters, dating from 712 A.D.) and the *Nihongi* or *Nihon shoki* (Chronicle of Japan, from 720 A.D.), the Japanese islands were created by the gods, two of whom— the male Izanagi and the female Izanami—descended from heaven to carry out the task. They also brought into being other *kami* (deities or supernatural forces), such as those influencing the sea, rivers, wind, woods, and mountains. Two of these deities, the Sun Goddess, Amaterasu Ōmikami, and her brother, the Storm God, Susano-o, warred against each other, with Amaterasu emerging victorious.

Subsequently Amaterasu sent her grandson, Ninigi, to rule over the sacred islands. Ninigi took with him what became the three imperial regalia—a curved jewel (*magatama*), a mirror, and a "sword of gathered clouds"—and ruled over the island of Kyūshū (see fig. 1). Ninigi's great-grandson, Jimmu, recognized as the first human emperor of Japan, set out to conquer Yamato. On the main island of Honshū, according to tradition, he established the unbroken line of imperial descent from the Sun Goddess and founded the Land of the Rising Sun in 660 B.C.

Archaeological evidence shows some human activity as early as 30,000 B.C., when the islands were connected glacially to the Asian mainland. The first modern inhabitants of Japan, however, are thought to have been relative latecomers, arriving from diverse points of the eastern Pacific rim by around 10,000 B.C.

Of these prehistoric people, those who left the clearest record were members of the heterogeneous Jōmon culture (ca. 10,000–300 B.C.) who made by 3,000 B.C. clay pottery impressed with rope or cord patterns (Jōmon means "patterns of plaited cord") with a growing sophistication. These people also used chipped stone tools and were hunters, gatherers, and skillful coastal and deepwater fishermen. They practiced a rudimentary form of agriculture and lived in caves and later in temporary shallow pit dwellings, leaving rich kitchen middens for modern anthropological study. Many elements of Japanese culture, such as Shinto mythology, marriage customs, and architectural styles, may date from the end

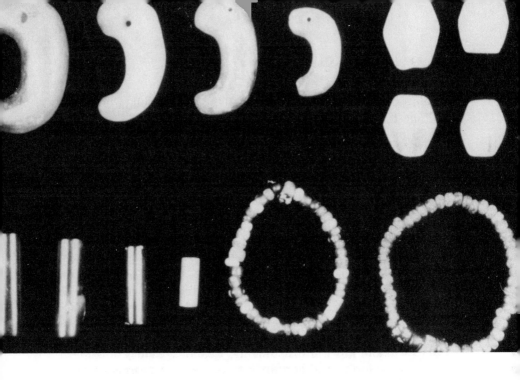

Ancient ornaments, including several magatama, *or "curved jewels"*
Courtesy The Mainichi Newspapers

of this period and reflect a mingled migration from northern Asian and southern Pacific areas.

Some developments of the next cultural period, the Yayoi, are attributed to Chinese and Korean influences. The Yayoi culture (named after the section of Tokyo where archaeological investigations uncovered its traces) flourished between about 300 B.C. and A.D. 300 from southern Kyūshū to northern Honshū. The earliest of these people, who are thought to have migrated from Korea to northern Kyūshū and intermixed with the Jōmon, also used chipped stone tools. Although the pottery of the Yayoi was more technologically advanced—produced on a potter's wheel—it was more simply decorated than Jōmon ware. The Yayoi made bronze ceremonial nonfunctional bells, mirrors, and weapons, and by the first century A.D., iron agricultural tools and weapons. They wove cloth, lived in permanent farming villages, constructed buildings of wood and stone, accumulated wealth through land ownership and the storage of grain, and developed distinct social classes. Their irrigated, wet-rice culture was similar to that of central and south China, requiring a heavy input of human labor, which led to the development and eventual growth of a highly sedentary society. Unlike China, which had to undertake massive public works and water-control projects, leading to a highly centralized government,

Japan had abundant water. In Japan, then, local political and social developments were relatively more important than the activities of the central authority and a stratified society.

Kofun Period, ca. A.D. 300–710

New continental influences, such as the extensive use of iron, characterized the next historical period. The Kofun, or old tomb, period (ca. A.D. 300–710, also known as the Yamato period), takes its name from the culture's distinctive earthen funeral mounds with large stone burial chambers, many of which were keyhole shaped. During this time, a highly aristocratic society with militaristic rulers developed. Its horse-riding warriors wore armor, carried swords and other weapons, and used advanced military methods like those of Northeast Asia. Evidence of these advances is seen in *haniwa* (literally, clay rings) funerary figures found in thousands of tombs scattered throughout the area. The figures are portrayed using a wide variety of musical instruments, weapons, modes of conveyance, and so forth. Another funerary piece, the *magatama,* became one of the symbols of the power of the imperial house.

The Kofun period was a critical stage in Japan's evolution toward a more cohesive and recognized state. This society was most developed in the easternmost part of the Inland Sea (Seto Naikai), and its armies established a foothold on the southern tip of Korea. Japan's rulers of the time even petitioned the Chinese court for confirmation of royal titles; the Chinese, in turn, recognized Japanese military control over parts of the Korean Peninsula. The earliest written records about Japan are from Chinese sources from this period. Wa (the Japanese pronunciation of an early Chinese name for Japan) was first mentioned in A.D. 57. Early Chinese historians described Wa as a land of hundreds of scattered tribal communities, not the unified land with a 700-year tradition as laid out in the *Nihongi,* which puts the foundation of Japan at 660 B.C. Third-century Chinese sources reported that the Wa people lived on raw vegetables, rice, and fish served on bamboo and wooden trays, had vassal-master relations, collected taxes, had provincial granaries and markets, clapped their hands in worship (something still done in Shinto shrines), had violent succession struggles, built earthen grave mounds, and observed mourning. Himiko, a female ruler of an early political federation known as Yamatai, flourished during the third century. While Himiko reigned as spiritual leader, her younger brother carried out affairs of state, which included diplomatic relations with the court of the Chinese Wei Dynasty (A.D. 220–65).

The Yamato polity, which emerged in the mid-Kofun period, was distinguished by powerful great clans or extended families, each

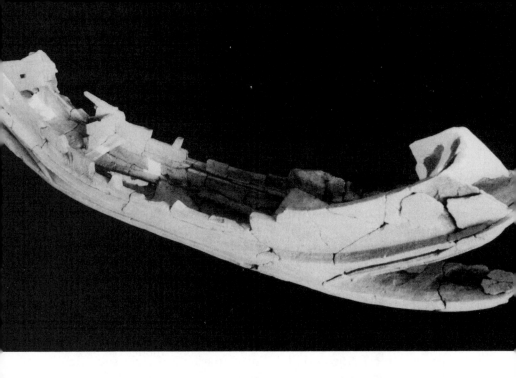

Haniwa *ship excavated at Ōsaka in 1988*
Courtesy Asahi Shimbun

with its dependents. Each clan was headed by a patriarch who performed sacred rites to the clan's *kami* to ensure the long-term welfare of the clan. Clan members were the aristocracy, and the kingly line that controlled the Yamato court was at its pinacle.

By the fifth century A.D., the Yamato court was concentrated in Asuka, near modern Nara, and exercised power over clans in Kyūshū and Honshū, bestowing titles, some hereditary, on clan chieftains. The Yamato name became synonomous with all of Japan as the Yamato rulers suppressed the clans and acquired agricultural lands. Based on Chinese models (including the adoption of the Chinese written language), they developed a central administration and an imperial court attended by subordinate clan chieftains but with no permanent capital. By the mid-seventh century, the agricultural lands had grown to a substantial public domain, subject to central policy. The basic administrative unit was the county, and society was organized into occupation groups. Most people were farmers; other were fishers, weavers, potters, artisans, armorers, and ritual specialists.

More exchange occurred between Japan and the continent of Asia late in the Kofun period. Buddhism was introduced from Korea, probably in A.D. 538, exposing Japan to a new body of religious doctrine. The Soga, a Japanese court family that rose to prominence with the accession of the Emperor Kimmei about A.D. 531, favored the adoption of Buddhism and of governmental and cultural models based on Chinese Confucianism. But some at the Yamato court—such as the Nakatomi family, which was responsible for performing Shinto rituals at court, and the Mononobe, a military clan—were set on maintaining their prerogatives and resisted the alien religious influence of Buddhism. The Soga introduced Chinese-modeled fiscal policies, established the first national treasury, and considered the Korean Peninsula a trade route rather than an object of territorial expansion. Acrimony continued between the Soga and the Nakatomi and Mononobe clans for more than a century during which the Soga temporarily emerged ascendant.

The Soga intermarried with the imperial family and by A.D. 587 Soga Umako, the Soga chieftain, was powerful enough to install his nephew as emperor and later to assassinate him and replace him with the Empress Suiko. Suiko, the first of eight sovereign empresses, was merely a figurehead for Umako and Prince Regent Shōtoku Taishi (A.D. 574–622). Shōtoku, recognized as a great intellectual of this period of reform, was a devout Buddhist well-read in Chinese literature. He was influenced by Confucian principles, including the Mandate of Heaven, which suggested that the sovereign ruled at the will of a supreme force. Under Shōtoku's direction, Confucian models of rank and etiquette were adopted, and his Seventeen Article Constitution (*Kenpō jūshichijō*) prescribed ways to bring harmony to a society chaotic in Confucian terms. In addition, Shōtoku adopted the Chinese calendar, developed a system of highways, built numerous Buddhist temples, had court chronicles compiled, sent students to China to study Buddhism and Confucianism, and established formal diplomatic relations with China.

Numerous official missions of envoys, priests, and students were sent to China in the seventh century. Some remained twenty years or more; many of those who returned became prominent reformers. In a move greatly resented by the Chinese, Shōtoku sought equality with the Chinese emperor by addressing a memorial "From the Son of Heaven in the Land of the Rising Sun to the Son of Heaven of the Land of the Setting Sun." Shōtoku's bold step set a precedent: Japan never again accepted a subordinate status in its relations with China. Although the missions continued the transformation of Japan through Chinese influences, the Korean influence on Japan declined despite the close connections there had been during the early Kofun period.

About twenty years after the deaths of Shōtoku (in A.D. 622), Soga Umako (in A.D. 626), and Empress Suiko (in A.D. 628), court intriques over the succession and the threat of a Chinese invasion led to a palace coup against the Soga oppression in 645. The revolt was led by Prince Naka and Nakatomi Kamatari, who seized control of the court from the Soga family and introduced the Taika Reform (Taika means great change) to centralize the state.

The Taika Reform—influenced by Chinese practices—started with land redistribution, aimed at ending the existing landholding system of the great clans and their control over domains and occupational groups. What were once called "private lands and private people" became "public lands and public people," as the court now sought to assert its control over all of Japan and to make the people direct subjects of the throne. Land was no longer hereditary but reverted to the state at the death of the owner. Taxes were levied on harvests and on silk, cotton, cloth, thread, and other products. A corvée (labor) tax was established for military conscription and building public works. The hereditary titles of clan chieftains were abolished, and three ministries were established to advise the throne (the minister of the left, minister of the right, and minister of the center, or chancellor). The country was divided into provinces headed by governors appointed by the court, and the provinces were further divided into districts and villages.

Naka assumed the position of minister of the center, and Kamatari was granted a new family name—Fujiwara—in recognition of his great service to the imperial family. Fujiwara Kamatari became the first in a long line of court aristocrats. Another, long-lasting change was the use of the name Nippon or Nihon (see Glossary), or sometimes Dai Nippon (Great Japan) in diplomatic documents and chronicles. Following the reigns of Naka's uncle and mother, Naka assumed the throne as Emperor Tenji in 662, taking the additional title *tennō* (heavenly sovereign). This new title was intended to improve the Yamato clan's image and to emphasize the divine origins of the imperial family in the hope of keeping it above political frays, such as those precipitated by the Soga clan. Within the imperial family, however, power struggles continued as the emperor's brother and son vied for the throne. The brother, who later reigned as Emperor Temmu, consolidated Tenji's reforms and state power in the imperial court.

Reforms were further consolidated and codified in A.D. 701 under the Taihō-ryōritsu (Great Treasure Code, known as the Taihō Code), which, except for a few modifications and being relegated to primarily ceremonial functions, remained in force until

1868. The Taihō Code provided for Confucian-model penal provisions (light rather than harsh punishments) and Chinese-style central administration through the Department of Rites, which was devoted to Shinto and court rituals, and the Department of State, with its eight ministries (for central administration, ceremonies, civil affairs, the imperial household, justice, military affairs, people's affairs, and the treasury). A Chinese-style civil service examination system based on the Confucian classics was also adopted. Tradition circumvented the system, however, as aristocratic birth continued to be the main qualification for higher position. The Taihō Code did not address the selection of the sovereign. Several empresses reigned from the fifth to the eighth centuries, but after 770 succession was restricted to males, usually from father to son, although sometimes to brother or uncle.

Nara and Heian Periods, A.D. 710-1185

Economic, Social, and Administrative Developments

Before the Taihō Code was established, the capital was customarily moved after the death of an emperor because of the ancient belief that a place of death was polluted. Reforms and bureaucratization of government led to the establishment of a permanent imperial capital at Heijōkyō, or Nara, in A.D. 710. (Previously the capital had been about twenty-five kilometers south of Nara, in and around Asuka, the name given by some historians to the pre-Nara period [538–710] and art style.) The capital at Nara, which gave its name to the new period (710–94), was styled after the grand Chinese Tang Dynasty (618–907) capital at Chang'an and was the first truly urban center in Japan. It soon had a population of 200,000, representing nearly 4 percent of the country's population, and some 10,000 people worked in government jobs.

Economic and administrative activity increased during the Nara period. Roads linked Nara to provincial capitals and taxes were collected more efficiently and routinely. Coins were minted, if not widely used. Outside the Nara area, however, there was little commercial activity, and in the provinces the old Shōtoku land reform systems declined. By the mid-eighth century, *shōen* (landed estates), one of the most important economic institutions in medieval Japan, began to rise as a result of the search for a more manageable form of landholding. Local administration gradually became more self-sufficient while the breakdown of the old land distribution system and the rise of taxes led to the loss or abandonment of land by many people who became the "wave people," or *rōnin* (see Glossary). Some of these formerly "public people" were privately employed by large landholders, and "public lands" increasingly reverted to the *shōen.*

Factional fighting at the imperial court continued throughout the Nara period. Imperial family members, leading court families, such as the Fujiwara, and Buddhist priests all contended for influence. In the late Nara period, financial burdens on the state increased, and the court began dismissing nonessential officials. In 792 universal conscription was abandoned, and district heads were allowed to establish private militia forces for local police work. Decentralization of authority became the rule despite the reforms of the Nara period. Eventually, to return control to imperial hands, the capital was moved in 784 to Nagaoka and in 794 to Heiankyō (Capital of Peace and Tranquility) or Heian, about twenty-six kilometers north of Nara. By the late eleventh century, the city was popularly called Kyōto (Capital City), the name it has had ever since.

Cultural Developments and the Establishment of Buddhism

Some of Japan's literary monuments were written during the Nara period including the *Kojiki* and *Nihongi,* the first national histories compiled in 712 and 720 respectively; the *Man'yōshū* (Collection of Ten Thousand Leaves), an anthology of poems; and the *Kaifūsō* (Fond Recollections of Poetry), an anthology written in Chinese by Japanese emperors and princes. Another major cultural development of the era was the permanent establishment of Buddhism in Japan. Buddhism had been introduced in the sixth century, but had a mixed reception until the Nara period, when it was heartily embraced by the Emperor Shōmu. Shōmu and his Fujiwara consort were fervent Buddhists and actively promoted the spread of Buddhism, making it the "guardian of the state" and strengthening Japanese institutions through still further Chinese acculturation. During Shōmu's reign, the Tōdaiji (Great East Temple) was built and within it was placed the Buddha Dainichi (Great Sun Buddha), a sixteen-meter-high, gilt-bronze statue. This Buddha was identified with the Sun Goddess, and from this point on a gradual syncretism of Buddism and Shinto ensued. Shōmu declared himself the "Servant of the Three Treasures" of Buddhism: the Buddha, the law or teachings of Buddhism, and the Buddhist community.

Although these efforts stopped short of making Buddhism the state religion, Nara Buddhism heightened the status of the imperial family. Buddhist influence at court increased under the two reigns of Shōmu's daughter. As Empress Kōken from 749 to 758, she brought many Buddhist priests into court. Kōken abdicated in 758 on the advice of her cousin, Fujiwara Nakamaro. When the retired empress came to favor a Buddhist faith healer named Dōkyō, Nakamaro rose up in arms in 764 but was quickly crushed. Kōken charged the ruling emperor with colluding with Nakamaro, and had him deposed and reascended the throne as Empress Shōtoku from 764 to 770. It was at this point that she commissioned the printing of 1 million prayer charms, many examples of which survive, and which were known as the earliest printing in the world until an earlier example dating 751 was discovered in Korea in 1966. Shōtoku had the charms printed to placate the Buddhist clergy. She may even have wanted to make Dōkyō emperor, but she died before she could act. Her actions shocked Nara society and led to the exclusion of women from imperial succession and the removal of Buddhist priests from positions of political authority.

Despite such machinations, Buddhism began to spread throughout Japan during the ensuing Heian period (794–1185) primarily through two major esoteric sects, Tendai (Heavenly Terrace) and Shingon (True Word). Tendai originated in China and is based on the *Lotus Sutra*. Shingon is an indigenous sect with close affiliations to original Indian, Tibetan, and Chinese Buddhist thought founded by Kūkai (also called Kōbō Daishi), who greatly impressed the emperors following Emperor Kammu (782–806) and generations of Japanese, not only with his holiness, but also with his poetry, calligraphy, painting, and sculpture. Kammu himself was a notable patron of the otherworldly Tendai sect, which rose to great power over the ensuing centuries. A close relationship developed between the Tendai monastery complex on Mount Hiei and the imperial court in its new capital at the foot of the mountain and, as a result, Tendai emphasized great reverence for the emperor and the nation.

The Fujiwara Regency

When Kammu moved the capital to Heian (Kyōto), which remained the imperial capital for the next 1,000 years, he did so not only to strengthen imperial authority but also to improve his seat of government geopolitically. Kyōto had good river access to the sea and could be reached by land routes from the eastern provinces. The early Heian period (794–967) continued Nara culture; the Heian capital was patterned on the Chinese capital at Chang'an, as was Nara, but on a larger scale. Despite the decline of the Taika-Taihō reforms, imperial government was vigorous during the early Heian period. Indeed, Kammu's avoidance of drastic reform decreased the intensity of political struggles, and he became recognized as one of Japan's most forceful emperors.

The eighth-century Nara Daibutsu, Tōdaiji
Courtesy Asahi Shimbun

Although Kammu had abandoned universal conscription in 792, he still waged major military offensives to subjugate the Ainu, a north Asian caucasoid people, sometimes referred to as Emishi, living in northern and eastern Japan. After making temporary gains in 794, in 797 Kammu appointed a new commander under the title *seii taishōgun* (barbarian-subduing generalissimo, often referred to as shogun). By 801 the shogun had defeated the Ainu and extended the imperial domains to the eastern end of Honshū. Imperial control over the provinces was tenuous at best, however, and in the ninth and tenth centuries much authority was lost to the great families who disregarded the Chinese-style land and tax systems imposed by the government in Kyōto. Stability came to Heian Japan, but, even though succession was ensured for the imperial family through heredity, power again concentrated in the hands of one noble family, the Fujiwara.

Following Kammu's death in 806 and a succession struggle among his sons, two new offices were established in an effort to adjust the Taika-Taihō administrative structure. Through the new Emperor's Private Office, the emperor could issue administrative edicts more directly and with more self-assurance than before. The new Metropolitan Police Board replaced the largely ceremonial imperial guard units. While these two offices strengthened the

13

emperor's position temporarily, soon they and other Chinese-style structures were bypassed in the developing state. Chinese influence effectively ended with the last imperial-sanctioned mission to China in 838. Tang China was in a state of decline, and Chinese Buddhists were severely persecuted, undermining Japanese respect for Chinese institutions. Japan began to turn inward.

As the Soga had taken control of the throne in the sixth century, the Fujiwara by the ninth century had intermarried with the imperial family, and one of their members was the first head of the Emperor's Private Office. Another Fujiwara became regent for his grandson, then a minor emperor, and yet another was appointed *kanpaku* (regent for an adult emperor). Toward the end of the ninth century, several emperors tried, but failed, to check the Fujiwara. For a time, however, during the reign of Emperor Daigo (897–930), the Fujiwara regency was suspended as he ruled directly.

Nevertheless, the Fujiwara were not demoted by Daigo, but actually became stronger during his reign. Central control of Japan had continued to decline, and the Fujiwara, along with other great families and religious foundations, acquired ever larger *shōen* and greater wealth during the early tenth century. By the early Heian period, the *shōen* had obtained legal status, and the large religious establishments sought clear titles in perpetuity, waiver of taxes, and immunity from government inspection of the *shōen* they held. Those people who worked the land found it advantageous to transfer title to *shōen* holders in return for a share of the harvest. People and lands were increasingly beyond central control and taxation, a de facto return to conditions before the Taika Reform.

Within decades of Daigo's death, the Fujiwara had absolute control over the court. By the year 1000 Fujiwara Michinaga was able to enthrone and dethrone emperors at will. Little authority was left for traditional officialdom, and government affairs were handled through the Fujiwara family's private administration. The Fujiwara had become what historian George B. Sansom has called "hereditary dictators."

Despite their usurpation of imperial authority, the Fujiwara presided over a period of cultural and artistic flowering at the imperial court and among the aristocracy. There was great interest in graceful poetry and vernacular literature. Japanese writing had long depended on Chinese ideograms (*kanji*), but these were now supplemented by *kana*, a phonetic Japanese script based on simplified Chinese ideograms; *katakana*, a mnemonic device using parts of Chinese ideograms; and *hiragana*, a cursive form of *katakana* writing and an art form in itself (see Arts, ch. 3). *Hiragana* gave written expression to the spoken word and, with it, to the rise in Japan's famous vernacular literature, much of it written by court women who had not been trained in Chinese as had their male counterparts. Three late tenth-century and early eleventh-century women presented their views of life and romance at the Heian court in *Kagerō nikki* (The Gossamer Years) by "the mother of Michitsuna," *Makura no sōshi* (The Pillow Book) by Sei Shōnagon, and *Genji monogatari* (Tale of Genji)—the world's first novel—by Murasaki Shikibu (see Literature, ch. 3). Indigenous art also flourished under the Fujiwara after centuries of imitating Chinese forms. Vividly colored *yamato-e* (Japanese style) paintings of court life and stories about temples and shrines became common in the mid- and late Heian periods, setting patterns for Japanese art to this day (see Art, ch. 3).

As culture flourished, so did decentralization. Whereas the first phase of *shōen* development in the early Heian period had seen the opening of new lands and the commending of lands to aristocrats and religious institutions, during the second phase patrimonial "house governments," as in the old clan system, arose. (In fact, the form of the old clan system had remained largely intact within the great old centralized government.) New institutions were now needed in the face of social, economic, and political changes. The Taihō Code lapsed, its institutions relegated to ceremonial functions. Family administrations now became public institutions. As the most powerful family, the Fujiwara governed Japan and determined the general affairs of state, such as succession to the throne. Family and state affairs were thoroughly intermixed, a pattern followed among other families, monasteries, and even the imperial family. Land management became the primary occupation of the aristocracy, not so much because direct control by the imperial family or central government had declined but more from strong family solidarity and a lack of a sense of Japan as a single nation.

The Rise of the Military Class

Under the early courts, when military conscription had been centrally controlled, military affairs had been taken out of the hands of the provincial aristocracy. But as the system broke down after 792, local power holders again became the primary source of military strength. *Shōen* holders had access to manpower and, as they obtained improved military technology (such as new training methods, more powerful bows, armor, horses, and superior swords) and faced worsening local conditions in the ninth century, military service became part of *shōen* life. Not only the *shōen,* but also civil and religious institutions formed private guard units to protect themselves. Gradually, the provincial upper class was transformed into a new military elite based on the ideals of the *bushi*

15

(warrior) or samurai (literally, "one who serves"; see The Bushidō Code, ch. 8).

Bushi interests were diverse, cutting across old power structures to form new associations in the tenth century. Mutual interests, family connections, and kinship were consolidated in military groups that became part of family administration. In time, large regional military families formed around members of the court aristocracy who had become prominent provincial figures. These military families gained prestige from connections to the imperial court and court-granted military titles and access to manpower. The Fujiwara, Taira, and Minamoto were among the most prominent families supported by the new military class.

Decline in food production, growth of the population, and competition for resources among the great families all led to the gradual decline of Fujiwara power and gave rise to military disturbances in the mid-tenth and eleventh centuries. Members of the Fujiwara, Taira, and Minamoto families—all of whom had descended from the imperial family—attacked one another, claimed control over vast tracts of conquered land, set up rival regimes, and generally broke the peace of the Land of the Rising Sun.

The Fujiwara controlled the throne until the reign of Emperor Go-Sanjō (1068-73), the first emperor not born of a Fujiwara mother since the ninth century. Go-Sanjō, determined to restore imperial control through strong personal rule, implemented reforms to curb Fujiwara influence. He also established an office to compile and validate estate records with the aim of reasserting central control. Many *shōen* were not properly certified, and large landholders, like the Fujiwara, felt threatened with the loss of their lands. Go-Sanjō also established the Inchō, or Office of the Cloistered Emperor, which was held by a succession of emperors who abdicated to devote themselves to behind-the-scenes governance, or *insei* (cloistered government).

The Inchō filled the void left by the decline of Fujiwara power. Rather than being banished, the Fujiwara were mostly retained in their old positions of civil dictator and minister of the center while being bypassed in decision making. In time, many of the Fujiwara were replaced, mostly by members of the rising Minamoto family. While the Fujiwara fell into disputes among themselves and formed northern and southern factions, the *insei* system allowed the paternal line of the imperial family to gain influence over the throne. The period from 1086 to 1156 was the age of supremacy of the Inchō and of the rise of the military class throughout the country. Military might rather than civil authority dominated the government.

A struggle for succession in the mid-twelfth century gave the Fujiwara an opportunity to regain their former power. Fujiwara Yorinaga sided with the retired emperor in a violent battle in 1158 against the heir apparent, who was supported by the Taira and Minamoto. In the end, the Fujiwara were destroyed, the old system of government supplanted, and the *insei* system left powerless as *bushi* took control of court affairs, marking a turning point in Japanese history. Within a year, the Taira and Minamoto clashed and a twenty-year period of Taira ascendancy began. The Taira were seduced by court life and ignored problems in the provinces. Finally, Minamoto Yoritomo (1147–99) rose from his headquarters at Kamakura (in the Kantō region, southwest of modern Tokyo) to defeat the Taira, and with them the child emperor they controlled, in the Genpei War (1180–85).

Kamakura and Muromachi Periods, 1185–1573

The Bakufu and the Hōjō Regency

The Kamakura period (1185–1333) marks the transition to the Japanese "medieval" era, a nearly 700-year period in which the emperor, the court, and the traditional central government were left intact, but were largely relegated to ceremonial functions. Civil, military, and judicial matters were controlled by the *bushi* class, the most powerful of whom was the de facto national ruler. The term *feudalism* is generally used to describe this period, being accepted by scholars as applicable to medieval Japan as well as medieval Europe. Both had land-based economies, vestiges of a previously centralized state, and a concentration of advanced military technologies in the hands of a specialized fighting class. Lords required the loyal services of vassals, who were rewarded with fiefs of their own. The fief holders exercised local military rule and public power related to the holding of land. This period in Japan differed from the old *shōen* system in its pervasive military emphasis.

Once Minamoto Yoritomo had consolidated his power, he established a new government at his family home in Kamakura. He called his government a *bakufu* (tent government), but because he was given the title *seii taishōgun* by the emperor, it is often referred to in Western literature as the shogunate. Yoritomo followed the Fujiwara form of house government and had an administrative board, a board of retainers, and a board of inquiry. After confiscating Taira estates in central and western Japan, he had the imperial court appoint stewards for the estates and constables for the provinces. As shogun, Yoritomo was both the steward and the constable-general. The Kamakura *bakufu* was not a national regime, however, and although it controlled large tracts of land, there was strong resistance to the stewards. The regime continued warfare against the Fujiwara in the north, but never brought either the north or the west under complete military control. The old court resided in Kyōto, continuing to hold the land over which it had jurisdiction, while newly organized military families were attracted to Kamakura.

Despite a strong beginning, Yoritomo failed to consolidate the leadership of his family on a lasting basis. Intrafamily contention had long existed within the Minamoto, although Yoritomo had eliminated most serious challengers to his authority. When he died suddenly in 1199, his son Yoriie became shogun and nominal head of the Minamoto, but Yoriie was unable to control the other eastern *bushi* families. By the early thirteenth century, a regency had been established for the shogun by his maternal grandparents—members of the Hōjō family, a branch of the Taira that had allied itself with the Minamoto in 1180. Under the Hōjō, the *bakufu* became powerless, and the shogun, often a member of the Fujiwara family or even an imperial prince, was merely a figurehead.

With the protector of the emperor a figurehead himself, strains emerged between Kyōto and Kamakura, and in 1221 a war—the Jōkyū Incident—broke out between the cloistered emperor and the Hōjō regent. The Hōjō forces easily won the war, and the imperial court was brought under direct *bakufu* control. The shogun's constables gained greater civil powers, and the court was obliged to seek Kamakura's approval for all of its actions. Although deprived of political power, the court was allowed to retain extensive estates with which to sustain the imperial splendor the *bakufu* needed to help sanction its rule.

Several significant administrative achievements were made during the Hōjō regency. In 1225 the Council of State was established, providing opportunities for other military lords to exercise judicial and legislative authority at Kamakura. The Hōjō regent presided over the council, which was a successful form of collective leadership. The adoption of Japan's first military code of law—the Jōei Code—in 1232 reflected the profound transition from court to militarized society. While legal practices in Kyōto were still based on 500-year-old Confucian principles, the Jōei Code was a highly legalistic document that stressed the duties of stewards and constables, provided means for settling land disputes, and established rules governing inheritances. It was clear and concise, stipulated punishments for violators of its conditions, and remained in effect for the next 635 years.

Burning of the Sanjō Palace, detail from illustration from
Heike monogatari *(Tale of Heike), thirteenth century*
Courtesy Museum of Fine Arts, Boston

As might be expected, the literature of the time reflected the unsettled nature of the period. The *Hōjōki* (An Account of My Hut)
describes the turmoil of the period in terms of the Buddhist concepts of impermanance and the vanity of human projects. The *Heike
monogatari* (Tale of the Heike) narrated the rise and fall of the Taira
(also known as the Heike), replete with tales of wars and samurai
deeds. A second literary mainstream was the continuation of
anthologies of poetry in the *Shin kokinshū wakashū* (New Collection
of Ancient and Modern Times), of which twenty volumes were
produced between 1201 and 1205.

The Flourishing of Buddhism

In the time of disunity and violence, deepening pessimism increased the appeal of the search for salvation. Kamakura was the
age of the great popularization of Buddhism with two new sects,
Jōdō (Pure Land) and Zen (Meditation), dominating the period.
The old Heian sects had been quite esoteric and more appealing
to intellectuals than to the masses. The Mount Hiei monasteries
had become politically powerful but appealed primarily to those
capable of systematic study of the sect's teachings. This situation
gave rise to the Jōdō sect, based on unconditional faith and devotion

and prayer to Amida Buddha. Zen rejected all temporal and scriptural authority, stressing moral character rather than intellectual attainments, an emphasis that appealed to the military class. Zen masters, regarded as embodiments of truth, were turned to by growing numbers of the military class.

Mongol Invasions

The repulsions of two Mongol invasions were momentous events in Japanese history. Japanese relations with China had been terminated in the mid-ninth century after the deterioration of late Tang China and the turning inward of the Heian court. Some commercial contacts were maintained with southern China in later centuries, but Japanese pirates made the open seas dangerous. At a time when the *bakufu* had little interest in foreign affairs and ignored communications from China and Koryŏ (as Korea was then known), news arrived in 1268 of a new Mongol regime in Beijing. Its leader, Khubilai Khan, demanded that the Japanese pay tribute to the new Yuan Dynasty (1279–1368) and threatened reprisals if they failed to do so. Unused to such threats, Kyōto raised the diplomatic counter of Japan's divine origin, rejected the Mongol demands, dismissed the Korean messengers, and started defensive preparations. After further unsuccessful entreaties, the first Mongol invasion took place in 1274. More than 600 ships carried a combined Mongol, Chinese, and Korean force of 23,000 troops armed with catapults, combustible missiles, and bows and arrows. In fighting, these soldiers grouped in close cavalry formations against samurai accustomed to one-on-one combat. Local Japanese forces at Hakata, on northern Kyūshū, defended against the superior mainland force, which, after one day of fighting was decimated by the onslaught of a sudden typhoon. Khubilai realized that nature, not military incompetence, had been the cause of his forces' failure so, in 1281, he launched a second invasion. Seven weeks of fighting took place in northwestern Kyūshū before another typhoon struck, again destroying the Mongol fleet.

Although Shinto priests attributed the two defeats of the Mongols to a "divine wind" (kamikaze), a sign of heaven's special protection of Japan, the invasion left a deep impression on the *bakufu* leaders. Long-standing fears of the Chinese threat to Japan were reinforced, and the Korean Peninsula became regarded as "an arrow pointed at the heart of Japan." The Japanese victory, however, gave the *bushi* a sense of fighting superiority that remained with Japan's soldiers until 1945. The victory also convinced the *bushi* of the value of the *bakufu* form of government.

The Mongol war had been a drain on the economy, and new taxes had to be levied to maintain defensive preparations for the future. The invasions also caused disaffection among those who expected recompense for their help in defeating the Mongols. There were no lands or other rewards to be given, however, and such disaffection, combined with overextension and the increasing defense costs, led to a decline of the Kamakura *bakufu*. Additionally, inheritances had divided family properties, and landowners increasingly had to turn to moneylenders for support. Roving bands of *rōnin* further threatened the stability of the *bakufu*.

Civil War

The Hōjō reacted to the ensuing chaos by trying to place more power among the various great family clans. To further weaken the Kyōto court, the *bakufu* decided to allow two contending imperial lines—known as the Southern Court or junior line and the Northern Court or senior line—to alternate on the throne. The method worked for several successions until a member of the Southern Court ascended to the throne as Emperor Go-Daigo (1318–39). Go-Daigo wanted to overthrow the *bakufu* and openly defied Kamakura by naming his own son his heir. In 1331 the *bakufu* exiled Go-Daigo, but loyalist forces rebelled. They were aided by Ashikaga Takauji (1305–58), a constable who turned against Kamakura when dispatched to put down Go-Daigo's rebellion. At the same time, another eastern chieftain rebelled against the *bakufu*, which quickly disintegrated, and the Hōjō were defeated.

In the swell of victory, Go-Daigo endeavored to restore imperial authority and tenth-century Confucian practices. This period of reform, known as the Kemmu Restoration (1333–36), aimed at strengthening the position of the emperor and reasserting the primacy of the court nobles over the *bushi*. The reality, however, was that the forces who had arisen against Kamakura had been set on defeating the Hōjō, not on supporting the emperor. Ashikaga Takauji finally sided with the Northern Court in a civil war against the Southern Court represented by Go-Daigo. The long War Between the Courts lasted from 1336 to 1392. Early in the conflict, Go-Daigo was driven from Kyōto, and the Northern Court contender was installed by Ashikaga, who became the new shogun.

Ashikaga Bakufu

The ensuing period of Ashikaga rule (1336–1573) was called Muromachi for the district in which its headquarters were in Kyōto after 1378. What distinguished the Ashikaga *bakufu* from that of Kamakura was that, whereas Kamakura had existed in equilibrium with the Kyōto court, Ashikaga took over the remnants of the imperial government. Nevertheless, the Ashikaga *bakufu* was not as strong as the Kamakura had been and was greatly preoccupied by the civil war. Not until the rule of Ashikaga Yoshimitsu (as third shogun, 1368–94, and chancellor, 1394–1408) did a semblance of order emerge.

Yoshimitsu allowed the constables, who had had limited powers during the Kamakura period, to become strong regional rulers, later called *daimyō* (from *dai*, great, and *myōden*, named lands). In time a balance of power evolved between the shogun and the *daimyō;* the three most prominent *daimyō* families rotated as deputies to the shogun at Kyōto. Yoshimitsu was finally successful in reunifying the Northern and Southern courts in 1392, but, despite his promise of greater balance between the imperial lines, the Northern line maintained control over the throne thereafter. The line of shoguns gradually weakened after Yoshimitsu and increasingly lost power to the *daimyō* and other regional strongmen. The shogun's decisions about imperial succession became meaningless, and the *daimyō* backed their own candidates. In time, the Ashikaga family had its own succession problems, resulting finally in the Ōnin War (1467–77), which left Kyōto devastated and effectively ended the national authority of the *bakufu*. The power vacuum that ensued launched a century of anarchy (see Provincial Wars and Foreign Contacts, this ch.).

Economic and Cultural Developments

Contact with Ming Dynasty (1368–1644) China was renewed during the Muromachi period after the Chinese sought support in suppressing Japanese pirates, or *wakō,* who controlled the seas and pillaged coastal areas of China. Wanting to improve relations with China and to rid Japan of the *wakō* threat, Yoshimitsu accepted a relationship with the Chinese that was to last for half a century. Japanese wood, sulfur, copper ore, swords, and folding fans were traded for Chinese silk, porcelain, books, and coins in what the Chinese considered tribute but the Japanese saw as profitable trade.

During the time of the Ashikaga *bakufu,* a new national culture, called Muromachi culture, emerged from the *bakufu* headquarters in Kyōto to reach all levels of society. Zen Buddhism played a large role in spreading not only religious but also artistic influences, especially those derived from Chinese painting of the Chinese Song (960–1279), Yuan, and Ming dynasties. The proximity of the imperial court and the *bakufu* resulted in a comingling of imperial family members, courtiers, *daimyō,* samurai, and Zen priests. Art of all kinds, architecture, literature, Nō drama, comedy, poetry, the tea ceremony, landscape gardening, and flower arranging, all flourished during Muromachi times.

There also was renewed interest in Shinto, which had quietly coexisted with Buddhism during the centuries of the latter's predominance. In fact, Shinto, which lacked its own scriptures and had few prayers, as a result of syncretic practices begun in the Nara period had widely adopted Shingon Buddhist rituals and, between the eighth and fourteenth centuries, was nearly totally absorbed by Buddhism and became known as Ryōbu Shinto (Dual Shinto). The Mongol invasions in the late thirteenth century, however, had evoked a national consciousness of the role of the kamikaze in defeating the enemy. Less than fifty years later (1339–43), Kitabatake Chikafusa (1293–1354), the chief commander of the Southern Court forces, wrote the *Jinnō shōtō ki* (Chronicle of the Direct Descent of the Divine Sovereigns). This chronicle emphasized the importance of maintaining the divine descent of the imperial line from Amaterasu to the current emperor, a condition that gave Japan a special national polity (*kokutai*). Besides reenforcing the concept of the emperor as a deity, the *Jinnō shōtō ki* provided a Shinto view of history, which stressed the divine nature of all Japanese and the country's spiritual supremacy over China and India. As a result, a change gradually occurred in the balance between the dual Buddhist-Shinto religious practice. Between the fourteenth and seventeenth centuries, Shinto reemerged as the primary belief system, developed its own philosophy and scripture (based on Confucian and Buddhist canons), and became a powerful nationalistic force.

Provincial Wars and Foreign Contacts

The Ōnin War led to serious political fragmentation and obliteration of domains: a great struggle for land and power ensued among *bushi* chieftains until the mid-sixteenth century. Peasants rose against their landlords and samurai against their overlords as central control virtually ceased. The imperial house was left impoverished, and the *bakufu* was controlled by contending chieftains in Kyōto. The provincial domains that emerged after the Ōnin War were smaller and easier to control. Many new small *daimyō* arose from among the samurai who had overthrown their great overlords. Border defenses were improved and well-fortified castle towns began to be built to protect the newly opened domains, for which land surveys were made, roads built, and mines opened. New house laws provided practical means of administration, stressing duties and rules of behavior. Emphasis was put on success in war, estate management, and finance. Threatening alliances were guarded against through strict marriage rules. Aristocratic society was overwhelmingly military in character, the rest of society controlled in a system of vassalage. The *shōen* were obliterated, and court nobles and absentee landlords were dispossessed. The new *daimyō* directly controlled the land, keeping the peasantry in permanent serfdom in exchange for protection.

Most wars of the period were short and localized, though they occurred throughout Japan. By 1500 the entire country was engulfed in civil wars. Rather than disrupting the local economies, however, the frequent movement of armies stimulated the growth of transportation and communications, which in turn provided additional revenues from customs and tolls. To avoid such fees, commerce shifted to the central region, which no *daimyō* had been able to control, and to the Inland Sea. Economic developments and the desire to protect trade achievements brought about the establishment of merchant and artisan guilds.

By the end of the Muromachi period, the first Europeans had arrived. The Portuguese landed in southern Kyōshū in 1543 and within two years were making regular port calls. The Spanish arrived in 1587, followed by the Dutch in 1609. The Japanese began to attempt studies of European civilization in depth, and new opportunities were presented for the economy along with serious political challenges. European firearms, fabrics, glassware, clocks, tobacco, and other Western innovations were traded for Japanese gold and silver. Wealth was accumulated on a major scale through trade, and lesser *daimyō,* especially in Kyūshū, greatly increased their power. Provincial wars were made more deadly with the introduction of firearms, such as muskets and cannons, and greater use of infantry.

Christianity had an impact on Japan, largely through the efforts of the Jesuits, led first by Saint Francis Xavier (1506–52), who arrived in Kagoshima in southern Kyūshū in 1549. Both *daimyō* and merchants seeking better trade arrangements as well as peasants were among the converts. By 1560 Kyōto had become another major area of missionary activity in Japan. In 1568 the port of Nagasaki was established by a Christian *daimyō,* and turned over to Jesuit administration in 1579. By 1582 there were as many as 150,000 converts (2 percent of the population) and 200 churches. But *bakufu* tolerance for this alien influence diminished as the country became more unified and the openness of the period decreased. Proscriptions against Christianity began in 1587 and outright persecutions in 1597. Although foreign trade was still encouraged, it was closely regulated, and by 1640 the exclusion and suppression of Christianity had become national policy (see Tokugawa Period, 1600–1867, this ch.; Religious and Philosophical Traditions, ch. 2).

Reunification, 1573–1600

Between 1560 and 1600, powerful military leaders arose to defeat the warring *daimyō* and unify Japan. Three major figures dominated the period in succession: Oda Nobunaga (1534–82), Toyotomi Hideyoshi (1536–98), and Tokugawa Ieyasu (1542–1616), each of whom emerged as a major overlord with large military forces under his command. As their power increased, they looked to the imperial court in Kyōto for sanction. In 1568 Nobunaga, who had defeated another overlord's attempt to attack Kyōto in 1560, marched on the capital, gained the support of the emperor, and installed his own candidate in the succession struggle for shogun. Backed by military force, Nobunaga was able to control the *bakufu*.

Initial resistance to Nobunaga in the Kyōto region came from the Buddhist monks, rival *daimyō*, and hostile merchants. Surrounded by his enemies, Nobunaga struck first at the secular power of the militant Tendai Buddhists, destroying their monastic center at Mount Hiei near Kyōto and killing thousands of monks in 1571. By 1573 he had defeated the local *daimyō*, banished the last Ashikaga shogun, and ushered in what historians call the Azuchi-Momoyama period (1573–1600), named after the castles of Nobunaga and Hideyoshi. Having taken these major steps toward reunification, Nobunaga then built a seven-story castle surrounded by stone walls at Azuchi on the shore of Lake Biwa. The castle was able to withstand firearms and became a symbol of the age of reunification. Nobunaga's power increased as he enfeoffed the conquered *daimyō*, broke down the barriers to free commerce, and drew the humbled religious communities and merchants into his military structure. He secured control of about one-third of the provinces through the use of large-scale warfare and he institutionalized administrative practices, such as systematic village organization, tax collection, and standardized measurements. At the same time, other *daimyō*, both those Nobunaga had conquered and those beyond his control, built their own heavily fortified castles and modernized their garrisons. In 1577 Nobunaga dispatched his chief general, Hideyoshi, to conquer twelve western Honshū provinces. The war was a protracted affair, and in 1582, when Nobunaga led an army to assist Hideyoshi, he was assassinated.

After destroying the forces responsible for Nobunaga's death, Hideyoshi was rewarded with a joint guardianship of Nobunaga's heir, who was a minor. By 1584 Hideyoshi had eliminated the three other guardians, taken complete control of Kyōto, and become the undisputed successor of his late overlord. A commoner by birth and without a surname, Hideyoshi was adopted by the Fujiwara family, given the surname Toyotomi, and granted the title *kanpaku,* representing civil and military control of all Japan. By the following year, he had secured alliances with three of the nine major *daimyō* coalitions and continued the war of reunification in Shikoku and northern Kyūshū. In 1590, with an army of 200,000 troops, Hideyoshi defeated his last formidable rival, who controlled the Kantō region of eastern Honshū. The remaining contending *daimyō* capitulated, and the military reunification of Japan was complete.

All of Japan was controlled by the dictatorial Hideyoshi either directly or through his sworn vassals, and a new national government structure had evolved: a country unified under one *daimyō* alliance but still decentralized. The basis of the power structure was again the distribution of territory. A new unit of land measurement and assessment—the *koku*—was instituted. One *koku* was equivalent to about 180 liters of rice; *daimyō* were by definition those who held lands capable of producing 10,000 *koku* or more of rice. Hideyoshi personally controlled 2 million of the 18.5 million *koku* total national assessment (taken in 1598). Tokugawa Ieyasu, a powerful central Honshū *daimyō* (not completely under Hideyoshi's control), held 2.5 million *koku.*

Despite Hideyoshi's tremendous strength and the fear in which he was held, his position was far from secure. He attempted to rearrange the *daimyō* holdings to his advantage, for example, reassigning the Tokugawa family to the conquered Kantō region and surrounding their new territory with more trusted vassals. He also adopted a hostage system for *daimyō* wives and heirs at his castle town at Ōsaka and used marriage alliances to enforce feudal bonds. He imposed the *koku* system and land surveys to reassess the entire nation. In 1590 Hideyoshi declared an end to any further class mobility or change in social status, reinforcing the class distinctions between cultivators and *bushi* (only the latter could bear arms). He provided for an orderly succession in 1591 by taking the title *taikō,* or retired *kanpaku,* turning the regency over to his son Hideyori. Only toward the end of his life did Hideyoshi try to formalize the balance of power by establishing the five-member Board of Regents (one of them Ieyasu), sworn to keep peace and support the Toyotomi, the five-member Board of House Administrators for routine policy and administrative matters, and the three-member Board of Mediators, who were charged with keeping peace between the first two boards.

Momoyama art (1573–1615), named after the hill on which Hideyoshi built his castle at Fushima, south of Kyōto, flourished during this period. It was a period of interest in the outside world, the development of large urban centers, and the rise of the merchant and leisure classes. Ornate castle architecture and interiors adorned with painted screens embellished with gold leaf reflected *daimyō* power and wealth of the period. Depictions of the "southern barbarians"—Europeans—were exotic and popular.

In 1577 Hideyoshi had seized Nagasaki, Japan's major point of contact with the outside world. He took control of the various trade associations and tried to regulate all overseas activities. Although China rebuffed his efforts to secure trade concessions, Hideyoshi succeeded in sending commercial missions to the Philippines, Malaya, and Siam (present-day Thailand). He was suspicious of Christianity, however, as potentially subversive to *daimyō* loyalties and he had some missionaries crucified.

Hideyoshi's major ambition was to conquer China, and in 1592, with an army of 200,000 troops, he invaded Korea, then a Chinese vassal state. His armies quickly overran the peninsula before losing momentum in the face of a combined Korean-Chinese force. During peace talks Hideyoshi demanded a division of Korea, free-trade status, and a Chinese princess as consort for the emperor. The equality with China sought by Japan was rebuffed by the Chinese and peace efforts ended. In 1597 a second invasion was begun, but it abruptly ended with Hideyoshi's death in 1598.

Tokugawa Period, 1600–1867
Rule of Shogun and Daimyō

An evolution had taken place in the centuries from the time of the Kamakura *bakufu,* which existed in equilibrium with the imperial court, to the Tokugawa, when the *bushi* became the unchallenged rulers in what historian Edwin O. Reischauer has called a "centralized feudal" form of government. Instrumental in the rise of the new *bakufu* was Tokugawa Ieyasu, the main beneficiary of the achievements of Nobunaga and Hideyoshi. Already powerful, Ieyasu profited by his transfer to the rich Kantō area. He maintained 2.5 million *koku* of land, had a new headquarters at Edo, a strategically situated castle town (the future Tokyo), and had an additional 2 million *koku* of land and thirty-eight vassals under his control. After Hideyoshi's death, Ieyasu moved quickly to seize control from the Toyotomi family.

Ieyasu's victory over the western *daimyō* at the Battle of Sekigahara (1600) gave him virtual control of all Japan. He rapidly abolished numerous enemy *daimyō* houses, reduced others, such as that of the Toyotomi, and redistributed the spoils of war to his family and allies. Ieyasu still failed to achieve complete control of the western *daimyō*, but his assumption of the title of shogun helped consolidate the alliance system. After further strengthening his power base, Ieyasu was confident enough to install his son Hidetada (1579–1632) as shogun and himself as retired shogun in 1605. The Toyotomi were still a significant threat, and Ieyasu devoted the next decade to their eradication. In 1615 the Toyotomi stronghold at Ōsaka was destroyed by the Tokugawa army.

The Tokugawa (or Edo) period brought 200 years of stability to Japan. The political system evolved into what historians call *bakuhan*, a combination of the terms *bakufu* and *han* (domains) to describe the government and society of the period. In the *bakuhan*, the shogun had national authority and the *daimyō* had regional authority, a new unity in the feudal structure, which had an increasingly large bureaucracy to administer the mixture of centralized and decentralized authorities. The Tokugawa became more powerful during their first century of rule: land redistribution gave them nearly 7 million *koku*, control of the most important cities, and a land assessment system reaping great revenues.

The feudal hierarchy was completed by the various classes of *daimyō*. Closest to the Tokugawa house were the *shinpan* or "related houses." They were twenty-three *daimyō* on the borders of Tokugawa lands, *daimyō* all directly related to Ieyasu. The *shinpan* held mostly honorary titles and advisory posts in the *bakufu*. The second class of the hierarchy were the *fudai*, or "house *daimyō*," rewarded with lands close to the Tokugawa holdings for their faithful service. By the eighteenth century, 145 *fudai* controlled such smaller *han*, the greatest assessed at 250,000 *koku*. Members of the *fudai* class staffed most of the major *bakufu* offices. Ninety-seven *han* formed the third group, the *tozama* (outside vassals), former opponents or new allies. The *tozama* were located mostly on the peripheries of the archipelago and collectively controlled nearly 10 million *koku* of productive land. Because the *tozama* were least trusted of the *daimyō*, they were the most cautiously managed and generously treated, although they were excluded from central government positions.

The Tokugawa not only consolidated their control over a reunified Japan, they also had unprecedented power over the emperor, the court, all *daimyō*, and the religious orders. The emperor was held up as the ultimate source of political sanction for the shogun, who ostensibly was the vassal of the imperial family. The Tokugawa helped the imperial family recapture its old glory by rebuilding its palaces and granting it new lands. To ensure a close tie between

The six-story Himeji Castle, built in 1601–9, considered one of the grandest of the surviving castles, Hyōgo Prefecture
Courtesy Eliot Frankeberger

the imperial clan and the Tokugawa family, Ieyasu's granddaughter was made an imperial consort in 1619.

A code of laws was established to regulate the *daimyō* houses. The code encompassed private conduct, marriage, dress, and types of weapons and numbers of troops allowed; required alternate-year residence at Edo; prohibited the construction of ocean-going ships; proscribed Christianity; and stipulated that *bakufu* regulations were the national law. Although the *daimyō* were not taxed per se, they were regularly levied for contributions for military and logistical support and such public works projects as castles, roads, bridges, and palaces. The various regulations and levies not only strengthened the Tokugawa but depleted the wealth of the *daimyō*, thus weakening their threat to the central administration. The *han*, once military-centered domains, became mere local administrative units. The *daimyō* did have full administrative control over their territory and complex systems of retainers, bureaucrats, and commoners. Loyalty was exacted from religious foundations, already greatly weakened by Nobunaga and Hideyoshi, through a variety of control mechanisms.

Seclusion and Social Control

Like Hideyoshi, Ieyasu encouraged foreign trade but also was

29

suspicious of outsiders. He wanted to make Edo a major port, but once he learned that the Europeans favored ports in Kyūshū and that China had rejected his plans for official trade, he moved to control existing trade and allowed only certain ports to handle specific kinds of commodities.

The "Christian problem" was, in effect, a problem in controlling both the Christian *daimyō* in Kyūshū and trade with the Europeans. By 1612 the shogun's retainers and residents of Tokugawa lands had been ordered to foreswear Christianity. More restrictions came in 1616 (the restriction of foreign trade to Nagasaki and Hirado, an island northwest of Kyūshū), 1622 (the execution of 120 missionaries and converts), 1624 (the expulsion of the Spanish), and 1629 (the execution of thousands of Christians). Finally, in 1635, an edict prohibited any Japanese from traveling outside Japan or, if someone left, from ever returning. In 1636 the Portuguese were restricted to Deshima, a man-made islet—and thus, not true Japanese soil—in Nagasaki's harbor.

The Shimabara Rebellion of 1637–38, in which discontented Christian samurai and peasants rebelled against the *bakufu*—and Edo called in Dutch ships to bombard the rebel stronghold—marked the end of the Christian movement. Soon thereafter the Portuguese were permanently expelled, members of the Portuguese diplomatic mission were executed, all subjects were ordered to register at a Buddhist or Shinto temple, and the Dutch and Chinese were restricted respectively to Deshima and a special quarter in Nagasaki. Besides small trade of some outer *daimyō* with Korea and the Ryūkyū Islands, to the southwest of Japan's main islands, by 1641 foreign contacts were limited to Nagasaki.

Japanese society of the Tokugawa period was influenced by Confucian principles of social order. At the top of the hierarchy, but removed from political power, were the imperial court families at Kyōto. The real political power holders were the samurai followed by the rest of society, in descending hierarchical order: farmers, who were organized into villages, artisans, and merchants. Urban dwellers, often well-to-do merchants, were known as *chōnin* (townspeople) and confined to special districts. The individual had no legal rights in Tokugawa Japan. The family was the smallest legal entity, and the maintenance of family status and privileges was of great importance at all levels of society.

Economic Development

Economic development during the Tokugawa period included urbanization, more shipping of commodities, a significant expansion of domestic and, initially, foreign commerce, and a diffusion of trade and handicraft industries. Edo had a population of more than 1 million and Ōsaka and Kyōto each had more than 400,000 inhabitants by the mid-eighteenth century. Many other castle towns grew as well. Ōsaka and Kyōto became busy trading and handicraft production centers while Edo was the center for the supply of food and essential urban consumer goods. The construction trades flourished along with banking facilities and merchant associations. Increasingly, *han* authorities oversaw the rising agricultural production and the spread of rural handicrafts.

Intellectual Trends

The flourishing of neo-Confucianism was the major intellectual development of the Tokugawa period. Confucian studies had long been kept active in Japan by Buddhist clerics, but during the Tokugawa period, Confucianism emerged from Buddhist religious control. This system of thought increased attention to a secular view of man and society. The ethical humanism, rationalism, and historical perspective of neo-Confucian doctrine appealed to the official class, and by the mid-seventeenth century, it was Japan's dominant legal philosophy and contributed directly to the development of the *kokugaku* (national learning) school of thought.

Advanced studies and growing applications of neo-Confucianism contributed to the transition of the social and political order from feudal norms to class-and large-group-oriented practices. The rule of the people or Confucian man was gradually replaced by the rule of laws. New laws were developed and new administrative devices were instituted. A new theory of government and a new vision of society emerged as a means of justifying more comprehensive governance by the *bakufu*. Each person had a distinct place in society and was expected to work to fulfill his mission in life. The people were to be ruled with benevolence by those whose assigned duty it was to rule. Government was all-powerful but responsible and humane. Although the class system was influenced by neo-Confucianism, it was not identical to it. Whereas soldiers and clergy were at the bottom of the hierarchy in the Chinese model, in Japan some members of these classes constituted the ruling elite.

Members of the samurai class adhered to *bushi* traditions with a renewed interest in Japanese history and cultivating the ways of Confucian scholar-administrators, resulting in the development of the concept of *bushidō* (the way of the warrior—see Glossary). Another special way of life—*chōnindō*—also emerged. *Chōnindō* (the way of the townspeople) was a distinct culture that arose in cities such as Ōsaka, Kyōto, and Edo. It encouraged aspiration to *bushidō* qualities—diligence, honesty, honor, loyalty, and frugality—while blending Shinto, neo-Confucian, and Buddhist beliefs. Study of mathematics, astronomy, cartography, engineering, and medicine were also encouraged. Emphasis was placed on quality of workmanship, especially in the arts. For the first time, urban populations had the means and leisure time to support a new mass culture. Their search for enjoyment became known as *ukiyo* (the floating world), an ideal world of fashion and popular entertainment. Professional female entertainers (geisha), music, popular stories, Kabuki and *bunraku* (puppet) theater, poetry, a rich literature, and art, exemplified by beautiful woodblock prints (known as *ukiyo-e*), were all part of this flowering culture (see Visual Arts, ch. 3). Literature also flourished with the talented examples of the playwright Chikamatsu Monzaemon (1653–1724) and the poet, essayist, and travel writer Matsuo Bashō (1644–94).

Buddhism and Shinto were both still important in Tokugawa Japan. Buddhism, combined with neo-Confucianism, provided standards of social behavior. Although not as powerful politically as it had been in the past, Buddhism was espoused by the upper classes. Proscriptions against Christianity benefited Buddhism in 1640 when the *bakufu* ordered everyone to register at a temple. The rigid separation of Tokugawa society into *han,* villages, wards, and households helped reaffirm local Shinto attachments. Shinto provided spiritual support to the political order and was an important tie between the individual and his community. Shinto also helped preserve a sense of national identity.

Shinto eventually assumed an intellectual form as shaped by neo-Confucian rationalism and materialism. The *kokugaku* movement emerged from the interactions of these two belief systems. *Kokugaku* contributed to the emperor-centered nationalism of modern Japan and the revival of Shinto as a national creed in the eighteenth and nineteenth centuries. The *Kojiki, Nihongi,* and *Man'yōshū* were all studied anew in the search for the Japanese spirit. Some purists in the *kokugaku* movement even criticized the Confucian and Buddhist influences—in effect, foreign ones—for contaminating Japan's ancient ways. Japan was the land of the *kami* and, as such, had a special destiny.

Knowledge of the West during the early Tokugawa was restricted to a tiny school of thought known as Rangaku (Dutch Learning). Its adherents were mostly in Nagasaki, where the Dutch outpost was located on Deshima Island.

Decline of the Tokugawa

The Tokugawa did not eventually collapse simply because of intrinsic failures. Foreign intrusions helped to precipitate a complex political struggle between the *bakufu* and a coalition of its critics. The continuity of the anti-*bakufu* movement in the mid-nineteenth century would finally bring down the Tokugawa. From the outset, the Tokugawa attempted to restrict families' accumulation of wealth and fostered a "back to the soil" policy, in which the farmer, the ultimate producer, was the ideal person in society. Despite these efforts to restrict wealth, and partly because of the extraordinary period of peace, the standard of living for urban and rural dwellers alike grew significantly during the Tokugawa period. Better means of crop production, transportation, housing, food, and entertainment were all available, as was more leisure time, at least for urban dwellers. The literacy rate was high for a preindustrial society, and cultural values were redefined and widely imparted throughout the samurai and *chōnin* classes. Despite the reappearance of guilds, economic activities went well beyond the restrictive nature of the guilds, and commerce spread and a money economy developed. Although government heavily restricted the merchants and viewed them as unproductive and usurious members of society, the samurai, who gradually became separated from their rural ties, depended greatly on the merchants and artisans for consumer goods, artistic interests, and loans. In this way, a subtle subversion of the warrior class by the *chōnin* took place.

A struggle arose in the face of political limitations that the shogun imposed on the entrepreneurial class. The government ideal of an agrarian society failed to square with the reality of commercial distribution. A huge government bureaucracy had evolved, which now stagnated because of its discrepancy with a new and evolving social order. Compounding the situation, the population increased significantly during the first half of the Tokugawa period. Although the magnitude and growth rates are uncertain, there were at least 26 million commoners and about 4 million members of samurai families and their attendants when the first nationwide census was taken in 1721. Drought, followed by crop shortages and starvation, resulted in twenty great famines between 1675 and 1837. Peasant unrest grew, and by the late eighteenth century, mass protests over taxes and food shortages had become commonplace. Newly landless families became tenant farmers while the displaced rural poor moved into the cities. As the fortunes of previously well-to-do families declined, others moved in to accumulate land, and a new, wealthy farming class emerged. Those people who benefited were able to diversify production and to hire laborers, while others were left discontented. Many samurai fell on hard times and were forced into handicraft production and wage jobs for merchants.

Western intrusions were on the increase in early nineteenth century. Russian warships and traders encroached on Karafuto (today the Soviet island of Sakhalin) and the Kuril Islands, the southernmost of which are considered by the Japanese as the northern islands of Hokkaidō. A British warship entered Nagasaki Harbor searching for enemy Dutch ships in 1808, and other warships and whalers were seen in Japanese waters with increasing frequency in the 1810s and 1820s. Whalers and trading ships from the United States also arrived on Japan's shores. Although the Japanese made some minor concessions and allowed some landings, they largely attempted to keep all foreigners out, sometimes using force. Rangaku became crucial not only in understanding the foreign "barbarians" but in using the knowledge gained from the West to fend them off.

By the 1830s, there was a general sense of crisis. Famines and natural disasters hit hard, and unrest led to a peasant uprising against officials and merchants in Ōsaka in 1837. Although it lasted only a day, the uprising made a dramatic impression. Remedies came in the form of traditional solutions that sought to reform moral decay rather than institutional problems. The shogun's advisers pushed for a return to the martial spirit, more restrictions on foreign trade and contacts, suppression of Rangaku, censorship of literature, and elimination of "luxury" in the government and samurai class. Others sought the overthrow of the Tokugawa and espoused the political doctrine of *sonnō-jōi* (revere the emperor, expel the barbarians), which called for unity under imperial rule and opposed foreign intrusions. The *bakufu* persevered for the time being amidst growing concerns over Western successes in establishing colonial enclaves in China following the Opium War of 1839–42. More reforms were ordered, especially in the economic sector, to strengthen Japan against the Western threat.

Japan turned down a demand from the United States, which was greatly expanding its own presence in the Asia-Pacific region, to establish diplomatic relations when Commodore James Biddle appeared in Edo Bay with two warships in July 1846. However, when Commodore Matthew C. Perry's four-ship squadron appeared in Edo Bay in July 1853, the *bakufu* was thrown into turmoil. The chairman of the senior councillors, Abe Masahiro (1819–57), was responsible for dealing with the Americans. Having no precedent to manage this threat to national security, Abe tried to balance the desires of the senior councillors to compromise with the foreigners, of the emperor who wanted to keep the foreigners out, and of the *daimyō* who wanted to go to war. Lacking consensus, Abe decided to compromise by accepting Perry's demands for opening Japan to foreign trade while also making military preparations. In March 1854, the Treaty of Peace and Amity (or Treaty of Kanagawa) opened two ports to American ships seeking provisions, guaranteed good treatment to shipwrecked American sailors, and allowed a United States consul to take up residence in Shimoda, a seaport on the Izu Peninsula, southwest of Edo. A commercial treaty, opening still more areas to American trade, was forced on the *bakufu* five years later.

The resulting damage to the *bakufu* was significant. Debate over government policy was unusual and had engendered public criticism of the *bakufu*. In the hope of enlisting the support of new allies, Abe, to the consternation of the *fudai*, had consulted with the *shinpan* and *tozama daimyō*, further undermining the already weakened *bakufu*. In the Ansei Reform (1854–56), Abe then tried to strengthen the regime by ordering Dutch warships and armaments from the Netherlands and building new port defenses. In 1855 a naval training school with Dutch instructors was set up at Nagasaki, and a Western-style military school was established at Edo; by the next year, the government was translating Western books. Opposition to Abe increased within *fudai* circles, which opposed opening *bakufu* councils to *tozama daimyō*, and he was replaced in 1855 as chairman of the senior councillors by Hotta Masayoshi (1810–64).

At the head of the dissident faction was Tokugawa Nariaki, who had long embraced a militant loyalty to the emperor along with antiforeign sentiments, and who had been put in charge of national defense in 1854. The Mito school—based on neo-Confucian and Shinto principles—had as its goal the restoration of the imperial institution, the turning back of the West, and the founding of a world empire under the divine Yamato Dynasty.

In the final years of the Tokugawa, foreign contacts increased as more concessions were granted. The new treaty with the United States in 1859 allowed more ports to be opened to diplomatic representatives, unsupervised trade at four additional ports, and foreign residences in Ōsaka and Edo. It also embodied the concept of extraterritoriality (foreigners were subject to the laws of their own countries but not to Japanese law). Hotta lost the support of key *daimyō*, and when Tokugawa Nariaki opposed the new treaty, Hotta sought imperial sanction. The court officials, perceiving the weakness of the *bakufu*, rejected Hotta's request and thus suddenly embroiled Kyōto and the emperor in Japan's internal politics for the first time in many centuries. When the shogun died without an heir, Nariaki appealed to the court for support of his own son, Tokugawa Yoshinobu (or Keiki), for shogun, a candidate favored by the *shinpan* and *tozama daimyō*. The *fudai* won the power struggle, however, installing Tokugawa Yoshitomi, arresting Nariaki and Keiki, executing Yoshida Shōin (1830–59, a leading *sonnō-jōi* intellectual who had opposed the American treaty and plotted a revolution against the *bakufu*), and signing treaties with the United States and five other nations, thus ending more than 200 years of exclusion.

The strong measures the *bakufu* took to reassert its dominance were not enough. Revering the emperor as a symbol of unity, extremists wrought violence and death against the *bakufu* and *han* authorities and foreigners. Foreign naval retaliation led to still another concessionary commercial treaty in 1865, but Yoshitomi was unable to enforce the Western treaties. A *bakufu* army was defeated when it was sent to crush dissent in Satsuma and Chōshū *han* in 1866. Finally, in 1867, the emperor died and was succeeded by his minor son Mutsuhito; Keiki reluctantly became head of the Tokugawa house and shogun. He tried to reorganize the government under the emperor while preserving the shogun's leadership role. Fearing the growing power of the Satsuma and Chōshū *daimyō*, other *daimyō* called for returning the shogun's political power to the emperor and a council of *daimyō* chaired by the former Tokugawa shogun. Keiki accepted the plan in late 1867 and resigned, announcing an ''imperial restoration.'' The Satsuma, Chōshū, and other *han* leaders and radical courtiers, however, rebelled, seized the imperial palace, and announced their own restoration on January 3, 1868. The *bakufu* was abolished, Keiki was reduced to the ranks of the common *daimyō*, and the Tokugawa army gave up without a fight (although other Tokugawa forces fought until November 1868, and *bakufu* naval forces continued to hold out for another six months).

The Emergence of Modern Japan, 1868–1919

The Meiji Restoration

Those people who wanted to end Tokugawa rule did not envision a new government or a new society; they merely sought the transfer of power from Edo to Kyōto while retaining all their feudal prerogatives. Instead, a profound change took place. The emperor emerged as a national symbol of unity in the midst of reforms that were much more radical than had been envisioned.

The first reform was the promulgation of the Charter Oath in 1868, a general statement of the aims of the Meiji leaders to boost morale and win financial support for the new government. Its five provisions were the establishment of deliberative assemblies, the involvement of all classes in carrying out state affairs, freedom of social and occupational mobility, replacement of "evil customs" with the "just laws of nature," and an international search for knowledge to strengthen the foundations of imperial rule. Implicit in the Charter Oath was an end to exclusive political rule by the *bakufu* and a move toward more democratic participation in government. To implement the Charter Oath, an eleven-article constitution was drawn up. Besides providing for a new Council of State, legislative bodies, and systems of ranks for nobles and officials, it limited office tenure to four years, allowed public balloting, provided for a new taxation system, and ordered new local administrative rules.

The Meiji government assured the foreign powers that it would abide by the old treaties negotiated by the *bakufu* and announced that it would act in accordance with international law. Mutsuhito, who was to reign until 1912, selected a new reign title—Meiji, or Enlightened Rule—to mark the beginning of a new era in Japanese history. To further dramatize the new order, the capital was relocated from Kyōto, where it had been situated since 794, to Tokyo (Eastern Capital), the new name for Edo. In a move critical for the consolidation of the new regime, most *daimyō* voluntarily surrendered their land and census records to the emperor, symbolizing that the land and people were under the emperor's jurisdiction. Confirmed in their hereditary positions, the *daimyō* became governors, and the central government assumed their administrative expenses and paid samurai stipends. The *han* were replaced with prefectures in 1871, and authority continued to flow to the national government. Officials from the favored former *han,* such as Satsuma, Chōshū, Tosa, and Hizen, staffed the new ministries. Formerly out-of-favor court nobles and lower-ranking but more radical samurai replaced *bakufu* appointees, *daimyō,* and old court nobles as a new ruling class appeared.

Inasmuch as the Meiji Restoration had sought to return the emperor to a preeminent position, efforts were made to establish a Shinto-oriented state much like the state of 1,000 years earlier. An Office of Shinto Worship was established, ranking even above the Council of State in importance. The *kokutai* ideas of the Mito school were embraced, and the divine ancestry of the imperial house emphasized. The government supported Shinto teachers, a small but important move. Although the Office of Shinto Worship was demoted in 1872, by 1877 the Home Ministry controlled all Shinto shrines and certain Shinto sects were given state recognition. Shinto was at last released from Buddhist administration and its properties restored. Although Buddhism suffered from state sponsorship of Shinto, it had its own resurgence. Christianity was also legalized and Confucianism remained an important ethical doctrine. Increasingly, however, Japanese thinkers identified with Western ideology and methods.

The Meiji oligarchy, as the new ruling class is known to historians, was a privileged clique that exercised imperial power, sometimes despotically. The members of this class were adherents to *kokugaku* and believed they were the creators of a new order as grand as that established by Japan's original founders. Two of the major figures of this group were Ōkubo Toshimichi (1832–78), son of a Satsuma retainer, and Satsuma samurai Saigō Takamori (1827–77), who had joined forces with Chōshū, Tosa, and Hizen to overthrow the Tokugawa. Ōkubo became minister of finance and Saigō a field marshal; both were imperial councillors. Kido Kōin (1833–77), native of Chōshū, student of Yoshida Shōin, and coconspirator with Ōkubo and Saigō, became minister of education and chairman of the Governors' Conference and pushed for constitutional government. Also prominent were Iwakura Tomomi (1825–83), a Kyōto native who had opposed the Tokugawa and was to become the first ambassador to the United States, and Ōkuma Shigenobu (1838–1922), of Hizen, a student of Rangaku, Chinese, and English, who held various ministerial portfolios, eventually becoming prime minister in 1898.

To accomplish the new order's goals, the Meiji oligarchy set out to abolish the Tokugawa class system through a series of economic and social reforms. *Bakufu* revenues had depended on taxes on Tokugawa and other *daimyō* lands, loans from wealthy peasants and urban merchants, limited customs fees, and reluctantly accepted foreign loans. To provide revenue and develop a sound infrastructure, the new government financed harbor improvements, lighthouses, machinery imports, schools, overseas study for students, salaries for foreign teachers and advisers, modernization of the army and navy, railroads and telegraph networks, and foreign diplomatic missions.

Difficult economic times, manifested by increasing incidents of agrarian rioting, led to calls for social reforms. Besides the old high rents, taxes, and interest rates, the average citizen was faced with cash payments for new taxes, military conscription, and tuition charges for compulsory education. The people needed more time for productive pursuits while correcting social abuses of the past. To achieve these reforms, the old Tokugawa class system of samurai, farmer, artisan, and merchant was abolished by 1871, and, even though old prejudices and status consciousness continued, all were theoretically equal before the law. Actually helping

Emperor Meiji and Empress Haruko in Western garb, a sign of the reform taken under his rule (1868–1912)
Courtesy Prints and Photographs Division, Library of Congress

to perpetuate social distinctions, the government named new social divisions: the former *daimyō* became nobility, the samurai became gentry, and all others became commoners. *Daimyō* and samurai pensions were paid off in lump sums, and the samurai later lost their exclusive claim to military positions. Former samurai found new pursuits as bureaucrats, teachers, army officers, police officials, journalists, scholars, colonists in the northern parts of Japan, bankers, and businessmen. These occupations helped stem some of the discontent this large group felt; some profited immensely, but many were not successful and provided significant opposition in the ensuing years (see Opposition to the Meiji Oligarchy, this ch.).

Additionally, between 1871 and 1873, a series of land and tax laws were enacted as the basis for modern fiscal policy. Private ownership was legalized, deeds were issued, and lands were assessed at a fair market value with taxes paid in cash rather than in kind as in pre-Meiji days and at slightly lower rates.

Undeterred by opposition, the Meiji leaders continued to modernize the nation through government-sponsored telegraph cable links to all major Japanese cities and the Asian mainland, and the construction of railroads, shipyards, munitions factories, mines, textile manufacturing facilities, factories, and experimental agriculture stations. Much concerned about national security, the leaders made significant efforts at military modernization, which included establishing a small standing army and a large reserve system, and compulsory militia service for all men (see Militarism Before 1945, ch. 8). Foreign military systems were studied, foreign advisers brought in, and Japanese cadets sent abroad to European and United States military and naval schools.

Foreign Relations

The Meiji leaders also modernized foreign policy, an important step in making Japan a full member of the international community. The traditional East Asia world view was based not on an international society of national units but on cultural distinctions and tributary relationships; monks, scholars, and artists, rather than professional diplomatic envoys, had generally served as the conveyors of foreign policy. Foreign relations were related more to the sovereign's desires than to the public interest. For Japan to emerge from the feudal period, it had to avoid the fate of other Asian countries by establishing genuine national independence and equality. The Meiji oligarchy was aware of Western progress, and ''learning missions'' were sent abroad to absorb as much of it as possible. One such mission, led by Iwakura, Kido, and Ōkubo, and containing forty-eight members in total, spent two years (1871–73) touring the United States and Europe, studying government institutions, courts, prison systems, schools, the import-export business, factories, shipyards, glass plants, mines, and other enterprises. Upon returning, mission members called for domestic reforms that would help Japan catch up with the West. The revision of unequal treaties forced on Japan became a top priority. The returned envoys also sketched a new vision for a modernized Japan's leadership role in Asia, but they realized that this role required that Japan develop its national strength, cultivate nationalism among the population, and carefully craft policies toward potential enemies. No longer could Westerners be seen as ''barbarians,'' for example. In time, Japan formed a corps of professional diplomats.

Although he never assumed a government post, another influential Meiji period figure was Fukuzawa Yukichi (1835–1901). He was a prolific writer on many subjects, the founder of schools and a newspaper, and, above all, an educator bent on impressing his fellow Japanese with the merits of Westernization.

Japan was shortly to test its new world outlook. Disputes with China over sovereignty of the Ryūkyū Islands, with Russia over sovereignty of the Kuril Islands and Sakhalin, and with Korea over the Korean court's refusal to recognize the new Meiji government and its envoys were all settled diplomatically between 1874 and 1876. Military threats had been made in the Chinese and Korean affairs, and it seemed to many that Japan would soon use military means to achieve its goals.

Opposition to the Meiji Oligarchy

The 1873 Korean crisis resulted in the resignation of military-expedition proponents Saigō and Councillor of State Etō Shimpei (1834–74). Etō, the founder of various patriotic organizations, conspired with other discontented elements to start an armed insurrection against government troops in Saga, the capital of his native prefecture in Kyūshū in 1874. Charged with suppressing the revolt, Ōkubo swiftly crushed Etō, who had appealed unsuccessfully to Saigō for help. Three years later, the last major armed uprising—but most serious challenge to the Meiji government—took shape in the Satsuma Rebellion, this time with Saigō playing an active role. The Saga Rebellion and other agrarian and samurai uprisings mounted in protest to the Meiji reforms had been easily put down by the army. Satsuma's former samurai were numerous, however, and they had a long tradition of opposition to central authority. Saigō, with some reluctance and only after more widespread dissatisfaction with the Meiji reforms, raised a rebellion in 1877. Both sides fought well, but the modern weaponry and better financing of the government forces ended the Satsuma Rebellion. Although he was defeated and committed suicide, Saigō was not branded a traitor and became a heroic figure in Japanese history. The suppression of the Satsuma Rebellion marked the end of serious threats to the Meiji regime but was sobering to the oligarchy. The fight drained the national treasury, led to serious inflation, and forced land values—and badly needed taxes—down. Most importantly, calls for reform were renewed.

The Development of Representative Government

The major institutional accomplishment after the Satsuma Rebellion was the start of the trend toward developing representative government. People who had been forced out or left out of the governing apparatus after the Meiji Restoration had witnessed or heard of the success of representative institutions in other countries of the world and applied greater pressure for a voice in government.

A major proponent of representative government was Itagaki Taisuke (1837–1919), a powerful leader of Tosa forces who had resigned from his Council of State position over the Korean affair in 1873. Itagaki sought peaceful rather than rebellious means to gain a voice in government. He started a school and a movement aimed at establishing a constitutional monarchy and a legislative assembly. Itagaki and others wrote the Tosa Memorial in 1874 criticizing the unbridled power of the oligarchy and calling for the immediate establishment of representative government. Dissatisfied with the pace of reform after having rejoined the Council of State in 1875, Itagaki organized his followers and other democratic proponents into the nationwide Aikokusha (Society of Patriots) to push for representative government in 1878. In 1881, in an action for which he is best known, Itagaki helped found the Jiyūtō (Liberal Party), which favored French political doctrines. In 1882 Ōkuma established the Rikken Kaishintō (Constitutional Progressive Party), which called for a British-style constitutional democracy. In response, government bureaucrats, local government officials, and other conservatives established the Rikken Teiseitō (Imperial Rule Party), a progovernment party, in 1882. Numerous political demonstrations followed, some of them violent, resulting in further government restrictions. The restrictions hindered the political parties and led to divisiveness within and among them. The Jiyūtō, which had opposed the Kaishintō, was disbanded in 1884, and Ōkuma resigned as Kaishintō president.

Government leaders, long preoccupied with violent threats to stability and the serious leadership split over the Korean affair, generally agreed that constitutional government should someday be established. Kido had favored a constitutional form of government since before 1874, and several proposals that provided for constitutional guarantees had been drafted. The oligarchy, however, while acknowledging the realities of political pressure, was determined to keep control. Thus, modest steps were taken. The Ōsaka Conference in 1875 resulted in the reorganization of government with an independent judiciary and an appointed Council of Elders (Genrōnin) tasked with reviewing proposals for a legislature. The emperor declared that "constitutional government shall be established in gradual stages" as he ordered the Council of Elders to draft a constitution. Three years later, the Conference of Prefectural Governors established elected prefectural assemblies. Although limited in their authority, these assemblies represented a move in the direction of representative government at the national level, and by 1880 assemblies also had been formed in villages and towns. In 1880 delegates from twenty-four prefectures held a national convention to establish the Kokkai Kisei Dōmei (League for Establishing a National Assembly).

Although the government was not opposed to parliamentary rule, confronted with the drive for "people's rights," it continued to try to control the political situation. New laws in 1875 prohibited press criticism of the government or discussion of national laws. The Public Assembly Law (1880) severely limited public gatherings by disallowing attendance by civil servants and requiring police permission for all meetings. Within the ruling circle, however, and despite the conservative approach of the leadership, Ōkuma continued as a lone advocate of British-style government, a government with political parties and a cabinet organized by the majority party, answerable to the national assembly. He called for elections to be held by 1882 and for a national assembly to be convoked by 1883; in doing so, he precipitated a political crisis that ended with an 1881 imperial rescript declaring the establishment of a national assembly in 1890 and dismissing Ōkuma.

Rejecting the British model, Iwakura and other conservatives borrowed heavily from the Prussian constitutional system. One of the Meiji oligarchy, Itō Hirobumi (1841–1909), a Chōshū native long involved in government affairs, was charged with drafting Japan's constitution. He led a Constitutional Study Mission abroad in 1882, spending most of his time in Germany. He rejected the United States Constitution as "too liberal" and the British system as too unwieldy and having a parliament with too much control over the monarchy; the French and Spanish models were rejected as tending toward despotism.

On Itō's return, one of the first acts of the government was to establish new ranks for the nobility. Five hundred persons from the old court nobility, former *daimyō*, and samurai who had provided valuable service to the emperor were organized in five ranks: prince, marquis, count, viscount, and baron. Itō was put in charge of the new Bureau for Investigation of Constitutional Systems in 1884, and the Council of State was replaced in 1885 with a cabinet headed by Itō as prime minister. The positions of chancellor, minister of the left, and minister of the right, which had existed since the seventh century as advisory positions to the emperor, were all abolished. In their place, the Privy Council was established in 1888, to evaluate the forthcoming constitution and to advise the emperor. To further strengthen the authority of the state, the Supreme War Council was established under the leadership of Yamagata Aritomo (1838–1922), a Chōshū native who has been credited with the founding of the modern Japanese army and was to become the first constitutional prime minister. The Supreme War Council developed a German-style general staff system with a chief of staff who had direct access to the emperor and could operate independently of the army minister and civilian officials.

When finally granted by the emperor as a sign of his sharing his authority and giving rights and liberties to his subjects, the 1889 Constitution of the Empire of Japan (the Meiji Constitution) provided for the Imperial Diet (Teikoku Gikai), composed of a popularly elected House of Representatives with a very limited franchise of male citizens who paid ¥15 (for value of the yen—see Glossary) in national taxes, about 1 percent of the population; the House of Peers, composed of nobility and imperial appointees; and a cabinet responsible to the emperor and independent of the legislature. The Diet could approve government legislation and initiate laws, make representations to the government, and submit petitions to the emperor. Nevertheless, in spite of these institutional changes, sovereignty still resided in the emperor on the basis of his divine ancestry. The new constitution specified a form of government that was still authoritarian in character, with the emperor holding the ultimate power and only minimal concessions made to popular rights and parliamentary mechanisms. Party participation was recognized as part of the political process. The Meiji Constitution was to last as the fundamental law until 1947.

The first national election was held in 1890 and 300 members were elected to the House of Representatives. The Jiyūtō and Kaishintō parties had been revived in anticipation of the election and together won over half of the seats. The House of Representatives soon became the arena for disputes between the politicians and the government bureaucracy over large issues, such as the budget, the ambiguity of the constitution on the Diet's authority, and the desire of the Diet to interpret the "will of the emperor" versus the oligarchy's position that the cabinet and administration should "transcend" all conflicting political forces. The main leverage the Diet had was in its approval or disapproval of the budget, and it successfully wielded its authority henceforth.

In the early years of constitutional government, the strengths and weaknesses of the Meiji Constitution were revealed. A small clique of Satsuma and Chōshū elite continued to rule Japan, becoming institutionalized as an extraconstitutional body of *genrō* (elder statesmen). Collectively, the *genrō* made decisions reserved for the emperor, and the *genrō,* not the emperor, controlled the government politically. Throughout the period, however, political problems were usually solved through compromise, and political parties gradually increased their power over the government and held an ever larger role in the political process as a result.

*Itō Hirobumi, major statesman
of the Meiji era
Courtesy Prints and Photographs
Division, Library of Congress*

Between 1891 and 1895, Itō served as prime minister with a cabinet composed mostly of *genrō* who wanted to establish a government party to control the House of Representatives. Although not fully realized, the trend toward party politics was well established.

Modernization and Industrialization

Japan emerged from the Tokugawa-Meiji transition as the first Asian industrialized nation. Domestic commercial activities and limited foreign trade had met the demands for material culture in the Tokugawa period, but the modernized Meiji era had radically different requirements. From the onset, the Meiji rulers embraced the concept of a market economy and adopted British and North American forms of free enterprise capitalism. The private sector—in a nation blessed with an abundance of aggressive entrepeneurs— welcomed such change.

Economic reforms included a unified modern currency based on the yen, banking, commercial and tax laws, stock exchanges, and a communications network. Establishment of a modern institutional framework conducive to an advanced capitalist economy took time, but was completed by the 1890s. By this time, the government had largely relinquished direct control of the modernization process, primarily for budgetary reasons. Many of the former *daimyō*, whose pensions had been paid in a lump sum, benefited greatly through investments they made in emerging industries, while

45

those who had been informally involved in foreign trade before the Meiji Restoration also flourished. Old *bakufu*-serving firms that clung to their traditional ways failed in the new business environment.

The government was initially involved in economic modernization, providing a number of "model factories" to facilitate the transition to the modern period. After the first twenty years of the Meiji period, the industrial economy expanded rapidly through to about 1920 with inputs of advanced Western technology and large private investments. Stimulated by wars and through cautious economic planning, Japan emerged from World War I as a major industrial nation.

Overseas Expansion

Historically, Japan's main foreign preoccupation has been China. The Korean Peninsula, a strategically located feature critical to the defense of the Japanese archipelago, greatly occupied Japan's attention in the nineteenth century. Earlier tension over Korea had been settled temporarily through the Treaty of Kanghwa in 1876, which opened Korean ports to Japan, and in 1885 the Tianjin Convention had provided for the removal from Korea of both Chinese and Japanese troops sent to support contending factions in the Korean court. In effect, the convention had made Korea a co-protectorate of Beijing and Tokyo at a time when Russian, British, and United States interests in the peninsula also were on the increase. A crisis was precipitated in 1894 when a leading pro-Japanese Korean political figure was assassinated in Shanghai with Chinese complicity. Prowar elements in Japan called for a punitive expedition, which the cabinet resisted. With assistance from several Japanese nationalistic societies, the illegal Tonghak (Eastern Learning) nationalistic religious movement in Korea staged a rebellion that was crushed by Chinese troops. Japan responded with force and quickly defeated China in the First Sino-Japanese War (1894–95). After nine months of fighting, a cease-fire was called and peace talks were held. The victor's demands were such that a Japanese protectorate over China seemed in the offing, but an assassination attempt on Li Hongzhang, China's envoy to the peace talks, embarrassed Japan, which then quickly agreed to an armistice. The Treaty of Shimonoseki recognized Korean independence; the end of Korean tribute to China; a 200-million-tael (Chinese ounces of silver, the equivalent in 1895 of US$150 million) indemnity; the ceding of Taiwan, the Penghu Islands, and the Liaodong Peninsula (the southern part of Manchuria) to Japan; and the opening of Chang Jiang (Yangtze River) ports to Japanese trade. It also assured Japanese rights to engage in industrial enterprises in China.

Having their own imperialist designs on China and fearing its impending disintegration, Russia, Germany, and France jointly objected to Japanese control of Liaodong. Threatened with a tripartite naval maneuver in Korean waters, Japan decided to give back Liaodong in return for a larger indemnity from China. Russia moved to fill the void by securing from China a twenty-five-year lease of Dalian (Dairen in Japanese, also known as Port Arthur) and rights to the South Manchurian Railway Company, a semiofficial Japanese company, to construct a railroad. St. Petersburg also wanted to lease more Manchurian territory, and, although Japan was loath to confront Russia over this issue, it did move to use Korea as a bargaining point: Japan would recognize Russian leaseholds in southern Manchuria if Russia would leave Korean affairs to Japan. The Russians only agreed not to impede the work of Japanese advisers in Korea, but Japan was able to use diplomatic initiatives to keep St. Petersburg from leasing Korean territory in 1899. At the same time, Japan was able to wrest a concession from China that the coastal areas of Fujian Province, across the strait from Taiwan, were within Japan's sphere of influence and could not be leased to other powers. In 1900 Japanese forces participated in suppressing the Boxer Uprising, exacting still more indemnity from China.

Japan then succeeded in attracting a Western ally to its cause. Japan and Britain, both of whom wanted to keep Russia out of Manchuria, signed a Treaty of Alliance in 1902, which was in effect until 1921, when the two signed the Four Power Treaty on Insular Possessions, which took effect in 1923. The British recognized Japanese interests in Korea and assured Japan they would remain neutral in case of a Russo-Japanese war but would become more actively involved if another power (probably an allusion to France) entered the war as a Russian ally. In the face of this joint threat, Russia became more conciliatory toward Japan and agreed to withdraw its troops from Manchuria in 1903. The new balance of power in Korea favored Japan and allowed Britain to concentrate its interests elsewhere in Asia. Hence, Tokyo moved to gain influence over Korean banks, opened its own financial institutions in Korea, and began constructing railroads and obstructing Russian and French undertakings on the peninsula.

When Russia failed to withdraw its troops from Manchuria by an appointed date, Tokyo issued a protest. St. Petersburg replied that it would agree to a partition of Korea at the thirty-ninth parallel, with a Japanese sphere to the south and a neutral zone to the north.

But Manchuria was to be outside Japan's sphere, and Russia would not guarantee the evacuation of its troops. Despite the urging of caution by most *genrō*, Japan's hardliners issued an ultimatum to Russia, which showed no signs of further compromise. War broke out in February 1904 with Japanese surprise attacks on Russian warships at Dalian and Chemulpo (in Korea, now called Inch'ŏn). Despite tremendous loss of life on both sides, the Japanese won a series of land battles and then decisively defeated Russia's Baltic Sea Fleet (renamed the Second Pacific Squadron) at the Battle of Tsushima in May 1905. At an American-mediated peace conference in Portsmouth, New Hampshire, Russia acknowledged Japan's paramount interests in Korea and agreed to avoid "military measures" in Manchuria and Korea. Both sides agreed to evacuate Manchuria, except for the Guandong Territory, a leasehold on the Liaodong Peninsula, and restore the occupied areas to China. Russia transferred its lease on Dalian and adjacent territories and railroads to Japan, ceded the southern half of Sakhalin to Japan, and granted Japan fishing rights in the Sea of Okhotsk and the Bering Sea.

Japanese nationalism intensified after the Russo-Japanese War and a new phase of continental expansion began after 1905. Politically and economically, Korea became a protectorate of Japan and in 1910 was formally annexed as a part of the empire. By means of the South Manchurian Railway, Japanese entrepreneurs vigorously exploited Manchuria. By 1907 Russia had entered into a treaty arrangement with Japan whereby both sides recognized the other's sphere of influence in Manchuria.

Political Rivalries

After the bitter political rivalries between the inception of the Diet and 1894, when the nation was unified for the war effort against China, there followed five years of unity, unusual cooperation, and coalition cabinets. From 1900 to 1912, the Diet and the cabinet cooperated even more directly, with political parties playing larger roles. Throughout the entire period, the old Meiji oligarchy retained ultimate control, but steadily yielded power to the opposition parties. The major figures of the period were Yamagata Aritomo, whose long tenure (1868–1922) as a military and civil leader, including two terms as prime minister, was characterized by his intimidation of rivals and resistance to democratic procedures; and Itō, who was a compromiser and, although overruled by the *genrō*, wanted to establish a government party to control the House during his first term. When Itō returned to the prime ministership in 1898, he again pushed for a government party, but when Yamagata and others refused, Itō resigned. With no willing successor among the *genrō*, the Kenseitō (Constitutional Party) was invited to form a cabinet under the leadership of Ōkuma and Itagaki, a major achievement in the opposition parties' competition with the *genrō*. This success was short-lived: the Kenseitō split into two parties, the Kenseitō led by Itagaki and the Kensei Hontō (Real Constitutional Party) led by Ōkuma, and the cabinet ended after only four months. Yamagata then returned as prime minister with the backing of the military and the bureaucracy. Despite broad support of his views on limiting constitutional government, Yamagata formed an alliance with Kenseitō. Reforms of electoral laws, an expansion of the House to 369 members, and provisions for secret ballots won Diet support for Yamagata's budgets and tax increases. He continued to use imperial ordinances, however, to keep the parties from fully participating in the bureaucracy and to strengthen the already independent position of the military. When Yamagata failed to offer more compromises to the Kenseitō, the alliance ended in 1900, beginning a new phase of political development.

Itō and a protégé, Saionji Kimmochi (1849–1940), finally succeeded in forming a progovernment party—the Seiyūkai (Association of Friends of Constitutional Government)—in September 1900, and a month later Itō became prime minister of the first Seiyūkai cabinet. The Seiyūkai held the majority of seats in the House, but Yamagata's conservative allies had the greatest influence in the House of Peers, forcing Itō to seek imperial intervention. Tiring of political infighting, Itō resigned in 1901. Thereafter, the prime ministership alternated between Yamagata's protégé, Katsura Tarō (1847–1913; prime minister 1901–5 and 1908–11), and Saionji (prime minister 1905–8 and 1911–12). The alternating of political power was an indication of the two sides' ability to cooperate and share power and helped foster the continued development of party politics.

The Meiji era ended with the death of the emperor in 1912 and the accession of Crown Prince Yoshihito as emperor of the Taishō period (Great Righteousness, 1912–26). The end of the Meiji era was marked by huge government domestic and overseas investments and defense programs, nearly exhausted credit, and a lack of foreign exchange to pay debts. The beginnning of the Taishō era was marked by a political crisis that interrupted the earlier politics of compromise. When Saionji tried to cut the military budget, the army minister resigned, bringing down the Seiyūkai cabinet. Both Yamagata and Saionji refused to resume office and the *genrō* were unable to find a solution. Public outrage over the military manipulation of the cabinet and the recall of Katsura for a third term led to still more demands for an end to *genrō* politics. Despite old guard opposition, the conservative forces formed a party of their own in 1913, the Rikken Dōshikai (Constitutional Association of Friends), a party that won a majority in the House over the Seiyūkai in late 1914.

World War I

Seizing the opportunity of Berlin's distraction with the European War, and wanting to expand its sphere of influence in China, Japan declared war on Germany in August 1914 and quickly occupied German-leased territories in China's Shandong Province and the Mariana, Caroline, and Marshall islands in the Pacific. With its Western allies heavily involved in the war in Europe, Japan sought further to consolidate its position in China by presenting the Twenty-One Demands to China in January 1915. Besides expanding its control over the German holdings, Manchuria, and Inner Mongolia, Japan also sought joint ownership of a major mining and metallurgical complex in central China, prohibitions on China's ceding or leasing any coastal areas to a third power, and miscellaneous other political, economic, and military controls, which if achieved, would have reduced China to a Japanese protectorate. In the face of slow negotiations with the Chinese government, widespread anti-Japanese sentiments in China, and international condemnation, Japan withdrew the final group of demands, and treaties were signed in May 1915.

Japan's hegemony in northern China and other parts of Asia was facilitated through other international agreements. One with Russia in 1916 helped further secure Japan's influence in Manchuria and Inner Mongolia, and agreements with France, Britain, and the United States in 1917 recognized Japan's territorial gains in China and the Pacific. The Nishihara Loans (named after Nishihara Kamezō, Tokyo's representative in Beijing) of 1917 and 1918, while aiding the Chinese government, put it still deeper into Japan's debt. Toward the end of the war, Japan increasingly filled orders for its European allies' needed war matériel, thus helping to diversify the country's industry, increase its exports, and transform Japan from a debtor to a creditor nation for the first time.

Japan's power in Asia grew with the demise of the tsarist regime in Russia and the disorder the 1917 Bolshevik Revolution left in Siberia. Wanting to seize the opportunity, the Japanese army planned to occupy Siberia as far west as Lake Baykal. To do so, Japan had to negotiate an agreement with China allowing the transit of Japanese troops through Chinese territory. Although the force was scaled back to avoid antagonizing the United States, more than 70,000 Japanese troops joined the much smaller units of the Allied Expeditionary Force sent to Siberia in 1918.

The year 1919 saw Japan sitting among the "Big Five" powers at the Versailles Peace Conference. Tokyo was granted a permanent seat on the Council of the League of Nations, and the peace treaty confirmed the transfer to Japan of Germany's rights in Shandong, a provision that led to anti-Japanese riots and a mass political movement throughout China. Similarly, Germany's former Pacific islands were put under a Japanese mandate. Despite its small role in World War I (and the Western powers' rejection of its bid for a racial equality clause in the peace treaty), Japan emerged as a major actor in international politics at its close.

Between the Wars, 1920–36

Two-Party System

The two-party political system that had been developing in Japan since the turn of the century finally came of age after World War I. This period has sometimes been called that of "Taishō democracy," after the reign title of the emperor. In 1918 Hara Takashi (1856–1921), a protégé of Saionji and a major influence in the prewar Seiyūkai cabinets, had become the first commoner to serve as prime minister. He took advantage of long-standing relationships he had throughout the government, won the support of the surviving *genrō* and the House of Peers, and brought into his cabinet as army minister Tanaka Giichi (1864–1929), who had a greater appreciation of favorable civil-military relations than his predecessors. Nevertheless, major problems confronted Hara: inflation, the need to adjust the Japanese economy to postwar circumstances, the influx of foreign ideas, and an emerging labor movement. Prewar solutions were applied by the cabinet to these postwar problems, and little was done to reform the government. Hara worked to ensure a Seiyūkai majority through time-tested methods, such as new election laws and electoral redistricting, and embarked on major government-funded public works programs.

The public grew disillusioned with the growing national debt and the new election laws, which retained the old minimum tax qualifications for voters. Calls were raised for universal suffrage and the dismantling of the old political party network. Students, university professors, and journalists, bolstered by labor unions and inspired by a variety of democratic, socialist, communist, anarchist, and other Western schools of thought, mounted large but orderly public demonstrations in favor of universal male suffrage in 1919 and 1920. New elections brought still another Seiyūkai majority, but barely so. In the political milieu of the day, there was a proliferation of new parties, including socialist and communist parties.

In the midst of this political ferment, Hara was assassinated by a disenchanted railroad worker in 1921 (see Diplomacy, this ch.). He was followed by a succession of nonparty prime ministers and coalition cabinets. Fear of a broader electorate, left-wing power, and the growing social change engendered by the influx of Western popular culture together led to the passage of the Peace Preservation Law (1925), which forbade any change in the political structure or the abolition of private property.

Unstable coalitions and divisiveness in the Diet led the Kenseikai (Constitutional Government Association) and the Seiyū Hontō (True Seiyūkai) to merge as the Rikken Minseitō (Constitutional Democratic Party) in 1927. The Minseitō platform was committed to the parliamentary system, democratic politics, and world peace. Thereafter, until 1932, the Seiyūkai and the Rikken Minseitō alternated in power.

Despite the political realignments and hope for more orderly government, domestic economic crises plagued whichever party held power. Fiscal austerity programs and appeals for public support of conservative government policies like the Peace Preservation Law—including reminders of the moral obligation to make sacrifices for the emperor and the state—were attempted as solutions. Although the world depression of the late 1920s and early 1930s had minimal effects on Japan—indeed Japanese exports grew substantially during this period—there was a sense of rising discontent that was heightened with the assassination of Minseitō prime minister Hamaguchi Osachi in 1931.

The events flowing from the Meiji Restoration in 1868 had seen not only the fulfillment of many domestic and foreign economic and political objectives—without Japan's first suffering the colonial fate of other Asian nations—but also a new intellectual ferment, in a time when there was interest worldwide in socialism and an urban proletariat was developing. Universal male suffrage, social welfare, workers' rights, and nonviolent protest were ideals of the early leftist movement. Government suppression of leftist activities, however, led to more radical leftist action and even more suppression, resulting in the dissolution of the Japan Socialist Party (Nihon Shakaitō), only a year after its 1906 founding, and in the general failure of the socialist movement.

The victory of the communists in Russia in 1917 and their hopes for a world revolution led to the establishment of the Comintern (a contraction of Communist International, the organization founded in Moscow in 1919 to coordinate the world communist movement). The Comintern realized the importance of Japan in achieving successful revolution in East Asia and actively worked to form the Japan Communist Party (Nihon Kyōsantō), which was founded in July 1922. An end to feudalism, the abolition of the monarchy, withdrawal of Japanese troops from Siberia, Sakhalin, China, Korea, and Taiwan, and recognition of the Soviet Union were the announced goals of the Japan Communist Party in 1923. A brutal suppression of the party followed. Radicals responded with an assassination attempt on Prince Regent Hirohito. The 1925 Peace Preservation Law was a direct response to the "dangerous thoughts" perpetrated by communist elements in Japan.

The liberalization of election laws, also in 1925, benefited communist candidates even though the Japan Communist Party itself was banned. A new Peace Preservation Law in 1928, however, further impeded communist efforts by banning the parties they had infiltrated. The police apparatus of the day was ubiquitous and quite thorough in attempting to control the socialist movement (see The Police System, ch. 8). By 1926 the Japan Communist Party had been forced underground, by the summer of 1929 the party leadership had been virtually destroyed, and by 1933 the party had largely disintegrated.

Diplomacy

Emerging Chinese nationalism, the victory of the communists in Russia, and the growing presence of the United States in East Asia all worked against Japan's postwar foreign policy interests. The four-year Siberian expedition and activities in China, combined with big domestic spending programs, had depleted Japan's wartime earnings. Only through more competitive business practices, supported by further economic development and industrial modernization, all accommodated by the growth of the *zaibatsu* (wealth groups—see Glossary), could Japan hope to become predominant in Asia. The United States, long a source of many imported goods and loans needed for development, was seen as becoming a major impediment to this goal because of its policies of containing Japanese imperialism.

An international turning point in military diplomacy was the Washington Conference of 1921–22, which produced a series of agreements that effected a new order in the Pacific region. Japan's economic problems made a naval buildup nearly impossible and, realizing the need to compete with the United States on an economic rather than a military basis, the Japanese government came to see rapprochement as inevitable. Japan adopted a more neutral attitude toward the civil war in China; joined the United States, Britain, and France in encouraging Chinese self-development; and dropped efforts to expand its hegemony into China proper.

In the Four Power Treaty on Insular Possessions (December 13, 1921), Japan, the United States, Britain, and France agreed to recognize the status quo in the Pacific, and Japan and Britain agreed to terminate formally their Treaty of Alliance. The Five Power Naval Disarmament Treaty (February 6, 1922) established an international capital ship ratio (5, 5, 3, 1.75, and 1.75, respectively, for the United States, Britain, Japan, France, and Italy) and limited the size and armaments of capital ships already built or under construction. In a move that gave the Japanese Imperial Navy greater freedom in the Pacific, Washington and London agreed not to build any new military bases between Singapore and Hawaii.

The goal of the Nine Power Treaty (February 6, 1922), signed by Belgium, China, the Netherlands, and Portugal along with the original five powers, was the prevention of war in the Pacific. The signatories agreed to respect China's independence and integrity, not to interfere in Chinese attempts to establish a stable government, to refrain from seeking special privileges in China or threatening the positions of other nations there, to support a policy of equal opportunity for commerce and industry of all nations in China, and to reexamine extraterritoriality and tariff autonomy policies. Japan also agreed to withdraw its troops from Shandong, relinquishing all but purely economic rights there, and to evacuate its troops from Siberia.

In 1928 Japan joined fourteen other nations in signing the Kellogg-Briand Pact, which denounced "recourse to war for the solution of international controversies." Thus, when Japan invaded Manchuria only three years later, its pretext was the defense of its nationals and economic interests there. The London Naval Conference in 1930 came at the time of an economic recession in Japan, and the Japanese government was amenable to further, cost-saving naval reductions. Although Prime Minister Hamaguchi Osachi (1870–1931) had civilian support, he bypassed the Naval General Staff and approved the signing of the London Naval Treaty. Hamaguchi's success was pyrrhic: ultranationalists called the treaty a national surrender, and navy and army officials girded themselves for defense of their budgets. Hamaguchi himself died from wounds suffered in an assassination attempt in November 1930, and the treaty, with its complex formula for ship tonnage and numbers aimed at restricting the naval arms race, had loopholes that made it ineffective by 1938.

The Rise of the Militarists

Ultranationalism had characterized right-wing politicians and conservative military men since the inception of the Meiji Restoration, contributing greatly to the prowar politics of the 1870s. Disenchanted former samurai had formed patriotic societies and intelligence-gathering organizations, such as the Gen'yōsha (Black Ocean Society, founded in 1881) and its later offshoot, the Kokuryūkai (Black Dragon Society, or Amur River Society, founded in 1901). These groups became active in domestic and foreign politics, helped foment prowar sentiments, and supported ultranationalist causes through the end of World War II. After Japan's victories over China and Russia, the ultranationalists concentrated on domestic issues and perceived domestic threats, such as socialism and communism.

After World War I and the intellectual ferment of the period, nationalist societies became numerous but had a minority voice during the era of two-party democratic politics. Diverse and angry groups called for nationalization of all wealth above a fixed minimal amount and for armed overseas expansion. The emperor was highly revered by these groups, and when Hirohito was enthroned in 1927 initiating the Shōwa period (Bright Harmony, 1926–89), there were calls for a "Shōwa Restoration" and a revival of Shinto. Emperor-centered neo-Shintoism, or State Shinto, which had long been developing, came to fruition in the 1930s and 1940s. It glorified the emperor and traditional Japanese virtues to the exclusion of the Western influences perceived as greedy, individualistic, bourgeois, and assertive. The ideals of the Japanese family-state and self-sacrifice in service of the nation were given a missionary interpretation, being thought by their ultranationalist proponents to be applicable to the modern world.

The 1930s were a decade of fear in Japan, characterized by the resurgence of right-wing patriotism, the weakening of democratic forces, domestic terrorist violence (including an assassination attempt on the emperor in 1932), and stepped-up military aggression abroad. A prelude to this state of affairs was Tanaka Giichi's term as prime minister from 1927 to 1929. Twice he sent troops to China to obstruct Chiang Kai-shek's unification campaign, and, in June 1928, adventurous officers of the Guandong Army, the Imperial Japanese Army unit stationed in Manchuria, embarked on unauthorized initiatives to protect Japanese interests, including the assassination of a former ally, Manchurian warlord Zhang Zuolin. The perpetrators hoped the Chinese would be prompted to take military action, forcing the Guandong Army to retaliate.

The Japanese high command and the Chinese, however, both refused to mobilize. The incident turned out to be a striking example of unchecked terrorism. Even though press censorship kept the Japanese public from knowing about these events, they led to the downfall of Tanaka and set the stage for a similar plot, the Manchurian Incident, in 1931.

A secret society founded by army officers seeking to establish a military dictatorship—the Sakurakai (Cherry Society, the cherry blossom being emblematic of self-sacrifice)—plotted to attack the Diet and political party headquarters, assassinate the prime minister, and declare martial law under a "Shōwa Restoration" government led by the army minister. Although the army cancelled its coup plans (to have been carried out in March 1931), no reprisals were taken and terrorist activity was again tacitly condoned.

The Manchurian Incident of September 1931 did not fail and it set the stage for the eventual military takeover of the Japanese government. Guandong Army conspirators blew up a few meters of South Manchurian Railway Company track near Mukden (now Shenyang), blamed it on Chinese saboteurs, and used the event as an excuse to seize Mukden. One month later, in Tokyo, military figures plotted the October Incident, which was aimed at setting up a national socialist state. The plot failed, but again the news was suppressed and the military perpetrators were not punished. Japanese forces attacked Shanghai in January 1932 on the pretext of Chinese resistance in Manchuria. Finding stiff Chinese resistance in Shanghai, the Japanese waged a three-month undeclared war there before a truce was reached in March 1932. Several days later, Manchukuo was established. Manchukuo was a Japanese puppet state headed by the last Chinese emperor, Puyi, as chief executive and later emperor. The civilian government in Tokyo was powerless to prevent these military happenings. Instead of being condemned, the Guandong Army's actions enjoyed popular support back home. International reactions were extremely negative, however. Japan withdrew from the League of Nations, and the United States became increasingly hostile.

The Japanese system of party government finally met its demise with the May 15th Incident in 1932, when a group of junior naval officers and army cadets assassinated Prime Minister Inukai Tsuyoshi (1855–1932). Although the assassins were put on trial and sentenced to fifteen years' imprisonment, they were seen popularly as having acted out of patriotism. Inukai's successors, military men chosen by Saionji, the last surviving *genrō,* recognized Manchukuo and generally approved the army's actions in securing Manchuria as an industrial base, an area for Japanese emigration, and a staging

Hirohito, the Emperor Shōwa,
124th Japanese sovereign, and
Empress Nagako in full
ceremonial dress, at their 1927
enthronement
Courtesy Prints and Photographs
Division, Library of Congress

ground for war with the Soviet Union. Various army factions contended for power amid increasing suppression of dissent and more assassinations. In the February 26th Incident of 1936, about 1,500 troops went on a rampage of assassination against the current and former prime ministers and other cabinet members, and even Saionji and members of the imperial court. The revolt was put down by other military units and its leaders executed after secret trials. Despite public dismay over these events and the discredit they brought to numerous military figures, Japan's civilian leadership capitulated to the army's demands in the hope of ending domestic violence. Increases were seen in defense budgets, naval construction (Japan announced it would no longer accede to the London Naval Treaty), and patriotic indoctrination as Japan moved toward a wartime footing.

In November 1936, the Anti-Comintern Pact, an agreement to exchange information and collaborate in preventing communist activities, was signed by Japan and Germany (Italy joined a year later). War was launched against China after the Marco Polo Bridge Incident of July 7, 1937, in which an allegedly unplanned clash took place near Beiping (as Beijing was then called) between Chinese and Japanese troops and quickly escalated into full-scale warfare. The Second Sino-Japanese War (1937–45) ensued, and relations with the United States, Britain, and the Soviet Union deteriorated. The increased military activities in China—and Japan's idea of establishing "Mengukuo" in Inner Mongolia and the Mongolian People's Republic—soon led to a major clash over rival Mongolia-Manchukuo border claims. When Japanese troops invaded eastern Mongolia, a major ground and air battle with a joint Soviet-Mongolian army took place between May and September 1939 at the Battle of Halhin Gol. The Japanese were severely defeated, sustaining as many as 80,000 casualties, and thereafter Japan concentrated its war efforts on its southward drive in China and Southeast Asia, a strategy that helped propel Japan ever closer to war with the United States, Britain, and their allies.

Under the prime ministership of Konoe Fumimaro (1891–1945)—the last head of the famous Fujiwara house—the government was streamlined and given absolute power over the nation's assets. In 1940, the 2,600th anniversary of the founding of Japan according to tradition, Konoe's cabinet called for the establishment of a "Greater East Asia Coprosperity Sphere," a concept building on Konoe's 1938 call for a "New Order in Greater East Asia," encompassing Japan, Manchukuo, China, and Southeast Asia. The Greater East Asia Coprosperity Sphere was to integrate Asia politically and economically—under Japanese leadership—against

Western domination. It was developed in recognition of the changing geopolitical situation emerging in 1940, and, eventually, a Greater East Asia Ministry was established (in 1942) and the Greater East Asia Conference was held in Tokyo in 1943. Also in 1940, political parties were ordered to dissolve, and the Imperial Rule Assistance Association, comprising members of all former parties, was established to transmit government orders throughout society. In September 1940, Japan joined the Axis alliance with Germany and Italy when it signed the Tripartite Pact, a military agreement to redivide the world that was directed primarily against the United States.

There had been a long-standing and deep-seated antagonism between Japan and the United States since the first decade of the twentieth century. Each perceived the other as a military threat, and trade rivalry was carried on in earnest. The Japanese greatly resented the racial discrimination perpetuated by United States immigration laws, and the Americans became increasingly wary of Japan's interference in the self-determination of other peoples. Japan's military expansionism and quest for national self-sufficiency eventually led the United States in 1940 to embargo war supplies, abrogate a long-standing commercial treaty, and put greater restrictions on the export of critical commodities. These American tactics, rather than forcing Japan to a standstill, made Japan more desperate. After the signing of the Japanese-Soviet Neutrality Pact in April 1941, and while still actively making war plans against the United States, Japan participated in diplomatic negotiations with Washington aimed at achieving a peaceful settlement. Washington was quite concerned about Japan's role in the Tripartite Pact and demanded the withdrawal of Japanese troops from China and Southeast Asia. Japan countered that it would not use force unless "a country not yet involved in the European war" (that is, the United States) attacked Germany or Italy, and demanded that the United States and Britain not interfere with a Japanese settlement in China (a pro-Japanese puppet government had been set up in Nanjing in 1940). Because certain Japanese military leaders were working at cross-purposes with officials seeking a peaceful settlement (including Konoe, other civilians, and some military figures), talks were deadlocked. On October 15, 1941, army minister Tōjō Hideki (1884–1948) declared the negotiations ended. Konoe resigned, replaced by Tōjō, and after one final United States rejection of Japan's terms of negotiation, on December 1, 1941, the Imperial Conference (an ad hoc meeting convened—and then rarely—in the presence of the emperor) ratified the decision to embark on a war of "self-defense and self-preservation" and to attack the United States naval base at Pearl Harbor.

World War II and the Occupation, 1941–52

After initial battlefield success and a tremendous overextension of its resources in the war (known to Japan as the Greater East Asia War, to the United States as the Pacific War) against a quickly mobilizing United States and Allied war effort, Japan was unable to sustain "Greater East Asia" (see fig. 2). As early as 1943, Konoe led a peace movement, and Tōjō was forced from office in July 1944. His successors sought peace mediation (Sweden and the Soviet Union were approached for help in such a process), but the enemy offered only unconditional surrender. After the detonation of atomic bombs over Hiroshima and Nagasaki on August 6 and 8, 1941, respectively, the emperor asked that the Japanese people bring peace to Japan by "enduring the unendurable and suffering what is insufferable" by surrendering to the Allied powers. The documents of surrender were signed on board the U.S.S. *Missouri* in Tokyo Bay, on September 2, 1945 (see World War II, ch. 8). The terms of surrender included the occupation of Japan by Allied military forces, assurances that Japan would never again go to war, restriction of Japanese sovereignty to the four main islands "and such minor islands as may be determined," and surrender of Japan's colonial holdings.

A period of demilitarization and democratization followed in Japan (1945–47). Under the direction of General Douglas MacArthur, the Supreme Commander for the Allied Powers (SCAP), Japan's army and navy ministries were abolished, munitions and military equipment were destroyed, and war industries were converted to civilian uses. War crimes trials found 4,200 Japanese officials guilty; 700 were executed, and 186,000 other public figures were purged. State Shinto was disestablished, and on January 1, 1946, Emperor Hirohito repudiated his divinity. MacArthur pushed the government to amend the 1889 Meiji Constitution, and on May 3, 1947, the new Japanese Constitution (often called the "MacArthur Constitution") came into force (see The Postwar Constitution, ch. 6). Constitutional reforms were accompanied by economic reforms, including agricultural land redistribution, the reestablishment of trade unions, and severe proscriptions on *zaibatsu* (see Patterns of Development, ch. 4).

Relatively rapid stabilization of Japan led to a relaxation of SCAP purges and press censorship. Quick economic recovery was encouraged, restrictions on former *zaibatsu* members eventually were lifted, and foreign trade was allowed. Finally, fifty-one nations met in San Francisco in September 1951 to reach a peace accord with Japan (formally known as the Treaty of Peace with Japan; China, India, and the Soviet Union participated in the conference but did not sign the treaty). Japan renounced its claims to Korea, Taiwan, Penghu, the Kuril Islands, southern Sakhalin, islands it gained by League of Nations mandate, South China Sea islands, and Antarctic territory, while agreeing to settle disputes peacefully according to the United Nations Charter. Japan's rights to defend itself and to enter into collective security arrangements were acknowledged. The 1952 ratification of the Japan-United States Mutual Security Assistance Pact also ensured a strong defense for Japan and a large postwar role in Asia for the United States (see Relations with the United States, ch. 7; Early Developments, ch. 8).

Toward a New Century, 1953-84

Political parties had begun to revive almost immediately after the occupation began. Left-wing organizations, such as the Japan Socialist Party and the Japan Communist Party quickly reestablished themselves, as did various conservative parties. The old Seiyūkai and Rikken Minseitō came back as, respectively, the Liberal Party (Nihon Jiyūtō) and the Japan Progressive Party (Nihon Shimpotō). The first postwar elections were held in 1946 (women were given the franchise for the first time), and the Liberal Party's vice president, Yoshida Shigeru (1878–1967), became prime minister. For the 1947 elections, anti-Yoshida forces left the Liberal Party and joined forces with the Progressive Party to establish the new Democratic Party (Minshutō). This divisiveness in conservative ranks gave a plurality to the Japan Socialist Party, which was allowed to form a cabinet that lasted less than a year. Thereafter the socialist party steadily declined in its electoral successes. After a short period of Democratic Party administration, Yoshida returned in late 1948 and continued to serve as prime minister until 1954.

Even before Japan regained full sovereignty, the government had rehabilitated nearly 80,000 people who had been purged, many of whom returned to their former political and government positions. A debate over limitations on military spending and the sovereignty of the emperor ensued, contributing to the great reduction in the Liberal Party's majority in the first postoccupation elections (October 1952). After several reorganizations of the armed forces, in 1954 the Self-Defense Forces were established under a civilian director (see The Self-Defense Forces, ch. 8). Cold War realities and the hot war in nearby Korea also contributed significantly to the United States-influenced economic redevelopment,

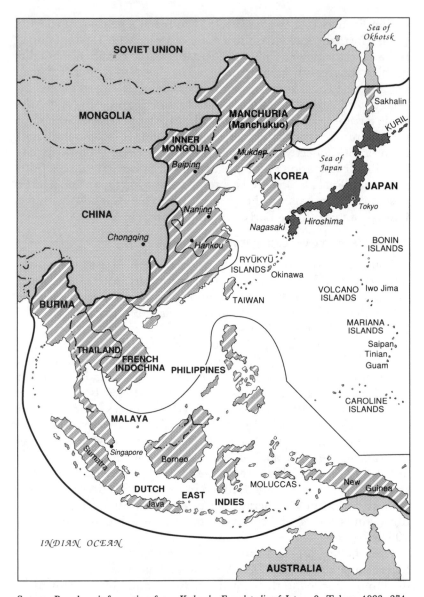

Source: Based on information from *Kodansha Encyclopedia of Japan,* 8, Tokyo, 1983, 274.

Figure 2. The Japanese Empire During World War II

the suppression of communism, and the discouragement of organized labor in Japan during this period.

Continual fragmentation of parties and a succession of minority governments led conservative forces to merge the Liberal Party

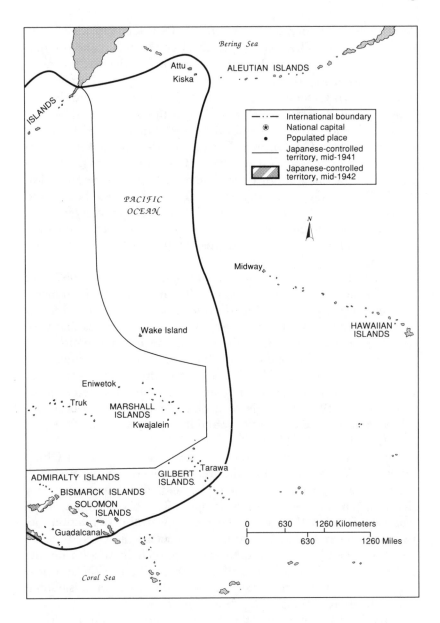

(Jiyūtō) with the Japan Democratic Party (Nihon Minshutō), an offshoot of the earlier Democratic Party, to form the Liberal Democratic Party (Jiyō-Minshutō; LDP) in November 1955. This party has continuously held power from 1955 through 1990 (see

The Liberal Democratic Party, ch. 6). Its leadership was drawn from the elite who had seen Japan through the defeat and occupation; it attracted former bureaucrats, local politicians, businessmen, journalists, other professionals, farmers, and university graduates. In October 1955, socialist groups reunited under the Japan Socialist Party, which emerged as the second most powerful political force. It was followed closely in popularity by the Kōmeitō (Clean Government Party), founded in 1964 as the political arm of the Sōka Gakkai (Value Creation Society), a lay organization of the Buddhist sect Nichiren Shōshū (see Kōmeitō, ch. 6). The Komeitō emphasized traditional Japanese beliefs and attracted urban laborers, former rural residents, and many women. Like the Japan Socialist Party, it favored the gradual modification and dissolution of the Japan-United States Mutual Security Assistance Pact.

Japan's biggest postwar political crisis took place in 1960 over the revision of this pact. As the new Treaty of Mutual Cooperation and Security was concluded, which renewed the United States role as military protector of Japan, massive street protests and political upheaval occurred, and the cabinet resigned a month after the Diet's ratification of the treaty. Thereafter political turmoil subsided. Japanese views of the United States, after years of mass protests over nuclear armaments and the mutual defense pact, improved by 1972, with the reversion of United States-occupied Okinawa to Japanese sovereignty and the winding-down of the Second Indochina War (1954–75).

Japan had reestablished relations with the Republic of China after World War II, and cordial relations were maintained with the nationalist government when it was exiled to Taiwan, a policy that won Japan the enmity of the People's Republic of China, which was established in 1949. After the general warming of relations between China and Western countries, especially the United States, which shocked Japan with its sudden rapprochement with Beijing in 1971, Tokyo established relations with Beijing in 1972 and close cooperation in the economic sphere followed (see Communist Countries, ch. 5; Relations with China, ch. 7).

Japan's relations with the Soviet Union continued to be problematic long after the war. The main object of dispute was the Soviet occupation of what Japan calls its Northern Territories, the two most southerly islands in the Kurils (Etorofu and Kunashiri) and Shikotan and the Habomai Islands (northeast of Hokkaidō), which were seized by the Soviets in the closing days of World War II (see Soviet Union, ch. 7).

Throughout the postwar period, Japan's economy continued to boom, with results far outstripping expectations. Japan rapidly caught up with the West in foreign trade, gross national product (GNP—see Glossary), and general quality of life (see Living Standards, ch. 4; Postwar Development, ch. 5). These achievements were underscored by the 1964 Tokyo Olympic Games and the Ōsaka International Exposition (Expo '70) world's fair in 1970.

The high economic growth and political tranquility of the mid-to-late 1960s were tempered by the quadrupling of oil prices by the Organization of Petroleum Exporting Countries in 1973. Almost completely dependent on imports for petroleum, Japan experienced its first and only recession since the war.

Despite its wealth and central position in the world economy, Japan has had little or no influence in global politics for much of the postwar period. Under the prime ministership of Tanaka Kakuei (1972–74), Japan took a stronger but still low-key stance by steadily increasing its defense spending and easing trade frictions with the United States. Tanaka's administration was also characterized by high-level talks with United States, Soviet, and Chinese leaders, if with mixed results. His visits to Indonesia and Thailand prompted riots, a manifestation of long-standing anti-Japanese sentiments (see Relations with other Asian Countries, ch. 7). Tanaka was forced to resign in 1974 because of his alleged connection to financial scandals and, in the face of charges of involvement in the Lockheed bribery scandal, he was arrested and jailed briefly in 1976.

By the late 1970s, the Kōmeitō and the Democratic Socialist Party had come to accept the Treaty of Mutual Cooperation and Security, and the Democratic Socialist Party even came to support a small defense buildup. The Japan Socialist Party, too, was forced to abandon its once strict antimilitary stance. The United States kept up pressure on Japan to increase its defense spending above 1 percent of its GNP, engendering much debate in the Diet, with most opposition coming not from minority parties or public opinion but from budget-conscious officials in the Ministry of Finance (see Defense Spending, ch. 8).

The fractious politics of the LDP hindered consensus in the Diet in the late 1970s. The sudden death of Prime Minister Ōhira Masayoshi just before the June 1980 elections, however, brought out a sympathy vote for the party and gave the new prime minister, Suzuki Zenkō, a working majority. Suzuki was soon swept up in a controversy over the publication of a textbook that appeared to many of Japan's former enemies as a whitewash of Japanese aggression in World War II. This incident, and serious fiscal problems, caused the Suzuki cabinet, composed of numerous LDP factions, to fall.

Nakasone Yasuhiro, a conservative backed by the still-powerful Tanaka and Suzuki factions, who once served as director general of the Defense Agency, became prime minister in November 1982. Several cordial visits between Nakasone and United States president Ronald Reagan were aimed at improving relations between their countries. Nakasone's more strident position on Japanese defense issues made him popular with some United States officials but not, generally, in Japan or among Asian neighbors. Although his characterization of Japan as an "unsinkable aircraft carrier," his noting the "common destiny" of Japan and the United States, and his calling for revisions to Article 9 of the Constitution (which renounced war as the sovereign right of the nation), among other prorearmament statements, produced negative reactions at home and abroad, a gradual acceptance emerged of the Self-Defense Forces and the mutual security treaty with the United States in the mid-1980s.

Another serious problem was Japan's growing trade surplus, which reached record heights during Nakasone's first term (see Foreign Trade Policies; Trade and Investment Relations, ch. 5). The United States pressured Japan to remedy the imbalance, demanding that Tokyo raise the value of the yen and open its markets further to facilitate more imports from the United States. Because Japan aids and protects its key industries, it was accused of creating an unfair competitive advantage. Tokyo agreed to try to resolve these problems, but generally defended its industrial policies and made concessions on its trade restrictions very reluctantly.

In November 1984, Nakasone was chosen for a second term as LDP president. His cabinet received an unusually high rating, a 50 percent favorable response in polling during his first term, while opposition parties reached a new low in popular support. As he moved into his second term, Nakasone thus held a strong position in the Diet and the nation. Despite being found guilty of bribery in 1983, Tanaka in the early to mid-1980s remained a power behind the scenes through his control of the party's informal apparatus and continued as an influential adviser to the more internationally minded Nakasone. Fluctuation in the popularity of the LDP and charges of corruption among political leaders continued as the decade progressed.

* * *

Many histories of Japan are available to Western readers. H. Paul Varley's *A Syllabus of Japanese Civilization* provides a structure for studying Japanese history while suggesting useful additional readings. Short general overview histories include Edwin O. Reischauer's *Japan: The Story of a Nation,* Reischauer and Albert M. Craig's *Japan: Tradition and Transformation,* Richard Storry's *A History of Modern Japan,* and Conrad Totman's *Japan Before Perry.* More detailed studies are John Whitney Hall's *Japan: From Prehistory to Modern Times,* Arthur E. Tiedemann's *An Introduction to Japanese Civilization,* and George B. Sansom's three-volume *History of Japan.* *Feudalism in Japan* by Peter Duus provides an excellent overview of the evolution from tribal rule to premodern Japan, while *Studies in the Institutional History of Early Modern Japan,* edited by Hall and Marius B. Jansen, is an excellent analytical collection on the Tokugawa period. A similar collection, covering the Meiji, Taishō, and Shōwa periods, is Harry Wray and Hilary Conroy's *Japan Examined.* Books by Donald Keene (*The Japanese Discovery of Europe, 1720–1830*) and Michael Cooper (*They Came to Japan*) are useful in understanding the dynamics of Japanese-Western relations starting in the sixteenth century. *The Rise of Modern Japan* by Duus, *The Modern History of Japan* by W.G. Beasley, and *Political Development in Modern Japan* by Robert E. Ward provide useful information on the nineteenth and twentieth centuries.

Analyses and translations of historical works are found in Ryusaku Tsunoda and colleagues' *Sources of Japanese Tradition.* Another excellent reference is the nine-volume *Kodansha Encyclopedia of Japan.* *The Cambridge History of Japan,* three of the six volumes of which have been published, provides in-depth analyses of many topics. (For further information and complete citations, see Bibliography.)

Chapter 2. The Society and Its Environment

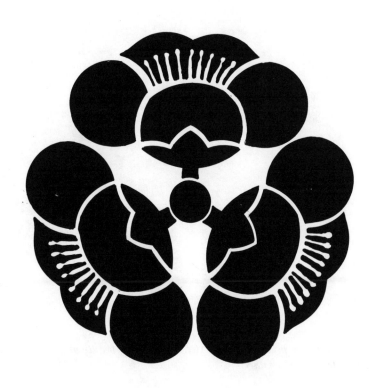

Family crest using plum blossoms (ume), *a sign of beauty and imperviousness to late winter weather*

JAPAN IS KNOWN throughout the world for its economic successes, yet Japanese society remains an enigma to many outside its borders. Those people who stress the nation's uniqueness, including many Japanese, often overlook the common human traits that make cross-cultural communication possible and rewarding. Those who stress Japan's convergence with the West miss the deeper differences that have allowed Japan to chart its own path through the unknowns of the postindustrial period.

Geography and climate do not determine social organization or values, but they do set parameters for human action. Leaders of this island nation historically have exerted close political control over their people and limited foreign influence to degrees not possible elsewhere. Mountainous terrain and wet-rice agriculture fostered—but did not ensure—attitudes of cooperation within the social unit and a sense of separateness from the outside. Extending nearly 3,800 kilometers from northeast to southwest, Japan has a generally mild, temperate climate with a rich variety of local habitats. This expansiveness resulted in regional variations in culture and economic development historically, but these differences decreased in importance (or were relegated to tourist attractions) in the twentieth century. With 77 percent of the population living in urban areas and a large majority of farm families earning most of their income from nonfarm labor, regional and rural-urban differences in life-style were minimal in the early 1990s. The large and stable national population, with low fertility and mortality rates, was aging rapidly.

Japanese society underwent great social changes after 1945. Families became smaller, women increasingly participated in paid labor, and urban life replaced the rural community as the common environment in which children were raised and human interaction took place. The changes brought new problems, such as industrial pollution, the entrance examination "hell," and social anomie. The government responded with new policies, and ordinary citizens utilized traditional customs to give meaning to the present. Japanese cities in the late twentieth century were convenient and safe. Surface prosperity masked an unequal distribution of wealth and discrimination against those perceived to be "different." Films, television, nightlife, and comic books (*manga*), sometimes garish and violent, offered an escape from the pressures of contemporary life. Categorization of social problems as medical syndromes tended

71

to focus attention on personal-problem solving and away from societal-level causes, such as poverty, gender roles, or the lack of assistance in caring for ill elderly relatives.

The pace and rhythm of life in 1990 Japan would have seemed familiar to Westerners. Yet the Japanese approached them with a world view eclectically derived from a variety of religious and secular traditions, emphasizing human relations. Many Japanese were willing to delay rewards, to put forth their best efforts for their teams, and to avoid open conflict. The outside world was an arena of intense competition. Family, neighborhood, and workplace represented ever-widening circles of social relations to which individuals adjusted and through which they grew as human beings.

Japan, with the world's second largest gross national product (GNP—see Glossary) and seventh largest population, played an increasingly important part in world affairs. As the government embarked on a policy of internationalization, individual Japanese creatively combined elements from their own history with foreign influences and new inventions, as they adapted to the postindustrial world.

Physical Setting

Composition, Topography, and Drainage

The mountainous islands of the Japanese Archipelago form a crescent off the eastern coast of Asia (see fig. 1). They are separated from the mainland by the Sea of Japan, which historically served as a protective barrier. Japan's insular nature, together with the compactness of its main territory and the cultural homogeneity of its people, enabled the nation to remain free of outside domination until its defeat in World War II (see World War II and the Occupation, 1941–52, ch. 1). The country consists of four principal islands: Hokkaidō, Honshū, Shikoku, and Kyūshū; more than 3,000 adjacent islands and islets, including Ōshima in the Nampō chain; and more than 200 other smaller islands, including those of the Amami, Okinawa, and Sakishima chains of the Ryūkyū Archipelago. The national territory also includes the small Bonin Islands (called Ogasawara by the Japanese), Iwō Jima, and the Volcano Islands (Kazan Rettō), stretching some 1,100 kilometers from the main islands. A territorial dispute with the Soviet Union, dating from the end of World War II, over the two southernmost of the Kuril Islands, Etorofu and Kunashiri, and the smaller Shikotan and Habomai island groups northeast of Hokkaidō remained a sensitive spot in Japan-Soviet Union relations throughout the 1980s (see Relations with the Soviet Union, ch. 7). Excluding

At the summit of Mount Fuji, overlooking Lake Yamanaka
Courtesy Prints and Photographs Division, Library of Congress

disputed territory, the archipelago covers about 377,000 square kilometers. No point in Japan is more than 150 kilometers from the sea.

The four major islands are separated by narrow straits and form a natural entity. The Ryūkyū Islands curve 970 kilometers southward from Kyūshū.

The distance between Japan and the Korean Peninsula, the nearest point on the Asian continent, is about 200 kilometers at the Korea Strait. Japan has always been linked with the continent through trade routes, stretching in the north toward Siberia, in the west through the Tsushima Islands to the Korean Peninsula, and in the south to the ports on the south China coast.

The Japanese islands are the summits of mountain ridges uplifted near the outer edge of the continental shelf. About 75 percent of Japan's area is mountainous, and scattered plains and intermontane basins (in which the population is concentrated) cover only about 25 percent. A long chain of mountains runs down the middle of the archipelago, dividing it into two halves, the "face," fronting on the Pacific Ocean, and the "back," toward the Sea of Japan. On the Pacific side are steep mountains 1,500 to 3,000 meters high ,with deep valleys and gorges. Central Japan is marked by the convergence of the three mountain chains—the Hida, Kiso, and Akaishi mountains—that form the Japanese Alps (Nihon Arupusu), several of whose peaks are higher than 3,000 meters. The highest point in the Japanese Alps is Kitadake at 3,192 meters. The highest point in the country is Mount Fuji (Fujisan, also called Fujiyama in the West but not in Japan), a volcano dormant since 1707 that rises to 3,776 meters above sea level in Shizuoka Prefecture. On the Sea of Japan side are plateaus and low mountain districts, with altitudes of 500 to 1,500 meters.

None of the populated plains or mountain basins is extensive in area. The largest, the Kantō Plain, where Tokyo is situated, covers only 13,000 square kilometers. Other important plains are the Nōbi Plain surrounding Nagoya, the Kinki Plain in the Ōsaka-Kyōto area, the Sendai Plain around the city of Sendai in northeastern Honshū, and the Ishikari Plain on Hokkaidō. Many of these plains are along the coast, and their areas have been increased by reclamation throughout recorded history.

The small amount of habitable land prompted significant human modification of the terrain over many centuries. Land was reclaimed from the sea and from river deltas by building dikes and drainage, and rice paddies were built on terraces carved into mountainsides. The process continued in the modern period with extension of shorelines and building of artificial islands for industrial and port development, such as Port Island in Kōbe and the new Kansai International Airport, which was under construction in Ōsaka Bay in 1990. Hills and even mountains have been razed to provide flat areas for housing.

Rivers are generally steep and swift, and few are suitable for navigation except in their lower reaches. Most rivers are less than 300 kilometers in length, but their rapid flow from the mountains provides a valuable, renewable resource: hydroelectric power generation. Japan's hydroelectric power potential has been exploited almost to capacity. Seasonal variations in flow have led to extensive development of flood control measures. Most of the rivers are very short. The longest, the Shinano, which winds through Nagano Prefecture to Niigata Prefecture and flows into the Sea of Japan, is only 367 kilometers long. The largest freshwater lake is Lake Biwa, northeast of Kyōto.

Extensive coastal shipping, especially around the Inland Sea (Seto Naikai) compensates for the lack of navigable rivers. The Pacific coastline south of Tokyo is characterized by long, narrow, gradually shallowing inlets produced by sedimentation, which has created many natural harbors. The Pacific coastline north of Tokyo, the coast of Hokkaidō, and the Sea of Japan coast are generally unindented, with few natural harbors (see fig. 3).

Geographic Regions

The country's forty-seven prefectures are grouped into eight regions frequently used as statistical units in government documents (see Local Government, ch. 6). The islands of Hokkaidō, Shikoku, and Kyūshū each form a region, and the main island of Honshū is divided into five regions.

Hokkaidō

Hokkaidō, about 83,500 square kilometers in area, constitutes more than 20 percent of Japan's land area. Like the other main islands, Hokkaidō is generally mountainous, but its mountains are lower than in other parts of Japan; many have leveled summits, and hills predominate. Valleys cut through the terrain, and communications are comparatively easy. Hokkaidō was long looked upon as a remote frontier area, and until the second half of the nineteenth century was left largely to the indigenous Ainu (see Minorities, this ch.). The Ainu in the 1980s numbered fewer than 20,000, and they were being rapidly assimilated into the main Japanese population. Since the movement of modern technology and development into the area in the late nineteenth century, Hokkaidō has been considered the major center of Japanese agriculture, forestry, fishing, and mining. Hokkaidō, with about 90 percent of Japan's pastureland, produced the same proportion of its dairy products in the late 1980s. Manufacturing industry played a smaller role compared to the other regions.

Hokkaidō's environmental quality and rural character were altered by industrial and residential development in the 1980s, with developments such as the completion of the Seikan Tunnel linking Hokkaidō and Honshū. Hokkaidō was both an important agricultural center and a growing industrial area, with most industrial development near Sapporo, the prefectural capital.

Tōhoku

The northeastern part of Honshū, called Tōhoku (literally "the northeast"), includes six prefectures. Tōhoku, like most of Japan, is hilly or mountainous. Its initial historical settlement occurred between the seventh and ninth centuries A.D., well after Japanese civilization and culture had become firmly established in central and southwestern Japan. Although iron, steel, cement, chemical, pulp, and petroleum-refining industries began developing in the 1960s, Tōhoku was traditionally considered the granary of Japan because it supplied Sendai and the Tokyo-Yokohama market with rice and other farm commodities. Tōhoku provided 20 percent of the nation's rice crop (see Agriculture, Forestry, and Fishing, ch. 4). The climate, however, is harsher than in other parts of Honshū and permits only one crop a year on paddy land. The inland location of many of the region's lowlands has led to a concentration of much of the population there. Coupled with coastlines that do not favor port development, this settlement pattern resulted in a much greater than usual dependence on land and railroad transportation. Low points in the central mountain range fortunately make communications between lowlands on either side of the range moderately easy. Tourism became a major industry in the Tōhoku region, with points of interest including the islands of Matsushima Bay, Lake Towada, the Rikuchu Coastline National Park, and the Bandai-Asahi National Park.

Kantō

The Kantō ("east of the barrier") region encompasses seven prefectures around Tokyo on the Kantō Plain. The plain itself, however, makes up only slightly more than 40 percent of the region. The rest consists of the hills and mountains that border it except on the seaward side. Once the heartland of feudal power, the Kantō became the center of modern development (see Tokugawa Period, 1600–1867, ch. 1). Within the Tokyo-Yokohama metropolitan area, the Kantō housed not only Japan's seat of government, but also the largest group of universities and cultural institutions in addition to the greatest population and a large industrial zone. Although most of the Kantō Plain was used for residential, commercial, or industrial construction, it was still farmed in the early 1990s. Rice was the principal crop, although the zone around Tokyo and Yokohama had been landscaped to grow garden produce for the metropolitan market.

The Kantō region in the late twentieth century was the most highly developed, urbanized, and industrialized part of Japan. Tokyo and Yokohama formed a single industrial complex with a concentration of light and heavy industry along Tokyo Bay. Smaller cities, farther away from the coast, housed substantial light industry. The average population density reached 5,471 persons per square kilometer in 1987 (see Population Density, this ch.).

Chūbu

The Chūbu or central region encompasses nine prefectures in the midland of Japan, west of the Kantō region. The region is the widest part of Honshū and is characterized by high, rugged mountains. The Japanese Alps divide the country into the sunnier Pacific side, known as the front of Japan or Omote-Nihon, and the colder Sea of Japan side, or Ura-Nihon, the back of Japan. The region comprises three distinct districts: Hokuriku, a coastal strip on the Sea of Japan that is a major wet-rice producing area; Tōsan, or the Central Highlands; and Tōkai, or the eastern seaboard, a narrow corridor along the Pacific Coast.

Hokuriku lies west of the massive mountains that occupy the central Chūbu region. The district has a very heavy snowfall and strong winds. Its turbulent rivers are the source of abundant hydroelectric power. Niigata Prefecture is the site of domestic gas and oil production. Industrial development is extensive, especially in the cities of Niigata and Toyama. Fukui and Kanazawa also have large manufacturing industries. Hokuriku developed largely independently of other regions, mainly because it remained relatively isolated from the major industrial and cultural centers on the Pacific Coast. Because port facilities were limited and road transport hampered by heavy winter snows, the district relied largely on railroad transportation (see Railroads and Subways, ch. 4).

The Tōsan district is an area of complex and high rugged mountains—often called the roof of Japan—that include the Japanese Alps. The population is chiefly concentrated in six elevated basins connected by narrow valleys. Tōsan was long a main silk-producing area, although output declined after World War II. Much of the labor formerly required in silk production was absorbed by the district's diversified manufacturing industry, which included precision instruments, machinery, textiles, food processing, and other light manufacturing.

The Tōkai district, bordering the Pacific Ocean, is a narrow corridor interrupted in places by mountains that descend into the sea. Since the Tokugawa period (1600–1867), this corridor has been important in linking Tokyo, Kyōto, and Osaka. One of old Japan's most famous roads, the Tōkaido, ran through it connecting Edo (Tokyo, since 1868) and Kyōto, the old imperial capital; in the twentieth century it became the route of new super-express highways and high-speed railroad lines.

A number of small alluvial plains are found in the corridor section. A mild climate, favorable location relative to the great metropolitan complexes, and the availability of fast transportation have made them truck-gardening centers for out-of-season vegetables. Upland areas of rolling hills are extensively given over to the growing of mandarin oranges and tea. The corridor also has a number of important small industrial centers. The western part of Tōkai includes the Nōbi Plain, where rice was grown by the seventh century A.D. Nagoya, facing Ise Bay, is a center for heavy industry, including iron and steel and machinery manufacturing.

Kinki

The Kinki region lies to the west of Tōkai and consists of seven prefectures forming a comparatively narrow area of Honshū, stretching from the Sea of Japan on the north to the Pacific Ocean on the south. It includes Japan's second largest industrial-commercial complex, centered on Ōsaka and Kōbe, and the two former capital cities of Nara and Kyōto, seats of the imperial family from the early eighth century A.D. until the Meiji Restoration in 1868 (see The Meiji Restoration, ch. 1). The area is rich in imperial and cultural history and attracts many Japanese and foreign tourists.

The Ōsaka Plain is the site of Ōsaka, Kōbe, and a number of intermediate-sized industrial cities, which together form the Hanshin commercial-industrial complex. The suburbs of Ōsaka were given over to farming, including vegetables, dairy farming, poultry raising, and rice cultivation in the 1980s. These areas were progressively reduced as the cities expanded and residential areas, including numerous so-called "new cities," were built, such as the developments north of Ōsaka resulting from the Ōsaka International Exposition (Expo '70) world's fair.

Chūgoku

The Chūgoku region, occupying the western end of Honshū encompasses five prefectures. It is characterized by irregular rolling hills and limited plain areas and is divided into two distinct parts by mountains running east and west through its center. The northern, somewhat narrower, district is known as San'in, or "shady side of the mountain," and the southern district, as San'yō, or "sunny side," because of their marked differences in climate. The whole Inland Sea region, including San'yo underwent rapid development in the late twentieth century. The city of Hiroshima, rebuilt after being destroyed by the atomic bomb in 1945, was an industrial metropolis of more than 2.8 million people by 1987. Overfishing and pollution reduced the productivity of the Inland Sea fishing grounds, and the area concentrated on heavy industry. San'in, on the other hand, was less industrialized and relied on agriculture.

Shikoku

The Shikoku region—comprising the entire island of Shikoku—covers about 18,800 square kilometers and consists of four prefectures. It is connected to Honshū by ferry and air, and since 1988 by the Seto-Ōhashi bridge network. Until completion of the bridges, the region was isolated from the rest of Japan, and the freer movement between Honshū and Shikoku was expected to promote economic development on both sides of the bridges.

Mountains running east and west divide Shikoku into a narrow northern subregion, fronting on the Inland Sea, and a southern part facing the Pacific Ocean. Most of the population lived in the north in the 1980s, and all but one of the island's few larger cites were located there. Industry was moderately well developed and included the processing of ores from the important Besshi copper mine. Land was used intensively. Wide alluvial areas, especially in the eastern part of the zone, were planted with rice and subsequently double cropped with winter wheat and barley. Fruit was grown throughout the northern area in great variety, including citrus fruits, persimmons, peaches, and grapes.

The larger southern section of Shikoku is mountainous and sparsely populated. The only significant lowland is a small alluvial plain at Kōchi, a prefectural capital. The section's mild winters stimulated some truck farming, specializing in growing out-of-season vegetables under plastic covering. Two crops of rice can be cultivated annually in the southern portion. The pulp and paper industry took advantage of the abundant forests and hydroelectric power.

Kyūshū

Kyūshū, meaning "nine provinces" (from its ancient administrative structure), is the southernmost of the main islands and in modern times comprises seven prefectures. It was the stepping stone to Honshū for early migrants from the Korean Peninsula and a channel for the spread of ideas from the Asian mainland (see Early Developments, ch. 1). Kyūshū lies at the western end of the Inland Sea. Its northern extremity is only about 1.6 kilometers from Honshū, and the two islands are connected by the Kammon Bridge and by three tunnels, including one for the Japan Railways Group's Shinkansen (bullet train). The region is divided not only geographically, but economically, by the Kyūshū Mountains, which run diagonally across the middle of the island. The north, including Kitakyūshū industrial region, became increasingly urbanized and industrialized after World War II, while the agricultural south became relatively poorer. The hilly northwestern part of the island has extensive coal deposits, the second largest in Japan, which formed the basis for a large iron and steel industry. An extensive lowland area, in the northwest, between Kumamoto and Saga, was an important farming district in the late 1980s.

The climate of Kyūshū is generally warm and humid, and the cultivation of vegetables and fruits was supplemented by cattle raising. The cities of Kitakyūshū and Sasebo were noted for iron and steel production, and Nagasaki for manufacturing. Nagasaki is a city of historical and cultural importance, a center for Chinese and Western influences from the sixteenth century on, and the only port open to foreign ships during most of the Tokugawa period. Like Hiroshima, it also was rebuilt after being devastated by an atomic bomb attack in 1945.

Ryūkyū Islands

The Ryūkyū Islands include more than 200 islands and islets— some little more than coral outcrops—of which fewer than half are populated. They extend in a chain generally southwestward from the Tokara Strait, which separates them from the outlying islands of Kyūshū, to within 120 kilometers of Taiwan. The Ryūkyūs are considered part of the Ryūshū region but historically have been quite distinctively separate from the rest of the region.

The islands are the tops of mountain ranges along the outer edge of the continental shelf. They are generally hilly or mountainous, with active volcanos occurring mainly in the northern part of the archipelago. Okinawa is the largest and economically the most important of the Ryūkyūs. There was little industry in the 1980s, and the economy relied heavily on tourism. Northern Okinawa is quite rugged and forested, while the southern part consists of rolling hills. Although agriculture and fishing remained the occupations of most of the population in the Ryūkyūs, the region experienced considerable industrial expansion during the period of United States occupation from 1945 to 1972.

Climate

Lying in the middle latitudes, covering about 22° of latitude in the northern hemisphere, Japan is generally a rainy country with high humidity. Because of its wide range of latitude, Japan has diverse climates, with a range often compared to that of the east coast of North America, from Nova Scotia to Georgia. Tokyo's latitude is about 36° north, comparable to that of Tehran, Athens, or Los Angeles. The generally humid, temperate climate exhibits marked seasonal variation celebrated in art and literature, as well as regional variations ranging from cool in Hokkaidō to subtropical in Kyūshū. Climate also varies with altitude and with location on the Pacific Ocean or on the Sea of Japan. Northern Japan has warm summers but long, cold winters with heavy snow. Central

Japan has hot, humid summers and short winters, and southwestern Japan has long, hot, humid summers and mild winters. Two primary factors influence Japanese climate: a location near the Asian continent and the existence of major oceanic currents. The climate from June to September is marked by hot, wet weather brought by tropical airflows from the Pacific Ocean and Southeast Asia. These airflows are full of moisture and deposit substantial amounts of rain when they reach land. There is a marked rainy season, beginning in early June and continuing for about a month. It is followed by hot, sticky weather. Five or six typhoons pass over or near Japan every year from early August to early September, sometimes resulting in significant damage. Annual precipitation, which averages between 100 and 200 centimeters, is concentrated in the period between June and September. In fact, 70 to 80 percent of the annual precipitation falls during this period. In winter, a high-pressure area develops over Siberia, and a low-pressure area over the northern Pacific Ocean. The result is a flow of cold air eastward across Japan that brings freezing temperatures and heavy snowfalls to the central mountain ranges facing the Sea of Japan, but clear skies to areas fronting on the Pacific.

Two major ocean currents affect this climatic pattern. The warm Kuroshio Current (Black Current; also known as the Japan Current) and the cold Oyashio Current (Parent Current; also known as the Okhotsk Current). The Kuroshio Current flows northward on the Pacific side of Japan and warms areas as far north as Tokyo; a small branch, the Tsushima Current, flows up the Sea of Japan side. The Oyashio Current, which abounds in plankton beneficial to cold-water fish, flows southward along the northern Pacific, cooling adjacent coastal areas. The meeting point of these currents at latitude 36° north is a bountiful fishing ground.

Earthquakes

Ten percent of the world's active volcanos—40 in the 1980s (another 148 were dormant)—are found in Japan, which lies in a zone of extreme crustal instability. As many as 1,500 earthquakes are recorded yearly, and magnitudes of four to six on the Richter scale are not uncommon. Minor tremors occur almost daily in one part of the country or another, causing slight shaking of buildings. Major earthquakes occur infrequently; the most famous in the twentieth century was the great Kantō earthquake of 1923, in which 130,000 people died. Undersea earthquakes also expose the Japanese coastline to danger from tsunami.

Japan has become a world leader in research on causes and prediction of earthquakes. The development of advanced technology has permitted the construction of skyscrapers even in earthquake-prone areas. Extensive civil defense efforts focus on training in protection against earthquakes, in particular against accompanying fire, which represents the greatest danger.

Pollution

As Japan changed from an agricultural society to an urbanized industrial power, much of its natural beauty was destroyed and defaced by overcrowding and industrial development. However, as the world's leading importer of both exhaustible and renewable natural resources and the second largest consumer of fossil fuels, Japan came to realize that it had a major international responsibility to conserve and protect the environment. By 1990 Japan had some of the world's strictest environmental protection regulations.

These regulations were the consequence of a number of well publicized environmental disasters. Cadmium poisoning from industrial waste in Toyama Prefecture was discovered to be the cause of the extremely painful *itai-itai* disease (*itai-itai* means ouch-ouch), which causes severe pain in the back and joints, contributes to brittle bones that fracture easily, and brings about degeneration of the kidneys. Recovery of cadmium effluent halted the spread of the disease, and no new cases have been recorded since 1946. In the 1960s, hundreds of inhabitants of Minamata City in Kumamoto Prefecture contracted "Minamata disease," a degeneration of the central nervous system caused by eating mercury-poisoned seafood from Minamata Bay (nearly 1,300 cases of Minamata disease had been diagnosed by 1979). In Yokkaichi, a port in Mie Prefecture, air pollution caused by sulfur oxide and nitrogen oxide emissions led to a rapid increase in the number of people suffering from asthma and bronchitis. In urban areas, photochemical smog from automotive and industrial exhaust fumes also contributed to the rise in respiratory problems. In the early 1970s, chronic arsenic poisoning attributed to dust from local arsenic mines (since shut down) was experienced in Shimane and Miyazaki prefectures. The incidence of polychlorobiphenyl (PCB) poisoning, caused by polluted cooking oil and food, particularly seafood, was also problematic.

Grass-roots pressure groups were formed in the 1960s and 1970s as a response to increasing environmental problems. These groups were independent of formal political parties and focused on single, usually local, environmental issues. Such citizens' movements were reminiscent of earlier citizen protests in the 1890s. As a result of this pressure, Japan began in the early 1970s to combat pollution on an official governmental level, with the establishment of the Environmental Agency. Although the agency lacked strong public influence and political power, it established effective regulations to curb pollution from photochemical smog through strict automotive emissions standards. It also worked to reduce noise from trains and airplanes, to remove mining, forestry, and tourist debris left on mountainsides and in national forests, and to monitor noise and air pollutant levels in major cities.

Groups also pressured the government and industry for a system of compensation for pollution victims. A series of lawsuits in the early 1970s established that corporations were responsible for damage cause by their products or activities. The Pollution Health Damage Compensation Law of 1973 provides industry funds for victims. Compensation, however, was slow, and awards small, while the establishment of a government fund helped industry diffuse public outrage. In 1984, it was reported that Japan had more than 85,000 recognized victims of environmental pollution, with an estimated rate of increase of 6 percent a year. The regulations aimed at business were not enough to solve Japan's environmental problems, according to the Environmental Agency's 1989 *White Paper on the Environment,* although public awareness and interest had grown and a number of civic and public interest groups had been established to combat pollution. Fewer public interest groups were engaged in the environmental debate than in antinuclear issues, and the peak of public interest in the environment occurred in the 1970s and early 1980s.

Japan had still not addressed worldwide environmental issues adequately. Japanese whaling continued in the late 1980s to be the object of international protest, and Japanese corporate involvement in the deforestation of Southeast Asia created concern among domestic and international groups.

The late 1980s saw the beginnings of change. In a 1984 public opinion poll conducted by the government, Japanese citizens had indicated less concern for environmental problems than their European counterparts. In the same year, the Environmental Agency had issued its first white paper calling for greater participation by Japan's public and private sectors in protecting the global environment. That challenge was repeated in the 1989 study. When citizens were asked in 1989 if they thought environmental problems had improved compared with the past, nearly 41 percent thought things had improved, 31 percent thought that they had stayed the same, and nearly 21 percent thought that they had worsened. Some 75 percent of those surveyed expressed concern about endangered species, shrinkage of rain forests, expansion of deserts, destruction of the ozone layer, acid rain, and increased water and air pollution in developing countries. Most believed that Japan, alone or in cooperation with other industrialized countries, had the responsibility to solve environmental problems. Although environmental public interest groups were not as numerous or active as they had been in the 1970s, the increased awareness of global environmental issues was likely to result in increased grass-roots activism.

Since the 1960s, Japan has made slow but significant progress in combating environmental problems. Efforts made in the late 1980s created a base of technology and concern that was expected to help the Japanese face the environmental issues of the 1990s.

Population

With a population of 122.6 million in 1988, Japan was three times more densely populated than Europe as a whole and twelve times more densely populated than the United States. The population has grown more than threefold since 1872, when it stood at 34.8 million. Beginning in the 1950s the birth rate declined, however, and by the late 1980s the rate of natural increase was 0.5 percent, the lowest in the world outside Europe. Both the density and the age structure of Japan's population are likely to influence the country's future.

Population Density

Japan had an average of 324 persons per square kilometer in 1988, high compared with China (115), the United States (26), or the Soviet Union (13), but lower than in some other Asian countries, such as the Republic of Korea (South Korea), which had 428 people per square kilometer. The population per square kilometer of *habitable* land in 1988 was 1,523 persons, however, compared with 384 in the Federal Republic of Germany (West Germany), 165 in France, and 54 in the United States. About 77 percent of the population lived in urban areas, and the Pacific Coast from Tokyo to Ōsaka was particularly densely populated. Well over 50 percent of the Japanese population lived on slightly over 2 percent of its land.

Japan's population density has helped promote extremely high land prices. Between 1955 and 1989, land prices in the six largest cities increased 15,456 percent. Urban land prices generally increased 40 percent from 1980 to 1987; in the six largest cities, the price of land doubled over that period. For many families, this trend put housing in central cities out of reach. The result was lengthy commutes for many workers; daily commutes of up to two hours each way were not uncommon in the Tokyo area in the late 1980s. Despite the large amount of forested land in Japan, parks in cities were smaller and scarcer than in major European or United States cities, which averaged ten times the amount of parkland per inhabitant. However, despite the high cost of urban housing, more people were likely to move back into central city areas, especially as the price of transportation and commuting time increased. National and regional governments devoted resources to making regional cities and rural areas more attractive by developing transportation networks, social services, industry, and education institutions in attempts to decentralize settlement and improve the quality of life. Nevertheless, major cities, especially Tokyo, remained attractive to young people seeking education and jobs.

Age Structure

Like other postindustrial countries, Japan in the 1980s faced the problems associated with an aging population (see Patterns of Development, ch. 4). In 1988, only 11.2 percent of the population was sixty-five years or older, but projections were that nearly 24 percent would be in that age category by 2020 (see table 2, Appendix). That shift will make Japan one of the world's most elderly societies, and the change will have taken place in a shorter span of time than in any other country.

This aging of the population was brought about by a combination of low fertility and high life expectancies. In 1988, the fertility rate was 11.9 per 1,000, and the average number of children born to a woman over her lifetime had been fewer than two since the late 1970s (the average number was 1.7 in the mid-1980s). Family planning was nearly universal, with condoms and legal abortions the main forms of birth control. A number of factors contributed to the trend toward small families: late marriage, increased participation of women in the labor force, small living spaces, and the high costs of children's education. Life expectancies at birth, 81.3 years for women and 75.5 years for men in 1988, were the highest in the world. (The expected life span at the end of World War II, for both men and women, was fifty years.) The mortality rate in 1988 was 6 per 1,000. The leading causes of death were cancer, heart disease, and cerebrovascular disease, a pattern common to postindustrial societies (see Health Care, this ch.).

Public policy, the media, and discussions with private citizens revealed a high level of concern for the implications of one in four persons in Japan being sixty-five or older. By 2025 the dependency ratio (the ratio of people under fifteen years plus those sixty-five and older to those aged fifteen to sixty-five, indicating in a general way the ratio of the dependent population to the working population) was expected to be two dependents for every three

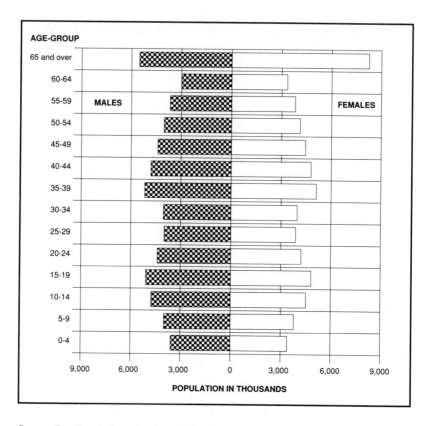

Source: Based on information from Hideo Tsuda (ed.), *Japan 1990: An International Comparison*, Tokyo, 1990. 8.

Figure 4. Age-Sex Distribution, 1988

workers. The aging of the population was already becoming evident in the aging of the labor force and the shortage of young workers in the late 1980s, with potential impacts on employment practices, wages and benefits, and the roles of women in the labor force (see The Structure of Japan's Labor Markets, ch. 4). The increasing proportion of elderly people in the population also had a major impact on government spending. As recently as the early 1970s, social expenditures amounted to only about 6 percent of Japan's national income. In 1989, that portion of the national budget was 18 percent, and it was expected that by 2025, 27 percent of national income would be spent on social welfare.

In addition, the median age of the elderly population was rising in the late 1980s (see fig. 4). The proportion of people aged seventy-five to eighty-five was expected to increase from 6 percent in 1985 to 15 percent in 2025. Because the incidence of chronic disease increases with age, the health-care and pension systems, too, were expected to come under severe strain. The government in the mid-1980s began to reevaluate the relative burdens of government and the private sector in health care and pensions, and it established policies to control government costs in these programs. Recognizing the lower probability that an elderly person will be residing with an adult child and the higher probability of any daughter or daughter-in-law's participation in the paid labor force, the government encouraged establishment of nursing homes, day-care facilities for the elderly, and home health programs. Longer life spans were altering relations between spouses and across generations, creating new government responsibilities, and changing virtually all aspects of social life.

Migration

Between 6 million and 7 million people moved their residences each year during the 1980s. About 50 percent of these moves were within the same prefecture; the others were relocations from one prefecture to another. During Japan's economic development in the twentieth century, and especially during the 1950s and 1960s, migration was characterized by urbanization as people from rural areas in increasing numbers moved to the larger metropolitan areas in search of better jobs and education. Out-migration from rural prefectures continued in the late 1980s, but more slowly than in previous decades.

In the 1980s, government policy provided support for new urban development away from the large cities, particularly Tokyo, and assisted regional cities to attract young people to live and work there. Regional cities offered familiarity to those from nearby areas, lower costs of living, shorter commutes, and, in general, a more relaxed life-style then could be had in larger cities. Young people continued to move to large cities, however, to attend universities and find work, but some returned to regional cities (a pattern known as U-turn) or to their prefecture of origin (a pattern known as J-turn).

Government statistics show that in the 1980s significant numbers of people left the largest cities (Tokyo and Ōsaka). In 1988, more than 500,000 people left Tokyo, which experienced a net loss through migration of nearly 73,000 for the year. Ōsaka had a net loss of nearly 36,000 in the same year. However, the prefectures showing the highest net growth were located near the major urban centers, such as Saitama, Chiba, Ibaraki, and Kanazawa around Tokyo, and Hyōgo, Nara, and Shiga near Ōsaka and Kyōto. This pattern suggests a process of suburbanization, people moving away from the cities for affordable housing but still commuting there for work and recreation, rather than a true decentralization.

Japanese economic success has led to an increase in certain types of external migration. In 1988, about 8.5 million Japanese went abroad. Over 80 percent of these people traveled as tourists, especially visiting other parts of Asia and North America. However, about 548,000 Japanese were living abroad, 48,000 of whom had permanent foreign residency, about four times the number who had that status in 1975. Nearly 200,000 Japanese went abroad in 1988 for extended periods of study, research, or business assignments. As the government and private corporations have stressed internationalization, greater numbers of individuals have been directly affected, decreasing Japan's historically claimed insularity. Despite the benefits of experiencing life abroad, individuals who have lived outside of Japan for extended periods often faced problems of discrimination upon their return because others might no longer consider them fully Japanese. By the late 1980s, these problems, particularly the bullying of returnee children in the schools, had become a major public issue both in Japan and in Japanese communities abroad (see Primary and Secondary Education, ch. 3).

Minorities

Japanese society, with its ideology of homogeneity, has traditionally been intolerant of ethnic and other differences. People identified as different might be considered "polluted"—the category applied historically to the outcasts of Japan, particularly the *burakumin*—and thus not suitable as marriage partners or employees. Men or women of mixed ancestry, those with family histories of certain diseases, atomic bomb survivors of Hiroshima and Nagasaki and their descendants, foreigners, and members of minority groups faced discrimination in a variety of forms.

Foreign Residents

If Japanese society was reluctant to readmit returnees in the 1980s, it was even less willing to accept those people who were not ethnic Japanese as full members of society. In 1988 there were 941,000 foreign residents in Japan, less than 1 percent of Japan's population (if illegal aliens were counted, the number of foreigners might be several times higher than the quoted figure). Of this number, 677,000 (about 72 percent) were Koreans, and 129,000 (some 14 percent) were Chinese. Many of these people were descendants of those brought to Japan during Japan's occupation of Taiwan (1895-1945) and of Korea (1905-45) to work at unskilled jobs, such as coal mining. Because Japanese citizenship was based on the nationality of the parent rather than the place of birth, subsequent generations were not automatically Japanese and had to be naturalized to claim citizenship, despite being born and educated in Japan and speaking only Japanese, as was the case with most Koreans in Japan. Until the late 1980s, people applying for citizenship were expected to use only the Japanese renderings of their names and, even as citizens, continued to face discrimination in education, employment, and marriage. Thus, few chose naturalization, and they faced legal restrictions as foreigners as well as extreme social prejudice.

All non-Japanese were required by law to register with the government and carry alien registration cards. From the early 1980s, a civil disobedience movement encouraged refusal of the fingerprinting that accompanied registration every five years. Those people who opposed fingerprinting argued that it was discriminatory since the only Japanese who were fingerprinted were criminals. The courts upheld fingerprinting, but the law was changed so that fingerprinting was done once rather than with each renewal of the registration. Some Koreans, often with the support of either the Republic of Korea (South Korea) or the Democratic People's Republic of Korea (North Korea), attempted to educate their children in Korean language, history, and culture and to instill pride in their Korean heritage. Most Koreans in Japan in 1990, however, had never been to the Korean Peninsula, and did not speak Korean. Many were caught in a vicious cycle of poverty and discrimination in a society that emphasized Japan's homogeneity and cultural uniqueness. Other Asians, too, whether students or permanent residents, faced prejudice and a strong "we-they" distinction. Europeans and North Americans might be treated with greater hospitality but nonetheless found it difficult to become full members of Japanese society. Public awareness of the place of foreigners (*gaijin*) in Japanese society was heightened in the late 1980s in debates over the acceptance of Vietnamese and Chinese refugees and the importing of Filipino brides for rural farmers.

Burakumin

Despite Japan's claim of homogeneity, two Japanese minority groups can be identified. The largest is known as *burakumin* (literally, residents of *buraku*, hamlets), descendants of premodern outcast hereditary occupational groups, such as butchers, leatherworkers, and certain entertainers. Discrimination against these occupational groups arose historically because of Buddhist prohibitions against killing and Shinto notions of pollution, as well as governmental attempts at social control. During the Tokugawa period, such people were required to live in special *buraku* and, like the rest of the population, were bound by sumptuary laws based on the inheritance of social class. The Meiji government abolished derogatory names applied to *burakumin* in 1871, but the new laws had little effect on the social discrimination faced by the former outcasts and their descendants. The laws, however, did eliminate the economic monopoly they had over certain occupations.

Burakumin in 1990, although physically indistinguishable from other Japanese, often lived in urban ghettoes or in the traditional special hamlets in rural areas. Some attempted to pass as ordinary Japanese, but the checks on family background that were often part of marriage arrangements and employment applications made this difficult. Estimates on the number of *burakumin* ranged from 2 million to 4 million, or about 2 to 3 percent of the national population.

Ordinary Japanese claimed that *burakumin* status can be surmised from the location of the family home, occupation, dialect, or mannerisms, and, despite legal equality, continued to discriminate against people they surmised to be *burakumin*. Past and current discrimination had resulted in lower educational attainment and socioeconomic status among *burakumin* than among the majority of Japanese. Movements with objectives ranging from ''liberation'' to encouraging integration have tried over the years to change this situation. As early as 1922, leaders of the *burakumin* community organized a movement, the Levelers Association of Japan (Suiheisha), to advance their rights. After World War II, the National Committee for Burakumin Liberation was founded, changing its name to the Burakumin Liberation League in the 1950s. The league, with the support of the socialist and communist parties, pressured government into making important concessions in the late 1960s and 1970s. One concession was the passing of a Special Measures Law for Assimilation Projects, which provided financial aid for *burakumin* communities. Another was the closing of nineteenth-century family registers, kept by the Ministry of Justice for all Japanese, which revealed the outcaste origins of *burakumin* families and individuals. These records could now be consulted only in legal cases, making it more difficult to identify or discriminate against *burakumin*. Even into the 1980s, however, the subjects of *burakumin* discrimination and liberation were taboo in public discussion. In the late 1970s, the Sayama incident, which involved a murder conviction of a *burakumin* based on circumstantial evidence, focused public attention on the problems of the *burakumin*. In the 1980s, some educators and local governments, particularly in areas with relatively large *burakumin* populations, began special education programs, which they hoped would encourage greater educational and economic success for young *burakumin* and decrease the discrimination they faced.

Ainu

The second minority group among Japanese citizens is the Ainu, who are thought to be related to Tungusic, Altaic, and Uralic peoples of Siberia. Historically, the Ainu (Ainu means human in the Ainu language) were an indigenous hunting and gathering population who occupied most of northern Honshū as late as the Nara period (A.D. 710–94). As Japanese settlement expanded, the Ainu were pushed northward, until by the Meiji period, they were confined by the government to a small area in Hokkaidō, in a manner similar to the placing of native Americans on reservations. Characterized as remnants of a primitive circumpolar culture, the fewer than 20,000 Ainu in 1990 were considered racially distinct and thus not fully Japanese. Disease and a low birth rate had severely diminished their numbers over the past two centuries and intermarriage had brought about an almost completely mixed population.

Although no longer in daily use, the Ainu language in 1990 was preserved in epics, songs, and stories transmitted orally over succeeding generations. Distinctive rhythmic music and dances and some Ainu festivals and crafts were preserved, but mainly in order to take advantage of tourism.

Values and Beliefs

Contemporary Japan is a secular society. Creating harmonious relations with others through reciprocity and the fulfillment of social obligations is more significant for most Japanese than an individual's relationship to a transcendent God. Harmony, order, and self-development are three of the most important values that underlie Japanese social interaction. Basic ideas about self and the nature of human society are drawn from several religious and philosophical traditions. Religious practice, too, emphasizes the maintenance of harmonious relations with others (both spiritual beings and other humans) and the fulfillment of social obligations as a member of a family and a community.

Values

Empathy and Human Relations

In Japanese mythology, the gods display human emotions, such as love and anger. In these stories, behavior that results in positive relations with others is rewarded, and empathy, identifying oneself with another, is highly valued. By contrast, those actions that are antisocial, or that harm others, are condemned. Hurtful behavior is punished in the myths by ostracizing the offender.

No society can exist that tolerates significant antisocial behavior in the long term, but Japan is among the societies that most strongly rely on social rather than supernatural sanctions and emphasize the benefits of harmony. Japanese children learn from their earliest days that human fulfillment comes from close association with others. Children learn early to recognize that they are part of an interdependent society, beginning in the family and later extending to larger groups such as neighborhood, school, community, and workplace. Dependence on others is a natural part of the human condition; it is viewed negatively only when the social obligations it creates are too onerous to fulfill.

In interpersonal relationships, most Japanese tend to avoid open competition and confrontation. Working with others requires self-control, but it carries the rewards of pride in contributing to the group, emotional security, and social identity. *Wa,* the notion of harmony within a group, requires an attitude of cooperation and a recognition of social roles. If each individual in the group understands personal obligations and empathizes with the situations of others, then the group as a whole benefits. Success can come only if all put forth their best individual efforts. Decisions are often made only after consulting with everyone in the group. Consensus does not imply that there has been universal agreement, but this style of consultative decision making involves each member of the group in an information exchange, reinforces feelings of group identity, and makes implementation of the decision smoother. Cooperation within a group also is often focused on competition between that group and a parallel one, whether the issue is one of educational success or market share. Symbols such as uniforms, names, banners, and songs identify the group as distinct from others both to outsiders and internally. Participation in group activities, whether official or unofficial, is a symbolic statement that an individual wishes to be considered part of the group. Thus, after-work bar hopping provides not only instrumental opportunities for the exchange of information and release of social tensions, but also opportunities to express nonverbally a desire for continued affiliation.

Working in a group in Japan requires the development of successful channels of communication, which reinforce group interdependence and the sense of difference from those who are not members of the group. Yet social interaction beyond that which occurs with individuals with whom one lives and works is a necessity in contemporary society. If the exchange is brief and relatively

Practitioners of Kendō—*the "way of the sword"—a form of spiritual discipline combined with ancient Chinese fencing techniques*
Courtesy Eliot Frankeberger

insignificant, such as buying a newspaper, anonymity will be maintained. But if the relationship is expected to continue over a long period, whether in business, marriage, employment, or neighborhood, great care is likely to be invested in establishing and maintaining good relationships. Such relationships are often begun by using the social networks of a relative, friend, or colleague who can provide an introduction to the desired person or serve as *nakōdo* (go-between). The *nakōdo* most often refers to the person (or people) who negotiates marriage arrangements, including checking each family's background, conveying questions and criticisms, and smoothing out difficulties. But this kind of personal mediation is common in many aspects of Japanese life.

Group membership in Japan provides enjoyment and fulfillment, but also causes tremendous tension. An ideology of group harmony does not ensure harmony in fact. Japan is an extremely competitive society, yet competition within the group must be suppressed. Minor issues are sometimes dealt with by appeals to higher authority, but they may well smolder unresolved for years. Major problems may be denied, especially to outsiders, but may result in factions or in the fissioning of the group (see Interest Groups, ch. 6). It is often the individual, however, who bears the burden of these interpersonal tensions. This burden is reflected in high rates of alcohol consumption and of minor, sometimes psychosomatic, illness. Many Japanese cope with these stresses by retreating into the private self or by enjoying the escapism offered by much of the popular culture (see The Arts, ch. 3).

The Public Sphere: Order and Status

It is difficult to imagine a Japanese vision of the social order without the influence of Confucianism, because prior to the advent of Chinese influence in the sixth century, Japan did not have a stratified society (see Religious and Philosophical Traditions, this ch.). Confucianism emphasizes harmony among heaven, nature, and human society achieved through each person's accepting his or her social role and contributing to the social order by proper behavior. An often quoted phrase from the Confucian essay "Da Xue" (The Great Learning) explains, "Their persons being cultivated, their families were regulated. Their families being regulated, their states were rightly governed. Their states being rightly governed, the whole kingdom was made tranquil and happy."

This view implies that hierarchy is natural. Relative status differences define nearly all social interaction. Age or seniority, gender, educational attainment, and place of employment are common distinctions that guide interaction. Without some knowledge of the other's background, age and gender may be an individual's only guidelines. A Japanese person may prefer not to interact with a stranger to avoid potential errors in etiquette. The business cards or calling cards so frequently exchanged in Japan are valuable tools of social interaction because they provide enough information about another person to facilitate normal social exchange. Japan scholar Edwin O. Reischauer noted that whereas Americans often act to minimize status differences, Japanese find it awkward, even unbecoming, when a person does not behave in accordance with status expectations.

The Japanese language is one means of expressing status differences and contributes to the assumption that hierarchy is natural. Verb endings regularly express relationships of superiority or inferiority. Japanese has a rich vocabulary of honorific and humble terms that indicate a person's status or may be manipulated to express what the speaker desires the relationship to be. Men and women employ somewhat different speech patterns, with women making greater use of polite forms. Certain words are identified with masculine speech and others with feminine. For example, there are a number of ways to say the pronoun "I," depending on the formality of the occasion, the gender of the speaker, and the relative

People and goods being ferried from Nagasaki
Courtesy The Mainichi Newspapers

status of the speaker and listener. As is appropriate in a culture that stresses the value of empathy, one person cannot speak without considering the other.

The term *hierarchy* implies a ranking of roles and a rigid set of rules, and Japan has its share of bureaucracy. But the kind of hierarchical sense that pervades the whole society is of a different sort, which anthropologist Robert Smith calls "diffuse order." For example, in premodern times, local leaders were given a great deal of autonomy in exchange for assuming total responsibility for affairs in their localities. In contemporary Japan also, responsibility is collective and authority diffuse. The person seeming to be in charge is, in reality, bound into the web of group interdependence as tightly as those who appear to be his subordinates. Leadership thus calls not for a forceful personality and sharp decision-making skills, but for sensitivity to the feelings of others and skills in mediation. Even in the early 1990s, leaders were expected to assume responsibility for a major problem occurring in or because of their groups by resigning their posts, although they may have had no direct involvement in the situation.

Status in Japan is based on specific relationships between individuals, often relationships of social dependency between those of unequal status. *Giri* (duty), the sense of obligation to those to

97

whom one is indebted, requires deferential behavior and eventually repayment of the favor, which in turn calls forth future favors. Relations of social dependence thus continue indefinitely, with their very inequality binding individuals to each other. Rules of hierarchy are tempered by the relationship itself. This tempering is known as *ninjō* (human emotion or compassion). The potential conflict between *giri* and *ninjō* has been a frequent theme in Japanese drama and literature (see Performing Arts; Literature, ch. 3). Although young Japanese in 1990 were less likely to phrase a personal dilemma in those terms, claiming that the concept of *giri* was old-fashioned, many continued to feel stress in doing what they should when it was not what they wanted. Social order exists in part because all members of the society are linked in relationships of social dependency, each involved in giving and receiving.

The Private Sphere: Goals and Self

Relative status may be seen as the basis of social organization and affiliation with others may be considered desirable, but these assumptions by no means negate a concept of self. An ideology of harmony with others does not automatically create a congruence of individual with group or institutional goals. Anthropologist Brian Moeran distinguishes Japanese attitudes toward individuality and individualism. Individuality, or the uniqueness of a person, is not only tolerated, but often admired if the person is seen as sincere, as acting from the heart. A work of art conveys strength as well as beauty from its "individuality." Individualism, on the other hand, is viewed negatively, for it is equated with selfishness, the opposite of the empathy that is so highly valued. While many modern Japanese deny the relevance of the concept of *seishin* (selfless spiritual strength, as in World War II soldiers), selfishness (especially "selfish mothers," because the behavior of mothers is commonly thought to effect the mental and physical health of children) takes the blame for many social problems of modern society. These problems include ones categorized as psychosomatic medical syndromes, such as kitchen syndrome (*dadokoro shōkōgun*), in which formerly meticulous housewives suddenly adopt odd behaviors and complain of aches and pains, nonverbally expressing their frustration with or rejection of the "good wife-wise mother" role, or school-refusal syndrome (*tōkō kyohi*), in which children complain of somatic problems, such as stomachaches, and thus miss school in an attempt to avoid academic or social failure.

Japan, like all other societies, has conflicts between individual and group. What is different from North American society is not that the Japanese have no sense of self, but rather that the self is defined through its interaction with others and not merely through the force of individual personality.

According to Japan scholar Edwin O. Reischauer, "The cooperative, relativistic Japanese is not thought of as the bland product of a social conditioning that has worn off all individualistic corners, but rather as the product of firm inner self-control that has made him master of his . . . anti-social instincts . . . . Social conformity . . . is no sign of weakness but rather the proud, tempered product of inner strength." This mastery is achieved by overcoming hardship, through self-discipline, and through personal striving for a perfection that one knows is not possible but remains a worthy goal. In this view, both the self and society can be improved, and in fact are interrelated, since the ideal of selfhood toward which many Japanese strive is one in which consideration of others is paramount. Whereas Americans attempt to cultivate a self that is unique, most Japanese place greater emphasis on cultivating "a self that can feel human in the company of others," according to David Plath. Maturity means continuing to care about what others are thinking but feeling confident in one's ability to judge and act effectively, acknowledging social norms while remaining true to self.

Religious and Philosophical Traditions

The values described in the preceding section are derived from a number of religious and philosophical traditions, both indigenous and foreign. Taken together, these traditions may be considered the Japanese world view, although the personal beliefs of an individual Japanese may incorporate some aspects and disregard others. The Japanese world view is eclectic, contrasting with a Western view in which religion is exclusive and defines one's identity. Contemporary Japanese society is highly secular. Cause and effect relations are frequently based in scientific models, and illness and death are explained by modern medical theories. Yet the scientific view is but one of the options from which an individual may draw in interpreting life's experiences.

The Japanese world view is characterized also by a pragmatic approach to problem solving, in which the technique may be less important than the results. Thus a Japanese who is ill may simultaneously or sequentially seek the assistance of a medical doctor, obtain medication from a person trained in the Chinese herbal tradition, and visit a local shrine. Each of these actions is based on a different belief in causation of the illness: the physician may say that the illness is due to a bacterial infection; the herbalist regards the body as being out of balance; and the basis of the shrine visit is the belief that the mind must be cleansed to heal the body. In the West, these explanations might be viewed as mutually exclusive, but the Japanese patient may hold all of these views simultaneously without a sense of discord. Similarly, a student studying for university entrance examinations knows that without extraordinary hard work, admission is impossible. Yet the student will probably also visit a special shrine to ask for the help of the spiritual world in assuring success.

The roots of the Japanese world view can be traced to several traditions. Shinto, the only indigenous religion of Japan, provided the base. Confucianism, from China, provided concepts of hierarchy, loyalty, and the emperor as the son of heaven. Daoism, also from China, helped give order and sanction to the system of government implied in Shinto. Buddhism brought with it not only its contemplative religious aspects but also a developed culture of art and temples, which had a considerable role in public life. Christianity brought an infusion of Western ideas, particularly those involving social justice and reform.

Shinto

Shinto (Way of the Gods) is the term used to refer to an assortment of beliefs and practices indigenous to Japan that predate the arrival of Buddhism, but have in turn been influenced by it. The Shinto world view is of a pantheistic universe of *kami,* spirits or gods with varying degrees of power.

Although each person is expected to continue existence as a *kami* after death, Shinto is concerned with this world rather than with the afterlife. This world contains defiling substances, and Shinto ritual often involves mental and physical purification of a person who has come into contact with a pollutant, such as death. Water or salt commonly serve as purifying agents. Some *kami* are guardian deities for villages, and thus they symbolize the unity of the human community as well as mediating in its relationship with the natural and supernatural worlds.

Japanese legends describe the activities and personalities of the *kami.* The most well-known legends describe the creation of the human world and trace the origins of the Japanese imperial family to the gods (see Ancient Cultures, ch. 1). The latter legend formed the basis of the wide acceptance of the concept of the emperor's divine descent in pre-1945 Japan.

In the fifth and sixth centuries, Shinto came under the influence of Chinese Confucianism and Buddhism. From the former, it borrowed the veneration of ancestors, and from the latter it adopted philosophical ideas and religious rites. Because of the popularity of things Chinese and the ethical and philosophical attraction of

Buddhism for the court and the imperial family, Shinto became somewhat less influential than Buddhism for more than a millennium. Many people, however, were adherents to both systems of belief. By the seventeenth century, Shinto began to emerge from Buddhism's shadow through the influence of neo-Confucian rationalism (see Intellectual Trends, ch. 1).

The emerging nationalism of the late Tokugawa period combined with the political needs of the Meiji Restoration (1868) oligarchs to reform Shinto into a state religion, and it flourished as such until 1945 under government patronage. Japan's defeat in World War II and the emperor's denial of his divinity brought an end to State Shinto (see The Status of the Emperor, ch. 6). Sometimes considered synonymous with State Shinto before 1945 was Shrine Shinto (Jinja Shintō), but after the war most Shinto traditions were observed in the home rather than in shrines. Most shrines, which had previously benefited from state sponsorship, were organized into the Association of Shinto Shrines after 1946. Sect Shinto (Kyōha Shintō) consists of more than eighty private religious sects, which conduct services in houses of worship or lecture halls rather than in shrines.

In 1987 there were more than 81,350 Shinto shrines and 102,000 clergy in Japan. After World War II, the requirement of membership in a shrine parish was revoked, but in 1990 local shrines still served as focal points for community identity for many Japanese, and occasional informal or ritual visits are common. Nearly 95 million Japanese citizens professed adherence to some form of Shinto. Some of the Sect Shinto groups are considered new religions.

Buddhism

Buddhism, which originated in India, was introduced into Japan in the sixth century A.D. from Korea and China. Buddhism introduced ideas into Japanese culture that have become inseparable from the Japanese world view: the concept of rebirth, ideas of karmic causation, and an emphasis on the unity of experience. It gained the patronage of the ruling class, which supported the building of temples and production of Buddhist art (see Cultural Developments and the Establishment of Buddhism, ch. 1). In the early centuries of Buddhism in Japan, scholarly esoteric sects were popular, and the Buddhist influence was limited mainly to the upper class. From the late Heian period (A.D. 794–1185) through the Kamakura period (1185–1333), Pure Land (Jōdo) and Nichiren Shōshū sects, which had much wider appeal, spread throughout all classes of society (see The Flourishing of Buddhism, ch. 1). These

101

The 160-meter-high torii *gate at Itsukushima Shrine, in Hiroshima Bay, dedicated to Shinto* kami, *who protect seafarers and oversee fishing*
Courtesy Jane T. Griffin

sects stressed experience and faith, promising salvation in a future world. Zen Buddhism, which encourages the attainment of enlightenment through meditation and an austere life style, had wide appeal among the *bushi* or samurai—the warrior class—who had come to have great political power (see The Rise of the Military Class, ch. 1). Under the sponsorship of the ruling military class, Zen had a major impact on Japanese aesthetics. In addition, Japan scholar Robert Bellah has argued, Buddhist sects popular among commoners in the Tokugawa period encouraged values such as hard work and delayed rewards, which, like Protestantism in Europe, helped lay the ideological foundation for Japan's industrial success.

Buddhist funerary and ancestral rites remained pervasive in Japan in the late 1980s. Although regular attendance at Buddhist temples was rare, partly because many Buddhist sects did not observe community worship, there were in 1987 more than 77,000 temples and 274,000 clergy. Buddhist as well as Shinto priests marry and often sons inherit the responsibility for their father's parish at his death. The Nichiren school, based on belief in the *Lotus Sutra* and its doctrine of universal salvation, was the largest sect in Japan in 1989, with 35,541,430 members. Its wide appeal was based on the broad range of religious and social thought and the lay activities it incorporates.

Confucianism

Although not practiced as a religion, Confucianism from China has deeply influenced Japanese thought. In essence, Confucianism is the practice of proper forms of conduct, especially in social and familial relationships. It is derived from compilations attributed to the fifth-century B.C. Chinese philosopher Kong Fuzi or Kongzi (Confucius; in Japanese, Kōshi). Confucian government was to be a moral government, bureaucratic in form and benevolent toward the ruled. Confucianism also provided an hierarchical system, in which each person was to act according to his or her status to create a harmoniously functioning society and ensure loyalty to the state. The teachings of filial piety and humanity continue to form the foundation for much of social life and ideas about family and nation.

Neo-Confucianism, introduced to Japan in the twelfth century, is an interpretation of nature and society based on metaphysical principles, and influenced by Buddhist and Daoist ideas. In Japan, where it is known as Shushigaku (Shushi School, after the Chinese neo-Confucian scholar Zhu Xi—Shushi in Japanese), it brought the idea that family stability and social responsibility are human obligations. The school used various metaphysical concepts to

Buddhist monk
Courtesy Sheila Page Gault

Buddhist nun
Courtesy Kelsey Saint

explain the natural and social order. Shushigaku, in turn, influenced the *kokutai* (national polity) theory, which emphasized the special national characteristics of Japan.

Daoism

Daoism (literally, the way) from China has also influenced Japanese thought, and has a special affinity for Zen Buddhism. Zen's praise of emptiness, exhortations to act in harmony with nature, and admonitions to avoid discrimination and duality all are parallel in Daoist beliefs. The lunar calendar, the selection of auspicious days for special events, the siting of buildings, and numerous folk medicinal treatments also have origins in Daoism and continue as customs to varying degrees in contemporary Japanese society. Daoism has also influenced native shamanistic traditions and rituals.

Christianity

Christianity was introduced in the sixteenth century by Portuguese and Spanish Roman Catholic missionaries, but, because it was associated with Western imperialism and considered a threat to Japanese political control, it was banned from the mid-seventeenth century to the mid-nineteenth century (see Seclusion and Social Control, ch. 1). With the reopening of Japan in the mid-1850s, missionaries again arrived. While fewer than 900,000 people (less than 1 percent of the population) considered themselves Christian in the late 1980s, Christianity was respected for its contributions to society, particularly in education and social action. In the late 1980s, about 64 percent of all Christians belonged to Protestant churches, about 32 percent to the Roman Catholic Church, and about 4 percent to other Christian denominations. There were more than 3,200 places of Christian worship in Japan.

New Religions

A number of religious organizations are generally labeled "new religions" (*shinkō shūkyō*), although some date back to the early nineteenth century. The largest are Sōka Gakkai (Value Creation Society), Risshō Kōseikai (Society for the Establishment of Justice and Community for the Rise [of Buddhism]), and Tenrikyō (Religion of Divine Wisdom), with more than 17 million, 6 million, and about 2.5 million members, respectively, in the late 1980s. Both Sōka Gakkai and Risshō Kōseikai are offshoots of the Nichiren Shōshū sect of Buddhism. Tenrikyō was once considered an offshoot of Sect Shinto but is now regarded as independent of other divisions of Shinto. Some of the larger of these new religions were active internationally as well as in Japan.

No one category can be used to describe all of the new religions. What distinguishes them from popular or folk religions is their claim to an organizational status equivalent to Shinto or Buddhism. Their teachings are diverse, but most syncretize elements of Buddhist, Shinto, Christian, and other beliefs. Most emphasize the dependence of the living on *kami,* the Buddha or Buddhist figures, or ancestors. Some, such as Tenrikyō, are monotheistic and stress individual salvation. For example, Risshō Kōseikai adherents gather in small groups to discuss religious issues and problems of daily life. Most of the new religions provide special support to their adherents through small group meetings, and encourage solving problems through ritual and proper behavior. Many stress harmonious relations with others, hard work, and sincerity as the way to a better life.

Most of the new religions were founded by charismatic lay people, often women, who had experienced transforming spiritual episodes and felt called upon to convey these experiences to others. They stressed lay participation, involving small, local, face-to-face groups as well as national organizations. They encouraged direct contact with the supernatural, and some groups practiced faith healing and mutual support techniques. People who joined these groups often did so in response to personal problems, but many found continuing fulfillment through their emphasis on returning to traditional values.

Religious Practice

Most Japanese participate in rituals and customs derived from several religious traditions (see table 3, Appendix). Life cycle events are often marked by visits to a Shinto shrine. The birth of a new baby is celebrated with a formal shrine visit at the age of about one month, as are the third, fifth, and seventh birthdays and the official beginning of adulthood at age twenty. Wedding ceremonies are often performed by Shinto priests, but Christian weddings are also popular. In the early 1980s, more than 8 percent of weddings were held in a shrine or temple and nearly 4 percent in a church. The most popular place for a wedding ceremony—chosen by 41 percent—was a wedding hall.

Funerals are most often performed by Buddhist priests, and Buddhist rites are also common on death day anniversaries of deceased family members. Some Japanese do not perform ancestral ceremonies at all, and some do so rather mechanically and awkwardly. But there have also been changes in these practices, such as more personal and private ceremonies and women honoring their own as well as their husband's ancestors, that make them more meaningful to contemporary participants.

There are two categories of holidays in Japan: *matsuri* (festivals), which are largely of Shinto origin and relate to the cultivation of rice and the spiritual well-being of the community; and *nenchū gyō* (annual events), mainly of Chinese or Buddhist origin. The *matsuri* were supplemented during the Heian period with more festivals added, and they were organized into a formal calendar. In addition to the complementary nature of the different holidays, there were later accretions during the feudal period. Very few *matsuri* or *nenchū gyō* are national holidays, but they are included in the national calendar of annual events (see table 4, Appendix).

Most holidays are secular in nature, but the two most significant for the majority of Japanese—New Year's Day for Shinto believers and Obon (also call Bon Festival) for Buddhists, which marks the end of the ancestors' annual visit to their earthly home—involve visits to Shinto shrines or Buddhist temples. The New Year's holiday (January 1–3) is marked by the practice of numerous customs and the consumption of special foods. These customs include time for getting together with family and friends, for special television programming, and for visiting Shinto shrines to pray for family blessings in the coming year. Dressing in a kimono, hanging out special decorations, eating noodles on New Year's Eve to show continuity into the new year, and playing a poetry card game are among the more "traditional" practices. During Obon season, in mid-August (or mid-July depending on the locale), *bon* (spirit altars) are set up in front of Buddhist family altars, which, along with ancestral graves, are cleaned in anticipation of the return of the spirits. As with the New Year holiday, people living away from their family homes return for visits with relatives. Celebrations include folk dancing and prayers at the Buddhist temple as well as family rituals in the home.

Many Japanese also participate, at least as spectators, in one of the many local *matsuri* celebrated throughout the country. *Matsuri* may be sponsored by schools, towns, or other groups, but are most often associated with Shinto shrines. As religious festivals, these strike a Western observer as quite commercialized and secular, but the many who plan the events, cook special foods, or carry the floats on their shoulders, find renewal of self and of community through participation.

Religion and the State

Article 20 of the 1947 Constitution states that, "Freedom of religion is guaranteed to all. No religious organization shall receive

Shinto presentation ceremony for girls ages seven and five
Courtesy Sheila Page Gault

any privileges from the State, nor exercise any political authority . . ." (see The Postwar Constitution, ch. 6). Contemporary religious freedom fits well with the tolerant attitude of most Japanese toward other religious beliefs and practices. Separation of religion and the state, however, is a more difficult issue.

Historically, there was no distinction between a scientific and a religious world view. In early Japanese history, the ruling class was responsible for performing propitiatory rituals, which later came to be identified as Shinto, and for the introduction and support of Buddhism. Later, religious organization was used by regimes for political purposes, as when the Tokugawa government required each family to be registered as a member of a Buddhist temple for purposes of social control. In the late nineteenth century, rightists created State Shinto, requiring that each family belong to a shrine parish and that the concepts of emperor worship and a national Japanese "family" be taught in the schools.

In the 1980s, the meaning of the separation of state and religion again became controversial. The issue came to a head in 1985 when Prime Minister Nakasone Yasuhiro paid an official visit to Yasukuni Shrine, which honors Japanese war dead, including leaders from the militarist period in the 1930s and 1940s (see The Rise of the Militarists, ch. 1). Supporters of Nakasone's action (mainly on the political right) argued that the visit was to pay homage to patriots; others claimed that the visit was an attempt to revive State Shinto and nationalistic extremism. The visit was protested by China, North Korea, South Korea, and other countries occupied by Japan in the first half of the twentieth century, and domestically by leftists, intellectuals, and the Japanese news media. Similar cases have occurred at local levels, and courts increasingly often have been asked to clarify the division between religion and government. Separating religious elements of the Japanese world view from what is merely "Japanese" is not easy, especially given the ambiguous role of the emperor, whose divinity was denied in 1945, but who continued to perform functions of both state and religion.

Social Organization

From birth Japanese are recognized as autonomous human beings. However, from the beginning infants are influenced by society's emphasis on social interdependence. In fact, Japanese human development may be seen as a movement toward mastery of an ever-expanding circle of social life, beginning with the family, widening to include school and neighborhood as children grow, and incorporating roles as colleague, inferior, and superior. Viewed in this perspective, socialization does not culminate with adolescence, for the individual must learn to be, for example, a section chief, a parent-teacher association member, or a grandparent at various points in life.

Many Westerners ask whether there is a Japanese self that exists apart from identification with a group. The answer lies in the Japanese distinction between *uchi* (inside) and *soto* (outside). These terms are relative, and the "we" implied in *uchi* can refer to the individual, the family, a work group, a company, a neighborhood, or even all of Japan. But it is always defined in opposition to a "they." The context or situation thus calls for some level of definition of self. When an American businessman meets a Japanese counterpart, the Japanese will define himself as a member of a particular company with which the American is doing business. However, if the American makes a cultural mistake, the Japanese is likely to define himself as Japanese as distinguished from a foreigner. The American might go away from his encounter with the belief that the Japanese think of themselves only as members of a group. The same person attending a school event with one of his children might be defined at the level of his family or household. Viewed relaxing at home or playing golf with former classmates, he would perhaps have reached a level of definition more similar to an American concept of self.

From childhood, however, Japanese are taught that this level of self should not be assertive, but rather considerate of the needs of others; the private emotions and perhaps the fun-loving, relaxed side of Japanese individuals are tolerated and even admired as long as these do not interfere with the performance of more public responsibilities. The proper performance of social roles is necessary to the smooth functioning of society. Individuals, aware of private inner selves (and even resistance to the very roles they perform), use a shifting scale of *uchi* and *soto* to define themselves in various situations.

Family

The family is the earliest locus of social life for an individual and provides a model of social organization for most later encounters with the wider world. Yet, as *uchi*, the Japanese family does not have clear boundaries. At times the term *family* may refer to a nuclear family of parents and unmarried children. On other occasions it refers to a line of descent, and on still others it refers to the household as a unit of production or consumption.

A great variety of family forms have existed historically in Japan, from the matrilocal customs of the Heian elite, which are described in *Genji monogatari* (Tale of Genji), to the extreme patrilineality of the samurai class in the feudal period. Numerous family forms, through which ran a common belief in the existence of the family-household beyond the life of its current members, coexisted, particularly in the countryside. Among the upper classes and wealthier merchant and artisan urban households of the Tokugawa period, the *chōnin*, providing for household continuity, and if possible enriching the household's estate, represented duty to one's ancestors and appreciation toward one's parents.

With the promulgation of the Domestic Relations and Inheritance Law in 1898, the Japanese government institutionalized more rigid family controls than most people had known in the feudal period. Individuals were registered in an official family registry. In the early twentieth century, each family was required to conform to the *ie* (household) system, with a multigenerational household under the legal authority of a household head. In establishing the *ie* system, the government moved the ideology of family in the opposite direction of trends resulting from urbanization and industrialization. The *ie* system took as its model for the family the Confucian-influenced pattern of the Tokugawa period upper classes. Authority and responsibility for all members of the *ie* lay legally with the household head. Each generation supplied a male and female adult, with a preference for first son inheritance and patrilocal marriage. When possible, daughters were expected to marry out and younger sons to establish their own households. Women could not legally own or control property or select spouses. The *ie* system thus artificially restricted the development of individualism, individual rights, women's rights, and the nuclearization of the family. It formalized patriarchy and emphasized lineal and instrumental rather than conjugal and emotional ties within the family.

After World War II, the Allied occupation forces established a new family ideology based on equal rights for women, equal inheritance by all children, and free choice of spouse and career. From the late 1960s, most marriages in Japan have been based on the mutual attraction of the couple and not the arrangement of parents. Moreover, arranged marriages in the 1980s might have begun with an introduction by a relative or family friend, but actual negotiations did not begin until all parties, including the bride and groom, were satisfied with the relationship.

Under the *ie* system, only a minority of households included three generations at a time, since nonsuccessor sons (those who were not-heirs) often set up their own household. From 1970 to 1983, the proportion of three-generation households fell from 19 percent to 15 percent of all households, while two-generation households consisting of a couple and their unmarried children increased only slightly, from 41 percent to 42 percent of all households. The greatest change has been the increase in couple-only households and in elderly single-person households.

Public opinion surveys in the late 1980s seemed to confirm the statistical movement away from the three-generation *ie* family model. Half of the respondents did not think that the first son had a special role to play in the family, and nearly two-thirds rejected the need for adoption of a son in order to continue the family. Other changes, such as an increase in filial violence and school refusal suggest a breakdown of strong family authority.

Official statistics, however, indicate that Japanese concepts of family continued to diverge from those in the United States in the 1980s. The divorce rate, although increasing slowly, remained at 1.3 per 1,000 marriages in 1987, low by international standards. Strong gender roles remained the cornerstone of family responsibilities. Most survey respondents said that family life should emphasize parent-child ties over husband-wife relations. Nearly 80 percent of respondents in a 1986 government survey believed that the ancestral home and family grave should be carefully kept and handed on to one's children. Over 60 percent thought it best for elderly parents to live with one of their children. This sense of family as a unit that continued through time was stronger among people who had a livelihood to pass down, such as farmers, merchants, owners of small companies, and physicians, than among urban salary and wage earners. Anthropologist Jane Bachnik noted the continued emphasis on continuity in the rural families she studied. *Uchi* (here, the contemporary family) were considered the living members of an *ie,* which had no formal existence. Yet, in each generation, there occurred a sorting of members into permanent and temporary members, defining different levels of *uchi.*

Various family life-styles exist side by side in contemporary Japan. In many urban families, the husband may commute to work and return late, having little time with his children except for Sundays, a favorite day for family outings. The wife might be a "professional housewife," with nearly total responsibility for raising children, assuring their careers and marriages, running the household, and managing the family budget. She also has primary responsibility for maintaining social relations with the wider circles of relatives, neighbors, and acquaintances, and for managing the family's reputation. Her social life remains separate from that of her husband. It is increasingly likely that in addition to these family responsibilities, she would also have a part-time job or participate in adult education or other community activities. The closest emotional ties within such families are between the mother and children.

In other families, particularly among the self-employed, husband and wife work side by side in a family business. Although gender-based roles are clear cut, they might not be as rigidly distinct as in a household where work and family are more separated. In such families, fathers are more involved in their children's development because they have more opportunity for interacting with them.

As women worked outside of the home with increasing frequency in the 1970s and 1980s, there was pressure on their husbands to take on more responsibility for housework and child care. Farm families, who depended on nonfarm employment for most of their income, were also developing patterns of interaction different from those of previous generations.

Neighborhood

Beyond the family, the next group to which children are introduced is the neighborhood. Although the loose, informal groups of children who wandered through villages of the past had no counterpart in contemporary heavily trafficked city streets, neighborhood playgrounds and the grounds of local shrines and temples are sites where young children, accompanied by mothers, begin to learn to get along with others.

Among neighbors, there is great concern for face. In old urban neighborhoods or rural villages, families might have been neighbors for generations, and thus expect relationships of assistance and cooperation to continue into the future. In newer company housing, neighbors represent both competition and stress at the workplace, which cannot be expressed. Extra care is taken to maintain proper relations while maximizing family privacy. Participation in neighborhood activities is not mandatory, but nonparticipants might lose face. If a family plans to stay in an area, people feel strong pressures to participate in public projects such as neighborhood cleanups or seasonal festivals. Concern for the family's reputation is real because background checks for marriage and employment might include asking neighbors their opinions about a family. More positively, neighbors become *uchi* for certain purposes, such as local merchants providing personal services, physicians responding to calls for minor ailments and emergency treatment, and neighbors taking care of children while their mother goes out.

People who work in the neighborhood where they live often have a different attitude from those who spend most of their waking hours at distant workplaces, creating differences in character between the central city and the suburbs. Central city areas, dominated by the old middle class of artisans, merchants, and small business owners, generally have more active neighborhood associations and other local groups, such as merchant associations and shrine associations. The neighborhood association's activities include public sanitation and health, volunteer firefighting, disaster preparedness, crime prevention, information exchange, and recreational activities, particularly for children and the elderly. In new urban or suburban developments, local governments might take a more active role in performing these functions. In neighborhoods with mixtures of new and old middle class residents, it is people with the time and interest, most likely those with businesses in the area, who are active in neighborhood affairs. The activities of women and children, however, might cut across such class distinctions. The emphasis on good relations with neighbors helps counteract the potential depersonalization of urban living. Working together on community projects, exchanging information, and cooperating in community rituals, such as festivals, helps maintain a sense of community.

The consequences of economic growth were examined more closely by 1980s consumers, who began to demand higher quality social services, more libraries and cultural centers, greater access to sports facilities, and more parkland. Attention was increasingly focused on the adverse effects of urban life on families: modern children were seen as more demanding and less disciplined than their forebears, who had experienced war and poverty.

Despite these problems, urban life was much safer and more convenient than in many other countries in the late twentieth century. In contrast to most industrialized nations, urban crime rates were declining. The streets of Tokyo were safe even at night, and a public campaign was more likely to urge residents to lock their doors than to suggest they install deadbolts. Public transportation was congested but convenient, clean, punctual, and relatively inexpensive (see Transportation and Communications, ch. 4). Complaints were heard, however, that railroad station parking lots were too small to accommodate all commuter bicycles. In urban areas, houses were close together; but at the same time shops were close by, and housewives could easily purchase fresh vegetables and fish daily. Urban life was made more attractive for many by a wide variety of cultural and sports activities, including the symphony orchestra, theater, sumo, professional baseball, museums, and art galleries (see The Arts, ch. 3).

Workplace

Entry into the labor force widens the circle of social relationships. For many adults, these contacts are important sources of friendships and resources. For men especially, the workplace is the focus of their social world. Many both in and outside of Japan share an image of the Japanese workplace that is based on a lifetime-employment model used by large companies. These employment practices came about as the result of labor shortage in the 1920s, when companies competed to recruit and retain the best workers by offering better benefits and job security. By the 1960s, employment at a large prestigious company had become the goal of children of the new middle class; the pursuit of which required mobilization of family resources and great individual perseverance in order to achieve success in the fiercely competitive education system.

Lifetime employment referred not to a worker's lifetime, but to the time from school graduation until mandatory retirement, in 1990 at age sixty for most men. Workers were recruited directly out of school, and large investments were made in training. Employees were expected to work hard and demonstrate loyalty to the firm, in exchange for some degree of job security and benefits, such as housing subsidies, good insurance, the use of recreational facilities, and bonuses and pensions. Wages began low, but seniority was rewarded with promotions based on a combination of seniority and ability. Leadership was not based on assertiveness or quick decision making, but on the ability to create consensus, taking into account the needs of subordinates. Surveys indicated continued preference for bosses who were demanding but showed concern for workers' private lives over less-demanding bosses interested only in performance on the job. This system rewarded behavior demonstrating identification with the team effort, indicated by singing the company song, not taking all of one's vacation days, and sharing credit for accomplishments with the work group. Pride in one's work was expressed through competition with other parallel sections in the company and between one's company and other companies in similar lines of business. Thus, individuals were motivated to maintain *wa* (harmony) and participate in group activities, not only on the job, but in after-hours socializing as well. The image of group loyalty, however, might have been more a matter of ideology than practice, especially for people who did not make it to the top.

Every worker did not enjoy the benefits of such employment practices and work environments in the 1980s. Although 64 percent of households in 1985 depended on wages or salaries for most of their income, most of these workers were employed by small and medium-sized firms that could not afford the benefits or achieve the successes of the large companies, despite the best intentions of owners. Even in the large corporations, distinctions between permanent and temporary employees made many workers, often women, ineligible for benefits and promotions. These workers were also the first to be laid off in difficult business conditions. Japan scholar Dorinne K. Kondo compares the status of permanent and temporary workers with Bachnik's distinctions between permanent and temporary members of an *ie,* creating degrees of inside and outside within a firm. Traditions of entrepreneurship and of inheritance of the means of livelihood continued among merchants, artisans, farmers, and fishermen, still nearly 20 percent of the work force in 1985. These workers gave up security for autonomy, and when economically necessary, supplemented household income with wage employment. Traditionally, such businesses used unpaid family labor, but in 1990 wives or even husbands were likely to go off to work in factories or offices and leave spouses or retired parents to work the farm or mind the shop. Policies of decentralization provided factory jobs locally for families that farmed part-time; on the other hand, unemployment created by deindustrialization affected rural as well as urban workers. Unemployment was low in Japan compared to other industrialized nations (less than 3 percent through the late 1980s), but an estimated 400,000 day laborers shared none of the security or affluence enjoyed by those employees with lifetime-employment benefits.

Although Japanese workers are known worldwide for their hard work and dedication to their firms, more than 50 percent of respondents of a 1988 government survey said that they would rather have more free time than increased income. The proportion preferring free time to increased income was greater among professionals, supervisors, and white-collar workers. There was also evidence of increased interfirm mobility among some types of workers in the late 1980s, as a result of a labor shortage and changing attitudes toward work among young people.

Popular Culture

Japanese popular culture not only reflects the attitudes and concerns of the present, but also provides a link to the past. Popular films, television programs, comics, and music all developed from older artistic and literary traditions, and many of their themes and styles of presentation can be traced to traditional art forms. Contemporary forms of popular culture, like the traditional forms, provide not only entertainment, but also an escape for the contemporary Japanese from the problems of an industrial world. When asked how they spent their leisure time, 80 percent of a sample of men and women surveyed by the government in 1986 averaged about two and one-half hours per weekday watching television, listening to the radio, and reading newspapers or magazines. Some

16 percent spent an average of two and one-quarter hours a day engaged in hobbies or amusements. Others spent leisure time participating in sports, socializing, and personal study. Teenagers and retired people reported more time spent on all of these activities than other groups.

In the late 1980s, the family was the focus of leisure activities, such as excursions to parks or shopping districts. Although Japan is often thought of as a hard-working society with little time for pleasure, the Japanese seek entertainment wherever they can. In the 1980s, it was common to see Japanese commuters riding the train to work, enjoying their favorite comic book or listening through earphones to the latest in popular music on cassette players.

In the mid-1980s, Japan had about 71 million television sets in use, and television was the main source of home entertainment and information for most of the population. The Japanese had a wide variety of programs to choose from, including the various dramas (police, crime, home, and samurai), cartoons, news, and game, quiz, and sports shows provided by the Japan Broadcasting Corporation (Nippon Hōsō Kyōkai—NHK) general station, the NHK educational station, and numerous commercial and independent stations. The violence of the samurai and police dramas and the scatological humor of the cartoons drew criticism from mothers and commentators. Characters in dramas and cartoons often reflected racial and gender stereotypes. Women news anchors were not given equal exposure in news broadcasts, and few women were portrayed on television in high career positions.

Individuals also could choose from a variety of types of popular entertainment. There was a large selection of musical tapes, films, television programs, and the products of a huge comic book industry, among other forms of entertainment, from which to choose in the late 1980s (see Performing Arts; Literature; and Films and Television, ch. 3).

Gender Stratification and the Lives of Women

Gender has been an important principle of stratification throughout Japanese history, but the cultural elaboration of gender differences has varied over time and among different social classes. In the twelfth century, for example, women could inherit property in their own names and manage it by themselves. Later, under feudal governments, the status of women declined. Peasant women continued to have de facto freedom of movement and decision-making power, but upper-class women's lives were subject to the patrilineal and patriarchal ideology supported by the government as part of its efforts at social control. With early industrialization,

The fourteenth-century Golden Pavilion in Kyōto
Courtesy Eliot Frankeberger
St. Mary's Cathedral in Tokyo, designed by Tange Kenzō
Courtesy St. Mary's Cathedral

119

young women participated in factory work under exploitative and unhealthy working conditions without gaining personal autonomy. In the Meiji period, industrialization and urbanization lessened the authority of fathers and husbands, but at the same time the Meiji Civil Code denied women legal rights and subjugated them to the will of household heads. Peasant women were less affected by the institutionalization of this trend, but it gradually spread even to remote areas. In the 1930s and 1940s, the government encouraged the formation of women's associations, applauded high fertility, and regarded motherhood as a patriotic duty to the Japanese Empire.

After World War II, the legal position of women was redefined by the occupation authorities, who included an equal rights clause in the 1947 Constitution and the revised Civil Code of 1948. Individual rights were given precedence over obligation to family. Women as well as men were guaranteed the right to choose spouses and occupations, to inherit and own property in their own names, to initiate divorce, and to retain custody of their children. Women were given the right to vote in 1946. Other postwar reforms opened education institutions to women and required that women receive equal pay for equal work. In 1986, an Equal Employment Opportunity Law took effect. Legally, few barriers to women's equal participation in the life of society remained.

Gender inequality, however, continued in family life, the workplace, and popular values. The notion expressed in the proverbial phrase "good wife, wise mother," continued to influence beliefs about gender roles. Most women may not have been able to realize that ideal, but many believed that it was in their own, their children's, and society's best interests that they stay home to devote themselves to their children, at least while the children were young. Many women found satisfaction in family life and in the accomplishments of their children, gaining a sense of fulfillment from doing good jobs as household managers and mothers. In most households, women were responsible for their family budgets and made independent decisions about the education, careers, and lifestyles of their families. On the other hand, women took the social blame for problems of family members.

Women's educational opportunities have increased in the twentieth century. Among new workers in 1989, 37 percent of women had received education beyond upper-secondary school, compared with 43 percent of men, but most women had received their postsecondary education in junior colleges and technical schools rather than in universities and graduate schools (see Higher Education, ch. 3).

Forty-seven percent of all women over fifteen years of age participated in the paid labor force in 1987. Two major changes in the female work force were under way. The first was a move away from household-based employment. Peasant women and those from merchant and artisan families had always worked. With self-employment becoming less common, however, the more usual pattern was separation of home and workplace, creating new problems of child care, care of the elderly, and housekeeping responsibilities. The second major change was the increased participation of married women in the labor force. In the 1950s, most women employees were young and single; 62 percent of the female labor force in 1960 had never been married. In 1987, 66 percent of the female labor force was married, and only 23 percent was made up women who had never married. Some women continued working after marriage, most often in professional and government jobs, but their numbers were small. Others started their own businesses, or took over family businesses. More commonly, women left paid labor after marriage, then returned after their youngest children were in school. These middle-age recruits generally took low-paying, part-time service or factory jobs. They continued to have nearly total responsibility for home and children, and often justified their employment as an extension of their responsibilities for the care of their families. Despite legal support for equality and some improvement in their status, married women understood that their husbands' jobs demanded long hours and extreme commitment. Because women earned an average of only 60 percent as much as men, most did not find it advantageous to take full-time, responsible jobs after marriage, if doing so left no one to manage the household and care for children (see Working Women, ch. 4).

Yet women's status in the labor force was changing in the late 1980s, most likely as a result of changes brought about by the aging of the population. Longer life expectancies, smaller families and bunched births, and lowered expectations of being cared for in old age by their children have all led women to participate more fully in the labor force. At the same time, service job opportunities in the postindustrial economy expanded, and there were fewer new male graduates to fill them.

Some of the same demographic factors—low birth rates and high life expectancies—also changed workplace demands on husbands. For example, men recognized their need for a different kind of relationship with their wives in anticipation of long post-retirement periods.

Age Stratification and the Elderly

Another key principle in the stratification of Japanese society is age. "Acting one's age" may be more important in Japan than in some other societies, resulting in relatively narrow age ranges for such life cycle events as university education, first job, or marriage. This pattern fits with the value placed on playing social roles appropriately.

Old age ideally represents a time of relaxation of social obligations, assisting with the family farm or business without carrying the main responsibility, socializing, and receiving respectful care from family and esteem from the community. In the late 1980s, high (although declining) rates of suicide among older people and the continued existence of temples where one could pray for quick death indicated that this ideal was not always fulfilled. Japan has a national holiday called Respect for the Aged Day, but for most people it is merely another day for picnics or an occasion when the commuter trains run on holiday schedules. True respect for the elderly may be questioned when buses and trains carry signs above specially reserved seats to remind people to give up their seats for elderly riders. Although the elderly might not have been accorded a generalized respect based on age, many older Japanese continued to live full lives that included gainful employment and close relationships with adult children.

Although the standard retirement age in Japan throughout most of the postwar period was fifty-five, people aged sixty-five and over in Japan were more likely to work than in any other developed country in the 1980s. In 1987, 36 percent of men and 15 percent of women in this age-group were in the labor force. With better pension benefits and decreased opportunities for agricultural or other self-employed work, however, labor force participation by the elderly has been decreasing since 1960. In 1986, 90 percent of Japanese surveyed said that they wished to continue working after age sixty-five. They indicated both financial and health reasons for this choice. Other factors, such as a strong work ethic and the centering of men's social ties around the workplace, may also be relevant. Employment was not always available, however, and men and women who worked after retirement usually took substantial cuts in salary and prestige. Between 1981 and 1986, the proportion of people sixty and over who reported that a public pension was their major source of income increased from 35 percent to 53 percent, while those relying most on earnings for income fell from 31 to 25 percent, and those relying on children decreased from 16 to 9 percent (see Aging and Retirement of the Labor Force, ch. 4).

As the 1990s approached, there was a major trend toward the elderly maintaining separate households rather than co-residing with the families of adult children. The proportion living with children decreased from 77 percent in 1970 to 65 percent in 1985, although this rate was still much higher than in other industrialized countries. The number of elderly living in Japan's retirement or nursing homes also increased from around 75,000 in 1970 to more than 216,000 in 1987; still, this group was a small portion of the total elderly population. People living alone or only with spouses constituted 32 percent of the sixty-five-and-over group. Less than half of those responding to a government survey believed that it was the duty of the eldest son to care for parents, but 63 percent replied that it was natural for children to take care of their elderly parents. The motive of co-residence seems to have changed, from being the expected arrangement of an agricultural society to being an option for coping with circumstances such as illness or widowhood in a postindustrial society.

In the late 1980s, concern for the health of the aged continued to receive a great deal of attention, and nearly free medical care for people over seventy years of age was a national policy. Responsibility for the care of the aged, bedridden, or senile, however, still devolved mainly on family members, usually daughters-in-law.

Health Care and Social Welfare

While most postwar Japanese relied on personal savings and the support of family, both the government and private companies have long provided assistance for the ill or otherwise disabled, and for the old. Beginning in the 1920s, the government enacted a series of welfare programs, based mainly on European models, to provide medical care and financial support. Government expenditures for all forms of social welfare increased from 6 percent of national income in the early 1970s to 18 percent in 1989. The mixtures of public and private funding have created complex pension and insurance systems.

Health Care

A person who becomes ill in Japan has a number of options. One may visit a Buddhist temple or Shinto shrine, or send a family member in their place. There are numerous folk remedies, including hot springs baths and chemical and herbal over-the-counter medications. A person may seek the assistance of traditional healers, such as herbalists, masseurs, and acupuncturists. However, Western biomedicine has dominated Japanese medical care in the postwar period.

Public health services, including free screening examinations for particular diseases, prenatal care, and infectious disease control were provided by national and local governments. Payment for personal medical services was offered through a universal medical insurance system that provided relative equality of access, with fees set by a government committee. People without insurance through employers could participate in a national health insurance program administered by local governments. Since 1973, all elderly persons were covered by government-sponsored insurance. Patients were free to select physicians or facilities of their choice.

There were more than 1,000 mental hospitals, 8,700 general hospitals, and 1,000 comprehensive hospitals with a total capacity of 1.5 million beds. Hospitals provided both out-patient and in-patient care. In addition, 79,000 clinics offered primarily out-patient services, and there were 48,000 dental clinics. Most physicians and hospitals sold medicine directly to patients, but there were 36,000 pharmacies where patients could purchase synthetic or herbal medication.

National health expenditures rose from about ¥1 trillion (for value of the yen—see Glossary) in 1965 to over ¥18 trillion in 1987, or from slightly more than 5 percent to almost 7 percent of Japan's national income. In addition to cost control problems, the system was troubled with excessive paperwork, long waits to see physicians, assembly-line care for out-patients (because few facilities made appointments), overmedication, and abuse of the system because of low out-of-pocket costs to patients. Another problem in the late 1980s was an uneven distribution of health personnel, with cities favored over rural areas.

In the late 1980s, government and professional circles were considering changing the system so that primary, secondary, and tertiary levels of care would be clearly distinguished within each geographical region, and facilities might be designated by level of care, with referrals required to obtain more complex care. Policy makers and administrators also recognized the need to unify the various insurance systems and control costs.

There were nearly 191,400 physicians, 66,800 dentists, and 333,000 nurses, plus more than 200,000 people licensed to practice massage, acupuncture, moxibustion, and other East Asian therapeutic methods. Since around 1900, Chinese-style herbalists have been required to be licensed medical doctors. Training was professionalized and, except for East Asian healers, was based on a biomedical model of disease. However, the practice of biomedicine was influenced as well by Japanese social organization and cultural expectations concerning education, the organization of the workplace, and social relations of status and dependency, decision-making styles, and ideas about the human body, causes of illness, gender, individualism, and privacy. Anthropologist Emiko Ohnuki-Tierney notes that "daily hygienic behavior and its underlying concepts, which are perceived and expressed in terms of biomedical germ theory, in fact are directly tied to the basic Japanese symbolic structure."

Although the number of cases remained small by international standards, public health officials were concerned in the late 1980s about the worldwide epidemic of acquired immune deficiency syndrome (AIDS). The first confirmed case of AIDS in Japan was reported in 1985. By August 1989, there were 108 confirmed cases and between 1,000 and 2,500 others infected with the virus. Officials anticipated a fourfold increase by 1992. Japanese statistics on patterns of transmission of the disease differ greatly from those of other countries. Fifty-eight percent of AIDS patients were hemophiliacs, who were infected with the AIDS virus by receiving tainted imported blood products. Another 29 percent were homosexual and the remaining 13 percent were infected through heterosexual intercourse. While frightened by the deadliness of the disease yet sympathetic to the plight of hemophiliac AIDS patients, most Japanese were unconcerned with contracting AIDS themselves. Various levels of government responded to the introduction of AIDS into the heterosexual population by establishing government committees, mandating AIDS education, and advising testing for the general public without targeting special groups. A fund, underwritten by pharmaceutical companies that distributed imported blood products, was established in 1988 to provide financial compensation for AIDS patients.

Social Welfare

The futures of Japan's health and welfare systems in 1990 were being shaped by the rapid aging of the population. Medical insurance, health care for the elderly, and public health expenses constituted about 60 percent of social welfare and social security costs in 1975, while government pensions accounted for 20 percent. By the early 1980s, pensions accounted for nearly 50 percent of social welfare and social security expenditures because people were living longer after retirement. A fourfold increase in workers' individual contributions was projected by the twenty-first century.

A major revision in the public pension system in 1986 unified several former plans into a single Employee Pension Insurance Plan. In addition to merging the former plans, the 1986 reform attempted to reduce benefits to hold down increases in worker contribution rates. It also established the right of women who did not work outside the home to pension benefits of their own, not only as a dependent of a worker. Everyone aged between twenty and sixty was a compulsory member of this Employee Pension Insurance Plan.

Despite complaints that these pensions amounted to little more than "spending money," an increasing number of people planning for their retirement counted on them as an important source of income. Benefits increased so that the basic monthly pension was about US$420 in 1987, with future payments adjusted to the consumer price index. Forty percent of elderly households in 1985 depended on various types of annuities and pensions as their only sources of income.

Some people were also eligible for corporate retirement allowances. About 90 percent of firms with thirty or more employees gave retirement allowances in the late 1980s frequently as lump sum payments, but increasingly often in the form of annuities.

Japan also had public assistance programs benefiting about 1 percent of the population. About 33 percent of recipients were elderly people, about 45 percent were households with sick or disabled members, about 14 percent were fatherless families, and about 8 percent were in other categories.

Japanese often claim to outsiders that their society is homogeneous. By world standards, the Japanese enjoy a high standard of living, and nearly 90 percent of the population consider themselves part of the middle class. Most people express satisfaction with their lives and take great pride in being Japanese and in their country's status as an economic power on a par with the United States and Western Europe. In folk crafts and in right-wing politics, in the new religions and in international management, the Japanese have turned to their past to interpret the present. In doing so, however, they may be reconstructing history as a common set of beliefs and practices that make the country look more homogeneous than it is.

In a society that values outward conformity, individuals may appear to take a back seat to the needs of the group. Yet it is individuals who create for themselves a variety of life-styles. They are constrained in their choices by age, gender, life experiences, and other factors, but they draw from a rich cultural repertoire of past and present through which the wider social world of families, neighborhoods, and institutions gives meaning to their lives. As Japan set out to internationalize itself in the 1990s, the identification of inherent Japanese qualities took on new significance, and the ideology of homogeneity sometimes masked individual decisions and life-styles of postindustrial Japan.

* * *

A good general introduction to Japanese society is Edwin O. Reischauer's *The Japanese Today*. The *Kodansha Encyclopedia of Japan* contains articles on numerous aspects of Japanese society. The Japanese government publishes excellent information in English on a variety of subjects as well as statistical reports, such as the *Japan Statistical Yearbook*. Japan's physical setting and its relation to society are discussed in Martin Collcutt and others' *Cultural Atlas of Japan*. Hori Ichiro and others' *Japanese Religion* and H. Byron Earhart's *Japanese Religion: Unity and Diversity* provide good introductions to religious life.

Analyses of Japanese culture and values can be found in *Japanese Society* by Robert J. Smith, *Long Engagements* by David Plath, *The Monkey as Mirror* by Emiko Ohnuki-Tierney, a variety of articles in *Japanese Culture and Behavior* edited by Takie Sugiyama Lebra and William P. Lebra, *The Chrysanthemum and the Sword* by Ruth Benedict, and *Conflict in Japan*, edited by Ellis S. Krauss and others. Social organization is described by Nakane Chie in *Japanese Society*, Ezra F. Vogel in *Japan's New Middle Class*, Harumi Befu in *Japan: An Anthropological Introduction*, and Joy Hendry in *Understanding Japanese Society*. (For further information and complete citations, see Bibliography.)

Chapter 3. Education and the Arts

Artist's rendition of Great Wave off the Coast of Kanagawa, *from the series* Thirty-six Views of Mount Fuji *by* ukiyo-e *artist Hokusai Katsushika (1760–1849)*

JAPANESE CULTURAL VALUES are deeply imbedded in the country's richly varied, ancient past. Rooted in the native religion of Shinto (Way of the Gods), these values are also heavily indebted to the continental influences of Buddhism and Confucianism. In Shinto, gods permeate the universe and are perceived as embodied in specific places, such as sacred Mount Fuji and the Nachi Falls, or as tutelary spirits of rocks and trees. Therefore, a reverence for nature and admiration for particular scenic places are pervasive in Japanese art, echoed in literary descriptions, and expressed in architectural concepts that remove walls to allow the outside in and in avant-garde smoke sculptures, which recreate mists. Shinto concepts of ritual cleanliness, purification, and renewal have played a role in preserving the forms of ancient shrines like that at Ise and have nurtured handicrafts. They also have shaped some funereal practices, for example, the clay sculptures or *haniwa* in the Kofun period (ca. A.D. 300–710), which provided the first real likeness of the ancient Japanese.

Buddhist thought was fundamental to the formulation of most of Japan's arts, blending and absorbing elements from the proto-historic Shinto. Basic to Buddhist thought is the comprehension of the universe as in constant flux, which results in emphasis on the idea that all living things perish or are transformed in the chain of existence. From this view comes a feeling for "the poignancy of things" (*mono no aware*), a frequent element in literature beginning in the Heian period (794–1185). Cherry blossoms are appreciated for their short-lived beauty, which symbolizes the samurai ideal of a brilliant life with a sudden, dramatic end. Zen Buddhism affirms the values of rustic simplicity and finding pleasure in the ordinary or minimal; it stresses austerity, simplicity, and brevity in all things and a life of solitude and contemplation, ideas which, together with Zen teaching devices, found expression in the tea ceremony, short poems, spontaneous ink paintings, and meditation gardens.

Chinese artistic forms and philosophical concepts have been variously integrated and modified over the centuries by the Japanese. Confucianism glorifies the cultivation of wisdom: the scholarly life is its ideal, as are the virtues of ethical behavior, sincerity, and a desire for social harmony. All these elements were embodied in the gentleman-scholar and his successors, the teacher-scholar and

131

the artist-writer, whose proficiency in language and use of the brush made literature and calligraphy the most admired art forms.

Japanese children are taught a reverence for learning and trained in the traditional arts both within the school system and outside. Instruction in music, calligraphy, flower arrangement, and the tea ritual may begin at home, but soon the child studies with a skilled practitioner. Only the martial arts, such as judo or Japanese fencing (*kendō*), are generally limited to men. Men often practice the other arts as well. Such early introduction to and widespread participation in different expressions of Japanese heritage lead to support for traditional cultural values and the appreciation throughout society of artistic qualities.

Education

Many of the historical and cultural characteristics that shape Japanese arts shape its education as well. Japanese tradition stresses respect for society and the established order and prizes group goals above individual interests. In the early 1990s, schooling emphasized in addition diligence, self-criticism, and well-organized study habits. More generally, the belief was ingrained that hard work and perseverance would yield success in life. Much of official school life was devoted directly or indirectly to teaching correct attitudes and moral values and to developing character, with the aim of creating a citizenry that was both literate and attuned to the basic values of culture and society.

At the same time, the academic achievement of Japanese students was extremely high by international standards. Japanese children consistently ranked at or near the top in successive international tests of mathematics. The system was characterized by high enrollment and retention rates throughout. An entrance examination system, particularly important at the college level, exerted strong influences throughout the entire system. The structure did not consist exclusively of government-sponsored, formal official education institutions. Private education also formed an important part of the educational landscape, and the role of schools outside the official school system could not be ignored.

A majority of children began their education by attending preschool, although it was not part of the official system. The official structure in the early 1990s provided compulsory free schooling and a sound and balanced education to virtually all children from grade one through grade nine. Upper-secondary school, from grades ten through twelve, though also not compulsory, attracted about 94 percent of those who completed lower-secondary school. About one-third of all Japanese upper-secondary school graduates advanced to postsecondary education—to full four-year universities, two-year junior colleges, or to other institutions.

Japan in the early 1990s remained a highly education-minded society. Education was esteemed, and educational achievement was often the prerequisite for success in work and in society at large.

Historical Background

Japan has had relations with other cultures since the dawn of its history (see Early Developments, ch. 1). Foreign civilizations have often provided new ideas for the development of Japan's own culture. Chinese teachings and ideas, for example, flowed into Japan from the sixth to ninth centuries. Along with the introduction of Buddhism came the Chinese system of writing and its literary tradition, and Confucianism (see Religious and Philosophical Traditions, ch. 2).

By the ninth century, Kyōto, the imperial capital, had five institutions of higher learning, and during the remainder of the Heian period (794–1185), other schools were established by the nobility and the imperial court. During the medieval period (1185–1600), Zen Buddhist monasteries were especially important centers of learning, and the Ashikaga School (Ashikaga Gakkō) flourished in the fifteenth century as a center of higher learning.

In the sixteenth and early seventeenth centuries, Japan experienced intense contact with the major European powers. Jesuit missionaries, who accompanied Portuguese traders, proselytized Christianity, opening a number of religious schools. Japanese students thus began to study Latin and Western music, as well as their own language.

By 1603 Japan had been reunified by the Tokugawa regime, and by 1640 foreigners had been ordered out of Japan, Christianity banned, and virtually all foreign contact prohibited. The nation then entered a period of isolation and relative domestic tranquility, which was to last 200 years. When the Tokugawa period began, few common people in Japan could read or write. By the period's end, learning had become widespread. Tokugawa education left a valuable legacy: an increasingly literate populace, a meritocratic ideology, and an emphasis on discipline and competent performance. Under subsequent Meiji leadership, this foundation would facilitate Japan's rapid transition from feudal country to modern nation (see Tokugawa Period, 1600–1867, ch. 1).

During the Tokugawa period, the role of many of the *bushi,* or samurai, changed from warrior to administrator, and as a consequence, their formal education and their literacy increased proportionally. Samurai curricula stressed morality and included both military and literary studies. Confucian classics were memorized, and their reading and recitation were common methods of study. Arithmetic and calligraphy were also studied. Most samurai attended schools sponsored by their *han* (domains), and by the time of the Meiji Restoration of 1868, more than 200 of the 276 *han* had established schools. Some samurai and even commoners also attended private academies, which often specialized in particular Japanese subjects or in Western medicine, modern military science, gunnery, or Rangaku (Dutch studies), as European studies were called (see Intellectual Trends; The Emergence of Modern Japan, 1868–1919, ch. 1).

Education of commoners was generally practically oriented, providing basic training in reading, writing, and arithmetic, emphasizing calligraphy and use of the abacus. Much of this education was conducted in so-called temple schools (*terakoya*), derived from earlier Buddhist schools. These schools were no longer religious institutions, nor were they, by 1867, predominantly located in temples. By the end of the Tokugawa period, there may have been more than 14,000 such schools. Teaching techniques included reading from various textbooks, memorizing, and repeatedly copying Chinese characters and Japanese script.

After 1868 new leadership set Japan on a rapid course of modernization. Realizing from the outset that education was fundamental to nation building and modernization, the Meiji leaders established a public education system to help Japan catch up with the West. Missions were sent abroad to study the education systems of leading Western countries. These missions and other observers returned with the ideas of decentralization, local school boards, and teacher autonomy. Such ideas and ambitious initial plans, however, proved very difficult to carry out. After some trial and error, a new national education system emerged. As an indication of its success, elementary school enrollments climbed from about 40 or 50 percent of the school-age population in the 1870s to over 90 percent by 1900.

By the 1890s, after earlier intensive preoccupation with Western, particularly United States, educational ideas, a much more conservative and traditional orientation evolved: the education system became more reflective of Japanese values. Confucian precepts were stressed, especially those concerning the hierarchical nature of human relations, service to the new state, the pursuit of learning, and morality. These ideals, embodied in the 1890 Imperial Rescript on Education, along with highly centralized government control over education, largely guided Japanese education until the end of World War II.

In the early twentieth century, education at the primary level was egalitarian and virtually universal, but at higher levels it was multitracked, highly selective, and elitist. College education was largely limited to the few national universities, where German influences were strong. Three of the imperial universities admitted women, and there were a number of women's colleges, some quite prestigious, but women had relatively few opportunities to enter higher education. During this period, a number of universities were founded by Christian missionaries, who also took an active role in expanding educational opportunities for women, particularly at the secondary level.

After 1919 several of the private universities received official status, being granted government recognition for programs they had conducted, in many cases, since the 1880s. In the 1920s, the tradition of liberal education briefly reappeared, particularly at the kindergarten level, where the Montessori method attracted a following. In the 1930s, education was subject to strong military and nationalistic influences.

By 1945 the Japanese education system had been devastated, and with the defeat came the discredit of much prewar thought. A new wave of foreign ideas was introduced during the postwar period of military occupation (see World War II and the Occupation, 1941–52, ch. 1).

Occupation policy makers and the United States Education Mission, set up in 1946, made a number of changes aimed at democratizing Japanese education: instituting the six-three-three grade structure (six years of elementary school, three of lower-secondary school, and three of upper-secondary school) and extending compulsory schooling to nine years. They replaced the prewar system of higher-secondary schools with comprehensive upper-secondary schools (high schools). Curricula and textbooks were revised, the nationalistic morals course was abolished and replaced with social studies, locally elected school boards were introduced, and teachers unions established (see Contemporary Setting, this ch.).

With the abolition of the elitist higher education system and an increase in the number of higher education institutions, the opportunities for higher learning grew. Expansion was accomplished initially by granting university or junior college status to a number of technical institutes, normal schools, and advanced secondary schools.

After the restoration of full national sovereignty in 1952, Japan immediately began to modify some of the changes in education,

to reflect Japanese ideas about education and educational administration. The postwar Ministry of Education regained a great deal
of power. School boards were appointed, instead of elected. A course
in moral education was reinstituted in modified form, despite substantial initial concern that it would lead to a renewal of heightened nationalism.

By the 1960s, postwar recovery and accelerating economic growth
brought new demands to expand higher education and greater stress
related to higher education quality and finances. In general, the
1960s was a time of great turbulence in higher education. Late in
the decade especially, universities in Japan were rocked by violent
student riots that disrupted many campuses. Campus unrest was
the confluence of a number of factors, including the anti-Vietnam
War movement in Japan, ideological differences between various
Japanese student groups, disputes over campus issues such as discipline, student strikes, and even general dissatisfaction with the
university system itself.

The government responded with the University Control Law
in 1969, and in the early 1970s, with further education reforms.
New laws governed the founding of new universities and teachers'
compensation, and public school curricula were revised. Private
education institutions began to receive public aid, and a nationwide standardized university entrance examination was added for
the national universities. Also during this period, strong disagreement developed between the government and teachers groups.

Despite the numerous educational changes that have occurred
in Japan since 1868, and especially since 1945, the education system in 1990 still reflected long-standing cultural and philosophical
ideas: that learning and education are esteemed and to be pursued
seriously, and that moral and character development are integral
to education. The meritocratic legacy of the Meiji period has endured, as has the centralized education structure. Interest remains
in adapting foreign ideas and methods to Japanese traditions and
in improving the system generally.

Education Reform

In spite of the admirable success of the education system since
World War II, there were still problems in the 1980s. Some of these
difficulties as perceived by domestic and foreign observers included
rigidity, excessive uniformity, lack of choices, undesirable influences
of the university examinations, and overriding emphasis on formal educational credentials. There was also a belief that education was responsible for some social problems and for the general
academic, behavioral, and adjustment problems of some students.

There was great concern too that Japanese education be responsive to the new requirements caused by international challenges of the changing world in the twenty-first century.

Flexibility, creativity, internationalization (*kokusaika*), individuality, and diversity thus became the watchwords of Japan's momentous education reform movement of the 1980s, although they echoed themes heard earlier, particularly in the 1970s (see Higher Education, this ch.). The proposals and potential changes of the 1980s were so significant that some are comparing them to the educational changes that occurred when Japan opened to the West in the nineteenth century and to those of the occupation.

Concerns of the new reform movement were captured in a series of reports issued between 1985 and 1987 by the National Council on Educational Reform. The final report outlined basic emphases in response to the internationalization of education, new information technologies, and the media; and emphases on individuality, lifelong learning, and adjustment to social change. To explore these new directions, the council suggested that eight specific subjects be considered: designing education for the twenty-first century, organizing a system of lifelong learning and reducing the emphasis on the educational background of individuals, improving and diversifying higher education, enriching and diversifying elementary and secondary education, improving the quality of teachers, adapting to internationalization, adapting to the information age, and conducting a review of the administration and finance of education. These subjects reflected both educational and social aspects of the reform, in keeping with the Japanese view about the relationship of education to society. Even as debate over reform took place, the government quickly moved to begin implementing changes in most of these eight areas.

Contemporary Setting

The late twentieth-century Japanese education system had a strong legal foundation. Three documents in particular—the Fundamental Law of Education, the School Education Law, and the new Constitution, all adopted in 1947—provided this legal basis (see The Postwar Constitution, ch. 6). The system was highly centralized, although three levels of government administration— national, prefectural, and municipal—had various responsibilities for providing, financing, and supervising educational services for the nation's more than 65,000 schools and the nearly 27 million students in 1989 (see table 5, Appendix). At the top of the system stood the Ministry of Education, Science, and Culture (hereafter, the Ministry of Education, or Monbushō), which had significant responsibility for funding, curricula, textbooks, and national education standards.

More general responsibilities of the Ministry of Education were the promotion and dissemination of education, scientific knowledge, academic research, culture, and sports. The ministry was supported by advisory bodies and standing councils, such as the Central Council on Education, and by ad hoc councils, such as the National Council on Educational Reform.

The ministry's authority and responsibilities were not limited to public institutions. Most of its regulations, particularly concerning compulsory education, also applied to private institutions. The ministry had power to approve the founding of universities and supervised the national universities. In addition, it provided financial assistance and guidance to lower levels of government on educational matters and was empowered to mandate changes in local policies.

The ministry drafted its annual budget and education-related legislation and submitted them to the Diet (see The Legislature, ch. 6). Monbushō administered the disbursement of funds and cooperated with other agencies concerned with education and its finance. In 1990 a main area of ministry activity was implementing reforms based on the reports and recommendations of the National Council on Educational Reform, whose final report was submitted to the prime minister in 1987.

Each of the forty-seven prefectures had a five-member board of education appointed by the governor with the consent of the prefectural assembly. The prefectural boards administered and operated public schools under their supervision, including most of the public upper-secondary schools, special schools for the handicapped, and some other public institutions in the prefecture (see Local Government, ch. 6). Prefectural boards were the teacher-licensing bodies; with the advice of municipal governments, they appointed teachers to public elementary and lower-secondary schools; they also licensed preschools and other schools in their municipalities and promoted social education.

Municipal-level governments operated the public elementary and lower-secondary schools in their jurisdictions. Supervision was conducted by the local board of education, usually a five-member organization appointed by the mayor with the consent of the local assembly. The board also made recommendations to the prefectures about the appointment or dismissal of teachers and adopted textbooks from the list certified by the Ministry of Education. Mayors also were charged with some responsibilities for municipal universities and budget coordination.

All three levels of government—national, prefectural, and municipal—provided financial support for education. National government was the largest source of direct funding, through the budget of the Ministry of Education, and a significant source of indirect funding of local education through a tax rebate to local government, in a tax allocation grant. The national government bore from one-third to one-half of the cost of education in the form of teachers' salaries, school construction, the school lunch program, and vocational education and equipment.

The ministry's budget between fiscal year (FY—see Glossary) 1980 and FY 1988 increased a total of about 7 percent (see The Role of Government and Business, ch. 4). But, as a percentage of the total national budget (before the deduction of mandated expenses and debt service), the ministry's share actually declined steadily throughout the 1980s, from about 10 percent in 1980 to about 7.7 percent in the budget proposed for FY 1989. The proposed FY 1989 budget asked for ¥4.637 trillion (for value of the yen—see Glossary), an increase of 1.34 percent over FY 1988's ¥4.576 trillion.

Teaching remained an honored profession, and teachers had high social status, stemming from the Japanese cultural legacy and public recognition of their important social responsibilities. Society expected teachers to embody the ideals they were to instill, particularly because teaching duties extended to the moral instruction and character development of children. Formal classroom moral education, informal instruction, and even academic classes were all viewed as legitimate venues for this kind of teaching. Teachers' responsibilities to their schools and students frequently extended beyond the classroom, off school grounds and after school hours.

In the 1980s, teachers were well paid, and periodic improvements also were made in teachers' salaries and compensation. Starting salaries compared favorably with those of other white collar professionals, and in some cases were higher. In addition to salary, there were many types of special allowances and a bonus (paid in three installments), which in the late 1980s amounted to about five months' salary. Teachers also received the standard health and retirement benefits available to most Japanese salaried workers.

Whether for economic reward, social status, or the desire to teach, the number of people wishing to enter teaching exceeded the number of new openings by as many as five or six applicants to every one position. Prefectural boards and other public bodies were able to select the best qualified from a large pool of applicants.

By the late 1980s, the great majority of new teachers were entering the profession with a bachelor's degree, but about 25 percent of the total teaching force at the elementary school level did not have a bachelor's degree. The program for prospective teachers at the undergraduate level included study in education as well as concentration in academic areas. Most new teachers majored in a subject other than education, and graduates of colleges of education were still in the minority. After graduation, a teacher had to pass a prefectural-level examination to be licensed by a prefectural board of education.

Changes also occurred during the 1980s in in-service training and supervision of new teachers. In-service training, particularly that conducted under the auspices of the Ministry of Education, had been questioned for many years. After considerable debate, and some opposition from the Japan Teachers Union (Nihon Kyōshokuin Kumiai—Nikkyōsō), a new system of teacher training was introduced in 1989. The new system established a one-year training program, required new teachers to work under the direction of a master teacher, and increased the required number of both in-school and out-of-school training days and the length of time new teachers were under probationary status.

The Japan Teachers Union, established in 1947, was the largest teachers union in the late 1980s. The union functioned as a national federation of prefectural teachers unions, although each of these unions had considerable autonomy and its own strengths and political orientation. Historically, there had been considerable antagonism between the union and the Ministry of Education, owing to a variety of factors. Some were political, because the stance of the union had been strongly leftist and it often opposed the more conservative ruling Liberal Democratic Party. Another factor was the trade union perspective that the teachers union had on the profession of teaching (see The Liberal Democratic Party, ch. 6). Additional differences on education issues concerned training requirements for new teachers, decentralization in education, school autonomy, curricula, textbook censorship, and, in the late 1980s, the reform movement.

The union tended to support the Japan Socialist Party, while a minority faction supported the Japan Communist Party (see The Opposition Parties, ch. 6). In the late 1980s, internal disagreements in the Japan Teachers Union on political orientation and on the union's relationships to other national labor organizations finally caused a rupture. The union thus became less effective than in previous years at a time when the national government and the ministry were moving ahead on reform issues. The union had opposed many reforms proposed or instituted by the ministry, but failed to forestall changes in certification and teacher training, two issues on which it was often at odds with the government. The new union leadership that emerged after several years of internal discord seemed to take a more conciliatory approach to the ministry and reform issues, but the union's future directions were not clear.

Preschool and Day Care

Early childhood education began at home, and there were numerous books and television shows aimed at helping mothers of preschool children to educate their children and to "parent" more effectively. Much of the home training was devoted to teaching manners, proper social behavior, and structured play, although verbal and number skills were also popular themes. Parents were strongly committed to early education and frequently enrolled their children in preschools.

Preschool education provided the transition from home to formal school for most children. Children's lives at home were characterized by indulgence, and the largely nonacademic preschool experience helped children make the adjustment to the group-oriented life of school and, in turn, to life in society itself (see Values, ch. 2).

Preschools (*yōchien*), predominantly staffed by young female junior college graduates, were supervised by the Ministry of Education in the 1980s, but were not part of the official education system. In addition to preschools, a well-developed system of government-supervised day-care centers (*hoikuen*), supervised by the Ministry of Labor, was an important provider of preschool education. Together, these two kinds of institutions enrolled well over 90 percent of all preschool-age children prior to their entrance into the formal system at first grade. The Ministry of Education's 1990 Course of Study for Preschools, which applied to both kinds of institutions, covered such areas as human relationships, environment, words (language), and expression. The 58 percent of preschools that were private accounted for 77 percent of all children enrolled.

Primary and Secondary Education

Education in postwar Japan was compulsory and free for all school children from the first through the ninth grades (see fig. 5). The school year began on April 1 and ended on March 31 of the following year. Schools used a trimester system demarcated by vacation breaks. Japanese children attended school five full weekdays and one-half day on Saturdays. The school year had a legal minimum of 210 days, but most local school boards added about 30 more days for school festivals, athletic meets, and ceremonies with nonacademic educational objectives, especially those encouraging cooperation and school spirit. With allowance made for the time

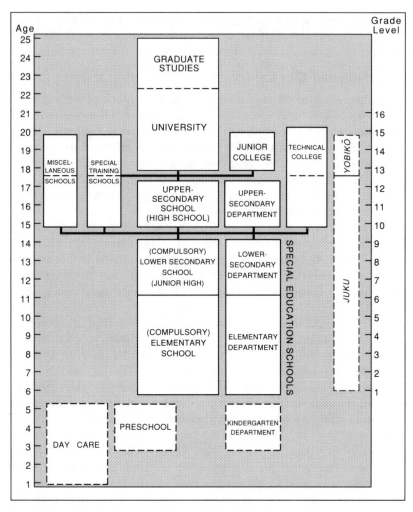

Source: Based on information from Robert Leestma et al., *Japanese Education Today,* Washington, 1987, 6; and Japan, Ministry of Education, Science, and Culture, *Education in Japan: A Graphic Presentation,* Tokyo, 1982, 14.

Figure 5. Structure of the Education System, 1987

devoted to such activities and the half day of school on Saturday, the number of days devoted to instruction was about 195 per year.

The Japanese hold several important beliefs about education, especially compulsory schooling: that all children have the ability to learn the material; that effort, perseverance, and self-discipline, not academic ability, determine academic success; and that these study and behavioral habits can be taught. Thus, students in elementary and lower-secondary schools were not grouped or taught on the basis of their ability, nor was instruction geared to individual differences.

The nationally designed curricula exposed students to balanced, basic education, and compulsory schooling was known for its equal educational treatment of students and for its relatively equal distribution of financial resources among schools. However, the demands made by the uniform curricula and approach extracted a price in lack of flexibility, including expected conformity of behavior. Little effort was made to address children with special needs and interests. Much of the reform proposed in the late 1980s, particularly that part emphasizing greater flexibility, creativity, and opportunities for greater individual expression, was aimed at changing these approaches.

Textbooks were free to students at compulsory school levels. New texts were selected by school boards or principals once every three years from the Ministry of Education's list of approved textbooks or from a small list of texts that the ministry itself published. The ministry bore the cost of distributing these books, in both public and private schools. Textbooks were small, paperbound volumes that could easily be carried by the students and that became their property.

Almost all schools had a system of access to health professionals. Educational and athletic facilities were good; almost all elementary schools had an outdoor playground, roughly 90 percent had a gymnasium, and 75 percent an outdoor swimming pool.

Elementary School

In the late 1980s, more than 99 percent of elementary school-age children were enrolled in school. All children entered first grade at age six, and starting school was considered a very important event in a child's life.

Virtually all elementary education took place in public schools; less than 1 percent of the schools were private. Private schools tended to be costly, although the rate of cost increases in tuition for these schools had slowed in the 1980s. Some private elementary schools were prestigious and served as a first step to higher-level private schools with which they were affiliated, and thence to a university. Competition to enter some of these "ladder schools" was quite intense.

Although public elementary education was free, some school expenses were borne by parents, for example, school lunches and supplies. For many families, there were also nonschool educational expenses, for extra books, or private lessons, or *juku* (see Glossary).

Such expenses rose throughout the decade, reaching an average of ¥184,000 (US$1,314) in FY 1987 for each child. Costs for private elementary schools were substantially higher.

Elementary school classes were large, about thirty-one students per class on average, but higher numbers were permitted. Students were usually organized into small work groups, which had both academic and disciplinary functions. Discipline also was maintained, and a sense of responsibility encouraged, by the use of student monitors and by having the students assume responsibility for the physical appearance of their classroom and school.

The ministry's Course of Study for Elementary Schools was composed of a wide variety of subjects, both academic and nonacademic, including moral education and "special activities." "Special activities" referred to scheduled weekly time given over to class affairs and to preparing for the school activities and ceremonies that were used to emphasize character development and the importance of group effort and cooperation. The standard academic curriculum included Japanese language, social studies, arithmetic, and science. Nonacademic subjects taught included art and handicrafts, music, homemaking, physical education, and moral education. Japanese language was the subject most emphasized. The complexity of the written language and the diversity of its spoken forms in educated speech require this early attention.

A new course of study was established in 1989, partly as a result of the education reform movement of the 1980s and partly because of ongoing curriculum review. Important changes scheduled were an increased number of hours devoted to Japanese language, the replacement of the social sciences course with a daily life course—instruction for children on proper interaction with the society and environment around them—and an increased emphasis on moral education. While evidence was still inconclusive, it appeared that at least some children were having difficulties with Japanese language. New emphasis also was to be given in the curriculum to the national flag and the national anthem. The ministry suggested that the flag be flown and the national anthem be sung at important school ceremonies. Because neither the flag nor the anthem had been legally designated as national symbols, and because of the nationalistic wartime associations the two had in the minds of some citizens, the suggestion from the ministry was greeted with some opposition. The revised history curriculum was to emphasize cultural legacies and events and the biographies of key figures. The ministry provided a proposed list of biographies, and there was some criticism surrounding particular suggestions.

Elementary teachers were generally responsible for all subjects, and classes remained in one room for most activities. Teachers were well prepared in the subjects they taught. Most teachers, about 60 percent of the total, were women; but most principals and head teachers in elementary schools were men.

Teachers had ample teaching materials and audiovisual equipment. There was an excellent system of educational television and radio, and almost all elementary schools used programs prepared by the School Education Division of Japan Broadcasting Corporation (Nippon Hōsō Kyōkai—NHK). In addition to broadcast media, schools increasingly were equipped with computers. Although only 6.5 percent of public elementary schools had personal computers in 1986, by 1989 the number had passed 20 percent. The ministry was greatly concerned with this issue and planned much greater use of such equipment.

Virtually all elementary schoolchildren received a full lunch at school. Although heavily subsidized by government, both directly and indirectly, the program was not altogether free. Full meals usually consisted of bread (or increasingly, of rice), a main dish, and milk. Though the program grew out of concern in the immediate postwar period for adequate nutrition, the school lunch was also important as a teaching device. Because there were relatively few cafeterias in elementary schools, meals were taken in the classroom with the teacher, providing another informal opportunity for teaching nutrition and health and good eating habits and social behavior. Frequently, students also were responsible for serving the lunch and cleanup.

Japanese elementary schooling was acknowledged both in Japan and abroad to be excellent, but not without some problems, notably increasing absenteeism and a declining but troublesome number of cases of bullying. In addition, special provision for the many young children returning to Japan from long absences overseas was an issue of major interest. The government also was concerned with the education of Japanese children residing abroad and sent teachers overseas to teach in Japanese schools.

Elementary school education was seen in Japan as fundamental in shaping a positive attitude toward lifelong education. Regardless of academic achievement, almost all children in elementary school were advanced to lower-secondary schools, the second of the two compulsory levels of education.

Lower-Secondary School

Lower-secondary school covered grades seven, eight, and nine—children between the ages of roughly twelve and fifteen—with increased focus on academic studies. Although it was still possible to leave the formal education system after completing lower-secondary school and find work, fewer than 4 percent did so by the late 1980s.

Like elementary schools, most lower-secondary schools in the 1980s were public, but 5 percent were private. Private schools were costly, averaging ¥558,592 (US$3,989) per student in 1988, about four times more than the ¥130,828 (US$934) that the ministry estimated as the parental cost for students enrolled in public lower-secondary schools.

The teaching force in lower-secondary schools was two-thirds male. Schools were headed by principals, 99 percent of whom were men in 1988. Teachers had often majored in the subjects they taught, and more than 80 percent had graduated from a four-year college. Classes were large, with thirty-eight pupils per class on average, and each class was assigned a homeroom teacher who doubled as counselor. Unlike elementary students, lower-secondary school students had different teachers for different subjects. The teacher, however, rather than the students, moved to a new room for each fifty-minute period.

Instruction in lower-secondary schools tended to rely on the lecture method. Teachers also used other media, such as television and radio, and there was some lab work. About 45 percent of all public lower-secondary schools had computers, including schools that used them only for administrative purposes. Classroom organization was still based on small work groups, although no longer for reasons of discipline. By lower-secondary school, students were expected to have mastered daily routines and acceptable behavior.

All course contents were specified in the Course of Study for Lower-Secondary Schools. Some subjects, such as Japanese language and mathematics, were coordinated with the elementary curriculum. Others, such as foreign-language study, usually English, began at this level. The curriculum covered Japanese language, social studies, mathematics, science, music, fine arts, health, and physical education. All students also were exposed to either industrial arts or homemaking. Moral education and special activities continued to receive attention.

Students also attended mandatory club meetings during school hours, and many also participated in after-school clubs. Most lower-secondary students said they liked school, although it was the chance to meet their friends daily—not the lessons—that was particularly attractive to them.

The ministry recognized a need to improve the teaching of all foreign languages, especially English. To improve instruction in spoken English, the government invited many young native speakers of English to Japan to serve as assistants to school boards and prefectures under its Japan Exchange and Teaching Program. By 1988, participants numbered over 1,000.

As part of the movement to develop an integrated curriculum and the education reform movement of the late 1980s, the entire Course of Study for Lower-Secondary Schools was revised in 1989 to take effect in the 1991–93 school years. A main aim of the reform was to equip students with the basic knowledge needed for citizenship. In some measure, this meant increased emphasis on Japanese history and culture, as well as understanding Japan as a nation and its relationships with other nations of the world. The course of study also increased elective hours, recommending that electives be chosen in light of individual student differences and with an eye toward diversification.

Two problems of great concern to educators and citizens began to appear at the lower-secondary level in the 1980s: bullying, which seemed rampant in the mid-1980s but had abated somewhat by the end of the decade, and the school-refusal syndrome (*tōkō kyohi*— manifested by a student's excessive absenteeism), which was on the rise. Experts disagreed over the specific causes of these phenomena, but there was general agreement that the system offered little individualized or specialized assistance, thus contributing to disaffection among those who could not conform to its demands or who were otherwise experiencing difficulties. Another problem concerned Japanese children returning from abroad. These students, particularly if they had been overseas for extended periods, often needed help not only in reading and writing, but in adjusting to rigid classroom demands. Even making the adjustment did not guarantee acceptance: besides having acquired a foreign language, many of these students had also acquired foreign customs of speech, dress, and behavior that marked them as different.

Special Education

Japanese special education at the compulsory level was highly organized in the late 1980s, even though it had been nationally mandated and implemented only in 1979. In 1990 there was still controversy over whether children with special needs could or should be "mainstreamed." In a society that stressed the group, many parents desired to have their children attend regular schools. Mainstreaming in Japan, however, did not necessarily mean attending regular classes; it often meant attending a regular school that had special classes for handicapped students. There were also special public schools for the handicapped, which had departments equivalent to the various levels of elementary and secondary schools, including kindergarten and upper-secondary departments in some cases. There were few private institutions for special education. Some students attended regular classes and also special classes for training for their particular needs. Some teachers were also dispatched to children who could not attend schools (see table 6, Appendix).

Upper-Secondary School

Even though upper-secondary school was not compulsory in Japan, 94 percent of all lower-secondary school graduates entered upper-secondary schools in 1989. Private upper-secondary schools accounted for about 24 percent of all upper-secondary schools, and neither public nor private schools were free. The Ministry of Education estimated that annual family expenses for the education of a child in a public upper-secondary school were about ¥300,000 (US$2,142) in both 1986 and 1987 and that private upper-secondary schools were about twice as expensive.

All upper-secondary schools, public and private, were informally ranked, based on their success in placing graduates in freshman classes of the most prestigious universities. In the 1980s, private upper-secondary schools occupied the highest levels of this hierarchy, and there was substantial pressure to do well in the examinations that determined the upper-secondary school a child entered. Admission also depended on the scholastic record and performance evaluation from lower-secondary school, but the examination results largely determined school entrance. Students were closely counseled in lower-secondary school, so that they would be relatively assured of a place in the schools to which they applied.

The most common type of upper-secondary schools had a full-time, general program that offered academic courses for students preparing for higher education and also technical and vocational courses for students expecting to find employment after graduation. More than 70 percent of upper-secondary school students enrolled in the general academic program in the late 1980s. A small number of schools offered part-time or evening courses or correspondence education.

The first-year programs for students in both academic and commercial courses were similar. They included basic academic courses, such as Japanese language, English, mathematics, and science. In upper-secondary school, differences in ability were first publicly acknowledged, and course content and course selection were far more individualized in the second year. However, there was a core of academic material throughout all programs.

Vocational-technical programs included several hundred specialized courses, such as information processing, navigation, fish farming, business English, and ceramics. Business and industrial courses were the most popular, accounting for 72 percent of all students in full-time vocational programs in 1989.

The upper-secondary curriculum also underwent thorough revision; and in 1989 a new Course of Study for Upper-Secondary Schools was announced that would be phased in beginning in 1994. Among noteworthy changes was the requirement that both male and female students take a course in home economics. The government was concerned with instilling in all students an awareness of the importance of family life, the various roles and responsibilities of family members, the concept of cooperation within the family, and the role of the family in society. The family continued to be an extremely important part of the social infrastructure, and the ministry clearly was interested in maintaining family stability within a changing society. Another change of note was the division of the old social studies course into history, geography, and civics courses.

Most upper-secondary teachers in the late 1980s were university graduates. Upper-secondary schools were organized into departments, and teachers specialized in their major fields although they taught a variety of courses within their disciplines. Although women composed about 20 percent of the teaching force, only 2.5 percent of principals were women.

Teaching depended largely on the lecture system, with the main goal of covering the very demanding curriculum in the time allotted. Approach and subject coverage tended to be uniform, at least in the public schools. As in lower-secondary school, the teachers, not the students, moved from room to room after each fifty-minute class period.

Upper-secondary students were subject to a great deal of supervision by school authorities and school rules even outside of school. Students' behavior and some activities were regulated by school codes that were known and obeyed by most children. School regulations often set curfews and governed dress codes, hairstyles, student employment, and even leisure activities. The school frequently was responsible for student discipline when a student ran afoul of the regulations, or occasionally, of the law. Delinquency, generally, and school violence, in particular, were troubling to Japanese authorities. Violations by upper-secondary school students included smoking and some substance abuse (predominantly of amphetamines). Use of drugs, although not a serious problem by international standards, was of concern to the police and civil authorities (see Public Order and Internal Security, ch. 8). Bullying and the drop-out rate were also subjects of attention. Upper-secondary students dropped out at a rate of between 2.0 and 2.5 percent per year. The graduation rates for upper-secondary schools stood at 87.5 percent in 1987.

Discrimination in education was prohibited, but the *burakumin* (outcast people), a group of people racially and culturally Japanese who had been discriminated against historically, were still disadvantaged in education to some degree (see Minorities, ch. 2). Their relatively poor educational attainment through the upper-secondary level in the 1960s was said to have been largely corrected by the 1980s, but reliable evidence was lacking.

There were some private schools for the children of the foreign community in Japan, and some Korean schools for children of Japan's Korean minority population, many of whom were second-generation or third-generation residents in Japan. Graduates of Korean schools faced some discrimination, particularly in entering higher education. Observers estimated that 75 percent of Korean children were attending Japanese schools in the early 1980s.

Training of handicapped students, particularly at the upper-secondary level, emphasized vocational education, to enable students to be as independent as possible within society. Vocational training varied considerably depending on the student's handicap, but the options were limited for some. It was clear that the government was aware of the necessity of broadening the range of possibilities for these students. Advancement to higher education was also a goal of the government, and it struggled to have institutions of higher learning accept more handicapped students.

Upper-secondary school students returning to Japan after living overseas presented another problem. The ministry was trying to get upper-secondary schools to accept these students more readily, and in the late 1980s had decided to allow credit for one upper-secondary school year spent abroad.

Upper-secondary school graduates choosing to enter the world of work were supported by a very effective system of job placement, which, combined with favorable economic conditions, kept the unemployment rate among new graduates quite low (see The Structure of Japan's Labor Market, ch. 4). For those students going on to college, the final phases of school life became increasingly dedicated to preparing for examinations, particularly in some of the elite private schools. About 31 percent of upper-secondary graduates advanced to some form of higher education directly after graduation.

After-school clubs provided an important upper-secondary school activity. Sports, recreational reading, and watching television were popular daily leisure activities, but schoolwork and other studies remained the focus of the daily lives of most children. The college entrance examinations greatly influenced school life and study habits, not only for college-bound students, but indirectly for all; the prospect of the examinations often imparted a seriousness to the tone of school life at the upper-secondary level.

After-School Education

Much debated, and often criticized in the late twentieth century, *juku* were special private schools that offered highly organized lessons conducted after regular school hours and on the weekends. Although best known and most widely publicized for their role as "cram schools," where children (sent by concerned parents) could study to improve scores on upper-secondary school entrance examinations, academic *juku* actually performed several educational functions. They provided supplementary education that many children needed just to keep up with the regular school curriculum, remedial education for the increasing numbers of children who fell behind in their work, and preparation for students striving to improve test scores and preparing for the all-important upper-secondary and university entrance examinations. In many ways, *juku* compensated for the formal education system's inability or unwillingness to address particular individual problems. Half of all compulsory school-age children attended academic *juku,* which offered instruction in mathematics, Japanese language, science, English, and social studies. Many other children, particularly younger children, attended nonacademic *juku* for piano lessons, art instruction, swimming, and abacus lessons. To some observers, *juku* represented an attempt by parents to exercise a meaningful measure of choice in Japanese education, particularly for children attending public schools. Some *juku* offered subject matter not available in the public school curricula, while others emphasized a special philosophical or ethical approach.

Juku also played a social role, and children in Japan said they liked going to *juku* because they were able to make new friends; many children asked to be sent because their friends attended. Some children seemed to like *juku* because of the closer personal contact they had with their teachers.

Juku attendance rose from the 1970s through the mid-1980s; participation rates increased at every grade level throughout the compulsory education years. This phenomenon was a source of great concern to the ministry, which issued directives to the regular schools that it hoped would reduce the need for after-school lessons, but these directives had little practical effect.

Some *juku* even had branches in the United States and other countries to help children living abroad to catch up with students in Japan. Because of the commercial nature of most *juku*, some critics argued that they had profit rather than education at heart, and not all students could afford to attend. *Juku* introduced some inequality into what had been a relatively egalitarian approach to education, at least in public schools through ninth grade. Yet, while some *juku* were expensive, the majority were affordable for most families; *juku* could not price themselves beyond the reach of their potential clientele. If rising enrollments in *juku* were any indication, costs were not yet a limiting factor for most parents, and *juku* clearly were given some priority in family budgeting.

If a student did not attend *juku,* it did not mean that he or she was necessarily at a disadvantage in school. Other avenues of assistance were available. For example, self-help literature and supplemental texts and study guides, some produced by publishing houses associated with *juku,* were widely available commercially. Most of these items were moderately priced. A correspondence course of the Upper-Secondary School of the Air was broadcast almost daily on the NHK educational radio and television channels. These programs were free, and costs for accompanying textbooks were nominal. In addition, about 1 percent of elementary school students and 7.3 percent of lower-secondary school students took extra lessons at home with tutors.

Higher Education

College Entrance

College entrance was based largely on the scores that students achieved in entrance examinations. Private institutions accounted for 73 percent of all university enrollments in 1988, but with a few exceptions, the public national universities were the most highly regarded. This distinction had its origins in historical factors—the long years of dominance of the select imperial universities, such as Tokyo and Kyōto universities, which trained Japan's leaders before the war—and also in differences in quality, particularly in facilities and faculty ratios. In addition, certain prestigious employers, notably the government and select large corporations, continued to restrict their hiring of new employees to graduates of the most esteemed universities. There was a close link between university background and employment opportunity. Because Japanese society placed such store in academic credentials, the competition

An elementary-level juku *poetry-reading class*
Courtesy The Mainichi Newspapers
Mathematics class, Fukuoka Upper-Secondary School, Iwate Prefecture
Courtesy Eliot Frankeberger

153

to enter the prestigious universities was keen. In addition, the eighteen-year-old population was still growing in the late 1980s, increasing the number of applicants.

Students applying to national universities took two entrance examinations, first a nationally administered uniform achievement test and then an examination administered by the university that the student hoped to enter. Applicants to private universities needed to take only the university's examination. Some national schools had so many applicants that they used the first test, the Joint First Stage Achievement Test, as a screening device for qualification to their own admissions test.

Such intense competition meant that many students could not compete successfully for admission to the college of their choice. An unsuccessful student could either accept an admission elsewhere, forego a college education, or wait until the following spring to take the national examinations again. A large number of students chose the last option. These students, called *rōnin* (see Glossary), spent an entire year, and sometimes longer, studying for another attempt at the entrance examinations.

Yobikō (see Glossary) are private schools that in current times, like many *juku*, help students prepare for entrance examinations. While *yobikō* have many programs for upper-secondary school students, they are best known for their specially designed full-time, year-long classes for *rōnin*. The number of applicants to four-year universities totalled almost 560,000 in 1988. *Rōnin* accounted for about 40 percent of new entrants to four-year colleges in 1988. Most *rōnin* were men, but about 14 percent were women. The *rōnin* experience was so common in Japan that the Japanese educational structure was often said to have an extra *rōnin* year built into it.

Yobikō sponsored a variety of programs, both full-time and part-time, and employed an extremely sophisticated battery of tests, student counseling sessions, and examination analysis to supplement their classroom instruction. The cost of *yobikō* education was high, comparable to first-year university expenses, and some specialized courses at *yobikō* were even more expensive. Some *yobikō* published modified commercial versions of the proprietary texts they used in their classrooms through publishing affiliates or by other means, and these were popular among the general population preparing for college entrance exams. *Yobikō* also administered practice examinations throughout the year, which they opened to all students for a fee.

In the late 1980s, the examination and entrance process were the subjects of renewed debate. In 1987 the schedule of the Joint First Stage Achievement Test was changed, and the content of the examination itself was revised for 1990. The schedule changes for the first time provided some flexibility for students wishing to apply to more than one national university. The new Joint First Stage Achievement Test was prepared and administered by the National Center for University Entrance Examination and was designed to accomplish better assessment of academic achievement.

The ministry hoped many private schools would adopt or adapt the new national test to their own admissions requirements and thereby reduce or eliminate the university tests. But, by the time the new test was administered in 1990, few schools had displayed any inclination to do so. The ministry urged universities to increase the number of students admitted through alternate selection methods, including admission of students returning to Japan from long overseas stays, admission by recommendation, and admission of students who had graduated from upper-secondary schools more than a few years before. Although a number of schools had programs in place or reserved spaces for returning students, only 5 percent of university students were admitted under these alternate arrangements in the late 1980s.

Other college entrance issues were proper guidance for college placement at the upper-secondary level and better dissemination of information about university programs. The ministry provided information through the National Center for University Entrance Examination's on-line information access system and encouraged universities, faculties, and departments to prepare brochures and video presentations about their programs.

Universities

In 1989 there were just over 2 million students enrolled in Japan's 490 universities. At the top of the higher education structure, these institutions provided four-year training leading to a bachelor's degree, and some offered six-year programs leading to a professional degree. There were two types of public four-year colleges: the 95 national universities (including the University of the Air) and the 38 local public universities, founded by prefectures and municipalities. The 357 remaining four-year colleges were private (see table 7, Appendix).

The overwhelming majority of college students attended full-time day programs. In 1988 the most popular courses, enrolling almost 40 percent of all undergraduate students, were in the social sciences, including business, law, and accounting. Other popular subjects were engineering (20 percent), the humanities (15 percent), and education (7.5 percent).

The average costs (tuition, fees, and living expenses) for a year of higher education in 1986 were ¥1.4 million (US$10,000), of which parents paid a little less than 80 percent, or about 20 percent of the average family's income in 1986. To help defray expenses, students frequently worked part-time or borrowed money through the government-supported Japan Scholarship Association. Assistance also was offered by local governments, nonprofit corporations, and other institutions.

In 1988 women accounted for about 26 percent of all university undergraduates, and their numbers were slowly increasing. Women's choices of majors and programs of study still tended to follow traditional patterns, with more than two-thirds of all women enrolled in education, social sciences, or humanities courses. Only 15 percent studied scientific and technical subjects, and women represented less than 3 percent of students in engineering, the most popular subject for men.

Junior Colleges

Junior colleges—mainly private institutions—were a legacy of the occupation period; many had been prewar institutions upgraded to college status at that time. More than 90 percent of the students in junior colleges were women, and higher education for women was still largely perceived as preparation for marriage or for a short-term career before marriage. Junior colleges provided many women with social credentials as well as education and some career opportunities. These colleges frequently emphasized home economics, nursing, teaching, the humanities, and social sciences in their curricula.

Special Training Schools

Advanced courses in special training schools required upper-secondary-school graduation. These schools offered training in specific skills, such as computer science and vocational training, and they enrolled a large number of men. Some students attended these schools in addition to attending a university; others went to qualify for technical licenses or certification. The prestige of special training schools was lower than that of universities, but graduates, particularly in technical areas, were readily absorbed by the job market.

Miscellaneous Schools

In 1988 there were about 3,700 predominantly private ''miscellaneous schools,'' whose attendance did not require upper-secondary school graduation. Miscellaneous schools offered a variety

Students at Shokutoku Junior College
Courtesy The Mainichi Newspapers

of courses in such programs as medical treatment, education, social welfare, and hygiene, diversifying practical postsecondary training and responding to social and economic demands for certain skills.

Technical Colleges

Most technical colleges were national institutions established to train highly skilled technicians in five-year programs in a number of fields, including the merchant marine. Sixty-two of these schools had been operating since the early 1960s. About 10 percent of technical college graduates transferred to universities as third-year students, and some universities, notably the University of Tokyo and Tokyo Institute of Technology, earmarked entrance places for these transfer students in the 1980s.

Graduate Education and Research

Graduate schools became a part of the formal higher education system only after World War II and were still not stressed in 1990. Even though 60 percent of all universities had graduate schools, only 7 percent of university graduates advanced to master's programs, and total graduate school enrollment was about 4 percent of the entire university student population.

The pattern of graduate enrollment was almost the opposite of that of undergraduates: the majority (63 percent) of all graduate students were enrolled in the national universities, and it appeared that the disparity between public and private graduate enrollments was widening. Graduate education was largely a male preserve, and women, particularly at the master's level, were most heavily represented in the humanities, social sciences, and education. Men, on the other hand, were frequently found in engineering programs where, at the master's level, women comprised only 2 percent of the students. At the doctoral level, the two highest levels of female enrollment were found in medical programs and the humanities, where in both fields 30 percent of doctoral students were women. Women accounted for about 13 percent of all doctoral enrollments.

The generally small numbers of graduate students and the graduate enrollment profile resulted from a number of factors, especially the traditional employment pattern of industry. The private sector frequently preferred to hire and train new university graduates, allowing them to develop their research skills within the corporate structure. Thus, the demand for students with advanced degrees was low.

The Ministry of Education, Science, and Culture

The Ministry of Education, Science, and Culture was the primary authority over higher education. It approved the establishment of all new institutions, both public and private, and directly controlled the budgets of all national institutions and their affiliated research institutes. In addition, the ministry regulated many aspects of the university environment, including standards for academics and physical plants and facilities. The ministry also provided subsidies to private higher education institutions for both operation and equipment and made long-term loans for physical plant improvement.

Government appropriations were the largest source of funds for national universities (over 75 percent), and tuition and fees provided most revenues for private schools (about 66 percent), with subsidies accounting for another 10 to 15 percent for the private schools. The 1975 Private School Promotion Law allowed the government to subsidize private education and increased the ministry's authority over private schools, but the ministry's own budgetary limits and general fiscal restraint have tended to limit such subsidies, which remained relatively low. In FY 1988, for example, only ¥244 billion of the total ministry budget of ¥4.6 trillion went for this purpose.

The Ministry of Education had two major areas of responsibility related to graduate education and research. In addition to being generally responsible for the national universities and establishing their research institutes, the ministry also promoted the research conducted at universities and funded both institutions and individuals. About a half-dozen research institutes, such as the National Institute for Educational Research and the National Institute for Special Education, were also under direct ministry supervision. Several types of research organizations were affiliated with universities: the national research institutes attached to national universities, independent research facilities affiliated with national universities but open to researchers from universities throughout Japan, other research centers, and other facilities at national, local, public, and private universities.

The ministry was not the exclusive agent for funding and promoting research, but it accounted for about half of the entire government budget for research throughout most of the 1980s. In addition to providing funds for research institutes and national universities, the ministry gave smaller amounts for scientific grants and programs in other public and private institutions.

The ministry could devote funds to particular areas of research that it considered important. In FY 1988, space science, particularly scientific satellites, rockets, and astronomy, high-energy physics and accelerator experiments, and the construction of a national research and development information network were programs that the ministry emphasized in its budget.

Reform

The quality of undergraduate and graduate education was the subject of widespread criticism in the 1980s, and its improvement was one of the focal points of university reform. One complaint was that students, once admitted, had little incentive to study because graduation was virtually automatic. There were few attendance requirements and, except for examinations, students were free to come and go as they pleased. There was poor teaching, and little study. Students and the system were accused of squandering the four years.

In response to the call for university reform in the reports of the National Council on Educational Reform, the ministry founded the University Council in 1987. High on the council's agenda were the diversification and reform of graduate education, improvement in the management and organization of universities, and the development of a policy for lifelong education and diversification in educational activities. The recommendations that had emerged by 1989 included improvements in the provision of private financial support to universities and modified personnel practices for college instructors in the national schools. There were calls for better information and data-processing education and for the establishment or reorganization of departments and research faculties in those fields. Finally, in the area of lifelong education, changes under discussion were the provision of more public lectures, expansion of university entrance opportunities for the general adult population, improvements in the University of the Air, and better school-community links.

The University of the Air, which had no entrance requirements, was originally designed to give all Japanese access to higher education through radio and television broadcasts. Although it was hampered by limited broadcast radius and frequencies, it had a potential leading role in promoting lifelong learning (see Social Education, this ch.).

Internationalization was an issue for every education level, but particularly for higher education. The number of students studying in Japan from foreign countries, especially Asian countries, was increasing, and the higher education structure was not particularly well-equipped to deal with them. In 1988 approximately 25,000 foreign students from more than 100 countries were studying in Japanese universities and colleges, and the ministry expected the figure to be 100,000 by the beginning of the twenty-first century. The ministry was also working to regulate and improve the standards for teaching Japanese to foreign students and trying to improve their financial and living arrangements. During the 1980s, Japanese universities established branches in the United States, and many American schools also set up Japanese branches. At least one Japanese women's university began to require its undergraduates to spend a semester on the campus of an affiliated school in the United States.

As in virtually every other area of education, debate over reform of graduate education and research was widespread at the end of the 1980s. The University Council established a subcommittee on graduate schools consisting of academics, researchers, and corporate executives. The subcommittee identified a number of critical issues: establishing graduate schools that were independent of traditional university structures, founding new and specialized graduate schools, reconsidering entrance and graduation criteria, increasing the international student population and internationalizing graduate education, addressing the qualifications of graduate school faculties, modifying the mission of doctoral courses, arranging for flexibility in admissions to graduate school, standardizing the length of graduate programs and reconciling the variations between degrees awarded by different schools and in different disciplines, establishing an accreditation and evaluation system, and reviewing the financial situation of graduate students. These recommendations were acknowledged in the ministry's FY 1988 budget, which included funds for expanding student aid programs, reforming graduate programs, and establishing a new Graduate School for Advanced Studies. Proposed reform of the research system concentrated on improving cooperation between universities and the private sector, and between universities and other institutions.

Finally, the subcommittee recommended greater Japanese participation and cooperation in international projects and greater efforts to make Japanese scientific and technical literature available in English. Although there were more programs for international scholarly exchange and more foreign researchers and foreign graduate students in Japan than in the past, Japanese society and education institutions were still having some difficulties in accommodating them smoothly.

Some of the urgency behind considering reforms in graduate education and research came from the recognition that Japan was increasingly involved in advanced research and was no longer assured of having foreign models to study. To remain competitive and to guarantee its future, Japan would need to make serious changes in its education and research structures. Its institutions would have to be more flexible and diverse, and encourage the creativity in education that would foster new technology. This need was seen to require a national effort, one not limited to the graduate sector.

Social Education

Modern Japan is unquestionably a society that values education highly. Nowhere in the 1980s was this better reflected than in "social education," as the Japanese called nondegree-oriented education. Diverse institutions, such as the miscellaneous schools, provided these services. Large newspaper companies sponsored cultural centers that offered ongoing programs of informal education, department stores organized curricula covering everything from cooking classes to music, English conversation, and Japanese poetry.

"Lifelong learning," another term for social education, was also a key phrase in the education reforms of the late 1980s. The responsibility for social education was shared by all levels of government, but especially local government. Local governments also were largely responsible for such public facilities as libraries and museums, basic resources in social education (see table 8, Appendix). The ministry was interested in increasing the use of public school facilities for lifelong learning activities, increasing the number of social education facilities, training staff, and disseminating information about lifelong learning opportunities.

The Japanese are voracious readers. In the 1980s, well-known bookstores were full from the moment they opened their doors each day with readers seeking books from a staggering range of foreign as well as Japanese titles. The top four national newspapers alone had a combined daily circulation (with two editions each day) of over 35 million, and there were four daily English-language papers as well.

Although education in Japan in 1990 was in transition in many regards, it still retained its postwar organizational structure. Even with growing pressure for reforms and for more emphasis on individuality and internationalization in education, it was clear that educational changes would be a unique amalgam of traditional values and modern innovations.

The Arts

The introduction of Western cultural values, which had flooded Japan by the late nineteenth century, led to a dichotomy developing between traditional values and the attempts to duplicate and assimilate a variety of clashing new ideas. This split remained evident in the late twentieth century, although much synthesis had occurred, which had created an international cultural atmosphere and stimulated contemporary Japanese arts toward ever more innovative forms.

Japan's aesthetic conceptions, deriving from diverse cultural traditions, have been formative in the production of unique art forms, all of which are characterized by an overwhelming technical perfection. Over the centuries, a wide range of artistic motifs developed and were refined, becoming imbued with symbolic significance and acquiring many layers of meaning. Japanese aesthetics provide a key to understanding artistic works perceivably different from those coming from Western traditions.

Within the East Asian artistic tradition, China has been the acknowledged teacher and Japan the devoted student. Nevertheless, Japanese arts developed their own style, which can be clearly differentiated from the Chinese. The monumental, symmetrically balanced, rational approach of Chinese art forms became miniaturized, irregular, and subtly suggestive in Japanese hands. Miniature rock gardens, diminutive plants (bonsai), and flower arrangements, in which the selected few represented a garden, were the favorite pursuits of refined aristocrats for a millennium, and they have remained a part of contemporary cultural life.

Daisen-in rock garden, Kyōto
Courtesy Jane T. Griffin

The diagonal, reflecting a natural flow, rather than the fixed tri-angle became the favored structural device, whether in painting, architectural or garden design, dance steps, or musical notations. Odd numbers replace even ones in the regularity of a Chinese master pattern, and a pull to one side allows a motif to turn the corner of a three-dimensional object, thus giving continuity and motion that is lacking in a static frontal design. Japanese painters used the devices of the cutoff, close-up, and fade-out by the twelfth century in *yamato-e,* or Japanese-style, scroll painting, perhaps one reason why modern filmmaking has been such a natural and successful art form in Japan. Suggestion is used rather than direct statement; oblique poetic hints, allusive, inconclusive melodies and thoughts—all have proved frustrating to the Westerner trying to penetrate the meanings of literature, music, painting, and even everyday language.

The Japanese began defining such aesthetic ideas in a number of evocative phrases by at least the tenth or eleventh centuries. The courtly refinements of the aristocratic Heian period evolved into the elegant simplicity seen as the essence of good taste in the under-stated art that is called *shibui* (see Nara and Heian Periods, 710–1185, ch. 1). Two terms originating from Zen Buddhist medita-tive practices describe degrees of tranquility: one, the repose found in humble melancholy (*wabi*), the other, the serenity accompany-ing the enjoyment of subdued beauty (*sabi*). Zen thought also contributed a penchant for combining the unexpected or startling, used to jolt one's consciousness toward the goal of enlightenment: in art, this approach was expressed in combinations of such unlikely materials as lead inlaid in lacquer and in clashing poetic imagery. Unexpectedly humorous and sometimes grotesque images and motifs also stem from the Zen *koan* (conundrum). Although the arts have been mainly secular since the Tokugawa period, traditional aesthetics and training methods, stemming generally from religious sources, continue to underlie artistic productions (see Tokugawa Period, 1600–1867, ch. 1).

In the Meiji period (1868–1912), Western art forms came into Japan and were studied with intense interest by Japanese artists, who quickly imitated a variety of European models. By the early twentieth century, a period of assimilation began as techniques were mastered and the new forms of literature and the visual and performing arts were adapted. Artists divided into two main camps, those continuing in traditional Japanese style and those who wholeheartedly studied the new Western culture. By the late 1920s, a generation of Japanese artists had synthesized Western and Japanese artistic conceptions. Oil painters used the calligraphic, black lines of traditional Japanese brushwork, and musicians used the Asian tonal system and instruments to create a concerto, while new theaters dealt with social themes in the allusive traditional literary style. Artists employing Western forms were accused of imitating rather than innovating. Yet, the age-old Asian cultural tradition has always entailed copying a master's style until it has been perfected, which explains why so much so-called "imitative art" was produced. Japan produced much vibrant and unique new art through such exchanges.

After World War II, many artists began working in art forms deriving from the international scene, moving away from local artistic developments into the mainstream of world art. But traditional Japanese conceptions endured, particularly in the use of modular space in architecture and certain spacing intervals in music and dance, and a propensity for certain color combinations and characteristic literary forms. The wide variety of art forms available to the Japanese in the 1990s reflected the vigorous state of the arts, widely supported by the Japanese people and promoted by the government.

Traditionally, the artist was a vehicle for expression and was personally reticent, in keeping with the role of an artisan or entertainer of low social status. The calligrapher—a member of the Confucian literati class, or samurai—did have a higher status, while artists of great genius were often recognized in the medieval period by receiving a name from a feudal lord and thus rising socially (see The Kamakura and Muromachi Periods, 1185–1573, ch. 1). The performing arts, however, were generally held in less esteem, and the purported immorality of actresses of the early Kabuki theater caused the Tokugawa government to bar women from the stage; female roles in Kabuki and Nō thereafter were played by men (see The Bakufu and the Hōjō Regency, ch. 1).

In the early 1990s, there were a number of specialized universities for the arts, led by the national universities. The most important was the prestigious Tokyo Arts University, said to be the most difficult of all national universities to enter. Another seminal center was Tama Arts University in Tokyo, which produced many of Japan's late twentieth-century innovative young artists. Traditional training in the arts remained: experts taught from their homes or headed schools working within a master-pupil relationship. A pupil did not experiment with a personal style until the top level of training, or graduation, or becoming head of a school. Many young artists have criticized this system as stifling creativity and individuality. A new generation of the avant-garde has broken with this tradition, often receiving its training in the West. In the traditional arts, however, the master-pupil system preserved the secrets and skills of the past. Some master-pupil lineages could be traced to the medieval period, from which they continued to use a great master's style or theme. Japanese artists considered technical virtuosity as the sine qua non of their professions, a fact recognized by the rest of the world as one of the hallmarks of Japanese art.

The national government has actively supported the arts through the Agency for Cultural Affairs, set up in 1968 as a special body of the Ministry of Education. The agency's budget for FY 1989 rose to ¥37.8 billion after five years of budget cuts, but still represented much less than 1 percent of the general budget. The agency's Cultural Affairs Division disseminated information about the arts within Japan and internationally, and the Cultural Properties Protection Division protected the nation's cultural heritage. The Cultural Affairs Division was concerned with such areas as art and culture promotion, arts copyrights, and improvements in the national language. It also supported both national and local arts and cultural festivals, and funded traveling cultural events in music, theater, dance, art exhibitions, and filmmaking. Special prizes were offered to encourage young artists and established practitioners, and some grants were given each year to enable them to train abroad. The agency funded national museums of modern art in Kyōto and Tokyo and the Museum of Western Art in Tokyo, which exhibited both Japanese and international shows. The agency also supported the Japan Academy of Arts, which honored eminent persons of arts and letters, appointing them to membership and offering ¥3.5 million in prize money. Awards were made in the presence of the emperor, who would personally bestow the highest accolade, the Cultural Medal. In 1989 the fifth woman ever to be so distinguished was cited for Japanese-style painting, while for the first time two women—a writer and a costume designer—were nominated for the Order of Cultural Merit, another official honor carrying the same stipend.

The Cultural Properties Protection Division originally was established to oversee restorations after World War II. In 1989 it was responsible for over 2,500 historic sites, including the ancient capitals of Asuka, Heijōkyō, and Fujiwara, more than 275 scenic places, and nearly 1,000 national monuments, and for such indigenous fauna as ibis and storks. As of 1989, some 1,000 buildings, paintings, sculptures, and other art forms had been designated National Treasures. In addition, about 11,500 items had the lesser designation of Important Cultural Properties, with buildings accounting for the largest share, closely followed by sculpture and craft objects.

The government also protected buried properties, of which some 300,000 had been identified. During the 1980s, many important prehistoric and historic sites were investigated by the archaeological institutes that the agency funded, resulting in about 2,000 excavations in 1989. The wealth of material unearthed shed new light on the controversial period of the formation of the Japanese state (see Early Developments, ch. 1).

A 1975 amendment to the Cultural Properties Protection Act of 1897 enabled the Agency for Cultural Affairs to designate traditional areas and buildings in urban centers for preservation. From time to time, various endangered traditional artistic skills were added to the agency's preservation roster, such as the 1989 inclusion of a kind of ancient doll making.

One of the most important roles of the Cultural Properties Protection Division was to preserve the traditional arts and crafts and performing arts through their living exemplars. Individual artists and groups, such as a dance troupe or a pottery village, were designated as *mukei bunkazai* (intangible cultural assets) in recognition of their skill. Major exponents of the traditional arts have been designated as *ningen kokuhō* (living national treasures). About seventy persons are so honored at any one time; in 1989 the six newly designated masters were a *kyōgen* (comic) performer, a chanter of *bunraku* (puppet) theater, a performer of the *nagauta samisen* (a special kind of stringed instrument), the head potter making Nabeshima decorated porcelain ware, the top pictorial lacquer-ware artist, and a metal-work expert. Each was provided a lifetime annual pension of ¥2 million and financial aid for training disciples.

The national museums of Japanese and Asian art in Tokyo, Kyōto, Nara, and Ōsaka, the cultural properties research institutes at Tokyo and Nara, the national theaters, the Ethnological Museum, the National Museum of History and Folk Culture, and the National Storehouse for Fine Arts all came under the aegis of the Cultural Properties Protection Division. During the 1980s, the National Nō Theater and the National Bunraku Theater were constructed by the government.

Arts patronage and promotion by the government were broadened to include a new cooperative effort with corporate Japan to provide funding beyond the tight budget of the Agency for Cultural Affairs. Many other public and private institutions participated, especially in the burgeoning field of awarding arts prizes. A growing number of large corporations joined major newspapers in sponsoring exhibitions and performances and in giving yearly prizes. The most important of the many literary awards given were the venerable Naoki Prize and the Akutagawa Prize, the latter being the equivalent of the Pulitzer Prize in the United States. In 1989 an effort to promote cross-cultural exchange led to the establishment of a Japanese "Nobel Prize" for the arts—the Premium Imperiale—by the Japan Art Association. This prize of US$100,000 was funded largely by the mass media conglomerate Fuji-Sankei and awarded on a world-wide selection basis.

A number of foundations promoting the arts arose in the 1980s, including the new Cultural Properties Foundation set up to preserve historic sites overseas, especially along the Silk Route in Inner Asia and at Dunhuang in China. Another international arrangement was made in 1988 with the United States Smithsonian Institution for cooperative exchange of high-technology studies of Asian artifacts. The government played a major role by funding the Japan Foundation, which provided both institutional and individual grants, effected scholarly exchanges, awarded annual prizes, supported publications and exhibitions, and sent traditional Japanese arts groups to perform abroad. The Arts Festival held for two months each fall for all the performing arts was sponsored by the Agency for Cultural Affairs. Major cities also provided substantial support for the arts; a growing number in the 1980s had built large centers for the performing arts and, stimulated by government funding, were offering prizes such as the Lafcadio Hearn Prize initiated by the city of Matsue. There were also a number of new municipal museums providing about one-third more facilities in the 1980s than were previously available. In the late 1980s, Tokyo added more than twenty new cultural halls, notably, the large Cultural Village built by Tōkyū Corporation and the reconstruction of Shakespeare's Globe Theater. All these efforts reflected a rising popular enthusiasm for the arts. Japanese art buyers swept the Western art markets in the late 1980s, paying record highs for impressionist paintings and US$51.7 million alone for one blue period Picasso.

After World War II, artists typically gathered in arts associations, some of which were long-established professional societies while others reflected the latest arts movement. The Japan Artists League, for example, was responsible for the largest number of major exhibitions including the prestigious annual Nitten (Japan Art Exhibition). The P.E.N. Club of Japan (P.E.N. stands for prose, essay, and narrative)—a branch of an international writers' organization—was the largest of some thirty major authors' associations. Actors, dancers, musicians, and other kinds of performing artists boasted their own major and minor societies, including the Kabuki Society, organized in 1987 to maintain this art's traditional high standards, which were thought to be endangered by modern innovation. By the 1980s, however, avant-garde painters and sculptors had eschewed all groups, and were "unattached" artists.

Visual Arts

Architecture

With the introduction of Western building techniques, materials, and styles into Meiji Japan, new steel and concrete structures were built in strong contrast to traditional styles. Japan played some role in modern skyscraper design because of its long familiarity with the cantilever principle to support the weight of heavy tiled temple roofs. Frank Lloyd Wright was strongly influenced by Japanese spatial arrangements and the concept of interpenetrating exterior and interior space, long achieved in Japan by opening up walls made of sliding doors. In the late twentieth century, however, only in domestic and religious architecture was Japanese style commonly employed. Cities bristled with modern skyscrapers, epitomized by Tokyo's crowded skyline, reflecting a total assimilation and transformation of modern Western forms.

The widespread urban planning and reconstruction necessitated by the devastation of World War II produced such major architects as Maekawa Kunio and Tange Kenzō. Maekawa, a student of world-famous architect Charles LeCorbusier, produced thoroughly international, functional modern works. Tange, who worked at first for Maekawa, supported this concept. Both were notable for infusing Japanese aesthetic ideas into starkly contemporary buildings, returning to the spatial concepts and modular proportions of tatami (sleeping mats), using textures to enliven the ubiquitous ferroconcrete and steel, and integrating gardens and sculpture into their designs. Tange used the cantilever principle in a pillar and beam system reminiscent of ancient imperial palaces; the pillar—a hallmark of Japanese traditional monumental timber construction—became fundamental to his designs. Maki Fumihiko advanced new city planning ideas based on the principle of layering or cocooning around an inner space (*oku*), a Japanese spatial concept that was adapted to urban needs. He also advocated the use of empty or open spaces (*ma*), a Japanese aesthetic principle reflecting Buddhist spatial ideas. Another quintessentially Japanese aesthetic concept was a basis for Maki designs, which focused on openings onto intimate garden views at ground level while cutting off ugly skylines. A dominant 1970s architectural concept, the "metabolism" of convertibility, provided for changing the functions of parts of buildings according to use, and has remained influential in the 1990s.

A major architect of the 1970s and 1980s was Isozaki Arata, originally a student and associate of Tange's, who also based his style on the LeCorbusier tradition and then turned his attention toward the further exploration of geometric shapes and cubic silhouettes. He synthesized Western high-technology building concepts with peculiarly Japanese spatial, functional, and decorative ideas to create a modern Japanese style. Isozaki's predilection for the cubic grid and trabeated pergola in large-scale architecture, for the semicircular vault in domestic-scale buildings, and for extended barrel vaulting in low, elongated buildings led to a number of striking variations. New Wave architects of the 1980s were influenced by his designs, either pushing to extend his balanced style, often into mannerism, or reacting against them.

A number of avant-garde experimental groups were encompassed in the New Wave of the late 1970s and the 1980s. They reexamined and modified the formal geometric structural ideas of modernism by introducing metaphysical concepts, producing some startling fantasy effects in architectural design. In contrast to these innovators, the experimental poetic minimalism of Andō Tadao embodied the postmodernist concerns for a more balanced, humanistic approach than that of structural modernism's rigid formulations. Andō's buildings provide a variety of light sources, including extensive use of glass bricks and opening up spaces to the outside air. He adapted the inner courtyards of traditional Ōsaka houses to new urban architecture, using open stairways and bridges to lessen the sealed atmosphere of the standard city dwelling. His ideas became ubiquitous in the 1980s, when buildings were commonly planned around open courtyards or plazas, often with stepped and terraced spaces, pedestrian walkways, or bridges connecting building complexes. In 1989 Andō became the third Japanese to receive France's Prix de L'Académie d'Architecture, an indication of the international strength of the major Japanese architects, all of whom produced important structures abroad during the 1980s. Japanese architects were not only skilled practitioners in the modern idiom but also enriched postmodern designs worldwide with innovative spatial perceptions, subtle surface texturing, unusual use of industrial materials, and a developed awareness of ecological and topographical problems.

Sculpture

Japanese sculpture derived from Shinto funerary and Buddhist religious arts, and developed portrait sculpture only as a memorial to a shrine patron or temple founder. Materials traditionally used were metal—especially bronze—and, more commonly, wood, often lacquered, gilded, or brightly painted. By the end of the Tokugawa period, such traditional sculpture—except for miniaturized works—had largely disappeared because of the loss of patronage by Buddhist temples and the nobility.

The stimulus of Western art forms returned sculpture to the Japanese art scene and introduced the plaster cast, outdoor heroic sculpture, and the school of Paris concept of sculpture as an "art form." Such ideas adapted in Japan during the late nineteenth century, together with the return of state patronage, rejuvenated sculpture. After World War II, sculptors turned away from the figurative French school of Rodin and Maillol toward aggressive modern and avant-garde forms and materials, sometimes on an enormous scale. A profusion of materials and techniques characterized these new experimental sculptures, which also absorbed the ideas of international "op" (optical illusion) and "pop" (popular motif) art. A number of innovative artists were both sculptors and painters or printmakers, their new theories cutting across material boundaries.

In the 1970s, the ideas of contextual placement of natural objects of stone, wood, bamboo, and paper into relationships with people and their environment were embodied in the *mono-ha* school. These artists emphasized materiality as the most important aspect of art and brought to an end the antiformalism that had dominated the avant-garde in the preceding two decades. This focus on the

Contemporary outdoor sculpture by Isamu Noguchi, Kagawa Prefecture
Courtesy Asahi Shimbun

relationships between objects and people was ubiquitous throughout the arts world and led to a rising appreciation of "Japanese" qualities in the environment and a return to native artistic principles and forms. Among these precepts were a reverence for nature and various Buddhist concepts brought into play by architects to treat time/space problems. Western ideology was carefully reexamined, and much was rejected as artists turned to their own environment—both inward and outward—for sustenance and inspiration. From the late 1970s through the late 1980s, artists began to create a vital new art, which was both contemporary and Asian in sources and expression but still very much a part of the international scene. These artists focused on projecting their own individualism and national styles rather than on adapting or synthesizing Western ideas exclusively.

Outdoor sculpture, which came to the fore with the advent of the Hakone Open-Air Museum in 1969, was widely used in the 1980s, and cities supported enormous outdoor sculptures for parks and plazas, and major architects planned for sculpture in their buildings and urban layouts. Outdoor museums and exhibitions burgeoned, stressing the natural placement of sculpture in the environment. Since hard sculpture stone is not native to Japan, most outdoor pieces were created from stainless steel, plastic, or aluminum for "tension and compression" machine constructions of mirror-surfaced steel or for elegant, polished-aluminum, ultramodern shapes. The strong influence of modern high technology on the artists resulted in experimentation with kinetic, tensile forms, such as flexible arcs and "info-environmental" sculptures using lights. Video components and video art developed rapidly from the late 1970s throughout the 1980s. The new Japanese experimental sculptors could be understood as working with Buddhist ideas of permeability and regeneration in structuring their forms, a contrast to the general Western conception of sculpture as something with finite and permanent contours.

In the 1980s, wood and natural materials were used prominently by many sculptors, who now began to place their works in inner courtyards and enclosed spaces. Also, a Japanese feeling for rhythmic motion, captured in recurring forms as a "systematic gestural motion," was used by both long-established artists like Kiyomizu Kyūbei and Nagasawa Hidetoshi and the younger generation spearheaded by Toya Shigeo. The 1970s search for a national identity led to a renewed understanding of Japanese forms, spatial perceptions, rhythms, and philosophical conceptions, which reinvigorated Japanese sculpture in the 1980s.

Painting

Painting is one of the oldest and most highly refined of Japanese arts, stemming from classic continental traditions of the early historical period (sixth-seventh centuries A.D.). Native Japanese traditions reached their apex in the Heian period (794-1185), producing many artistic devices still in use in the 1990s. During periods of strong Chinese influence, new art forms were adapted, such as Buddhist works in Nara, ink painting in the Muromachi period, and landscape painting by literati in the Tokugawa era. When Western painting theories were introduced in the Meiji period, Japan already had a long history of adaptation of imported ideas and had established a copy process ranging from emulation to synthesis. But it was not until well into the twentieth century that the Japanese were able to assimilate the new medium of oil paints with new ideas of three-dimensional projections on flat surfaces.

Most contemporary Japanese artists could be divided into those who worked in a broadly international style and those who maintained Japanese artistic traditions, though usually within a modern idiom. After World War II, painters, calligraphers, and printmakers flourished in the big cities, particularly Tokyo, and became preoccupied with the mechanisms of urban life, reflected in the flickering lights, neon colors, and frenetic pace of their abstractions. All the "isms" of the New York-Paris art world were fervently embraced. After the abstractions of the 1960s, the 1970s saw a return to realism strongly flavored by the "op" and "pop" art movements, embodied in the 1980s in the explosive works of Shinohara Ushio. Many such outstanding avant-garde artists worked both in Japan and abroad, winning international prizes. These artists felt that there was "nothing Japanese" about their works, and indeed they belonged to the international school. By the late 1970s, the search for Japanese qualities and a national style caused many artists to reevaluate their artistic ideology and turn away from what some felt were the empty formulas of the West. Contemporary paintings within the modern idiom began to make conscious use of traditional Japanese art forms, devices, and ideologies. A number of *mono-ha* artists turned to painting to recapture traditional nuances in spatial arrangements, color harmonies, and lyricism.

Japanese-style painting (*nihonga*) had continued in a modern fashion, updating traditional expressions while retaining their intrinsic character. Some artists within this style still painted on silk or paper with traditional colors and ink, while others used new materials, such as acrylics. Many of the older schools of art, most notably those of the Tokugawa period, were still practiced. For example, the decorative naturalism of the *rimpa* school, characterized by brilliant, pure colors and bleeding washes, was reflected in the work of many postwar artists and in the 1980s art of Hikosaka Naoyoshi. The realism of the Maruyama-Ōkyo school and the calligraphic and spontaneous Japanese style of the gentlemen-scholars were both widely practiced in the 1980s. Sometimes all of these schools, as well as older ones, such as the Kanō ink traditions, were drawn on by contemporary artists in the Japanese style and in the modern idiom. Many Japanese-style painters were honored with awards and prizes, as the late 1970s and the 1980s saw a renewed popular demand for Japanese-style art. More and more, the international modern painters also drew on the Japanese schools as they turned away from Western styles in the 1980s. The tendency had been to synthesize East and West. But new artistic approaches were less in favor of a conscious blending than of recapturing the Japanese spirit within a modern idiom. Thus, the 100-year split between Japanese-style and Western-style art began to heal. Some artists had already leapt the gap between the two, as did the outstanding painter, Shinoda Tōko. Her bold *sumi* ink abstractions were inspired by traditional calligraphy but realized as lyrical expressions of modern abstraction.

173

Calligraphy

Calligraphy, the art of beautiful writing, had long been highly esteemed, intensively studied, and avidly collected. The writing of Chinese ideograms (*kanji*) in a wide variety of styles was inherited from the Chinese scholarly tradition, which at one extreme became the nearly indecipherable grass-style writing and at the other geometric abstractions. There are famous exponents of all these styles in contemporary Japan who have spent lifetimes perfecting their skills. The most widely used mode is called *kana*, referring to the Japanese syllabary, which provides an opportunity to depict both ideograms and Japanese phonetic sounds in set phrases. There are many ways in which this kind of writing may be done: with fine, delicate strokes or bold, splashy ones, carefully controlled or in uninhibited freedom, and on a scale ranging from large to minuscule. Traditional Japanese poetry is usually classified in the *kana* group, while modern poetry is placed in a group by itself. Zen Buddhism promoted a spontaneous style of writing in its *koan*, which includes some pictorial additions.

Because calligraphy lends itself so well to modern abstract painting, some artists have used it in this form; the Bokusho abstract school has developed some outstanding masters. Calligraphers are greatly revered not only for their skill and scholarship but also for their attainment of a high spiritual level, which produces the meditative calm considered necessary for truly creative brushwork. Calligraphy is widely collected at enormous prices. Even those who cannot read the script, which is not uncommon because some is nearly abstract, treasure writing by well-known persons in various fields, such as politics or the military.

Prints

Outstanding among the contemporary arts for vitality and originality are the works of the creative printmakers, which have brought worldwide recognition. The twentieth-century Japanese print evolved from the Western idea of a single artist's conceiving, executing, and producing one individual work. In contrast, the classic *ukiyo-e* (floating world art) print approach was of a team production by an artist designer, craftsman carver, colorist, printer, and publisher, who promoted sales of multiple copies. The modern print movement so stressed the creative process that even in the 1980s, editions of prints were seldom very large and were apt to differ in color or even design elements from one printing to the next.

In the late twentieth century, a broad spectrum of artistic styles from traditional to experimental was practiced in a multiplicity of media and techniques. Munakata Shikō, a major force in gaining

Aristocratic lady reading, early Edo period, ukiyo-e *school, attributed to
Iwasa Matabei (1578–1650)
Courtesy Freer Gallery of Art (69.15), Smithsonian Institution, Washington*

recognition for creative printmaking, drew deeply on Japanese artistic sources, from folk art to Zen poetry-paintings, combining *kanji* with free-floating Chagall-like figures. He influenced many other celebrated print artists who drew on folk art and used natural earth and mineral colors to depict traditional village scenes and lively local festivals. Artists such as Sekino Jun'ichirō and Saitō Kiyoshi were inspired to update famous views, as of the Tōkaidō, while others played with traditional themes derived from sumo, the theater, or geisha. At the opposite pole are the works of the abstractionists, the exponents of all the "isms" of the day, and the experimental essays of some consummate designers. Most avant-garde artists worked in mixed media, often using engraving techniques with silk-screened colors or monochromatic metal prints with soldered wires. They experimented freely with photomontage, photo-prints made with an electric scanner, and lithographs. Photography as an art form came into its own in the 1980s, and major international exhibitions displayed the stunning products of artist photographers such as Namikawa Banri, Kurigama Kazumi, and Hashi. In the 1980s, a trend among many young printmakers was towards the use of black and white for somber, often superrealistic, themes, captured with exquisite technical and artistic precision.

Ceramics

One of Japan's oldest art forms, ceramics, reaches back to the Neolithic period (ca. 10,000 B.C.), when the earliest soft earthenware was coil-made, decorated by hand-impressed rope patterns (Jōmon ware), and baked in the open. Continental emigrants of the third century B.C. introduced the use of the wheel along with the metal age (Yayoi) and, eventually (in the third to fourth centuries A.D.), a tunnel kiln in which stoneware fired at high temperatures embellished with natural ash glaze was produced. Medieval kilns enabled more refined production of stoneware, which was still produced in the late twentieth century at a few famous sites, especially in central Honshū around the city of Seto, the wares of which were so widely used that Seto-mono became the generic term for ceramics in Japan. The overlord Toyotomi Hideyoshi's Korean campaigns of the late sixteenth century were dubbed the "ceramic wars," since the importation of Korean potters appeared to be their major contribution. These potters introduced a variety of new techniques and styles in their artifacts that were greatly admired for the tea ceremony. They also discovered in northern Kyūshū the proper ingredients needed to produce porcelain and were soon dazzling the guests at *daimyō* banquets with the first Japanese-made porcelain (see Ashikaga Bakufu, ch. 1).

The modern masters of these famous traditional kilns still bring the ancient formulas in pottery and porcelain to new heights of achievement at Shiga, Ige, Karatsu, Hagi, and Bizen. Yamamoto Masao of Bizen and Miwa Kyūsetsu of Hagi were designated as *mukei bunkazai*. By 1989 only a half-dozen potters were so honored, either as representatives of famous kiln wares or for the creation of superlative techniques in glazing or decoration, while two groups were designated for preserving the wares of distinguished ancient kilns.

In the old capital of Kyōto, the Raku family continued to produce the famous rough tea bowls that had so delighted Hideyoshi, while experiments continued to reconstruct the classic formulas of Momoyama-era Seto-type tea wares at Minō, such as the famous Oribe copper-green glaze and Shino ware's prized milky glaze. Artist potters experimented endlessly at the Kyōto and Tokyo arts universities to recreate traditional porcelain and its decorations under such outstanding ceramic teachers as Fujimoto Yoshimichi, a *mukei bunkazai*. Ancient porcelain kilns around Arita in Kyūshū were still maintained by the lineage of the famous Sakaida Kakiemon and Imaizume Imaiemon, hereditary porcelain makers to the Nabeshima clan; both were heads of groups designated *mukei bunkazai*.

By the end of the 1980s, many master potters no longer worked at major or ancient kilns, but were making classic wares in various parts of Japan or in Tokyo, a notable example being Tsuji Seimei, who brought his clay from Shiga but potted in the Tokyo area. A number of artists were engaged in reconstructing famous Chinese styles of decoration or glazes, especially the blue-green celadon and the watery-green *qingbai*. One of the most beloved Chinese glazes in Japan is the chocolate-brown *tenmoku* glaze that covered the peasant tea bowls brought back from Southern Song China (in the twelfth and thirteenth centuries) by Zen monks. For their Japanese users, these chocolate-brown wares embodied the Zen aesthetic of *wabi* (rustic simplicity).

Interest in the humble art of the village potter was revived in a folk movement of the 1920s by such master potters as Hamada Shōji and Kawai Kanjirō. These artists studied traditional glazing techniques to preserve native wares in danger of disappearing. The kilns at Tamba, overlooking Kobe, continued to produce the daily wares used in the Tokugawa period, while adding modern shapes. Most of the village wares were made anonymously by local potters for utilitarian purposes. Local styles, whether native or imported, tended to be continued without alteration into the present. In Kyūshū, kilns set up by Korean potters in the sixteenth century, such as at Kōishibara and its offshoot at Onta, perpetuated sixteenth-century Korean peasant wares. In Okinawa, the production of village ware continued under several leading masters, with Kaneshiro Jirō honored as a *mukei bunkazai*.

Handicrafts

The many and varied traditional handicrafts of Japan enjoyed official recognition and protection and, owing to the folk art movement, were much in demand. Each craft demanded a set of specialized skills. Textile crafts, for example, included silk, hemp, and cotton, woven (after spinning and dyeing) in forms ranging from timeless folk designs to complex court patterns. Village crafts evolving from ancient folk traditions also continued in weaving and indigo dyeing in Hokkaidō by the Ainu peoples, whose distinctive designs had prehistoric prototypes and by other remote farming families in northern Japan. Silk-weaving families can be traced to the fifteenth century in the famous Nishijin weaving center of Kyōto, where elegant fabrics worn by the emperor and the aristocracy were produced. In the seventeenth century, designs on textiles were applied using stencils and rice paste, in the *yūzen* or paste-resist method of dyeing. The *yūzen* method provided an imitation of aristocratic brocades, which were forbidden to commoners by sumptuary laws. Moriguchi Kako of Kyōto has continued to create works of art in his *yūzen*-dyed kimonos, which were so sought after that the contemporary fashion industry designed an industrial method to copy them for use on Western-style clothing. Famous designers, such as Hanae Mori, borrowed extensively from kimono patterns for their couturier collections. By the late 1980s, an elegant, handwoven, dyed kimono had become extremely costly, running to US$25,000 for a formal garment. In Okinawa, the famous *yūzen*-dyeing method was especially effective where it was produced in the *bingata* stencil-dyeing techniques, which produced exquisitely colored, striking designs as artistic national treasures.

Lacquer, the first plastic, was invented in Asia, and its use in Japan can be traced to prehistoric finds. Lacquer ware is most often made from wooden objects, which receive multiple layers of refined lac juices, each of which must dry before the next is applied. These layers make a tough skin impervious to water damage and breakage-resistant, providing lightweight, easy to clean utensils of every sort. The decoration on such lacquers, whether carved through different colored layers or in surface designs, applied with gold or inlaid with precious substances, has been a prized art form since the Nara period (A.D. 710–94).

Papermaking is another contribution of Asian civilization; the Japanese art of making paper from the mulberry plant is thought

*Rimpa school painting, Edo period, showing a screen,
garments, and other objects
Courtesy Freer Fallery of Art (07.127), Smithsonian Institution, Washington*

to have begun in the sixth century. Dyeing paper with a wide
variety of hues and decorating it with designs became a major
preoccupation of the Heian court, and the enjoyment of beautiful paper and its use has continued thereafter, with some modern
adaptations. The traditionally made paper called Izumo (after the
shrine area where it is made) was especially desired for *fusuma*
(sliding panels) decoration, artists' papers, and elegant letter paper.
Some printmakers have their own logo made into their papers,
and since the Meiji period, another special application has been
Western marbleized end papers (made by the Atelier Miura in
Tokyo).

Metalwork is epitomized in the production of the Japanese sword,
of extremely high quality. These swords originated before the first
century B.C. and reached their height of popularity as the chief
possession of warlords and samurai. The production of a sword
has retained something of the religious quality it once had in embodying the soul of the samurai and the martial spirit of Japan.
For many Japanese, the sword, one of the "three jewels" of the
nation, remained a potent symbol; possessors would treasure a
sword and it would be maintained within the family, its loss sig-
nifying their ruin (see Ancient Cultures, ch. 1).

Performing Arts

A remarkable number of the traditional forms of music, dance, and theater have survived in the contemporary world, enjoying some popularity through reidentification with Japanese cultural values. Traditional music and dance, which trace their origins to ancient religious use—Buddhist, Shinto, and folk—have been preserved in the dramatic performances of Nō, Kabuki, and *bunraku* theater. Ancient court music and dance forms deriving from continental sources were preserved through imperial household musicians and temple and shrine troupes. Some of the oldest musical instruments in the world have been in continuous use in Japan from the Jōmon period, as shown by finds of stone and clay flutes and zithers with between two and four strings, to which Yayoi-period metal bells and gongs were added to create early musical ensembles. By the early historical period (sixth to seventh centuries A.D.), there were a variety of large and small drums, gongs, chimes, flutes, and stringed instruments, such as the imported mandolin-like *biwa*, and the flat six-stringed zither, which evolved into the thirteen-stringed *koto*. These instruments formed the orchestras for the seventh-century continentally derived ceremonial court music, which, together with the accompanying *bugaku* (a type of court dance), are the most ancient of such forms still performed at the imperial court, ancient temples, and shrines. Buddhism introduced the rhythmic chants, still used in the 1990s, that were joined with native ideas and underlay the development of vocal music, such as in Nō.

The oldest dramatic form preserved in Japan is Nō theater, which attained its contemporary form at the fourteenth-century Ashikaga court. In the 1980s, there were five major Nō groups and a few notable regional troupes performing several hundred plays from a medieval repertoire for a popular audience, not just for an elite. A Nō play unfolds around the recitation and dancing of a principal and secondary figure, while a seated chorus chants a story, accentuated by solemn drum and flute music. The dramatic action is mimed in highly stylized gestures symbolizing intense emotions, which are also evoked by terse lyrical prose and dance. Standardized masks and brilliant costumes stand out starkly against the austere, empty stage with its symbolic pine tree backdrop. The stories depict legendary or historical events of a tragic cast, infused with Buddhist ideas. The foreboding atmosphere is relieved by comic interludes (*kyōgen*) played during the intermission. A few experimental plays have been developed by authors such as Mishima Yukio (1925–70), and in the 1980s a Christian Nō play was written

Shinoda Tōko, a leading modern abstract painter, at work Courtesy The Phillips Collection, Washington

"Unseen Forms," a two-panel sumi *screen by Shinoda Tōko Courtesy Chase Manhattan Bank*

by a Sophia University philosophy professor and daringly performed at the Vatican for Pope John Paul II. The National Nō Theater has revived popular interest in this ancient art form by supporting experimental Nō plays in the late 1980s.

Kabuki and *bunraku* theater developed as popular forms of entertainment in the seventeenth century. Kabuki combined contemporary music, acrobatics, and mimicry like that of Nō, and was originally performed by troupes that included actresses. Women were soon barred from appearing, so the often large casts consisted entirely of male performers. Classical Kabuki somewhat resembles Western drama, except that dialogue is supplemented by chanting and accompanied by music provided by the *samisen,* a three-stringed lute perfected during the seventeenth century. The plot was often clarified by the use of a storyteller who recounted the major action, as was also customary in Nō.

Kabuki conventions include the use of artificially high-pitched voices, exaggerated gestures and miming, and flamboyant costumes and makeup, but no masks. Elaborate stage devices—trapdoors, revolving stages, and runways through the theater—heighten the excitement. Historical and legendary themes were extended to include events from the urban life of the seventeenth and eighteenth centuries, such as a townsman's dislike for the samurai. A common theme in the late seventeenth-century and early eighteenth-century works of Chikamatsu Monzaemon, "the Shakespeare of Japan," is the conflict between personal desires and the Confucian sense of loyalty and duty. By the early 1990s, there were two national Kabuki theaters in Tokyo, as the major performance centers for this classical art, featuring a growing repertoire of lesser known as well as classic work. Among contemporary masters working to "update" Kabuki and attract modern audiences were Ichikawa Ennosuke III, whose deft acting, clever acrobatics, and swift costume changes evoked nearly magical illusions, and Tamasaburō Bandō, the top player of a wide range of feminine roles. These and other superb Kabuki actors brought record audiences to performances in the late 1980s.

Bunraku, puppet theater native to Ōsaka, was regarded as a serious dramatic medium for adults (unlike puppetry in many Western countries), and has flourished along with Kabuki since the Tokugawa period. Chikamatsu turned to writing for the *bunraku* when he became dissatisfied with the liberties some Kabuki actors took with his plays. A narrator, who sings all the parts, and a *samisen*-playing chorus are the main elements of *bunraku.* The narrator-singer conveys the emotional content of the play and generates the illusion of life into the large puppets, who move realistically in complex roles, manipulated by a master and black-hooded, robed assistants. These narrator-singers derive from the ancient tradition of storytellers, whose exponents continue to flourish in modern forms, now including women and such uproarish comics as Katsura Shijaku.

Traditional music, song, and dance have been performed by women, notably the geisha of Tokyo and Kyōto. Theatrical performances by Kyōto geisha can be seen in the spring and autumn Miyako Odori dance performances. A *nagauta* (lyric music) singing group has a full orchestral ensemble, consisting of drums, flutes, *samisen,* and *koto.* The traditional musical notation is based on a five-tone scale, with semitones often ending on a rising note. Famous performers may play the *samisen* or *koto* only, or play together with a singer or dancer. The dances come from Nō, Kabuki, and folk sources, featuring large ensemble dances as highlights of these brilliant spectacles.

Folk music and dance deriving from regional festivals and ceremonies began to become well-known in Japan through radio, television, and recordings. Folk festivals, concerts, and contests, and taverns specializing in folk singing contributed to the rising popularity of these ancient forms, revitalized by the growing desire of the young in the 1980s to learn traditional agrarian songs and dances, while the Japan Folkloric Dance Ensemble performed them internationally. Some thirty outstanding performers from all the traditional performing arts were designated as *mukei bunkazai* at the end of the 1980s.

Classical Western music has become a fundamental part of Japanese musical education since its introduction in the nineteenth century. The Tōhō School of Music in Tokyo has produced many outstanding international performers on the piano and stringed instruments. Children commonly studied piano or violin, and the famous Suzuki violin method of training children from the age of two had produced a generation of virtuosos, some, such as Midori, enjoyed an international reputation.

Symphony orchestras played in Tokyo and most major cities, also making international tours. Japanese musicians and conductors gained international recognition, some performing regularly with top foreign orchestras overseas and on tour in Japan. Contemporary Japanese composers have experimented widely with instruments: using Japanese and Western instruments together, using only Asian instruments, and capturing traditional sounds with electronic synthesizers and Western instruments. The Ensemble Nipponica, Music Today, and Sound Space Ark were among the major groups promoting modern Japanese music.

Classical Western opera enjoyed a boom, with many foreign companies performing, and even local companies rose to new heights with the development of leading operatic singers. Further evidence of interest in Japanese themes was shown by a major competition to write a new opera about Chikamatsu, with music composed by Hara Kazuko, a Doshisha University professor.

Popular music was enjoyed in many forms. Musical comedies and revues were standard urban entertainment. Broadway and London hits were quickly adapted by Tokyo theater troupes, often using foreign directors for notable productions and sometimes featuring Western actors who spoke their lines in Japanese. Japanese youth everywhere enjoyed popular music: highly international jazz, rock, heavy metal, folk, new music, pop, synthesized music, instrumental music, and Japanese folk songs. Springing from popular music were the works of experimental composers like Hosono Haruomi and Sakamoto Ryūichi, who blended Middle Eastern or Chinese sounds for the huge recording industry and film sound tracks. In 1988 Sakamoto was Japan's first Oscar-winning musician for his score for *The Last Emperor.*

Live jazz in concert halls, open air, and hundreds of disco coffee shops and pianobars was enthusiastically embraced. While American jazz greats were acclaimed, veteran Japanese instrumentalists Watanabe Sadao and Hino Teramasu also commanded major audiences at jazz festivals. Kitarō was the leading composer in synthesized sounds, providing sometimes exotic, but generally soothing, music dear to the frazzled urbanite. While percussionist Tsuchitori Toshi recreated the *Mahabharata* and other ethnic works, an indigenous kind of jazz poured from the Sado Island Kodō drummers, whose prodigious athletic performances mesmerized all and made their home a new music festival center. Singing and dancing at amateur open nights (*karaoke*) at a growing number of pubs was an activity in which everyone could shine by singing along with prerecorded tapes. In the late 1980s, the *kawaiko-chan,* the new girl singers, also were popular. Records, tapes, and compact discs spread every type of music nationwide and provided common experience for music appreciation.

Twentieth-century Japanese dance draws on various traditional styles and Western classical and avant-garde forms, all interpretated with the high standards of Japanese schools. Many famous dance studios grew from training centers for Kabuki actor-dancers or derived from famous Kabuki families. Women dancers drawing their art from *butoh* (classical Japanese dance) were trained by the Hanayagi school, whose top dancers performed internationally. Ichinohe Sachiko choreographed and performed traditional dances

Kyōgen *master Shigeyama
Sengoro in Kyōto, 1989
Courtesy* Asahi Shimbun

in Heian court costumes, characterized by the slow, formal, and elegant motions of this classical age of Japanese culture.

Western schools covered classical ballet, jazz-dance, and modern dance, and influenced the *butoh* avant-garde dance movement. Ballet was said to have replaced traditional Japanese arts, such as flower arrangement and the tea ceremony in the hearts of young girls. Prima ballerina Morishita Yōko sat on the jury for the Prix de Lausanne Ballet Competition in 1989, held for the first time in Tokyo, and marking the arrival of Japanese classical ballet in the international community. Horiuchi Gen, a 1980 Prix de Lausanne winner, became a major soloist with the New York City Ballet, and Japanese performers noted for their superb technique were members of many major international companies. Modern dance was performed early after the war and was later taught by such famous dancers as Eguchi Takaya. The Tokyo Modern Dance School and the Ozawa Hisako Modern Dance Company also promoted avant-garde modern dance. A wide experimental range within modern dance occurred from which choreographer Teshigawara Saburo skillfully drew to create multifaceted works for his KARAS Company.

The vital avant-garde *butoh* dance was a major development after the war: at least five major schools performed in the 1985 Butoh Festival, and there were numerous creative offshoots. Hijikata Tatsumi was a charismatic dancer who experimented with different

185

kinds of creative dance to capture expressive motions he considered expressly suited to the Japanese physiognomy and psyche. He combined eroticism, social criticism, and avant-garde theater ideas, and considered the body to be a repository for "stored memories," which could be metamorphosed into dance forms. His theories and choreography were carried on by a number of famous dancers, who eventually formed their own major companies, which were strong in the 1980s and made tours abroad.

Modern drama in the late twentieth century consisted of *shingeki* (experimental Western-style theater), which employed naturalistic acting and contemporary themes in contrast to the stylized conventions of Kabuki and Nō. In the postwar period, there was a phenomenal growth in creative new dramatic works, which introduced fresh aesthetic concepts that revolutionized the orthodox modern theater. Challenging the realistic, psychological drama focused on "tragic historical progress" of the Western-derived *shingeki,* young playwrights broke with such accepted tenets as conventional stage space, placing their action in tents, streets, and open areas, and, at the extreme, in scenes played out all over Tokyo. Plots became increasingly complex, with play-within-a-play sequences, moving rapidly back and forth in time, and intermingling reality with fantasy. Dramatic structure was fragmented, with the focus on the performer, who often used a variety of masks to reflect different personae. Playwrights returned to common stage devices perfected in Nō and Kabuki to project their ideas, such as employing a narrator, who could also use English for international audiences. Major playwrights in the 1980s were Kara Jōrō, Shimizu Kunio, and Betsuyaku Minoru, all closely connected to specific companies. In the 1980s, stagecraft was refined into a more sophisticated, complex format than in the earlier postwar experiments but lacked their bold critical spirit.

Many Western plays, from those of the ancient Greeks to Shakespeare and from those of Fyodor Dostoevsky to Samuel Beckett, were performed in Tokyo. An incredible number of performances, perhaps as many as 3,000, were given each year, making Tokyo one of the world's leading theatrical centers. The opening of the replica of the Globe Theater was celebrated by importing an entire British company to perform all of Shakespeare's historical plays, while other Tokyo theaters produced other Shakespearean plays including various new interpretations of *Hamlet* and *King Lear.*

Suzuki Tadashi's Togo troupe developed a unique kind of "method acting," integrating avant-garde concepts with classical Nō and Kabuki devices, an approach that became a major creative

Botoh *dance group Sankai Juku performing "Jomon Sho"*
Courtesy Kiyomi Yamaji, Sankai Juku, and Jomon Sho

force in Japanese and international theater in the 1980s. Another highly original East-West fusion occurred in the inspired production *Nastasya*, taken from Dostoevsky's *The Idiot*, in which Bandō Tamasaburō, a famed Kabuki *onnagata* (female impersonator), played the roles of both the prince and his fiancée.

Literature

Japanese literature dates from about the fifth century A.D., when the Chinese writing system began to be used by scribes at the Yamato court. As soon as the Japanese courtiers learned to read, they began to write, compiling between the sixth century and the eighth century both a state history of epic proportions, the *Kojiki* (Record of Ancient Matters) and one of the world's oldest poetry anthologies, the *Man'yōshū* (Collection of Ten Thousand Leaves), both of which contain many older works. They also composed Chinese-style poetry, which they found suitable for more difficult, lengthy, and profound thoughts. By the eighth century, the elite had already come to grips with the problem of assimilating difficult foreign ideas in a complex new language. The dichotomy between native expression and the use of prestigious imported forms became a pattern of Japanese artistic life. Buddhist commentary appeared after several centuries of copying, translation, and study.

In the ninth century it found a strong voice and skilled brush in the monk Kūkai, through whose inspiration religious themes became a part of the literary fabric.

Prose works had reached a high level by the tenth century, when the literary diary made its appearance, and in the eleventh the world's first novel, *Genji monogatari* (Tale of Genji), was composed by a court lady, Murasaki Shikibu. Her acute psychological observations molded by a subtle feminine sensibility wove a deft picture of the hothouse Heian court society. It remains a matchless source for all subsequent writers and an important part of the classical education of every Japanese. In the medieval period, women's vernacular writing dominated prose in the form of diaries of court ladies, supplemented by recollections of courtiers, the wry comments and musings of monks, and a wide variety of tales and legends, both secular and profane. *Heike monogatari* (Tale of the Heike) captured the samurai spirit of the Kamakura warriors' age, while the melancholy thirty-one syllable *waka* poems (in a five-seven-five-seven-seven syllables-per-line arrangement) of the twelfth-century monk Saigyō reflected the mood of a militant era. Exiles from the capital and monastic authors who contemplated the fleeting vanities of this world, and the theme of death and the spirit world characterized writing of the Muromachi period, setting the tone for the Nō plays of Zeami Motokiyo (1363–1443). Comic relief was provided by *kyōgen*, using the vernacular to reveal something of the life of the commoner.

The peace and prosperity of the Tokugawa age produced a new mercantile class—the *chōnin*—whose antics were humorously described in the vigorous seventeenth-century novels of Ihara Saikaku, dispelling the lingering melancholy of the late feudal period. A major poet of this age, Matsuo Bashō, lifted his voice to extol the qualities of loneliness, of getting away from the new crowded towns by taking the "narrow road to the deep north," a celebrated journey whose three-hundredth anniversary was widely commemorated in the late 1980s. Bashō's matchless *renku* (linked poems) of thirty-six verses and his lighthearted seventeen-syllable haiku (five-seven-five) set a norm for modern emulators. A third literary genius of this period was the great dramatist, Chikamatsu Monzaemon, whose historical and domestic plays formed the soul of the Kabuki theater. In the eighteenth century, Chinese novels were translated into Japanese, the poet Yosa Buson infused a new romantic spirit into haiku poems, and Kobayashi Issa made interesting subjects out of the "ordinariness" of the common folk and the ugly, starveling sparrow.

A noble spying on two princesses playing a koto *and a lute. Watercolor, nineteenth century, Tosa school, from* Genji monogatari *(Tale of Genji)*
Courtesy Barbara L. Dash

Japanese literature clearly draws on a tradition rich in poetic and prose forms. The writing of poetry in both the classic thirty-one syllable *waka* and the seventeen-syllable haiku remained a national pastime and a skill expected of the educated, among whom competitions were frequently held. Japanese *renga* parties, at which poets and the intelligentsia composed poetry in groups, continued as a major literary pursuit. Haiku poets were among the most honored of all creative artists, and a haiku museum was established in 1976 as a public center for poetry study. The ancient *waka* in modern usage is called a *tanka,* or short song (also with a five-seven-five-seven-seven syllabic formula). Many writers continued to use this form for less profound thoughts. Even more striking were the modern permutations of older literary forms: such experiments as two syllable haiku, *tanka* in *romaji* (romanized form of *kana*), and Zen ideas expressed in Western-style "free verse."

The introduction of European literature in the late nineteenth century brought "free verse" into the poetic repertoire; it became widely used for longer works embodying new intellectual themes. Young Japanese prose writers and dramatists have struggled with a whole galaxy of new ideas and artistic schools, but novelists were the first to successfully assimilate some of these concepts. A new colloquial literature developed centering around the ''I novel,'' with some unusual protagonists as in Natsume Sōseki's *Wagahai wa neko de aru* (I Am a Cat). Two modern literary giants whose works were deeply rooted in Japanese sensibilities were Tanizaki Jun'ichirō, who captured the East-West value struggle in Japanese life prior to World War II and Kawabata Yasunari, a master of psychological fiction during the mid-century and a Nobel Prize winner. Capturing the immediate postwar atmosphere were Dazai Osamu and Mishima Yukio, both of whom committed suicide. Dazai's writing reflected the quiet desperation of living with defeat, while Mishima provided a glowing vision of traditional morality, gradually overcome by new Western values.

Prominent writers of the 1970s and 1980s, such as Ōe Kensaburō, were identified with intellectual and moral issues in their attempts to raise social and political consciousness. Inoue Mitsuaki had long been concerned with the atomic bomb and continued in the 1980s to write on problems of the nuclear age, while Endō Shusaku depicted the religious dilemma of Roman Catholics in feudal Japan, as a springboard to address spiritual problems. Inoue Yasushi also turned to the past in masterful historical novels of Inner Asia and ancient Japan, in order to portray present human fate.

Avant-garde writers, such as Abe Kōbō, who wanted to express the Japanese experience in modern terms without using either international styles or traditional conventions, developed new inner visions. Furui Yoshikichi tellingly related the lives of alienated urban dwellers coping with the minutiae of daily life, while the psychodramas within such daily life crises have been explored by a rising number of important women novelists. The 1988 Naoki Prize went to Tōdō Shizuko for *Ripening Summer*, a story capturing the complex psychology of modern women. Other award-winning stories at the end of the decade dealt with current issues of the elderly in hospitals, the recent past (*Pure-Hearted Shopping District in Kōenji, Tokyo*), and the life of a Meiji *ukiyo-e* artist. In international literature, Ishiguro Kazuo, a native of Japan, had taken up residence in Britain and won Britain's prestigious Booker Prize.

Although modern Japanese writers covered a wide variety of subjects, one particularly Japanese approach stressed their subjects' inner lives, widening the earlier novel's preoccupation with the narrator's consciousness. In Japanese fiction, plot development and action have often been of secondary interest to emotional issues. In keeping with the general trend toward reaffirming national characteristics, many old themes reemerged, and some authors turned consciously to the past. Strikingly, Buddhist attitudes about the importance of knowing oneself and the poignant impermanence of things formed an undercurrent to sharp social criticism of this material age. There was a growing emphasis on women's roles, the Japanese persona in the modern world, and the malaise of common people lost in the complexities of urban culture.

Popular fiction, nonfiction works, and children's literature all flourished in urban Japan in the 1980s. Many popular works fell between "pure literature" and pulp novels, including all sorts of historical serials, information-packed docudramas, science fiction, mysteries, business stories, war journals, and animal stories. Bestsellers in the late 1980s were several books by a young woman, "Banana" Yoshimoto, and Murakami Haruki's spectacularly successful *Norwegian Wood* and *A Wild Sheep Chase*. Nonfiction covered everything from crime to politics. Although factual journalism predominated, many of these works were interpretive, reflecting a high degree of individualism. Children's works reemerged in the 1950s, and the newer entrants into this field, many of them younger women, brought new vitality to it in the 1980s. *Manga* (comic books) have penetrated almost every sector of the popular market. Widely used for soft pornography, they also have included a multivolume high-school history of Japan and, for the adult market, a *manga* introduction to economics, which was also available in English. *Manga* represented between 20 and 30 percent of annual publications at the end of the 1980s, in sales of some ¥400 billion per year.

Films and Television

Reeling from television's overwhelming success, the cinema industry retreated in the 1980s to the tried-and-true formulas, the comedies, romances, detective stories, and youth films that always had sure audiences. Production at the four major film companies dwindled to some 200 films a year, of which only a handful were quality productions. Pornographic films grew to constitute about half of films made. The animated format used for children's films did show promising originality, but truly creative productions could be found only among independent film directors. A burgeoning number of art films, both domestic and imported, found homes in intimate art theaters in the cities. Foreign films were often the major draws in urban areas, which had record runs for European and North American hits. Some top directors produced major films with foreign funding or in foreign locations. In a return to Japanese production at the end of the 1980s, Akira Kurosawa, the acknowledged old master of cinematic art, summarized his remembrance of things past in his movie *Dreams*. A nostalgic look at past views of family life was seen in Ichikawa Kon's remake of Tanizaki Jun'ichirō's *The Makioka Sisters*, a visually beautiful color film

191

portraying the nearly vanished world of early twentieth-century upper-class women. A major historical offering was Teshigawara Hiroshi's *Rikyū* (1989), which marked the return of this major director after a seventeen-year absence from films, in a pictorially magnificent presentation of the life of the famous Momoyama tea master and his moral conflict with the political overlord Hideyoshi.

Although there was virtually no market in Japan for documentaries, a major docudrama, *Tōkyō saiban* (Tokyo Judgment), directed by Kobayashi Masaki, and taken directly from footage of tribunal proceedings against alleged Japanese war criminals, had a rapt audience. Outstanding among the newer independent directors were Itami Jūzō and Morita Yoshimitsu, whose *The Family Game* set a new pattern for satirical comedies on urban dilemmas. By the mid-1980s, Itami's savage new satires showed unprecedented originality. Although these films addressed the anomalies and excesses of Japanese life, their subjects were mirrored around the world, and they had a strong international following.

Popular comedy was led by the beloved Tora-san series about the travel adventures of an avuncular, bumbling everyman, played by the ever-popular Atsumi Kiyoshi, whose forty-first feature film in 1989 took the hero to Vienna in a telling display of internationalization. Another hoary favorite was the monster series starring Godzilla. The most sophisticated youth movie of the 1980s may have been Yamakawa Naoto's *The New Morning of Billy the Kid,* a fantasy set in a Tokyo theme-bar, which was embraced by the young worldwide. A much-loved children's classic *Kaze no matasaburō* (Children of the Wind) written by Miyazawa Kenji, was filmed by award-winning director Ito Shunya as a skillful fantasy. Animated full-length features ranged from a gorgeously interpreted selection from *Tale of Genji* to Otomoto Katsushiro's *Akira,* a violent, provocative futuristic fantasy. Such animated features had their origins in the wildly popular *manga* action cartoons. Television also produced a substantial number of cartoons, including the ever popular "Sazae-san," which had the highest rating in the late 1980s.

Television had attained virtually 100 percent penetration by 1990, and only 1 percent of households were without a color television set, making Japan a major information society. Programming consisted of about 50 percent pure entertainment and nearly 25 percent cultural shows, the remainder being news reports and educational programs. There were two main broadcasting systems: the public NHK and five private networks. The major system, NHK, was publicly subsidized by mandatory subscription fees. Leading newspapers were among the financial supporters of the most important private channels. International programs were transmitted by satellite for instant replay after the government, in 1979, set up the Communications and Broadcasting Satellite Organization. Japan's first operational broadcast satellite was launched in 1984. Commercial television stations had become a major vehicle for advertising in place of newspapers and received huge revenues, far surpassing those of NHK.

Samurai and *yakuza* (Japanese underworld) themes were now almost solely the provenance of television, as were those of family life, ubiquitous in daytime soaps. The biggest hit of the 1980s overall was the television drama "Oshin," a tale of a mother's struggles and suffering. The longest-running series since 1981 was "From the North Country," in which a divorced father and his two children survive in the backwoods of Hokkaidō.

Criticisms continued concerning the vulgarity of some commercial programs, but these programs still appeared in the early 1990s. Major problems perceived were the high level of violence and the lack of moral values in children's shows. All television and radio stations, however, were required to devote a certain proportion of broadcast time to educational programs to retain their licenses, and these programs grew steadily in response to popular demand. All networks have to comply with the Broadcasting Law of 1950, while several councils oversee general programming, although compliance with their recommendations is voluntary.

Japan's traditional arts and their modern counterparts found wide expression at home and internationally in the 1980s, reflecting the strong continuing creativity of its artists, performers, and writers. Major trends were seen in the search for characteristic cultural values and modes of expression, on the one hand, and the growing awareness of internationalism, on the other, affirming Japan's strong economic position in the world.

*   *   *

A good general work on contemporary education is *Japanese Education Today,* by Robert Leestma and others. Both Benjamin Duke's *The Japanese School* and *Educational Policies in Crisis,* by William K. Cummings and others, offer useful insights into the Japanese educational system and its differences from that of the United States. Historical information can be found in Ronald S. Anderson's *Education in Japan* and Ronald P. Dore's *Education in Tokugawa Japan.* Of particular interest is the winter 1989 special issue of the *Journal of Japanese Studies,* containing a symposium devoted largely to preschool and early education. On secondary education, Thomas P.

Rohlen's *Japan's High Schools* provides excellent coverage. The Ministry of Education is a rich source of statistical data; in English, information can be obtained from the annual *Statistical Abstract of the Ministry of Education, Science, and Culture,* but the Japanese-language annual *Gakkō kihon chōsa hōkokusho* (Fundamental School Survey) is more complete.

A useful work on the arts is *Sources of Japanese Tradition,* by Tsunoda Ryūsaku and others, which translates primary materials on cultural and aesthetic values. *Cultural Affairs and Administration in Japan, 1988* from the Agency for Cultural Affairs and *Artist and Patron in Postwar Japan* and "Government and the Arts in Contemporary Japan" by Thomas R.H. Havens outline the government's participation in the arts. Helpful specialized works include Takashina Shūji, Yoshiaki Tono, and Nakahara Yūsuke's *Art in Japan,* David B. Stewart's *The Making of a Modern Japanese Architecture,* Kodansha's *Contemporary Japanese Prints,* the Library of Congress's *Words in Motion: Contemporary Japanese Calligraphy,* Hayashiya Seizo's *Japanese Ceramics Today,* J. Thomas Rimer's *A Reader's Guide to Japanese Literature,* the essays on Japan in *Cinema and Cultural Identity* edited by Wimal Dissanayake, Makoto Ueda's *Modern Japanese Poets,* the P.E.N. Club's *Survey of Japanese Literature Today,* edited by Isoda Kōichi, and *The Handbook of Japanese Popular Culture* edited by Richard Gid Powers and Kato Hidetoshi. (For further information and complete citations, see Bibliography.)

Chapter 4. The Character and Structure of the Economy

Family crest with a flying phoenix (hō'ō), *the bird of immortality*

THE JAPANESE ECONOMY entered the 1990s in excellent shape. Japan had the world's second largest gross national product (GNP—see Glossary) throughout the 1970s and ranked first among major industrial nations in 1989 in per capita GNP, at US$23,616, up sharply from US$8,900 in 1980. After a mild economic slump in the mid-1980s, Japan's economy began a period of expansion in 1986 that was continuing in 1990. Economic growth averaging 5 percent between 1987 and 1989 revived industries, such as steel and construction, which had been relatively dormant in the mid-1980s, and brought record salaries and employment (see table 9, Appendix). Unlike the economic booms of the 1960s and 1970s, however, when increasing exports played the key role in economic expansion, domestic demand propelled the Japanese economy in the late 1980s. This development involved fundamental economic restructuring, from export dependence to reliance on domestic demand. The boom that started in 1986 was generated by the decisions of companies to increase private plant and equipment spending and of consumers to go on a buying spree. Japan's imports grew at a faster rate than exports.

During the 1980s, the Japanese economy shifted its emphasis away from primary and secondary activities (notably agriculture, manufacturing, and mining) to processing, with telecommunications and computers becoming increasingly vital. Information became an important resource and product, central to wealth and power. The rise of an information-based economy was led by major research in highly sophisticated technology, such as advanced computers. The selling and use of information became very beneficial to the economy. Tokyo became a major financial center, home of some of the world's major banks, financial firms, insurance companies, and the world's largest stock exchange.

A national effort in the 1980s involved both government and business in increasing Japan's influence in the area of high technology. One important development area was industrial automation. Automotive producers, such as Toyota and Nissan, relied increasingly on robotics in their factories. Japan planned a much-touted Fifth Generation artificial intelligence computer project, boasted a new but active space program, and designated new towns as research centers and production hubs for new technologies. In the area of semiconductors, by 1989 Japan was outproducing the United States, which had enjoyed a nearly two-to-one lead in world market

197

share in the mid-1980s. Japan became a world leader in technological research and production.

Japanese postwar technological research was carried out for the sake of economic growth rather than military development. The growth in high-technology industries in the 1980s resulted from heightened domestic demand for high-technology products and for higher living, housing, and environmental standards, better health, medical, and welfare opportunities, better leisure-time facilities, and improved ways to accommodate a rapidly aging society.

The development of a postindustrial economy did not mean the end of Japan's importance as a major manufacturing center. Traditional industries, such as iron and steel, automobiles, and construction, experienced strong growth in the late 1980s, and there was every indication that these industries would continue to grow in the 1990s. Only the primary sector (agriculture, forestry, and fishing) and mining showed signs of decline in the 1980s.

Patterns of Development

Revolutionary Change

Since the mid-nineteenth century, when the Tokugawa government first opened the country to Western commerce and influence, Japan has gone through two periods of economic development (see Decline of the Tokugawa; The Emergence of Modern Japan, 1868–1919; and World War II and the Occupation, 1941–52, ch. 1). The first began in 1854 and extended through World War II; the second began in 1945 and continued into the early 1990s. In both periods, the Japanese opened themselves to Western ideas and influence; experienced revolutionary social, political, and economic changes; and became a world power with carefully developed spheres of influence. During both periods, the Japanese government encouraged economic change by fostering a national revolution from above, planning and advising in every aspect of society. The national goal each time was to make Japan so powerful and wealthy that its independence would never again be threatened.

In the Meiji period (1868–1912), leaders inaugurated a new Western-based education system for all young people, sent thousands of students to the United States and Europe, and hired more than 3,000 Westerners to teach modern science, mathematics, technology, and foreign languages in Japan (see Historical Background, ch. 3). The government also built railroads, improved roads, and inaugurated a land reform program to prepare the country for further development.

To promote industrialization, government decided that, while it should help private business to allocate resources and to plan, the private sector was best equipped to stimulate economic growth. The greatest role of government was to help provide the economic conditions in which business could flourish. In short, government was to be the guide, and business the producer. In the early Meiji period, the government built factories and shipyards that were sold to entrepreneurs at a fraction of their value. Many of these businesses grew rapidly into the larger conglomerates that still dominated much of the business world in the early 1990s. Government emerged as chief promoter of private enterprise, enacting a series of probusiness policies, including low corporate taxes.

Before World War II, Japan built an extensive empire that included Taiwan, Korea, Manchuria, and parts of northern China (see Diplomacy, ch. 1). The Japanese regarded this sphere of influence as a political and economic necessity, preventing foreign states from strangling Japan by blocking its access to raw materials and crucial sea-lanes. Japan's large military force was regarded as essential to the empire's defense. The colonies were lost as a result of World War II, but since then the Japanese have extended their economic influence throughout Asia and beyond. Japan's Constitution, promulgated in 1947, forbids an offensive military force, but Japan still maintained its formidable Self-Defense Forces and ranked third in the world in military spending behind the United States and the Soviet Union in the late 1980s (see The Postwar Constitution, ch. 6; Defense Spending, ch. 8).

Rapid growth and structural change have characterized Japan's two periods of economic development since 1868. In the first period, the economy grew only moderately at first and relied heavily on traditional agriculture to finance modern industrial infrastructure. By the time the Russo-Japanese War (1904–5) began, 65 percent of employment and 38 percent of gross domestic product (GDP—see Glossary) was still based on agriculture, but modern industry had begun to expand substantially. By the late 1920s, manufacturing and mining contributed 23 percent of GDP, compared to 21 percent for all of agriculture. Transportation and communications had developed to sustain heavy industrial development.

In the 1930s, the Japanese economy suffered less from the Great Depression than other industrialized nations, expanding at the rapid rate of 5 percent of GDP per year, while manufacturing and mining came to account for more than 30 percent of GDP, more than twice the value for the agricultural sector. Most industrial growth, however, was geared toward expanding the nation's military power.

World War II wiped out many of Japan's gains since 1868. About 40 percent of the nation's industrial plants and infrastructure was destroyed, and production reverted to levels of about fifteen years earlier. The people were shocked by the devastation and swung into action. New factories were equipped with the best modern machines, giving Japan an initial competitive advantage over the victor states, who now had older factories. As Japan's second period of economic development began, millions of former soldiers joined a well-disciplined and highly educated work force to rebuild Japan.

Japan's highly acclaimed postwar education system contributed strongly to the modernizing process. The world's highest literacy rate and high education standards were major reasons for Japan's success in achieving a technologically advanced economy. Japanese schools also encouraged discipline, another benefit in forming an effective work force.

The early postwar years were devoted to rebuilding lost industrial capacity: major investments were made in electric power, coal, iron and steel, and chemical fertilizers. By the mid-1950s, production matched prewar levels. Released from the demands of military-dominated government, the economy not only recovered its lost momentum, but also surpassed the growth rates of earlier periods. Between 1953 and 1965, GDP expanded by over 9 percent per year, manufacturing and mining by 13 percent, construction by 11 percent, and infrastructure by 12 percent. In 1965 these sectors employed over 41 percent of the labor force while only 26 percent remained in agriculture.

The mid-1960s ushered in a new type of industrial development as the economy opened itself to international competition in some industries and developed heavy and chemical manufactures. Whereas textiles and light manufactures maintained their profitability internationally, other products, such as automobiles, ships, and machine tools, assumed new importance. Manufacturing and mining value-added grew at the rate of 17 percent per year between 1965 and 1970. Growth rates moderated to about 8 percent and evened out between the industrial and service sectors between 1970 and 1973, as retail trade, finance, real estate, information, and other service industries streamlined their operations.

Japan faced severe economic challenge in the mid-1970s. The world oil crisis in 1973 shocked an economy that had become virtually dependent on foreign petroleum (see The Value of the Yen, ch. 5). Japan experienced its first postwar decline in industrial production together with severe price inflation. The recovery that followed the first oil crisis revived the optimism of most business leaders, but the maintenance of industrial growth in the face of high energy costs required shifts in the industrial structure.

Changing price conditions favored conservation and alternative sources of industrial energy. Although the investment costs were high, many energy-intensive industries successfully reduced their dependence on oil during the late 1970s and 1980s and enhanced their productivity. Advances in microcircuitry and semiconductors in the late 1970s and 1980s also led to new growth industries in consumer electronics and computers and to higher productivity in already established industries. The net result of these adjustments was to increase the energy efficiency of manufacturing and to expand so-called knowledge-intensive industry. The service industries expanded in an increasingly postindustrial economy.

Structural economic changes, however, were unable to check the slowing of economic growth, as the economy matured in the late 1970s and 1980s, attaining annual growth rates no better than 4 to 6 percent. But, these rates were remarkable in a world of expensive petroleum and in a nation of few domestic resources. Japan's average growth rate of 5 percent in the late 1980s, for example, was far higher than the 3.8 percent growth rate of the United States.

Despite more petroleum price increases in 1979, the strength of the Japanese economy was apparent. It expanded without the double-digit inflation that afflicted other industrial nations and that had bothered Japan itself after the first oil crisis in 1973. Japan experienced slower growth in the mid-1980s, but its demand-sustained economic boom of the late 1980s revived many troubled industries.

Complex economic and institutional factors affected Japan's postwar growth. First, the nation's prewar experience provided several important legacies. The Tokugawa period (1600–1867) bequeathed a vital commercial sector in burgeoning urban centers, a relatively well-educated elite (although one with limited knowledge of European science), a sophisticated government bureaucracy, productive agriculture, a closely unified nation with highly developed financial and marketing systems, and a national infrastructure of roads. The buildup of industry during the Meiji period to the point where Japan could vie for world power was an important prelude to postwar growth and provided a pool of experienced labor following World War II.

Second, and more important, was the level and quality of investment that persisted through the 1980s. Investment in capital equipment, which averaged more than 11 percent of GNP during the prewar period, rose to some 20 percent of GNP during the 1950s and to more than 30 percent in the late 1960s and 1970s. During the economic boom of the late 1980s, the rate still kept to around 20 percent. Japanese businesses imported the latest technologies to develop the industrial base. As a latecomer to modernization,

Japan was able to avoid some of the trial and error earlier needed by other nations to develop industrial processes. In the 1970s and 1980s, Japan improved its industrial base through technology licensing, patent purchases, and the imitation and improvement of foreign inventions. In the 1980s, industry stepped up its research and development, and many firms became famous for their innovations and creativity.

Japan's labor force contributed importantly to economic growth, not only because of its availability and literacy, but also because of its reasonable wage demands. Before and immediately after World War II, the transfer of numerous agricultural workers to modern industry resulted in rising productivity and only moderate wage increases. As population growth slowed and the nation became increasingly industrialized in the mid-1960s, wages rose significantly. But labor union cooperation generally kept salary increases within the range of productivity gains.

High productivity growth played a key role in postwar economic growth. The highly skilled and educated labor force, extraordinary savings rates and accompanying levels of investment, and the low growth of Japan's labor force were major factors in the high rate of productivity growth.

The nation has also benefited from economies of scale. Although medium-sized and small enterprises generated much of the nation's employment, large facilities were most productive. Many industrial enterprises consolidated to form larger, more efficient units. Before World War II, large holding companies formed wealth groups, or *zaibatsu* (see Glossary), which dominated most industry. The *zaibatsu* were dissolved after the war, but *keiretsu*—large and modern industrial enterprise groupings—emerged. The coordination of activities within these groupings and the integration of smaller subcontractors into the groups enhanced industrial efficiency.

Japanese corporations developed strategies that contributed to their immense growth. Growth-oriented corporations that took chances competed successfully. Product diversification became an essential ingredient of the growth patterns of many *keiretsu*. Japanese companies added plant and human capacity ahead of demand. Seeking market share rather than quick profit was another powerful strategy.

Finally, circumstances beyond Japan's direct control contributed to its success. International conflicts tended to stimulate the Japanese economy until the devastation at the end of World War II. The Russo-Japanese War (1904–5), World War I (1914–18), the Korean War (1950–53), and the Second Indochina War (1954–75) brought economic booms to Japan. In addition, benign treatment from the United States after World War II facilitated the nation's reconstruction and growth. The United States occupation of Japan (1945–52) resulted in the rebuilding of the nation and the creation of a democratic state. United States assistance totaled about US$1.9 billion during the occupation, or about 15 percent of the nation's imports and 4 percent of GNP in that period. About 59 percent of this aid was in the form of food; 15 percent in industrial materials, and 12 percent in transportation equipment. United States grant assistance, however, tapered off quickly in the mid-1950s. United States military procurement from Japan peaked at a level equivalent to 7 percent of Japan's GNP in 1953 and fell below 1 percent after 1960. A variety of United States-sponsored measures during the occupation, such as land reform, contributed to the economy's later performance by increasing competition. In particular, the postwar purge of industrial leaders allowed new talent to rise in the management of the nation's rebuilt industries. Finally, the economy benefited from foreign trade, as it was able to expand exports rapidly enough to pay for imports of equipment and technology without falling into debt as have a number of developing nations in the 1980s, (see Level and Commodity Composition of Trade, ch. 5).

The consequences of Japan's economic growth were not always positive. Large advanced corporations existed side-by-side with the smaller and technologically less-developed firms, creating a kind of economic dualism in the late twentieth century. Often the smaller firms, which employed more than two-thirds of Japan's workers, worked as subcontractors directly for larger firms, supplying a narrow range of parts and temporary workers. Excellent working conditions, salaries, and benefits, such as permanent employment, were provided by most large firms, but not by the smaller firms. Temporary workers, mostly women, received much smaller salaries and had less job security than permanent workers. Thus, despite the high living standards of many workers in larger firms, Japan in 1990 remained in general a low-wage country whose economic growth was fueled by highly skilled and educated workers who accepted poor salaries, often unsafe working conditions, and poor living standards (see table 10, Appendix).

Additionally, Japan's preoccupation with boosting the rate of industrial growth during the 1950s and 1960s led to the relative neglect of consumer services and also to the worsening of industrial pollution. Housing and urban services, such as water and sewage systems, and social security benefits, lagged behind the development of industry, and despite considerable improvement in the 1970s and 1980s, still lagged well behind other industrialized nations at the end of the 1980s. Agricultural subsidies and a complex and outmoded distribution system also kept the prices of some essential consumer goods very high by world standards (see Living Standards, this ch.). Industrial growth came at the expense of the environment. Foul air, heavily polluted water, and waste disposal became critical political issues in the 1970s and again in the late 1980s (see Pollution, ch. 2).

The Evolving Occupational Structure

As late as 1955, some 40 percent of the labor force still worked in agriculture, but this figure had declined to 17 percent by 1970 and to 8.3 percent by 1988. The government estimated in the late 1980s that this figure would decline to 4.9 percent by 2000, as Japan imported more and more of its food and small family farms disappeared.

Japan's economic growth in the 1960s and 1970s was based on the rapid expansion of heavy manufacturing in such areas as automobiles, steel, shipbuilding, chemicals, and electronics. The secondary sector (manufacturing, construction, and mining) expanded to 35.6 percent of the work force by 1970. By the late 1970s, however, the Japanese economy began to move away from heavy manufacturing toward a more service-oriented (tertiary sector) base. During the 1980s, jobs in wholesaling, retailing, finance and insurance, real estate, transportation, communications, and government grew rapidly, while secondary sector employment remained stable. The tertiary sector grew from 47 percent of the work force in 1970 to 58 percent in 1987 and was expected to grow to 62 percent by 2000, when the secondary sector will probably employ 33 percent of Japan's workers.

The Role of Government and Business

Although Japan's economic development was primarily the product of private entrepreneurship, the government has directly contributed to the nation's prosperity. Its actions have helped initiate new industries, cushion the effects of economic depression, create a sound economic infrastructure, and protect the living standards of the citizenry. Indeed, so pervasive has government influence in the economy seemed that many foreign observers have popularized the term "Japan Incorporated" to describe its alliance of business and government interests. Whether Japan in 1990 actually fit this picture seemed questionable, but there was little doubt that government agencies continued to influence the economy through a variety of policies.

Japanese attitudes towards government have historically been shaped by Confucianism (see Cultural Developments and the Establishment of Buddhism, ch. 1; and Religious and Philosophical Traditions, ch. 2). Japan often has been defined as a Confucian country, but one in which loyalty is more important than benevolence. Leadership stemmed from the government and authority in general, and business looked to government for guidance. These attitudes, coupled with the view of the nation as a family, allowed government to influence business, and businesses worked hard not only for their own profits, but also for national well-being. There was a national consensus that Japan must be an economic power and that the duty of all Japanese was to sacrifice themselves for this national goal. Thus, the relationship between government and business was as collaborators rather than as mutually suspicious adversaries.

Government-business relations were conducted in many ways and through numerous channels. The most important conduits in the postwar period were the economic ministries: the Ministry of Finance and the Ministry of International Trade and Industry, known as MITI (see Trade and Investment Institutions, ch. 5). The Ministry of Finance had operational responsibilities for all fiscal affairs, including the preparation of the national budget (see table 11, Appendix). It initiated fiscal policies and, through its indirect control over the Bank of Japan, the central bank, was responsible for monetary policy as well. The Ministry of Finance allocated public investment, formulated tax policies, collected taxes, and regulated foreign exchange.

The Ministry of Finance established low interest rates, and by thus reducing the cost of investment funds to corporations, promoted industrial expansion. MITI was responsible for the regulation of production and the distribution of goods and services. It was the "steward" of the Japanese economy, developing plans concerning the structure of Japanese industry. MITI had several special functions in the late 1980s: controlling Japan's foreign trade and supervising international commerce, ensuring the smooth flow of goods in the national economy, promoting the development of manufacturing, mining, and distribution industries, and supervising the procurement of a reliable supply of raw materials and energy resources.

The Ministry of Transportation was responsible for oversight of all land, sea, and air transport. The Ministry of Construction was charged with supervising all construction in Japan and Japanese-supported construction abroad. Its responsibilities also included land acquisition for public use and environmental protection as it related to construction. The Ministry of Health and Welfare was responsible for supervising and coordinating all health and welfare services, and the Ministry of Posts and Telecommunications was responsible for the postal service and electronic communications.

Industrial Policy

After World War II and especially in the 1950s and 1960s, the Japanese government devised a complicated system of policies to promote industrial development and cooperated closely for this purpose with private firms. The objective of industrial policy was to shift resources to specific industries, to gain international competitive advantage for Japan. These policies and methods were used primarily to increase the productivity of inputs and to influence, directly or indirectly, industrial investment.

Administrative guidance (*gyōsei shidō*) was a principal instrument of enforcement used extensively throughout the Japanese government to support a wide range of policies. Influence, prestige, advice, and persuasion were used to encourage both corporations and individuals to work in directions judged desirable. The persuasion was exerted and the advice was given by public officials, who often had the power to provide or withhold loans, grants, subsidies, licenses, tax concessions, government contracts, import permits, foreign exchange, and approval of cartel arrangements. The Japanese used administrative guidance to buffer market swings, anticipate market developments, and enhance market competition (see Foreign Trade Policies, ch. 5).

Mechanisms used by the Japanese government to affect the economy typically related to trade, labor markets, competition, and tax incentives. They included a broad range of trade protection measures, subsidies, de jure and de facto exemptions from antitrust statutes, labor market adjustments, and industry-specific assistance to enhance the use of new technology. Rather than producing a broad range of goods, the Japanese selected a few areas in which they could develop high-quality goods that they could produce in vast quantities at competitive prices. A good example is the camera industry, which since the 1960s has been dominated by Japan.

Historically, there have been three main elements in Japanese industrial development. The first was the development of a highly competitive manufacturing sector. The second was the deliberate restructuring of industry toward higher value-added, high-productivity industries. In the late 1980s, these were mainly knowledge-intensive tertiary industries. The third element was aggressive domestic and international business strategies.

Japan has few natural resources and depends on massive imports of raw materials. It must export to pay for its imports, and manufacturing and the sales of its services, such as banking and finance, were its principal means of doing so. For these reasons, the careful development of the producing sector was a key concern of both government and industry throughout most of the twentieth century. Government and business leaders generally agreed that the composition of Japan's output must continually shift if living standards were to rise. Government played an active role in making these shifts, often anticipating economic developments rather than reacting to them.

After World War II, the initial industries that policy makers and the general public felt Japan should have were iron and steel, shipbuilding, the merchant marine, machine industries in general, heavy electrical equipment, and chemicals. Later they added the automobile industry, petrochemicals, and nuclear power, and in the 1980s, such industries as computers and semiconductors. Since the late 1970s, the government has strongly encouraged the development of knowledge-intensive industries. Government support for research and development grew rapidly in the 1980s, and large joint government-industry development projects in computers and robotics were started. At the same time, government promoted the managed decline of competitively troubled industries, including textiles, shipbuilding, and chemical fertilizers, through such measures as tax breaks for corporations that retrained workers to work at other tasks.

Although industrial policy remained important in Japan in the 1970s and 1980s, thinking began to change. Government seemed to intervene less and become more respective of price mechanisms in guiding future development. During this period, trade and direct foreign investment were liberalized, tariff and nontariff trade barriers were lowered, and the economies of the advanced nations became more integrated, with the growth of international trade and international corporations. In the late 1980s, knowledge-intensive and high-technology industries became prominent. The government showed little inclination to promote such booming parts of the economy as fashion design, advertising, and management consulting. The question at the end of the 1980s was whether the government would become involved in such new developments or whether it would let them progress on their own.

Monetary and Fiscal Policy

Monetary policy pertained to the regulation, availability, and cost of credit, while fiscal policy dealt with government expenditures, taxes, and debt. Through management of these areas, the Ministry of Finance regulated the allocation of resources in the economy, affected the distribution of income and wealth among the citizenry, stabilized the level of economic activities, and promoted economic growth and welfare.

The Ministry of Finance played an important role in Japan's postwar economic growth. It advocated a "growth first" approach, with a high proportion of government spending going to capital accumulation, and minimum government spending overall, which kept both taxes and deficit spending down, making more money available for private investment. Most Japanese put money into savings accounts (see table 12, Appendix).

In the postwar period, the government's fiscal policy centered on the formulation of the national budget, which was the responsibility of the Ministry of Finance. The ministry's Budget Bureau prepared expenditure budgets for each fiscal year (FY—see Glossary) based on the requests from government ministries and affiliated agencies. The ministry's Tax Bureau was responsible for adjusting the tax schedules and estimating revenues. The ministry also issued government bonds, controlled government borrowing, and administered the Fiscal Investment and Loan Program, which is sometimes referred to as the "second budget."

Three types of budgets were prepared for review of the National Diet each year (see The Legislature, ch. 6). The general account budget included most of the basic expenditures for current government operations. Special account budgets, of which there were about forty, were designed for special programs or institutions where close accounting of revenues and expenditures was essential: for public enterprises, state pension funds, and public works projects financed from special taxes. Finally, there were the budgets for the major public enterprises, including public service corporations, loan and finance institutions, and the special public banks (see table 13, Appendix). Although these budgets were usually approved before the start of each fiscal year, they were usually revised with supplemental budgets in the fall. Local jurisdiction budgets depended heavily on transfers from the central government.

Government fixed investments in infrastructure and loans to public and private enterprises were about 15 percent of GNP. Loans from the Fiscal Investment and Loan Program, which were outside the general budget and funded primarily from postal savings, represented more than 20 percent of the general account budget, but their total effect on economic investment was not completely accounted for in the national income statistics. Taxes, representing 14 percent of GNP in 1987, were low compared to those in other developed economies. Taxes provided 87.8 percent of revenues in 1990. Income taxes were graduated and progressive. The principal structural feature of the tax system was the tremendous elasticity of the individual income tax. Because inheritance and property taxes were low, there was a slowly increasing concentration of wealth in the upper tax brackets. In 1989, the government introduced a major tax reform, including a 3 percent consumption tax.

The Financial System

In the mid-1980s, while the United States was becoming a debtor nation, Japan became the world's largest creditor and Tokyo a major international financial center. Four of the biggest banks in the world were Japanese at that time and Japan had the world's largest insurance company, advertising firm, and stock market. In the remainder of the 1980s, Japan's financial and banking industries grew at unprecedented rates.

The main elements of Japan's financial system were much the same as those of other major industrialized nations: a commercial banking system, which accepted deposits, extended loans to businesses, and dealt in foreign exchange; specialized government-owned financial institutions, which funded various sectors of the domestic economy; securities companies, which provided brokerage services, underwrote corporate and government securities, and dealt in securities markets; capital markets, which offered the means to finance public and private debt and to sell residual corporate ownership; and money markets, which offered banks a source of liquidity and provided the Bank of Japan with a tool to implement monetary policy.

Japan's traditional banking system was segmented into clearly defined components in the late 1980s: commercial banks (thirteen major and sixty-four smaller regional banks), long-term credit banks (seven), trust banks (seven), mutual loan and savings banks (sixtynine), and various specialized financial institutions. During the 1980s, a rapidly growing group of nonbank operations, such as consumer loan, credit card, leasing, and real estate organizations began performing some of the traditional functions of banks, such as the issuing of loans.

In the early postwar financial system, city banks provided short-term loans to major domestic corporations while regional banks took deposits and extended loans to medium-sized and small businesses. Neither engaged much in international business. In the 1950s and 1960s, a specialized bank, the Bank of Tokyo, took care of most of the government's foreign exchange needs and functioned as the nation's foreign banking representative. Long-term credit banks were intended to complement rather than to compete with the commercial banks. Authorized to issue debentures rather than take ordinary deposits, they specialized in long-term lending to major *kaisha,* or corporations. Trust banks were authorized to conduct retail and trust banking and often combined the work of commercial and long-term credit banks. Trust banks not only managed portfolios but also raised funds through the sale of negotiable loan trust certificates. Mutual loan and savings banks, credit associations, credit cooperatives, and labor credit associations collected individual deposits from general depositors. These deposits were then loaned to cooperative members and to the liquidity-starved city banks via the inter-bank money markets or were sent to central cooperative banks, which in turn loaned the funds to small businesses and corporations. More than 8,000 agricultural, forestry, and fishery cooperatives performed many of the same functions for the cooperatives. Many of their funds were transmitted to their central bank, the Norinchukin Bank, which was the world's largest bank in terms of domestic deposits.

A group of government financial institutions paralleled the private banking sector. The Japan Export-Import Bank, the Japan Development Bank, and a number of finance corporations, such as the Housing Loan Corporation, promoted the growth of specialized sectors of the domestic economy. These institutions derived their funding from deposits collected by the postal savings system and deposited with the Trust Fund Bureau. The postal savings system, through the 24,000 post offices, accepted funds in various forms, including savings, annuities, and insurance. The post offices offered the highest interest rates for regular savings accounts (8 percent for time deposits in 1990) and tax free savings until 1988, thereby collecting more deposits and accounts than any other institution in the world.

Japan's securities markets increased their volume of dealings rapidly during the late 1980s, led by Japan's rapidly expanding securities firms. There were three categories of securities companies in Japan, the first consisting of the "Big Four" securities houses (among the six largest such firms in the world): Nomura, Daiwa, Nikko, and Yamaichi. The Big Four played a key role in international financial transactions and were members of the New York Stock Exchange. Nomura was the world's largest single securities firm; its net capital, in excess of US$10 billion in 1986, exceeded that of Merrill Lynch, Salomon Brothers, and Shearson Lehman combined. In 1986 Nomura became the first Japanese member of the London Stock Exchange. Nomura and Daiwa were primary

A busy moment on the Tokyo Securities and Stock Exchange
Courtesy The Mainichi Newspapers

dealers in the United States Treasury bond market. The second tier of securities firms contained ten medium-sized firms and the third all the smaller securities firms registered in Japan. Many of these smaller firms were affiliates of the Big Four, while some were affiliated with banks. In 1986 eighty-three of the smaller firms were members of the Tokyo Securities and Stock Exchange. Japan's securities firms derived most of their incomes from brokerage fees, equity and bond trading, underwriting, and dealing. Other services included the administration of trusts. In the late 1980s, a number of foreign securities firms, including Salomon Brothers and Merrill Lynch, became players in Japan's financial world.

Japanese insurance companies became important leaders in international finance in the late 1980s. More than 90 percent of the population owned life insurance, and the amount held per person was at least 50 percent greater than in the United States. Many Japanese used insurance companies as savings vehicles. Insurance companies' assets grew at a rate of over 20 percent per year in the late 1980s, reaching nearly US$694 billion in 1988. These assets permitted the companies to become major players in international money markets. Nippon Life Insurance Company, the world's largest insurance firm, was reportedly the biggest single holder of United States Treasury securities in 1989.

The Tokyo Securities and Stock Exchange became the largest in the world in 1988, in terms of the combined market value of outstanding shares and capitalization, while the Ōsaka Stock Exchange ranked third after those of Tokyo and New York. Although there are eight stock exchanges in Japan, the Tokyo stock exchange represented 83 percent of the nation's total equity in 1988. Of the 1,848 publicly traded domestic companies in Japan at the end of 1986, about 80 percent were listed on the Tokyo stock exchange.

Two developments in the late 1980s helped in the rapid expansion of the Tokyo Securities and Stock Exchange. The first was a change in the financing of company operations. Traditionally, large firms obtained funding through bank loans rather than capital markets, but in the late 1980s they began to rely more on direct financing. The second development came in 1986 when the Tokyo exchange permitted non-Japanese brokerage firms to become members for the first time. By 1988 the exchange had sixteen foreign members. The Tokyo Securities and Stock Exchange had 124 member companies all told in mid-1990.

Japan's stock market dealings exploded in the 1980s, with increased trading volume and rapidly rising stock prices. The Nikkei Stock Average grew from 6,850 in October 1982 to nearly 39,000 in early 1990. During one six-month period in 1986, total trade volume on the Tokyo exchange increased by 250 percent with wild swings in the Nikkei average. After the plunge of the New York Stock Exchange in October 1987, the Tokyo average dropped by 15 percent, but there was a sharp recovery by early 1988. In 1990 five types of securities were traded on the Tokyo exchange: stocks, bonds, investment trusts, rights, and warrants alone.

Public Corporations

Although the Japanese economy is largely based on private enterprise, it does have a number of government-owned (public) corporations, which are more extensive and, in some cases, different in function from what exists in the United States. In 1988 there were 97 public corporations, reduced from 111 in the early 1980s as a result of administrative reforms. Public companies at the national level were normally affiliated with one of the economic ministries, although the extent of direct management and supervision varied. The government divided the national-level corporations into several categories. The first included the main public service and monopoly corporations: Nippon Telegraph and Telephone Corporation, Japanese National Railways, and Japan Tobacco and Salt Public Corporation. However, Nippon Telegraph and Telephone Corporation was privatized in 1985, the Japanese National

Railways in 1987, and the Japan Tobacco and Salt Corporation in 1988. The second category included the major development corporations devoted to housing, agriculture, highways, water resources, ports, energy resources, and urban development projects. Other categories of corporations included those charged with special government projects, loans and finance, and special types of banking. Local public corporations were involved with utilities.

Public corporations benefited the economy in several ways. Some, like Nippon Telegraph and Telephone Corporation before privatization, were important sources of technology development funds or centers around which private industry could cluster. Others provided vital public services that private industry would find impossible to finance. The development banks, particularly the Japan Development Bank, were sources of long-term investment funds and instrumental in shaping the pattern of industry, especially in the early postwar period. Because public corporations also added revenue to the national budget and were, theoretically, self-financing, they required little from the government in the way of financial support. They also provided employment for retired bureaucrats. The reemployment of retired bureaucrats as advisors to these corporations as well as many private-sector firms was rather common, especially in the late 1960s and early 1970s, under the title *amakudari* (descent from heaven). The practice was most prevalent in the highregulated banking, steel, and transportation industries, but was found throughout the Japanese economy.

Public corporations also had a negative side. Their operations were apt to be less efficient than those of the private sector, and in some corporations, close government supervision impeded corporate responsibility. Conflicts between corporate heads, who were retired from competing ministries, and envy among career employees, who saw their advancement blocked by the influx of retired officials, also created frequent management problems. Labor relations were also less harmonious in the public sector than the private sector. Some of Japan's most debilitating strikes and work slowdowns have been launched by public transportation workers.

Private Enterprise

The engine of Japanese economic growth has been private initiative and enterprise, together with strong support and guidance from the government and from labor. The most numerous enterprises were single proprietorships, of which there were over 4 million in the late 1980s. The dominant form of organization, however, was the corporation: in 1988 some 2 million corporations employed more than 30 million workers, or nearly half of the total labor force of 60.1 million people. Corporations ranged from large to small, but the favored type of organization was the joint-stock company, with directors, auditors, and yearly stockholders' meetings.

Japan's postwar business order dates back to the dissolution of the *zaibatsu* during the Allied occupation. Central holding companies were dissolved and families and other owners were compensated with non-negotiable government bonds. Individual operating firms were then freed to act independently. At the same time, the government instituted antimonopoly legislation and formed the Fair Trade Commission. Together with agricultural land reform and the start of the labor movement, these measures helped introduce a degree of competition into markets that had not previously existed.

It was not long, however, before the spirit and letter of these reform laws were neglected. During the 1950s, government guidance of industry often sidestepped the provisions of the law. While market forces determined the course of the vast majority of enterprise activities, adjustments in the allocation of bank credit and the formation of cartels favored the reemergence of conglomerate groupings. These groups competed vigorously with one another for market shares both within and outside Japan, but they dominated lesser industry.

In contrast to the dualism of the prewar era—featuring a giant gap between modern, large enterprises and the smaller, traditional firms—the postwar system was more graduated. Interlocking production and sales arrangements between greater and smaller enterprises characterized corporate relations in most markets. The average Japanese business executive was well aware of the firms that led production and sales in each industry and sensitive to minute differentiations of rank among the many corporations.

At the top of the corporate system were three general types of corporate groupings. The first included the corporate heirs of the *zaibatsu* (including many of the same firms), and the second consisted of corporations that formed around major commercial banks. The nation's six largest groupings were in these categories. Mitsui, Mitsubishi, and Sumitomo were former *zaibatsu,* while other groupings were formed around the Fuji-Sankei, Sanwa, and Dai-Ichi Kangyo banking giants. A third type of corporate grouping developed around large industrial producers.

The relations among the members of the first two types of groups were flexible, informal, and quite different from the holding company pattern of the prewar days. Coordination took place at periodic gatherings of corporation presidents and chief executive officers. The purpose of these meetings was to exchange information and ideas rather than to command group operations in a formal way. The general trading firms associated with each group could also be used to coordinate group finance, production, and marketing policies although none of these relationships was entirely exclusive (see Trading Companies, ch. 5). The practice of cross-holding shares of group stock further cemented these groups, and such holdings usually made up about 30 percent of the total group equity. Member corporations would typically, though not exclusively, borrow from group banks.

Similar relationships characterized the third type of corporate group, which established around a major industrial producer. Members of this group were often subsidiaries or affiliates of the parent firm, or regular subcontractors. Subsidiaries and contracting corporations normally built components for the parent firm and, because of their smaller size, afforded several benefits to the parent. The larger firm could concentrate on final assembly and high value-added processes, while the smaller firm could perform specialized and labor-intensive tasks. Cash payments to the subcontractors were supplemented by commercial bills whose maturity could be postponed when the need arose. In the late 1980s, subcontracting firms accounted for over 60 percent of Japan's 6 million small and medium-sized enterprises (those having fewer than 300 employees).

This characterization of the economy as consisting of neat, hierarchical corporate groupings is somewhat simplistic. In the 1970s and 1980s, a number of independent middle-sized firms—especially in the services and retail trade—were busy catering to increasingly diversified and specialized markets. Unaffiliated with the nation's large conglomerates, these corporations dueled each other in a highly competitive market. Bankruptcies among such companies and the smaller firms were much more common than among the large enterprises. Small business was the main provider of employment for the Japanese—two-thirds of Japanese workers were employed by small firms throughout the 1980s—and thereby the source of consumer demand; it engaged in almost half of business investment as well.

The issue of who controlled the enterprise system was complex. While theoretically corporations were owned by stockholders, individual stock-ownership fell throughout the 1970s and 1980s, and in 1990 was less than 30 percent. Financial corporations accounted for the remaining 70 percent or so. Relative to capital, almost all large corporations carried enormous debt, a phenomenon known as overborrowing. Such an unbalanced capital structure resulted from the easy availability of credit from the main group bank and the network of corporate relations, which reduced the need to resort to capital markets. Corporate shareholder meetings were often only window dressing. Thugs sometimes terrorized stockholders, demanding payments to vote for management or refrain from exposing scandals. The auditing system also was not well developed. Until the late 1980s, few companies engaged outside auditors, and accounting practices gave corporations room to mislead both the public and shareholders. The law was changed in 1981 to control this kind of excess, to enhance the power of auditors, and to reduce the number of stockholders in the employ of management. But in general, it seemed that business management held the reins of corporate control, often with little public accountability. The corporate system maintained itself by smoothing relations with the government bureaucracy, expanding benefits to workers and consumers, and public relations and philanthropy.

The Culture of Japanese Management

The culture of Japanese management so famous in the West was generally limited to Japan's large corporations. These flagships of the Japanese economy provided their workers with excellent salaries and working conditions and secure employment. These companies and their employees were the business elite of Japan. A career with such a company was the dream of many young people in Japan, but only a select few attained the jobs. Qualification for employment was limited to the men and the few women who graduated from the top thirty colleges and universities in Japan.

In the late twentieth century, placement and advancement of Japanese workers was heavily based on educational background. Students who did not gain admission to the most highly rated colleges only rarely had the chance to work for a large company. Instead, they had to seek positions in small and medium-sized firms that could not offer comparable benefits and prestige. The quality of one's education and, more importantly, the college attended, played decisive roles in a person's career (see Higher Education, ch. 3).

Few Japanese attended graduate school, and graduate training in business per se was rare in the 1980s. There were only a few business school programs in Japan. Companies provided their own training and showed a strong preference for young men who could be trained in the company way. Interest in a person whose attitudes and work habits were shaped outside the company was low. When young men were preparing to graduate from college, the attempt to find a suitable employer began. This process had been very difficult: there were only a few positions in the best government ministries, and quite often entry into a good firm was determined by competitive examination. In the 1990s, the situation was becoming less competitive with a gradual decrease in the number of candidates. New workers enter their companies as a group on April 1 each year.

One of the prominent features of Japanese management was the practice of permanent employment (*shūshin koyō*). Permanent employment covered the minority of the work force that worked for the major companies. Management trainees, traditionally nearly all of whom were men, were recruited directly from colleges when they graduated in the late winter and, if they survived a six-month probationary period with the company, were expected to stay with the companies for their entire working careers. Employees were not dismissed thereafter on any grounds, except for serious breaches of ethics.

Permanent employees were hired as generalists, not as specialists for a specific positions. A new worker was not hired because of any special skill or experience; rather, the individual's intelligence, educational background, and personal attitudes and attributes were closely examined. On entering a Japanese corporation, the new employee would train from six to twelve months in each of the firm's major offices or divisions. Thus, within a few years a young employee would know every facet of company operations, knowledge which allowed companies to be more productive.

Another unique aspect of Japanese management in the late twentieth century was the system of promotion and reward. An important criterion was seniority. Seniority was determined by the year an employee's class entered the company. Career progression was highly predictable, regulated, and automatic. Compensation for young workers was quite low, but they accepted low pay with the understanding that their pay would increase in regular increments and be quite high by retirement. Compensation consisted of a wide range of tangible and intangible benefits, including housing assistance, inexpensive vacations, good recreational facilities, and, most importantly, the availability of low-cost loans for such things as housing and a new car. Regular pay was often augmented by generous semiannual bonuses. Members of the same graduating class usually started with similar salaries, and salary increases and promotions each year were generally uniform. The purpose was to maintain harmony and avoid stress and jealousy within the group.

Individual evaluation, however, did occur. Early in a worker's career (by age thirty) distinctions were made in pay and job assignments. During the latter part of a worker's career another weeding took place: the best workers were selected for accelerated advancement into upper management. Those employees who failed to advance were forced to retire from the company in their mid-to late fifties. Retirement did not necessarily mean a life of leisure. Poor pension benefits and modest social security meant that many people had to continue working after retiring from a career. Many management retirees worked for the smaller subsidiaries of the large companies, with another company, or with the large company itself at substantially lower salaries.

A few major corporations in the late 1980s were experimenting with variations of permanent employment and automatic promotion. Some rewarded harder work and higher production with higher raises and more rapid promotions, but most retained the more traditional forms of hiring and advancement. A few companies that experienced serious reverses laid off workers, but such instances were rare.

Another aspect of Japanese management was the company union, which most regular company employees were obliged to join. The worker did not have a separate skill identification outside of the company. Despite federations of unions at the national level, the union did not exist as an entity separate from, or with an adversarial relationship to, the company. The linking of the company with the worker put severe limits on independent union action and the worker did not wish to harm the economic well-being of the company. Strikes were rare and usually brief.

Japanese managerial style and decision making in large companies emphasized the flow of information and initiative from the bottom up, making top management a facilitator rather than the source of authority, while middle management was both the impetus for and shaper of policy. Consensus was stressed as a way of arriving at decisions, and close attention was paid to workers' well-being. Rather than serve as an important decision maker, the ranking officer of a company had the responsibility of maintaining harmony so that employees could work together. A Japanese chief executive officer was a consensus builder.

Employment and Labor Relations

Rising labor productivity, particularly in the manufacturing industries, contributed significantly to the nation's economic development. Labor productivity was unusually high in the late 1970s, when Japan's wages first became competitive with other industrialized nations. But, productivity rose at an annual average rate of only 2.6 percent between 1978 and 1987 (see table 14, Appendix). At the same time, Japan was able to keep its unemployment rate between 2.3 and 3.0 percent from 1985 to 1990. The structure of the nation's employment system and relatively harmonious labor-management relations were two of the reasons for this enviable performance.

Employment, Wages, and Working Conditions

Japan's work force grew by less than 1 percent per year in the 1970s and 1980s. In 1990 it stood at nearly 63 percent of the total population over fifteen years of age, a level little changed since 1970. Labor force participation differed within age and gender groupings and was similar to that in other industrialized nations in its relative distribution among primary, secondary, and tertiary industries. The percentage of people employed in the primary sector (agriculture, forestry, and fishing) dropped from 17.4 in 1970 to 8.3 in 1987 and was projected to fall to 4.9 by 2000. The percentage of the Japanese labor force employed in heavy industry was 33.7 in 1970; it dropped to 33.1 in 1987 and was expected to be 27.7 in 2000. Light industry employed 47 percent of the work force in 1970 and 58 percent in 1987. The sector was expected to employ 62 percent by 2000. Throughout the 1970s and 1980s, well over 95 percent of all men between the ages of twenty-five and fifty-four in the work force, but the proportion dropped sharply after the usual retirement age of fifty-five (by 1990 the retirement age for most men had risen to sixty). Women participated most actively in the job market in their early twenties and between the ages of thirty-five and fifty-four (see Gender Stratification and the Lives of Women, ch. 2). The unemployment rate (2.3 percent in 1989) was considerably lower than in the other industrialized nations.

Wages varied by industry and type of employment. Regular workers in firms with more than thirty employees, those in finance, real estate, public service, petroleum, publishing, and emerging high-technology industries earned the highest wages. The lowest paid were those in textiles, apparel, furniture, and leather products industries. The average farmer fared even worse. During the period of strong economic growth from 1960 to 1973, wage levels rose rapidly. Nominal wages increased an average of 13 percent per year while real wages rose 7 percent each year. Wage levels then stagnated as economic growth slowed. Between 1973 and 1987 annual nominal and real wage increases dropped to 8 percent and 2 percent, respectively. Wages began rising in 1987 as the value of the yen sharply appreciated. In 1989 salaried workers receiving the highest average pay hikes over the previous year were newspaper employees (6.7 percent), followed by retail and wholesale workers (6 percent) and hotel employees (5.7 percent). Workers in the steel

(2.5 percent) and shipbuilding (4.2 percent) industries fared worse. The salaries of administrative and technical workers were about 20 percent higher than those of production workers. In the late 1980s, with wages in manufacturing firms having 500 or more workers indexed at 100, enterprises with 100 to 499 employees were indexed at 79, those with 30 to 99 employees at 64, and those with 5 to 29 employees at 56.6. The gap between wages paid to secondary school and college graduates was slight, but widened as they grew older and peaked at the age of fifty-five, when the former received only 60 to 80 percent of the wages of the latter.

Workers received two fairly large bonuses as well as their regular salary, one mid-year and the other at year's end. In 1988 workers in large companies received bonuses equivalent to their pay for 1.9 months while workers in the smallest firms gained bonuses equal to 1.2 months' pay. In addition to bonuses, Japanese workers received a number of fringe benefits, such as living allowances, incentive payments, remuneration for special job conditions, allowances for good attendance, and cost-of-living allowances.

Working conditions varied from firm to firm. On average, employees worked a forty-six-hour week in 1987; employees of most large corporations worked a modified five-day week with two Saturdays a month, while those in most small firms worked as much as six days each week. In the face of mounting international criticism of excessive working hours in Japan, in January 1989 public agencies began closing two Saturdays a month. Labor unions made reduced working hours an important part of their demands, and many larger firms responded in a positive manner. In 1986 the average employee in manufacturing and production industries worked 2,150 hours in Japan, compared to 1,924 hours in the United States and 1,643 in France. The average Japanese worker was entitled to fifteen days of paid vacation a year, but actually took only seven days.

The Structure of Japan's Labor Market

The structure of Japan's labor market was experiencing gradual change in the late 1980s and was expected to continue this trend throughout the 1990s. Labor market structure was affected by the aging of the working population, increasing numbers of women in the labor force, and workers' rising education level. There was the prospect of increasing numbers of foreign nationals in the labor force. And, finally, the labor market faced possible changes owing to younger workers who sought to break away from traditional career paths to those that stressed greater individuality and creativity.

Japan Airlines Boeing 747
Courtesy Japan Airlines

Working Women

In the early 1990s, Japanese women were joining the labor force in unprecedented numbers. In 1987 there were 23.6 million working women (40 percent of the labor force), and they accounted for 59 percent of the increase in employment from 1975 to 1987. The participation rate for women in the labor force (the ratio of those working to all women aged fifteen and older) rose from 45.7 percent in 1975 to 48.6 percent in 1987 and was expected to reach 50 percent by 2000.

The growing participation of women reflected both supply and demand factors. Industries such as wholesaling, retailing, banking, and insurance have expanded, in large part because of the effective use of women as part-time employees (see Age Structure; ch. 2).

Foreign Workers

Traditionally Japan has had strict laws regarding the employment of foreigners, although exceptions were made for certain occupational categories. Excepted categories have included executives and managers engaged in commercial activities, full-time scholars associated with research and education institutions, professional entertainers, engineers and others specializing in advanced

221

technology, foreign-language teachers, and others with special skills unavailable among Japanese nationals.

The problems of foreign workers in the labor force were expected to continue in the 1990s. Despite the long-term upward trend in the unemployment rate, many unpopular jobs went unfilled and the domestic labor market was sluggish. Imported labor was seen as a solution to this situation by some employers, who hired low-paid foreign workers, who were, in turn, enticed by comparatively high Japanese wages. The strict immigration laws were expected to remain on the books, however, although the influx of illegal aliens from nearby Asian countries to participate in the labor market was likely to increase (see table 16, Appendix).

Workers' Changing Attitudes

The success of corporations in Japan was attributable to the remarkable motivation of its workers. Also behind this corporate prosperity was the workers' strong sense of loyalty to and identification with their employers. While many theories have evolved to explain the extraordinary attitude of Japanese workers, perhaps the most noteworthy is that of personnel management. This view holds that loyalty to the company has developed as a result of job security and a wage system in which those with the greatest seniority reap the highest rewards. Such corporate structure presumably fostered not only a determined interest in the company, but a low percentage of workers who changed jobs.

During the postwar economic reconstruction, the backbone of the labor force was, of course, made up of people born before World War II. These people grew up in a Japan that was still largely an agriculturally based economy and had little material wealth. Moreover, they suffered the hardships of war and accepted hard work as a part of their lives. In the late twentieth century, these people were being replaced by generations born after the war, and there were indications that the newcomers had different attitudes toward work. Postwar generations were accustomed to prosperity, and they were also much better educated than their elders.

As might be expected, these socioeconomic changes have affected workers' attitudes. Prior to World War II, surveys indicated that the aspect of life regarded as most worthwhile was work. During the 1980s, the percentage of people who felt this way was declining. Workers' identification with their employers was weakening as well. A survey by the Management and Coordination Agency revealed that a record 2.7 million workers changed jobs in the one-year period beginning October 1, 1986, and the ratio of those who switched jobs to the total labor force matched the previous high recorded in 1974. This survey also showed that the percentage of workers indicating an interest in changing jobs increased from 4.5 percent in 1971 to 9.9 percent in 1987.

Another indication of changing worker attitudes was the number of people meeting with corporate scouts to discuss the possibility of switching jobs. Corporations' treatment of older workers also affected attitudes: there were fewer positions for older workers, and many found themselves without the rewards that their predecessors had enjoyed.

Aging and Retirement of the Labor Force

Japan's population was aging in the late twentieth century. During the 1950s, the percentage of the population in the sixty-five-and-over group remained steady at around 5 percent. Throughout subsequent decades, however, that age-group expanded, and by 1987 it had grown to almost 11 percent of the population. It was expected to have reached 16 percent by 2000 and almost 24 percent by 2020 (see Population, ch. 2). Perhaps the most outstanding feature of this trend was the speed with which it was occurring in comparison to trends in other industrialized nations. In the United States, expansion of the sixty-five-and-over age-group from 7 percent to 14 percent took seventy-five years; in Britain and the Federal Republic of Germany (West Germany) this expansion took forty-five years. The same expansion in Japan was expected to take only twenty-six years.

As Japan's population aged, so did its work force. In 1988 the Ministry of Labor projected that, by 1990, 20 percent of the work force would be made up of workers aged fifty-five and over. By 2000, the ministry predicted, 24 percent of the working population (almost one in four workers) would be in this age-group. This demographic shift was expected to bring about both macroeconomic and microeconomic problems. At the national level, Japan may have trouble in financing the pension system. At the corporate level, problems will include growing personnel costs and the shortage of senior positions. If such problems become severe, government will be forced to develop countermeasures.

In most Japanese companies, salaries rose with worker age. Because younger workers were paid less, they were more attractive to employers, and the difficulty in finding employment increased with age. This pattern was evidenced by the unemployment rates for different age-groups and by the number of applicants per job vacancy for each age-group in openings handled by public employment offices. As the Japanese population ages, such trends may grow.

Most Japanese companies required that employees retire upon reaching a specified age. During most of the postwar period, that age was fifty-five. Since government social security payments normally began at age sixty, workers were forced to find reemployment to fill the five-year gap. However, in 1986 the Diet passed the Law Concerning the Stabilization of Employment for Elderly People, to provide various incentives for firms to raise their retirement age to sixty. Many Japanese companies raised the retirement age they set, partly in response to this legislation. And despite mandatory retirement policies, many Japanese companies allowed their employees to continue working beyond the age of sixty—although generally at reduced wages. Reasons that people over sixty continued to work varied: some did so to supplement inadequate pension incomes, while others simply wanted to give meaning to their lives or to keep in touch with society (see table 17, Appendix).

As Japan's population aged, the financial health of the public pension plan deteriorated. To avoid massive premium increases, government reformed the system in 1986 by cutting benefit levels and raising the plan's specified age at which benefits began from sixty to sixty-five. Under the revised system, contributions paid in equal share by employer and employee were expected to be equivalent to about 30 percent of wages, as opposed to 40 percent of wages under the old system. However, problems now arose in securing employment opportunities for the sixty-to-sixty-five age-group.

In 1990, some 90 percent of companies paid retirement benefits to their employees in the form of lump-sum payments and pensions. Some companies based the payment amount on the employee's base pay, while others used formulas independent of base pay. Since the system was designed to reward long service, payment rose progressively with the number of years worked.

Social Insurance and Minimum Wage Systems

Companies in Japan were responsible for enrolling their employees in various social insurance systems, including health insurance, employee pension insurance, employment insurance, and workers' accident compensation insurance. The employer covered all costs for workers' accident compensation insurance, but payments to the other systems were shared by both employer and employee.

The Minimum Wage Law, introduced in 1947 but not enacted until 1959, was designed to protect low-income workers. Minimum wage levels have been determined, according to both region and industry, by special councils composed of government, labor, and employment representatives.

Labor Unions

Japan's over 74,500 trade unions were represented by four main labor federations in the mid-1980s: the General Council of Trade Unions of Japan (Nihon Rōdō Kumiai Sōhyōgikai, commonly known as Sōhyō), with 4.4 million members—a substantial percentage representing public sector employees; the Japan Confederation of Labor (Zen Nihon Rōdō Sōdōmei, or Dōmei for short), with 2.2 million members; the Federation of Independent Labor Unions (Churitsu Roren), with 1.6 million members; and the National Federation of Industrial Organizations (Shinsanbetsu), with only 61,000 members. In 1987 Dōmei and Churitsu Roren were dissolved and amalgamated into the newly established National Federation of Private Sector Unions (Rengō); and in 1990 Sōhyō affiliates merged with Rengō to form a new entity, Shin Rengō. Local labor unions and work unit unions, rather than the federations, conducted the major bargaining. Unit unions often banded together for wage negotiations, but federations did not control their policies or actions. Federations also engaged in political and public relations activities (see Interest Groups, ch. 6).

The rate of labor union membership, which was 35.4 percent in 1970, had declined considerably by the end of the 1980s. The continuing long-term reduction in union membership was caused by several factors, including the restructuring of Japanese industry away from heavy industries. Many people entering the work force in the 1980s joined smaller companies in the tertiary sector, where there was a general disinclination toward joining labor organizations.

The relationship between the typical labor union and the company was unusually close. Both white- and blue-collar workers joined the union automatically in most major companies. Temporary and subcontracting workers were excluded, and managers with the rank of section chief and above were considered part of management. In most corporations, however, many of the managerial staff were former union members. In general, Japanese unions were sensitive to the economic health of the company, and company management usually briefed the union membership on the state of corporate affairs.

Any regular employee below the rank of section chief was eligible to become a union officer. Management, however, often pressured the workers to select favored employees. Officers usually maintained their seniority and tenure while working exclusively on union activities and being paid from the union's accounts, and union offices were often located at the factory site. Many union officers went on to higher positions within the corporation if they were particularly effective (or troublesome), but few became active in organized labor activities at the national level.

During prosperous times, the spring labor offensives were highly ritualized affairs, with banners, sloganeering, and dances aimed more at being a show of force than a crippling job action. Meanwhile, serious discussions took place between the union officers and corporate managers to determine pay and benefit adjustments. If the economy turned sour, or if management tried to reduce the number of permanent employees, however, disruptive strikes often occurred. The number of working days lost to labor disputes peaked in the economic turmoil of 1974 and 1975 at around 9 million workdays in the two-year period. In 1979, however, there were fewer than 1 million days lost. Since 1981 the average number of days lost per worker each year to disputes was just over 9 percent of the number lost in the United States (see table 18, Appendix). After 1975, when the economy entered a period of slower growth, annual wage increases moderated, and labor relations were conciliatory. During the 1980s, workers received pay hikes that on average closely reflected the real growth of GNP for the preceding year. In 1989, for example, workers received an average 5.1 percent pay hike, while GNP growth had averaged 5 percent between 1987 and 1989. The moderate trend continued in the early 1990s, as the country's national labor federations were reorganizing themselves.

Infrastructure and Technology

A mountainous, insular nation, Japan has inadequate natural resources to support its growing economy and large population (see Energy, this ch.). Although many kinds of minerals were extracted throughout the country, most mineral resources had to be imported in the postwar era. Local deposits of metal-bearing ores were difficult to process because they were of a low grade. The nation's large and varied forest resources, which covered 70 percent of the country in the late 1980s, were not utilized extensively. Because of the precipitous terrain, underdeveloped road network, and high percentage of young trees, domestic sources were able to supply only between 25 and 30 percent of the nation's timber needs. Agriculture and fishing were the best developed resources, but only through years of painstaking investment and toil. The nation therefore built up the manufacturing and processing industries to convert raw materials imported from abroad. This strategy of economic development necessitated the establishment of a strong economic infrastructure to provide the needed energy, transportation, communications, and technological know-how.

Construction

The mainstay of infrastructure development was the construction industry, which employed slightly less than 10 percent of the labor force in 1985 and contributed some 8.5 percent of GDP. After the two oil crises in the 1970s, construction investment turned sluggish and the share of construction investment in GNP decreased gradually. In 1987, however, business expanded through investors' confidence, continued increase in corporate earnings, improvement of personal income, and rapid rise in land prices. The share of construction investment in GNP rose sharply, especially for more sophisticated and higher value-added private housing and private nonhousing structures.

Construction starts in FY 1988 covered a total area of 258 million square meters, the second highest area on record, while housing starts numbered 1.66 million, the third highest on record. Total investment in construction exceeded US$483 billion. Growing demand for private housing and new industry plants and equipment led to Japan's fifty largest construction companies experiencing double-digit growth in FY 1988.

Although demand for new private housing was expected to grow in the early 1990s, even greater growth was expected for new urban office buildings. A number of large urban development projects, including those for Tokyo's waterfront, other urban redevelopment, highway construction, and new or expanded airports, suggested continued work for the construction industry through the 1990s.

Japan's construction technology, which includes advanced earthquake-resistant designs, was among the most developed in the world (see Visual Arts, ch. 3). Major firms competed to improve quality control over all phases of design, management, and execution. Research and development focused especially on energy-related facilities, such as nuclear power plants and liquid natural gas (LNG) storage tanks. The largest firms were also improving their underwater construction methods.

Mining

Mining was a rapidly declining industry in the 1980s. Domestic coal production shrank from a peak of 55 million tons in 1960 to slightly more than 16 million tons in 1985, while coal imports grew to nearly 91 million tons in 1987. Domestic coal mining companies faced cheap coal imports and high production costs, which caused them chronic deficits in the 1980s. In the late 1980s, Japan's approximately 1 million tons of coal reserves were mostly hard coal used for coking. Most of the coal Japan consumed was used to produce electric power.

Japanese coal is found at the extreme ends of the country, in Hokkaidō and Kyūshū, which have, respectively, 45 and 40 percent of the country's coal deposits. Kyūshū's coal is generally of poor quality and hard to extract, but the proximity of the Kyūshū mines to ports facilitates transportation. In Hokkaidō, the coal seams are wider and can be worked mechanically, and the quality of the coal is good. Unfortunately, these mines are located well inland, making transportation difficult. In most Japanese coal mines, inclined galleries, which extended in some places to 9.7 kilometers underground, were used instead of pits. This arrangement was costly, despite the installation of moving platforms. The result was that a miner's daily output was far less than in Western Europe and the United States and domestic coal cost far more than imported coal.

Energy

Japan lacks any significant domestic sources of energy except coal and must import substantial amounts of crude oil, natural gas, and other energy resources, including uranium. In 1986 the country's dependence on imports for primary energy stood at nearly 92 percent. Its rapid industrial growth since the end of World War II had doubled energy consumption every five years. The use of power had also changed qualitatively. In 1950, coal supplied half of Japan's energy needs, hydroelectricity one-third, and oil the rest. In 1987 oil provided Japan with 56.6 percent of energy needs. Coal provided 18 percent of energy needs, natural gas 9.7 percent, nuclear power 10 percent, hydroelectic power 4.1 percent, geothermal 0.1 percent, and 1.5 percent came from other sources. During the 1960–72 period of accelerated growth, energy consumption grew much faster than GNP, doubling Japan's consumption of world energy. By 1976, with only 3 percent of the world's population, Japan was consuming 6 percent of global energy supplies.

After the two oil crises of the 1970s, the pattern of energy consumption in Japan changed from heavy dependence on oil to some diversification to other forms of energy resources. Japan's domestic oil consumption dropped slightly, from around 5.1 million barrels of oil per day in the late 1970s to 4.9 million barrels per day in 1990. While the country's use of oil was declining, its consumption of nuclear power and LNG rose substantially. Because domestic natural gas production is minimal, rising demand was met by greater imports. Japan's main LNG suppliers in 1987 were Indonesia (51.3 percent), Malaysia (20.4 percent), Brunei (17.8 percent),

Abu Dhabi (7.3 percent), and the United States (3.2 percent). Several Japanese industries, including electric power companies and steelmakers, switched from petroleum to coal, most of which was imported.

In 1987, the latest year for which complete statistics were available, Japan's total energy requirements were tabulated at 372 million tons of petroleum equivalent. Of this total, 85 percent was imported. Consumption totalled 263.8 million tons, 45.9 percent of which was used by industry; 23.6 percent by the transportation sector; 26.8 percent for agricultural, residential, services, and other uses; and 3.7 percent for non-energy uses, such as lubricating oil or asphalt.

In 1989 Japan was the world's third largest producer of electricity. Most of the more than 3,300 power plants were thermoelectric. About 75 percent of the available power was controlled by the ten major regional power utilities, of which Tokyo Electric Power Company was the world's largest. Electricity rates in Japan were among the world's highest.

The Japanese were working to increase the availability of nuclear power in 1985. Although Japan was a late starter in this field, it finally imported technology from the United States and obtained uranium from Canada, France, South Africa, and Australia. By 1987 the country had thirty-three nuclear reactors in operation, with seventeen additional reactors planned or under construction. The ratio of nuclear power generation to total electricity production increased from 2 percent in 1973 to 26 percent in 1987.

During the 1980s, Japan's nuclear power program was strongly opposed by environmental groups, particularly after the Three Mile Island accident in the United States. Other problems for the program were the rising costs of nuclear reactors and fuel, the huge investments necessary for fuel enrichment and reprocessing plants, reactor failures, and nuclear waste disposal. Nevertheless, Japan continued to build nuclear power plants. Of alternative energy sources, Japan has effectively exploited only geothermal energy. The country had six geothermal power stations with a combined capacity of 133,000 kilowatts per hour in 1989 (see table 19, Appendix).

Research and Development

As its economy matured in the 1970s and 1980s, Japan gradually shifted away from dependence on foreign research. Japan's ability to conduct independent research and development became a decisive factor in boosting the nation's competitiveness. As early as 1980, the Science and Technology Agency, a component of the

Office of the Prime Minister, announced the commencement of "the era of Japan's technological independence." By 1986 Japan had come to devote a higher proportion of its GNP to research and development than the United States. In 1989 nearly 700,000 Japanese were engaged in research and development, more than the number of French, Britons, and West Germans combined. At the same time Japan was producing more engineers than any country except the Soviet Union and the United States. Similar trends were seen in the use of capital resources. Japan spent US$39.1 billion on government and private research and development in 1987, equivalent to 2.9 percent of its national income (the highest ratio in the world). Although the United States spent around US$108.2 billion on research and development in 1987, only 2.6 percent of its income was devoted to that purpose, ranking it third behind Japan and West Germany.

The Japanese reputation for originality also increased. Of the 1.2 million patents registered worldwide in 1985, 40 percent were Japanese, and Japanese citizens took out 19 percent of the 120,000 patent applications made in the United States. In 1987, around 33 percent of computer-related patents in the United States were Japanese, as were 30 percent of aviation-related and 26 percent of communications patents.

Despite its advances in technological research and development and its major commitment to applied research, however, Japan significantly trailed other industrialized nations in basic scientific research. In 1989 around 13 percent of Japanese research and development funds were devoted to basic research. The proportion of basic research expenses borne by government was also much lower in Japan than in the United States, as was Japan's ratio of basic research expenses to GNP. In the late 1980s, the Japanese government attempted to rectify national deficiencies in basic research through a broad "originality" campaign in schools, generously funding research, and encouraging private cooperation in various fields.

Most research and development was private, although government support to universities and laboratories aided industry greatly. In 1986, private industry provided 76 percent of the funding for research and development, which was especially strong in the late 1980s in electrical machinery (with a ratio of research costs to total sales of 5.5 percent in 1986), precision instruments (4.6 percent), chemicals (4.3 percent), and transportation equipment (3.2 percent).

As for government research and development, the national commitment to greater defense spending in the 1980s translated into increased defense-related research and development. Meanwhile, government moved away from supporting large-scale industrial technology, such as shipbuilding and steel. Research emphases in the 1980s were in alternative energy, information processing, life sciences, and modern industrial materials.

Industry

The nation's industrial activities (including mining, manufacturing, and power, gas, and water utilities) contributed 46.6 of total domestic industrial production in 1989, up slightly from 45.8 percent in 1975. This steady performance of the industrial sector in the 1970s and 1980s was a result of the growth of high-technology industries (see table 20, Appendix). During this period, some of the older heavy industries, such as steel and shipbuilding, either declined or simply held stable. Together with the construction industry, those older heavy industries employed 34.9 of the work force in 1989 (relatively unchanged from 34.8 percent in 1980). The service industry sector grew the fastest in the 1980s in terms of GNP, while the greatest losses occurred in agriculture, forestry, mining, and transportation. Most industry catered to the domestic market, but exports were important for several key commodities. In general, industries relatively geared toward exports over imports in 1988 were transportation equipment (with a 24.8 percent ratio of exports over imports), motor vehicles (54 percent), electrical machinery (23.4 percent), general machinery (21.2 percent), and metal and metal products (8.2 percent).

Industry was concentrated in several regions, which were in order of importance: the Kantō region surrounding Tokyo, especially the prefectures of Chiba, Kanagawa, Saitama, and Tokyo (the Keihin industrial region); the Nagoya metropolitan area, including Aichi, Gifu, Mie, and Shizuoka prefectures (the Chukyo-Tōkai industrial region); Kinki (the Keihanshin industrial region); the southwestern part of Honshū and northern Shikoku around the Inland Sea (the Setouchi industrial region); and the northern part of Kyūshū (Kitakyūshū). In addition, a long narrow belt of industrial centers was found between Tokyo and Hiroshima, established by particular industries, that had developed as mill towns. These included Toyota City, near Nagoya, the home of the automobile manufacturer.

The fields in which Japan enjoyed relatively high technological development included semiconductor manufacturing, optical fibers, optoelectronics, video discs and videotex, facsimile and copy machines, industrial robots, and fermentation processes. Japan lagged slightly in such fields as satellites, rockets, and large aircraft, where advanced engineering capabilities were required, and in such fields as computer-aided design and computer-aided manufacturing (CAD/CAM), databases, and natural resources exploitation, where basic software capabilities were required.

Basic Manufactures

Japan's major export industries included automobiles, consumer electronics, computers, semiconductors, and iron and steel (see Major International Industries, ch. 5). Additionally, key industries in Japan's economy were mining, nonferrous metals, petrochemicals, pharmaceuticals, bioindustry, shipbuilding, aerospace, textiles, and processed foods.

As the coal-mining industry declined, so did the general importance of domestic mining in the whole economy. Only 0.2 percent of the labor force was engaged in mining operations in 1988, and the value added from mining was about 0.3 percent of the total for all mining and manufacturing. Domestic production contributed most to the supply of such nonmetals as silica sand, pyrophyllite clay, dolomite, and limestone. Domestic mines were contributing declining shares of the requirements for the metals zinc, copper, and gold. Almost all of the ores used in the nation's sophisticated processing industries were imported.

The nonferrous metals industry fared very well in the late 1980s, as domestic demand for these metals reached record levels. Japan's consumption of the main nonferrous metals, such as copper, lead, zinc, and aluminum, was the second highest in the noncommunist world after the United States. In 1989, sales of copper products exceeded 1.5 million tons for the first time. Production of electric wire and cable, which accounted for 70 percent of Japan's copper demand, and brass mills, which use the other 30 percent, experienced sharp growth, as did the demand for aluminum.

The petrochemical industry experienced moderate growth in the late 1980s because of steady economic expansion. The highest growth came in the production of plastics, polystyrene, and polypropylene. Prices for petrochemicals remained high because of increased demand in the newly developing economies of Asia, but the construction of factory complexes to make ethylene-based products in the Republic of Korea (South Korea) and Thailand by 1990 was expected to increase supplies and reduce prices. In the long term, the Japanese petrochemical industry was likely to face intensifying competition due to the integration of domestic and international markets, and efforts by other Asian countries to catch up with Japan.

The pharmaceutical industry and bioindustry experienced strong growth in the late 1980s. Pharmaceuticals production grew an estimated 8 percent in 1989, because of increased expenditures by Japan's rapidly aging population. Leading producers actively developed new drugs, such as those for degenerative and geriatric diseases, while internationalizing operations. Pharmaceutical companies were establishing tripolar networks connecting Japan, the United States, and Western Europe to coordinate product development. They also increased merger and acquisition activity overseas. Biotechnology research and development was progressing steadily, including the launching of marine biotechnology projects, with full-scale commercialization expected to take place in the early 1990s. Biotechnology research covered a wide variety of fields: agriculture, animal husbandry, pharmaceuticals, chemicals, food processing, and fermentation. Human hormones and proteins for pharmaceutical products were sought through genetic recombination using bacteria. Biotechnology also was used to enhance bacterial enzyme properties to further improve amino-acid fermentation technology, a field in which Japan was the world leader. The government cautioned Japanese producers, however, against overoptimism regarding biotechnology and bioindustry. The research race both in Japan and abroad intensified in the 1980s, leading to patent disputes and forcing some companies to abandon research. Also, researchers began to realize that such drug development continually showed new complexities, requiring more technical breakthroughs than first imagined. Yet despite these problems, research and development, especially in leading companies, were still expected to be successful and end in product commercialization in the mid-term.

Japan dominated world shipbuilding in the late 1980s, filling more than half of all orders worldwide. Its closest competitors were South Korea and Spain, with 9 percent and 5.2 percent of the market, respectively. Japan's shipyards replaced their West European competitors as world leaders in production, through advanced design, fast delivery, and low production costs. The Japanese shipbuilding industry was hit by a lengthy recession from the late 1970s through most of the 1980s, which resulted in a drastic cutback in the use of facilities and in the work force, but there was a sharp revival in 1989. The industry was helped by a sudden rise in demand from other countries that needed to replace their aging fleets and from a sudden decline in the South Korean shipping industry. In 1988 Japanese shipbuilding firms received orders for 4.8 million gross tons of ships, but this figure grew to 7.1 million tons in 1989.

The aerospace industry received a major boost in 1969 with the establishment of the National Space Development Agency, which was charged with the development of satellites and launch vehicles (see Telecommunications, this ch.). Japan's aircraft industry was only one-twentieth the size of that of the United States and one-twelfth that of Western Europe, and its technological level lagged as well. However, in the late 1980s Japan began to participate in new international aircraft development projects as its technical capabilities developed. The Asuka fanjet-powered short takeoff and landing (STOL) aircraft made a successful test flight in 1985. In 1988 Japan signed an accord with the United States to cooperate in building Japan's next-generation fighter aircraft, the FSX (see Defense Industry, ch. 8).

The textile industry showed a strong revival in the late 1980s because of increased domestic demand from the construction, automobile, housing, and civil engineering industries for various synthetic fibers. The clothing industry also fared well in the late 1980s, thanks to the expansion of consumer demand, especially in the area of women's apparel. Production of high value-added fashionable clothes became the mainstay of this industry.

The production value of the food industry ranked third among manufacturing industries after electric and transport machinery. It produced a great variety of products, ranging from traditional Japanese items, such as soybean paste (miso) and soy sauce, to beer and meat. The industry as a whole experienced mild growth in the 1980s, primarily from the development of such new products as "dry beer" and precooked food, which was increasingly used because of the tendency of family members to dine separately, the trend toward smaller families, and convenience. A common feature of all sectors of the food industry was their internationalization. As domestic raw materials lost their price competitiveness following the liberalization of imports, food makers more often produced foodstuffs overseas, promoted tie-ups with overseas firms, and purchased overseas firms.

Domestic Trade and Services

The nation's service industries were the major contributor to GNP and employment, generating about 58 percent of the national totals in 1987. Moreover, services were the fastest growing sector, outperforming manufacturing in the 1980s. The service sector covered many diverse activities. Wholesale and retail trade was dominant, but advertising, data processing, publishing, tourism, leisure industries, entertainment, and other industries grew rapidly in the 1980s. Most service industries were small and labor-intensive, but became more technologically sophisticated as computer and electronic products were incorporated by management.

The operation of wholesale and retail trades has often been denigrated by other nations as a barrier to foreign participation in the Japanese market, as well as being called antiquated and inefficient. Small retailers and "mom-and-pop" stores predominated. In 1985 there were 1.6 million retail outlets in Japan, slightly more than the total number of retail outlets in the United States (1.5 million in 1982), even though Japan has only half the population of the United States and is smaller than California.

There were several changes in wholesaling and retailing in the 1980s. Japan's distribution system was becoming more efficient. Retail outlets and wholesale establishments both peaked in number in 1982 and were down 5.4 percent and 3.7 percent, respectively, in 1985. The main casualties were sole proprietorships, especially mom-and-pop stores and wholesale locations with fewer than ten employees. Almost 96,000 of the 1,036,000 mom-and-pop stores in operation in 1982 were out of business three years later. Government estimates for the late 1980s show additional consolidation in both wholesale and retail sectors, including a continued sharp decline in mom-and-pop store operations. A further decline in mom-and-pop stores was expected as a result of the Large-Scale Retail Store Law of 1990, which greatly reduced the power of small retailers to block the establishment of large retail stores. Soaring land prices were a major cause of the decline of mom-and-pop stores, but an even more important reason was the growth of convenience and discount stores. Discount stores were not much bigger than the traditional small shops, but their distribution networks gave them a big pricing edge. Moreover, Japanese consumers were discovering the advantages of catalog shopping, which offered not only convenience, but also greater selection and lower prices. According to a Nikkei survey, the mail-order business expanded 13 percent between April 1987 and March 1988 to more than US$8.9 billion in annual sales. Specialty chains, particularly those handling men's and women's clothing, shoes, and consumer electronics, were also doing better than the overall industry. Department stores, supermarkets, and superstores (hybrid supermarket-discount stores) and other big retail operations were gaining business at the expense of small retailers, although their progress was quite slow. Between 1980 and 1988, department stores increased their share of total retail sales by only 1 percentage point to 8.4 percent. Supermarkets and superstores increased in market share from 6.5 to 7.3 percent. Between 1980 and 1988, the number of department stores grew from

325 to just 371, and other big self-service stores only increased in number by 62 units between 1984 and 1988.

Among service industries, the restaurant, advertising, real estate, hotel and leisure business, and data-processing industries grew rapidly in the 1980s. The fast-food industry has been profitable for both foreign and domestic companies. By 1989 family restaurants and fast-food chains had grown into a US$138 billion business. Overall growth declined in the late 1980s because of the sharp rise of rents and a proliferation of restaurants in many areas. The number of hotel and guest rooms grew from 189,654 in 1981 to 342,695 in 1988.

Because much of the sales competition in Japan was of the nonprice variety, advertising was extremely important. Consumers had to see the suitability of products and services for their lifestyles. The intense competition for the domestic market spurred the growth of the world's largest advertising agency, Dentsu, as well as other advertisers.

Transportation and Communications

Railroads and Subways

Railroads were long the most important means of passenger and freight transportation, ever since they were established in the late nineteenth century, but from the 1960s they were rivalled in usage by road transportation (see Roads, this ch.; table 21, Appendix). The relative share of railroads in total passenger-kilometers fell from 66.7 percent in 1965 to 42 percent in 1978, and to 37.1 percent in 1987. By contrast, passenger cars and domestic airlines were carrying ever-larger shares of the passenger traffic in the late 1980s (see Civil Aviation, this ch.; table 22, Appendix).

At the heart of Japan's railroad system is the Japan Railways Group, a government-subsidized group of eight companies that took over most of the assets, operations, and liabilities of the government-owned Japanese National Railways in 1987. Initially, the companies remained in the public domain with privatization planned, at least for some of the companies, by the early 1990s. There were six passenger companies: the East Japan, West Japan, and Central Japan railway companies, which operated in Honshū, and the Kyūshū, Shikoku, and Hokkaidō railway companies, which operated on the islands for which the companies were named. In addition, the East Japan Railway Company, since the opening of the Seikan Tunnel between Honshū and Hokkaidō in 1988, also provided express service to Sapporo. Similarly, the Central Japan Railway Company started serving Shikoku after the 1990 completion

A trunk line of the Japan Railways Group, opened in 1986
Courtesy The Mainichi Newspapers
The Tokyo subway, one of the world's busiest metro systems
Courtesy The Mainichi Newspapers

of the Seto-Ōhashi bridges, a system of seven bridges linking Honshū and Shikoku. The six companies had 18,800 kilometers of routes (mostly 1.1-meter track) in use in the late 1980s. About 25 percent of the routes were in double-track and multi-track sections, and the rest were single-track. In 1988, 51 percent of the six companies' 1,000 locomotives were diesel and the rest were electric. Another company, Japan Freight Railway Company, owned its locomotives (295 diesel and 569 electric locomotives in 1988), rolling stock, and stations but hired track from the six passenger companies. It ran fewer trains on less track than Japanese National Railways freight service did before its demise but at increased revenues and higher productivity. The eighth company, the Shinkansen Property Corporation, leased Shinkansen (''bullet'' train) railroad facilities— including 2,100 kilometers of 1.4-meter gauge high-speed track—to the passenger companies on Honshū. Some of the Shinkansen electric-powered trains operated at speeds up to 240 kilometers per hour.

Another nearly 3,400 kilometers of routes, mostly 1.1-meter-gauge, were operated by major private railroads, and by what are known in Japan as third sector railroads—new companies, financed with private and local government funds—that absorbed some of Japanese National Railways' rural lines. There were twenty-seven private and third sector companies in 1989.

What remained of the debt-ridden Japanese National Railways after its 1987 breakup was named the Japanese National Railways Settlement Corporation. Its purpose was to dispose of assets not absorbed by the successor companies and to execute other activities relating to the breakup, such as reemployment of former personnel. The demise of the government-owned system came after charges of serious management inefficiencies, profit losses, and fraud. By the early 1980s, passenger and freight business had declined, and fare increases failed to keep up with higher labor costs. The new companies introduced competition, cut their staffing, and made reform efforts. Initial public reaction to these moves was good: the combined passenger travel on the Japan Railways Group passenger companies in 1987 was 204.7 billion passenger-kilometers, up 3.2 percent from 1986, while the passenger sector previously had been stagnant since 1975. The growth in passenger transport of private railroads in 1987 was 2.6 percent, which meant that the Japan Railways Group's rate of increase was above that of the private-sector railroads for the first time since 1974. Demand for rail transport was improved, although it still accounted for only 37 percent of passenger transportation and only 5 percent of cargo transportation in 1987. Rail passenger transportation was superior to automobiles in terms of energy efficiency and on speed of long-distance transportation.

In addition to its extensive railroads, Japan has an impressive number of subway systems. The largest was in Tokyo, where the subway network in 1989 consisted of 211 kilometers of track serving 205 stations. Two subway systems served the capital: one run by the Teito Rapid Transit Authority, with seven lines (the oldest of which was built in 1927), and the other operated by the Tokyo metropolitan government's Transportation Bureau, with three lines. Outlying and suburban areas were served by seven private railroad companies whose lines intersected at major stations with the subway system. More than sixty additional kilometers of subway were under construction in 1990 by the two companies. As of 1989, there also were full subway systems in Fukuoka, Kōbe, Kyōto, Nagoya, Ōsaka, Sendai, and Yokohama. Hiroshima and Kōbe had light rail systems, and Ōsaka, in addition to its subway, had an intermediate capacity transit system (rubber-tired motor cars running on concrete guideways). Like Tokyo, all of these cities also were well served by public and private railroads.

Roads

Road passenger and freight transport expanded considerably during the 1980s as private ownership of motor vehicles greatly increased along with the quality and extent of the nation's roads. Passenger transport by motor vehicles in 1987 totaled 540.7 billion passenger-kilometers, up 8.2 percent over the previous year. The Japan Railways Group companies operated long-distance bus service in the late 1980s on the nation's expanding expressway network. In addition to relatively low fares and deluxe seating, the buses were well utilized because they continued service during the night when air and train services were limited. The cargo sector also grew rapidly in the 1980s, recording 224.1 billion ton-kilometers in 1987. The freight handled by motor vehicles, mainly trucks, in 1989, was over 5 billion tons, accounting for 90 percent of domestic freight tonnage and about 50 percent of ton-kilometers.

The total length of roads in Japan reached about 1,098,900 kilometers in 1987 (see fig. 6). Sixty-five percent of the roads were paved, compared to only about 40 percent in 1978. Efforts to upgrade roads, however, have not kept up with increases in automobile ownership. In the late 1980s, many roads had reached a saturation point and traffic jams were especially serious in large urban areas. There was a vigorous government plan to improve the situation by constructing an additional 14,000 kilometers of highways in the 1990s. The 1988 opening of the Seto-Ōhashi section of the Honshū-Shikoku Bridge project provided a long-awaited direct link between Honshū and relatively undeveloped Shikoku.

Maritime Transportation

In 1986 the Japanese merchant fleet included 10,011 ships with a total displacement of 38.5 million gross tons, a steady decrease from 10,425 ships with a total gross tonnage of 40.4 million in 1984. Of the nearly 1,200 Japanese ships of 1,000 gross registered tons and over, there were more than 300 bulk carriers; more than 250 petroleum, oils, and lubricants tankers; some 240 vehicle and cargo carriers; and more than 150 refrigerated cargo ships. The remainder were passenger and passenger-cargo ships, container ships, roll-on/roll-off cargo ships, chemical tankers, combination ore and oil carriers, and other specialized types of large ships.

Japanese ports, mainly Yokohama, Nagoya, and Kōbe, received 40,129 ships in 1986, loaded 88.1 million tons of cargo, and unloaded 598.9 million tons. Other major ports included Chiba, Hakodate, Kitakyūshū, Kushiro, Ōsaka, Tokyo, and Yokkaichi.

Almost all shipping operated from coastal ports. Japans' rivers were short and were unnavigable except in the lower reaches.

Civil Aviation

The civil aviation industry grew steadily during the 1980s, with increased demand for both domestic and international services. Increases in the number of passengers on each type of route reached more than 10 percent per year. Direct service was provided between the New Tokyo International Airport at Narita-Sanrizuka, seventy kilometers northeast of Tokyo, and nearly every country in the world via Japan Airlines, All Nippon Airways, and most other international carriers. Tokyo International Airport at Haneda and Ōsaka, Nagoya, Nagasaki, Fukuoka, Kagoshima, and Naha airports also handled some international flights in the late 1980s, and the new Kansai International Airport was under construction in Ōsaka Bay with a projected completion date of 1993. Japan Airlines, All Nippon Airways, and Japan Air System also provided connections between most major Japanese cities, and South-West Air Lines operated scheduled flights to major islands in the Ryūkyūs. In 1986 Japanese carriers served more than 53.6 million passengers. Although air cargo accounted for only for a small proportion of all cargo transported both domestically and internationally—approximately 3.5 trillion ton-kilometers in 1986—the rate of air cargo growth was very high.

Telecommunications

In 1990 no other nation in the world was as literate (with a literacy rate of 99 percent) and dominated by the mass media as Japan (see Literature; Films and Television, ch. 3; The Mass Media and Politics, ch. 6). Japan's telecommunications system is excellent both in domestic and foreign service. The rapid spread of television sets in the 1960s, and advances in satellite communications in the 1970s, which permitted rapid improvements in television broadcasting, were major postwar factors in Japan's new information society.

The broadcast industry has been dominated by the Japan Broadcasting Corporation (Nippon Hōsō Kyōkai—NHK) since its founding in 1925. It operated two public television and three radio networks nationally, producing about 1,700 programs per week in the late 1980s. Its general and education programs were broadcast through more than 6,900 television and nearly 330 AM and more than 500 FM radio transmitting stations. Comprehensive service in twenty-one languages was available throughout the world. Although NHK's budget and operations are under the purview of the Ministry of Posts and Telecommunications, the Broadcasting Law of 1950 provides for independent management and programming by NHK.

Television broadcasting began in 1953, and color television was introduced in 1960. Cable television was introduced in 1969. In 1978 an experimental broadcast satellite with two color television channels was launched. Operational satellites for television use were launched between 1984 and 1990. Television viewing spread so rapidly that, by 1987, 99 percent of Japan's households had color television sets and the average family had its set on at least five hours a day. Starting in 1987, NHK began full-scale experimental broadcasting on two channels using satellite-to-audience signals, thus bringing service to remote and mountainous parts of the country that earlier had experienced poor reception. The new system also provided twenty-four hours a day, nonstop service.

In the late 1980s, Japan also had more than 100 commercial television companies, which operated more than 6,300 stations, and the country had more than 140 commercial radio companies operating about 630 medium wave, short wave, and FM stations, including several national as well as many local stations. Broadcasting innovations in the 1980s included sound multiplex (two-language or stereo) broadcasting, satellite broadcasting, and in 1985 the University of the Air and teletext services were inaugurated.

Rapid improvements, innovations, and diversification in communications technology, including optical fiber cables, communications satellites, and facsimile machines, led to rapid growth of the communications industry in the 1980s. Nippon Telegraph and Telephone Corporation, government-owned until 1985, had dominated the communications industry until April 1985, when new common carriers, including Daini Denden, were permitted to enter the field. Kokusai Denshin Denwa Company lost its monopoly hold on international communications activities in 1989, when Nihon Kokusai Tsushin and other private overseas communications firms began operations.

Japan's first satellite was launched in 1970, followed by subsequent launches of experimental and applications satellites in fields such as communications, broadcasting, meteorology, and earth observation. Satellites were launched from Japan's Tanegashima Space Center on the island of Tanegashima in Kagoshima Prefecture. Japanese space scientists have successfully launched three H-I rockets that accommodate a payload of 550 kilograms each. Japan also cooperated with the United States, Western Europe, and Canada to construct an earth-orbiting space station. In 1990 a consortium of Japanese firms led by Mitsubishi Heavy Industries was planning to enter the commercial rocket industry by the mid-1990s, but unexpectedly high costs and the need to further improve the H-II booster, the first rocket designed and developed entirely in Japan, meant that Japanese commercial launch services would probably not begin until the late 1990s.

Japan's burgeoning high-technology communications system included the widespread use of telephones. In 1989 there were 64 million telephones in Japan, nearly one for every two people.

Agriculture, Forestry, and Fishing

Agriculture, forestry, and fishing dominated the Japanese economy through the 1940s, but thereafter declined in relative importance. In the 1870s, these sectors accounted for more than 82 percent of employment. Employment in agriculture declined in the prewar period, but the sector was still the largest employer (about 50 percent of the work force) by the end of World War II. It further declined to 23.5 percent in 1965, 11.9 percent in 1977, and to 8.3 percent in 1988. The importance of agriculture in the national economy later continued its rapid decline, with the share of net agricultural production in GNP finally reduced between 1975 and 1989 from 4.1 to 3 percent. In the late 1980s, 85.5 percent of Japan's farmers were also engaged in occupations outside of farming, and most of these part-time farmers earned most of their income from nonfarming activities (see table 23, Appendix).

Japan's economic boom that began in the 1950s left farmers far behind both in income and agricultural technology. Farmers were determined to close this income gap as quickly as possible. They were attracted to the government's food control policy under which high rice prices were guaranteed and farmers were encouraged to increase the output of any crops of their own choice. Farmers became mass producers of rice, even turning their own vegetable gardens into rice fields. Their output swelled to over 14 million tons in the late 1960s, a direct result of greater cultivated acreage and increased yield per unit area owing to improved cultivation techniques.

Three types of farm households developed: those engaging exclusively in agriculture (14.5 percent of the 4.2 million farm households in 1988, down from 21.5 percent in 1965); those deriving more than half their income from the farm (14.2 percent, down from 36.7 percent in 1965); and those mainly engaged in jobs other than farming (71.3 percent, up from 41.8 percent in 1965). As more and more farm families turned to nonfarming activities, the farm population declined (down from 4.9 million in 1975 to 4.8 million in 1988). The rate of decrease slowed in the late 1970s and 1980s, but the average age of farmers rose to fifty-one years by 1980, twelve years older than the average industrial employee.

The most striking feature of Japanese agriculture was the shortage of farmland. The 4.9 million hectares under cultivation constituted just 13.2 percent of the total land area in 1988. However, the land was intensively cultivated. Rice paddies occupied most of the countryside, whether on the alluvial plains, the terraced slopes, or the swampland and coastal bays. Nonrice farmlands shared such terraces and lower slopes and were planted with wheat and barley in the autumn and with sweet potatoes, vegetables, and dry rice in the summer. Intercropping was common: such crops were alternated with beans and peas.

Japanese agriculture has been characterized as a "sick" sector because it must contend with a variety of constraints, such as the rapidly diminishing availability of arable land and falling agricultural incomes. Nevertheless, the Japanese managed production at high levels. Agriculture was maintained through the use of technically advanced fertilizers and farm machinery, and a vast array of price supports. The nation's many agricultural cooperatives were in charge of purchasing grain according to prices indexed to the average wage rates in the nonagricultural sector. As a result, rice, wheat, and barley prices followed productivity trends in industry rather than in agriculture. This type of support system, enacted in 1960 along with the Basic Agricultural Law, resulted in large government rice stockpiles and high agricultural prices. Excessive rice production had an adverse effect on other crop production.

Japan's self-sufficiency ratio for grains other than rice fell below 10 percent in the 1970s and but rose to 14 percent in the mid- to late 1980s. The problem of surplus rice was further aggravated by extensive changes in the diets of many Japanese in the 1970s and 1980s. Even a major rice crop failure did not reduce the accumulated stocks by more than 25 percent of the reserve. In 1987, Japan was 71 percent self-sufficient in food, but only provided about 30 percent of its cereals and fodder needs.

Livestock raising was a minor activity. Demand for beef rose strongly in the 1980s and farmers often shifted from dairy farming to production of high-quality (and high-cost) beef. Throughout the 1980s, domestic beef production met over 60 percent of demand. In 1991, as a result of heavy pressure from the United States, Japan ended import quotas on beef as well as citrus fruit (see Import Policies, ch. 5). Milk cows were numerous in Hokkaidō, where 25 percent of farmers ran dairies, but milk cows were also raised in Iwate, in Tōhoku, and near Tokyo and Kōbe. Beef cattle were mostly concentrated in western Honshū, and Kyūshū. Hogs, the oldest domesticated animals raised for food, were found everywhere. Pork was the most popular meat.

The nation's forest resources, although abundant, had not been well developed to sustain a large lumber industry. Of the 24.5 million hectares of forests, 19.8 million were classified as active forests. Most often forestry was a part-time activity for farmers or small companies. About a third of all forests were owned by the government. Production was highest in Hokkaidō and in Aomori, Iwate, Akita, Fukushima, Gifu, Miyazaki, and Kagoshima prefectures. Nearly 33.5 million cubic meters of roundwood were produced in 1986, of which 98 percent was destined for industrial uses.

Japan was the world's largest fishing nation in tonnage of fish caught—12.5 million tons in 1987, up from 9.3 million tons in 1970 and 11.12 million tons in 1980. After the 1973 energy crisis, deep-sea fishing in Japan declined, with the annual catch in the 1980s averaging 2 million tons. Offshore fisheries accounted for an average of 50 percent of the nation's total fish catches in the late 1980s, although they experienced repeated ups and downs during that period. Coastal fisheries had smaller catches than northern sea fisheries in 1986 and 1987. As a whole, Japan's fish catches registered a slower growth in the late 1980s. By contrast, Japan's import of marine products increased greatly in the 1980s, surpassing 2 million tons in 1987. Japan also introduced the "culture and breed" fishing system or sea farming. In this system, artificial insemination and hatching techniques are used to breed fish and shellfish,

Mechanized agriculture at harvesttime
Courtesy The Mainichi Newspapers

which are then released into rivers or seas. These fish and shellfish are caught after they grow bigger. Salmon was one cultured fish. Japan is also one of the world's few whaling nations. As a member of the International Whaling Commission, the government pledged that its fleets would restrict their catch to international quotas, but it attracted international opprobrium for its failure to sign an agreement placing a moratorium on sperm whaling. Japan has more than 2,000 fishing ports, including Nagasaki, in southwest Kyūshū; Otaru, Kushiro, and Abashiri in Hokkaidō; and Yaezu and Misaki on the east coast of Honshū.

Living Standards

In general, Japanese consumers have benefited from the nation's economic growth, while in turn they have stimulated the economy through demand for sophisticated products, loyalty to domestically produced goods, and saving and pooling investment funds. But personal disposable income has not risen as fast as the economy as a whole in many years—at 1 percentage point less than average GNP growth in the late 1980s. Despite the hard work and sacrifice that have made Japan one of the wealthiest nations in the world, some Japanese feel they are "a rich nation, but a poor people." Such a negative view of the economy was prompted by the fact that the average consumer had to pay dearly for goods and services that were much cheaper elsewhere.

Real household expenditures did rise during Japan's economic growth. Living standards improved sharply in the 1970s and 1980s. The share of total family living expenses devoted to food dropped from 35 percent in 1970 to 27 percent in 1986, while net household savings, which averaged slightly over 20 percent in the mid-1970s, averaged between 15 and 20 percent in the 1980s. Japanese households thus had greater disposable income to pay for improved housing and other consumer items. The increase in disposable income partly explained the economic boom of the 1980s, which was pushed by explosive domestic demand.

Japanese income distribution in the 1980s, both before and after taxes, was among the most equitable in the world. An important factor in income distribution was that the lower income group was better off than in most industrialized countries.

Japanese homes, although they were relatively new, were much smaller and often had fewer amenities than those in other industrialized nations. Even though the percentage of residences with flush toilets jumped from 31.4 percent in 1973 to 65.8 percent in 1988, this figure was still far lower than in other industrialized states. In some primarily rural areas of Japan, it was still under 30 percent. Even 9.7 percent of homes built between 1986 and 1988 did not have flush toilets. People in other industrialized countries took central heating and either a shower or bath for granted, but many Japanese homes were lacking in all three. However, by 1988 only 9 percent of Japanese residences had no bathtub, a figure that had improved from nearly 27 percent in 1973. The alternative for many Japanese remained public baths, although these were gradually disappearing. Additionally, 81 percent of Japanese households used kerosene heaters as the main source of heat.

Japanese housing in the early 1990s was very expensive relative to annual income, but the high cost was somewhat offset by low interest rates and probable future income gains, making Japanese housing more affordable than it might appear. There were also many urban apartments found near public transportation that rented for as little as US$600 to US$800 a month in early 1990.

The Westernization of many areas of Japanese life included consuming a greater diversity of foods. After World War II, Japanese dietary patterns changed radically and came to resemble those of the West. While older Japanese still preferred a breakfast with traditional dishes—boiled rice, miso soup, and pickled vegetables—younger Japanese had toast and coffee. The Japanese diet improved along with other living standards. Average intake per day was 2,084

With more than 5 million units in use, vending machines have become a ubiquitous feature of Japanese daily life.
Courtesy Kenji Nachi and Hitachi

calories and 77.9 grams of protein, in the late 1980s. Of total protein intake, 26.5 percent came from cereals (including 18.4 percent from rice), 9.6 percent from pulses, 23.1 percent from fish, 14.8 percent from livestock products, 11 percent from eggs and milk, and 15 percent from other sources. Before World War II, the average annual consumption of rice was 140 kilograms per capita, but it fell to 72 kilograms in 1987. This development further exacerbated the problem of rice oversupply, leading to a huge rice stock and creating great deficits in the government's foodstuff control account. The government inaugurated several policies to switch to nonrice crops, but they met with limited success and rice remained in oversupply.

A negative aspect of Japan's economic growth was industrial pollution. Until the mid-1970s, both public and private sectors pursued economic growth with such single-mindedness that prosperity was accompanied by severe degradation of both the environment and quality of life (see Pollution, ch. 2).

Typically, Japanese consumers have been savers as well as buyers, partly because of habit, but by 1980 the consumer credit industry began to flourish. Younger families were particularly prone to take on debt. Housing was the largest single item for which consumers contracted loans. In 1989 families annually borrowed an estimated US$17,000 or about 23 percent of their average savings. Those who wished to buy houses and real estate needed an average US$242,600, of which they borrowed about US$129,000. But many younger families in the 1980s were giving up the idea of ever buying a house. This change led many young Japanese to spend part of their savings on trips abroad, expensive consumer items, and other luxuries. As one young worker put it, "If I can never buy a house, at least I can use my money to enjoy life now." As credit card and finance agency facilities expanded, the use of credit to procure other consumer durables was spreading. By 1989 the number of credit cards issued in Japan reached virtual parity with the population.

Japanese families still feel that saving for retirement is critical because of the relative inadequacy of official social security and private pension plans. The average family in 1989 had US$76,500 in savings, a figure far short of what was needed to cover the living expenses for retired individuals, although official pensions and retirement allowances did help cover the financial burdens of senior citizens. The annual living expenses for retired individuals in 1989 were estimated at US$22,800, half of which was received from government pensions and the rest from savings and retirement allowances. Senior citizens in their seventies had the largest savings, including deposits, insurance, and negotiable securities worth an estimated US$113,000 per person. In 1989 individuals in their twenties had savings amounting to US$23,800, while salaried workers in their thirties had US$66,000 in savings.

The Japanese consumer benefited most from the availability of compact, sophisticated consumer products that were popular exports. Television sets, watches, clothing, automobiles, household appliances, and personal computers were quality items that industry provided in quantity. In the late 1980s, virtually every Japanese family had one or more television sets, a washing machine, a refrigerator, small space heaters, and cameras. Sixty percent of Japanese homes in 1989 had air conditioning of some kind. Other popular items in the 1980s included electric ranges, video cassette recorders, video cameras, compact disc players, and personal computers. Most families had an automobile.

It is difficult to make cross-cultural comparisons, but one Japanese social scientist ranked Japan among a group of ten other industrialized nations according to a variety of variables. In this comparison, for which there is data from the mid-1970s to the late 1980s, Japan was better than average in terms of overall income distribution, per capita disposable income, traffic safety and crime, life expectancy and infant mortality, proportion of owner-occupied homes, work stoppages and labor unrest, worker absenteeism, and air pollution. Japan was below average for wage differentials by gender and firm size, labor's share of total manufacturing income, social security and unemployment benefits, weekly workdays and daily work hours, overall price of land and housing, river pollution, sewage facilities, and recreational park areas in urban centers. Some of these variables, especially pollution and increased leisure time, improved in the 1980s, and, in general, living standards in Japan were comparable to those of the world's wealthiest economies.

* * *

There are numerous excellent works on the Japanese economy from a variety of perspectives. Studies charting the nation's modernization from the prewar era include William W. Lockwood's *The State and Economic Enterprise in Japan,* G. C. Allen's *Japan's Economic Policy,* and Allen's *A Short Economic History of Modern Japan.* The best source for prewar data is *Patterns of Japanese Economic Development,* edited by Ohkawa Kazushi and Miyohei Shinohara. Among general works on the postwar economy are *Asia's New Giant,* edited by Hugh Patrick and Henry Rosovsky, and *The Japanese Economic System,* by Haitani Kanji. Both works are out of date, but give an accurate appraisal of the Japanese economy through the 1970s. More up-to-date works include *The Political Economy of Japan,* edited by Kozo Yamamura and Yasukichi Yasuba, Frank Gibney's *Miracle by Design,* Daniel A. Metraux's *The Japanese Economy and the American Businessman,* Edward J. Lincoln's *Japan: Facing Economic Maturity,* and Kunio Yoshihara's *Japanese Economic Development.* Rodney Clark's *The Japanese Company* is an excellent summary of research on the Japanese corporate system and labor-management relations. Some of the better books on Japanese management and labor include Michael A. Cusumano's *The Japanese Automobile Industry,* W. Mark Fruin's *Kikkoman: Company, Clan, and Community,* R. P. Dore's classic, *British Factory, Japanese Factory,* Andrew Gordon's *The Evolution of Labor Relations in Japan,* and Taishiro Shirai's *Contemporary Industrial Relations in Japan.* An excellent study of government-business relations is found in *Industrial Policy of Japan,* edited by Ryūtarō Komiya, Masahiro Okuno, and Kotaro Suzumura. An equally comprehensive work is Chalmers Johnson's *MITI and the Japanese Miracle.* Excellent coverage of Japan's financial and corporate worlds is found in Robert J. Ballon and Iwao Tomita's *The Financial Behavior of Japanese Corporations,* Aron Viner's *Inside Japan's Financial Markets,* and James C. Abeggleu and George Stalk, Jr.'s *Kaisha:*

The Japanese Corporation. The *Japan Statistical Yearbook* produced by Japan's Management and Coordination Agency provides up-to-date statistics. For up-to-date and sophisticated analyses, see the publications of the Washington-based Japan Economic Institute of America (JEI). Regular JEI publications include the monthly *Japan Economic Survey* and the weekly *JEI Report.* For a Japanese perspective on the economy, see articles in the English-language *Japan Economic Journal, Journal of Japanese Trade & Industry, Mitsubishi Bank Review, Japan Times Weekly, Japan Echo,* and *The Japan Economic Review* [all published in Tokyo]. There are frequent articles on the Japanese economy in *Far Eastern Economic Review* [Hong Kong] and *Asian Survey.* (For further information and complete citations, see Bibliography).

Chapter 5. International Economic Relations

Family crest using bamboo (take) leaves and stems, symbols of endurance and resilience

JAPAN IS BOTH a major trading nation and one of the largest international investors in the world. In many respects, international trade is the lifeblood of Japan's economy, and it is the window through which most people in the United States view Japan. Imports and exports totaling the equivalent of US$452 billion in 1988 meant that Japan was the world's third largest trading nation after the United States and the Federal Republic of Germany (West Germany). Trade was once the primary form of Japan's international economic relationships, but in the 1980s, its rapidly rising foreign investments added a new and increasingly important dimension, broadening the horizons of Japanese businesses and giving Japan new world prominence.

Japan's international economic relations in the first three decades after World War II were shaped largely by two factors: a relative lack of domestic raw materials and a determination to catch up with the industrial nations of the West. Because of Japan's lack of raw materials, its exports have consisted almost exclusively of manufactured goods, and raw materials have represented a large share of its imports. The country's sense of dependency and vulnerability has also been strong because of its lack of raw materials. Japan's determination to catch up with the West encouraged policies to move away from simple labor-intensive exports toward more sophisticated export products (from textiles in the 1950s to automobiles and consumer electronics in the 1980s), and pursue protectionist policies to limit foreign competition for domestic industries.

The sense of dependence on imported raw materials was especially strong in Japan during the 1970s, when crude petroleum and other material prices rose and supply was uncertain. Throughout much of the postwar period, in fact, Japanese government policy has aimed at generating sufficient exports to pay for raw material imports. During the 1980s, however, raw material prices fell and the feeling of vulnerability lessened. The 1980s also brought rapidly rising trade surpluses, so that Japan could export far more than was needed to balance its imports. With these developments, some of the resistance to manufactured imports, long considered luxuries in the relative absence of raw materials, began to dissipate.

By the 1980s, Japan had caught up. Now an advanced industrial nation, it faced new changes in its economy, on both domestic and international fronts, including demands to supply more foreign aid and to open its markets for imports. It had become a leader in the international economic system, through its success in certain export markets, its leading technologies, and its growth as a major investor around the world. These were epochal changes for Japan, after a century in which the main national motivation was to catch up with the West. These dramatic changes also fed domestic developments that were lessening the society's insularity and parochialism.

The processes through which Japan was becoming a key member of the international economic community were expected to continue in the 1990s—productivity continued to grow at a healthy pace, the country's international leadership in a number of industries remained unquestioned, and investments abroad continued to expand. Pressures were likely to lead to further openness to imports, increased aid to foreign countries, and involvement in the running of major international institutions, such as the International Monetary Fund (IMF—see Glossary). As Japan achieved a more prominent international position during the 1980s, it also generated considerable tension with its trade partners, and especially with the United States. These tensions will likely remain, but should be manageable as both sides continue to see economic benefits from the relationship.

Postwar Development

After the end of World War II, Japan's economy was in a shambles, and its international economic relations almost completely disrupted. Initially, imports were limited to essential food and raw materials, mostly financed by economic assistance from the United States. Because of extreme domestic shortages, exports did not begin to recover until the Korean War (1950–53), when special procurement by United States armed forces created boom conditions in indigenous industries. By 1954 economic recovery and rehabilitation were essentially complete. For much of the 1950s, however, Japan had difficulty exporting as much as it imported, leading to chronic trade and current account deficits. Keeping these deficits under control, so that Japan would not be forced to devalue its currency under the Bretton Woods System (see Glossary) of fixed exchange rates that prevailed at the time, was a primary concern of government officials. Stiff quotas and tariffs on imports were part of the policy response. By 1960, Japan accounted for 3.6 percent of all exports of noncommunist countries.

During the 1960s, the dollar value of exports grew at an average annual rate of 16.9 percent, more than 75 percent faster than the average rate of all noncommunist countries. By 1970 exports had risen to nearly 6.9 percent of all noncommunist-world exports.

The rapid productivity growth in manufacturing industries made Japanese products more competitive in world markets at the fixed exchange rate for the yen (for value of the yen—see Glossary) during the decade, and the chronic deficits that the nation faced in the 1950s had disappeared by the middle of the 1970s. International pressure to dismantle quota and tariff barriers mounted, and Japan began moving in this direction.

The 1970s brought major, wrenching changes for Japan's external relations. The decade began with the end of the fixed exchange rate for the yen (a change brought about mainly by rapidly rising Japanese trade and current account surpluses) and with a strong rise in the value of the yen under the new system of floating rates. Japan also faced sharply higher bills for imports of energy and other raw materials. The new exchange rates and the rise in raw material prices meant that the surpluses of the decade's beginning were lost, and large trade deficits followed in the wake of the oil price shocks of 1973 and 1979. Expanding the country's exports remained a priority in the face of these raw material supply shocks, and during the decade exports continued to expand at a high annual average rate of 21 percent (see Balance of Merchandise Trade, this ch.).

Most of the concerns of the 1970s diminished in the 1980s. Oil and other raw material prices fell dramatically, and Japan's trade deficits turned quickly to enormous trade surpluses by the middle of the decade. In response to these surpluses, the value of the yen rose against that of other currencies in the last half of the decade, but the surpluses proved surprisingly resilient to this change. The large surpluses, combined with foreign perceptions that Japan's import markets were still relatively closed, exacerbated tension between Japan and a number of its principal trading partners, especially the United States. A rapid increase in imports of manufactured goods after 1987 eased some of these tensions, but as the decade ended friction still continued.

Through most of the postwar period, foreign investment was not a significant part of Japan's external economic relations. Both inward and outward investments were carefully controlled by government regulations, which kept the investment flows small. These controls applied to direct investment in the creation of subsidiaries under the control of a parent company, portfolio investment, and lending. Controls were motivated by the desire to prevent foreigners (mainly Americans) from gaining ownership of the economy when Japan was in a weak position after World War II, and by concerns over the balance of payments deficits (see Capital Flows, this ch.). Beginning in the late 1960s, these controls were gradually loosened, and the process of deregulation accelerated and continued throughout the 1980s. The result was a dramatic increase in capital movements, with the biggest change occurring in outflows—investments by Japanese in other countries. By the end of the 1980s, Japan had become a major international investor. Because the country was a newcomer to the world of overseas investment, this development led to new forms of tension with other countries, including criticism of highly visible Japanese acquisitions in the United States and elsewhere.

Trade and Investment Institutions

The Ministry of International Trade and Industry

Japan's Ministry of International Trade and Industry (MITI) was formed in 1949 from the union of the Trade Agency and the Ministry of Commerce and Industry, in an effort to curb postwar inflation and provide government leadership and assistance for the restoration of industrial productivity and employment.

MITI has held primary responsibility for formulating and implementing international trade policy, although it has done so by seeking a consensus among interested parties, including the Ministry of Foreign Affairs, and the Ministry of Finance (see The Role of Government and Business, ch. 4). MITI has also coordinated trade policy with the Economic Planning Agency, the Bank of Japan, and the ministries of agriculture, forestry and fisheries, health and welfare, construction, transportation, and posts and telecommunications on issues affecting their interests. As trade issues broadened in scope, these other ministries became more important in international negotiating, so that in the late 1980s MITI had less control in formulating international trade policy than it had had in the 1950s and 1960s. The prime minister, the National Diet (Japan's legislature), and the Fair Trade Commission have also circumscribed MITI's operations.

MITI has been responsible not only in the areas of exports and imports, but also for all domestic industries and businesses not specifically covered by other ministries, for investments in plant and equipment, pollution control, energy and power, some aspects of foreign economic assistance, and consumer complaints. This span has allowed MITI to integrate conflicting policies, such as those on pollution control and export competitiveness, to minimize damage to export industries.

MITI has served as an architect of industrial policy, an arbiter on industrial problems and disputes, and a regulator. A major objective of the ministry has been to strengthen the country's industrial base. It has not managed Japanese trade and industry along the lines of a centrally planned economy, but it has provided industries with administrative guidance and other direction, both formal and informal, on modernization, technology, investments in new plants and equipment, and on domestic and foreign competition.

The close relationship between MITI and Japanese industry has led to foreign trade policy that often complements the ministry's efforts to strengthen domestic manufacturing interests. MITI facilitated the early development of nearly all major industries by providing protection from import competition, technological intelligence, help in licensing foreign technology, access to foreign exchange, or assistance in mergers.

These policies to promote domestic industry and to protect it from international competition were strongest in the 1950s and 1960s. As industry became stronger and as MITI lost some of its policy tools, such as control over allocation of foreign exchange, MITI's policies also changed. The success of Japanese exports and the tension it has caused in other countries led MITI to provide guidance on limiting exports of particular products to various countries. Starting in 1981, MITI presided over the establishment of voluntary restraints on automobile exports to the United States, to allay criticism from American manufacturers and their unions.

Similarly, MITI was forced to liberalize import policies, despite its traditional protectionist focus. During the 1980s, the ministry helped to craft a number of market-opening and import-promoting measures, including the creation of an import promotion office within the ministry. The close relationship between MITI and industry allowed the ministry to play such a role in fostering more open markets but conflict remained between the need to open markets and the desire to continue promoting new and growing domestic industries.

The Japan External Trade Organization

The Japan External Trade Organization (JETRO) was established by MITI in 1958 to consolidate Japan's efforts in export promotion. The government has provided more than half of JETRO's annual operating budget. As of 1989, JETRO maintained seventy-eight offices in fifty-seven countries, as well as thirty offices in Japan, with a total staff of 1,200.

Initially, JETRO's activities focused mainly on promoting exports to other countries. As exporters established themselves in world markets and the balance of trade turned from deficit to surplus, however, JETRO's role shifted to encompass more varied activities. These have included the furtherance of mutual understanding with trading partners, import promotion, liaison between small businesses in Japan and their overseas counterparts, and data dissemination. Import promotion services have included publications, promotion of trade fairs, seminars, and trade missions.

Trading Companies

A major Japanese innovation in international trade has been the development of large integrated general trading companies. These corporations were first organized during the late nineteenth century as part of the effort to replace the foreign companies dominating Japan's trade and to provide foreign marketing services to Japanese firms unfamiliar with the outside world.

At first, trading companies acted as specialized wholesalers for Japanese manufacturers in domestic and foreign markets and bought raw materials and other inputs for manufacturing operations. Later, trading companies also served as financial intermediaries, absorbed foreign exchange risk for their customers, provided technical advice to small firms whose products might be exported, and engaged in direct investment overseas, often to secure stable sources of supply.

After World War II, the trading companies developed some third-country trade, some of which did not involve Japanese products or firms. Such transactions included arranging for the sale of a United States chemical plant to the Soviet Union and importing Romanian urea into Bangladesh. By 1988, such offshore trade accounted for almost 20 percent of total sales of the nine largest trading companies in Japan.

In the 1980s, several thousand trading companies existed in Japan. The top nine companies, however, accounted for the bulk of the transactions. In fiscal year (FY—see Glossary) 1988, C. Itoh led with sales of ¥15.6 trillion, followed by Mitsui (¥14.8 trillion), Sumitomo (¥14.6 trillion), Marubeni (¥14.2 trillion), and Mitsubishi (¥13.8 trillion). Others in the top nine were Nissho Iwai, Tomen, Nichimen, and Kanematsu-Gosho. These companies were very important in Japan's foreign trade: in 1988 they together handled 42 percent of exports and 74 percent of imports.

These companies were best at handling large-volume bulk products, such as raw materials. They faced some difficulties in the 1970s and 1980s with fluctuations in international raw material markets, but they continued to play a very important role in Japan's international trade. During the 1980s, they increasingly acted through direct investment.

Financial Institutions

For most of the postwar period, Japan's financial institutions operated in a severely regulated environment: most interest rates were controlled, the type of business these institutions could engage in was narrowly circumscribed, and few international transactions were possible. Beginning in the 1970s, these controls began to loosen, and financial institutions rapidly expanded their international activities. By the end of the 1980s, they were major international players.

The major international players were "city" banks (the thirteen largest banks in Japan, which operated nationwide branches), investment houses, and life insurance companies, which invested heavily in pension funds abroad in the 1980s (see The Financial System, ch. 4). In 1988, the nine largest banks in the world, measured by total assets, were Japanese banks. These banks opened branches abroad, acquired existing foreign banks, and became engaged in new activities, such as underwriting Euro-yen bond issues. The investment houses also increased overseas activities, especially participating in the United States Treasury bond market (where as much as 25 to 30 percent of each new issue was purchased by Japanese investors in the late 1980s). The life insurance companies moved heavily into foreign investments as deregulation allowed them to do so and as their resources increased through the spread of fully funded pension funds.

As of March 1989, the five largest city banks in Japan (in order of total fund volume) were Dai-Ichi Kangyo Bank, Sumitomo Bank, Fuji Bank, Mitsubishi Bank, and Sanwa Bank. The four largest investment houses, which dominated the securities business, were Nomura, Daiwa, Nikko, and Yamaichi.

Besides these private institutions, there were a number of government-owned financial institutions in the late 1980s. Of these, the Japan Export-Import Bank (Exim Bank) was the only one with an international focus. The Exim Bank provided financing for trade between Japan and developing countries, performing the function of export-import banks run by governments in other countries (including the United States), although its participation was possibly greater.

As Japan became a more important international financial power, Tokyo became a world financial center. In April 1989, the average daily volume of transactions in the Tokyo foreign exchange market was US$115 billion, not far behind the US$129 billion in New York. The Tokyo Securities and Stock Exchange also rivaled the New York Stock Exchange in daily volume, overtaking New

York in 1988 to become the world's largest stock exchange in terms of the combined market value of outstanding shares and capitalization.

Foreign Aid Institutions

In 1990 Japan had three government institutions involved in disbursing foreign aid: the Japan International Cooperation Agency (JICA), the Overseas Economic Cooperation Fund (OECF), and the Exim Bank. JICA was responsible for technical cooperation; the OECF was responsible for soft loans; and the Exim Bank had not only a trade-financing role but also became increasingly involved in lending for aid programs. The Exim Bank, for example, was the government agency chosen to carry out US$10 billion in cofinancing with the World Bank (see Glossary) and IMF in the 1989 Brady Plan for partial relief of Mexico's international debt.

International Trade and Development Institutions

Japan was a member of the United Nations (UN), IMF, Organisation for Economic Co-operation and Development (OECD), and General Agreement on Tariffs and Trade (GATT—see Glossary). It also participated in the international organizations focusing on economic development, including the World Bank and the Asian Development Bank.

As a member of the IMF and World Bank, for example, Japan played a role in the effort during the 1980s to address the international debt crisis brought on by the inability of certain developing countries to service their foreign debts as raw material prices fell and their economies stagnated. As a member of the IMF, Japan also cooperated with other countries in moderating the short-run volatility of the yen and participated in discussions on strengthening the international monetary system.

Japan's membership in the OECD has constrained its foreign economic policy to some extent. When Japan joined the OECD in 1966, it was obliged to agree to OECD principles on capital liberalization, an obligation that led Japan to begin the process of liberalizing its many tight controls on investment flows into and out of Japan. Japan was also a participant in the OECD's "gentlemen's agreement" on guidelines for government-supported export credits, which placed a floor on interest rates and other terms for loans to developing countries from government-sponsored export-import banks.

GATT has provided the basic structure through which Japan has negotiated detailed international agreements on import and

A Japanese tuna-fishing ship on the open sea
Courtesy The Mainichi Newspapers

export policies. Although Japan had been a member of GATT since 1955, it retained reservations to some GATT articles, permitting it to keep in place stiff quota restrictions until the early 1960s. Japan took its GATT obligations seriously, however, and a number of American disputes with Japan over its import barriers were successfully resolved by obtaining GATT rulings, with which Japan complied. Japan also negotiated bilaterally with countries on economic matters of mutual interest.

The international organization with the strongest Japanese presence has been the Asian Development Bank, the multilateral lending agency established in 1966 that made soft loans to developing Asian countries. Japan and the United States have had the largest voting rights in the Asian Development Bank and Japan has traditionally filled the presidency.

As Japan became a greater international financial power in the 1980s, its role in financing these trade and development institutions grew. Previously, the government had been a very quiet participant in these organizations, but as its financial role increased, pressure to expand voting rights and play a more active policy role mounted. By the end of the 1980s, Japan's voting rights in the World Bank had increased, and discussions were proceeding on a similar change in the IMF.

Foreign Trade Policies

Export Policies

For many years, export promotion was a large issue in Japanese government policy. Government officials recognized that Japan needed to import to grow and develop, and it needed to generate exports to pay for those imports. After the war, Japan had difficulty exporting enough to pay for its imports until the mid-1960s, and resulting deficits were the justification for export promotion programs and import restrictions.

The belief in the need to promote exports was strong and part of Japan's self-image as a ''processing nation.'' A processing nation must import raw materials, but is able to pay for the imports by adding value to them and exporting some of the output. Nations grow stronger economically by moving up the industrial ladder to produce products with greater value added to the basic inputs. Rather than letting markets accomplish this movement on their own, the Japanese government felt the economy should be guided in this direction through industrial policy.

Japan's methods of promoting exports took two paths. The first was to develop world-class industries that could initially substitute for imports and then compete in international markets. The second was to provide incentives for firms to export.

During the first two decades after World War II, export incentives took the form of a combination of tax relief and government assistance to build export industries. After joining the IMF in 1964, however, Japan had to drop its major export incentive—the total exemption of export income from taxes—to comply with IMF procedures. It did maintain into the 1970s, however, special tax treatment of costs for market development and export promotion.

Once chronic trade deficits came to an end in the mid-1960s, the need for export promotion policies diminished. Virtually all export tax incentives were eliminated over the course of the 1970s. Even JETRO, whose initial function was to assist smaller firms with overseas marketing, saw its role shift toward import promotion and other activities. In the 1980s, Japan continued to use industrial policy to promote the growth of new, more sophisticated industries, but direct export promotion measures were no longer part of the policy package.

The 1970s and 1980s saw the emergence of policies to restrain exports in certain industries. The great success of some Japanese export industries created a backlash in other countries, either because of their success per se or because of allegations of unfair competitive practices. Under GATT guidelines, nations have been reluctant to raise tariffs or impose import quotas—quotas violate the guidelines and raising tariffs goes against the general trend among industrial nations. Instead, they have resorted to convincing the exporting country to "voluntarily" restrain exports of the offending product. In the 1980s, Japan was quite willing to carry out such export restraints. Among Japan's exports to the United States, steel, color television sets, and automobiles all were subject to such restraints at various times.

Import Policies

Japan began the postwar period with heavy import barriers. Virtually all products were subject to government quotas, many faced high tariffs, and MITI had authority over the allocation of the foreign exchange companies needed to pay for any import. These policies were justified at the time by the weakened position of Japanese industry and the country's chronic trade deficits.

By the late 1950s, Japan's international trade had regained its prewar level, and its balance of payments displayed sufficient strength for its rigid protectionism to be increasingly difficult to justify. The IMF and GATT strongly pressured Japan to free its commerce and international payments system. Beginning in the 1960s, the government adopted a policy of gradual trade liberalization, easing import quotas, reducing tariff rates, freeing transactions in foreign exchange, and admitting foreign capital into Japanese industries, which has continued through the 1980s.

The main impetus for change throughout has been international obligation, response to foreign, rather than domestic, pressure. The result has been a prolonged, reluctant process of reducing barriers, which has frustrated many of Japan's trading partners.

Japan has been a participant in the major rounds of tariff-cutting negotiations under the GATT framework—the Kennedy Round completed in 1967, the Tokyo Round completed in 1979, and the Uruguay Round, which began in the 1980s and was scheduled for completion in 1990. As a result of these agreements, tariffs in Japan fell to a low level on average. Upon complete implementation of the Tokyo Round agreement, Japan had the lowest average tariff level among industrial countries—2.5 percent, compared with 4.2 percent for the United States and 4.6 percent for the European Community.

Japan's quotas also dropped. From 490 items under quota in 1962, Japan had only 27 items under quota in the mid-1980s, and that number dropped again late in the decade to 22 with further agreements scheduled to come into effect in the early 1990s, which would reduce the number again. But those products still under quota proved to be highly visible and were the object of complaints by exporting countries. The reduction of controlled items in the late 1980s resulted from Japan's loss of a GATT case brought by the United States concerning import restrictions on twelve agricultural products. In addition, heavy pressure from the United States led to an agreement that Japan would end import quotas on beef and citrus fruit in 1991. The one restricted product that continued to prompt objections from other countries at the end of the decade was rice, imports of which were prohibited. Rice has traditionally been the mainstay of the Japanese diet, and farm organizations have played upon the theme's deep cultural importance as a reason for prohibiting imports. Farm organizations also have a disproportionate political voice because of the shift of the population to the cities without any significant redistricting for seats in the Diet (see The Electoral System, ch. 6). Even on rice, however, it appeared by 1990 that political forces were moving, under foreign pressure, in the direction of a gradually opening to trade.

Despite Japan's rather good record on tariffs and quotas, it continued to be the target of complaints and pressure from its trading partners during the 1980s. Many complaints revolved around nontariff barriers other than quotas—standards, testing procedures, government procurement, and other policies that could be used to restrain imports. These barriers, by their very nature, were often difficult to document, but complaints were frequent.

In 1984 the United States government initiated intensive talks with Japan on four product areas: forest products, telecommunications equipment and services, electronics, and pharmaceuticals and medical equipment. The Market Oriented Sector Selective (MOSS) talks aimed at routing out all overt and informal barriers to imports in these areas. The negotiations lasted throughout 1985 and achieved modest success.

Supporting the view that Japanese markets remained difficult to penetrate, statistics showed that the level of manufactured imports in Japan as a share of gross national product (GNP—see Glossary) was still far below the level in other developed countries during the 1980s. Frustration with the modest results of the MOSS process and similar factors led to provisions in the United States Trade Act of 1988 aimed at Japan. Under the "Super 301" provision, nations were to be named as unfair trading partners and specific products chosen for negotiation, as appropriate, with retaliation against the exports of these nations should negotiations fail to provide satisfactory results. Japan was named an unfair trading nation in 1989, and negotiations began on forest products, supercomputers, and telecommunications satellites (see United States and Canada, this ch.).

By the end of the 1980s, however, some internally generated changes in import policy appeared to be under way in Japan. The rapid appreciation of the yen after 1985, which made imports more attractive, stimulated a domestic debate over nontariff barriers and other structural features of the economy impeding imports. Greater openness in policies and structures began to be sought in response to domestic pressures rather than in response to foreign pressure and international obligation.

External pressure for change also increased when the United States initiated a series of bilateral talks in 1989 parallel to negotiations under the "Super 301" provision. These new talks, known as the Structural Impediments Initiative, focused on structural features in Japan that seemed to impede imports in ways outside the normal scope of trade negotiations. Issues raised in the Structural Impediments Initiative, and by the Japanese themselves in domestic discussions, included the distribution system (in which manufacturers continued to have unusually strong control over wholesalers and retailers handling their products, inhibiting newcomers, especially foreign ones) and investment behavior that made it very difficult for foreign firms to acquire Japanese firms. These discussions highlighted some of the fundamental differences in the Japanese and United States economies, but how quickly change might result from the talks was unclear.

Level and Commodity Composition of Trade

Exports

Japanese exports grew rapidly in the 1960s and 1970s, but growth slowed considerably during the 1980s. Over these decades, both the composition and the reputation of products from Japan changed profoundly.

Because of the success of certain exports, Japan was often viewed as a heavily export-dependent nation. As a percentage of GNP, however, the country exports less than other major trading countries of the world. In 1988, for example, it exported 9.3 percent of its GNP compared with 15.6 percent for Italy, 16.9 percent for France, 17.8 percent for Britain, 24.4 percent for Canada, 26.8 percent for West Germany, and 43.4 percent for the Netherlands. The United States exported a smaller share of its GNP at 6.6 percent. Japan was, therefore, less dependent on foreign trade than many other industrialized countries of the world. In certain industries, however, export dependence was high. In 1988, for example, just over half of all automobiles produced in Japan were exported.

The growth of Japanese exports during the 1960s and 1970s was truly phenomenal. Beginning in 1960 at US$4.1 billion, merchandise exports grew at an average annual rate of 16.9 percent in the 1960s and at one of 21 percent in the 1970s. From 1981 to 1988, however, export growth was 7.4 percent, about one-third the level of the 1970s. By 1988 merchandise exports reached US$264.9 billion (see table 24, Appendix).

The growth in exports can be viewed in terms of both pull and push factors. The pull came from increasing demand for Japanese products as the United States and other foreign markets grew and as trade barriers in major market countries were reduced. Another pull factor was the price competitiveness of Japanese products. From 1960 to 1970, Japan's export price index increased by only 4 percent, reflecting the high rate of productivity growth in the manufacturing industries producing export products. Inflation was higher in the 1970s, but export prices were still only 45 percent higher in 1980 than in 1970 (growing at an average annual rate of less than 4 percent), considerably lower than world inflation. The 1980s began with another short burst of inflation because of oil price increases in 1979, but by 1988 Japanese export prices were actually 23 percent lower than in 1980, offsetting much of the price increase of the 1980s. This record enhanced the international price competitiveness of Japanese products.

During the 1950s, Japanese export products had a reputation for poor quality. However, this image changed dramatically during the 1970s. Japanese steel, ships, watches, television receivers, automobiles, semiconductors, and many other goods developed a reputation for being manufactured to high standards and under strict quality control. The Japanese were the acknowledged world leaders for quality and design in the 1980s for some of these products. This rise in product quality also increased demand for Japanese exports.

The push behind Japan's exports came from manufacturers. Many recognized that to reach efficient levels of production they needed to adopt a global approach. Manufacturers concentrated on the domestic market (often protected from foreign products) until they reached internationally competitive levels and domestic markets were saturated. Often helped by the large general trading companies, manufacturers aggressively attacked foreign markets when they felt able to compete globally. This push factor partially accounted for the extraordinarily high level of export growth in the 1970s, when the domestic economy slowed; increasing exports was

JT-60 critical plasma equipment used in nuclear fusion testing
Courtesy Embassy of Japan, Washington

a way for manufacturers to continue expanding despite the more sluggish domestic market.

Exports included a wide variety of products, virtually all of which were processed to some degree (see table 25; table 26, Appendix). After the war, the composition of exports shifted through technological progression. Primary products, light manufactures, and crude items, which predominated during the 1950s, were gradually eclipsed by heavy industrial goods, complex machinery and equipment, and consumer durables, which required large capital investments and advanced technology to produce. This process was illustrated vividly in the case of textiles, which composed more than 30 percent of Japanese exports in 1960, but less than 3 percent by 1988. Iron and steel products, which grew rapidly in the 1960s to become nearly 15 percent of exports by 1970, also declined to less than 6 percent of exports by 1988. Over the same period, however, exports of motor vehicles rose from under 2 percent to over 18 percent of the total. In 1988 Japan's major exports were motor vehicles, office machinery, iron and steel, semiconductors and other electronic components, and scientific and optical equipment.

Imports

During the 1960s and 1970s, imports grew in tandem with

exports, at an average annual rate of 15.4 percent during the 1960s and 22.2 percent during the 1970s. In a sense, import growth over much of this period was constrained by exports because exports generated the foreign exchange to purchase the imports. During the 1980s, however, import growth lagged far behind exports, at an average annual rate of only 2.9 percent from 1981 to 1988. This low level of import growth led to the large trade surpluses that emerged in the 1980s.

In general, Japan has not imported an unusually large amount as a share of its GNP, but it has been highly dependent on imports for a variety of critical raw materials. Japan has by no means been the only industrialized nation dependent on imported raw materials, but it has depended on imports for a wider variety of materials, and often for a higher share of its needs for these materials. The country imported, for example, 50 percent of its caloric intake of food and about 30 percent of the total value of food consumed in the late 1980s. It also depended on imports for about 85 percent of its total energy needs (including all of its petroleum and 89 percent of its coal) and nearly all of its iron, copper, and lead ore and nickel.

The long-term growth in imports was facilitated by several major factors. The most important was general growth in the Japanese economy and income levels. Rising real incomes increased demand for imports, both those consumed directly and those entering into production. Another factor was the shift in the economy toward greater reliance on imported raw materials. Primary energy sources in the late 1940s, for example, were domestic coal and charcoal. The shift to imported oil and coal as major energy sources did not come until the late 1950s and 1960s. The small size and poor quality of many of the mineral deposits in Japan, combined with innovations in ocean transportation, such as bulk ore carriers, meant that as the economy grew, demand outstripped domestic supply and cheaper imports were utilized.

The price of imports was also a factor in their growth. In 1973 Japan's import price index was at essentially the same level as in 1955, partly because of the appreciation of the yen after 1971, which reduced the yen price of imports, but also because of the reduced costs of ocean shipping and stable prices for food and raw materials. For the rest of the 1970s, however, import prices skyrocketed, climbing 219 percent from 1973 to 1980. This dramatic price rise, especially for petroleum but by no means confined to it, was responsible for the rapid growth of the dollar value of imports during the 1970s, despite the slower growth of the economy. During the 1980s, import prices fell again, especially for petroleum, dropping by 44 percent from 1980 to 1988. Reflecting these price movements, the dollar value of petroleum imports rose from about US$2.8 billion in 1970 to nearly US$58 billion in 1980, and then fell by half, to less than US$26 billion by 1988 (see table 27; table 28, Appendix).

A third factor affecting imports was trade liberalization. Reduced tariff rates and a weakening of other overt trade barriers meant that imports should have been able to compete more fully in Japan's markets. The extent to which this was true, however, was subject to much debate among analysts. The share of manufactured imports in the GNP changed very little from 1970 to 1985, suggesting that falling import barriers had little impact on the propensity to purchase foreign products. Falling trade barriers might become more significant in the 1990s as liberalization continues.

Yet another factor determining import levels was the exchange rate. After the ending of the Bretton Woods System in 1971, the yen appreciated against the dollar and other currencies. The appreciation of the yen made imports less expensive to Japan, but it had a complex effect on total imports. Demand for raw material imports was not affected much by price changes (at least in the short run). Demand for manufactured goods, however, was more responsive to price changes. Much of the rapid increase in imports of manufactures after 1985, when the yen began to appreciate rapidly, can be attributed to this exchange rate effect.

All factors combined led to the rapid growth of imports in the 1960s and 1970s and their very slow growth in the 1980s. Rapid economic growth combined with stable import prices and the shift toward imported raw materials brought high import growth in the 1960s. The big jump in raw material prices in the 1970s kept import growth high despite lower economic growth. In the 1980s, falling raw material prices, a relatively weak yen, and continued modest economic growth kept import growth low in the first half of the decade. Import growth finally accelerated in the second half of the 1980s, when raw material prices stopped falling and as the rise in the value of the yen encouraged manufactured imports.

Japan imported a wide range of products, although energy sources, raw materials, and food were the major items. Mineral fuels, for example, rose from under 17 percent of all imports in 1960 to a high of nearly 50 percent in 1980. They had declined to under 21 percent by 1988. These shifts show the enormous impact of price changes on imports. Swings in imports of other raw materials were far less dramatic, and many declined over time as a share of total imports. Metal ores and scrap, for example, declined steadily from 15 percent in 1960 to less than 5 percent in 1988, reflecting the changing structure of the economy, which moved away from basic metal manufactures to higher value-added industries. Textile materials also dropped from 17 percent of total imports in 1960 to under 2 percent in 1988, as the textile industry became less important and imports of finished textiles increased. Foodstuffs, on the other hand, were relatively steady as a share of imports, rising from just over 12 percent in 1960 to less than 16 percent in 1988.

Manufactured goods—chemicals, machinery and equipment, and miscellaneous commodities—gained as a share of imports, but the variation among them was considerable. Manufactures were about 22 percent of total imports in 1960, remained at just under 23 percent in 1980, and then expanded to 49 percent by 1988. Imports of textiles, nonferrous metals, and iron and steel products all showed significant gains, for the same reasons that the raw material imports to produce them had declined. However, chemical and machinery and equipment imports showed little increase in share until after 1985.

The heavy dependency on raw materials that characterized Japan until the mid-1980s reflected both their absence in Japan and the process of import-substitution in which Japan favored domestic industries over imports. The desire to restrict manufactured imports was intensified by the knowledge that the nation needed strong manufacturing industries to generate exports to pay for needed raw material imports. Only with the appreciation of the yen after 1985, and the drop in petroleum and other raw material prices, did this sense of vulnerability ease. These trends were reflected in the rising share of manufactures in imports in the late 1980s.

Balance of Merchandise Trade

Between 1960 and 1964, Japan incurred annual trade deficits (based on a customs clearance for imports) ranging from US$0.4 billion to US$1.6 billion. The era of chronic trade deficit ended in 1965, and by 1969, with a positive balance of almost US$1 billion, Japan was widely regarded as a surplus trading nation. In 1971 the surplus reached US$4 billion, and its rapid increase was a main factor behind the United States decision to devalue the dollar and pressure Japan to revalue the yen—events that led quickly to the end of the Bretton Woods System of fixed exchange rates. By 1972 Japan's surplus had climbed to US$5 billion, despite the revaluation of the yen in 1971.

The jump in prices of petroleum and other raw materials during 1973 plunged the balance of trade into deficit, and in 1974 the deficit reached US$6.6 billion. With strong export growth, however, this was reversed to a surplus of US$2.4 billion by 1976. The surplus reached a record US$18.2 billion in 1978, promoting considerable tension between the United States and Japan.

In 1979 petroleum prices jumped again, and Japan's trade balance again turned to deficit, reaching US$10.7 billion in 1980. Once again rapid export growth and stagnant imports returned Japan quickly to surplus by 1981. From that time through 1986, Japan's trade surplus grew explosively, to a peak of US$82.7 billion. This unprecedented trade surplus resulted from the moderate annual rise in exports and drop in imports noted above. Underlying these trade developments was the weakness of the yen against other currencies, which enhanced export price competitiveness and dampened import demand.

After 1986 the dollar value of Japan's trade surplus declined, to US$77.6 billion in 1988. This decline came as the yen finally appreciated strongly against the dollar (beginning in 1985) and as a rapid rise in manufactured imports began to offset the large drop in the value of raw material imports. Nevertheless, the surplus showed surprising resilience in the face of the strengthening of the yen.

Underlying trends throughout the 1970s and 1980s was the fundamental strength of Japan's export sector. Under the fixed exchange rates of the 1960s, exports became progressively more competitive on world markets, lifting the country out of the persistent trade deficits that had continued into the early years of the decade. During the 1970s, rapid export expansion extricated the country from the deficits immediately following the two oil price shocks of 1973 and 1979. Continuing export strength then drove the nation to the extraordinary trade surpluses of the 1980s, as the temporary burden of costly oil imports waned.

Japan's fundamental strength in world markets required its fear of vulnerability and opposition to manufactured imports to be reassessed. In the early 1980s, fear of vulnerability remained strong and fed the continuation of policies and behavior that kept manufactured imports unusually low compared with those of other industrial nations. Only with the large decline in raw material prices and the explosion of trade surpluses did policies and behavior begin to change. These changes would not necessarily bring down the trade surplus, but would help diminish tension between Japan and its trading partners.

Balance of Payments Accounts

Services and the Current Account

Japan has traditionally run a deficit in services. Trade in services includes transportation (freight and passenger fares), insurance, travel expenditures, royalties, licensing fees, and income from investments. The steadily rising deficit in services from 1960 through 1980, from US$99 million in 1960, to nearly US$1.8 billion in 1970 and to more than US$11 billion in 1980, can be attributed to rising royalty and licensing payments for Japan's acquisition of technology from other industrial countries and to rising deficits in the trade-related services of transportation and insurance. The transportation deficit rose after the 1960s, as rapidly climbing labor costs made Japanese-flag vessels less competitive, leading to greater use of foreign-flag carriers (including many flag-of-convenience vessels actually owned by Japanese interests).

Beginning in the late 1970s, however, rapidly growing overseas investments began to increase the inflow of investment income. The investments themselves are part of capital flows in the balance of payments, but repatriation of earnings on those investments is part of the services account. From a small surplus of US$900 million in 1978, the balance on investment income (earnings from abroad minus the earnings of foreigners in Japan) grew to US$21 billion by 1988. The tremendous growth in Japanese investments abroad had not been matched by any such growth of foreign investment in Japan.

Despite the rapid growth in Japan's investment income surplus, the country's total services account remained in deficit in the 1980s. It did diminish in the first half of the decade, but then total deficits increased again, from US$4.9 billion in 1986 to nearly US$11.2 billion in 1988. Offsetting the rising surpluses in investment income were an enormous jump in the deficit on overseas travel and purchases by Japanese citizens while abroad. The net balance on passenger transportation deteriorated from a net deficit of US$1.3 billion in 1985 to US$3.7 billion by 1988, and foreign travel and spending (purchases of goods and services by individuals while abroad) increased from US$3.7 billion to US$15.8 billion over the same short time. This burst of overseas travel and spending came as the movement in the exchange rate made foreign travel more attractive to the Japanese. It also reflected the rising perception among Japanese consumers that prices for a wide range of manufactured items were substantially lower abroad than at home, giving them an incentive to purchase these items while out of their country. By the end of the decade, the number of Japanese taking overseas trips approached 10 million annually.

One other nonmerchandise transaction is included in the current account balance—net transfers. These represent the flow of foreign aid from Japan. As the country supplied more foreign aid, the deficit in this account rose. Much of the change occurred in the 1980s, with the deficit growing from US$1.5 billion in 1980

Mitsubishi Heavy Industries launches the mail steamer California Mercury. *Courtesy The Mainichi Newspapers*

to US$4.1 billion by 1988. It was expected to grow further, with Japan's foreign aid expanding in the 1990s.

Adding net exports of services and net transfers to the merchandise trade balance, with imports measured free on board (f.o.b.), rather than as customs, insurance, and freight (c.i.f.), gives the balance on current account. Movements in Japan's current account balance have generally mirrored those of the merchandise trade balance considered above, although deficits in services and net transfers have offset the surpluses somewhat. Japan began to register surpluses in the current account in 1965, which later continued to rise, though they were punctuated by short-term deficits following the two oil price hikes in 1973 and 1979.

During the 1980s Japan's current account balance shot from a record deficit of US$10.7 billion in 1980 to a record surplus of US$87 billion in 1987. As a share of GNP, this surplus reached a peak of 4.4 percent in 1985, a large value for a current account surplus. The appreciation of the yen against the dollar and other currencies beginning in 1985 was slow to have any impact on the dollar value of the current account surplus, although it did decline by US$8 billion in 1988.

Capital Flows

Capital movements offset the surpluses or deficits in the current account. A current account surplus, for example, implies that rather than using all the foreign currency earned by selling exports to buy imports, corporations and individuals chose to invest the money in foreign-currency-denominated assets instead. As measured in Japan's balance of payments data, capital movements consist of long- and short-term investments, and movements in official foreign exchange reserves and private bank accounts. Capital movements include loans, portfolio investments in corporate stock, and direct investment (establishment or purchase of subsidiaries abroad). A capital outflow occurs when a Japanese individual or corporation makes a loan, buys foreign stock, or establishes a subsidiary abroad. A capital inflow occurs when foreigners engage in these operations in Japan.

After World War II, Japan's return to world capital markets as a borrower was slow and deliberate. Even before the war, Japan did not participate in world capital markets to the same extent as the United States or West European countries. Caution and control remained strong until well into the 1970s, when the nation was no longer a net debtor. Since that time, deregulation has proceeded steadily and capital flows have grown rapidly. The rapid growth of investment abroad in the 1980s had made Japan the largest net investor in the world by the end of the decade.

As might be expected of a country recovering from a major wartime defeat, Japan remained a net debtor nation until the mid-1960s, although it was never as far in debt as many of the more recently developing countries. By 1967, however, Japanese investments overseas had begun to exceed foreign investments in Japan, changing Japan from a net debtor to a net creditor nation. The country remained a modest net creditor until the 1980s, when its creditor position expanded explosively, altering Japan's relationship to the rest of the world.

In the Japanese balance of payments data, these changes are most readily seen in the long-term capital account. During the first half of the 1960s, this account generally showed small net inflows of capital (as did the short-term capital account). From 1965 on, however, the long-term capital account consistently showed an outflow, ranging from US$1 billion to US$12 billion during the 1970s. The sharp shift in the balance of payments brought about by the oil price hike at the decade's end produced an unusual net inflow of long-term capital in 1980 of US$2.3 billion, but thereafter the outflow resumed and grew enormously. From nearly US$10 billion in 1981, the annual net outflow of long-term capital reached nearly US$137 billion in 1987 and then dropped slightly, to just over US$130 billion, in 1988 (see table 29, Appendix).

Short-term capital flows in the balance of payments do not show so clear a picture. These more volatile flows have generally added to the net capital outflow, but in some years movements in international differentials in interest rates or other factors led to a net inflow of short-term capital.

The other significant part of capital flows in the balance of payments is the movement in gold and foreign exchange reserves held by the government, which represent the funds held by the Bank of Japan to intervene in foreign exchange markets to affect the value of the yen. In the 1970s, the size of these markets became so large that any government intervention was only a small share of total transactions, but Japan and other governments used their reserves to influence exchange rates when necessary. In the second half of the 1970s, for example, foreign exchange reserves rose rapidly, from a total of US$12.8 billion in 1975 to US$33 billion by 1978, as the Bank of Japan sold yen to buy dollars in foreign exchange markets to slow or stop the rise in the yen's value, fearful that such a rise would adversely affect Japanese exports. The same operation occurred on a much larger scale after 1985. From US$26.5 billion in 1985 (a level little changed from the decade's beginning), exchange reserves had climbed to almost US$98 billion by 1988. This intervention was similarly inspired by concern about the yen's high value.

The combination of net outflows of long- and short-term capital and rising holdings of foreign exchange by the central government produced enormous change in Japan's accumulated holdings of foreign assets, compared to foreigners' holdings of assets in Japan. As a result, from a net asset position of US$11.5 billion in 1980 (meaning that Japanese investors held US$11.5 billion more in foreign assets than foreigners held in Japan), Japan's international net assets had grown to nearly US$292 billion by 1988 (see table 30, Appendix). Japanese assets abroad grew from nearly US$160 billion in 1980 to almost US$1.5 trillion by 1988, a ninefold increase. Liabilities—investments by foreigners in Japan—expanded somewhat more slowly, about sevenfold, from US$148 billion in 1980 to US$1.1 trillion in 1988. Dramatic shifts were seen in portfolio securities purchases—stocks and bonds—in both directions. Japanese purchases of foreign securities went from only US$4.2 billion in 1976 to over US$21 billion in 1980 and to US$427 billion by 1988. Although foreign purchases of Japanese securities also expanded, the growth was much slower, and the total was still under US$255 billion in 1988.

Capital flows have been heavily affected by government policy. During the 1950s and the first half of the 1960s, when Japan faced chronic current account deficits, concern over maintaining a high credit rating in international capital markets and fear of having to devalue the currency and of foreign ownership of Japanese companies all led to tight controls over both inflow and outflow of capital. As part of these controls, for example, government severely restricted foreign direct investment in Japan, but encouraged licensing agreements with foreign firms to obtain access to their technology. As Japan's current account position strengthened in the 1960s, however, the nation came under increasing pressure to liberalize its tight controls.

When Japan became a member of the OECD in 1966, it also had to agree to liberalize its capital markets. This process began in 1967 and continued in the early 1990s. Decontrol of international capital flows was aided in 1980, when the new Foreign Exchange and Foreign Control Law went into effect. In principle, all external economic transactions were free of control, unless specified otherwise. In practice, a wide range of transactions continued to be subject to some form of formal or informal control by the government.

Because of continuing capital controls, negotiations between Japan and the United States were held, producing an agreement in 1984, the Yen-Dollar Accord. This agreement led to additional liberalizing measures that were implemented over the next several years. Many of these changes concerned the establishment and functioning of markets for financial instruments in Japan (such as a short-term treasury bill market) rather than the removal of international capital controls per se. This approach was taken because of American concerns that foreign investment in Japan was impeded by a lack of various financial instruments in the country and by the government's continued control of interest rates for many of those instruments that did exist. As a result of the agreement, for example, interest rates on large bank deposits were decontrolled, and the minimum denomination for certificates of deposit was lowered.

By the end of the 1980s, barriers to capital flow were no longer a major issue in United States-Japan relations. However, imbalances in the flows and in accumulated totals of capital investment, with Japan becoming a large world creditor, were emerging as new areas of tension. This tension was exacerbated by the fact that the United States became the world's largest net debtor at the same time that Japan became its largest net creditor. Nevertheless, no policy decisions had been made by the end of the 1980s that would restrict the flow of Japanese capital to the United States.

One important area of capital flows is direct investment—outright ownership or control (as opposed to portfolio investment). Japan's direct foreign investment has grown rapidly, although not as dramatically as portfolio investment. Data collected by its Ministry of Finance show the accumulated value of Japanese foreign direct investment growing from under US$3.6 billion in 1970 to US$36.5 billion in 1980 and to over US$186 billion by 1988 (see table 31, Appendix). Direct investment tends to be very visible, and the rapid increase of Japan's direct investments in countries such as the United States, combined with the large imbalance between Japan's overseas investment and foreign investment in Japan was a primary cause of tension at the end of the 1980s.

The location of Japan's direct investments abroad has been shifting. In 1970, 21 percent of its investments were in Asia and nearly 22 percent in the United States. By 1988, the share of investments in Asia had dropped slightly, to under 18 percent, while that in the United States had risen sharply, to nearly 39 percent of the total. During this period, Japan's share of investments in Latin America held rather steady (from nearly 16 percent in 1970 to nearly 17 percent in 1988), as it did in Europe (down slightly from nearly 18 percent to over 16 percent in that period), and Africa (where it was under 3 percent in both years). Both the Middle East (down from over 9 percent to under 2 percent) and the Pacific (down from roughly 8 percent to 5 percent) became relatively less important locations for Japanese investments. However, because of the rapid growth in the dollar amounts of the investments, these shifts were all relative. Even in the Middle East, the dollar value of Japanese investments had grown.

The drive to invest overseas stemmed from several motives. A major reason for many early investments was to obtain access to raw materials. As Japan became more dependent on imported raw materials, energy, and food during the 1960s and 1970s, direct investments were one way of ensuring supply. The Middle East, Australia, and some Asian countries (such as Indonesia) were major locations for such investments by 1970. Second, rising labor costs during the 1960s and 1970s led certain labor-intensive industries, especially textiles, to move abroad.

Investment in other industrial countries, such as the United States, was often motivated by barriers to exports from Japan. The restrictions on automobile exports to the United States, which went into effect in 1981, became a primary motivation for Japanese automakers to establish assembly plants in the United States. The same situation had occurred earlier, in the 1970s, for plants manufacturing television sets. Japanese firms exporting from developing countries, moreover, often received preferential tariff treatment in developed countries (under the Generalized System of Preferences). In short, protectionism in developed countries often motivated Japanese foreign direct investment.

After 1985, a new and important incentive materialized for such investments. The rapid rise in the value of the yen seriously undermined the international competitiveness of many products manufactured in Japan. While this situation had been true for textiles in the 1960s, it now also affected a much wider range of more sophisticated products. Japanese manufacturers began actively seeking lower cost production bases. This factor, rather than any increase in foreign protectionism, appeared to lie behind the acceleration of overseas investments after 1985.

This cost disadvantage also led more Japanese firms to think of their overseas factories as a source of products for the Japanese market itself. Except for the basic processing of raw materials, manufacturers had previously regarded foreign investments as a substitute for exports rather than as an overseas base for home markets. The share of output from Japanese factories in the lower-wage-cost countries of Asia that was destined for the Japanese market (rather than for local markets or for export) rose from 10 percent in 1980 to 16 percent in 1987.

The Value of the Yen

The relative value of the yen is determined in foreign exchange markets by the forces of demand and supply. The demand for the yen is governed by the desire of foreigners to buy goods and services in Japan and by their interest in investing in Japan (buying yen-denominated real and financial assets). The supply of the yen in the market is governed by the desire of yen holders to exchange their yen for other currencies to purchase goods, services, or assets.

In 1949 the value of the yen was set at ¥360 per US$1 through an American plan, which was part of the Bretton Woods System, to stabilize prices in the Japanese economy. That exchange rate was maintained until 1971, when the United States abandoned the convertibility of the dollar to gold, which had been a key element of the Bretton Woods System, and imposed a 10 percent surcharge on imports, and set in motion changes that eventually led to floating exchange rates in 1973.

By 1971 the yen had become undervalued (see table 32, Appendix). Japanese exports were costing too little in international markets, and imports from abroad were costing the Japanese too much. This undervaluation was reflected in the current account balance, which had risen from the deficits of the early 1960s to a then-large surplus of US$5.8 billion in 1971. The belief that the yen, and several other major currencies, were undervalued motivated the United States actions in 1971.

Following the United States measures to devalue the dollar in the summer of 1971, the Japanese government agreed to a new, fixed exchange rate as part of the Smithsonian Agreement, signed at the end of the year. This agreement set the exchange rate at ¥308 per US$1. However, the new fixed rates of the Smithsonian Agreement were difficult to maintain in the face of supply and demand pressures in the foreign exchange market. In early 1973, the rates were abandoned, and the major nations of the world allowed their currencies to float.

In the 1970s, Japanese government and business people were very concerned that a rise in the value of the yen would hurt export growth by making Japanese products less competitive and would damage the industrial base. The government, therefore, continued to intervene heavily in foreign exchange marketing (buying or selling dollars), even after the 1973 decision to allow the yen to float.

Despite intervention, market pressures caused the yen to continue climbing in value, peaking temporarily at an average of ¥271 per US$1 in 1973 before the impact of the oil crisis was felt. The increased costs of imported oil caused the yen to depreciate to a range of ¥290 to ¥300 between 1974 and 1976. The reemergence of trade surpluses drove the yen back up to ¥211 in 1978. This currency strengthening was again reversed by the second oil shock, with the yen dropping to ¥227 by 1980.

During the first half of the 1980s, the yen failed to rise in value even though current account surpluses returned and grew quickly. From ¥221 in 1981, the average value of the yen actually dropped to ¥239 in 1985. The rise in the current account surplus generated stronger demand for yen in foreign exchange markets, but this trade-related demand for yen was offset by other factors. A wide differential in interest rates, with United States interest rates much higher than those in Japan, and the continuing moves to deregulate the international flow of capital, led to a large net outflow of capital from Japan. This capital flow increased the supply of yen in foreign exchange markets, as Japanese investors changed their yen for other currencies (mainly dollars) to invest overseas. This situation kept the yen weak relative to the dollar and fostered the rapid rise in the Japanese trade surplus that took place in the 1980s.

In 1985 a dramatic change began. Finance officials from major nations signed an agreement (the Plaza Accord) affirming that the dollar was overvalued (and, therefore, the yen undervalued). This agreement, and shifting supply and demand pressures in the markets, led to a rapid rise in the value of the yen. From its average of ¥239 per US$1 in 1985, the yen rose to a peak of ¥128 in 1988, virtually doubling its value relative to the dollar. After 1988 the yen's value declined slightly to ¥145 in September 1989, but remained much stronger than in 1985.

The yen's increased value made Japanese exports less price competitive and imports more price competitive, which should have brought down the value of trade and current account surpluses. The current account figures discussed above, however, indicated that such a response was slow. The strong appreciation of the yen began in 1985, but the current account continued to rise until 1987, and its decline in 1988 was rather small.

Trade and Investment Relations

Japan was engaged in trade and investment with nearly every country in the world. Generally speaking, however, its greatest economic interaction was with other developed countries, and over time this interaction grew.

In 1988 about 61 percent of exports went to developed countries, 34 percent to developing countries, and 5 percent to communist countries. The largest single destination of Japanese exports was the United States, which accounted for an extraordinary 33.8 percent of all exports. The United States was the major growth market for Japanese exports in the 1980s; it had accounted for only 24 percent of the total in 1980. West Germany, Britain, the Republic of Korea (South Korea), and Taiwan were the next largest markets, at the much lower level of about 6 percent each (see table 33, Appendix).

Of imports, 51 percent came from developed countries in 1988, 42 percent from developing countries, and 7 percent from communist countries, with the developed countries' share rising over the course of the 1980s as raw materials, which predominate in developing country sales to Japan, declined in price. Despite Japan's dependence on foreign sources of energy and raw materials, the United States was the largest single source of imports, accounting for 22.4 percent in 1988, larger than the combined share (10 percent) for all Middle Eastern countries, the suppliers of much of Japan's oil. Over time, however, dependence on United States imports had slipped rather steadily, from 34.6 percent in 1960, as sources of supply diversified. Other major sources of 1988 imports were South Korea (6.3 percent), Australia (5.5 percent), China (5.3

percent), Indonesia (5.1 percent), Taiwan (4.7 percent), Canada (4.4 percent), and West Germany (4.3 percent).

Historically, Japan has had trade deficits with raw material suppliers and surpluses with other countries. In the 1980s, however, balances with all trading partners shifted somewhat in Japan's favor. Its surplus in trade with developed countries rose from US$12 billion in 1980 to US$67 billion by 1988, while the balance with developing countries shifted from a deficit of US$25 billion in 1980 to a surplus of nearly US$11 billion in 1988. Its deficit in trade with the Middle East, peaked at about US$30 billion in 1980, sinking to only US$10.5 billion by 1988.

Partly because of this rapid shift toward surplus, and because of continued problems of access to Japanese markets, Japan faced increased tensions with a number of its trading partners during the 1980s. The decade was marked by contentious negotiations especially with the United States. Complicating the nature of all these relationships was the very swift rise of Japan as a major investor in the domestic assets of its major trading partners.

United States and Canada

The United States has been Japan's largest economic partner, taking 33.8 percent of its exports, supplying 22.4 percent of its imports, and accounting for 38.6 percent of its direct investment abroad in 1988. The United States also supplied 47 percent accumulated direct investment by foreign firms in Japan.

Japanese imports from the United States included both raw materials and manufactured goods. American agricultural products were a leading import in 1988 (US$9.1 billion as measured by United States export statistics), made up of meat (US$1.4 billion), fish (US$1.6 billion), grains (US$2.3 billion), and soybeans (US$1.0 billion). Imports of manufactured goods were mainly in the category of machinery and transportation equipment, rather than consumer goods. In 1988 Japan imported US$6.9 billion of machinery from the United States, of which computers and computer parts (US$2.4 billion) formed the largest single component. In the category of transportation equipment, Japan imported US$2.2 billion of aircraft and parts (automobiles and parts accounted for only US$500 million).

Japanese exports to the United States were almost entirely manufactured goods. Automobiles were by far the largest single category, amounting to US$21 billion in 1988, or 23 percent of total Japanese exports to the United States. Automotive parts accounted for another US$5 billion. Other major items were office machinery (including computers), which totaled US$10.6 billion in 1988, telecommunications equipment (US$10.4 billion), power generating equipment (US$3.3 billion), iron and steel (US$2.9 billion), and metalworking machinery (US$1.7 billion).

From the mid-1960s, the trade balance has been in Japan's favor. According to Japanese data, its surplus with the United States grew from US$380 million in 1970 to nearly US$48 billion in 1988. United States data on the trade relationship (which differ slightly because each nation includes transportation costs on the import but not the export side) also show a rapid deterioration of the imbalance in the 1980s, from a Japanese surplus of US$10 billion in 1980 to one of US$60 billion in 1987, with a slight improvement, to one of US$55 billion, in 1988.

This general deterioration, and the very modest improvement in trade balance after the yen rose in value after 1985, contributed greatly to strained economic relations. The United States had pressured Japan to open its markets since the early 1960s, but the intensity of the pressure increased through the 1970s and 1980s.

Tensions were exacerbated by issues specific to particular industries perhaps more than by the trade imbalance in general. Beginning with textiles in the 1950s, a number of Japanese exports to the United States were subject to opposition from American industry. These complaints generally alleged unfair trading practices, such as dumping (selling at a lower cost than at home, or selling below the cost of production) and patent infringement. The result of negotiations was often Japan's agreement "voluntarily" to restrain exports to the United States. Such agreements applied to a number of products, including color television sets in the late 1970s and automobiles in the 1980s.

Some innovative approaches emerged in the 1980s as United States companies strove to achieve greater access to Japanese markets. MOSS negotiations in 1985 addressed access problems related to four industries: forest products, pharmaceuticals and medical equipment, electronics, and telecommunications equipment and services.

Problems of access to Japanese markets were among the motivations for the United States Trade Act of 1988, which included a provision calling on the president to identify unfair trading partners of the United States and to specify products for negotiation with these countries. In the spring of 1989, Japan was named under this provision and three areas—forest products, telecommunications satellites, and supercomputers—were selected for negotiations. This action exemplified the continuing mood of dissatisfaction over access to Japanese markets at the end of the decade (see Import Policies, this ch.).

At the same time, the United States initiated broad talks concerning the structural factors inhibiting manufactured imports in Japan, in the Structural Impediments Initiative. These talks addressed such areas as the law restraining the growth of large discount store chains in Japan, weak antitrust law enforcement, land taxation that encouraged inefficient farming, and high real estate prices.

As elsewhere, Japanese direct investment in the United States expanded rapidly and had become an important new dimension in the countries' relationship. The total value of cumulative investments of this kind was US$8.7 billion in 1980; it had grown by more than eight times by 1988 to US$71.9 billion. United States data identified Japan as the second largest investor in the United States; it had about half the value of investments of Britain, but more than those of the Netherlands, Canada, or West Germany. Much of Japan's investment in the United States in the late 1980s was in the commercial sector, providing the basis for distribution and sale of Japanese exports to the United States. Wholesale and retail distribution accounted for 35 percent of all Japanese investments in the United States in 1988, while manufacturing accounted for 23 percent. Real estate became a popular investment during the 1980s, with cumulative investments rising to US$10 billion by 1988, 20 percent of the total.

Japan's balance of trade with Canada tended to be in deficit because Canada was a supplier of raw materials to Japan. In 1988 Canada was the destination for 2.4 percent of Japan's exports and the source of 4.4 percent of its imports. Canada was a major supplier of food (particularly wheat), wood and wood pulp, and coal. Japan's deficit with Canada in 1988 was US$1.9 billion.

Noncommunist Asia

The developing nations of Asia grew rapidly as suppliers to and buyers from Japan. In 1988 these countries (including South Korea, Taiwan, Hong Kong, Singapore, Indonesia, and other countries in Southeast Asia) accounted for 25 percent of Japan's exports, a share well below the 34 percent value of 1960, but one that had been roughly constant since 1970. In 1988 developing Asian countries provided 26 percent of Japan's imports, a share that had risen slowly, from 16 percent in 1970 and 23 percent in 1980.

As a whole, Japan had run a surplus with noncommunist Asia, and this surplus rose quickly in the 1980s. From a minor deficit in 1980 of US$841 million (mostly caused by a peak in the value of oil imports from Indonesia), Japan showed a surplus of nearly US$3 billion with these countries in 1985 and of over US$19 billion in 1988. The shift was caused by the fall in the prices of oil and other raw materials that Japan imported from the region and to the rapid growth in Japanese exports as the region's economic growth continued at a high rate.

Indonesia and Malaysia both continued to show a trade surplus because of their heavy raw material exports to Japan. However, falling oil prices caused trade in both directions between Japan and Indonesia to decline in the 1980s. Trade similarly declined with the Philippines, owing to the political turmoil and economic contraction there in the 1980s.

South Korea, Taiwan, Hong Kong, and Singapore constituted the newly industrialized economies (NIEs) in Asia, and all four exhibited high economic growth during the 1970s and 1980s. Like Japan, they lacked many raw materials and mainly exported manufactured goods. Their deficits with Japan increased from 1980 to 1988 when the deficits of all four were sizeable. Over the 1970s and 1980s, they evolved a pattern of importing components from Japan and exporting assembled products to the United States.

Japanese direct investment in Asia also expanded, with the total cumulative value reaching over US$32 billion by 1988. Indonesia, at US$9.8 billion in 1988 was the largest single location for these investments. As rapid as the growth of investment was, however, it did not keep pace with Japan's global investment, so the share of Asia in total cumulative investment slipped, from 26.5 percent in 1975 to 17.3 percent in 1988.

Western Europe

Japan's trade with Western Europe grew steadily, but had been relatively small well into the 1980s considering the size of this market. In 1980 Western Europe supplied only 7.4 percent of Japan's imports and took 16.6 percent of its exports. However, the relationship began to change very rapidly after 1985. West European exports to Japan increased two and one-half times in just the three years from 1985 to 1988 and rose as a share of all Japanese imports to 16 percent. (Much of this increase came from growing Japanese interest in European consumer items, including luxury automobiles.) Likewise, Japan's exports to Europe rose rapidly after 1985, more than doubling by 1988 and accounting for 21 percent of all Japanese exports.

In 1988 the major European buyers of Japanese exports were West Germany (US$15.8 billion) and Britain (US$10.6 billion) (see table 34, Appendix). The largest European suppliers to Japan were West Germany (US$8.1 billion), France (US$4 billion), and Britain (US$4.2 billion) (see table 35, Appendix). Traditionally, West

European countries had trade deficits with Japan, and this continued to be the case in 1988, despite the surge in Japan's imports from them after 1985. From 1980 to 1988, the deficit of the West European countries as a whole expanded from US$11 billion to US$25 billion, with much of the increase coming after 1985.

Trade relations with Western Europe were strained during the 1980s. Policies varied among the individual countries, but many imposed restrictions on Japanese imports. Late in the decade, as discussions proceeded on the trade and investment policies that would prevail with European economic integration in 1992, many Japanese officials and business people became concerned that protectionism directed against Japan would increase. Domestic content requirements (specifying the share of local products and value added in a product) and requirements on the location of research and development facilities and manufacturing investments appeared likely.

Fear of a protectionist Western Europe accelerated Japanese direct investment in the second half of the 1980s. Total accumulated Japanese direct investments in the region grew from US$4.5 billion in 1980 to over US$30 billion in 1988, from 12.2 percent to more than 16 percent of such Japanese investments. Rather than being discouraged by protectionist signals from Europe, Japanese businesses appeared to be determined to play a significant role in what promised to be a large, vigorous, and integrated market in the 1990s. Investment offered the surest means of circumventing protectionism, and Japanese business appeared to be willing to comply with whatever domestic content or other performance requirements the European Communities might impose.

The Middle East

The importance of the Middle East expanded dramatically in the 1970s with the jumps in crude oil prices. Japan was deeply concerned with maintaining good relations with these oil-producing nations to avoid a debilitating cut in oil supplies. During the 1980s, however, oil prices fell and Japan's concerns over the security of its oil supply diminished greatly.

The Middle East represented only 7.5 percent of total Japanese imports in 1960 and 12.4 percent in 1970, with the small rise resulting from the rapid increase in the volume of oil consumed by the growing Japanese economy. By 1980, however, this share had climbed to a peak of 31.7 percent because of the two rounds of price hikes in the 1970s. Falling oil prices after 1980 brought this share back down to 10.5 percent by 1988—actually a lower percentage than in 1970, before the price hikes had started. The major oil suppliers to Japan in 1988 were Saudi Arabia and the United Arab Emirates. Iran, Iraq, and Kuwait were also significant, but smaller, sources. These three countries became less important oil suppliers after 1980 because of the Iran-Iraq war (1980–88) and resulting damage to loading facilities and shipping.

As imports from the Middle East surged in the 1970s, so did Japanese exports to the region. Paralleling the pattern for imports, however, this share fell in the 1980s. Equalling 1.8 percent in 1960, exports to this region rose to 11.1 percent of total Japanese exports in 1980, but then declined to 3.6 percent by 1988.

Part of Japan's strategy to assure oil supplies was to encourage investment in oil-supplying countries. However, such investment never kept pace with Japan's investments in other regions. The country's expanding need for oil helped push direct investment in the Middle East to 9.3 percent of total direct investments abroad by Japanese companies in 1970, but this share had fallen to 6.2 percent by 1980 and to only 1.8 percent by 1988. The Iran-Iraq war was a major factor in the declining interest of Japanese investors, exemplified by the fate of a large US$3 billion petrochemical complex in Iran, which was almost complete when the revolution took place in 1979. Completion was delayed first by political concerns (when United States embassy personnel were held hostage) and then by repeated Iraqi bombing raids. The project was finally cancelled in 1989, with losses for both Japanese companies and the Japanese government, which had provided insurance for the project.

Oceania

Australia and New Zealand were predominantly sources of food and raw materials for Japan. In 1988 Australia accounted for 5.5 percent of total Japanese imports, a share that held relatively steady in the late 1980s, while New Zealand accounted for less than 1 percent. Because they provided raw materials, both nations had trade surpluses with Japan. Australia was the largest single supplier of coal, iron ore, wool, and sugar to Japan in 1988, while New Zealand was the second largest supplier of wool.

Resource development projects in Australia attracted Japanese capital, as did trade protectionism by necessitating local production for the Australian market. Investments in Australia totaled US$8.1 billion in 1988, accounting for 4.4 percent of Japanese direct investment abroad. But, because of the broadening reach of Japan's foreign investment, this share had been declining, down from 5.9 percent in 1980. During the 1980s, Japanese real estate investment increased in Australia, particularly in the ocean resort area known as the Gold Coast, where Japanese presence was strong enough to create some backlash.

The trade of both Australia and New Zealand had shifted away from other Commonwealth of Nations countries toward Asia. Japan in particular had emerged as the leading trading partner for these two countries. Faced with growing interdependence with Asia, Australia joined Japan in actively calling for greater consultation and cooperation among Pacific nations. Still, Australia and New Zealand faced quotas, high tariffs, and unusual standards barriers in exporting agricultural products including beef, butter, and apples, to Japan.

Latin America

In the 1970s, Japan briefly showed enthusiasm over Brazilian prospects. A vast territory richly endowed with raw materials and with a sizable Japanese-Brazilian minority in the population, Brazil appeared to Japanese business to offer great opportunities for trade and investment. However, none of those expectations have been realized, and Japanese financial institutions became caught up in the international debt problems of Brazil and other Latin American countries.

In 1988 Japan received US$8.3 billion of imports from Latin America as a whole, and exported US$9.3 billion to the region, for a surplus of US$1 billion. Although the absolute value of both exports and imports had grown over time, Latin America had declined in importance as a Japanese trading partner. The share of Japan's total imports coming from this region dropped from 7.3 percent in 1970 to 4.1 percent in 1980, remaining at 4.4 percent in 1988. Japanese exports to Latin America also declined, from 6.9 percent in 1980 to 3.5 percent in 1988.

Despite this relative decline in trade, Japanese direct investment in the region continued to grow quickly, reaching US$31.6 billion in 1988, or 16.9 percent of Japan's total foreign direct investment. This share was only slightly below that of 1975 (18.1 percent) and was almost equal to the share in Asian countries. However, over US$11 billion of this investment was in Panama—mainly for Panamanian-flag shipping, which does not represent true investment in the country. The Bahamas also attracted US$1.9 billion in investment, mainly from Japanese financial institutions, but in arrangements to secure favorable tax treatment rather than real investments. Brazil absorbed US$5 billion in Japanese direct investment, Mexico US$1.6 billion, and other Latin American countries amounts below US$1 billion in the late 1980s.

Latin American countries lie at the heart of the Third World debt problems that plagued international financial relations in the 1980s. Japanese financial institutions became involved as lenders to these nations, although they were far less exposed than United States banks. Because of this financial involvement, the Japanese government was actively involved in international discussions of how to resolve the crisis. In 1987, Minister of Finance Miyazawa Kiichi put forth a proposal on resolving the debt issue. Although that initiative did not go through, the Brady Plan that emerged in 1989 contained some elements of the Miyazawa Plan. The Japanese government supported the Brady Plan by pledging US$10 billion in cofinancing with the World Bank and IMF.

Africa

Africa has been the least important world region for Japanese trade and investment. Japan had little historical experience with Africa and little interest in economic ties with the region, except for development of raw material supplies.

In 1988 Africa accounted for just over 1 percent of Japan's imports and for 1 percent of its exports. Japan's largest trading partner in Africa in 1988 was South Africa, which accounted for 34 percent of Japanese exports to Africa and 45 percent of Japan's imports from the region. Because of trading sanctions imposed on South Africa by the United States and other countries, Japan emerged as South Africa's largest trading partner during the 1980s. This position proved embarrassing to Japan and led it to downgrade some diplomatic and economic relations with the country. Despite the fact that South Africa remained Japan's largest trading partner in the region, both exports and imports in 1988 had declined by more than one-third from their value in 1980.

Africa was the location of only US$4.6 billion or 2.5 percent of Japanese foreign direct investment in 1988, of which most (US$3.6 billion) was in Liberia. As in Panama, this investment was mainly in the form of flag-of-convenience shipping. Japanese data showed virtually no direct investment in South Africa (US$1 million), and no new investment in this country during the 1980s.

Communist Countries

Japan's experience with communist countries was quite limited in the years after the war. In the 1980s, its patterns of interaction with China and the Soviet Union diverged sharply, its relations with China growing quickly, those with the Soviet Union stagnating. Other communist areas, such as Eastern Europe, continued to be only tiny trade and investment partners for Japan.

Exports to communist countries totaled US$13.8 billion in 1988, or 5.2 percent of Japan's exports. Imports from these countries totaled nearly US$13.9 billion, yielding a virtual balance in trade. Imports from the Soviet Union declined during the first half of the 1980s, from nearly US$1.9 billion to less than US$1.5 billion, and then recovered to almost US$2.8 billion by 1988, representing a modest growth for the entire period. Imports from China, on the other hand, more than doubled in this time, from just over US$4.3 billion in 1980 to nearly US$9.9 billion in 1988. Export trade followed a similar pattern: exports to the Soviet Union stagnated and then grew modestly, to over US$3.1 billion in 1988, while those to China expanded rapidly, from nearly US$5.1 billion in 1980 to just under US$9.5 billion in 1988.

China and Japan have geographic proximity, extensive cultural ties, and a long history of commercial relations. However, Japan's trade relationship with China was severely constrained in the 1950s and 1960s because of its support for the United States policy of containment. Japanese business did not expand such commercial relations significantly until the United States-China rapprochement in the early 1970s and Japan's subsequent establishment of diplomatic relations with China (see Relations with China, ch. 7). Japan recognized the Beijing government in 1972. After Mao Zedong's death in 1976, China pursued economic contacts with the West, and trade with Japan expanded rapidly. The new relationship was reinforced by the signing of a Long-Term Trade Agreement in 1978. In 1980 Japan granted China reduced tariff treatment under the Generalized System of Preferences.

Investment in China also expanded once relations improved in the 1970s. Japanese data show some US$2 billion of cumulative direct investment in China by 1988. China also became the largest single recipient of foreign aid from Japan during the 1980s. However, a treaty establishing a firm legal framework for direct investment, remained to be completed at the end of the 1980s. Furthermore, the massacre of Chinese prodemocracy demonstrators in Beijing's 1989 Tiananmen Incident, and subsequent political and economic tightening in China discouraged new Japanese investment.

Commercial relations with the Soviet Union also paralleled strategic developments. Japan was very interested in Siberian raw materials in the early 1970s as prices were rising and détente persisted. The challenges to détente, especially the invasion of Afghanistan in 1979 and falling raw material prices, put strong constraints on Japanese trade and investment relations with the Soviet Union. Only after Soviet policy began to change under

Mikhail Gorbachev's leadership, beginning in 1985, did Japanese trade resume its growth.

Further complicating economic relations with the Soviet Union was the dispute over four small northern islands occupied by the Soviets toward the end of World War II. No progress had taken place on this issue during three decades of intermittent negotiations. However, the 1980s ended with new hope that a settlement would emerge. Were this to occur, economic relations with the Soviet Union might expand more rapidly (see Relations with the Soviet Union, ch. 7).

Japan's trade was also constrained by the Coordinating Committee for Multilateral Export Controls (CoCom), which controlled exports of strategic high technology. In 1987 the United States discovered that Toshiba Machine Tool had shipped machine tools on the restricted list to the Soviet Union, tools used to manufacture quieter submarine propellers. Although the Japanese government moved reluctantly to punish Toshiba (and the United States imposed sanctions on Toshiba exports to the United States in response), the final outcome was stronger surveillance and punishment for CoCom violations in Japan.

Japanese investment loans and trade credits went mainly to Siberian resource development. But this development never expanded as originally expected. Soviet interest in revitalizing the economy in the late 1980s suggested that future Japanese investment would be concentrated in the western regions of the Soviet Union rather than in Siberia.

Japan's trade and investment relations with other communist countries in Eastern Europe and Asia were very limited. In 1988 exports to Eastern Europe were less than US$1 billion, as were imports from the region. The reunification of Germany and the rapid disintegration of communist regimes in other East European countries may open the prospect of expanded trade and investment during the 1990s, but economic problems within the region as these nations grappled with moving toward market-oriented economies were likely to continue to limit trade with Japan. Trade with other Asian communist countries was even less significant. The Democratic Republic of Korea (North Korea) is geographically close to Japan, but that nation's default on trade debt in the 1960s, combined with the political tension between it and the Republic of Korea (South Korea) kept North Korean trade with Japan at a minimum.

International Economic Cooperation and Aid

Japan emerged as one of the largest aid donors in the world during the 1980s. In 1988 Japan was the second largest foreign aid donor worldwide, behind the United States. Japan's ratio of foreign aid to GNP in this year was 0.32 percent behind the 0.35 percent average for the OECD's Development Assistance Committee member countries, but ahead of the United States ratio of 0.20 percent.

The foreign aid program began in the 1960s out of the reparations payments Japan was obliged to pay to other Asian countries for war damage. The program's budget remained quite low until the late 1970s, when Japan came under increasing pressure from other industrial countries to play a larger role. During the 1980s, Japan's foreign aid budget grew quickly, despite the budget constraints imposed by the effort to reduce the fiscal deficit. From 1984 to 1988, the Official Development Assistance (ODA) budget increased at an average annual rate of 22.5 percent, reaching US$9.1 billion by 1988. Part of this rise was due to exchange rate movements (with given yen amounts committed in the budget becoming larger dollar amounts). In the Japanese government budget, foreign aid rose at a lower, but still strong rate, of between 4 percent and 12 percent each year during the 1980s, with an average annual rate of growth from 1979 to 1988 of 8.6 percent.

Such assistance consisted of grants and loans, and support for multilateral aid organizations. In 1988 Japan allocated US$6.4 billion of its aid budget to bilateral assistance and US$2.7 billion to multilateral agencies. Of the bilateral assistance, US$2.9 billion went for grants and US$3.5 billion for concessional loans.

Japan's foreign aid program has been criticized for better serving the interests of Japanese corporations than those of developing countries. In the past, tied aid (grants or loans tied to the purchase of merchandise from Japan) was high, but untied aid expanded rapidly in the 1980s, reaching 71 percent of all aid by 1986. This share compared favorably with other Development Assistance Committee countries and with the United States corresponding figure of 54 percent. Nevertheless, complaints continued that even Japan's untied aid tended to be directed toward purchases from Japan. Aid in the form of grants (the share of aid disbursed as grants rather than as loans) was low relative to other Development Assistance Committee countries, and remained so late in the 1980s.

Bilateral assistance was concentrated in the developing countries of Asia, although modest moves took place in the 1980s to expand the geographical scope of aid. In 1988 some 62.8 percent of bilateral development assistance was allocated to Asia, 13.8 percent to Africa, 9.1 percent to the Middle East, and 6.2 percent to Latin America. Asia's share was down somewhat, from 75 percent in 1975 and 70 percent in 1980, but still accounted for by far the largest share of bilateral aid. During the 1980s, increased aid went to Pakistan and Egypt, partly in response to pressure from the United States to provide such aid for strategic purposes. Japan had little involvement in Africa, but the severe drought of the 1980s brought an increase in the share of development assistance for that continent.

The five largest recipients of Japanese ODA in 1988 were in Asia: Indonesia (US$985 million), China (US$674 million), the Philippines (US$535 million), Thailand (US$361 million), and Bangladesh (US$342 million). Earlier in the 1980s, China had been the largest single recipient for several successive years. These large aid amounts made Japan the largest single source of development assistance for most Asian countries. For the Association of Southeast Asian Nations (ASEAN) countries, for example, Japan supplied 55 percent of net ODA received in 1987, compared with 11 percent from the United States and only 10 percent from the multilateral aid agencies.

The largest use of Japan's bilateral aid was for economic infrastructure (transportation, communications, river development, and energy development), which accounted for 39 percent of the total in 1988. Smaller shares went to development of the production sector (19 percent) and social infrastructure (16 percent). In general, large construction projects predominated in Japan's bilateral foreign aid. Even within the category of social infrastructure, water supply and sanitation, which involved major construction projects, absorbed the largest amount of money (5.8 percent of the bilateral aid in 1988, compared with 4.7 percent for education and only 2 percent for health). Food aid (0.5 percent of total bilateral aid in 1988) and debt relief (2.7 percent) were not important parts of Japan's official development assistance.

Major International Industries

As in most countries, a relatively small number of industries dominated Japan's trade and investment interaction with the rest of the world. In the late 1980s, those industries were motor vehicles, consumer electronics, computers, semiconductors and other electronic components, and iron and steel.

Motor Vehicles

The motor vehicle industry was the most successful industry in Japan in the 1980s. In 1988 Japan produced 8.2 million passenger cars, making it the largest producer in the world (the United States in that year produced 7.1 million), and 54 percent of that output was exported. Passenger cars, other motor vehicles, and automotive parts were the largest class of Japanese exports throughout the

1980s. In 1988 they accounted for 18 percent of all Japanese exports, a meteoric rise from only 1.9 percent in 1960.

Fear of protectionism in the United States also led to major direct foreign investments there by Japanese auto producers. By the end of the decade, all the major Japanese producers had automotive assembly lines operating in the United States: Honda, Toyota, Nissan, Mazda, and Isuzu (in a joint plant with Subaru). Following the major assembly firms, Japanese auto parts producers also began investing in the United States in the late 1980s.

Automobiles were a major area of contention for the United States-Japan relationship during the 1980s. When the price of oil rose in 1979, demand for small automobiles increased, which worked to the advantage of Japanese exports in the United States market. As the Japanese share of the market increased, to 21.8 percent in 1981, pressures rose to restrict imports from Japan. The result of these pressures was a series of negotiations in early 1981, which produced a "voluntary" export agreement limiting Japanese shipments to the United States to 1.68 million units (excluding certain kinds of specialty vehicles and trucks). This agreement remained in effect for the rest of the decade, with the limit reset at 2.3 million units in 1985. As Japanese assembly lines in the United States came on line, imports of Japanese automobiles in 1988 actually fell below the limit.

Similar restraints on Japanese exports were imposed by Canada and several West European countries. Japan's investment increased in Western Europe as well, but it faced pressure to achieve high local value added as discussion proceeded on the European Economic Community unification slated for 1992.

Foreign penetration of the automotive market in Japan was less successful. Imports of foreign automobiles were very low during the forty years prior to 1985, never exceeding 60,000 units annually, or 1 percent of the domestic market. Trade and investment barriers restricted imported cars to an insignificant share of the market in the 1950s, and as barriers were finally lowered, strong control over the distribution networks made penetration difficult. The major American automobile manufacturers acquired minority interests in some Japanese firms when investment restrictions were relaxed, Ford obtaining a 25 percent interest in Toyo Kogyo (Mazda), General Motors a 34 percent interest in Isuzu, and Chrysler a 15 percent interest in Mitsubishi Motors. This ownership did not provide a means for American cars to penetrate the Japanese market until the end of the 1980s.

After the strong appreciation of the yen in 1985, however, Japanese demand for foreign automobiles increased. The greater sense of affluence in Japanese society was accompanied by a rising interest in European design. In 1988 automobile imports totaled 150,629 units, of which 127,309 were European, mostly West German. Only 21,124 units were imported from the United States in 1988.

Consumer Electronics

The industries producing consumer electronics—audio receivers, compact disc players, and other audio components; tape recorders, television receivers, video cassette recorders, and video cameras—were major exporters, and in the 1980s they invested overseas as well. In 1988, 34 percent of color televisions produced in Japan were exported, as were 79 percent of video cassette recorders. Some of these products had too small an export share to show up separately in summary trade data, but audio tape recorders represented 2.9 percent of total Japanese exports in 1988, video cassette recorders 2.3 percent, radio receivers 0.8 percent, and television receivers 0.7 percent, for a total of 6.7 percent.

All of these industries built on Japan's success in developing commercial applications for the transistor in the 1950s and the succeeding generations of semiconductor devices of the 1970s and 1980s. Most of this output came from large integrated electronics firms, which manufactured semiconductor devices, consumer electronics, and computers. Their international success came from continually pushing miniaturization and driving down manufacturing costs through innovations in the manufacturing process.

Mainly because of Japanese industry's success, the American consumer electronics industry withered. During the 1970s, Japanese inroads in the American market for color television receivers sparked charges of dumping and other predatory practices. These disputes led to an orderly marketing agreement or voluntary export restraint by Japan in 1977, which limited exports of color televisions to 1.75 million units annually between 1977 and 1980. While this agreement afforded some protection to the domestic industry, Japanese firms responded by investing in the United States. By the end of the 1980s, only one American-owned television manufacturer remained; the others had disappeared or been bought by West European or Japanese firms.

Other products for the consumer electronics market did not become as controversial as color televisions, partly because the Japanese had pioneered the products. Video cassette recorders, video cameras, and compact disc players were all developed for the consumer market by Japanese firms, and no American-owned firms were involved in their manufacture in the 1980s.

An assembly line at an 8mm video camera plant
Courtesy Embassy of Japan, Washington

Radio component manufacturing, Yokohama
Courtesy The Mainichi Newspapers

Japanese overseas investment in the consumer electronics industry was motivated by protectionism and labor costs. Protectionism was the main motivation for Japanese firms to establish color television plants in the United States. By 1980, after the three years of voluntary export restraints, seven Japanese firms had located plants in the United States. In addition, Japanese firms retained production of the most technologically advanced products at home, while shifting production of less advanced products to developing countries such as Taiwan. For these reasons, Japanese export of color televisions fell during the 1980s, from 2 percent of total exports in 1970 to only 0.7 percent in 1988.

Computers

Japan was a latecomer to computer manufacturing. IBM Japan, a wholly owned subsidiary of IBM, along with other foreign subsidiaries, originally dominated the Japanese market. Until the 1980s, Japanese computer manufacturers viewed their marketing battle as one of capturing Japan's domestic market from IBM Japan, not of penetrating world markets. However, Japan's industry developed with extraordinary speed and moved into international markets. The leading computer manufacturers in Japan at the end of the 1980s (by sales in the domestic market) were Fujitsu, IBM Japan, Hitachi, NEC, and Unisis, in mainframes, and NEC, Fujitsu, Seiko Epson, Toshiba, and IBM Japan in personal computers. Despite the benefits extended by Japanese industrial policy to the domestic computer industry, IBM was able to maintain a significant market position in Japan—a 24 percent share of the mainframe market and a 6 percent share of the personal computer market in 1988.

In 1988 Japan exported US$1.5 billion of computer equipment, up more than twelve-fold from the US$122 million in 1980. Japanese firms were not very successful in exporting mainframe computers, but did very well in peripheral equipment, such as printers and tape drives. In the rapidly growing personal computer market, the Japanese achieved a modest market share in the United States during the 1980s. Imports of computer equipment, in 1988, came to US$3.2 billion (including parts). However, much of the computer equipment produced by foreign-owned firms that was used in Japan was manufactured domestically by subsidiaries rather than imported.

The special treatment extended to the computer industry became the subject of trade disputes with the United States in the 1980s, in particular, government procurement practices for supercomputers (the fastest, top-of-the-line computers). At issue was the inability of American manufacturers to sell these machines to government-funded agencies in Japan. Some rules were changed in 1987, but supercomputers remained one of three products singled out for further negotiation by the United States in 1989 under the provisions of the 1988 Trade Act. Earlier, conflict ensued over a Japanese proposal to protect computer software under patent law rather than under copyright law, a move that the United States felt would reduce protection for American-designed software in the Japanese market. This issue was resolved when the patent law proposal was dropped.

Semiconductors

Semiconductor devices are the key components of computers and of a wide variety of other electronic equipment. Inasmuch as the entire electronics industry was considered vital to the health and growth of the economy, semiconductors received significant attention in Japan during the 1970s and 1980s. By the end of the 1980s, Japanese firms dominated world production and trade in certain segments of the semiconductor industry. In particular, they came to dominate the world market in dynamic random-access memory units (DRAMs). The Japanese share of the world merchant market for 1-megabit DRAMs at the end of the decade, for example, was estimated at 90 percent, while other estimates put the Japanese share of all semiconductor devices at 48 percent. Trade data showed that in 1988 Japan exported more than US$12 billion in semiconductor devices (and vacuum tubes), representing a dramatic increase from US$6 million in 1960 and just over US$2 billion in 1980. Such imports, on the other hand, totaled only US$2.2 billion in the same year.

The rise of Japanese competition and the decline in the world market share held by American manufacturers, coupled with allegations of unfair trade practices, made semiconductors a contentious issue between the United States and Japan throughout the 1980s. The allegations included charges of dumping in the United States market and of import barriers artificially limiting the market share of American firms selling in Japan. Negotiations in 1986 produced an agreement that led to an increase in Japanese DRAM export prices and that also included a provision to increase the American share of the Japanese market (from the 10 percent that prevailed at that time to 20 percent by 1991). United States complaints that the Japanese failed to carry out the agreement in good faith led to retaliation, the imposition of punitive 100 percent tariffs on US$300 million of Japanese exports to the United States. Evidence that the export prices of DRAMs had risen led to partial elimination of the sanctions, but others remained until compliance was seen in increasing the American market share in Japan. This entire episode remained very controversial at the end of the decade, particularly the question of specifying an acceptable market share for American products in Japan.

Iron and Steel

Iron and steel had been a leading industry in Japan and had been considered critical to economic growth by the Japanese government in the 1950s. This attitude, exemplified by government loans offered at favorable rates, led to rapid modernization and expansion of the domestic industry. By 1970 iron and steel were the leading exports from Japan, accounting for over US$2.8 billion or 14.7 percent of total exports. This export share peaked in 1974, at 19 percent. Because of both the domestic industry's strength and import barriers, imports of iron and steel represented a minimal US$276 million in 1974. Japan's success in this industry, however, did generate large imports of raw materials—iron ore and concentrates, and coking coal. Iron and steel were a classic case of a processing trade, with Japan importing raw materials, building state-of-the-art, integrated steel plants at harborside, and exporting part of the output to the rest of the world.

Iron and steel products were the object of major trade disputes in the 1970s. The United States steel industry alleged that the Japanese engaged in dumping to increase their market share in the United States. These disputes led to various responses. In 1978, the United States government instituted the ''trigger price mechanism'': when iron and steel imports reached a certain low price it would initiate dumping investigations, effectively setting a minimum price for imports. These prices were based on estimates of Japanese production costs because the Japanese were assumed to be the lowest-cost producer in the world. This system lasted until the early 1980s and was replaced in 1984 by a set of voluntary export restraints negotiated separately with major suppliers of iron and steel to the United States. Japanese shipments to the United States remained subject to these restraints for the rest of the decade.

Despite the emphasis placed on the iron and steel industry in the Japanese economy and its export success, the industry proved to be mature and declining in the 1980s. Its share of total Japanese exports slipped to only 5.8 percent by 1988. Imports of iron and steel to Japan rose rapidly in the 1980s, reaching US$4.6 billion or 2.5 percent of total imports. South Korea, for example, was rapidly moving into certain parts of the industry and managed to penetrate Japanese markets despite opposition from the Japanese industry. As a leader in steelmaking technology by the late 1970s, Japan had also become an important source of technology for South Korea, China, and other developing nations building their own steel industries.

Industries of the Future

The Japanese government remained actively involved in shaping Japan's economic future. Electronics were in the forefront in the 1980s, but the importance of other industries appeared to be rising by the end of the decade. These industries included composite materials, industrial ceramics, space development (including satellites and launch vehicles), and superconductors (and products using them, such as magnetic levitation trains). The government's strong belief that such industries will be critical for the nation's future will likely foster active participation in these industries by Japanese firms. As these industries develop, they are also likely to become the subject of trade disputes insofar as industrial policy concerns might limit imports and result in an export push that other nations would resent. On the other hand, because Japan is at the technological frontier with other nations in these industries, Japanese development might produce more original technologies that other nations would be eager to acquire, perhaps creating greater mutual dependence.

* * *

Information and analysis in English on Japanese international economic relations are widely available. Excellent survey articles can be found in *The Political Economy of Japan: Vol. 2, The International Dimension,* edited by Takeshi Inoguchi and Daniel Okimoto. Bela Belassa and Marcus Noland's *Japan in the World Economy* discusses both macroeconomic and microeconomic dimensions of Japan's foreign economic relations, and Edward J. Lincoln's *Japan's Unequal Trade* focuses on Japanese import behavior. Each year the Ministry of International Trade and Industry publishes a review of international economic relations in its *Tsūshō Hakusho* (Trade White Paper), abridged versions of which are available in English translation.

Current information is also available in a variety of specialized periodicals, including the *Japan Economic Journal, Tokyo Business Today, Far Eastern Economic Review,* and *Asian Wall Street Journal.*

Detailed trade and other international data are published in both Japanese and English in the Bank of Japan's *Economic Statistics Annual,* and the *Japan Statistical Yearbook* of the Prime Minister's Office.

Balance of payments data are available through the Bank of Japan's *Balance of Payments Monthly* (which also gives annual data), and trade data are available in the Japan Tariff Association's *Summary Report, Trade of Japan*. More detailed trade data are provided by the Japan Tariff Association's *Japan's Exports and Imports*. (For further information and complete citations, see Bibliography.)

Chapter 6. The Political System

Family crest of a double-petal chrysanthemum (kiku), a blossom that symbolizes nobility and purity; used by the imperial family

IN 1990, JAPAN'S oldest living person was Fujisawa Mitsu, 113 years old. In the year of her birth, 1876 (the ninth year of the 1868–1912 Meiji era), the government ended the special status of the samurai, taking away their stipends and prohibiting them from wearing swords. Members of the new ruling elite traveled to Europe and the United States to study Western political ideas and institutions. Mitsu was thirteen when the Meiji Constitution was promulgated, a constitution combining traditional nationalistic thought with German legal and political concepts. The most influential Meiji-era advocate of Anglo-American liberalism, Fukuzawa Yukichi, died in 1901 when Mitsu was twenty-five. She was middle-aged when political parties controlled the government during the "Taishō democracy" era of the early to middle 1920s and revolutionary Marxism was popular among university students and intellectuals. The "Shōwa fascism" of the 1930s and 1940s was in large measure a reaction against these Westernizing trends. When General Douglas MacArthur landed in Japan and began the United States occupation in 1945, Mitsu was sixty-nine years old. Her robust old age witnessed the reintroduction of Western-style liberalism, the emergence of a stable parliamentary system under the dominance of the Liberal Democratic Party (LDP—Jiyū-Minshutō), the rise of the new left, and postwar Japan's most dramatic episode of romantic rightist theater, writer Mishima Yukio's self-immolation in 1970.

That the lifespan of a single person could encompass such dramatic and abrupt changes suggests the heterogeneity of contemporary Japanese political values. The country has been host to a wide range of often conflicting foreign influences: Prussian statism, French radicalism, Anglo-American liberalism, Marxism and Marxism-Leninism, and European fascism. Mitsu lived to see the *kokutai* (national polity) ideology enshrined in the Meiji Constitution and overthrown in the postwar Constitution. The fact that a person living in 1990 had been born in the twilight of Japan's feudal regime suggests that some of the older values remained viable. Certainly Japan's economic dynamism is often explained in terms of the coupling of feudal values with the efficiency of modern organization. Political scientists seeking to describe the distinctive features of Japanese politics also point to the feudal legacy behind them. These features include the nature of decision making, the generally pragmatic spirit of Japanese politics and, especially, the post-1955 successes of the conservative LDP, which has epitomized feudal personalism.

Maintaining power uninterruptedly for nearly four decades, the LDP was able to promote a highly stable policy-making process. Its leaders functioned as brokers, joining the expertise of the elite civil service with the demands of important interest groups. The role of these leaders, however, was not passive. Since the 1960s, the party's policy-making power has increased while that of the bureaucracy has declined. Although political scandals were frequent, tarnishing the general image of politicians, the system succeeded in providing most groups in society with adequate representation and a share of prosperity. The Japanese middle-class in the early 1990s was large and stable.

At the same time, opposition parties were divided and generally ineffectual. Although they performed an important monitoring function, they seemed in the early 1990s incapable of joining forces or providing a credible alternative to the ruling party. The general election of February 18, 1990 still gave the scandal-shaken LDP a stable majority in the lower house, making it likely that not only Mitsu's great-great-grandchildren, but also her great-great-great grandchildren, would grow to maturity under a LDP prime minister.

The Postwar Constitution

On July 26, 1945, Allied leaders Winston Churchill, Harry S. Truman, and Joseph Stalin issued the Potsdam Declaration, which demanded Japan's unconditional surrender. This declaration also defined the major goals of the postsurrender Allied occupation: "The Japanese government shall remove all obstacles to the revival and strengthening of democratic tendencies among the Japanese people. Freedom of speech, of religion, and of thought, as well as respect for the fundamental human rights shall be established" (Section 10). In addition, this document stated: "The occupying forces of the Allies shall be withdrawn from Japan as soon as these objectives have been accomplished and there has been established in accordance with the freely expressed will of the Japanese people a peacefully inclined and responsible government" (Section 12). The Allies sought not merely punishment or reparations from a militaristic foe, but fundamental changes in the nature of its political system. In the words of political scientist Robert Ward: "The occupation was perhaps the single most exhaustively planned operation of massive and externally directed political change in world history."

The wording of the Potsdam Declaration—"The Japanese Government shall remove all obstacles . . ."—and the initial post-surrender measures taken by MacArthur, the Supreme Commander for the Allied Powers (SCAP), suggest that neither he nor his superiors in Washington intended to impose a new political system on Japan unilaterally. Instead, they wished to encourage new Japanese leaders to initiate democratic reforms on their own. But by early 1946, MacArthur's staff and Japanese officials were at odds over the most fundamental issue, the writing of a new constitution. Prime Minister Shidehara Kijūrō and many of his colleagues were extremely reluctant to take the drastic step of replacing the 1889 Meiji Constitution with a more liberal document. In late 1945, Shidehara appointed Matsumoto Jōji, state minister without portfolio, head of a blue-ribbon committee of constitutional scholars to suggest revisions. The Matsumoto Commission's recommendations, made public in February 1946, were quite conservative (described by one Japanese scholar in the late 1980s as "no more than a touching-up of the Meiji Constitution"). MacArthur rejected them outright and ordered his staff to draft a completely new document. This was presented to surprised Japanese officials on February 13, 1946.

The MacArthur draft, which proposed a unicameral legislature, was changed at the insistence of the Japanese to allow a bicameral legislature, both houses being elected. In most other important respects, however, the ideas embodied in the February 13 document were adopted by the government in its own draft proposal of March 6. These included the Constitution's most distinctive features: the symbolic role of the emperor, the prominence of guarantees of civil and human rights, and the renunciation of war. The new document was approved by the Privy Council, the House of Peers, and the House of Representatives, the major organs of government in the 1889 constitution, and promulgated on November 3, 1946, to go into effect on May 3, 1947. Technically, the 1947 Constitution was an amendment to the 1889 document rather than its abrogation.

The new Constitution would not have been written as it was had MacArthur and his staff allowed Japanese politicians and constitutional experts to resolve the issue as they wished. The document's foreign origins have, understandably, been a focus of controversy since Japan recovered its sovereignty in 1952. Yet in late 1945 and 1946, there was much public discussion on constitutional reform, and the MacArthur draft was apparently greatly influenced by the ideas of certain Japanese liberals. The MacArthur draft did not attempt to impose an American-style presidential or federal system.

Instead, the proposed Constitution conformed to the British model of parliamentary government, which was seen by the liberals as the most viable alternative to the European absolutism of the Meiji Constitution.

After 1952 conservatives and nationalists attempted to revise the Constitution to make it more "Japanese," but these attempts were frustrated for a number of reasons. One was the extreme difficulty of amending it. Amendments require approval by two-thirds of the members of both houses of the National Diet (see Glossary; The Legislature, this ch.), before they can be presented to the people in a referendum (Article 96). Also, opposition parties, occupying more than one-third of the Diet seats, were firm supporters of the constitutional status quo. Even for members of the ruling LDP, the Constitution was not disadvantageous. They had been able to fashion a policy-making process congenial to their interests within its framework. Nakasone Yasuhiro, a strong advocate of constitutional revision during much of his political career, for example, downplayed the issue while serving as prime minister between 1982 and 1987.

The Status of the Emperor

In the Meiji Constitution, the emperor was sovereign and the locus of the state's legitimacy: as the preamble stated, "The rights of sovereignty of the State, We have inherited from Our Ancestors, and We shall bequeath them to Our descendants." In the postwar Constitution, the emperor's role in the political system was drastically redefined. A prior and important step in this process was Emperor Hirohito's 1946 New Year's speech, made at the prompting of MacArthur, renouncing his status as a divine ruler. Hirohito declared that relations between the ruler and his people cannot be based on "the false conception that the emperor is divine or that the Japanese people are superior to other races."

In the first article of the new Constitution, the newly "humanized" ruler is described as "the symbol of the State and of the unity of the people, deriving his position from the will of the people with whom resides sovereign power." The authority of the emperor as sovereign in the 1889 constitution was broad and undefined. His functions under the postwar system are narrow, specific, and largely ceremonial, confined to such activities as convening the Diet bestowing decorations on deserving citizens, and receiving foreign ambassadors (Article 7). He does not possess "powers related to government" (Article 4). The change in the emperor's status was designed to preclude the possibility of military or bureaucratic cliques exercising broad and irresponsible powers "in

Emperor Akihito and Empress Michiko at a press conference, 1989
Courtesy The Mainichi Newspapers

the emperor's name"—a prominent feature of 1930s extremism. The Constitution defines the Diet as the "highest organ of state power" (Article 41), accountable not to the monarch but to the people who elected its members.

The use of the Japanese word *shōchō,* meaning symbol, to describe the emperor is unusual and—depending upon one's viewpoint—conveniently or frustratingly vague. The emperor is neither head of state nor sovereign, as are many European constitutional monarchs, although in October 1988 Japan's Ministry of Foreign Affairs claimed, controversially, that the emperor is the country's sovereign in the context of its external relations. Nor does the emperor have an official priestly or religious role. Although he continues to perform ancient rituals, such as ceremonial planting of the rice crop in spring, he does so in a private capacity.

Laws relating to the imperial house must be approved by the Diet. Under the old system, the Imperial House Law was separate from and equal with the constitution. After the war, the imperial family's extensive estates were confiscated and its finances placed under control of the Imperial Household Agency, part of the Office of the Prime Minister and theoretically subject to the Diet. In practice, the agency in the early 1990s remained a bastion of conservatism, its officials shrouding the activities of the emperor and his family behind a "chrysanthemum curtain" (the chrysanthemum being the crest of the imperial house) to maintain an aura of sanctity. Despite knowledge of his illness among the press corps and other observers, details about the late Emperor Hirohito's state of health in 1988 and 1989 were tightly controlled. In the early 1990s, the use of the masculine pronoun to describe the emperor was appropriate because the Imperial Household Law still restricted the succession to males—despite the fact that in earlier centuries some of Japan's rulers had been women (see Nara and Heian Periods, A.D. 710–1185, ch. 1).

The emperor's constitutional status became a focus of renewed public attention following news of Hirohito's serious illness in late 1988. Crown Prince Akihito became the first person to ascend the throne under the postwar system. One important symbolic issue was the choice of a new reign title under the *gengō* system—borrowed originally from imperial China and used before 1945—which enumerates years beginning with the first year of a monarch's reign. Thus 1988 was Shōwa 63, the sixty-third year of the reign of Hirohito, the Shōwa Emperor. The accession of a new monarch is marked by the naming of a new era that consists of two auspicious Chinese characters. *Shōwa,* for example, means bright harmony. Critics deplored the secrecy with which such titles were chosen in the past, the decision being left to a government-appointed committee of experts, and advocated public discussion of the choice as a reflection of Japan's democratic values. Although the *gengō* system was accorded official status by a bill the Diet passed in June 1979, some favored the system's abandonment altogether in favor of the Western calendar. But on January 7, 1989, the day of Hirohito's death, the government announced that Heisei (Achieving Peace) was the new era name. The first year of Heisei thus was 1989, and all official documents were so dated.

Still more controversial were the ceremonies held in connection with the late emperor's funeral and the new emperor's accession. State support of these activities would have violated Article 20 of the Constitution on the separation of state and religious activities. Rightists, such as members of the Society to Protect Japan (Nihon o Mamoru Kai), a nationwide lobbying group, demanded full public support of the ceremonies as expression of the people's love for their monarch. Walking a tightrope between pro-Constitution and rightist groups, the government chose to divide Hirohito's state funeral, held February 24, 1989, into official and religious components. Akihito's accession to the throne in November 1990 also had religious (Shinto) and secular components: the Sokui-no-rei, or Enthronement Ceremony, was secular; the Daijōsai, or Great

Thanksgiving Festival—traditionally, a communion between the new monarch and the gods in which the monarch himself became a deity—was religious. The government's decision to use public funds not only for the Sokui-no-rei but also for the Daijōsai, justified in terms of the "public nature" of both ceremonies, was seen by religious and opposition groups as a serious violation of Article 20.

In the early 1990s, an array of such symbolic political issues brought attention to the state's role in religious or quasi-religious activities. Defenders of the Constitution, including Japanese Christians, followers of new religions, leftists, and many members of the political opposition, considered any government involvement in religious aspects of the enthronement to be a conservative attempt to undermine the spirit, if not the letter, of the Constitution. They also strongly criticized the 1989 Ministry of Education, Science, and Culture's controversial directive, which called for the playing of the prewar national anthem ("Kimigayo," or "The Sovereign's Reign") and display of the rising sun flag (Hinomaru, the use of which dates to the early nineteenth century) at public school ceremonies. Although since the late 1950s, these activities had been described by the ministry as "desirable," neither had legal status under the postwar Constitution.

Another issue was state support for the Yasukuni Shrine. This shrine, located in Tokyo near the Imperial Palace, was established during the Meiji era as a repository for the souls of soldiers and sailors who died in battle, thus a holy place rather than simply a war memorial. Conservatives introduced bills five times during the 1970s to make it a "national establishment," but none was adopted. On the fortieth anniversary of the end of World War II, August 15, 1985, Prime Minister Nakasone Yasuhiro and members of his cabinet visited the shrine in an official capacity, an action viewed as a renewed conservative effort, outside the Diet, to invest the shrine with official status.

Despite the veneer of Westernization and Article 20's prohibition of state support of the emperor's religious or ceremonial activities, his postwar role was in some ways more like that of traditional rather than prewar emperors. During the Meiji (1868–1912), Taishō (1912–26), and early Shōwa (1926–89) eras, the emperor himself was not actively involved in politics. His political authority, however, was immense, and military and bureaucratic elites acted in his name. The "symbolic" role of the emperor after 1945, however, recalled feudal Japan, where political power was monopolized and exercised by the shoguns, and the imperial court carried on a leisurely, apolitical existence in the ancient capital of Kyōto and served as patrons of culture and the arts (see Kamakura and Muromachi Periods, 1185–1573, ch. 1; Religious and Philosophical Traditions, ch. 2).

Emperor Akihito, in an effort to put a modern face on the Japanese monarchy, held a press conference on August 7, 1989, his first since ascending to the throne. He expressed his determination to respect the Constitution and promote international understanding.

The Article 9 "No War" Clause

Another distinctive feature of the Constitution, and one that has generated as much controversy as the status of the emperor, is the Article 9 "No War" clause. It contains two paragraphs: the first states that the Japanese people "forever renounce war as a sovereign right of the nation and the threat or use of force as a means of settling international disputes," the second that "land, sea, and air forces, as well as other war potential will never be maintained." Some historians attribute the inclusion of Article 9 to Charles Kades, one of MacArthur's closest associates, who was impressed by the spirit of the 1928 Kellogg-Briand Pact renouncing war (see Diplomacy, ch. 1). MacArthur himself claimed that the idea had been suggested to him by Prime Minister Shidehara. The article's acceptance by the Japanese government may in part be explained by the desire to protect the imperial throne. Some Allied leaders saw the emperor as the primary factor in Japan's warlike behavior. His assent to the "No War" clause weakened their arguments in favor of abolishing the throne or trying the emperor as a war criminal.

Article 9 has had broad implications for foreign policy, the institution of judicial review as exercised by the Supreme Court, the status of the Self-Defense Forces, and the nature and tactics of opposition politics (see Major Foreign Policy Goals and Strategies, ch. 7; The Self-Defense Forces, ch. 8). During the late 1980s, increases in government appropriations for the Self-Defense Forces averaged more than 5 percent per year. By the early 1990s, Japan was ranked third, behind the Soviet Union and the United States, in total defense expenditures, and the United States urged Japan to assume a larger share of the burden of defense of the western Pacific. Given these circumstances, some have viewed Article 9 as increasingly irrelevant. It has remained, however, an important brake on the growth of Japan's military capabilities. Despite the fading of bitter wartime memories, the general public, according to opinion polls, continued to show strong support for this constitutional provision.

The cenotaph for victims of the atomic bomb, Peace Memorial Park, Hiroshima. The Atomic Bomb Dome, at the epicenter of the 1945 detonation, is seen through the arch.
Courtesy Jane T. Griffin

Rights and Duties of Citizens

"The rights and duties of the people" are prominently featured in the postwar Constitution. Altogether, 31 of its 103 articles are devoted to describing them in considerable detail, reflecting the commitment to "respect for the fundamental human rights" of the Potsdam Declaration. Although the Meiji Constitution had a section devoted to the "rights and duties of subjects," which guaranteed "liberty of speech, writing, publication, public meetings, and associations," these rights were granted "within the limits of law." Freedom of religious belief was allowed "insofar as it does not interfere with the duties of subjects" (all Japanese were required to acknowledge the emperor's divinity, and those, such as Christians, who refused to do so out of religious conviction were accused of lèse-majesté).

Such freedoms are delineated in the postwar Constitution without qualification. In addition, the later Constitution guarantees freedom of thought and conscience; academic freedom; the prohibition of discrimination based on race, creed, social status, or family origin; and a number of what could be called welfare rights: the

313

right to "minimum standards of wholesome and cultured living," the right to "equal education," the "right and obligation to work" according to fixed standards of labor and wages, and the right of workers to organize. Equality of the sexes and the right of marriage based on mutual consent (in contrast to arranged marriage in the most traditional sense, in which families decide on the match) are also recognized. Limitations are placed on personal freedoms only insofar as they are not abused (Article 12) or interfere with public welfare (Article 13). The bestowal of the power of judicial review on the Supreme Court (Article 81) is in part meant to serve as a means of defending individual rights from infringement by public authorities (see The Judicial System, this ch.).

Some United States origins of the Constitution are revealed in the phraseology of Article 13, which states that the right of the people to "life, liberty, and the pursuit of happiness" shall be the "supreme consideration in legislation and other governmental affairs." It was with some awkwardness that such concepts were translated into Japanese. Yet the document goes further in enumerating rights than do the United States and many other Western constitutions. For example, the article pertaining to equality of the sexes (Article 14) bans sexual (as well as racial, religious, and social) discrimination "in political, economic, or social relations" as clearly as the proposed United States equal rights amendment, which failed to be ratified during the 1970s and 1980s. Unlike their Japanese counterparts, United States schoolteachers and university professors are not protected by a special provision on academic freedom (Article 23). Instead, American teaching and research activities are subsumed under the more general guarantee of freedom of speech in the First Amendment.

The Structure of Government

The Legislature

Article 41 of the Constitution describes the National Diet, or national legislature, as "the highest organ of state power" and "the sole law-making organ of the State" (see fig. 7). This statement is in forceful contrast to the Meiji Constitution, which described the emperor as the one who exercised legislative power with the consent of the Diet. The Diet's responsibilities include not only the making of laws but also the approval of the annual national budget that the government submits and the ratification of treaties. It can also initiate draft constitutional amendments, which, if approved, must be presented to the people in a referendum. The Diet may conduct "investigations in relation to government" (Article

62). The prime minister must be designated by Diet resolution, establishing the principle of legislative supremacy over executive government agencies (Article 67). The government can also be dissolved by the Diet if it passes a motion of no confidence introduced by fifty members of the House of Representatives, the lower chamber. Government officials, including the prime minister and cabinet members, are required to appear before Diet investigative committees and answer inquiries. The Diet also has the power to impeach judges convicted of criminal or irregular conduct.

Japan's legislature is bicameral. Both the upper house, the House of Councillors, and the lower house, the House of Representatives, are elective bodies. The Constitution's Article 14 declares that "peers and peerages shall not be recognized." Upon its enactment, the old House of Peers was abolished. Members of the two new houses are elected by universal adult suffrage, and secrecy of the ballot is guaranteed (Article 15). The term of the House of Representatives is four years. It may be dissolved earlier, however, if the prime minister or members of the House of Representatives decide to hold a general election before the expiration of that term (Article 7). Multiple representatives are elected from 130 constituencies based theoretically on population (see The Electoral System, this ch.). In 1990 the House of Representatives had 512 members.

Members of the House of Councillors have six-year terms. One half of these terms expire every three years. There are two types of constituencies in the upper house: prefectural constituencies, for the forty-seven prefectures and districts, represented by 152 councillors, apportioned according to the district populations; and a national "proportional representation" constituency, represented by 100 councillors, which yields a total of 252. The proportional representation system, introduced in 1982, was the first major electoral reform under the postwar Constitution. Instead of choosing national constituency candidates as individuals, as had previously been the case, voters cast ballots for parties. Individual councillors, listed officially by the parties before the election, are selected on the basis of the parties' proportions of the total national constituency vote. The system was introduced to reduce the excessive money spent by candidates for the national constituencies. Critics charged, however, that this new system benefited the two largest parties, the LDP and Japan Socialist Party (Nihon Shakaitō), which in fact had sponsored the reform.

The House of Representatives has the greater power of the two contemporary houses, in contrast to the prewar system in which the two houses had equal status. According to Article 59, a bill

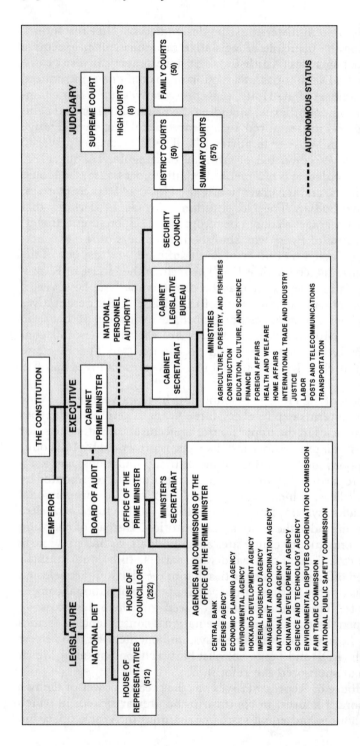

Source: Based on information from *Who's Who in Japanese Government, 1988–1989,* Tokyo, 1988, 4–5, 258–59, 260–61; and United States, Central Intelligence Agency, Directorate of Intelligence, *Chiefs of State and Cabinet Members of Foreign Governments: A Reference Aid,* Washington: July–August 1990, 41.

Figure 7. Structure of National Government, 1990

that is approved by the House of Representatives but turned down by the House of Councillors returns to the House of Representatives. If the latter passes the bill with a two-thirds or higher majority on this second ballot, the bill becomes law. However, three important exceptions to the principle exist, covering the approval of the budget, adoption of treaties with foreign countries, and the selection of the prime minister. In all three cases, if the upper and lower houses have a disagreement that is not resolved by a joint committee of the two houses, then after a lapse of thirty days "the decision of the House of Representatives shall be the decision of the Diet" (Articles 60, 61, and 67). Budgeting is an important annual political function, setting both taxes and the allowable expenditures of all segments of the central government, and the impotence of the upper house has been demonstrated on a number of occasions. Nevertheless, the House of Councillors, with its fixed terms, cannot be dissolved by the prime minister. In times of emergency, the cabinet may convene the House of Councillors rather than the House of Representatives (Article 54).

In the July 23, 1989, election for half the members of the House of Councillors, the LDP lost its majority. It won only 36 of the 126 seats contested in the prefectural and national constituencies, while the opposition parties together won 90; the largest opposition party, the Japan Socialist Party, won 46 (see table 36, Appendix). This result gave an admittedly unstable coalition of opposition groups the opportunity to use the limited powers of the upper house to delay or frustrate initiatives taken in the LDP-dominated lower house. On August 9, 1989, for the first time in forty-one years, the two houses nominated two different candidates for prime minister—Kaifu Toshiki of the LDP and Doi Takako of the Japan Socialist Party. Although Kaifu was finally chosen because of the principle of lower house supremacy, the events showed how opposition control of the upper house could complicate the political process. In March 1990, the upper house rejected a supplementary budget bill for fiscal year (FY—see Glossary) 1989 that had been proposed by the lower house. Although the bill was eventually approved despite upper house rejection, the wrangling caused some minor inconvenience to the country's more than 1 million national civil servants whose monthly salary payments were delayed. The more serious upheaval, that might have occurred had there been a real deadlock or a potential shift in fiscal policies brought about by the opposition parties, was avoided.

The Cabinet and Ministries

In the postwar political system, executive power is vested in the cabinet. The cabinet head is the prime minister, responsible for appointing and dismissing other cabinet members. Cabinet ministers include those appointed to head the ministries, twelve in number, and ministers of state placed in charge of the commissions and agencies of the Office of the Prime Minister, which itself has the status of a ministry. They include the director general of the Defense Agency, equivalent to a minister of defense but lacking ministerial status (a reflection of the Article 9 renunciation of war). Also among the ministers of state are the chief cabinet secretary, who coordinates the activities of the ministries and agencies, conducts policy research, and prepares materials to be discussed at cabinet meetings, and the director of the Cabinet Legislative Bureau, who advises cabinet members on drafting the legislation to be proposed to the Diet. Although the chief cabinet secretary does not have ministerial rank, the position is influential within the cabinet because of its coordination role.

The Board of Audit reviews government expenditures and submits an annual report to the Diet. The 1947 Board of Audit Law gives this body substantial independence from both cabinet and Diet control. The Security Council advises the prime minister on salaries and other matters pertaining to national government civil servants. Semiautonomous public corporations—including public housing corporations, financial institutions, and Japan Broadcasting Corporation (Nippon Hōsō Kyōkai—NHK, which was the sole, noncommercial public radio and television broadcasting system)—had been reduced in number by the privatization of Japan Airlines, the Japanese National Railways, the Japan Tobacco and Salt Public Corporation, and Nippon Telegraph and Telephone Corporation during the 1980s, but there still remained ninety-seven such organizations in 1988.

National government civil servants are divided into "special" and "regular" categories. Appointments in the special category are governed by political or other factors and do not involve examinations. This category includes cabinet ministers, heads of independent agencies, members of the Self-Defense Forces, Diet officials, and ambassadors. The core of the civil service is composed of members of the regular category, who are recruited through competitive examinations. This group is further divided into junior service and upper professional levels, the latter forming a well-defined civil service elite (see The Civil Service, this ch.).

Local Government

As of 1990, Japan was divided into forty-seven administrative divisions: one metropolitan district (*to*—Tokyo), two urban prefectures (*fu*—Kyōto and Ōsaka), forty-three regular prefectures (*ken*), and one district (*dō*—Hokkaidō) (see fig. 8). Large cities were sub-divided into wards (*ku*), and further split into precincts (*machi* or *chō*), or subdistricts (*shichō*) and counties (*gun*).

Each of the forty-seven local jurisdictions has a governor and a unicameral assembly, both elected by popular vote every four years. All are required by national law to maintain departments of general affairs, finance, welfare, health, and labor. Departments of agriculture, fisheries, forestry, commerce, and industry are optional, depending on local needs. The governor is responsible for all activities supported through local taxation or the national government.

Cities (*shi*) are self-governing units administered independently of the larger jurisdictions within which they are located. In order to attain *shi* status, a jurisdiction must have at least 30,000 inhabitants, 60 percent of whom are engaged in urban occupations. City government is headed by a mayor elected for four years by popular vote. There are also popularly elected city assemblies. The wards (*ku*) of larger cities also elect their own assemblies, which select ward superintendents.

The terms *machi* and *chō* designate self-governing towns outside the cities as well as precincts of urban wards. Like the cities, each has its own elected mayor and assembly. Villages (*son* or *mura*) are the smallest self-governing entities in rural areas. They often consist of a number of rural hamlets (*buraku*) containing several thousand people connected to one another through the formally imposed framework of village administration. Villages have mayors and councils elected to four-years terms.

Japan has a unitary rather than federal system of government, in which local jurisdictions largely depend on national government both administratively and financially. Although much less powerful than its prewar counterpart, the Home Ministry, the postwar Ministry of Home Affairs, and other national ministries as well, have the authority to intervene significantly in regional and local government. The result of this power is a high level of organizational and policy standardization among the different local governments. Because local tax revenues are insufficient to support prefectural and city governments, these bodies depend on central government for subsidies. The term "30 percent autonomy" is frequently used to describe local government because that amount of revenues is derived from local taxation. Yet local governments are not entirely passive. People have a strong sense of local community, are highly suspicious of central government, and wish to preserve the uniqueness of their prefecture, city, or town. Some of the more progressive jurisdictions, such as Tokyo and Kyōto,

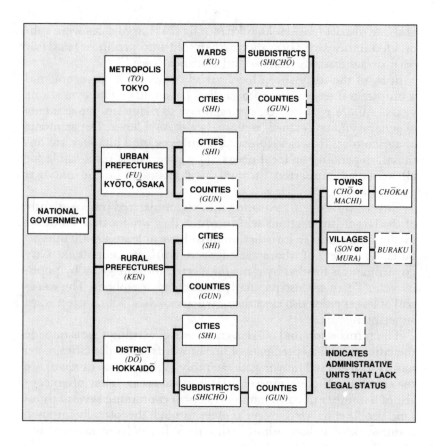

Figure 8. Structure of Local Government, 1990

have experimented with policies in such areas as social welfare that later were adopted by the national government.

The Electoral System

The Japanese political system has three types of elections: general elections to the House of Representatives held every four years (unless the lower house is dissolved earlier), elections to the House of Councillors held every three years to choose one-half of its members, and local elections held every four years for offices in prefectures, cities, and villages. Elections are supervised by election committees at each administrative level under the general direction of the Central Election Administration Committee. The minimum voting age for persons of both sexes is twenty years; voters must satisfy a three-month residency requirement before being allowed to cast a ballot. For those seeking office, there are two sets of age requirements: twenty-five years of age for admission to the House of Representatives and most local offices, and thirty years of age for admission to the House of Councillors and the prefectural governorship.

In the general election of February 18, 1990, the thirty-ninth held since the first parliamentary election in July 1890, the 130 multiple-seat election districts of the House of Representatives returned two to five representatives, depending on their population. There were two exceptions: the district encompassing the Amami Islands, south of Kyūshū, elected only one representative to the lower house, while the first district of Hokkaidō elected six. Successful candidates were those who won at least the fifth largest aggregation of votes in a five-person district, the fourth largest in a four-person district, and so on. Voters cast their ballots for only one candidate. Competition for lower house seats in the February 1990 general election varied from district to district. Tokyo's fourth district had seventeen candidates running for five seats, while the second district in Ibaraki Prefecture had only four persons running for three seats. In Okinawa Prefecture's single five-seat district, there were only six candidates.

In House of Councillors elections, the prefectural constituencies elect from two to eight councillors depending on their population. Each voter casts one ballot for a prefectural candidate and a second one for a party in the national constituency system.

Percentages of eligible voters casting ballots in postwar elections for the House of Representatives have varied within a rather narrow range, from 76.9 percent in May 1958 to 67.9 percent in December 1983. The figure for the February 18, 1990, general election was 72.4 percent. Although interest in politics is greater in urban than rural areas, voter turnout in the latter is generally higher, probably because constituents have a greater personal stake in such elections.

Elections and Political Funding

Partly as a result of revelations following the Recruit scandal of 1988–89, the problem of political funding was intensely debated during the late 1980s and early 1990s. The scandal arose through the dealings of Ezoe Hiromasa, ambitious chairman of the board of the Recruit Corporation (a professional search service that had diversified into finance and real estate, and had become involved in politics), who sold large blocks of untraded shares in a subsidiary, Recruit Cosmos, to seventy-six individuals. When the stock was traded over the counter in 1986, its price jumped, earning individual investors as much as ¥100 million (for value of the yen—see Glossary) in after-sales profits. The persons involved included the most influential leaders of the LDP (usually through their aides or spouses) and a smaller number of opposition party figures. Although such insider trading was not strictly illegal, it caused public outrage at a time when the ruling party was considering a highly controversial consumption tax. Before the scandal ran its weary course, Takeshita Noboru was obliged to resign as prime minister in April 1989, a senior aide committed suicide in expiation for his leader's humiliation, and former Prime Minister Nakasone Yasuhiro resigned from the LDP—becoming an "independent" Diet member—to spare the much-tainted party further shame.

Regarding the background issue of political funding, a group of parliamentarians belonging to the ruling LDP estimated in 1987 that annual expenses for ten newly elected members of the Diet averaged ¥120 million each, or about $US800,000 (see table 34, Appendix). This figure, which included expenses for staff and constituent services in a member's home district, was less than the average for Diet members as a whole, because long-term incumbents tend to incur higher expenses. Yet in the late 1980s, the government provided each Diet member with only ¥20 million for annual operating expenses, leaving ¥100 million to be obtained through private contributions, political party faction bosses, or other means (see The Liberal Democratic Party, this ch.). The lack of public funding meant that politicians—especially, but not exclusively, members of the LDP—needed constant infusions of cash to stay in office.

Maintaining staff and offices in Tokyo and the home district constituted the biggest expense. Near-obligatory attendance at the weddings and funerals of constituents and their families, however, was another large financial drain: the Japanese custom requires that attendees contribute cash, handed over discreetly in elaborately decorated envelopes, to the parents of the bride and groom or to the bereaved.

After revelations of corrupt activities forced the resignation of Prime Minister Tanaka Kakuei, postwar Japan's most skillful practitioner of "money politics," in 1974, the 1948 Political Funds Control Law was amended to establish ceilings for contributions from corporations, other organizations, and individuals. This change forced Diet members to seek a larger number of smaller contributions to maintain cash flow. Fund-raising parties to which tickets were sold were a major revenue source during the 1980s, and the abuse of these ticket sales became a public concern. Another related problem was the secrecy surrounding political funds and their use. Although many politicians, including members of newly appointed cabinets, voluntarily disclosed their personal finances, such disclosure was not compulsory in the early 1990s and many sources of revenue remained obscure.

Proposals for system reform in the early 1990s included compulsory full disclosure of campaign funding, more generous public allowances for Diet members to reduce (or, ideally, to eliminate) their reliance on under-the-table contributions, and stricter penalties for violators, including lengthy periods of being barred from running for public office. Some commentators advocated replacement of the lower house's multiple-seat election district system with single-seat constituencies like those found in Britain and the United States. It was argued that the multiple-seat districts made election campaigning more expensive because party members from the same district had to compete among themselves for the votes of the same constituents. It was hoped that the smaller size of single-seat districts would also reduce the expense of staff, offices, and constituent services. Critics argued, however, that the creation of single-seat constituencies would virtually eliminate the smaller opposition parties and would either create a United States-style two-party system or give the LDP an even greater majority in the lower house than it enjoyed under the multiple-seat system.

In contrast with multimillion-dollar United States political campaigns, direct expenses for the comparatively short campaigns before Japanese general, upper house, and local elections were relatively modest. The use of posters and pamphlets was strictly regulated, and candidates appeared on the noncommercial public television station, NHK, to give short campaign speeches. Most of this activity was publicly funded. Campaign sound-trucks wove their way through urban and rural streets, often bombarding residents with earsplitting harangues from candidates or their supporters. No politician, however, could expect to remain in office without considering expenses for constituent services the most important component of campaign expenses.

Electoral Districts

The apportionment of electoral districts in the early 1990s still reflected the distribution of the population in the years following World War II, when only one-third of the people lived in urban areas and two-thirds lived in rural areas. In the next forty-five years, the population became more than three-quarters urban, as people deserted rural communities to seek economic opportunities in Tokyo and other large cities (see Migration, ch. 2). The lack of reapportionment led to a serious underrepresentation of urban voters. Urban districts in the House of Representatives were increased by five in 1964, bringing nineteen new representatives to the lower house; in 1975, six more urban districts were established, with a total of twenty new representatives allocated to them and to other urban districts. Yet great inequities remained between urban and rural voters.

In the early 1980s, as many as five times the votes were needed to elect a representative from an urban district, as compared to a rural district. Similar disparities existed in the prefectural constituencies of the House of Councillors. The Supreme Court had ruled on several occasions that the imbalance violated the constitutional principle of one person-one vote. The Supreme Court mandated the addition of eight representatives to urban districts and the removal of seven from rural districts in 1986. Several lower house districts' boundaries were redrawn. Yet the disparity was still as much as three urban votes to one rural vote in the early 1990s.

After the 1986 change, the average number of total persons per lower house representative was 236,424. However, the figure varied from 427,761 persons per representative in the fourth district of Kanagawa Prefecture, which contains the large city of Yokohama, to 142,932 persons in the third district of largely rural and mountainous Nagano Prefecture. A major reapportionment seemed unlikely in the near future, since rural voters remained a major source of support for the LDP (see Interest Groups, this ch.).

The Judicial System

In contrast to the prewar system, in which executive bodies had much control over the courts, the postwar Constitution guarantees that "all judges shall be independent in the exercise of their conscience and shall be bound only by this Constitution and the Laws" (Article 76). They cannot be removed from the bench "unless judicially declared mentally or physically incompetent to perform official duties" and they cannot be disciplined by executive agencies (Article 78). A Supreme Court justice, however, may be removed by a majority of voters in a referendum that occurs at the first general election following the justice's appointment and every ten years thereafter. As of the early 1990s, however, the electorate had not used this unusual system to dismiss a justice.

The Supreme Court, the highest court, is the final court of appeal in civil and criminal cases. The Constitution's Article 81 designates it "the court of last resort with power to determine the constitutionality of any law, order, regulation, or official act." The Supreme Court is also responsible for nominating judges to lower courts, determining judicial procedures, overseeing the judicial

The Diet building completed in 1936; the House of Representatives is in the left wing, the House of Councillors in the right.
Courtesy Jane T. Griffin

system including the activities of public prosecutors, and disciplining judges and other judicial personnel. It renders decisions from either a grand bench of fifteen justices or a petty bench of five. The grand bench is required for cases involving constitutionality. The court includes twenty research clerks, whose function is similar to that of the clerks of the United States Supreme Court.

The judicial system is unitary: there is no independent system of prefectural level courts equivalent to the state courts of the United States. Below the Supreme Court, the Japanese system included eight high courts, fifty district courts, and fifty family courts in the late 1980s. Four of each of the last two types of courts were located in Hokkaidō, and one of each in the remaining forty-six rural prefectures, urban prefectures, and the Tokyo Metropolitan District. Summary courts, located in 575 cities and towns in the late 1980s, performed the functions of small courts and justices of the peace in the United States, having jurisdiction over minor offenses and civil cases.

Judicial Review

The Supreme Court was generally reluctant to exercise the powers of judicial review given to it by the Constitution, in large part because of unwillingness to become involved in politically sensitive issues. When decisions were rendered on such matters as the constitutionality of the Self-Defense Forces, the sponsorship of Shinto ceremonies by public authorities, or the Ministry of Education, Science, and Culture's right to determine the content of school textbooks or teaching curricula, the court generally took a conservative, progovernment stance.

In the words of political scientist T.J. Pempel, the Supreme Court "has been an important, if frequently unrecognized, vehicle for preserving the status quo in Japan and for reducing the capacity of the courts to reverse executive actions." Important exceptions to this conservative trend, however, were the rulings on the unconstitutionality of the electoral district apportionment system, discussed above.

The Role of Law in Japanese Society

As in other industrialized countries, law plays a central role in Japanese political, social, and economic life. Fundamental differences between Japanese and Western legal concepts, however, have often led Westerners to believe that Japanese society is based more on quasi-feudalistic principles of paternalism (the *oyabun-kobun* relationship) and social harmony, or *wa,* (see Values, ch. 2). Japan has a relatively small number of lawyers, about 13,000 practicing in the mid-1980s compared with 667,000 in the United States, a country with only twice Japan's population. This fact has been offered as evidence that the Japanese are strongly averse to upsetting human relationships by taking grievances to court. In cases of liability, such as the crash of a Japan Airlines jetliner in August 1985, which claimed 520 lives, Japanese victims or their survivors were more willing than their Western counterparts would be to accept the ritualistic condolences of company presidents (including officials' resignations over the incident) and nonjudicially determined compensation, which in many cases was less than they might have received through the courts.

Factors other than a cultural preference for social harmony, however, explain the court-shy behavior of the Japanese. The Ministry of Justice closely screened university law faculty graduates and others who wished to practice law or serve as judges. Only about 2 percent of the approximately 25,000 persons who applied annually to the Ministry's Legal Training and Research Institute two-year required course were admitted in the late 1980s. The institute graduated only a few hundred new lawyers each year. Plagued by shortages of attorneys, judges, clerks, and other personnel, the court system was severely overburdened. Presiding judges often strongly advised plaintiffs to seek out-of-court settlements. The progress of cases through even the lower courts was agonizingly slow, and appeals carried to the Supreme Court could take decades. Faced with such obstacles, most individuals chose not to seek legal remedies. If legal personnel were dramatically increased, which seemed unlikely in the early 1990s, use of the courts might approach rates found in the United States and other Western countries.

In the English-speaking countries, law has been viewed traditionally as a framework of enforceable rights and duties designed to protect the legitimate interests of private citizens. The judiciary is viewed as occupying a neutral stance in disputes between individual citizens and the state. Legal recourse is regarded as a fundamental civil right. The reformers of the Meiji era (1868–1912), however, were strongly influenced by legal theories that had evolved in Germany and other continental European states. The Meiji reformers viewed the law primarily as an instrument through which the state controls a restive population and directs energies to achieving the goals of *fukoku kyōhei* (wealth and arms).

The primary embodiment of the spirit of the law in modern Japan has not been the attorney representing private interests but the bureaucrat who exercises control through what the sociologist Max Weber has called "legal-rational" methods of administration. Competence in law, acquired through university training, consists of implementing, interpreting, and, at the highest levels, formulating law within a bureaucratic framework. Many functions performed by lawyers in the United States and other Western countries are the responsibility of civil servants in Japan. The majority of the country's ruling elite, both political and economic, has been recruited from among the graduates of the Law Faculty of the University of Tokyo and other prestigious institutions, people who have rarely served as private attorneys.

Legal-bureaucratic controls on many aspects of Japanese society were extremely tight. The Ministry of Education, Science, and Culture, for example, closely supervised both public and private universities. Changes in undergraduate or graduate curricula, the appointment of senior faculty, and similar actions required ministry approval in conformity with very detailed regulations. Although this "control-oriented" use of law did not inhibit the freedom of teaching or research (protected by Article 23 of the Constitution), it severely limited the universities' scope for reform and innovation. Controls were even tighter on primary and secondary schools (see Education, ch. 3).

Human Rights

Compared to most of its Asian neighbors and countries in most other parts of the world, Japan's record on human rights was commendable, if not exemplary. With some important exceptions, most observers considered informal social pressures a greater factor in limiting individual freedom than the coercive actions of the authorities. The ancient Japanese adage that "the nail that sticks up gets hammered down" captures the sense that Japanese people are pressured more to conform than are people in the more "individualistic" societies of the West. Some Japanese lower- and upper-secondary schools, for example, have adopted extremely strict dress codes, determining not only apparel but also the length of hair to the exact centimeter. Although defended by conservative educators as a way of cultivating discipline and self-control, these codes have been widely criticized as violations of students' rights. In another example, shopkeepers and local community groups throughout Japan canceled sales promotions and festivals in the wake of Emperor Hirohito's illness in late 1988, for fear of being labelled unpatriotic. This self-restraint movement cost them billions of yen.

Although freedom of expression was, for the most part, respected, certain matters—particularly those relating to the emperor—were widely considered taboo subjects for public figures. Nagasaki City mayor Motoshima Hitoshi, a member of the LDP, said in December 1988 that Hirohito bore some responsibility for World War II; he was later ostracized by influential, mainstream politicians, his life was threatened on several occasions, and in January 1990, he was seriously wounded outside his office by a right-wing extremist. Despite the affront to his father, Emperor Akihito visited Motoshima after the attempt on his life.

Despite Article 14's guarantee of sexual equality, women faced systematic discrimination in the workplace. They were generally expected to quit work after getting married or having children. However, the number of lifelong career women grew steadily during the 1980s and early 1990s. The Diet's passage of the Law for Equal Opportunity in Employment for Men and Women in 1985 was of some help in securing women's rights, even though the law was a "guideline" and entailed no legal penalties for employers who discriminated. The law has, however, been used by women in several court cases seeking equal treatment in such areas as retirement age (see Gender Stratification and the Lives of Women, ch. 2).

Human rights had also become an issue because of the police practice of obtaining confessions from criminal suspects. Although torture was rarely used, suspects were placed under tremendous psychological and physical pressures to confess. In several cases, the courts acknowledged that confessions were forced and ordered prisoners released (see The Criminal Justice System, ch. 8).

The greatest controversy concerning human rights, however, has focused on the social and legal treatment of minorities. Although the Japanese considered themselves to be a homogeneous people, minorities did exist, and they often suffered severe discrimination. The largest group, numbering from 2 million to 4 million in the 1980s, was the *burakumin,* descendants of the outcast communities of feudal Japan. The Ainu, indigenous inhabitants of northern Japan; the people of Okinawa; and ethnic Koreans also have suffered discrimination (see Minorities, ch. 2).

Contemporary Political Values

Japanese politics are generally described as pragmatic, limited by particularistic loyalties, and based on human relations rather than ideology or principles. The quintessential Japanese leader is a network builder rather than the embodiment of charisma or ideals; more like the crafty and resourceful founder of the Tokugawa *bakufu,* Tokugawa Ieyasu, than the ruthless but heroic Oda Nobunaga (see Reunification, 1573–1600; Tokugawa Period, 1600–1867, ch. 1). Such political dynamics are evident, for example, in the workings of the LDP, which has held power without interruption since 1955.

Yet the pragmatic, personalistic view of politics cannot explain Japan's militaristic past, the political crises of the 1960s, the controversies surrounding the emperor, Article 9, or the unwillingness of many in the Japan Socialist Party, despite a huge political cost, to abandon their antiwar and revolutionary commitment in the early 1990s. It also fails to account for the apparently sincerely held ideological beliefs of the wartime period. The "New Order in Greater East Asia" was legitimized on the basis of universal principles, such as "pan-Asianism," "international justice," and "permanent peace," even if the results were quite the opposite (see The Rise of the Militarists, ch. 1). The nonideological nature of mainstream Japanese politics in the postwar period reflects defeat in war, the failure after 1945 to find a national ideological consensus to replace discredited wartime beliefs, and the commitment of both elite and ordinary Japanese to expanding the economy and raising living standards. As these goals were attained, a complacent, largely apolitical "middle mass society" (a term coined by economist Murakami Yasusuke) emerged, in which 90 percent of the people in opinion polls consistently classified themselves as "middle class."

Community and Leadership

Certain distinctive features of Japanese politics can be identified, although this is not to say that they are unique to Japan. Rather, qualities also found in other political systems, such as the importance of personal connections and consensus building, played an extraordinarily important role in Japanese politics. These features have deep historical roots and reflect values that pervade the society as a whole.

In both feudal and modern eras, a major problem for Japanese political leaders has been reconciling the goals of community survival and the welfare and self-respect of individuals in an environment of extreme scarcity. In recent centuries, Japan lacked the natural resources and space to accommodate its population comfortably. With the exception of Hokkaidō and colonial territories in Asia between 1895 and 1945, there was no "frontier" to absorb excess people. One solution was to ignore the welfare of large sectors of the population (poor peasants and workers) and to use force when they expressed their discontent. Such coercive measures, common during both the Tokugawa and World War II periods, largely, although not entirely, disappeared in the postwar "welfare state" (for example, farmers were evicted from their land to construct the New Tokyo International Airport at Narita-Sanrizuka in the 1970s after long negotiations failed). But noncoercive, or mostly noncoercive, methods of securing popular compliance had developed to an extraordinary degree in social and political life.

The most important such method is the promotion of a strong sense of community consciousness and group solidarity. Japanese individuals are often characterized as having a strong sense of self-sacrifice and community dedication. Historians and sociologists note that both traditional and modern Japanese communities—the *buraku,* the feudal domain with its retinue of samurai, the large commercial houses found in Edo (the future Tokyo), Ōsaka, and Kyōto before 1868, and modern corporations and bureaucracies with their cohorts of lifetime employees—have striven to be all-inclusive. Such groups serve a variety of functions for the individual, providing not only income and sustenance but also emotional support and individual identity. Japanese called such community inclusiveness the "octopus-pot way of life" (*takotsubo seikatsu*). Large pots with narrow openings at the top are used by fishermen to capture octopuses, and the term is used to refer to people so wrapped up in their particular social group that they cannot see the world outside its confines.

The "group consciousness" model of Japanese social life, however, has been overstressed at times. A person may often go along

Grass-roots politics, a candidate's parade in Iwate Prefecture
Courtesy Eliot Frankeberger

with group demands because they serve self-interest in the long run (for example, political contributions may help secure future favors from those in office). Historically, democratic concepts of individual rights and limited government have been deeply appealing because they, too, promise protection of individual autonomy. Despite very different ethical and political traditions, the Japanese people were very receptive to imported liberal ideas both before and after 1945. John Stuart Mill's essay *On Liberty,* for example, was extremely popular during the Meiji era.

Because individual, usually passive, resistance to group demands occurred, Japanese leaders have found the creation of a strong community sense to be a difficult and time-consuming task. Harmony (*wa*), that most prized social value, is not easily attained. One mechanism for achieving *wa* is the use of rituals to develop a psychological sense of group identity. Political parties and factions, the offices of national and local governments, businesses, university departments, research groups, alumni associations, and other groups sponsor frequent ceremonies and more informal parties for this purpose. A group's history and identity are carefully constructed through the use of songs and symbols (often resembling, in miniature, the Meiji government's creation of symbols of *kokutai* in the late nineteenth century). Often, an organization's founder, especially if deceased, is regarded as something of a Confucian sage or a Shinto *kami* (deity). Group members, however, may find that pervasive ritualism allows them to "go through the motions" (such as the chanting of *banzai* (ten thousand years) at the end of political rallies, without having to make a deeper commitment to the group.

A second mechanism to promote community solidarity is the building of hierarchical relationships. In this practice, the influence of premodern ethics is readily apparent. In what the anthropologist Nakane Chie calls Japan's "vertical society," human relationships are defined in terms of inequality, and people relate to each other as superiors and inferiors along a minutely differentiated gradient of social status, not only within bureaucratic organizations, where it might be expected, but also in academic, artistic, and especially, political worlds.

Hierarchy expresses itself along two dimensions: first, an internal community differentiation of rank by seniority, education, and occupational status; and second, the distinction between "insiders" and "outsiders," between members and nonmembers of the community, along with the ranking of whole groups or communities along a vertical continuum. Although internal hierarchy can cause alienation as inferiors chafe under the authority of their superiors, the external kind of hierarchy tends to strengthen group cohesion as individual members work to improve their group's relative ranking. The Japanese nation as a whole has been viewed as a single group by its people in relation to other nations. Intense nationalism has frequently been a manifestation of group members' desire to "catch up and overtake" the advanced ("superior") nations of the West, while the rights of non-Western nations, like China or Korea, often viewed as "inferior," have been ignored.

Like group consciousness, however, the theme of hierarchy has been overstressed. Contemporary Japanese politics show a strong consciousness of equality, and even traditional communities, such as rural villages, were often egalitarian rather than hierarchical. Citizens' movements of the 1960s and 1970s differed from older political organizations in their commitment to promoting intragroup democracy. In addressing the nation, Emperor Akihito used colloquial Japanese terms that stressed equality, rather than the formal, hierarchy-laden language of his predecessors.

Two mechanisms for lessening the hierarchy-generated tensions are the seniority principle and early retirement. As men or women grow older, gaining seniority within an organization, they acquire authority and higher status. The seniority principle is reinforced by the traditional reluctance to place younger persons in positions of authority over older ones. The institution of early retirement (top-ranked businesspeople and bureaucrats commonly retired at age fifty-five or sixty) helps to the keep the promotion of others smooth and predictable. The system also helps to enable talented individuals to succeed to the most responsible positions and prevents a small group of older persons (what the Japanese call "one-man leaders") from monopolizing leadership positions and imposing increasingly outmoded ideas on the organization. Elite retirees, however, often continue to wield influence as advisers and usually pursue second careers in organizations affiliated with the one from which they retired.

The circulation of elites that results from the seniority and early retirement principles ensures that everyone within the upper ranks of the hierarchy has a turn at occupying a high-status position, such as a cabinet post in the national government. This principle, in turn, enables people to reward their followers. There has been, for example, a regular turnover of LDP leaders. No individual has served as party president (and prime minister) longer than Satō Eisaku, the incumbent between 1964 and 1972. The average tenure of party presidents/prime ministers between 1964 and 1987 was slightly more than three years. Frequent cabinet reshuffling meant that the average tenure of other cabinet ministers in the same period was a little less than a year. Japan has not been beset with leaders in their seventies and eighties unwilling to give up their powerful positions.

Another mechanism reducing intragroup tensions is the strong personal, rather than legalistic or ideological, ties between superior and subordinate. These ties are typically characterized in terms of fictive familial relationships, analogous to the bonds between parents and children (the *oyabun-kobun* relationship). The ideal leader is viewed as a paternalistic one, with a warm and personal concern for the welfare of his followers. For followers, loyalty is both morally prescribed and emotionally sustained by the system. In the political world, *oyabun-kobun* relationships are pervasive despite the formal commitment to universalistic, democratic values. At the same time, younger people find such relationships less appealing than their elders. The so-called *shinjinrui* (new human beings), born in the affluent 1960s and 1970s, were often criticized by older Japanese for being self-absorbed, egoistic, and "cool," in the 1980s. The younger generation is inclined to view with disdain the emotional expression of paternalistic ties, such as in the 1989 television broadcasts of former Prime Minister Tanaka Kakuei's supporters weeping profusely over his political retirement.

Consensus Building

The community is often demanding, but it is also fragile, because social ties are sustained not only through legal norms and common self-interest, but also through the affective patron-client relationship. Open conflict poses a danger to the survival of this sort of community, and thus policy making requires elaborate consultation and consensus building, usually involving all the parties concerned. According to political scientist Lewis Austin, "Everyone must be consulted informally, everyone must be heard, but not in such a way that the hearing of different opinions develops into opposition. The leader and his assistants 'harmonize opinion'. . . in advance, using go-betweens to avert the confrontation of opposing forces." After a preliminary agreement among all has been reached, a formal meeting is held in which the agreed-upon policy will be proposed and adopted.

This process is called *nemawashi* (root trimming or binding), evoking the image of a gardener preparing a tree or shrub for transplanting, that is, a change in policy. Austin points out that a common Japanese verb meaning "to decide" (*matomeru*) literally means to gather or bring together. Decisions are "the sum of the contributions of all." Although consensus building is, for leaders, a time-consuming and emotionally exhausting process, it is necessary not only to promote group goals but also to respect and protect individual autonomy. In fact, the process represents reconciliation of the two. In the political system as a whole, most groups played some role in the *nemawashi* process in the early 1990s. Exceptions were those groups or individuals, such as Koreans or *burakumin*, who were viewed as outsiders.

Political leaders have to maintain solidarity and harmony within a single group and also secure the cooperation of different groups who are often in bitter conflict. *Takotsubo seikatsu* can promote destructive sectionalism. During World War II, rivalry between the Imperial Army and the Imperial Navy was so intense that it was nearly impossible to coordinate their strategic operations. In the postwar political system, prime ministers have often been unable to persuade different ministries, all self-sufficient and intensely jealous "kingdoms," to go along with reforms in such areas as trade liberalization. Observers such as journalist Karel G. van Wolferen, have concluded that Japan's political system is empty at the center, lacking real leadership or a locus of responsibility: "Statecraft in Japan is quite different from that in the rest of Asia, Europe, and the Americas. For centuries it has entailed the preservation of a careful balance of semiautonomous groups that share power. . . .

334

These semiautonomous components, each endowed with great discretionary powers, are not represented in one central ruling body.'' This view is probably exaggerated. Leadership in other countries, including the United States, has been paralyzed from time to time by powerful interest groups and some policies in Japan requiring decisive leadership, such as the creation of social welfare and energy conservation policies in the 1970s and the privatization of state enterprises in the 1980s, have been reasonably successful.

Interest Groups

The emphasis on consensus in Japanese politics is seen in the role of interest groups in policy making. In the early 1990s, these groups ranged from those with economic interests, such as occupational and professional associations, to those with strong ideological commitments, such as the right-wing Society to Protect Japan and the left-wing Japan Teachers Union (Nihon Kyōshokuin Kumiai—Nikkyōsō). There were groups representing minorities (the Burakumin Liberation League, the Central Association of Korean Residents in Japan [Chōsōren], and Utari Kyōkai in Hokkaidō, representing the Ainu community), groups representing war veterans and postwar repatriates from Japan's overseas colonies (the Military Pensions Association and the Association of Repatriates), the victims of the atomic bombings of Hiroshima and Nagasaki, and women opposed to prostitution and the threat to public morals posed by businesses offering ''adult'' entertainment (the Japan Mothers League). Mayors' and prefectural governors' associations promoted regional development. Residents' movements near United States military installations in Okinawa and elsewhere pressured local authorities to support reductions in base areas and to exert more control over United States military personnel off base. The great majority of Japanese were connected, either directly or indirectly, to one or more of these bodies.

In the postwar period, extremely close ties emerged among major interest groups, political parties, and the bureaucracy. Many groups identified so closely with the ruling LDP that it was often difficult to discern the borders between party and group membership. Officers of agricultural, business, and professional groups were elected to the Diet as LDP legislators. Groups of LDP parliamentarians formed *zoku* (tribes), which represented the interests of occupational constituencies, such as farmers, small businesses, and the construction industry. The *zoku,* interest groups, and bureaucrats worked together closely in formulating policy in such areas as agriculture (see Bureaucrats and the Policy-making Process, this ch.).

In the case of the Japan Socialist Party, Democratic Socialist Party, Japan Communist Party (Nihon Kyōsantō), and Kōmeitō (Clean Government Party), the links with interest groups were even more intimate. Before the Japanese Trade Union Confederation (Shin Rengō) was established in 1989, most leaders of the Japan Socialist Party and Democratic Socialist Party and many socialist Diet members had been officers of the confederation's predecessors, the General Council of Trade Unions of Japan (Nihon Rōdō Kumiai Sōhyōgikai, or Sōhyō for short) founded in 1950, and the Japan Confederation of Labor (Zen Nihon Rōdō Sōdōmei, or Dōmei for short), established in 1964. Despite repeated disavowals, the Kōmeitō remained, in the early 1990s, related to its parent body, the Sōka Gakkai (Value Creation Society), an organization of lay followers of the Buddhist sect, Nichiren Shōshū, founded before World War II and one of Japan's most successful new religions (see Kōmeitō, this ch.; Religious and Philosophical Traditions, ch. 2). The communists had their own unions and small business groups, which competed with conservative small business associations. Japan's relatively few lawyers divided their allegiance among three professional groups separately affiliated with the LDP, the Japan Socialist Party, and the Japan Communist Party.

Both the LDP and the opposition parties, which had weak regional organizations, depended on the interest groups to win elections. The interest groups provided funding, blocks of loyal voters (although these could not be manipulated as easily as in the past), and local organizational networks.

One important question concerning interest groups in any country is how well they represent the diverse concerns of all the citizens. A second is whether government responds evenhandedly to their demands. Japan's postwar record on both counts was generally good. Both major and minor groups in society were well represented. And the government has implemented policies to spread the blessings of economic growth among the population at large. Such arrangements helped to ensure political stability, and to explain why, in repeated public opinion polls, 90 percent of respondents viewed themselves as "middle class."

After the war, for example, there were major policy changes on agriculture. Despite prewar nationalistic idealization of the rural village, the government at that time squeezed the farmers for taxes and rice. Political scientist Kent Calder observed that "the prewar state took heavily from the countryside, without providing much in return." Historians describe how many farm families starved, or were forced to sell their daughters into prostitution. Responding to the threat of vigorous leftist movements in the countryside, conservative governments after 1945 initiated price supports for rice and other measures that brought the farmers not just a decent standard of living but affluence. By the 1970s, it was not uncommon to encounter group tours of farmers who had never visited Tokyo taking holidays in Hawaii or New York City. In Calder's view, conservative governments were stoutly probusiness but were also willing to coopt other interests such as agriculture at the expense of business to ensure social stability and prevent socialist electoral victories. Sometimes government adopted policies first espoused by the opposition (for example, medical insurance and other social welfare policies).

Business Interests

Links between the corporate world and government were maintained through three national organizations: the Federation of Economic Organizations (Keizai Dantai Rengōkai—Keidanren), established in 1946; the Japan Committee for Economic Development (Keizai Dōyū Kai), established in 1946; and the Japan Federation of Employers Association (Nihon Keieishadantai Renmei—Nikkeiren), established in 1948. In the early 1990s, Keidanren was considered the most important. Its membership included 750 of the largest corporations and 110 manufacturers associations. Its Tokyo headquarters served as a kind of "nerve center" for the country's most important enterprises, and it worked closely with the powerful Ministry of International Trade and Industry (MITI). There was evidence, however, suggesting that the federation's power in the 1990s was not what it had been, partly because major corporations, which had amassed huge amounts of money by the late 1980s, were increasingly capable of operating without its assistance.

Nikkeiren was concerned largely with labor-management relations and with organizing a united business front to negotiate with labor unions on wage demands during the annual "Spring Struggle." The Keizai Dōyū Kai, composed of younger and more liberal business leaders, assigned itself the role of promoting business's social responsibilities. Whereas Keidanren and Nikkeiren were "peak organizations," whose members themselves were associations, members of the Keizai Dōyū Kai, were individual business leaders (see Labor Unions, ch. 4).

Because of financial support from companies, business interest groups were generally more independent of political parties than other groups. Both Keidanren and the Keizai Dōyū Kai, for example, indicated a willingness to talk with the socialists in the wake of the political scandals of 1988–89 and also suggested that the LDP might form a coalition government with an opposition party. Yet through an organization called the People's Politics Association (Kokumin Seiji Kyōkai), they and other top business groups provided the LDP with its largest source of party funding.

Small Business

Japan's streets are lined with small shops, grocery stores, restaurants, and coffeehouses. Although supermarkets and large discount department stores were more common in the early 1990s than a decade earlier, the political muscle of small business associations was reflected in the success with which they blocked the rationalization of the country's distribution system. The Large-Scale Retail Store Law of 1973, amended in 1978, made it very difficult in the late 1980s for either Japanese or foreign retailers to establish large, economically efficient outlets in local communities.

Many light industrial goods, such as toys, footwear, pencils, and kitchen utensils, were still manufactured by small local companies rather than imported from the Republic of Korea (South Korea), Taiwan, or Hong Kong. Traditional handicrafts, such as pottery, silk weaving, and lacquerware, produced using centuries-old methods in small workshops, flourished in every part of the country. Apart from protectionism of the "nontariff barrier" variety, the government assured the economic viability of small enterprises through lenient tax policies and access to credit on especially favorable terms.

Major associations representing small and medium-sized enterprises included the generally pro-LDP Japan Chamber of Commerce and Industry (Nihon Shōkō Kaigisho, or Nisshō for short), which was established in 1922 but whose origins are traced to the establishment of the Tokyo Chamber of Commerce and Industry in 1878, the National Central Association of Medium and Small Enterprise Associations, the Japan League of Medium and Small Enterprise Organizations, and the Japan Communist Party-sponsored Democratic Merchants and Manufacturers Association.

Although small enterprises in services and manufacturing preserved cultural traditions and enlivened urban areas, a major motivation for government nurture of small business was social welfare. In Kent Calder's words, "Much of small business, particularly in the distribution sector, serves as a labor reservoir. Its inefficiencies help absorb surplus workers who would be unemployed if distribution, services, and traditional manufacturing were uniformly as efficient as the highly competitive and modernized export sectors."

Agricultural Cooperatives

Observers have suggested that the great influence of the Central Union of Agricultural Cooperatives (Nōkyō) in policy making partly resulted from a widespread feeling of gratitude to the dwindling agricultural sector, which in the past supported the country's industrial modernization. Nōkyō spokespersons were vociferous in their claims that agriculture is somehow intimately connected with the spirit of the nation. They argued that self-sufficiency, or near self-sufficiency, in food production, resulting from government support of the nation's farmers, was central to Japan's security. The public in general was receptive to their arguments: an opinion poll in 1988, for example, revealed that 70 percent of respondents preferred paying a higher price for rice to importing it.

Nōkyō, organized in 1947 at the time of the land reform, had local branches in every rural village in the late 1980s. Its constituent local agricultural cooperatives included practically all of the population for which farming was the principal occupation. Since its founding, Nōkyō had been preoccupied with maintaining and increasing government price supports on rice and other crops and with holding back the import of cheaper agricultural products from abroad. Self-sufficient in rice, Japan in the late 1980s imported only a tiny quantity. A special variety of Thai rice, for example, is used specifically to make the traditional Okinawan liquor, *awamori*. Nōkyō's determination to preserve "Fortress Japan" in the agricultural realm had brought it into conflict with business groups such as Keidanren, which advocated market liberalization and cheaper food prices.

Although closely allied to the LDP in the past, Nōkyō and other agricultural groups were outraged by the government's concessions to the United States on imports of oranges and beef in 1988. Local cooperatives threatened to defect to the Japan Socialist Party if government continued to give in to American demands. The Japan Socialist Party chairwoman, Doi Takako, made agricultural protectionism a major component of her party's platform.

Labor Organizations

Postwar labor unions were established with the blessings of the occupation authorities. The mechanism for collective bargaining was set up, and unions were organized by enterprise: membership was determined by company affiliation rather than by skill or industry type. In general, membership was also limited to permanent, nonsupervisory personnel. Observers in the late 1980s viewed labor unions' role in the policy-making process as less powerful

339

than that of business and agricultural organizations because the unions' enterprise-based structure made national federations weak and unions were closely associated with parties that remained out of power.

The Japan Socialist Party largely depended on Sōhyō for funding, organizational support, and membership during most of the postwar period. Dōmei performed similar functions for the Democratic Socialist Party. Sōhyō was composed primarily of public sector unions such as those organized for national civil servants, municipal workers, and public school teachers. Dōmei's constituent unions were principally in the private sector. In the late 1980s, however, the labor movement saw significant change. In November 1987, the National Federation of Private Sector Trade Unions (Rengō), an amalgamation of Dōmei and smaller groups, was formed with a membership of 5.5 million workers. After two years of intense negotiations, it joined with 2.5 million members of public sector unions largely affiliated with Sōhyō to establish a new entity, Shin Rengō. With 8 million members, Shin Rengō included 65 percent of Japan's unionized workers and was, after the American Federation of Labor-Congress of Industrial Organizations (AFL–CIO) and the British Trades Union Congress, the world's third largest noncommunist union federation.

Shin Rengō was a moderate, nonideological movement that shunned involvement with Marxist Japan Communist Party-affiliated unions. Two leftist union confederations emerged in the wake of Shin Rengō: the 1.2-million-member Japan Confederation of Trade Unions (Zenrōren), and the 500,000-member National Trade Union Council (Zenrōkyō). The powerful Nikkyōsō, with 675,000 members in the country's public primary and secondary schools, was divided between adherents and opponents of Shin Rengō.

In the early 1990s, the relationship of Shin Rengō to the socialist political parties remained somewhat unclear. It was likely that many old support networks would remain in place. Some noted the new confederation's potential for promoting opposition party unity because it encompassed supporters of the two socialist parties and the small Social Democratic League. In the House of Councillors election on July 23, 1989, the three parties agreed to support twelve Shin Rengō candidates. Eleven of them won.

Professional Associations and Citizen and Consumer Movements

Physicians, dentists, lawyers, academics, and other professionals organized associations for the exchange of knowledge, supervision of professional activities, and influence of government policy, like those found in other developed countries. The Japan Medical Association has used its influence to preserve a highly profitable system in which physicians, rather than pharmacists, sell prescription drugs.

Citizens and consumer movements, which became prominent during the 1960s and 1970s, were organized around issues relating to the quality of life, the protection of the environment from industrial pollution, and the safety (although not the cost) of consumer goods. In the late 1960s, industrial pollution, symbolized by the suffering of victims of mercury poisoning caused by the pollution of Minamata Bay in Kumamoto Prefecture by a chemical company, was viewed as a national crisis. The Satō government responded by establishing the Environmental Agency in the Office of the Prime Minister in 1970, instituting tough penalties for polluters, and extending compensation to the victims of pollution. In the early 1990s, environmental issues continued to be the focus of intense local activity. Communities on Ishigaki Island in Okinawa Prefecture were divided over whether to construct a new airport to handle wide-bodied aircraft on land reclaimed from the sea. Supporters viewed the project as essential to the island's tourist development, while opponents claimed that construction would destroy offshore colonies of rare blue coral and would ruin the local fishing industry. Another environmental issue in many parts of Japan was the use of powerful chemicals on golf courses, which in some cases harmed nearby residents (see Pollution, ch. 2).

Women's groups were in the forefront of the consumer movement. In the early 1990s, they included the National Federation of Regional Women's Associations, the Housewives Association, and the National Association of Consumer Cooperatives. Their activities depended on the support of neighborhood women's associations, the women's sections of local agricultural and fishing cooperatives, and government-sponsored consumer education groups. Although boycotts had been organized against companies making products that the groups viewed as dangerous (for example, canned foods containing carcinogenic cyclamates), they did not, for the most part, demand lower prices for food or other goods. In tandem with agricultural interests, consumer groups opposed increased food imports on the grounds that supply was unpredictable and that they were laced with dangerous additives.

The Mass Media and Politics

Japan is a society awash in information. In the early 1990s, newspaper readership was, by a wide margin, the highest in the world. The six largest and most influential newspapers were *Yomiuri*

Shimbun, Mainichi Shimbun, Asahi Shimbun, Seikyo Shimbun, Sankei Shimbun, and *Nihon Keizai Shimbun.* There were also more than 100 local newspapers. The population, almost 100 percent literate, also consumed record numbers of books and magazines. The latter ranged from high-quality comprehensive general circulation intellectual periodicals such as *Sekai* (World), *Chūō Kōron* (Central Review), and *Bungei Shunjū* (Literary Annals) to *sarariman manga* (salaryman comics), comic books for adults that depict the vicissitudes and fantasies of contemporary office workers, and weeklies specializing in scandals. Japan probably also led the world in the translation of works by foreign scholars and novelists. Most of the classics of Western political thought, such as *The Republic* by Plato and *Leviathan* by Thomas Hobbes, for example, were available in Japanese.

News programs and special features on television, moreover, gave viewers detailed reports on political, economic, and social developments both at home and abroad. The sole noncommercial public radio and television broadcasting network, the Japan Broadcasting Corporation (Nippon Hōsō Kyōkai—NHK) provided generally balanced coverage. Unlike their counterparts in the United States, however, Japanese newscasters on NHK and commercial stations usually confined themselves to relating events and did not offer opinions or analysis.

The major magazines and newspapers were vocal critics of government policies and took great pains to map out the personnel and financial ties that held the conservative establishment together. Readers were regularly informed of matrimonial alliances between families of top politicians, civil servants, and business leaders, which in some ways resembled those of the old European aristocracy. The important print media were privately owned.

Observers in the early 1990s, however, pointed out that the independence of the established press had been compromised by the pervasive "press club" system. Politicians and government agencies each had one of these clubs, which contained from 12 to almost 300 reporters from the different newspapers, magazines, and broadcast media. Club members were generally described as being closer to each other than they were to their employers. They also established a close and collaborative working relationship with the political figures or government agencies to which they were attached. There was little opportunity for reporters to establish a genuinely critical, independent stance because reporting distasteful matters might lead to exclusion from the club and thus inability to gain information and write. Although the media has played a major role in exposing political scandals, some critics have accused the large newspapers, ostensibly oppositionist, of being little more than a conduit of government ideas to the people. Free-lance reporters, working outside the press club system, often made the real break-throughs in investigative reporting. For example, a free-lance jour-nalist published the first public accounts of Tanaka Kakuei's personal finances in a monthly magazine in 1974, even though the established press had access to this information.

The Liberal Democratic Party

The LDP has dominated the political system since 1955, when it was established as a coalition of smaller conservative groups. All of Japan's prime ministers since then have come from its ranks as have, with one exception, other cabinet ministers. The party's fortunes have risen and ebbed: a low point was reached in the July 23, 1989, election to the upper house, when it became, for the first time, a minority party (see The Structure of Government, The Liberal Democratic Party in National Elections, this ch.). But no opposition party, whether singly or in coalition, was able to oust the LDP from power and form a government of its own.

By the early 1990s, the LDP's nearly four decades in power al-lowed it to establish a highly stable process of policy formation. This process would not have been possible if other parties had se-cured parliamentary majorities. LDP strength was based on an en-during, although not unchallenged, coalition of big business, small business, agriculture, professional groups, and other interests. Elite bureaucrats collaborated closely with the party and interest groups in drafting and implementing policy. In a sense, the party's suc-cess was a result not of its internal strength but of its weakness. It lacked a strong, nationwide organization or consistent ideology with which to attract voters. Its leaders were rarely decisive, charis-matic, or popular. But it has functioned efficiently as a locus for matching interest group money and votes with bureaucratic power and expertise. This arrangement resulted in a great deal of cor-ruption, but the party could claim credit for helping to create eco-nomic growth and a stable, middle-class Japan.

Party History and Basic Principles

The LDP has a complex genealogy. Its roots can be traced to the groups established by Itagaki Taisuke and Ōkuma Shigenobu in the 1880s (see The Development of Representative Government, ch. 1). It attained its present form in November 1955, when the conservative Liberal Party (Jiyūtō) and Japan Democratic Party (Nihon Minshutō) united in response to the threat posed by a uni-fied Japan Socialist Party, which had been established the month before. The union of the two has often been described as a "shotgun marriage." Both had strong leaders and had previously competed with each other. The Japan Democratic Party, which had been established only a year before, in November 1954, was itself a coalition of different groups in which farmers were prominent. The result of the new amalgamation was a large party that represented a broad spectrum of interests but had minimal organization compared with the socialist and other leftist parties. In 1976, in the wake of the Lockheed bribery scandal, a handful of younger LDP Diet members broke away and established their own party, the New Liberal Club (Shin Jiyū Kurabu). A decade later, however, it was reabsorbed by the LDP.

Unlike the leftist parties, the LDP did not espouse a well-defined ideology or political philosophy. Its members held a variety of positions that could be broadly defined as being to the right of the opposition parties, yet more moderate than those of Japan's numerous rightist splinter groups (see Political Extremists, this ch.). The LDP traditionally identified itself with a number of general goals: rapid, export-based economic growth, close cooperation with the United States in foreign and defense policies, and several newer issues, such as administrative reform. Administrative reform encompassed several themes: simplification and streamlining of government bureaucracy, privatization of state-owned enterprises, and the adoption of measures, including tax reform, needed to prepare for the strain on the economy posed by an aging society. Other priorities in the early 1990s included promoting a more active and positive role for Japan in the rapidly developing Asia-Pacific region, internationalizing Japan's economy by liberalizing and promoting domestic demand, creating a high-technology information society, and promoting scientific research. A business-inspired commitment to free enterprise was tempered by the insistence of important small business and agricultural constituencies on some form of protectionism.

Party Structure

At the apex of the LDP's formal organization was the president, who served a two-year renewable term. Because of the party's parliamentary majority, the president has been the prime minister. The choice was formally that of a party convention composed of Diet members and local LDP figures, but in most cases, they merely approved the joint decision of the most powerful party leaders. To make the system more democratic, Prime Minister Miki Takeo introduced a "primary" system in 1978, which opened the balloting to some 1.5 million LDP members. The process was so costly and acrimonious, however, that it was subsequently abandoned in favor of the old "smoke-filled room" method.

The LDP was the most "traditionally Japanese" of the political parties because it relied on a complex network of patron-client (*oyabun-kobun*) relationships on both national and local levels. Nationally, a system of factions in both the House of Representatives and the House of Councillors tied individual Diet members to powerful party leaders. Locally, Diet members had to maintain *kōenkai* (local support groups) to keep in touch with public opinion and gain votes and financial backing. The importance and pervasiveness of personal ties between Diet members and faction leaders and between citizens and Diet members gave the party a pragmatic, "you scratch my back, I'll scratch yours" character. Its success depended less on generalized mass appeal than on *jiban* (a strong, well-organized constituency), *kaban* (a briefcase full of money), and *kanban* (prestigious appointment, particularly on the cabinet level).

Factions

In a sense, the LDP was not a single organization but a conglomeration of competitive factions, which, despite the traditional emphasis on consensus and harmony, engaged in bitter infighting. Over the years, factions numbered from 6 to 13, with as few as 4 members and as many as 120, counting those in both houses. The system was operative in both houses, although it was more deeply entrenched in the House of Representatives than in the less powerful House of Councillors. Faction leaders usually were veteran LDP politicians. Many, but not all, had served as prime minister.

Faction leaders offered their followers services without which the followers would have found it difficult, if not impossible, to survive politically. Leaders provided funds for the day-to-day operation of Diet members' offices and staff as well as financial support during expensive election campaigns. As discussed earlier, the operating allowances provided by the government were inadequate. The leader also introduced his followers to influential bureaucracts and business people, which made it much easier for the followers to satisfy their constituents' demands.

Historically, the most powerful and aggressive faction leader in the LDP was Tanaka Kakuei, whose dual-house strength in the early 1980s exceeded 110. His followers remained loyal despite the fact that he had been convicted of receiving ¥500 million (nearly US$4 million) in bribes from the American aircraft manufacturer, Lockheed, to facilitate the purchase of its passenger aircraft by All Nippon Airways, and had formally withdrawn from the LDP.

Tanaka and his bitterest factional rival, Fukuda Takeo, were a study in contrasts. Tanaka was a rough-hewn wheeler-dealer with a primary school education who had made a fortune in the construction industry; Fukuda was an elite product of the University of Tokyo Law Faculty and a career bureaucrat.

In the face of Fukuda's strong opposition, Tanaka engineered the selections of prime ministers Ōhira Masayoshi (1978–80) and Suzuki Zenkō (1980–82). The accession of Nakasone Yasuhiro to the prime ministership in 1982 would also not have occurred without Tanaka's support and, as a result, Nakasone, at that time a politically weak figure, was nicknamed "Tanakasone." But Tanaka's faction was dealt a grave blow when one of his subordinates, Takeshita Noboru, decided to form a breakaway group. Tanaka suffered a stroke in November 1985, but four years passed before he formally retired from politics.

The LDP faction system was closely fitted to the House of Representatives' medium-sized, multiple-member election districts. The party usually ran more than one candidate in each of these constituencies to maintain its lower house majority, and these candidates were from different factions. During an election campaign, the LDP, in a real sense, ran not only against the opposition but also against itself. In fact, intraparty competition within one election district was often more bitter than interparty competition, with two or more LDP candidates vying for the same block of conservative votes. For example, in the general election of February 18, 1990, three LDP and three opposition candidates competed for five seats in a southwestern prefecture. Two of the LDP candidates publicly expressed bitterness over the entry of the third, a son of the prefectural governor. Local television showed supporters of one of the LDP candidates cheering loudly when the governor's son was edged out for the fifth seat by a Kōmeitō candidate.

Local Support Groups

In the early 1990s, *kōenkai* (local support groups) were perhaps even more important than faction membership to the survival of LDP Diet members. These *kōenkai* served as pipelines through which funds and other support were conveyed to legislators and through which the legislators could distribute favors to constituents in return. To avoid the stringent legal restrictions on political activity outside of designated campaign times, *kōenkai* sponsored year-round cultural, social, and "educational" activities. In the prewar years, having an invincible, or "iron," constituency depended on gaining the support of landlords and other local notables. These people delivered blocks of rural votes to the candidates they favored.

In the more pluralistic postwar period, local bosses were much weaker and building a strong constituency base much more difficult and costly. Tanaka used his "iron constituency" in rural Niigata Prefecture to build a formidable, nationwide political machine; but other politicians, like Itō Masayoshi, were so popular in their districts that they could refrain, to some extent, from money politics and promote a "clean" image. *Kōenkai* remained particularly important in the overrepresented rural areas, where paternalistic, old-style politics flourished and where the LDP, despite disaffection during the late 1980s over agricultural liberalization policies, had its strongest support.

In the classic *oyabun-kobun* manner, local people who were consistently loyal to a figure like Tanaka become favored recipients of government largesse. In the 1980s, his own third electoral district in Niigata was the nation's top beneficiary in per capita public works spending. Benefits included stops on the Shinkansen bullet train to Tokyo and the cutting of a tunnel through a mountain to serve a hamlet of sixty people (see Transportation and Communications, ch. 4). Another fortunate area was Takeshita Noboru's district in Shimane Prefecture on the Sea of Japan.

The importance of local loyalties was also reflected in the widespread practice of a second generation's "inheriting" Diet seats from fathers or fathers-in-law. This trend was found predominantly, though not exclusively, in the LDP. In the February 1990 general election, for example, forty-three second-generation candidates ran: twenty-two, including twelve LDP candidates, were successful. They included the sons of former prime ministers Suzuki Zenkō and Fukuda Takeo, although a son-in-law of Tanaka Kakuei lost in a district different from his father-in-law's.

The Liberal Democratic Party in National Elections

Election statistics show that, while the LDP had been able to secure a majority in the twelve House of Representatives elections from May 1958 to February 1990, with only three exceptions (December 1976, October 1979, and December 1983), its share of the popular vote had declined from a high of 57.8 percent in May 1958 to a low of 41.8 percent in December 1976, when voters expressed their disgust with the party's involvement in the Lockheed scandal (see fig. 9; table 37, Appendix). The LDP vote rose again between 1979 and 1990. Although the LDP won an unprecedented 300 seats in the July 1986 balloting, its share of the popular vote remained just under 50 percent. The figure was 46.2 percent in February 1990. Following the three occasions when the LDP found itself a handful of seats shy of a majority, it was obliged to form

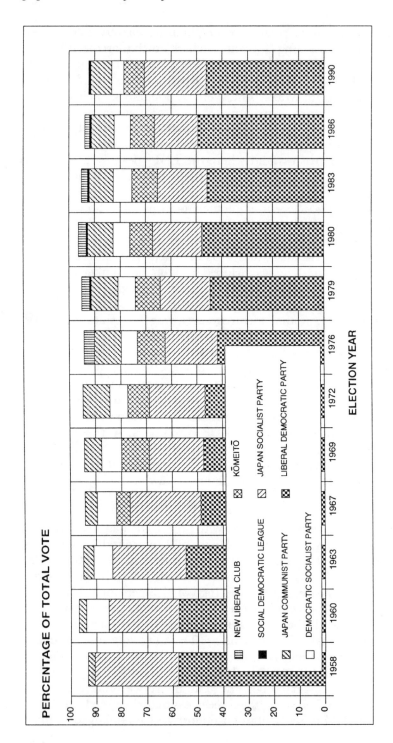

Figure 9. House of Representatives Elections, 1958–90

alliances with conservative independents and the breakaway New Liberal Club. In a cabinet appointment after the October 1983 balloting, a non-LDP minister, a member of the New Liberal Club, was appointed for the first time.

In the upper house, the July 1989 election represented the first time that the LDP was forced into a minority position. In previous elections, it had either secured a majority on its own or recruited non-LDP conservatives to make up the difference of a few seats.

The political crisis of 1988–89 was testimony to both the party's strength and its weakness. In the wake of a succession of issues— the pushing of a highly unpopular consumption tax through the Diet in late 1988, the Recruit insider trading scandal, which tainted virtually all top LDP leaders and forced the resignation of Prime Minister Takeshita Noboru in April (a successor did not appear until June), the resignation in July of his successor, Uno Sōsuke, because of a sex scandal, and the poor showing in the upper house election—the media provided the Japanese with a detailed and embarrassing dissection of the political system. By March 1989, popular support for the Takeshita cabinet as expressed in public opinion polls had fallen to 9 percent. Uno's scandal, covered in magazine interviews of a ''kiss and tell'' geisha, aroused the fury of female voters.

Yet Uno's successor, the eloquent if obscure Kaifu Toshiki, was successful in repairing the party's battered image. By January 1990, talk of the waning of conservative power and a possible socialist government had given way to the realization that, like the Lockheed affair of the mid-1970s, the Recruit scandal did not signal a significant change in who ruled Japan. The February 1990 general election gave the LDP, including affiliated independents, a comfortable, if not spectacular, majority: 286 of 512 total representatives.

In light of radical changes in other parts of the world during the late 1980s and early 1990s, particularly the collapse of the communist status quo in Eastern Europe, the LDP's durability seemed odd to outsiders. One explanation is that the LDP has grown quite skillful in manipulating the rituals of repentance. In 1989 Takeshita and other leaders expressed *kejime* (a very difficult term to translate, although ''knowing how to act under the circumstances'' indicates some of its meaning), begging the voters to accept their promise that they would do better in the future and would implement ''political reform.'' Before the general election, the ruling party also promised to consider revision, although not abolition, of the consumption tax. The overall economic well-being of most of the population, particularly in comparison with their own lives, or those of their parents, in the immediate postwar period, is another factor contributing to LDP sustainability. But the election results suggested to many that, despite the furor, the voters were less interested in "throwing the rascals out" than, in the quintessentially Confucian way, having them "reflect" on their errors.

An additional factor of major importance was the perceived inability of the opposition parties, some of whom were also tarnished by the Recruit scandal, to form a competent alternative government (see The Opposition Parties, this ch.). The strongly interest-oriented nature of Japanese politics, moreover, meant that many people were tied to local patronage networks that would suffer if the socialists or other opposition groups gained power. Many voters admitted, "I don't like the LDP, but I really had no choice."

Bureaucrats and the Policy-Making Process

The Japanese had been exposed to bureaucratic institutions at least by the early seventh century A.D., when the imperial court adopted the laws and government structure of Tang China (see Nara and Heian Periods, A.D. 710–1185, ch. 1). The distinctive Chinese institution of civil service examinations never took root, and the imported system was never successfully imposed on the country at large. But by the middle of the Tokugawa period (1600–1867), the samurai class functions had evolved from warrior to clerical and administrative functions. Following the Meiji Restoration (1868), the new elite, which came from the lower ranks of the samurai, established a Western-style civil service (see The Emergence of Modern Japan, 1868–1919, ch. 1).

Although the United States occupation dismantled both the military and *zaibatsu* (see Glossary) establishments, it did little, outside of abolishing the prewar Home Ministry, to challenge the power of the bureaucracy. There was considerable continuity—in institutions, operating style, and personnel—between the civil service before and after the occupation, partly because MacArthur's staff ruled indirectly and depended largely on the cooperation of civil servants. A process of mutual cooptation occurred. Also, United States policy planners never regarded the civil service with the same opprobrium as the military or economic elites. The civil service's role in Japan's militarism was generally downplayed. Many of the occupation figures themselves were products of President Franklin D. Roosevelt's New Deal and had strong faith in the merits of civil service "professionalism." Finally, the perceived threat of the Soviet Union in the late 1940s created a community of interests for the occupiers and conservative, social order-conscious administrators.

The Civil Service

In trying to discover "who's in charge here," many analysts have pointed to the elite bureaucracy as the people who really governed Japan, although they composed only a tiny fraction of the country's more than 1 million national government employees. In the early 1990s, several hundred of the elite were employed at each national ministry or agency. Although entry into the elite through open examinations did not require a college degree, the majority of its members were alumni of Japan's most prestigious universities. The University of Tokyo Law Faculty remained in the early 1990s the single most important source of elite bureaucrats. After graduation from college and, increasingly, some graduate-level study, applicants took a series of extremely difficult higher civil service examinations: in 1988, for example, 28,833 took the tests, but only 1,814, or 6.3 percent, were successful. Of the successful number, 721 were actually hired. Like the scholar-officials of imperial China, successful candidates were hardy survivors of a grueling education and testing process that necessarily began in early childhood and demanded total concentration. The typical young bureaucrat, who in the early 1990s was in most cases male, was an intelligent, hardworking, and dedicated individual. Some bureaucrats lacked imagination and, perhaps, compassion for people whose way of life was different from their own.

The public's attitude toward the elite was ambivalent. The elite enjoyed tremendous social prestige, but members were also resented. They lived in a realm that was at least partly public yet far removed from the lives of ordinary people. Compared with politicians, they were generally viewed as honest. Involvement of top officials in scandals such as the Recruit affair, however, had, to some extent, tarnished their image.

Japan's elite bureaucrats were insulated from direct political pressure because there were very few political appointments in the civil service. Cabinet ministers were usually career politicians, but they were moved in and out of their posts quite frequently (with an average tenure of under a year), and usually had little opportunity to develop a power base within a ministry or force their civil service subordinates to adopt reforms. Below the cabinet minister was the administrative vice minister. Administrative vice ministers and their subordinates were career civil servants whose appointments were determined in accordance with an internally established principle of seniority.

In a 1975 article, political scientist Chalmers Johnson quotes a retired vice minister of the Ministry of International Trade and Industry (MITI), who said that the Diet was merely "an extension of the bureaucracy.'' The official claimed that ''the bureaucracy drafts all the laws. . . . All the legislature does is to use its powers of investigation, which for about half the year keeps most of the senior officials cooped up in the Diet.''

In the years since this official made his proud boast, however, it has become apparent that there are limits to the bureaucrats' power. The most important check was the LDP's growing role in policy formation. Political scientist B.C. Koh suggested that in many cases members of the LDP policy-oriented tribes (*zoku*) had greater expertise in their fields than elite bureaucrats. Before the latter drafted legislation, they had to consult and follow the initiatives of the party's Policy Research Council. Many analysts consider the role of the bureaucracy in drafting legislation to be no greater than that of its counterparts in France, the Federal Republic of Germany (West Germany), and other countries. Also, the decision of many retired bureaucrats to run as LDP candidates for the Diet might not reflect, as had been previously assumed, the power of the officials but rather the impatience of ambitious men who wanted to locate themselves, politically, ''where the action is.''

An intense rivalry among the ministries came into play whenever major policy decisions were formulated. Elite civil servants were recruited by and spent their entire careers in a single ministry. As a result, they developed a strong sectional solidarity and zealously defended their turf. Nonbureaucratic actors—the politicians and interest groups—could use this rivalry to their own advantage.

The Ministry of Finance was generally considered the most powerful and prestigious of the ministries. Its top officials were regarded as the cream of the elite. Although it was relatively unsuccessful in the 1970s when the deficit rose, the ministry was very successful in the 1980s in constraining government spending and raising taxes, including a twelve-year battle to get a consumption tax passed. The huge national debt in the early 1990s, however, may turn out to be evidence that this budget-minded body had been unsuccessful in the previous decade in curbing demands for popular policies such as health insurance, rice price supports, and the unprofitable nationwide network of the privatized Japan Railways Group. MITI frequently encountered obstacles in its early post-occupation plans to reconsolidate the economy. It was not always successful in imposing its will on private interests, politicians, or other ministries. According to law professor John O. Haley, writing in the late 1980s, MITI's practice of *gyōsei shidō,* or administrative guidance, often described as evidence of the bureaucracy's hidden power, was in fact a second-best alternative to ''express statutory authority that would have legitimated its exercise of authority.'' Administrative reform policies in the 1980s imposed ceilings on civil service staff and spending that probably contributed to a deterioration of morale and working conditions.

Still another factor limiting bureaucratic power was the emergence of an affluent society. In the early postwar period, the scarcity of capital made it possible for the Ministry of Finance and MITI to exert considerable influence over the economy through control of the banking system (see The Financial System, ch. 4). To a decreasing extent, this scarcity remained until the 1980s because most major companies had high debt-equity ratios and depended on the banks for infusions of capital. Their huge profits and increasing reliance on securities markets in the late 1980s, however, meant that the Ministry of Finance had less influence. The wealth, technical sophistication, and new confidence of the companies also made it difficult for MITI to exercise administrative guidance. The ministry could not restrain aggressive and often politically controversial purchases by Japanese corporate investors in the United States, for example, Mitsubishi Estate's October 1989 purchase of Rockefeller Center in New York City, which, along with the Sony Corporation's acquisition of Columbia Pictures several weeks earlier, heated up trade friction between the two countries.

The whole issue of trade friction and foreign pressure tended to politicize the bureaucracy and promote unprecedented divisiveness in the late 1980s and early 1990s. During the Structural Impediments Initiative talks held by Japan and the United States in early 1990, basic changes in Japan's economy were discussed: reforms of the distribution and pricing systems, improvement of the infrastructure, and elimination of official procedures that limited foreign participation in the economy (see Trade and Investment Relations, ch. 5). Although foreign pressure of this sort was resented by many Japanese as an intrusion on national sovereignty, it also provided an opportunity for certain ministries to make gains at the expense of others. There was hardly a bureaucratic jurisdiction in the economic sphere that was not in some sense affected.

Repeatedly, internationally minded political and bureaucratic elites found their market-opening reforms, designed to placate American demands, sabotaged by other interests, especially agriculture. Such reactions intensified American pressure, which in turn created a sense of crisis and a siege mentality within Japan. The ''internationalization'' of Japan's society in other ways also divided the bureaucratic elite. MITI, the Ministry of Labor, and the Ministry of Justice had divergent views on how to respond to the influx of unskilled, usually South Asian and Southeast Asian, laborers into the labor-starved Japanese economy. An estimated 300,000 to 400,000 of them worked illegally for small Japanese firms in the late 1980s. Ministry of Education, Science, and Culture revision of guidelines on the writing of history textbooks, ostensibly a domestic matter, aroused the indignation of Japan's Asian neighbors because the changes tended to soften accounts of wartime atrocities.

Policy-Making Dynamics

Despite an increasingly unpredictable domestic and international environment, policy making in the early 1990s conformed to well-established postwar patterns. The close collaboration of the ruling party, the elite bureaucracy, and important interest groups often made it difficult to tell who exactly was responsible for specific policy decisions. The tendency for insiders to guard information on such matters carefully compounded the difficulty, especially for foreigners wishing to understand how domestic decision making could be influenced to reduce trade problems.

The Human Factor

The most important human factor in the policy-making process was the homogeneity of the political and business elites. In the early 1990s, they still tended to be graduates of a relatively small number of top-ranked universities. Regardless of these individuals' regional or class origins, their similar educational backgrounds encouraged their feeling of community, as was reflected in the finely meshed network of marriage alliances between top official, LDP and financial circle (*zaikai*) families. The institution of early retirement also fostered homogeneity. In the practice of *amakudari,* or descent from heaven, as it is popularly known, bureaucrats retiring in their fifties often assumed top positions in public corporations and private enterprise. They also became LDP politicians. By the late 1980s, most postwar prime ministers had had civil service backgrounds.

This homogeneity facilitated the free flow of ideas among members of the elite in informal settings. Bureaucrats and business people associated with a single industry, such as electronics, often held regular informal meetings in Tokyo hotels and restaurants. Political scientist T.J. Pempel has pointed out that the concentration of political and economic power in Tokyo—particularly the small geographic area of its central wards—made it easy for leaders, who were almost without exception denizens of the capital, to have repeated personal contact. Another often overlooked factor was the tendency of elite males not to be family men. Late night work and bar-hopping schedules gave them ample opportunity to hash and rehash policy matters and engage in *haragei* (literally, belly art), or intimate, often nonverbal communication. Like the warriors of ancient Sparta, who lived in barracks apart from their families during much of their adulthood, the business and bureaucratic elites were expected to sacrifice their private lives for the national good.

Formal Policy Development

After a largely informal process within elite circles in which ideas were discussed and developed, steps might be taken to institute more formal policy development. This process often took place in deliberation councils (*shingikai*). There were about 200 *shingikai*, each attached to a ministry; their members were both officials and prominent private individuals in business, education, and other fields. The *shingikai* played a large role in facilitating communication among those who ordinarily might not meet. Given the tendency for real negotiations in Japan to be conducted privately (in the *nemawashi*, or root binding, process of consensus building), the *shingikai* often represented a fairly advanced stage in policy formulation in which relatively minor differences could be thrashed out and the resulting decisions couched in language acceptable to all. These bodies were legally established, but had no authority to oblige governments to adopt their recommendations.

The most important deliberation council during the 1980s was the Provisional Commission for Administrative Reform, established in March 1981 by Prime Minister Suzuki Zenkō. The commission had nine members, assisted in their deliberations by six advisers, twenty-one "expert members," and around fifty "councillors" representing a wide range of groups. Its head, Keidanren president Dokō Toshio, insisted that government agree to take its recommendations seriously and commit itself to reforming the administrative structure and the tax system. In 1982 the commission had arrived at several recommendations that by the end of the decade had been actualized. These implementations included tax reform; a policy to limit government growth; the establishment, in 1984, of the Management and Coordination Agency to replace the Administrative Management Agency in the Office of the Prime Minister; and privatization of the state-owned railroad and telephone systems. In April 1990, another deliberation council, the Election Systems Research Council, submitted proposals that included the establishment of single-seat constituencies in place of the multiple-seat system.

Another significant policy-making institution in the early 1990s was the LDP's Policy Research Council. It consisted of a number of committees, composed of LDP Diet members, with the committees corresponding to the different executive agencies. Committee members worked closely with their official counterparts, advancing the requests of their constituents, in one of the most effective means through which interest groups could state their case to the bureaucracy through the channel of the ruling party.

The Budget Process

Despite the increasingly apparent limits of bureaucratic power, the Budget Bureau of the Ministry of Finance was at the heart of the political process because it drew up the national budget each year. This responsibility made it the ultimate focus of interest groups, through the medium of the LDP and of other ministries that competed for limited funds. The budgetary process generally began soon after the start of a new fiscal year on April 1. Ministries and government agencies prepared budget requests in consultation with the Policy Research Council. In the fall of each year, Budget Bureau examiners reviewed these requests in great detail, while top Ministry of Finance officials worked out the general contours of the new budget and the distribution of tax revenues. During the winter, after the release of the ministry's draft budget, campaigning by individual Diet members for their constituents and different ministries for revisions and supplementary allocations became intense. LDP and Ministry of Finance officials consulted on a final draft budget, which was generally passed by the Diet in late winter.

In broad outline, the process revealed a basic characteristic of Japanese political dynamics: that despite the oft-stated ideals of "harmony" and "consensus," interests, including bureaucratic interests, were in strong competition for resources. LDP leaders and Budget Bureau officials needed great skill to reach mutually acceptable compromises. The image of "Japan Incorporated," in which harmony and unanimity were virtually automatic, belied the reality of intense rivalry. The late twentieth-century system was successful insofar as superior political skills and appreciation of common interests minimized antagonisms and maintained an acceptable balance of power among groups. Whether this system would continue, as Japan faced such problems as growing social inequality, an aging society, and the challenge of "internationalization" of its society and economy, in the early 1990s remained unclear.

The Opposition Parties

With the exception of the period from May 1947 to March 1948, when a socialist, Katayama Tetsu, was prime minster, heading a coalition of socialists and conservatives, opposition parties failed to gain enough national electoral support to participate in forming a cabinet or to form one of their own. In 1990, major opposition parties with representation in the Diet were the Japan Socialist Party, the Kōmeitō, the Japan Communist Party, and the Democratic Socialist Party (Minshatō). Two smaller opposition parties were the Socialist Democratic League and the Progressive Party (Shimpotō). None had a sufficiently broad base of support to challenge the LDP at the polls, and in the early 1990s, they had not been able to form workable coalitions. An exception occurred in some local elections, where "progressive" coalitions were more effective in electing opposition candidates than on the national level.

The opposition parties were separated by ideology, with the Japan Communist Party and a significant faction of the Japan Socialist Party espousing Marxist revolution; the others were moderate and pragmatic. In many cases, the programs of the Kōmeitō and Democratic Socialist Party differed little from those of the LDP. Unlike the Japan Socialist Party, smaller opposition parties lacked the resources to run candidates in all the country's constituencies.

On occasions in the 1970s and 1980s, it seemed that the end of conservative power was at hand. One such time was following the Lockheed scandal of the mid-1970s (a journalist at the time described it as "conservative power self-destructs"); another was the combined furor over the 3 percent consumption tax and the Recruit scandal in 1988–89. When the LDP was pushed into the minority in the July 1989 upper-house election, many commentators believed that Doi Takako, chairwoman and leader of the Japan Socialist Party, was within striking distance of forming a government, probably in coalition with other opposition groups, in the upcoming, more important general election for the lower house. That this situation failed to materialize suggested not so much popular contentment with the LDP as the opposition's inability to present a viable alternative to voters.

The opposition was important if only because its existence legitimized Japan's claim to be a modern, democratic state. Moreover, the Japan Socialist Party and Japan Communist Party played a major role in the 1950s and 1960s in protecting the democratic institutions promoted by the United States occupation. The opposition's control of more than one-third of the seats in the Diet meant that amendments revising the Constitution (such as the proposed rewording or abolition of Article 9) could not be passed. If conservatives had had their way in the early postwar years, some of Japan's prewar symbols and military power would have been restored, a move that most likely would have greatly affected relations with East Asian and Southeast Asian countries, where bitter memories of Japanese wartime occupation remained fresh.

In a political system where the ruling party habitually swept embarrassing matters under the carpet and the established press club system inhibited investigative reporting, the opposition functioned reasonably well, to use film scholar Donald Richie's phrase, as "carpet picker-uppers." They exposed and demanded parliamentary investigations of scandals like the Recruit affair. Routinely, they used meetings of the Budget Committee and other committees in the Diet to question cabinet ministers and government officials, and these sessions received wide media publicity.

Ideas first proposed by the opposition, such as national health insurance and other social welfare measures, were frequently adopted and implemented by the ruling party. The "Eda Vision" of moderate socialist leader Eda Saburō in the early 1960s—"An American standard of living, Soviet levels of social welfare, a British parliamentary system, and Japan's peace constitution"—were largely realized under LDP auspices.

Although opposition control of the upper house after the July 1989 election represented a change, the opposition had little impact on the legislative process. Regulations in the Diet Law and the rules of the two houses gave presiding House of Representatives officers the power to convene plenary sessions, fix agendas, and limit debates. Because these officers were elected by the LDP majority, they used these powers to constrain opposition party activity. Although the opposition could not filibuster, the lack of a time limit for formal balloting allowed them to use the *gyūho senjutsu* (cow's pace tactics) to cause excruciating delays in the passage of LDP-sponsored bills, walking so slowly to cast their individual votes that the process took several hours, sorely trying the tempers of LDP Diet members.

Japan Socialist Party

The Japan Socialist Party was the largest opposition party in the early 1990s. Like the LDP, it resulted from the union of two smaller groups in 1955. The new opposition party had its own factions, although organized according to left-right ideological commitments rather than what it called the "feudal personalism" of the conservative parties. In the House of Representatives election of 1958, the Japan Socialist Party gained 32.9 percent of the popular vote and 166 out of 467 seats. After that, its percentage of the popular vote and number of seats gradually declined. In the double election of July 1986 for both Diet houses, the party suffered a rout by the LDP under Nakasone: its seats in the lower house fell from

112 to an all-time low of 85 and its share of the vote from 19.5 percent to 17.2 percent. But its popular chairwoman, Doi Takako, led it to an impressive showing in the February 1990 general election: 136 seats and 24.4 percent of the vote. Some electoral districts had more than one successful socialist candidate. Doi's decision to put up more than one candidate for each of the 130 districts represented a controversial break with the past, because, unlike their LDP counterparts, many Japan Socialist Party candidates did not want to run against each other. But the great majority of the 149 socialist candidates who ran were successful, including seven of eight women.

Doi, a university professor of constitutional law before entering politics, had a tough, straight-talking manner that appealed to voters tired of the evasiveness of other politicians. Many women found her a refreshing alternative to submissive female stereotypes, and in the late 1980s the public at large, in opinion polls, voted her their favorite politician (the runner-up in these surveys was equally tough-talking conservative LDP member Ishihara Shintarō). Doi's popularity, however, was of limited aid to the party. The powerful Shakaishugi Kyōkai (Japan Socialist Association), which was supported by a hard-core contingent of the party's 76,000-strong membership, remained committed to doctrinaire Marxism, impeding Doi's efforts to promote what she called *perestroika* and a more moderate program with greater voter appeal.

In 1983 Doi's predecessor as chairman, Ishibashi Masashi, began the delicate process of moving the party away from its strong opposition to the Self-Defense Forces. While maintaining that these forces were unconstitutional in light of Article 9, he claimed that, because they had been established through legal procedures, they had a "legitimate" status (this phrasing was changed a year later to say that the Self-Defense Forces "exist legally"). Ishibashi also broke past precedent by visiting Washington to talk with United States political leaders.

By the end of the decade, the party had accepted the Self-Defense Forces and the 1962 Japan-United States Treaty of Mutual Cooperation and Security as facts of life. It advocated strict limitations on military spending (no more than 1 percent of GNP annually), a suspension of joint military exercises with United States forces, and a reaffirmation of the "three nonnuclear principles" (no production, possession, or introduction of nuclear weapons into Japanese territory). Doi expressed support for "balanced ties" with the Democratic People's Republic of Korea (North Korea) and the Republic of Korea (South Korea). In the past, the Japan Socialist Party had favored the Kim Il Song regime in P'yŏngyang, and in the early 1990s it still refused to recognize the 1965 normalization of relations between Tokyo and Seoul. In domestic policy, the party demanded the continued protection of agriculture and small business in the face of foreign pressure, abolition of the consumer tax, and an end to the construction and use of nuclear power reactors. As a symbolic gesture to reflect its new moderation, at its April 1990 convention the party dropped its commitment to "socialist revolution" and described its goal as "social democracy": creation of a society in which "all people fairly enjoy the fruits of technological advancement and modern civilization and receive the benefits of social welfare." Delegates also voted Doi a third term as party chairwoman.

Because of the party's self-definition as a class-based party and its symbiotic relationship with Sōhyō, the public sector union confederation, few efforts were made to attract nonunion constituencies. Although some Sōhyō unions supported the Japan Communist Party, the Japan Socialist Party remained the representative of Sōhyō's political interests until the merger with private sector unions formed the noncommunist Shin Rengō in 1989. Because of declining union financial support during the 1980s, some Japan Socialist Party Diet members turned to dubious fund-raising methods. One was involved in the Recruit affair. The Japan Socialist Party, like others, sold large blocks of fund-raising party tickets, and the LDP even gave individual Japan Socialist Party Diet members funds from time to time to persuade them to cooperate in passing difficult legislation.

Kōmeitō

In 1990, the Kōmeitō (the euphemistic English translation of the Japanese name is Clean Government Party) was the second largest opposition party, with forty-five legislators in the House of Representatives after the February election, although the party lost eleven seats compared with its July 1986 showing. The Kōmeitō was an offshoot of the Sōka Gakkai, which had been founded in 1930 as an independent lay organization of the Nichiren Shōshū sect of Buddhism, whose numbers were estimated at 750,000 in 1958 and more than 35 million in the late 1980s. In 1962 the Sōka Gakkai, established a League for Clean Government, which became a regular political party, the Kōmeitō, two years later. Ties between the Kōmeitō and the Sōka Gakkai were formally dissolved in 1970, and the image of an "open party" was promoted. But the resignation in 1989 of a Kōmeitō Diet member, Ōhashi Toshio, following his criticism of the religious leader Ikeda Daisaku, suggested that the Sōka Gakkai's influence over the party remained substantial. Public suspicions concerning the religious connection (in principle a violation of the Constitution's Article 20), and the involvement of several Kōmeitō Diet members in the Recruit scandal accounted for the party's poor electoral showing in February 1990.

The party's supporters tended to be people who were largely outside the privileged labor union and "salarymen" circles of lifetime employment in large enterprises. The Kōmeitō's programs were rather vague. They emphasized welfare and quality of life issues. In foreign policy, they had dropped their previous opposition to the Japan-United States security treaty and the Self-Defense Forces. Given the party's aversion to the leftism of the Japan Socialist Party, and despite its occasional cooperation with the leftists, it was judged unlikely to enter into a lasting coalition with the largest opposition group, despite protracted negotiations. In fact, the LDP worked hard to gain the Kōmeitō's cooperation in the upper house to pass legislation, and most commentators considered the Kōmeitō, along with the Democratic Socialist Party, as a likely coalition partner should the LDP lose its parliamentary majority in the lower house.

Japan Communist Party

The Japan Communist Party was first organized in 1922, in the wake of the Russian Revolution, and remained part of the international, Moscow-controlled communist movement until the early 1960s. Although the party won a large percentage of the popular vote in Diet elections in 1949, it became extremely unpopular after 1950, when Moscow ordered it to cease being a "lovable party" and to engage in armed struggle. It was forced to go underground, and in the election lost all its seats in the Diet. A self-reliant party line, stressing independence from both Moscow and Beijing, evolved during the 1960s. The party's chairman, Miyamoto Kenji, a tough veteran of prewar struggles and wartime prisons, promoted the "parliamentary road" of nonviolent, electoral politics. Thereafter, the fortunes of the Japan Communist Party gradually revived. Representation in the lower house reached a high point of thirty-nine in the 1979 election, but declined to between twenty-six and twenty-nine seats in the 1980s and to sixteen in the February 1990 election. The party's program promoted unarmed neutrality, the severing of security ties with the United States, defense of the postwar Constitution, and socialism. It also voiced concern for welfare and quality of life issues.

Both organizationally and financially, the party was stronger than its opposition rivals and even the LDP. Revenues from its publishing enterprises, especially the popular newspaper *Akahata* (Red

Flag), which had the eighth largest circulation in the country, provided adequate support for its activities. As a result, the Japan Communist Party was the party least mired in money politics. This fact earned it the reluctant respect of voters. But suspicions about its ultimate intentions remained strong in the early 1990s. It was excluded from opposition party negotiations on coalitions. Its loss of ten seats in the February 1990 general election was partly the result of voter disgust with the party's Chinese counterpart following repression of prodemocracy demonstrators in Beijing's Tiananmen Incident in 1989. In the election campaigns of 1989–90, the LDP eagerly smeared the party with this association, forcing the communists in their publicity to emphasize that the Chinese and Japanese parties were different and that the Japanese party sincerely supported the struggle for democracy in China and Eastern Europe. Ironically, the Japan Communist Party had strongly condemned the Beijing incident, while the LDP government, ever conscious of business interests with big investments in China, had reacted lamely to the killings by describing them as "regrettable."

Democratic Socialist Party

The Democratic Socialist Party was established in January 1960 when right-wing members of the Japan Socialist Party broke away to form their own group. In the past, the Democratic Socialist Party derived much of its financial and organizational support from the Dōmei private sector labor confederation. Like the LDP and the Kōmeitō, it supported the security treaty with the United States and the Self-Defense Forces. As the most conservative of the opposition parties, it had formed coalitions with the LDP and viewed an opposition coalition with the Japan Socialist Party with distaste. In the February 1990 general election, the Democratic Socialist Party won fourteen seats, down from the twenty-six won in the July 1986 election. The party's chairman, Tsukamoto Saburō, was forced to resign in 1988, after it was revealed that he received 5,000 shares of stock from Recruit.

Other Parties and Independents

Like the Democratic Socialist Party, the tiny Social Democratic League was formed, in 1978, by defectors from the Japan Socialist Party. A non-Marxist party in the social democratic tradition, it won four seats in the February 1990 general election. In February 1990, the Progressive Party (Shimpotō) won one seat.

Largely to contest upper house elections, a large number of "miniparties" had emerged. In the July 1989 election, these included the Salaryman's New Party, which supported a more equitable tax system for salaried workers; the Global Club, devoted to women's rights; the Pension Party, concerned with inequities in the national pension system; and the People Opposed to Nuclear Power Party. The UFO Party advocated a government project to make contact with intelligent beings from outer space.

A relatively large number of candidates ran as independents in general elections. Twenty-one of them were elected in the February 1990 balloting, but the majority later affiliated themselves with the LDP, as was the custom. Their number has included powerful former members of the LDP such as Tanaka Kakuei and Nakasone Yasuhiro, who had resigned from the party because of scandals but continued to lead LDP factions.

Political Extremists

According to the 1989 *Asahi Nenkan,* there were 14,400 activist members of the "new left" organized into five major "currents" (*ryū*) and 27 or 28 different factions. Total membership was about 35,000. New left activity focused on the New Tokyo International Airport at Narita-Sanrizuka. In the early 1970s, radical groups and normally conservative farmers formed a highly unusual alliance to oppose expropriation of the latter's land for the airport's construction. Confrontations at the construction site, which pitted thousands of farmers and radicals against riot police, were violent but generally nonlethal. Although the airport was completed and began operations during the 1980s, the resistance continued, on a reduced scale, in the early 1990s. Radicals attempted to halt planned expansion of the airport by staging guerrilla attacks on those directly or indirectly involved in promoting the plan. By 1990, this activity had resulted in some deaths. There were also attacks against places associated with the emperor. In January 1990, leftists fired homemade rockets at imperial residences in Tokyo and Kyōto.

In terms of terrorist activities, the most important new left group was the Japanese Red Army (Nihon Sekigun). Formed in 1969, it was responsible for, among other acts, the hijacking of a Japan Airlines jet to P'yŏngyang in 1970 and the murder of twenty-six people at Lod International Airport in Tel Aviv in 1977. Its activists developed close connections with international terrorist groups, including Palestinian extremists (see Civil Disturbances, ch. 8). The Japanese Red Army also had close ties with the Kim Il Song regime in North Korea, where several of its hijackers resided during the early 1990s. The group was tightly organized, and one scholar has suggested that its "managerial style" resembled that of major Japanese corporations.

Right-wing extremists were diverse. In 1989 there were 800 such groups with about 120,000 members altogether. By police count, however, only about 50 groups and 23,000 individuals were considered active. Right-wing extremists indulged in a heady romanticism with strong links to the prewar period. They tended to be fascinated with the macho charisma of blood, sweat, and steel, and promoted (like many nonradical groups) traditional samurai values as the antidote to the spiritual ills of postwar Japan. Their preference for violent direct action rather than words reflected the example of the militarist extremists of the 1930s and the heroic "men of strong will" of the late Tokugawa period of the 1850s and 1860s. The modern right-wing extremists demanded an end to the postwar "system of dependence" on the United States, restoration of the emperor to his prewar, divine status, and repudiation of Article 9. Many, if not most, right-wingers had intimate connections with Japan's gangster underground, the *yakuza*.

The ritual suicide of one of Japan's most prominent novelists, Mishima Yukio, following a failed attempt to initiate a rebellion among Self-Defense Forces units in November 1970 shocked and fascinated the public. Mishima and his small private army, the Shield Society (Tate no Kai), hoped that a rising of the Self-Defense Forces would inspire a nationwide affirmation of the old values and put an end to the postwar "age of languid peace." Although rightists were also responsible for the assassination of socialist leader Asanuma Inejirō in 1960 and an attempt on the life of former prime minster Ōhira Masayoshi in 1978, most of them, unlike their prewar counterparts, largely kept to noisy street demonstrations, especially harassment campaigns aimed at conventions of the leftist Japan Teachers Union. In the early 1990s, however, there was evidence that a "new right" was becoming more violent. In May 1987, a reporter working for the liberal *Asahi Shimbun* was killed by a gunman belonging to the Nippon Minzoku Dokuritsu Giyugun Betsudō Sekihōtai (Blood Revenge Corps of the Partisan Volunteer Corps for the Independence of the Japanese Race), known as Sekihōtai (Blood Revenge Corps). The Sekihōtai also threatened to assassinate former Prime Minister Nakasone for giving in to foreign pressure on such issues as the revision of textbook accounts of Japan's war record. In January 1990, a member of the Seikijuku (translatable, ironically, as the Sane Thinkers School) shot and seriously wounded Nagasaki mayor Motoshima Hitoshi. The attack may have been provoked by the leftist rocket attacks on imperial residences in Tokyo and Kyōto a few days earlier as well as the mayor's critical remarks concerning Emperor Hirohito.

Despite the threat from political extremists on both left and right, periodic increases in the strength of opposition parties, and factionalism and the taint of scandal in its own ranks, the LDP continued to maintain a strong government. In the February 1990 election, Japan's economically stable citizenry continued to support the government that had ruled for nearly forty years.

* * *

Democratizing Japan, a collection of essays edited by Robert Ward and Sakamoto Yoshikazu, describes the writing of the postwar Constitution and other effects of the United States occupation on Japan's political system. Theodore Cohen's *Remaking Japan,* and *From a Ruined Empire,* edited by Otis Cary, depict the occupation from participants' points of view. Although most of the essays in Maruyama Masao's *Thought and Behavior in Modern Japanese Politics* were composed in the late 1940s and early 1950s, this volume still provides perhaps the best discussion of Japanese political values. *Authority and the Individual in Japan,* edited by J. Victor Koschmann, discusses changes in values from the Meiji period to the 1970s and has many interesting things to say about how Japanese view authority. *Against the State* by David Apter and Nagayo Sawa challenges the conventional view of the value placed on harmony (*wa*) in describing farmer and radical resistance to the construction of the New Tokyo International Airport. Although published in 1969, Nathaniel B. Thayer's *How the Conservatives Rule Japan* remained relevant in the early 1990s. More recent discussions of the political system include Bradley M. Richardson's *The Political Culture of Japan,* Kyōgoku Jun'ichi's *The Political Dynamics of Japan,* T.J. Pempel's *Policy and Politics in Industrial States,* and J.A.A. Stockwin and others' *Dynamic and Immobilist Politics in Japan.* Kent E. Calder's *Crisis and Compensation,* however, is especially illuminating because of its avoidance of cultural explanations (which are typically overused) and its abundance of comparisons with other countries. B.C. Koh's *Japan's Administrative Elite* provides a clear and concise discussion of the elite civil service and its policy-making role. Karel G. van Wolferen's controversial *The Enigma of Japanese Power,* which Japanese critics have called "a textbook for Japan-bashing," is filled with interesting details, even if its main thesis about the leaderless nature of the political system is questionable.

English-language journals and periodicals with useful articles on the political system include *Journal of Japanese Studies, Journal of Asian Studies, Asian Survey, Pacific Affairs* [Vancouver], *Japan Quarterly* [Tokyo], *Japan Echo* [Tokyo], and *Far Eastern Economic Review* [Hong

Kong]. One of the best, *Japan Interpreter* [Tokyo], ceased publication in 1980 but its articles from the 1960s and 1970s are still illuminating. (For further information and complete citations, see Bibliography.)

Chapter 7. Foreign Relations

Family crest using Chinese seal-style ideograph for longevity and stylized old pine trees (matsu)

JAPAN'S FOREIGN POLICY was facing new challenges and difficult decisions in 1990. The 1980s had seen enormous changes in the distribution of international economic power and the political influence that accompanies it. Japan had become the world's largest creditor nation and the second largest donor of foreign aid. Japanese industries and enterprises were among the most capable in the world. High savings and investment rates and high-quality education were expected to solidify the international leadership of these enterprises in the decade to come. Its economic power gave Japan a steadily growing role in the World Bank (see Glossary), the International Monetary Fund (IMF—see Glossary), and other international financial institutions. Investment and trade flows gave Japan by far the dominant economic role in Asia, and Japanese aid and investment were widely sought after in other parts of the world. It appeared to be only a matter of time before such economic power would be translated into greater political power.

The collapse of the Soviet domination of Eastern Europe and the growing Soviet preoccupation with internal political and economic problems increased the importance of economic competition, rather than military power, to Japan. The Soviet Union, a military superpower, was often depicted as a large Third World country trying desperately to stave off economic disaster and anxiously seeking aid, trade, and technical benefits from the developed countries, such as Japan. The power of Japan's ally, the United States, was also seen by many as waning. The United States's status in the 1980s had gone from the world's largest creditor to the world's largest debtor, and its economic position had weakened relative to some other developed countries, notably Japan. The United States was forced to look increasingly to Japan and others to shoulder the financial burdens entailed in the transformation of former communist economies in Eastern Europe and other urgent international requirements that fall upon the shoulders of world leaders.

Inside Japan, both elite and popular opinion expressed growing support for a more prominent international role, proportionate to the nation's economic power, foreign assistance, trade, and investment. But the traditional post-World War II reluctance to take a greater military role in the world remained. A firm consensus continued to support the 1960 Treaty of Mutual Cooperation and Security and other bilateral agreements with the United States as the keystones of Japan's security policy. However, Japanese officials were increasingly active in using their economic and financial resources in seeking a greater voice in international financial and political organizations, and in shaping the policies of the developed countries toward international trouble spots, especially in Asia. Meanwhile, there was some doubt in both Japan and the United States as to whether Japan-United States security arrangements, predicated on the Soviet threat, could be transformed to meet the new strategic realities of the 1990s.

Throughout the post-World War II period, Japan concentrated on economic growth. It accommodated itself flexibly to the regional and global policies of the United States while avoiding major initiatives of its own; adhered to pacifist principles embodied in the 1947 Constitution, referred to as the "peace constitution"; and generally took a passive, low-profile role in world affairs. Relations with other countries were governed by what the leadership called "omnidirectional diplomacy," which was essentially a policy of maintaining political neutrality in foreign affairs while expanding economic relations wherever possible. This policy was highly successful and allowed Japan to prosper and grow as an economic power, but it was feasible only while the country enjoyed the security and economic stability provided by its ally, the United States.

The need for a revamping of Japan's foreign policy posture had become apparent during the 1970s and particularly following the middle of the decade, as major changes in the international situation and the nation's own development into an economic world power made the old diplomacy obsolete. Japan's burgeoning economic growth and expansion into overseas markets had given rise to foreign charges of "economic aggression" and demands that it adopt more balanced trade policies. Changes in the power relationships in the Asia-Pacific quadrilateral—made up of Japan, China, the United States, and the Soviet Union—also called for reexamination of policies. The deepening Sino-Soviet split and confrontation, the dramatic rapprochement between the United States and China, the rapid reduction of the United States military presence in Asia following the Second Indochina War (1954–75), and the 1970s expansion of Soviet military power in the western Pacific all required a reevaluation of Japan's security position and overall role in Asia. Finally, the oil crises of the 1970s sharpened Japanese awareness of the country's vulnerability to cutoffs of raw material and energy supplies, underscoring the need for a less passive, more independent foreign policy.

Japanese thinking on foreign policy was also influenced by the rise of a new postwar generation to leadership and policy-making positions. The differences in outlook between the older leaders still in positions of power and influence and the younger generation that was replacing them complicated formulation of foreign policy.

By 1990 Japan's foreign policy choices often challenged the leadership's tendency to avoid radical shifts and to rely on incremental adjustments. Although still generally supportive of close ties, including the alliance relationship with the United States, Japanese leaders were well aware of strong American frustrations with Japanese economic practices and Japan's growing economic power relative to the United States in world affairs. Senior United States leaders were calling upon Japanese officials to work with them in crafting "a new conceptual framework" for Japan-United States relations that would take account of altered strategic and economic realities and changes in Japanese and United States views about the bilateral relationship. The results of this effort were far from clear. Some optimistically predicted "a new global partnership" in which the United States and Japan would work together as truly equal partners in dealing with global problems. Pessimists predicted that negative feelings generated by the realignment in United States and Japanese economic power and persistent trade frictions would prompt Japan to strike out more on its own, without the "guidance" of the United States. Given the growing economic dominance of Japan in Asia, Tokyo was seen as most likely to strike out independently there first, translating its economic power into political and perhaps, eventually, military influence.

Major Foreign Policy Goals and Strategies

Japan's geography—particularly its insular character, its limited endowment of natural resources, and its exposed location near potentially hostile giant neighbors—has played an important role in the development of its foreign policy. In premodern times, Japan's semi-isolated position on the periphery of the Asian mainland was an asset (see Physical Setting, ch. 2). It permitted the Japanese to exist as a self-sufficient society in a secure environment. It also allowed them to borrow selectively from the rich civilization of China while maintaining their own cultural identity. Insularity promoted a strong cultural and ethnic unity, which underlay the early development of a national consciousness that has influenced Japan's relations with outside peoples and cultures throughout its history.

Early Developments

In the early sixteenth century, a feudally organized Japan came into contact with Western missionaries and traders for the first time.

Westerners introduced important cultural innovations into Japanese society during more than a century of relations with various feudal rulers. But when the country was unified at the beginning of the seventeenth century, the Tokugawa government decided to expel the foreign missionaries and strictly limit intercourse with the outside world. National seclusion—except for contacts with the Chinese and Dutch—was Japan's foreign policy for more than two centuries (see Seclusion and Social Control, ch. 1).

When the Tokugawa seclusion was forcibly breached in 1853–54 by Commodore Matthew C. Perry of the United States Navy, Japan found that geography no longer ensured security—the country was defenseless against military pressures and economic exploitation by the Western powers. After Perry's naval squadron had compelled Japan to enter into relations with the Western world, the first foreign policy debate was over whether Japan should embark on an extensive modernization to cope with the threat of the "eastward advance of Western power," which had already violated the independence of China, or expel the "barbarians" and return to seclusion. The latter alternative—although it appealed to many—was never seriously considered. Beginning with the Meiji Restoration of 1868, which ushered in a new, centralized regime, Japan set out to "gather wisdom from all over the world" and embarked on an ambitious program of military, social, political, and economic reforms that transformed it within a generation into a modern nation-state and major world power.

Modern Japan's foreign policy was shaped at the outset by its need to reconcile its Asian identity with its desire for status and security in an international order dominated by the West. The principal foreign policy goals of the Meiji period (1868–1912) were to protect the integrity and independence of the nation against Western domination and to win equality of status with the leading nations of the West by reversing the unequal treaties. Since fear of Western military power was the chief concern of the Meiji leaders, their highest priority was building up the basic requirements for national defense, under the slogan "wealth and arms" (*fukoku kyōhei*). They saw that a modern military establishment required national conscription drawing manpower from an adequately educated population, a trained officer corps, a sophisticated chain of command, and strategy and tactics adapted to contemporary conditions (see The Modernization of the Military, 1868–1931, ch. 8). Finally, it required modern arms together with the factories to make them, sufficient wealth to purchase them, and a transportation system to deliver them (see The Emergence of Modern Japan, 1868–1919, ch. 1).

A Japanese view of the West, an 1850s woodblock print of a
contemporary American merchant ship by Hiroshige II
Courtesy Chadbourne Collection, Library of Congress

An important objective of the military buildup was to gain the respect of the Western powers and achieve equal status for Japan in the international community. Inequality of status was symbolized by the treaties imposed on Japan when the country was first opened to foreign intercourse. The treaties were objectionable to the Japanese not only because they imposed low fixed tariffs on foreign imports and thus handicapped domestic industries, but also because their provisions gave a virtual monopoly of external trade to foreigners and granted extraterritorial status to foreign nationals in Japan, exempting them from Japanese jurisdiction and placing Japan in the inferior category of uncivilized nations. Many of the social and institutional reforms of the Meiji period were designed to remove the stigma of backwardness and inferiority represented by the "unequal treaties," and a major task of Meiji diplomacy was to press for early treaty revision.

Once created, the Meiji military machine was used to extend Japanese power overseas, for many leaders believed that national security depended on expansion and not merely a strong defense. Within thirty years, the country's military forces had fought and defeated imperial China in the First Sino-Japanese War (1894–95), winning possession of Taiwan and Chinese recognition of Korea's independence. Ten years later, in the Russo-Japanese War (1904–5), Japan defeated tsarist Russia and won possession of southern Sakhalin as well as a position of paramount influence in Korea and southern Manchuria. By this time, Japan had been able to negotiate revisions of the unequal treaties with the Western powers and had in 1902 formed an alliance with the world's leading power, Britain. After World War I, in which it sided with the Western Allies, Japan, despite its relatively small role in the war (with little effort it gained possession of former German territories in the Pacific), sat with the victors at Versailles and enjoyed the status of a great power in its own right.

Between World War I and World War II, the nation embarked on a course of imperialist expansion, using both diplomatic and military means to extend its control over more and more of the Asian mainland. It began to see itself as the protector and champion of Asian interests against the West, a point of view that brought it increasingly into conflict with the Western powers (see Diplomacy, ch. 1). When its aggressive policies met firm resistance from the United States and its allies, Japan made common cause with the Axis partnership of Germany and Italy and launched into war with the United States and the Western Alliance (see World War II, ch. 8).

After Japan's devastating defeat in World War II, the nation came under an Allied occupation in which the United States, as the principal occupying power, was charged with the demilitarization and democratization of the state. Major changes were made in political, social, and economic institutions and practices. During the seven-year occupation, the country had no control over its foreign affairs and became in effect the ward of the United States on the international scene. It adopted a new Constitution whereby, in Article 9, the "Japanese people forever renounce war as a sovereign right of the nation and the threat or use of force as mean of settling international disputes" (see The Postwar Constitution, ch. 6).

Postwar Developments

When Japan regained its sovereignty in 1952 and reentered the international community as an independent nation, it found itself in a world dominated by the Cold War between East and West, in which the Soviet Union and the United States headed opposing camps. By virtue of the Treaty of Peace with Japan signed in San Francisco on September 8, 1951 (effective April 28, 1952), ending the state of war between Japan and most of the Allied powers except the Soviet Union and China, and the Mutual Security Assistance Pact between Japan and the United States, signed in San Francisco the same day, Japan was now essentially a dependent ally of the United States, which continued to maintain bases and troops on Japanese soil.

Japan's foreign policy goals during most of the early postwar period were essentially to regain economic viability and establish its credibility as a peaceful member of the world community. National security was entrusted to the protective shield and nuclear umbrella of the United States, which was permitted under the security pact that came into effect in April 1952, to deploy its forces in and about Japan. The pact provided a framework governing the use of United States forces against military threats—internal or external—in the region. A special diplomatic task was to assuage the suspicions and alleviate the resentments of Asian neighbors who had suffered from Japanese colonial rule and imperialist aggression in the past. Japan's diplomacy toward its Asian neighbors, therefore, tended to be extremely low-key, conciliatory, and non-assertive. With respect to the world at large, the nation avoided political issues and concentrated on economic goals. Under its omnidirectional diplomacy, it sought to cultivate friendly ties with all nations, proclaimed a policy of "separation of politics and economics," and adhered to a neutral position on some East-West issues.

During the 1950s and 1960s, foreign policy actions were guided by three basic principles: close cooperation with the United States for both security and economic reasons; promotion of a free trade system congenial to Japan's own economic needs; and international cooperation through the United Nations (UN)—to which it was admitted in 1956—and other multilateral bodies. Adherence to these principles worked well and contributed to phenomenal economic recovery and growth during the first two decades after the end of the occupation.

In the 1970s, the basic postwar principles remained unchanged, but were approached from a new perspective, owing to the pressure of practical politics at home and abroad. There was growing domestic pressure on the government to exercise more foreign policy initiatives independent of the United States, without, however, compromising vital security and economic ties. The so-called Nixon "shock," involving the surprise United States opening to China and other regional issues, also argued for a more independent Japanese foreign policy. The nation's phenomenal economic growth had made it a ranking world economic power by the early 1970s and had generated a sense of pride and self-esteem, especially among the younger generation. The demand for a more independent foreign policy reflected this enhanced self-image.

Changes in world economic relations during the 1970s also encouraged a more independent stance. Japan had become less dependent on the Western powers for resources. Oil, for example, was obtained directly from the producing countries and not from the Western-controlled multinational companies. Other important materials also came increasingly from sources other than the United States and its allies, while trade with the United States as a share of total trade dropped significantly during the decade of the 1970s. Thus, political leaders began to argue that in the interests of economic self-preservation, more attention should be paid to the financial and development needs of other countries, especially those that provided Japan with vital energy and raw material supplies.

The move toward a more autonomous foreign policy was accelerated in the 1970s by the United States decision to withdraw troops from Indochina. Japanese public opinion had earlier favored some distance between Japan and the United States involvement in war in Vietnam. The collapse of the war effort in Vietnam was seen as the end of United States military and economic dominance in Asia and brought to the fore a marked shift in Japanese attitudes about the United States. This shift, which had been developing since the early 1970s, took the form of questioning the credibility of the United States's nuclear umbrella, as well as its ability to underwrite a stable international currency system, guarantee Japanese access to energy and raw materials, and secure Japanese interests in a stable political order. The shift therefore required a reassessment of omnidirectional diplomacy.

Japan's leaders welcomed the reassertion of United States military power in Asian and world affairs following the revolution in

Iran, the United States hostage crisis, and the Soviet military invasion of Afghanistan, all of which occurred in 1979. Japanese leaders played a strong supporting role in curbing economic and other interaction with the Soviet Union and its allies, to help check the expansion of Soviet power in sensitive Third World areas. Under Prime Minister Nakasone Yasuhiro, Japan built up a close political-military relationship with the United States as part of a de facto international front of a number of developed and developing countries intent on checking Soviet expansion. Japan's defense spending continued to grow steadily despite overall Japanese budget restraint. Japan became increasingly active in granting foreign assistance to countries of strategic importance in East-West competition (see Strategic Considerations; Defense Spending, ch. 8).

The realignment of United States and Japanese currencies in the mid-1980s increased the growth of Japanese trade, aid, and investment, especially in Asia. It also accelerated the reversal of the United States fiscal position, from one of the world's largest creditors in the early 1980s to the world's largest debtor at the end of the decade. Japan became the world's largest creditor, an increasingly active investor in the United States, and a major contributor to international debt relief, financial institutions, and other assistance efforts.

The crucial issue for the United States and many other world governments in the 1990s centered on how Japan would employ this growing economic power. The strategic framework of the Japan-United States alliance also was called into question by the ending of the Cold War and collapse of the Soviet empire. Could a new rationale be found to sustain the active security tie that had been the basis for Japan's foreign affairs in the postwar period? Had Japan's foreign interactions become so broad and multifaceted that new mechanisms were needed? Were new ways of thinking about Japan's foreign policy being formulated and implemented in Japan? It appeared clear to observers in Japan in 1990 that the majority of the Japanese public and elite were satisfied with the general direction of Japanese foreign policy. That policy direction was characterized by continued close ties with the United States, to sustain world stability and prosperity that were so beneficial to Japan, and incrementally more assertive Japanese policies, especially regarding international economic and political institutions and Asian affairs. Yet, the world order was changing rapidly, and there were deep frustrations in some quarters in the United States, China, and Western Europe over Japanese practices. There also was some evidence of deep frustrations in Japan over Tokyo's seeming slowness in taking a more active world role. The possibility of more radical change in Japanese foreign policy, perhaps in directions more independent of the United States, remained a distinct possibility.

Foreign Policy Formulation

Institutional Framework

Under the 1947 Constitution, the cabinet exercises the primary responsibility for the conduct of foreign affairs, subject to the overall supervision of the Diet (see The Legislature, ch. 6). The prime minister is required to make periodic reports on foreign relations to the Diet, whose upper and lower houses each have a foreign affairs committee. Each committee reports on its deliberations to plenary sessions of the chamber to which it belongs. Ad hoc committees are formed occasionally to consider special questions. Diet members have the right to raise pertinent policy questions—officially termed interpellations—to the minister of foreign affairs and the prime minister. Treaties with foreign countries require ratification by the Diet. As the symbol of the state, the emperor performs the ceremonial function of receiving foreign envoys and attesting to foreign treaties ratified by the Diet.

As the chief executive and constitutionally the dominant figure in the political system, the prime minister has the final word in major foreign policy decisions. The minister of foreign affairs, a senior member of the cabinet, acts as the prime minister's chief adviser in matters of planning and implementation. The minister in 1990 was assisted by two vice ministers: one in charge of administration, who was at the apex of the Ministry of Foreign Affairs structure as its senior career official, and the other in charge of political liaison with the Diet. Other key positions in the ministry included members of the ministry's Secretariat which in 1989 had divisions handling consular, emigration, communications, and cultural exchange functions, and the directors of the various regional and functional bureaus in the ministry (see fig. 10).

The Ministry of Foreign Affairs staff included an elite career foreign service corps, recruited on the basis of a competitive examination and thereafter trained by the ministry's Foreign Service Training Institute. The handling of specific foreign policy issues was usually divided between the geographic and functional bureaus to minimize overlaps and competition. In general, bilateral issues were assigned to the geographic bureaus, and multilateral problems to the functional bureaus. The Treaties Bureau, with its wide-ranging responsibilities, tended to get involved in the whole spectrum of issues. The Information Analysis, Research, and Planning

Bureau in the ministry's Secretariat engaged in comprehensive and coordinated policy investigation and planning.

Long a profession of high social prestige, diplomatic service from the Meiji period through World War II was a preserve of the upper social strata. In addition to formal qualifications, proper social origin, family connections, and graduation from Tokyo Imperial University were important prewar requirements for admission. After World War II, these requirements were changed as part of democratic reform measures but foreign service continued to be a highly regarded career. Most career foreign service officers had passed the postwar Higher Foreign Service Examination before entry into the service. Many of these successful examinees were graduates of the prestigious Law Faculty of the University of Tokyo. Almost all ambassadorial appointments since the 1950s have been made from among veteran diplomats.

Diplomacy in postwar Japan was not a monopoly of the Ministry of Foreign Affairs. Given the overriding importance of economic factors in foreign relations, the ministry worked closely with the Ministry of Finance on matters of customs, tariffs, international finance, and foreign aid; with the Ministry of International Trade and Industry (MITI) on exports and imports; and with the Ministry of Agriculture, Forestry, and Fisheries on questions of foreign agricultural imports and fishing rights. The Ministry of Foreign Affairs also consulted other agencies, such as the Defense Agency, the Fair Trade Commission, the Japan Export-Import Bank, the Japan External Trade Organization, the Overseas Economic Cooperation Fund, and the Overseas Technical Cooperation Agency. On many issues affecting the country's foreign economic activities—and thus its diplomatic relations as well—the Ministry of Foreign Affairs and sometimes MITI and the Ministry of Finance were known to favor liberalizing import restrictions. On the other hand, the Ministry of Agriculture, Forestry, and Fisheries and other domestic ministries took a more protectionist stand, evidently because of pressures from special interest groups (see Trade and Investment Institutions, ch. 5).

The vital importance of foreign affairs expanded to affect virtually every aspect of national life in postwar Japan, and the multiplicity of agencies involved in external affairs continued to be a source of confusion and inefficiency in the formulation of foreign policy. On the other hand, as the postwar generation of leaders and policymakers began to assume a greater role in government decision making and as public attitudes on foreign policy issues matured, there were indications that foreign affairs were being conducted on the basis of a more stable consensus.

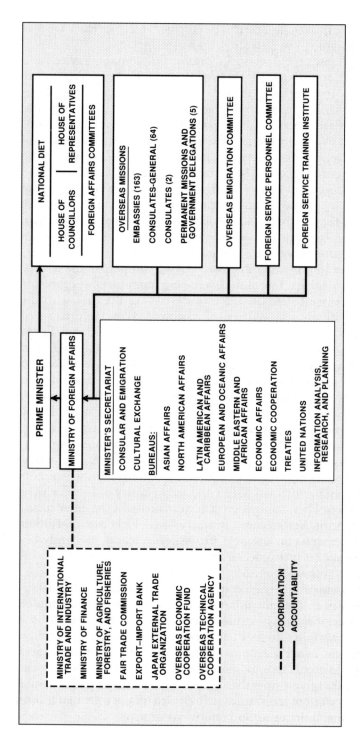

Source: Based on information from Japan, Ministry of Foreign Affairs, *Gaikō seisho* (Foreign Affairs Blue Paper), Tokyo, 1988.

Figure 10. Principal Organizations, Foreign Policy Formulation and Execution, 1988

The Role of Domestic Politics

The influence of Japanese domestic politics on the conduct of foreign affairs changed in the mid-1970s. Up to that time, the foreign policy debate in Japan had been between "progressives," who favored advances toward socialist countries and more independence from the United States, and "conservatives," who tended to identify Japanese interests closely with the United States-led alignment of Western countries. The ruling Liberal Democratic Party (LDP) was closely associated with the conservative, pro-United States position, while opposition parties often staked out positions at odds with the status quo (see The Liberal Democratic Party, ch. 6).

General satisfaction in Japan with the peace and prosperity that had been brought to the country made it hard for opposition parties to garner much support for a radical move to the left in Japan's foreign policy. The collapse of communism in Eastern Europe and the widely publicized brutalities of communist regimes in Asia in the late 1980s further dampened popular Japanese interest in shifting foreign policy to the left.

Meanwhile, the ruling LDP modified its base of political power. By the 1980s, it had markedly shifted the social composition of LDP support away from the traditional conservative reliance on business and rural groups, to include every category of the electorate. This shift resulted from efforts by LDP politicians to align various local interests in mutually advantageous arrangements in support of LDP candidates. The LDP had brought together various candidates and their supporting interest groups and had reached a policy consensus to pursue economic development while depending strongly on the United States security umbrella.

Domestic political challenges to LDP dominance waxed and waned later in the 1980s as the party faced major influence-peddling scandals with weak and divided leadership. In 1989 the opposition Japan Socialist Party won control of the Diet's House of Councillors. But the Japan Socialist Party's past ideological positions on foreign policy appeared to be more of a liability than an asset going into the lower-house elections in 1990, and the party attempted to modify a number of positions that called for pushing foreign policy to the left. In contrast, the LDP standard bearer, Prime Minister Kaifu Toshiki, used identification with the United States and the West to his advantage in the successful LDP effort to sustain control of the House of Representatives in February 1990 (see The Electoral System, ch. 6).

In 1990 the government, under the LDP, continued to popularize its policy of economic and security ties with the United States; of responding to domestic and international expectations of greater

Japanese political and economic contributions; and of international cooperation through the UN and other international organizations in the cause of world peace, disarmament, aid to developing countries, and educational and technical cooperation. Foreign policy speeches by the prime minister and the minister of foreign affairs were widely disseminated, and pamphlets and booklets on major foreign policy questions were issued frequently.

Political groups opposing the government's foreign policy presented their views freely through political parties and the mass media, which took vocal and independent positions on wide-ranging external issues. Some of the opposing elements were leftists who sought to exert influence through their representatives in the Diet, through mass organizations, and sometimes through rallies and street demonstrations. In contrast, special interest groups supporting the government—including the business community and agricultural interests—brought pressure to bear on the prime minister, cabinet members, and members of the Diet, usually through behind-the-scenes negotiations and compromises (see Interest Groups; The Mass Media and Politics, ch. 6).

Partisan political activities of all ideological tendencies were undertaken freely and openly, but the difference in foreign policy perspectives appeared increasingly in the 1980s to derive less from ideology than from more pragmatic considerations. Broadly stated, the partisan disagreement among the various groups competing for power had centered on the question of Japan's safety from external threat or attack. The dominant view was that, although the Japanese should be responsible for defending their homeland, they should continue their security ties with the United States, at least until they could gain sufficient confidence in their own self-defense power, which has been interpreted as not being proscribed by Article 9 of the Constitution. Proponents of this view agreed that this self-defense capability should be based on conventional arms and that any nuclear shield should be provided by the United States under the 1960 security treaty.

The Sino-United States rapprochement of the 1970s and the stiffening of Japan-Soviet relations in the 1980s caused the opposition parties to be less insistent on the need to terminate the security treaty. The Democratic Socialist Party and the Kōmeitō (Clean Government Party) indicated their readiness to support the treaty, while the Japan Socialist Party dropped its demand for immediate abrogation. Only the Japan Communist Party remained adamant.

Despite partisan differences, all political parties and groups were nearly unanimous during the 1970s and 1980s that Japan should exercise more independence and initiative in foreign affairs and not appear so ready to follow the United States on matters affecting Japan's interests. They also agreed that Japan should continue to prohibit the introduction of nuclear weapons into the country. These shared views stemmed from the resurgence of nationalism during the post-World War II era and from Japanese people's pride in their own heritage and in the economic achievements of the postwar decades. Although there were indications that the "nuclear allergy" produced by Japan's traumatic experience with the atomic bombings of Hiroshima and Nagasaki in August 1945 was beginning to moderate, nuclear weapons remained a sensitive political issue in 1990.

Except for security-related matters, most foreign affairs issues involved economic interests and mainly attracted the attention of the specific groups affected. The role of interest groups in formulating foreign policy varied with the issue at hand. Because trade and capital investment issues were involved, for example, in relations with China and with the Republic of Korea (South Korea), the business community increasingly became an interested party in the conduct of foreign affairs. Similarly, when fishing rights or agricultural imports were being negotiated, representatives of the industries affected worked with political leaders and the foreign affairs bureaucracies in shaping policy.

Because of the continuous control of the government enjoyed by the LDP since its formation in 1955, the policy-making bodies of the LDP had become the centers of government policy formulation. Because the unified will of the majority party almost invariably prevailed in the Diet, some observers believed that that body, had been reduced to a mere sounding board for government policy pronouncements and a rubber-stamp ratifier of decisions made by the prime minister and his cabinet. This situation meant that significant debate and deliberations on foreign policy matters generally took place not in the Diet but in closed-door meetings of the governing LDP, for example, between representatives of the Foreign Affairs Section of the LDP's Policy Research Council and officials of the Ministry of Foreign Affairs, MITI, or leaders of major LDP support groups, such as the Federation of Economic Organizations (Keizai Dantai Rengōkai—better known as Keidanren; see Business Interests, ch. 6).

The role of public opinion in the formulation of foreign policy throughout the postwar period has been difficult to determine. Japan continued to be extremely concerned with public opinion, and opinion polling became a conspicuous feature of national life. The large number of polls on public policy issues, including foreign policy matters, conducted by the Office of the Prime Minister, the

Ministry of Foreign Affairs, other government organizations, and the media led to the presumption by analysts that the collective opinions of voters do exert significant influence on policymakers. The public attitudes toward foreign policy that had held throughout much of the postwar period appeared to have shifted in the 1980s. Opinion polls reflected a marked increase in national pride and self-esteem. Moreover, public discussion of security matters by government officials, political party leaders, press commentators, and academics had become markedly less volatile and doctrinaire and more open and pragmatic, suggesting indirectly that public attitudes on this subject had evolved as well.

The mass media, and particularly the press, as the champion of the public interest and critic of the government, continued to mold public attitudes strongly. The media was the chief source of demands that the government exercise a more independent and less ''weak-kneed'' diplomacy in view of the changing world situation and Japan's increased stature in the world.

An Overview of Japan's Foreign Relations
Relations with the United States

Japan-United States relations were more uncertain in 1990 than at any time since World War II. As long-standing military allies and increasingly interdependent economic partners, Japan and the United States cooperated closely to build a strong, multifaceted relationship based on democratic values and interests in world stability and development. Japan-United States relations improved enormously in the 1970s and 1980s, as the two societies and economies became increasingly intertwined. In 1990 their combined gross national product (GNP—see Glossary) totaled about one third of the world's GNP. Japan received about 11 percent of United States exports (a larger share than any other country except Canada), and the United States bought about 34 percent of Japan's exports (see United States and Canada, ch. 5). Japan had US$65 billion in direct investment in the United States in 1990, while the United States had more than US$17 billion invested in Japan. Some US$100 billion in United States government securities held by institutions in Japan helped finance much of the United States budget deficit. Economic exchanges were reinforced by a variety of scientific, technical, tourist, and other exchanges. Each society continued to see the other as its main ally in Asia and the Pacific. Certain developments in the late 1980s damaged bilateral relations. Nevertheless, public opinion surveys continued to reveal that substantial majorities of Japanese and Americans believed that the bilateral relationship was vital to both countries.

Growing interdependence was accompanied by markedly changing circumstances at home and abroad that were widely seen to
have created a crisis in Japan-United States relations in the late
1980s. United States government officials continued to emphasize
the positive aspects of the relationship but warned that there was
a need for "a new conceptual framework." The *Wall Street Journal*
publicized a series of lengthy reports documenting changes in the
relationship in the late 1980s and reviewing the considerable debate in Japan and the United States over whether a closely cooperative relationship was possible or appropriate for the 1990s.
An authoritative review of popular and media opinion, published
in 1990 by the Washington-based Commission on US-Japan Relations for the Twenty First Century, was concerned with preserving
a close Japan-United States relationship. It warned of a "new ortho-
doxy" of "suspicion, criticism and considerable self-justification,"
which it said was endangering the fabric of Japan-United States
relations.

Three sets of factors stood out as most important in explaining
the challenges facing Japan-United States relations in the 1990s.
They were economic, political-military, and domestic in nature.

The relative economic power of Japan and the United States was
undergoing sweeping change, especially in the 1980s. This change
went well beyond the implications of the United States trade deficit
with Japan, which had remained between US$40 billion and US$48
billion annually since the mid-1980s. The persisting United States
trade and budget deficits of the early 1980s led to a series of decisions in the middle of the decade that brought a major realignment
of the value of Japanese and United States currencies. The stronger
Japanese currency gave Japan the ability to purchase more United
States goods and to make important investments in the United
States. By the late 1980s, Japan was the main international creditor.

Japan's growing investment in the United States—it was the second largest investor after Britain—led to complaints from some
American constituencies. Moreover, Japanese industry seemed well
positioned to use its economic power to invest in the high-technology
products in which United States manufacturers were still leaders.
The United States's ability to compete under these circumstances
was seen by many Japanese and Americans as hampered by heavy
personal, government, and business debt and a low savings rate.

In the late 1980s, the breakup of the Soviet bloc in Eastern Europe and the growing preoccupation of Soviet leaders with massive internal political and economic difficulties forced the Japanese
and United States governments to reassess their longstanding alliance against the Soviet threat. Officials of both nations had tended

to characterize the security alliance as the linchpin of the relationship, which should have priority over economic and other disputes. Some Japanese and United States officials and commentators continued to emphasize the common dangers to Japan-United States interests posed by the continued strong Soviet military presence in Asia (see Relations with the Soviet Union, this ch.). They stressed that until Moscow followed its moderation in Europe with major demobilization and reductions in its forces positioned against the United States and Japan in the Pacific, Washington and Tokyo needed to remain militarily prepared and vigilant.

Increasingly, however, other perceived benefits of close Japan-United States security ties were emphasized. The alliance was seen as deterring other potentially disruptive forces in East Asia, notably the Democratic People's Republic of Korea (North Korea). Ironically, some United States officials noted that the alliance helped keep Japan's potential military power in check and under the supervision of the United States.

The post-Cold War environment strengthened the relative importance of economic prowess over military power as the major source of world influence in the 1990s. This shift affected the perceived relative standing of Japan, the United States, and other powers. Increasingly, Japan was expected to shoulder international aid and economic responsibilities that in the past were discharged by the United States and other Western countries.

The declining Soviet threat, the rising power of the Japanese economy, increasingly close United States interaction (and related disputes) with Japan, and other factors led by 1990 to a decided shift in United States opinion about Japan, and less marked but nonetheless notable shifts in Japanese opinion. In the United States, this shift was reflected in questions about which was the more serious, the military threat from the Soviets or the economic challenge from Japan. In a series of polls in 1989 and 1990, most respondents considered the challenge from Japan the more serious. Similarly, poll data from early 1990 showed that most Japanese considered negative United States attitudes toward Japan a reflection of United States anger at "America's slipping economic position." Meanwhile, Japanese opinion was showing greater confidence in Japan's ability to handle its own affairs without constant reference—as in the past—to the United States. Japanese belief in United States reliability as a world leader also lessened.

In both countries, new or "revisionist" views of the Japan-United States relationship were promoted. In Japan, some commentators argued that the United States was weak, dependent on Japan, and unable to come to terms with world economic competition. They urged Japan to strike out on a more independent course. In the United States, prominent commentators warned of a Japanese economic juggernaut, out of control of the Japanese government, which needed to be "contained" by the United States.

At the same time, it was easy to overstate the changes in opinion in both countries. Japanese still considered the United States positively as their closest friend, the principal guardian of their external security, their most important economic partner and market, and the exemplar of a life-style that had much to offer—and much to envy. Moreover, the vast majority of Americans still viewed Japan positively, had high respect for Japanese accomplishments, and supported the United States defense commitment to Japan.

In the years after World War II, Japan's relations with the United States were placed on an equal footing for the first time at the end of the occupation by the Allied forces in April 1952. This equality, the legal basis of which was laid down in the peace treaty signed by forty-eight Allied nations and Japan, was initially largely nominal, because in the early postoccupation period Japan required direct United States economic assistance. A favorable Japanese balance of payments with the United States was achieved in 1954, mainly as a result of United States military and aid spending in Japan.

The Japanese people's feeling of dependence lessened gradually as the disastrous results of World War II subsided into the background and trade with the United States expanded. Self-confidence grew as the country applied its resources and organizational skill to regaining economic health. This situation gave rise to a general desire for greater independence from United States influence. During the 1950s and 1960s, this feeling was especially evident in the Japanese attitude toward United States military bases on the four main islands of Japan and in Okinawa Prefecture, occupying the southern two-thirds of the Ryūkyū Islands (see fig. 1).

The government had to balance left-wing pressure advocating disassociation from the United States against the realities of the need for military protection. Recognizing the popular desire for the return of the Ryūkyūs and the Bonin Islands (also known as the Ogasawara Islands), the United States as early as 1953 voluntarily relinquished its control of the Amami Island group at the northern end of the Ryūkyūs. But the United States made no commitment to return Okinawa, which was then under United States military administration for an indefinite period as provided in Article 3 of the peace treaty. Popular agitation culminated in a unanimous resolution adopted by the Diet in June 1956, calling for a return of Okinawa to Japan.

Bilateral talks on revising the 1952 security pact began in 1959, and the new Treaty of Mutual Cooperation and Security was signed in Washington on January 19, 1960. When the pact was submitted to the Diet for ratification on February 5, it became the subject of bitter debate over the Japan-United States relationship and the occasion for violence in an all-out effort by the leftist opposition to prevent its passage. It was finally approved by the House of Representatives on May 20. Japan Socialist Party deputies boycotted the lower house session and tried to prevent the LDP deputies from entering the chamber; they were forcibly removed by the police. Massive demonstrations and rioting by students and trade unions followed. These outbursts prevented a scheduled visit to Japan by President Dwight D. Eisenhower and precipitated the resignation of Prime Minister Kishi Nobusuke, but not before the treaty was passed by default on June 19, when the House of Councillors failed to vote on the issue within the required thirty days after lower house approval.

Under the treaty, both parties assumed an obligation to assist each other in case of armed attack on territories under Japanese administration. (It was understood, however, that Japan could not come to the defense of the United States because it was constitutionally forbidden to send armed forces overseas. In particular, the Constitution forbids the maintenance of "land, sea, and air forces." It also expresses the Japanese people's renunciation of "the threat or use of force as a means of settling international disputes." Accordingly, the Japanese find it difficult to send their "self-defense" forces overseas, even for peace-keeping purposes.) The scope of the new treaty did not extend to the Ryūkyū Islands, but an appended minute made clear that in case of an armed attack on the islands, both governments would consult and take appropriate action. Notes accompanying the treaty provided for prior consultation between the two governments before any major change occurred in the deployment of United States troops or equipment in Japan. Unlike the 1952 security pact, the new treaty provided for a ten-year term, after which it could be revoked upon one year's notice by either party. The treaty included general provisions on the further development of international cooperation and on improved future economic cooperation.

Both countries worked closely to fulfill the United States promise, under Article 3 of the peace treaty, to return all Japanese territories acquired by the United States in war. In June 1968 the United States returned the Bonin Islands (including Iwo Jima) to Japanese administrative control. In 1969 the Okinawa reversion issue and Japan's security ties with the United States became the focal points of partisan political campaigns. The situation calmed considerably when Prime Minister Satō Eisaku visited Washington in November 1969, and in a joint communiqué signed by him and President Richard M. Nixon, announced the United States agreement to return Okinawa to Japan in 1972. In June 1971, after eighteen months of negotiations, the two countries signed an agreement providing for the return of Okinawa to Japan in 1972.

The Japanese government's firm and voluntary endorsement of the security treaty and the settlement of the Okinawa reversion question meant that, two major political issues in Japan-United States relations were eliminated. But new issues arose. In July 1971, the Japanese government was surprised by Nixon's dramatic announcement of his forthcoming visit to the People's Republic of China. Many Japanese were chagrined by the failure of the United States to consult in advance with Japan before making such a fundamental change in foreign policy. The following month, the government was again surprised to learn that, without prior consultation, the United States had imposed a 10 percent surcharge on imports, a decision certain to hinder Japan's exports to the United States. Relations between Tokyo and Washington were further strained by the monetary crisis involving the December 1971 revaluation of the Japanese yen (for value of the yen—see Glossary).

These events of 1971 marked the beginning of a new stage in relations, a period of adjustment to a changing world situation that was not without episodes of strain in both political and economic spheres, although the basic relationship remained close. The political issues between the two countries were essentially security-related and derived from efforts by the United States to induce Japan to contribute more to its own defense and to regional security. The economic issues tended to stem from the ever-widening United States trade and payments deficits with Japan, which began in 1965 when Japan reversed its imbalance in trade with the United States and, for the first time, achieved an export surplus.

The United States withdrawal from Indochina in 1975 and the end of the Second Indochina War meant that the question of Japan's role in the security of East Asia and its contributions to its own defense became central topics in the dialogue between the two countries. United States dissatisfaction with Japanese defense efforts began to surface in 1975 when Secretary of Defense James A. Schlesinger publicly stigmatized Japan as a passive defense partner.

United States pressures continued and intensified, particularly as events in Iran and elsewhere in the Middle East after 1979 caused the United States to relocate more than 50 percent of its naval strength from East Asian waters to the Indian Ocean. Japan was repeatedly pressed not only to increase its defense expenditures and build up its antisubmarine and naval patrol capabilities, but to play a more active and positive security role generally.

The Japanese government, constrained by constitutional limitations and strongly pacifist public opinion, responded slowly to pressures for a more rapid buildup of its Self-Defense Forces (SDF). It steadily increased its budgetary outlays for those forces, however, and indicated its willingness to shoulder more of the cost of maintaining the United States military bases in Japan. In 1976 the United States and Japan formally established a subcommittee for defense cooperation, in the framework of a bilateral Security Consultative Committee provided for under the 1960 security treaty. This subcommittee, in turn, drew up new Guidelines for Japan-United States Defense Cooperation, under which military planners of the two countries have conducted studies relating to joint military action in the event of an armed attack on Japan.

On the economic front, Japan sought to ease trade frictions by agreeing to Orderly Marketing Arrangements, which limited exports on products whose influx into the United States was creating political problems. In 1977 an Orderly Marketing Arrangement limiting Japanese color television exports to the United States was signed, following the pattern of an earlier disposition of the textile problem. Steel exports to the United States were also curtailed, but the problems continued as disputes flared over United States restrictions on Japanese development of nuclear fuel-reprocessing facilities, Japanese restrictions on certain agricultural imports, such as beef and oranges, and liberalization of capital investment and government procurement within Japan.

To respond to the call, from its allies and from within the country as well, for a greater and more responsible role in the world, Japan developed what Ōhira Masayoshi, after he became prime minister in December 1978, called a "comprehensive security and defense strategy to safeguard peace." Under this policy, Japan sought to place its relations with the United States on a new footing—one of close cooperation but on a more reciprocal and autonomous basis, and on a global scale.

This policy was put to the test in November 1979, when radical Iranians seized the United States embassy in Tehran, taking sixty hostages. Japan reacted by condemning the action as a violation of international law. At the same time, Japanese trading firms and oil companies reportedly purchased Iranian oil that had become available when the United States banned oil imported from Iran. This action brought sharp criticism from the United States of Japanese government "insensitivity" for allowing the oil purchases and led to a Japanese apology and agreement to participate in sanctions against Iran in concert with other United States allies.

Following that incident, the Japanese government took greater care to support United States international policies designed to preserve stability and promote prosperity. Japan was prompt and effective in announcing and implementing sanctions against the Soviet Union following the Soviet invasion of Afghanistan in December 1979. In 1981, in response to United States requests, it accepted greater responsibility for defense of seas around Japan, pledged greater support for United States forces in Japan, and persisted with a steady buildup of the SDF.

A qualitatively new stage of Japan-United States cooperation in world affairs appeared to be reached in late 1982 with the election of Prime Minister Nakasone Yasuhiro. Officials of the Ronald Reagan administration worked closely with their Japanese counterparts to develop a personal relationship between the two leaders based on their common security and international outlook. Nakasone reassured United States leaders of Japan's determination against the Soviet threat, closely coordinated policies with the United States toward such Asian trouble spots as the Korean Peninsula and Southeast Asia, and worked cooperatively with the United States in developing China policy. The Japanese government welcomed the increase of United States forces in Japan and the Western Pacific, continued the steady buildup of the SDF, and positioned Japan firmly on the side of the United States against the threat of Soviet international expansion. Japan continued to cooperate closely with United States policy in these areas following Nakasone's term of office, although the political leadership scandals in Japan in the late 1980s made it difficult for newly elected President George Bush to establish the same kind of close personal ties that marked the Reagan years.

A specific example of Japan's close cooperation with the United States included its quick response to the United States call for greater host nation support from Japan following the rapid realignment of Japan-United States currencies in the mid-1980s. The currency realignment resulted in a rapid rise of United States costs in Japan, which the Japanese government, upon United States request, was willing to offset. Another set of examples was provided by Japan's willingness to respond to United States requests for foreign assistance to countries considered of strategic importance to the West. During the 1980s, United States officials voiced appreciation for Japan's "strategic aid" to countries such as Pakistan, Turkey, Egypt, and Jamaica. Prime Minister Kaifu Toshiki's pledges of support for East European and Middle Eastern countries in 1990 fit the pattern of Japan's willingness to share greater responsibility for world stability.

Despite complaints from some Japanese businesses and diplomats, the Japanese government remained in basic agreement with United States policy toward China and Indochina. The government held back from large-scale aid efforts until conditions in China and Indochina were seen as more compatible with Japanese and United States interests. Of course, there also were instances of limited Japanese cooperation. Japan's response to the United States decision to help to protect tankers in the Persian Gulf during the Iran-Iraq war in the late 1980s was subject to mixed reviews. Some United States officials stressed the positive, noting that Japan was unable to send military forces because of constitutional reasons but compensated by supporting the construction of a navigation system in the Gulf, providing greater host nation support for United States forces in Japan, and providing loans to Oman and Jordan (see The Article 9 "No War" Clause, ch. 6). Japan's refusal to join even in a mine-sweeping effort in the Gulf was an indication to some United States officials of Tokyo's unwillingness to cooperate with the United States in areas of sensitivity to Japanese leaders at home or abroad.

The main area of noncooperation with the United States in the 1980s was Japanese resistance to repeated United States efforts to get Japan to open its market more to foreign goods and to change other economic practices seen as adverse to United States economic interests. A common pattern was followed here. The Japanese government was sensitive to political pressures from important domestic constituencies that would be hurt by greater openness. In general, these constituencies were of two types—those representing inefficient or "declining" producers, manufacturers, and distributors, who could not compete if faced with full foreign competition; and those up-and-coming industries that the Japanese government wished to protect from foreign competition until they could compete effectively on world markets. To deal with domestic pressures while trying to avoid a break with the United States, the Japanese government engaged in protracted negotiations. This tactic bought time for declining industries to restructure themselves and new industries to grow stronger. Agreements reached dealt with some aspects of the problems, but it was common for trade or economic issues to be dragged out in talks over several years, involving more than one market-opening agreement. Such agreements were sometimes vague and subject to conflicting interpretations in Japan and the United States (see Import Policies, ch. 5).

During the 1970s and 1980s, United States administrations had favored an issue-by-issue approach in negotiating such economic disputes with Japan. This approach ostensibly limited the areas of dispute. But it resulted in widespread negative publicity, at a time when changing economic and security circumstances were causing both countries to reevaluate the relationship. Notable outpourings of United States congressional and media rhetoric critical of Japan accompanied the disclosure in 1987 that Toshiba had illegally sold sophisticated machinery of United States origin to the Soviet Union, which reportedly allowed Moscow to make submarines quiet enough to avoid United States detection, and the United States congressional debate in 1989 over the Japan-United States agreement to develop a new fighter aircraft—the FSX—for Japan's Air Self-Defense Force (see The Defense Industry, ch. 8).

A new approach was added in 1989. The so-called Structural Impediments Initiative was a series of talks designed to deal with domestic structural problems limiting trade on both sides. After several rounds of often contentious talks, agreements were reached in April and July 1990 that promised major changes in such sensitive areas as Japanese retailing practices, land use, and investment in public works. The United States pledged to deal more effectively with its budget deficit and to increase domestic savings. United States supporters saw the Structural Impediments Initiative talks as addressing fundamental causes of Japan-United States economic friction. Skeptics pointed to them as ways for officials to buy time and avoid an acute crisis in Japan-United States relations.

Relations with China

The priority that policy toward China has commanded in Japanese foreign affairs has varied over time. During the period of United States-backed "containment" of China, there was a sharp divergence between official policy and popular attitudes in Japan. As a loyal ally of the United States, the Japanese government was committed to nonrecognition, whereas popular sentiments favored diplomatic relations and expanded trade. The Japan Communist Party and the Japan Socialist Party sought to capitalize on this situation in their propaganda efforts to promote closer relations with Beijing. Pro-Chinese sentiment found support not only in the desire of the business community for a new source of raw materials and a profitable market, but also in the popular feeling of cultural affinity with the Chinese. Japanese leaders spent considerable effort trying to manage this tension.

The unanticipated United States opening to China in 1971 undermined the administration of Prime Minister Satō, but the subsequent government of Prime Minister Tanaka Kakuei quickly adjusted policy by normalizing diplomatic relations in 1972. Throughout the next decade, policy toward China continued to receive high priority as Japanese officials dealt with competing pressures from the Chinese and Soviet governments. Beijing and Moscow pressed Tokyo to side with their respective positions in the intense Sino-Soviet competition for influence in Asia following the substantial United States military withdrawal and the fall of United States-backed regimes in Indochina.

China's economic importance to Japanese policymakers rose in tandem with the market-oriented reforms and increased foreign interaction associated with the post-Mao Zedong policies of Chinese leader Deng Xiaoping. Unrealistic Japanese expectations of economic benefit in China were ended by the zigzag course of Chinese development in the 1980s. Japanese decision makers by the end of the decade were able to settle on a balanced policy toward China that required less attention from Japanese leaders and received lower priority than in the past. The massacre of prodemocracy demonstrators in Beijing's Tiananmen Incident and collapse of communist regimes in Eastern Europe and parts of Asia in 1989 discredited China's communist leaders in the minds of Japanese people and made it more difficult for Chinese officials or opposition Japanese politicians to raise China-related issues in Japanese domestic politics. The effect was to reduce further the need to make special government concessions on China-related issues.

The early post-World War II political differences between the two countries related especially to China's insistence that Japan end its official relations with the Guomindang (Chinese Nationalist Party) government on Taiwan and abrogate its security treaty with the United States. Initially, neither country allowed its political differences to stand in the way of broadening unofficial contacts, and in the mid-1950s they exchanged an increasing number of cultural, labor, and business delegations.

In 1958, however, China suspended its trade with Japan—apparently convinced that trade concessions were ineffective in achieving political goals. Thereafter, in a plan for improving political relations, China requested that the Japanese government not be hostile toward it, not obstruct any effort to restore normal relations between itself and Japan, and not join in any conspiracy to create two Chinas.

Coincident with its dispute with the Soviet Union, China resumed its trade with Japan in late 1960. Important provisions were attached to the arrangement, however, stipulating that trade was to be based on formal government-to-government agreements and private trade was to be sanctioned indirectly by the Japanese government. Only Japanese firms that pledged to support the three political principles of 1958 were to be allowed to participate.

In November 1962, Sino-Japanese relations were elevated to semiofficial status—still far short of diplomatic recognition—with the signing in Beijing of a five-year trade memorandum (1963–67), better known as the Liao-Takasaki Agreement. Under its terms, Chinese purchases of industrial plants were to be financed partly through medium-term credits from the Japan Export-Import Bank. The accord also permitted China to open a trade mission in Tokyo and in 1963 paved the way for Japanese government approval of the export to China of a synthetic textile manufacturing plant valued at around US$20 million, guaranteed by the bank. Subsequent protest from Taiwan caused Japan to shelve further deferred-payment plant exports. China reacted to this change by downgrading its Japan trade and intensified propaganda attacks against Japan as a "lackey" of the United States.

Relations cooled noticeably during the massive political and economic chaos that prevailed during the radical phases of the Cultural Revolution in China, from 1966 to 1969. As the turmoil subsided, however, the Japanese government—already under pressure both from the pro-China factions in the LDP and from opposition elements—sought to adopt a more forward posture. Japan's efforts to set its own China policy became particularly evident after July 1971 when Nixon, according to Japanese sources, "shocked" the Japanese by announcing his forthcoming visit to Beijing. Relations remained complicated, however, because of Japan's diplomatic and substantial economic ties with Taiwan and the presence of a powerful pro-Guomindang faction in the LDP.

The September 1972 visit to Beijing of Japan's newly elected prime minister, Tanaka Kakuei, culminated in the signing of a historic joint statement that ended nearly eighty years of enmity and friction between the two countries. In this statement, Tokyo recognized the Beijing regime as the sole legal government of China, stating at the same time that it understood and respected China's position that Taiwan was "an inalienable part of the territory of the People's Republic of China." For its part, China waived its demand for war indemnities from Japan. (This demand was first made in the mid-1950s; the war reparations claims totaled as much as the equivalent of US$50 billion.) Diplomatic relations were to be established as of September 29, 1972. Japan and China also agreed to hold negotiations aimed at the conclusion not only of a treaty of peace and friendship but also at agreements on trade, shipping, air transportation, and fisheries. Sino-Japanese trade grew rapidly after 1972. In January 1974, a three-year trade agreement—

the first of several working agreements covering civil air transportation, shipping, fisheries, and trademarks—was signed. Arrangements for technical cooperation, cultural exchange, and consular matters were also undertaken.

Negotiations for a Sino-Japanese peace and friendship treaty also began in 1974 but soon encountered a political problem Japan wished to avoid. China insisted on including in the treaty an antihegemony clause, clearly directed at the Soviet Union. Japan, wishing to adhere to its "equidistant" or neutral stance in the Sino-Soviet confrontation, objected. The Soviet Union made clear that a Sino-Japanese treaty would prejudice Soviet-Japanese relations. Japanese efforts to reach a compromise with China over this issue failed, and the talks were broken off in September 1975.

Matters remained at a standstill until political changes in China after the death of Mao Zedong in 1976 brought to the fore a leadership dedicated to economic modernization and interested in accommodation with Japan, whose aid was essential. A changing climate of opinion in Japan that was more willing to ignore Soviet warnings and protests and accept the idea of "antihegemonism" as an international principle also helped lay the groundwork for new efforts to conclude the treaty.

In February 1978, a long-term private trade agreement led to an arrangement by which trade between Japan and China would increase to a level of US$20 billion by 1985, through exports from Japan of plants and equipment, technology, construction materials, and machine parts in return for coal and crude oil. This long-term plan, which gave rise to inflated expectations, proved overly ambitious and was drastically cut back the following year as China was forced to reorder its development priorities and scale down its commitments. However, the signing of the agreement reflected the wish on both sides to improve relations. In April 1978, a dispute involving the intrusion of armed Chinese fishing boats into the waters off the Senkaku Islands, a cluster of barren islets north of Taiwan and south of the Ryūkyū Islands, flared up and threatened to disrupt the developing momentum toward a resumption of peace treaty talks. Restraint on both sides led to an amicable resolution. (The Senkakus are claimed by Japan, China, and Taiwan, but the question of territorial rights was finessed in this case.) Talks on the peace treaty were resumed in July, and agreement was reached in August on a compromise version of the antihegemony clause. The Treaty of Peace and Friendship was signed on August 12 and came into effect October 23, 1978.

Chinese domestic political problems and uneven progress in China's reform programs at times dampened Japanese enthusiasm for economic relations with China. Yet Sino-Japanese relations made considerable progress in the 1980s. In 1982 there was a serious political controversy over revision of Japanese textbooks dealing with the history of imperial Japan's war against China in the 1930s and 1940s. Beijing also registered concern in 1983 about the reported shift in United States strategic emphasis in Asia, away from China and in favor of more reliance on Japan, under the leadership of the more "hawkish" Prime Minister Nakasone Yasuhiro, warning anew against possible revival of Japanese militarism. By mid-1983, however, Beijing had decided—coincidentally with its decision to improve relations with the Reagan administration—to solidify ties with Japan. Chinese Communist Party general secretary Hu Yaobang visited Japan in November 1983, and Prime Minister Nakasone reciprocated by visiting China in March 1984.

The Chinese had long looked on Japan—by then a major trading partner—as a leading source of assistance in promoting economic development in China. The growth of Soviet military power in East Asia in the early 1980s prompted them to consult with Japan more frequently on security issues and to pursue parallel foreign policies designed to check Soviet influence and promote regional stability. While Japanese enthusiasm for the Chinese market waxed and waned, broad strategic considerations in the 1980s steadied Tokyo's policy toward Beijing. In fact, Japan's heavy involvement in China's economic modernization reflected in part a determination to encourage peaceful domestic development in China, to draw China into gradually expanding links with Japan and the West, to reduce China's interest in returning to its more provocative foreign policies of the past, and to obstruct any Sino-Soviet realignment against Japan.

Thus, common strategic concerns, as well as economic interests, held the two nations together. Until the late 1970s, the Chinese appeared more alarmed than Japan about the Soviet military buildup in Asia. But as Moscow increasingly sought to impede strategic cooperation among Japan, the United States, and possibly China, in part by stepped-up intimidation of Japan, the Nakasone government became more concerned about the Soviet military buildup.

Many of Tokyo's concerns about the Soviet Union duplicated Chinese worries. They included the increased deployment in East Asia of Soviet SS–20 missiles, Tu-22M Backfire bombers, and ballistic missile submarines; the growth of the Soviet Pacific fleet; the Soviet invasion of Afghanistan and the potential threat it posed to Persian Gulf oil supply routes; and an increased Soviet military presence in Vietnam.

In response, Japan and China adopted strikingly complementary foreign policies, designed to isolate the Soviet Union and its allies politically and to promote regional stability. In Southeast Asia, both countries provided strong diplomatic backing for the efforts of the Association of Southeast Asian Nations (ASEAN—see Glossary) to bring about a Vietnamese withdrawal from Cambodia. Japan cut off all economic aid to Vietnam and provided substantial economic assistance to Thailand to help with resettling Indochinese refugees. China was a key supporter of Thailand and of the Cambodian resistance groups. In Southwest Asia, both nations backed the condemnation of the Soviet occupation of Afghanistan, refused to recognize the Soviet-backed Kabul regime, and sought through diplomatic and economic means to bolster Pakistan. In Northeast Asia, Japan and China sought to moderate the behavior of their Korean partners—South Korea and North Korea, respectively—to reduce tensions. In 1983 both China and Japan strongly criticized the Soviet proposal to redeploy some of their European-based SS–20 missiles to Asia.

Complementary economic interests also strengthened Sino-Japanese relations. Japan was a major source of capital, technology, and equipment for China's modernization drive. In fact, Japan had been China's largest trading partner since the mid-1960s, accounting for more than 20 percent of China's total trade. Bilateral trade exploded in the 1970s and early 1980s, from US$1 billion in the early 1970s to over US$8 billion in 1982. Japan became China's largest creditor, accounting for nearly half of the estimated US$30 billion in credit China lined up from 1979 to 1983.

Although its share of Japan's global trade was still small (3 percent in 1982), China became Japan's sixth largest trading partner. Japan regarded China as a significant source of coal, oil, and strategic minerals, such as tungsten and chromium, and as an important market for Japanese steel, machinery plant equipment, chemical products, and synthetic textile fibers.

The optimism that marked the economic relationship in the late 1970s had given way to a greater degree of realism on both sides by the early 1980s. China's decision to curtail imports of heavy industrial goods in 1981 and 1982 had a sobering effect on the Japanese. Businesspeople in Japan came to appreciate the problems China faced, and revised their expectations of the growth of economic ties as the Chinese experimented with various economic policies. The Japanese continued to hope that they would profit from China's potentially huge domestic market, whenever its modernization began to pick up speed.

Japanese economic interests in China focused on developing energy resources and infrastructure and on promoting commercial trade. As of 1983, the Overseas Economic Cooperation Fund, Tokyo's official aid organization, had agreed to grant US$3.5 billion in loans to China for basic infrastructure projects, such as port and rail modernization. In addition, the Japan Export-Import Bank extended US$2 billion for oil exploration and coal mining at a 6.25 percent annual interest rate, the lowest rate China had gained from any country at that time. The Japanese were heavily involved in China's oil industry, and Japanese drilling in the Bohai Gulf appeared promising.

Japan encountered a number of episodes of friction with China during the rest of the 1980s. In late 1985, Chinese officials complained harshly about Prime Minister Nakasone's visit to the Yasukuni Shrine, which commemorates Japan's war dead, and in mid-1986 they complained about the latest revision of Japan's history textbooks to soften accounts of World War II atrocities. Economic issues centered on Chinese complaints that the influx of Japanese products into China had produced a serious trade deficit for China. Nakasone and other Japanese leaders were able to reduce these official concerns during visits to Beijing and in other talks with Chinese officials. Notably, they assured the Chinese of Japan's continued large-scale development and commercial assistance. At the popular level in China, it was not easy to allay concerns. Student-led demonstrations against Japan, on the one hand, helped reinforce Chinese officials' warnings to their Japanese counterparts. On the other hand, it was more difficult to change popular opinion in China than it was to change the opinions of the Chinese officials. Meanwhile, the removal of party chief Hu Yaobang in early 1987 was detrimental to smooth Sino-Japanese relations, since Hu had built personal relationships with Nakasone and other Japanese leaders.

The Chinese government's harsh crackdown on prodemocracy demonstrations in the spring of 1989 caused Japanese policymakers to realize that the new situation in China was extremely delicate and required careful handling to avoid Japanese actions that would push China farther away from reform. At the same time, these policymakers were loathe to break ranks with the United States and other Western countries, where popular opinion and domestic pressures to varying degrees required that officials condemn the crackdown and take action to restrict economic or other interaction of benefit to the Chinese regime. Beijing leaders reportedly judged at first that the industrialized countries would relatively quickly resume normal business with China after a brief period of complaint over the Tiananmen Incident. When that did not happen, the Chinese officials made strong suggestions to Japanese officials that they break from most industrialized nations by pursuing normal economic intercourse with China, consistent with Tokyo's longterm interests in China. Japanese leaders—like West European and United States leaders—were careful not to isolate China, and continued trade and other relations generally consistent with the policies of other industrialized democracies. But they also followed the United States lead in limiting economic relations notably advantageous to China. In particular, they held back for one year the disbursement of ¥810 billion in aid, which Japan had promised in 1988 to give China in the 1990–95 period.

Relations with the Soviet Union

The 1980s saw a decided hardening in Japanese attitudes toward the Soviet Union. Japan was pressed by the United States to do more to check the expansion of Soviet power in the Third World following the December 1979 Soviet invasion of Afghanistan. It responded by cutting off contacts beneficial to the Soviet regime and providing assistance to "front line" Third World states, such as Pakistan and Thailand. Under Nakasone, Japan worked hard to demonstrate a close identity of views with the Reagan administration on the Soviet threat. Japan steadily built up its military forces, welcomed increases in United States forces in Japan and the Western Pacific, and pledged close cooperation to deal with the danger posed by Soviet power.

Although public and media opinion remained skeptical of the danger to Japan posed by Soviet forces in Asia, there was strong opposition in Japan to Moscow's refusal to accede to Japan's claims to the Northern Territories, known to the Japanese as Etorofu and Kunashiri, at the southern end of the Kuril Island chain, and the smaller Shikotan Island and the Habomai Islands, northeast of Hokkaidō, which were seized by the Soviets in the last days of World War II (see fig. 11). The stationing of Soviet military forces on the islands gave tangible proof of the Soviet threat, and provocative maneuvers by Soviet air and naval forces in Japanese-claimed territory served to reinforce Japanese official policy of close identification with a firm United States-backed posture against Soviet power. In 1979, the Japanese government specifically protested a build up in Soviet forces in Etorofu, Kunashiri, and Shikotan.

The advent of the Mikhail Gorbachev regime in Moscow in the mid-1980s saw a replacement of hard-line Soviet government

diplomats who were expert in Asian affairs with more flexible spokesmen calling for greater contact with Japan. Gorbachev took the lead in promising new initiatives in Asia, but the substance of Soviet policy changed more slowly. In particular, throughout the rest of the 1980s, Soviet officials still seemed uncompromising regarding the Northern Territories, Soviet forces in the Western Pacific still seemed focused on and threatening to Japan, and Soviet economic troubles and lack of foreign exchange made prospects for Japan-Soviet Union economic relations appear poor. By 1990, Japan appeared to be the least enthusiastic of the major Western-aligned developed countries in encouraging greater contacts with and assistance to the Soviet Union.

Strains in Japan-Soviet Union relations had deep historical roots going back to the competition of the Japanese and Russian empires for dominance in Northeast Asia. In 1990, forty-five years after the end of World War II, a state of war between Japan and the Soviet Union existed technically because the Soviet Union had refused in the intervening years to sign the 1951 peace treaty. The main stumbling block in all Japan's subsequent efforts to establish bilateral relations on what it called "a truly stable basis" was the territorial dispute over the Northern Territories.

During the first half of the 1950s, other unsettled problems included Japanese fishing rights in the Sea of Okhotsk and off the coast of the Soviet maritime provinces and repatriation of Japanese prisoners of war, who, the Japanese claimed, were still being held in the Soviet Union. Negotiation of these issues broke down early in 1956 because of tension over territorial claims.

Negotiations soon resumed, however, and the two countries issued a joint declaration in October 1956 providing for the restoration of diplomatic relations. The two parties also agreed to continue negotiations for a peace treaty, including territorial issues. In addition, the Soviets pledged to support Japan for UN membership and waive all World War II reparations claims. The joint declaration was accompanied by a trade protocol that granted reciprocal most-favored-nation treatment and provided for the development of trade.

Except for admission to the UN in 1956, Japan derived few apparent gains from the normalization of diplomatic relations. The second half of the 1950s saw an increase in cultural exchanges. Soviet propaganda, however, had little success in Japan, where it encountered a longstanding antipathy stemming from the Russo-Japanese rivalry in Korea, Manchuria, and China proper in the late nineteenth century, from the Russo-Japanese War of 1904–5, and from the Soviet declaration of war on Japan in the last days

403

of World War II, in violation of the Japanese-Soviet Neutrality Pact of 1941.

The Soviet Union sought to induce Japan to abandon its territorial claims by alternating threats and persuasion. As early as 1956, it hinted at the possibility of considering the return of the Habomai Islands and Shikotan Island if Japan abandoned its alliance with the United States. In 1960 the Soviet government warned Japan against signing the Treaty of Mutual Cooperation and Security with the United States, and after the treaty was signed declared that it would not hand over the Habomai Islands and Shikotan Island under any circumstances unless Japan abrogated the treaty forthwith. In 1964 the Soviet government offered to return these islands unconditionally if the United States ended its military presence on Okinawa and the main islands of Japan.

Despite divergence on the territorial question, on which neither side was prepared to give ground, Japanese relations with the Soviet Union improved appreciably after the mid-1960s. The Soviet government began to seek Japanese cooperation in its economic development plans, and the Japanese responded positively. The two countries signed a five-year trade agreement in January 1966 and a civil aviation agreement as well.

Economic cooperation expanded rapidly during the 1970s, despite an often strained political relationship. The two economies were complementary, for the Soviet Union needed Japan's capital, technology, and consumer goods, while Japan needed Soviet natural resources, such as oil, gas, coal, iron ore, and timber. By 1979 overall trade had reached US$4.4 billion annually and had made Japan, next to the Federal Republic of Germany (West Germany), the Soviet Union's most important nonsocialist trading partner.

This economic cooperation was interrupted by Japan's decision in 1980 to participate in sanctions against the Soviet Union for its invasion of Afghanistan and by its actions to hold in abeyance a number of projects being negotiated, to ban the export of some high-technology items, and to suspend Siberian development loans. Subsequently, Japanese interest in economic cooperation with the Soviet Union waned as Tokyo found alternative suppliers and remained uncertain about the economic viability and political stability of the Soviet Union under Gorbachev. Japan-Soviet trade in 1988 was valued at nearly US$6 billion.

Japan-Soviet political relations during the 1970s were characterized by the frequent exchange of high-level visits to explore the possibility of improving bilateral relations and by repeated discussions of a peace treaty, which were abortive because neither side was prepared to yield on the territorial issue. Minister of Foreign

Affairs Andrei Gromyko of the Soviet Union visited Tokyo in January 1972—one month before United States president Nixon's historic visit to China—to reopen ministerial-level talks after a six-year lapse. Other high-level talks, including an October 1973 meeting between Prime Minister Tanaka Kakuei and Leonid I. Brezhnev, general secretary of the Communist Party of the Soviet Union, were held in Moscow during the next three years, but the deadlock on the territorial issue continued and prospects for a settlement dimmed. Moscow began to propose a treaty of friendship and goodwill as an interim step while peace treaty talks were continued. This proposal was firmly rejected by Japan.

After 1975 the Soviet Union began openly to warn that the Japanese peace treaty with China might jeopardize Soviet-Japan relations. In January 1976, Gromyko again visited Tokyo to resume talks on the peace treaty. When the Japanese again refused to budge on the territorial question, Gromyko, according to the Japanese, offered to return two of the Soviet-held island areas—the Habomai Islands and Shikotan Island—if Japan would sign a treaty of goodwill and cooperation. He also reportedly warned the Japanese, in an obvious reference to China, against "forces which come out against the relaxation of tension and which try to complicate relations between states, including our countries."

The signing of the Sino-Japanese peace treaty in mid-1978 was a major setback to Japanese-Soviet relations. Despite Japanese protestations that the treaty's antihegemony clause was not directed against any specific country, Moscow saw it as placing Tokyo with Washington and Beijing firmly in the anti-Soviet camp. Officially, both sides continued to express the desire for better relations, but Soviet actions served only to alarm and alienate the Japanese side. The 1980s Soviet military buildup in the Pacific was a case in point.

Changes in Soviet policy carried out under Gorbachev beginning in the mid-1980s, including attempts at domestic reform and the pursuit of détente with the United States and Western Europe, elicited generally positive Japanese interest, but the Japanese government held that the Soviet Union had not changed its policies on issues vital to Japan. The government stated that it would not conduct normal relations with the Soviet Union until Moscow returned the Northern Territories. The government and Japanese business leaders stated further that Japanese trade with and investment in the Soviet Union would not grow appreciably until the Northern Territories issue was resolved.

By 1990 the Soviet government had altered its tactics. The Soviets now acknowledged that the territorial issue was a problem and talked about it with Japanese officials at the highest levels and in working-level meetings. Soviet officials reportedly floated a proposal to lease the Northern Territories and part of Sakhalin—once a colonial holding of Japan's—to Japan. Gorbachev and others also referred to a 1956 Soviet offer to return one of the three main islands (Shikotan, the smallest of the three) and the Habomai Islands, and there were indications that Moscow might be prepared to revive the offer. The Soviets emphasized that they would not return all the islands because of Soviet public opposition and the possible reawakening of other countries' territorial claims against the Soviet Union. The Soviet military reportedly opposed a return, because the Kuril chain provided a protective barrier to the Sea of Okhotsk, where the Soviet navy deployed submarines carrying long-range ballistic missiles.

The Soviet government also stepped up its diplomacy toward Japan with the announcement in 1990 that Gorbachev would visit Japan in 1991. Soviet officials asserted that their government would propose disarmament talks with Japan and might make more proposals on the Northern Territories in connection with the visit. Observers believed that Gorbachev might propose a package dealing with the islands, arms reduction, and economic cooperation. In January 1990, the Japanese Ministry of Foreign Affairs shifted its position, which previously had rejected negotiations with the Soviet Union on arms reductions, indicating that Japan would be willing to negotiate. Ministry officials stated that the government would formulate policy on arms reduction in close coordination with the United States.

Relations with Other Asia-Pacific Countries

Japan's rapid rise as the dominant economic power in Asia in the 1980s helped to define Japanese policy toward this diverse region, stretching from South Asia to the islands in the South Pacific Ocean. The decline in East-West and Sino-Soviet tensions during the 1980s suggested that economic rather than military power would determine regional leadership. During the decade, Japan displaced the United States as the largest provider of new business investment and economic aid in the region, although the United States market remained a major source of Asia-Pacific dynamism. Especially following the rise in value of the yen relative to the dollar in the late-1980s, Japan's role as a capital and technology exporter and as an increasingly significant importer of Asian manufactured goods made it the core economy of the Asia-Pacific region.

From the mid-1950s to the late 1960s, Japan's relations with the rest of Asia were concerned mainly with promoting its far-flung,

Poster protesting the Soviet presence in the Northern Territories, Tokyo. The date on the poster—August 9—recalls the Soviet Union's 1945 entry into war against Japan. Courtesy Robert L. Worden

multiplying economic interests in the region through trade, technical assistance, and aid. Its main problems were the economic weakness and political instability of its trading partners and the growing apprehension of Asian leaders over Japan's "overpresence" in their region.

Japan began to normalize relations with its neighbors during the 1950s after a series of intermittent negotiations, which led to the payment of war reparations to Burma, Indonesia, the Philippines, and the Republic of Vietnam (South Vietnam). Thailand's reparations claims were not settled until 1963. Japan's reintegration into the Asian scene was also facilitated early by its joining the Colombo Plan for Cooperative Economic and Social Development in Asia and the Pacific in December 1954 and by its attendance at the April 1955 Afro-Asian Conference in Bandung, Indonesia. In the late 1950s, Japan made a limited beginning in its aid program. In 1958 it extended the equivalent of US$50 million in credits to India, the first Japanese loan of its kind in post-World War II years. As in subsequent cases involving India, as well as Sri Lanka, Malaysia, Taiwan, Pakistan, and South Korea, these credits were rigidly bound to projects that promoted plant and equipment purchases from Japan. In 1960 Japan officially established the Institute of Asian Economic Affairs (renamed the Institute of Developing Economies in 1969) as the principal training center for its specialists in economic diplomacy.

407

In the early 1960s, the government adopted a more forward posture in seeking to establish contacts in Asia. In 1960 the Institute of Asian Economic Affairs was placed under the jurisdiction of the Ministry of International Trade and Industry (MITI). In 1961 the government established the Overseas Economic Cooperation Fund as a new lending agency. The following year the Overseas Technical Cooperation Agency made its debut.

By the mid-1960s, Japan's role had become highly visible in Asia as well as elsewhere in the world. In 1966 Japan became a full member of the Organisation for Economic Co-operation and Development (OECD—see Glossary). As economic and trade expansion burgeoned, leaders began to question the propriety and wisdom of what they variously described as "mere economism," an "export-first policy," and the "commercial motives of aid." They wanted to contribute more to the solution of the North-South problem, as they dubbed the issue—the tenuous relationship between the developed countries and the developing countries.

Efforts since the beginning of the 1970s to assume a leading role in promoting peace and stability in Asia, especially Southeast Asia, by providing economic aid and by offering to serve as a mediator in disputes, faced two constraints. Externally there was fear in parts of Asia that Japan's systematic economic penetration into the region would eventually lead to something akin to its pre-World War II scheme to exploit Asian markets and materials. Internally, foreign policymakers were apprehensive that Japan's political involvement in the area in whatever capacity would almost certainly precipitate an anti-Japanese backlash and adversely affect its economic position.

After a reassessment of policy, the Japanese leadership appeared to have decided that more emphasis ought to be given to helping the developing countries of the region modernize their industrial bases to increase their self-reliance and economic resilience. In the late 1970s, Japan seemed to have decided that bilateral aid in the form of yen credits, tariff reductions, larger quota incentives for manufactured exports, and investments in processing industries, energy, agriculture, and education would be the focus of its aid programs in Asia.

By 1990, Japan's interaction with the vast majority of Asia-Pacific countries, especially its burgeoning economic exchanges, was multifaceted and increasingly important to the recipient countries. The developing countries of ASEAN (Brunei, Indonesia, Malaysia, the Philippines, and Thailand; Singapore was treated as a newly industrialized economy, or NIE) regarded Japan as critical to their development. Japanese aid to the ASEAN countries totaled US$1.9

billion in Japanese fiscal year (FY—see Glossary) 1988 versus about US$333 million for the United States during United States FY 1988. Japan was the number one foreign investor in the ASEAN countries, with cumulative investment as of March 1989 of about US$14.5 billion, more than twice that of the United States. Japan's share of total foreign investment in ASEAN countries ranged from 70–80 percent in Thailand to 20 percent in Indonesia.

South Asia

In South Asia, Japan's role was mainly that of an aid donor. Japanese aid to seven South Asian countries totaled US$1.1 billion in 1988, about the same as the United States gave. Except for Pakistan, which received heavy inputs of aid from the United States, all other South Asian countries received most of their aid from Japan. Four South Asian nations—India, Pakistan, Bangladesh, and Sri Lanka—were in the top ten list of Tokyo's aid recipients worldwide.

Prime Minister Kaifu signaled a broadening of Japan's interest in South Asia with his swing through the region in April 1990. In an address to the Indian parliament, Kaifu stressed the role of free markets and democracy in bringing about "a new international order," and emphasized the need for a settlement of the Kashmir territorial dispute between India and Pakistan, and for economic liberalization to attract foreign investment and promote dynamic growth. To India, which was very short of hard currency, Kaifu pledged a new concessional loan of ¥100 billion (about US$650 million) for the coming year.

Newly Industrialized Economies

Japan's relationships with the NIEs (South Korea, Taiwan, Hong Kong, and Singapore—often called the Four Tigers) were marked by both cooperation and competition. After the early 1980s, when Tokyo extended a large financial credit to South Korea for essentially political reasons, Japan avoided significant aid relationships with the NIEs. Relations instead involved capital investment, technology transfer, and trade. Increasingly, the NIEs came to be viewed as Japan's rivals in the competition for export markets for manufactured goods, especially the vast United States market (see International Economic Cooperation and Aid, ch. 5).

Australia, New Zealand, and the Pacific Islands

Japan's economic involvement in Australia was heavily tilted toward extraction of natural resources and in-country manufacturing for the Australian domestic market. Japanese investment by 1988 made Australia the single largest source of Japanese regional imports. Japan's trade with New Zealand was a small fraction of its trade with Australia.

Politically, Japan's relations with Australia and New Zealand had elements of tension as well as acknowledged mutuality of interest. Memories of World War II lingered among the public, as did a contemporary fear of Japanese economic domination. At the same time, government and business leaders saw Japan as a vital export market and an essential element in Australia's and New Zealand's future growth and prosperity.

By 1990 commercial and strategic interests prompted a strong surge in Japanese involvement in the newly independent island nations of the Pacific. Japan's rapidly growing aid to the South Pacific was seen by many as a response to United States calls for greater burden-sharing, and to the adoption of the 1982 Convention on Law of the Sea, which gave states legal control over fishery resources within their 200-nautical-mile economic zones. Japan was second after Australia as an aid donor to the region. The US$93 million it provided in 1988 was more than three times the United States aid of US$26.7 million in FY 1988. Japanese companies also invested heavily in the tourism industry in the island nations.

The Koreas

Japan's policies toward the two Koreas reflected the importance this area had for Asian stability, which was seen as essential to Japanese peace and prosperity. In 1990 Japan remained one of four major powers (along with the United States, the Soviet Union, and China) that had important security interests on the Korean Peninsula. However, Japan's involvement in political and security issues on the Korean Peninsula was more limited than that of the other three powers. Japan's relations with North Korea and South Korea had a legacy of bitterness stemming from harsh Japanese colonial rule over Korea from 1910 to 1945. Polls during the postwar period in Japan and South Korea showed that the people of each nation had a profound dislike of the other country and people.

Article 9 of Japan's Constitution is interpreted to bar Japan from entering into security relations with countries other than the United States. Consequently, Japan had no substantive defense relationship with South Korea, and military contacts were infrequent. The Japanese government supported noncommunist South Korea in other ways. It backed United States contingency plans to dispatch United States armed forces in Japan to South Korea in case of a North Korean attack on South Korea. It also acted as an intermediary between South Korea and China. It pressed the Chinese government to open and expand relations with South Korea in the 1980s.

Japan's trade with South Korea was US$27.25 billion in 1988, with a surplus of US$3.63 billion on the Japanese side. Japanese direct private investment in South Korea totaled US$3.25 billion in 1988. Japanese and South Korean firms often had interdependent relations, which gave Japan advantages in South Korea's growing market. Many South Korean products were based on Japanese design and technology. A surge in imports of South Korean products into Japan in 1990 was due partly to production by Japanese investors in South Korea.

Japan-North Korean relations remained antagonistic in the late 1980s. The two governments did not maintain diplomatic relations and had no substantive contacts. The opposition Japan Socialist Party, however, had cordial relations with the North Korean regime.

Issues in Japan-North Korean relations that produced tensions included North Korean media attacks on Japan, Japan's imposition of economic sanctions on North Korea for terrorist acts against South Korea in the 1980s, and unpaid North Korean debts to Japanese enterprises of about US$50 million. Japan allowed trade with North Korea through unofficial channels. This unofficial trade reportedly came to more than US$200 million annually in the 1980s.

Vietnam and Cambodia

Stability in Indochina also was very important to Japanese interests. During the Vietnam war of the 1960s and 1970s, Japan had consistently encouraged a negotiated settlement at the earliest possible date. Even before the hostilities ended, it had made contact with the Democratic Republic of Vietnam (North Vietnam) government and had reached an agreement to establish diplomatic relations in September 1973. Implementation, however, was delayed by North Vietnamese demands that Japan pay the equivalent of US$45 million in World War II reparations in two yearly installments, in the form of "economic cooperation" grants. Giving in to the Vietnamese demands, Japan paid the money and opened an embassy in Hanoi in October 1975 following the unification of North Vietnam and South Vietnam into the Socialist Republic of Vietnam. Recognition of the communist Khmer Rouge regime in Cambodia came in 1975, and diplomatic relations with that country were established in August 1976.

This Indochina policy was justified at home and to the member countries of ASEAN—some of which were hostile to and suspicious of Vietnam—on the grounds that official contacts and eventually aid to Vietnam would promote the peace and stability of Southeast Asia as a whole. In December 1978, after a visit to Tokyo by Vietnam's minister of foreign affairs, Nguyen Duy Trinh, Japan agreed to give Vietnam US$195 million in grant aid, as well as commodity loans and food shipments. When Vietnam launched its invasion of Cambodia later that same month, Japan was embarrassed and irritated. It joined ASEAN in condemning the invasion, supported the UN resolution calling for immediate withdrawal of Vietnamese forces, and suspended the aid commitments it had made with Hanoi.

Japan and the United States shared common ground in opposing the Soviet-backed Vietnamese invasion of Cambodia in December 1978. Japan's policy of restricting aid and other economic cooperation with Vietnam reinforced international pressures on Hanoi to pull back its forces and seek a comprehensive Cambodian settlement. Faced with international isolation, waning Soviet bloc support, continued armed resistance in Cambodia, and large-scale economic problems at home, Hanoi withdrew most if not all of its combat troops from Cambodia in 1989. It appealed to developed countries to open channels of economic cooperation, trade, and aid. Although some Japanese businesses were interested in investment and trade with Vietnam and Cambodia, the Japanese government still opposed economic cooperation with those countries until there was a comprehensive settlement in Cambodia. This stand was basically consistent with United States policy of the time.

Meanwhile, Japan gave informal assurances that Tokyo was prepared to bear a large share of the financial burden to help with reconstruction aid to Cambodia, whenever a comprehensive settlement was reached, and to help fund UN or other international peacekeeping forces, should they be required.

Relations with Other Countries

Japan had diplomatic relations with nearly all independent nations and had been an active member of the UN since December 1956. Its relations with countries other than those discussed above were mainly commercial and economic. It had few major political differences with any of them but was under continuing pressure from many to limit its exports and to remove restrictions imposed on the import of foreign goods and capital. It was also being pressed to contribute more to the socioeconomic betterment of the nations of the Third World.

During the 1970s, the government took positive measures to increase its Official Development Assistance (ODA) to developing countries and to contribute to the stabilization of the international

Prime ministers Kaifu Toshiki and Margaret Thatcher in Tokyo, 1989
Courtesy Asahi Shimbun

trade and monetary system. These measures were generally welcomed abroad, although some countries felt that the steps taken were not executed as rapidly or were not as extensive as similar efforts by some other advanced industrialized nations. Japan's ODA increased tenfold during the decade and stood at US$3.3 billion in 1980, but this ODA as a percentage of GNP was still below the average of other donor countries.

In the 1980s, Japan's ODA continued to rise rapidly. ODA net disbursements, in nominal terms, averaged around US$3 billion per year in the early 1980s, and jumped to US$5.6 billion in 1986 and US$9.1 billion in 1988. Japan's share of total disbursements from major aid donors also grew significantly, from 11.76 percent in 1979 to about 15 percent in the mid-1980s, and to nearly 19 percent in 1988. Japan's ODA as a percentage of its GNP, however, did not increase substantially during the 1980s, remaining at about 0.3 percent.

Japan continued to concentrate its economic assistance in Asia (about 72 percent of total commitments in 1987–88), reflecting its historical and economic ties to the region. Japan made modest increases in aid to Africa with the announcement in 1989 of a US$600 million grant program for the next three years. In early 1990, Japan also pledged large amounts of assistance to Eastern Europe, but

413

most of that aid was to be in the form of market rate credits and investment insurance, which did not qualify as ODA. In other regions, Japan appeared likely to continue allocating relatively small shares of assistance. Nevertheless, by 1987 Japan had become the largest bilateral donor in twenty-nine countries, nearly double the number in which that had been the case ten years earlier.

The continued growth of Japan's foreign aid appeared to be motivated by two fundamental factors. First, Japanese policy aimed at assuming international responsibilities commensurate with its position as a global economic power. Second, many believed, the growing Japanese foreign aid program came largely in response to pressure from the United States and other allies for Japan to take on a greater share of the financial burdens in support of shared security, political, and economic interests.

Although cultural and noneconomic ties with Western Europe grew significantly during the 1980s, the economic nexus remained by far the most important element of Japanese-West European relations throughout the decade. Events in West European relations, as well as political, economic, or even military matters, were topics of concern to most Japanese commentators because of the immediate implications for Japan. The major issues centered on the effect of the coming West European economic unification on Japan's trade, investment, and other opportunities in Western Europe. Some West European leaders were anxious to restrict Japanese access to the newly integrated European Community, but others appeared open to Japanese trade and investment. In partial response to the strengthening economic ties among nations in Western Europe and to the 1989 United States-Canada free trade agreement, Japan and other countries along the Asia-Pacific rim began moving in the late 1980s toward greater economic cooperation.

International Cooperation

United Nations

At the beginning of the 1990s, Japan continued to regard international cooperation within the UN framework as a basic foreign policy principle. When Japan joined the UN in 1956, it did so with great enthusiasm and broad public support, for the international organization was seen to embody the pacifist country's hopes for a peaceful world order. Membership was welcomed by many Japanese who saw the UN as a guarantor of a policy of unarmed neutrality for their nation. To others, support for the UN would be useful in masking or diluting Japan's almost total dependence on the United States for its security. The government saw the UN as an ideal arena for its risk-minimizing, omnidirectional foreign policy.

After the late 1950s, Japan participated actively in the social and economic activities of the UN's various specialized agencies and other international organizations concerned with social, cultural, and economic improvement. During the 1970s, as it attained the status of an economic superpower, Japan was called on to play an increasingly large role in the UN. As Japan's role increased and its contributions to UN socioeconomic development activities grew, many Japanese began to ask whether their country was being given an international position of responsibility commensurate with its economic power. There was even some sentiment, expressed as early as 1973, that Japan should be given a permanent seat on the UN Security Council with the United States, the Soviet Union, Britain, France, and China.

By 1990 Japan's international cooperation efforts had reached a new level of involvement and activism. Japan contributed about 11 percent of the regular UN budget, second only to the United States, which contributed 25 percent. Japan was particularly active in UN peacekeeping activities and in 1989, for the first time, sent officials to observe and participate in UN peacekeeping efforts (in Afghanistan, Iran, Iraq, and Namibia). Japan sent a small team to observe the February 1990 elections in Nicaragua, and planned to offer more than 100 people to help supervise elections in Cambodia if the UN were to establish a presence there.

Other Organizations

In addition to its UN activities and its participation in Asian regional groupings, such as the Colombo Plan and the Asian Development Bank, Japan was also involved, beginning in the 1950s, in worldwide economic groupings largely made up of, or dominated by, the industrialized nations of Western Europe and North America. In 1952 Japan became a member of the IMF and of the World Bank, where it played an increasingly important role. In 1955, it joined the General Agreement on Tariffs and Trade (GATT—see Glossary). In 1966 Japan was admitted to the OECD, which brought it into what was essentially a club of leading industrialized nations. Japan has participated actively since 1975 in the annual summit meetings of the seven largest capitalist countries—the Group of Seven—Canada, Federal Republic of Germany, France, Italy, Japan, Britain, and the United States.

International Banks

Based on its economic power and performance, Japan steadily expanded its role in the World Bank, the IMF, and other international

415

financial institutions. Investment and trade flows made Japan by far the dominant economic nation in Asia. Japanese aid and investment became widely sought after in other parts of the world, and it appeared to be only a matter of time before such economic power would translate into greater political influence.

In the multilateral development banks, Japan's financial and policy positions became more prominent. Tokyo had assumed a leading role at the Asian Development Bank for a number of years. At the World Bank, Japan's voting share represented about 9.4 percent, compared with 16.3 percent for the United States. Japan also made several "special" contributions to particular World Bank programs that raised its financial status but did not alter its voting position. Japan planned to participate in the East European Development Bank, making a contribution of 8.5 percent, the same as the United States and major West European donors. Japan also displayed a growing prominence in IMF deliberations, helping ease the massive debt burdens of Third World countries, and generally supported efforts at the GATT 1990 Uruguay Round of trade negotiations to liberalize world trade and investment.

Policy after the Cold War

The post-Cold War world promised an important position for Japan. Japanese leaders and popular opinion remained tentative and uncertain as to how Japan would use its remarkable economic power in order to preserve and enhance Japanese national interests. There seemed to be little alternative to a continued close strategic relationship with the United States and a general international outlook designed to promote global peace, development, and access to world markets and resources. Japanese leaders and public opinion were often anxious to see Japan assert a more pronounced position in world affairs, but the tradition of caution in Japanese foreign policy was reinforced by the still unclear outlines of the post-Cold War environment that would affect Japanese foreign policy in the years ahead.

* * *

There is voluminous literature in English on Japan's postwar foreign policy. James W. Morley's *Japan's Foreign Policy, 1868–1941,* Frank C. Langdon's *Japan's Foreign Policy,* Reinhard Drifte's *Japan's Foreign Policy,* Robert A. Scalapino's *The Foreign Policy of Modern Japan,* and William R. Nester's *Japan's Growing Predominance Over East Asia and the World Economy* are worthwhile monographs. The most useful current assessments appear in publications such as the

Far Eastern Economic Review, Asian Survey, Current History, Foreign Affairs, and *Foreign Policy.* Feature articles also appear in such important news sources as the *Asian Wall Street Journal.* Among United States government publications, the most useful are the Foreign Broadcast Information Service's *Daily Report: East Asia* and various publications of the United States Congress. (For further information and complete citations, see Bibliography.)

Chapter 8. National Security

Family crest consisting of three Chinese-style round fans (uchiwa), once used to direct troops in battle and the symbol of the god of war

JAPAN IN THE EARLY 1990s was in the unusual position of being a major world economic and political power, with an aggressive military tradition, resisting the development of strong armed forces. A military proscription is included as Article 9 of the 1947 Constitution, which states, "The Japanese people forever renounce war as a sovereign right of the nation and the threat or use of force as a means of settling international disputes." In 1990 that article, along with the rest of the "Peace Constitution," retained strong government and citizen support and was interpreted as permitting the Self-Defense Forces (SDF), but prohibiting those forces from possessing nuclear weapons or other offensive arms or being deployed outside of Japan.

The SDF were under control of the civilian Defense Agency, subordinate to the prime minister. Although highly trained and fully qualified to perform the limited missions assigned to them, the SDF were small, understaffed, and underequipped for more extensive military operations, and as of 1990 had never seen action in any operation other than disaster relief.

Japan's national defense policy has been based on maintaining the 1960 Treaty of Mutual Cooperation and Security with the United States, under which Japan assumed unilateral responsibility for its own internal security and the United States agreed to join in Japan's defense in the event that Japan or its territories were attacked. Although the size and capability of the SDF have always limited their role, until 1976 defense planning focused on developing forces adequate to deal with the conventional capabilities of potential regional adversaries. Beginning in 1976, government policy held that the SDF would be developed only to repel a small-scale, limited invasion and that the nation would depend on the United States to come to its aid in the event of a more serious incursion.

The Soviet invasion of Afghanistan in 1979 and the buildup of military forces in the Soviet Far East, including a group of islands to the north of Hokkaidō, which are occupied by the Soviet Union but claimed by Japan, led Japan to develop a program to modernize and improve the SDF in the 1980s, especially in air defense and antisubmarine warfare. In 1990 the government was reevaluating its security policy based on reduced East-West tensions and improving Soviet-Japanese relations.

The Japanese government valued its close relations with the United States and remained dependent on the United States nuclear umbrella. Thus, it worked to facilitate military contacts and to support the United States diplomatically whenever possible. Both the government and the public, however, supported only limited increases in self-defense capability. National security, it was believed, is fostered by international diplomacy and economic aid as much as by militai y might.

There were few critical issues for Japan's internal security in 1990. Conditions of public order compared favorably with those elsewhere in the world. The crime rate was remarkably low, kept that way by well-organized and efficient police assisted by general citizen cooperation and support.

Militarism Before 1945

The Bushidō Code

Japanese aversion for things military is of recent origin. For centuries before 1945, military men and a strong martial tradition exerted a powerful and, at times, dominant influence on national life. Although the development of a modern army and navy came only during the Meiji period (1868–1912), reverence for the art of war and its practitioners had long been characteristic of Japanese society.

In the middle of the seventh century, under the Taika Reform, the Yamato court used military forces, conscripted from the peasants and led by court-appointed aristocrats, to extend its realm and maintain order (see Early Developments, ch. 1). Military leaders initially were loyal to the emperors, but with the rise of the great private estates, or *shōen*, in the mid-eighth century, imperial control waned (see Nara and Heian Periods A.D. 710–1185, ch. 1). National conscription was abandoned in A.D. 792. Decreased imperial authority gave rise to chaotic conditions and lawlessness in the countryside. Provincial officials and *shōen* holders used local militias, civil officials under arms, and soldiers of the *shōen* holders to secure their land and compete for power.

By the mid-twelfth century, these local armed forces had developed into a distinct warrior class (*bushi,* or samurai), completely overshadowing the military strength of the imperial government. Empowered by a nationwide, feudal, military dictatorship, the chief national figure, the shogun, ruled in the name of a figurehead emperor. By the end of the sixteenth century, samurai dominated the social and political hierarchy that existed under the shogun and developed into a hereditary elite. After 1603 they alone were granted the right to bear the sword, which subsequently became the symbol of their superior status. During the sixteenth century, a wide variety of firearms also was introduced from Europe, and used quite effectively, particularly against some of the outer *daimyō,* or feudal lords.

In time, a customary ethical code, *bushidō* (see Glossary), was developed. According to this doctrine, the samurai was bound to accept death in battle rather than flight or surrender and, seeing corruption or disloyalty in another, was expected to slay the guilty party and then commit *seppuku* (see Glossary) lest his honorable intentions be questioned. As an ideal of conduct, the code emphasized personal honesty, reverence and respect for parents, willingness to sacrifice oneself for family honor, consideration for the feelings of others, indifference to pain, loyalty to one's superiors, and unquestioning obedience to duty in the face of any hardship or danger. Although a reality that often fell short of the ideal, *bushidō* had a profound and lasting impact on the nation. Its effects were still seen in the conduct of battle in World War II. *Banzai* (a rallying cry meaning 10,000 years) charges against stronger enemy forces and the tenacity of resistance under severe duress testified to the strength and persistence of the samurai tradition.

The Modernization of the Military, 1868–1931

When Western powers began to use their superior military strength to press Japan for trade relations in the 1850s, the country's decentralized and, by Western standards, antiquated military forces were unable to provide an effective defense against their advances. After the fall of the Tokugawa government in 1867 and the restoration of the Meiji emperor, de facto political and administrative power shifted to a group of younger samurai who had been instrumental in forming the new system and were committed to modernizing the military. They introduced drastic changes, which cleared the way for the development of modern, European-style armed forces.

Conscription became universal and obligatory in 1872 and, although samurai wedded to the traditional prerogatives of their class resisted, by 1880 a conscript army was firmly established. The Imperial Army General Staff Office was established directly under the emperor in 1878 and given broad powers for military planning and strategy. The new force eventually made the samurai spirit its own. Loyalties formerly accorded to feudal lords were transferred to the state and to the emperor. Upon release from service, soldiers carried these ideals back to their home communities, extending military-derived standards to all classes.

An imperial rescript of 1882 called for unquestioning loyalty to the emperor by the new armed forces and asserted that commands from superior officers were equivalent to commands from the emperor himself. Thenceforth, the military existed in an intimate and privileged relationship with the imperial institution. Top-ranking military leaders were given direct access to the emperor and the authority to transmit his pronouncements directly to the troops. The sympathetic relationship between conscripts and officers, particularly junior officers, who were drawn mostly from the peasantry, tended to draw the military closer to the people (see The Meiji Restoration, ch. 1). In time, most people came to look more for guidance in national matters to military commanders than to political leaders.

The first test of the nation's new military capabilities, a successful punitive expedition to Taiwan in 1874, was followed by a series of military ventures unmarred by defeat until World War II. Japan moved against Korea, China, and Russia, to secure by military means the raw materials and strategic territories it believed necessary for the development and protection of the homeland. Territorial gains were achieved in Korea, the southern half of Sakhalin (renamed Karafuto), and Manchuria. As an ally of Britain in World War I, Japan assumed control over Germany's possessions in Asia, notably in China's Shandong Province, and the Mariana, Caroline, and Marshall islands in the Pacific Ocean (see World War I, ch. 1).

The Naval General Staff, independent from the supreme command from 1893, became even more powerful after World War I. At the 1921–22 Washington Conference, the major powers signed the Five Power Naval Disarmament Treaty, which set the international capital ship ratio for the United States, Britain, Japan, France, and Italy at 5, 5, 3, 1.75, and 1.75 respectively. The Imperial Navy insisted that it required a ratio of seven ships for every eight United States naval ships, but settled for three to five, a ratio acceptable to the Japanese public (see Diplomacy, ch. 1). The London Naval Treaty of 1930 brought about further reduction but, by the end of 1935, Japan had entered a period of unlimited military expansion and ignored its previous commitments. By the late 1930s, the proportion of Japanese to United States naval forces was 70.6 percent in total tonnage and 94 percent in aircraft carriers, and Japanese ships slightly outnumbered those of the United States.

World War II

Establishment of Manchukuo

The power of the military grew when, in September 1931, without the knowledge or approval of the civil government, members of the

Imperial Army unit stationed in Manchuria—the Guandong, or Kwantung, Army—dynamited a short section of the South Manchurian Railway near Shenyang (called Mukden by the Japanese). Blaming the incident on Chinese saboteurs, the Guandong Army declared a state of emergency and quickly occupied all the principal cities in the region. In March 1932 this army formed the puppet state of Manchukuo (see Rise of the Militarists, ch. 1). At home, this quick and inexpensive victory greatly increased the confidence of the young nationalist officers, who could rightly claim credit for it, but other officers were sobered by the precedent for insubordination. Their apprehension was well founded: in the early 1930s a series of assassinations and conspiracies occurred within the nation and armed forces. In 1936 a force from the Tokyo garrison rose in open revolt. Although the rebels were suppressed on orders of the emperor, the stage was set for more radical military leaders to assume gradual control of the government, a process that was completed by 1940 and lasted until a few weeks before Japan's 1945 surrender in World War II.

Sino-Japanese War

On July 17, 1937, a new wave of expansion on the Asian mainland began with a skirmish between Chinese and Japanese troops at Marco Polo Bridge outside of Beiping (now Beijing). Although the Japanese commander had committed his troops without prior knowledge or consent of the government in Tokyo, he was promptly provided with reinforcements by the general staff, which by this time was strongly influenced by the younger officers. The fighting quickly spread, and the Second Sino-Japanese War (1937–45) had begun. On July 28 Chinese forces evacuated Beiping. Two days later the Japanese army occupied Tianjin, and on August 13 Japanese forces attacked China's financial center, Shanghai. Chinese forces resisted for three months, but finally succumbed to the better-armed and better-trained Japanese forces. The fall of Shanghai left China's capital, Nanjing, unprotected, and the Chinese government moved its capital to the southwestern mountain city of Chongqing. Japanese forces quickly occupied Nanjing, indiscriminately massacring about 100,000 civilians in the infamous "Rape of Nanjing." In mid-1938 the Japanese set their sights on the central Chinese industrial city of Wuhan. Wuhan held out for four and one-half months, but finally surrendered on December 25, 1938. The fall of Wuhan, coupled with the earlier fall of Guangzhou on October 21, left most urban areas in central and eastern China in the hands of the Japanese. To the north, however,

Japanese forces were defeated after a protracted battle with a joint Soviet-Mongolian force in 1939.

At home, the Japanese armed forces were portrayed as benevolent crusaders striving to free Asia from European colonial domination. The military's control over almost every phase of Japanese life was by now complete, and opposition to its policies was tantamount to treason. The top military commanders enjoyed direct access to the emperor, bypassing civilian authority completely.

War in the Pacific

In September 1940, with the permission of the pro-Nazi Vichy government of France, Japan moved into northern Indochina, establishing a foothold in strategically important Southeast Asia. A few days later, Japan signed a mutual defense agreement, the Tripartite Pact, with Germany and Italy, putting it on a collision course with the United States. The German invasion of the Soviet Union in June 1941 relieved the Japanese of the Soviet threat in East Asia. As a result, in July 1941 Japan decided to move its troops into southern Indochina for possible operations against the oil-rich Dutch East Indies. The United States responded by freezing Japanese assets in the United States and imposing an oil embargo on Japan. Britain, the British Commonwealth of Nations countries, and the government of the Dutch East Indies quickly followed suit, cutting 90 percent of Japan's oil imports. Faced with a choice of submitting to United States demands for a return to the pre-1931 status quo or confronting the United States, Japan determined to strike out boldly. Beginning with a devastating attack against the United States fleet at Pearl Harbor, Hawaii, on December 7, 1941, it quickly took advantage of superior air and naval power to occupy the Philippines, the Dutch East Indies, Malaya, and Singapore. An overland offensive brought Burma and Thailand under Japanese control, and a string of amphibious operations established Japan's control of the South Pacific. By mid-1942 Japanese forces appeared to be in control of most of their objectives (see fig. 2).

It was at this point that the superior economic and industrial power of the United States began to turn the tide. In June 1942 the Japanese directed the bulk of their navy to Midway, a tiny atoll at the northern tip of the Hawaiian chain, expecting to destroy the rest of the United States Pacific fleet. Instead, the Americans, forewarned of the attack, used carrier-based aircraft to devastate the Japanese fleet. The United States counteroffensive had begun. In the South Pacific, after six months of heavy fighting, Japanese forces evacuated Guadalcanal in February 1943. From there, revitalized United States and Allied forces retook most of the South Pacific

Japanese marines and armored cars, Shanghai, 1937
Courtesy Prints and Photographs Division, Library of Congress

islands occupied by the overextended Japanese forces. By June 1944, United States and Allied forces had reached Saipan, in the Mariana Islands, putting their bombers within range of the Japanese homeland.

When United States air, ground, and sea power began to reverse the tide of Japanese victories, the authority of the Japanese forces began to wane in the captured territories. At home in Japan, however, respect remained high until intensive United States aerial bombardment there raised popular doubt about the military's ability to win the war. It was not until the last days of the war, after the United States had dropped atomic bombs on Hiroshima and Nagasaki, that the emperor, in an unprecedented political act, compelled the general staff to accept the terms for surrender.

The Self-Defense Forces

Japan's defeat in World War II, the only major military defeat in the country's history, had a profound and lasting effect on national attitudes toward war, the armed forces, and military involvement in politics. These attitudes were immediately apparent in the public's willing acceptance of total disarmament and demobilization after the war and in the alacrity with which all military leaders were removed from positions of influence in the state. Under

General Douglas MacArthur of the United States Army, serving as the Supreme Commander of the Allied Powers, and in concert with the wishes of most Japanese, occupation authorities were committed to the demilitarization and democratization of the nation. All clubs, schools, and societies associated with the military and martial skills were eliminated. The general staff was abolished, along with army and navy ministries and the Imperial Army and Imperial Navy. Industry serving the military also was dismantled.

The trauma of defeat produced strong pacifist sentiments that found expression in the United States-fostered 1947 Constitution, which forever renounces war as an instrument for settling international disputes and declares that Japan will never again maintain "land, sea, or air forces or other war potential" (see The Postwar Constitution, ch. 6). Later cabinets interpreted these provisions as not denying the nation the right to self-defense and, with the encouragement of the United States, developed the SDF. Antimilitarist public opinion, however, remained a force to be reckoned with on any defense-related issue. The constitutional legitimacy of the SDF was challenged well into the 1970s, and even in the 1980s government acted warily on defense matters lest residual antimilitarism be aggravated and a backlash result.

Early Development

Deprived of any military capability after 1945, the nation had only occupation forces and a few domestic police on which to rely for security. Rising Cold War tensions in Europe and Asia, coupled with leftist-inspired strikes and demonstrations in Japan, prompted some conservative leaders to question the unilateral renunciation of all military capability. These sentiments were intensified in 1950 when most occupation troops were transferred to the Korean War (1950–53) theater, leaving Japan virtually helpless to counter internal disruption and subversion, and very much aware of the need to enter into a mutual defense relationship with the United States to guarantee the nation's external security. Encouraged by the occupation authorities, the Japanese government in July 1950 authorized the establishment of the National Police Reserve, consisting of 75,000 men equipped with light infantry weapons.

Under the terms of the Mutual Security Assistance Pact, ratified in 1952 along with the peace treaty Japan had signed with the United States and other countries, United States forces stationed in Japan were to deal with external aggression against Japan while Japanese forces, both ground and maritime, would deal with internal threats and natural disasters. Accordingly, in mid-1952 the

National Police Reserve was expanded to 110,000 men and named the National Safety Force. The Coastal Safety Force, which had been organized in 1950 as a waterborne counterpart to the National Police Reserve, was transferred with it to the National Safety Agency to constitute an embryonic navy (see Military Relations with the United States, this ch.).

As Japan perceived a growing external threat without adequate forces to counter it, the National Safety Force underwent further development that entailed difficult political problems. The war renunciation clause of the Constitution was the basis for strong political objections to any sort of force other than conventional police. In 1954, however, separate land, sea, and air forces for purely defensive purposes were created, subject to the Office of the Prime Minister (see The Cabinet and Ministries, ch. 6).

To avoid the appearance of a revival of militarism, Japan's leaders emphasized constitutional guarantees of civilian control of the government and armed forces and used nonmilitary terms for the organization and functions of the forces. The overall organization was called the Defense Agency rather than the Ministry of Defense. The armed forces were designated the Ground Self-Defense Force (GSDF), the Maritime Self-Defense Force (MSDF), and the Air Self-Defense Force (ASDF), instead of the army, navy, and air force.

Although possession of nuclear weapons is not forbidden in the Constitution, Japan, as the only nation to experience the devastation of atomic attack, early expressed its abhorrence of nuclear arms and determined never to acquire them. The Basic Atomic Energy Law of 1956 limits research, development, and utilization of nuclear power to peaceful uses, and from 1956 national policy has embodied "three non-nuclear principles"—forbidding the nation to possess or manufacture nuclear weapons or to allow them to be introduced into the nation. In 1976 Japan ratified the Treaty on the Non-Proliferation of Nuclear Weapons (adopted by the United Nations Security Council in 1968) and reiterated its intention never to develop, use, or allow the transportation of nuclear weapons through its territory.

Strategic Considerations

The expansion of military capabilities in the Soviet Far East beginning in 1970 was of grave concern to Japan, and Japanese authorities regularly monitored the activities of the Soviet Pacific fleet and Soviet aircraft in the waters and air space around Japan. Despite a general lessening of world tensions and Soviet overtures for improved bilateral relations, in 1990 the Soviet Union still maintained a variety of units, including a division headquarters, on the southernmost Kuril Islands claimed by Japan as its Northern Territories. The Soviet Union also operated about 100 major surface war ships and 140 submarines (about 75 nuclear powered) out of Vladivostok and other Pacific ports. Soviet naval combatants had passed through the Sōya, Tsugarū, and Korea straits and had sailed in the Sea of Japan and the Sea of Okhotsk and in Pacific Ocean areas adjacent to Japan (see fig. 1). Japan also was within range of Tu-22M Backfire bombers and sea- and air-launched cruise missiles and tactical nuclear weapons based in the Soviet Union.

Another area of strategic interest to the nation was the Korean Peninsula. The Democratic People's Republic of Korea (North Korea) and the Republic of Korea (South Korea) had remained implacable enemies since the Korean War, and in 1990 the border between them was one of the most heavily fortified in the world. Stable and peaceful relations between the two were considered vital to Japan's interest: an outbreak of hostilities would involve United States forces stationed in Japan, presenting political and possibly security problems for the nation, in addition to interrupting flourishing trade with South Korea. Although Japan maintained formal diplomatic relations only with South Korea, it had refused to contribute to that nation's defense, stating that any aid to a foreign military establishment would violate its own Constitution.

Events on the Asian mainland could also affect Japan. From the early 1970s, China possessed a nuclear force capable of striking Japan and a large standing army and substantial navy, even if the latter were geared primarily to coastal defense. China itself was unlikely to present a direct military threat to Japan, but Chinese internal unrest or China's conflicts with its neighbors could have an indirect impact on Japanese security and trade (see Trade and Investment Relations, ch. 5).

The nation was vitally dependent on maintaining access to regional and worldwide shipping lanes and fishing areas, but it was incapable of defending the sea routes on which it relied. Its energy supplies came primarily from Middle Eastern sources, and its tankers had to pass through the Indian Ocean, the Strait of Malacca, and the South China Sea, making them vulnerable to hostilities in Southeast Asia. Vulnerability to interception of oceangoing trade remained the country's greatest strategic weakness. Efforts to overcome this weakness, beginning with Prime Minister Suzuki Zenkō's statement in May 1981 that Japan would attempt to defend its sea lines of communication (SLOC) to a distance of 1,000 nautical miles, met with controversy. Within the Defense Agency itself, some viewed a role for the MSDF in defending the SLOC as "unrealistic, unauthorized, and impossible." Even the strongest supporters of this program allowed that constitutional and other legal restrictions would limit active participation of the MSDF to cases where Japan was under direct attack. Japan could, however, provide surveillance assistance, intelligence sharing, and search and rescue support to United States naval forces.

Japan's small size, its geographically concentrated industry, and the close proximity of potentially hostile powers all rendered the country vulnerable to a major nuclear strike. As for defense against conventional aggression, strategy was determined by the nation's elongated insular geography, its mountainous terrain, and the nearness of the Asian mainland. The terrain favors local defense against invasion by ground forces, but protection of the approximately 15,800 kilometer coastline of the four main islands would present unique problems in the event of a large-scale invasion. Potentially hostile aircraft and missile bases were so close that timely warning even by radar facilities might be difficult to obtain.

Maneuver space was limited to such an extent that ground defenses would have to be virtually in place at the onset of hostilities. No point of the country is more than 150 kilometers from the sea. Moreover, the straits separating Honshū from the other main islands restrict the rapid movement of troops from one island to another, even though all major islands are now connected by bridges and tunnels. Within each island, mountain barriers and narrow roads restrict troop and supply movements. The key strategic region was densely populated and highly industrialized central Honshū, particularly the area from Tokyo to Kōbe (see Physical Setting, ch. 2).

Place in National Life

The Defense Agency, aware that it could not accomplish its programs without popular support, paid close attention to public opinion. Although the people retained a lingering suspicion of the armed services, in the late 1980s antimilitarism had moderated, compared to its form in the early 1950s when the SDF was established. At that time, fresh from the terrible defeat of World War II, most people had ceased to believe that the military could maintain peace or serve the national interest. By the mid-1970s, memories of World War II had faded, and a growing number of people believed that Japan's military and diplomatic roles should reflect its rapidly growing economic strength. At the same time, United States-Soviet strategic contention in the area around Japan had increased. In 1976 Defense Agency Director General Sakata Michita called upon the cabinet to adopt the National Defense Program Outline to improve the quality of the armed forces and more clearly define their strictly defensive role. For this program to gain acceptance, Sakata had to agree to a ceiling on military expenditures of 1 percent of the gross national product (GNP—see Glossary) and a prohibition on exporting weapons and military technology. The outline was adopted by the cabinet and, according to public opinion polls, was approved by approximately 60 percent of the people. Throughout the remainder of the 1970s and into the 1980s, the quality of the SDF improved and public approval of the improved forces went up.

In November 1982, when the Defense Agency's former director general, Nakasone Yasuhiro, became prime minister, he was under strong pressure from the United States and other Western nations to move toward a more assertive defense policy in line with Japan's status as a major world economic and political power. Strong antimilitarist sentiment remained in Japanese public opinion, however, especially in the opposition parties. Nakasone chose a compromise solution, gradually building up the SDF and steadily increasing defense spending while guarding against being drawn beyond self-defense into collective security. In 1985 he developed the Mid-Term Defense Estimate (see Missions, this ch.). Although that program had general public backing, its goals could not be met while retaining the ceiling of 1 percent of GNP on military spending, which still had strong public support. At first the government tried to get around the problem by deferring payment, budgeting only the initial costs of major military hardware. But by late 1986, it had become obvious that the 1 percent ceiling had to be superseded. Thus, on January 24, 1987, in an extraordinary night meeting, the cabinet abandoned this ceiling. A March 1987 *Asahi Shimbun* poll indicated that this move was made in defiance of public opinion: only 15 percent approved the removal of the ceiling and 61 percent disapproved. But a January 1988 poll conducted by the Office of the Prime Minister reported that 58 percent approved the defense budget of 1.004 percent of GNP for Fiscal Year (FY— see Glossary) 1987.

During 1987 the Japanese government reviewed ways in which it could assist friendly forces in protecting shipping in the Persian Gulf. Several possibilities were seriously considered, including sending minesweepers to the gulf. But, in the end, the government determined that sending any military forces to the gulf would be unacceptable to the Japanese people. Instead the Japanese government agreed to fund the installation of radio navigation guides for gulf shipping.

Armored exercises in Shizuoka Prefecture
Courtesy Asahi Shimbun

Appreciation of the SDF continued to grow in the 1980s, with over half of the respondents in a 1988 survey voicing an interest in the SDF and over 76 percent indicating that they were favorably impressed. Although the majority (63.5 percent) of respondents were aware that the primary purpose of the SDF was maintenance of national security, an even greater number (77 percent) saw disaster relief as the most useful SDF function. The SDF therefore continued to devote much of its time and resources to disaster relief and other civic action. Between 1984 and 1988, at the request of prefectural governors, the SDF assisted in approximately 3,100 disaster relief operations, involving about 138,000 personnel, 16,000 vehicles, 5,300 aircraft, and 120 ships and small craft. In addition, the SDF participated in earthquake disaster prevention operations and disposed of a large quantity of World War II explosive ordnance, especially in Okinawa. The forces also participated in public works projects, cooperated in managing athletic events, took part in annual Antarctic expeditions, and conducted aerial surveys to report on ice conditions for fishermen and on geographic formations for construction projects. Especially sensitive to maintaining harmonious relations with communities close to defense bases, the SDF built new roads, irrigation networks, and schools in those areas. Soundproofing was installed in homes and public buildings near airfields. Despite these measures, in some areas local resistance to military installations remained strong.

Missions

Despite the nation's status as a major world power, Japan eschewed responsibility for regional defense. Having renounced war, the possession of war potential, the right of belligerency, and the possession of nuclear weaponry, it held the view that it should possess only the minimum defense necessary to face external threats. Within those limits, the Self-Defense Forces Law of 1954 provides the basis from which various formulations of SDF missions have been derived. The law states that ground, maritime, and air forces are to preserve the peace and independence of the nation and to maintain national security by conducting operations on land, at sea, and in the air to defend the nation against direct and indirect aggression.

The general framework through which these missions are to be accomplished was set forth in the Basic Policy for National Defense adopted by the cabinet in 1957; it remained in force in 1990. According to this document, the nation's security would be achieved by supporting the United Nations (UN) and promoting international cooperation, by stabilizing domestic affairs and enhancing public welfare, by gradually developing an effective self-defense capability, and by dealing with external aggression on the basis of Japan-United States security arrangements, pending the effective functioning of the UN.

The very general terms in which military missions were couched left specifics open to wide interpretation and prompted the criticism that the nation did not possess a military strategy. In the 1976 National Defense Program Outline, the cabinet sought to define missions more specifically by setting guidelines for the nation's readiness, including specific criteria for the maintenance and operation of the SDF. Under these guidelines, in cases of limited and small-scale attack, Japanese forces would respond promptly to control the situation. If enemy forces attacked in greater strength than Japan could counter alone, the SDF would engage the attacker until the United States could come to its aid. Against nuclear threat, Japan would rely on the nuclear deterrence of the United States. To accomplish its missions, the SDF would maintain surveillance, be prepared to respond to direct and indirect attacks, be capable of providing command, communication, logistics, and training support, and be available to aid in disaster relief.

The outline specified quotas of personnel and equipment that were deemed necessary for each force to meet its tasks. Particular elements of each force's mission were also identified. The GSDF was to defend against ground invasion and threats to internal security, be able to deploy to any part of the nation, and protect the bases of all three services of the Self-Defense Forces. The MSDF was to meet invasion by sea, guard and defend coastal waters, ports, bays, and major straits, sweep mines, and patrol and survey the surrounding waters. The ASDF was to render aircraft and missile interceptor capability, provide support fighter units for maritime and ground operations, supply air reconnaissance and air transport for all forces, and maintain airborne and stationary early warning units.

The Mid-Term Defense Estimate for FY 1986 through FY 1990 envisioned a modernized SDF with an expanded role. While maintaining Japan-United States security arrangements and the exclusively defensive policy mandated by the Constitution, this program undertook moderate improvements in Japanese defense capabilities. Among its specific objectives were bettering air defense by improving and modernizing interceptor-fighter aircraft and surface-to-air missiles, improving antisubmarine warfare capability with additional destroyers and fixed-wing antisubmarine patrol aircraft, and upgrading intelligence, reconnaissance, and command, control, and communications.

The SDF disaster relief role is defined in Article 83 of the Self-Defense Forces Law of 1954, requiring units to respond to calls for assistance from prefectural governors to aid in fire fighting, earthquake disasters, searches for missing persons, rescues, and reinforcement of embankments and levees in the event of flooding. As of 1990, the SDF had not been used in police actions nor was it likely to be assigned any internal security tasks in the future.

Organization, Training, and Equipment

Based on the Self-Defense Forces Law of 1954, the nation's defense establishment was organized to ensure civilian control of the armed forces. The result has been a unique military system. All SDF personnel were technically civilians: those in uniform were classified as special civil servants and were subordinate to the ordinary civil servants who ran the Defense Agency. There was no military secrets law, and offenses committed by military personnel—whether on base or off base, on duty or off duty, of military or nonmilitary nature—were all adjudicated under normal procedures by civil courts in appropriate jurisdictions (see The Criminal Justice System, this ch.).

The Defense Agency

In 1990 the Defense Agency, as part of the Office of the Prime Minister, was required by Article 66 of the Constitution to be completely subordinate to civilian authority. Its head, the director general, had the rank of minister of state. He was assisted by two vice directors general (vice ministers), one parliamentary and one administrative; the Defense Facilities Office; and the Internal Bureaus (see fig. 12). The highest figure in the command structure was the prime minister, who was responsible directly to the Diet (see Glossary; The Legislature, ch. 6). In a national emergency, the prime minister was authorized to order the various components of the Self-Defense Forces into action, subject to the consent of the Diet. In times of extreme emergency, that approval might be obtained after the fact.

In July 1986, the Security Council was established. The council was presided over by the prime minister and included the ministers of state specified in advance in Article 9 of the Cabinet Law, the foreign minister, the finance minister, the chief cabinet secretary, the chairman of the National Public Safety Commission, the director general of the Defense Agency, and the director general of the Economic Planning Agency. The chairman of the Security Council also could invite the chairman of the Joint Staff Council and any other relevant state minister or official to attend. Replacing the National Defense Council, which had acted as an advisory group on defense-related matters since 1956, the Security Council addressed a wider range of military and nonmilitary security issues, including basic national defense policy, the National Defense Program Outline, the outline on coordinating industrial production and other matters related to the National Defense Program Outline, and decisions on diplomatic initiatives and defense operations.

The internal bureaus, especially the Bureau of Defense Policy, Bureau of the Finance, and the Bureau of Equipment, were often headed by officials from other ministries and were the main centers of power and instruments of civilian control in the Defense Agency. The Bureau of Defense Policy was responsible for drafting defense policy and programs, for determining day-to-day operational activities, and for information gathering and analysis in the SDF. The Bureau of Finance was instrumental in developing the Defense Agency budget and in establishing spending priorities for the Defense Agency and the SDF. The Bureau of Equipment, organized into subunits for each of the military services, focused on equipment procurement. Before any major purchase was recommended to the Diet by the Defense Agency, it had to be reviewed by each of these important bureaus.

Below these civilian groups was the uniformed SDF. In 1990 its senior officer was the chairman of the Joint Staff Council, a body that included the chiefs of staff of the ground, maritime, and air arms of the Self-Defense Forces. Its principal functions were to advise the director general and to plan and execute joint exercises. The three branches maintained staff offices to manage operations in their branches. Although rank established echelons of command within the SDF, all three branches were immediately responsible to the director general and were coequal bodies with the Joint Staff Council and the three staff offices.

This structure precluded the concentration of power of the pre-1945 general staffs, but it impeded interservice coordination, and there were few formal exchanges among commanders from various branches. Moreover, some dissatisfaction was reported by high-ranking officers who felt they had little power compared with younger civilian officials in the bureaus, who most often had no military experience. To rectify this situation and to increase input by the SDF in policy matters, in the early 1980s the Joint Staff Council was enlarged to establish better lines of communication between the internal bureaus and the three staff offices. A computerized central command and communications system and various tactical command and communications systems were established, linking service and field headquarters with general headquarters at the Defense Agency and with one another.

In the 1980s, efforts were also under way to facilitate a clear and efficient command policy in the event of a crisis. The government stood by the principle that military action was permitted only under civilian control, but in recognition that delay for consultation might prove dangerous, ships of the MSDF began to be armed with live torpedoes, and fighter-interceptors were allowed to carry missiles at all times. Although aircraft had long been allowed to force down intruders without waiting for permission from the prime minister, ships were still required to receive specific orders before interdicting invading vessels. The Defense Agency had recommended drawing up more complete guidelines to clarify what action SDF combat units could take in emergencies.

Cooperation between the SDF and other civilian agencies in contingency planning was limited. No plans existed to ensure the support of civilian aircraft and merchant fleets in times of crisis, even though the SDF transportation capabilities were generally judged inadequate. In 1990 legislation was being studied to provide the SDF with the ability to respond in emergency situations not specifically covered by Article 76 of the Self-Defense Forces Law.

SDF training included instilling a sense of mission. Personnel were provided with the scientific and technical education to operate and maintain modern equipment and with the physical training necessary to accomplish their missions.

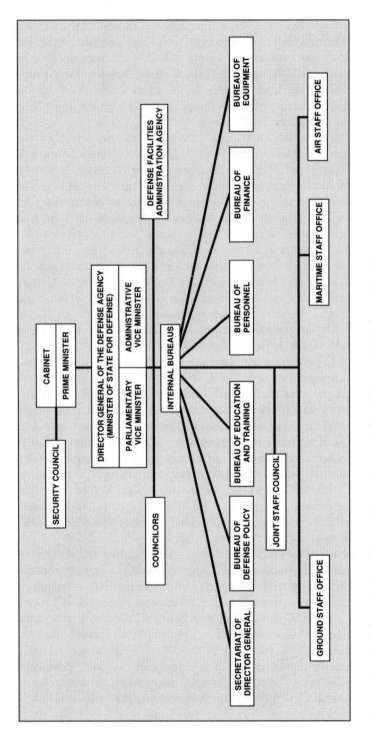

Source: Based on information from Japan, Defense Agency, *Defense of Japan, 1990*, Tokyo, 1990, 309.

Figure 12. Organization of the Defense Establishment, 1990

Modern equipment was gradually replacing obsolescent matériel in the SDF. In 1987 the Defense Agency replaced its communications system (which formerly had relied on telephone lines of the Nippon Telegraph and Telephone Corporation) with a microwave network incorporating a three-dimensional transmission system using a communications satellite. Despite efforts to increase stocks, however, supplies of ammunition and maintenance and repair parts in 1990 remained at less than satisfactory levels.

The Ground Self-Defense Force

The largest of the three services, the GSDF, operated under the command of the chief of the ground staff, based in the city of Ichikawa, east of Tokyo. Although allotted 180,000 slots for uniformed personnel, in 1989 the force was maintained at about 86 percent of that level (with approximately 156,200 personnel), because of funding constraints. The GSDF consisted of one armored division, twelve infantry divisions, one airborne brigade, two combined brigades, one training brigade, one artillery brigade with four groups, eight antiaircraft artillery groups, one helicopter brigade with twenty-four squadrons, and two antitank helicopter squadrons, with a third being formed, and five engineer brigades (see table 38, Appendix).

In 1989 the GSDF was divided into five regional armies, each containing two to four divisions, antiaircraft artillery units, and support units (see fig. 13). The largest, the Northern Army, was headquartered on Hokkaidō, where population and geographic constraints were less limiting than elsewhere. It had four divisions and artillery, antiaircraft artillery, and engineering brigades. The Northeastern and Eastern armies, headquartered in Sendai and Ichikawa, respectively, each had two divisions, and the Central Army, headquartered in Itami, had three divisions in addition to a combined brigade located on Shikoku. The Western Army, with two divisions, was headquartered at Kengun and maintained a combined brigade on Okinawa.

Intended to deter attack, repulse a small invasion, or provide a holding action until reinforced by United States armed forces, the ground element in 1990 was neither equipped nor staffed to offer more than a show of conventional defense by itself. Antitank artillery, ground-to-sea firepower, and mobility were being improved and surface-to-ship missiles were being acquired in the Mid-Term Defense Program scheduled for completion in FY 1990 (see table 39, Appendix). The number of uniformed personnel was insufficient to enable an immediate shift onto emergency footing. Instead, the ratio of officers to enlisted personnel was high, requiring

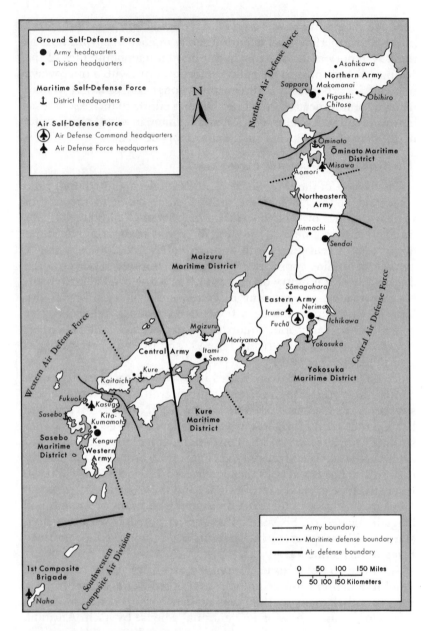

Source: Based on information from Japan, Defense Agency, *Defense of Japan, 1990,* Tokyo,
1990, 309.

Figure 13. Deployment of the Ground, Maritime, and Air Self-Defense Forces,
1990

augmentation by reserves or volunteers in times of crisis. In late 1989, however, GSDF reserve personnel, numbering 48,000, had received little professional training.

In 1989 basic training for lower-secondary and upper-secondary school graduates began in the training brigade and lasted approximately three months. Specialized enlisted and noncommissioned officer (NCO) candidate courses were available in branch schools, and qualified NCOs could enter an eight-to-twelve-week second lieutenant candidate program. Senior NCOs and graduates of an eighty-week NCO pilot course were eligible to enter officer candidate schools, as were graduates of the National Defense Academy at Yokosuka and of four-year universities. Advanced technical, flight, medical, and command staff officer courses were also run by the GSDF. Like the maritime and air forces, the GSDF ran a youth cadet program offering technical training to lower-secondary school graduates below military age in return for a promise of enlistment.

Because of population density on the Japanese islands, only limited areas were available for large-scale training and, even in these areas, noise restrictions were a problem (see Population, ch. 2). The GSDF tried to adapt to these conditions by conducting command post exercises and map maneuvers and by using simulators and other training devices. In live firing during training, propellants were reduced to shorten shell ranges. Such restriction diminished the value of combat training and troop morale.

The Maritime Self-Defense Force

The MSDF had an authorized strength in 1989 of 46,000 and maintained some 44,400 personnel and operated 149 major combatants, including 14 submarines, 56 destroyers and frigates, 47 mine warfare vessels, 14 patrol craft, and 6 amphibious ships. It also flew some 181 fixed-wing aircraft and 102 helicopters. Most of these aircraft were used in antisubmarine and mine warfare operations.

The MSDF was commanded by the chief of the maritime staff and included the maritime staff office, the self-defense fleet, five regional district commands, the air-training squadron, and various support units, such as hospitals and schools. The maritime staff office, located in Tokyo, served the chief of staff in command and supervision of the force. The self-defense fleet, headquartered at Yokosuka, was charged with defense of all waters around the Japanese Archipelago. It commanded four escort flotillas (two based in Yokosuka and one each in Sasebo and Maizuru), the fleet air force headquartered at Atsugi, two submarine flotillas based at Kure and Yokosuka, two mine-sweeping flotillas based at Kure and Yokosuka, and the fleet training command at Yokosuka.

Five district units acted in concert with the fleet to guard the waters of their jurisdictions and provide shore-based support. District headquarters were located in Ōminato, Maizuru, Yokosuka, Kure, and Sasebo.

MSDF recruits received three months of basic training followed by courses in patrol, gunnery, mine sweeping, convoy operations, and maritime transportation. Flight students, all upper-secondary school graduates, entered a two-year course. Officer candidate schools offered six-month courses to qualified enlisted personnel and those who had completed flight school. Graduates of four-year universities, the four-year National Defense Academy, and particularly outstanding enlisted personnel underwent a one-year officer course at the Officer Candidate School at Eta Jima (site of the former Imperial Naval Academy). Special advanced courses for officers were also available in such fields as submarine duty and flight training. The MSDF operated its own staff college in Tokyo for senior officers.

The large volume of coastal commercial fishing and maritime traffic limited in-service sea training, especially in the relatively shallow waters required for mine laying, mine sweeping, and submarine rescue practice. Training days were scheduled around slack fishing seasons in winter and summer—providing about ten days during the year. The MSDF maintained two oceangoing training ships and conducted annual long-distance on-the-job training for graduates of the one-year officer candidate school.

The naval force's capacity to perform its defense missions varied according to the task. MSDF training emphasized antisubmarine and antiaircraft warfare. Defense planners believed the most effective approach to combating submarines entailed mobilizing all available weapons, including surface combatants, submarines, aircraft, and helicopters, and the numbers and armament of these weapons were being increased in the Mid-Term Defense Program. A critical weakness remained, however, in the ability to defend such weapons against air attack. Because most of the MSDF's air arm was detailed to antisubmarine warfare, the ASDF had to be relied on to provide air cover, an objective that competed unsuccessfully with the ASDF's primary mission of air defense of the home islands. Extended patrols over sea lanes were also beyond the ASDF's capabilities. The fleet's capacity to provide ship-based anti-air-attack protection was limited by the absence of aircraft carriers and the inadequate number of shipborne long-range surface-to-air missiles and close-range weapons. The fleet was also short

Maritime
Self-Defence Force ships on
patrol in Tokyo Bay
Courtesy Asahi Shimbun

of underway replenishment ships and seriously deficient in all areas of logistic support (see table 40, Appendix). These weaknesses seriously compromised the ability of the MSDF to fulfill its mission and to operate independently of the United States Air Force and the United States Seventh Fleet.

The Air Self-Defense Force

The ASDF was the major aviation arm of the SDF. It had an authorized strength of 47,000 and maintained some 46,400 personnel and approximately 390 combat aircraft in 1989. Front-line formations included three ground-attack squadrons, nine fighter squadrons, one reconnaissance squadron, and five transport squadrons.

Major units of the ASDF were the Air Defense Command, the Flight Support Command, Flying Training Command, Air Developing and Proving Command, and Air Matériel Command. The Air Support Command was responsible for direct support of operational forces in rescue, transportation, control, weather monitoring, and inspection. The Flying Training Command was responsible for basic flying and technical training. The Air Developing and Proving Command, in addition to overseeing equipment research and development, was also responsible for research and development in such areas as flight medicine. The Air Defense Command had Northern, Central, and Western regional commands located at Misawa,

Iruma, and Kasuga, and a Southwestern Composite Air Division based at Naha on Okinawa. All four regional headquarters controlled surface-to-air missile units of both the ASDF and the GSDF located in their respective areas.

For its air defense of the nation, the ASDF in 1989 maintained an integrated network of twenty-eight radar installations and air defense direction centers known as the Basic Air Defense Ground Environment. In the late 1980s, the system was modernized and augmented with E–2C airborne early-warning aircraft.

The nation relied on fighter-interceptor aircraft and surface-to-air missiles to intercept hostile aircraft. In 1989 both of these systems were undergoing improvement. Outmoded aircraft were being replaced with more sophisticated models, and Nike-J missiles were being replaced with new Patriot systems (see table 41, Appendix). Essentially, however, the nation relied on United States forces to provide interceptor capability.

The ASDF also provided air support for ground and sea operations of the GSDF and the MSDF and air defense for bases of all the forces. Although support fighter squadrons were being modernized in 1989, they lacked precision-guided weapons for support of ground operations and attacks on hostile ships, and ASDF pilots received little flight training over oceans to prepare for maritime operations. The ASDF had a poor base defense capability, consisting mainly of outmoded antiaircraft guns and portable shelters to house aircraft. Base defenses were being upgraded in the late 1980s with new surface-to-air missiles, modern antiaircraft artillery, and new fixed and mobile aircraft shelters.

After passing an entrance examination, recruits could enter several training programs. Lower-secondary school graduates were eligible to enter the ASDF's four-year youth cadet program to earn upper-secondary school equivalency and NCO status, or they could undergo twelve-week recruit training courses followed by technical training lasting from five to fifty weeks. Upper-secondary school graduates could also enter either two-year NCO or four-year flight courses. Specialized training was available for all NCOs, as were opportunities to enroll in officer and flight officer candidate courses. Graduates of the four-year National Defense Academy or four-year universities received thirty to forty weeks of instruction in officer candidate schools. Advanced technical, flight, and command staff officer programs were available for officers.

Recruitment and Conditions of Service

The total authorized strength in the three branches of the SDF was approximately 274,000 in 1989. In addition, the SDF maintained a total of about 48,000 reservists attached to the three services. Even when Japan's active and reserve components were combined, however, the country maintained a lower ratio of military personnel to its population than did any member nation of the North Atlantic Treaty Organization (NATO) or the Warsaw Treaty Organization (Warsaw Pact). Of the major Asian nations, only India and Indonesia kept a lower ratio of personnel in arms.

The SDF was an all-volunteer force. Conscription per se was not forbidden by law, but many citizens considered Article 18 of the Constitution, which proscribes involuntary servitude except as punishment for a crime, as a legal prohibition of any form of conscription. Even in the absence of so strict an interpretation, however, a military draft appeared politically impossible.

SDF uniformed personnel were recruited as private, E-1, seaman recruit, and airman basic for a fixed term. Ground forces recruits normally enlisted for two years; those seeking training in technical specialties enlisted for three. Naval and air recruits normally enlisted for three years. Officer candidates, students in the National Defense Academy and National Defense Medical College, and candidate enlisted students in technical schools were enrolled for an indefinite period. The National Defense Academy and enlisted technical schools usually required an enrollment of four years and the National Defense Medical College six years.

When the SDF was originally formed, women were recruited exclusively for the nursing services. Opportunities were expanded somewhat when women were permitted to join the GSDF communication service in 1967 and the MSDF and ASDF communication services in 1974. In 1989 about 77 percent of service areas were open to women, and there were 4,924 women in the SDF: 1,046 nurses, 35 physicians, and 3,843 general service personnel.

In the face of some continued post-World War II public apathy or antipathy toward the armed services, the SDF in 1990 had difficulties in recruiting personnel. The forces had to compete for qualified personnel with well-paying industries and most enlistees were "persuaded" volunteers who signed up after solicitation from recruiters. Predominantly rural prefectures supplied military enlistees far beyond the proportions of their populations. In areas such as southern Kyūshū and Hokkaidō, where employment opportunities were limited, recruiters were welcomed and supported by the citizens. In contrast, little success or cooperation was encountered in urban centers such as Tokyo and Ōsaka.

Because the forces were all volunteer and legally civilian, members could resign at any time, and retention was a problem. Many enlistees were lured away by the prospects of highly paying civilian jobs, and Defense Agency officials complained of private industries looting their personnel. The agency attempted to stop these practices by threats of sanctions for offending firms that held defense contracts and by private agreements with major industrial firms. Given the nation's labor shortage, however, the problem promised to continue.

Some older officers considered the members of the modern forces unequal to personnel of the former Imperial Army and Imperial Navy, but the SDF were generally regarded as professional and able. Compared with their counterparts in other nations, members of the SDF were remarkably well educated and in good physical condition. Literacy was universal, and school training extensive. Personnel were trained in the martial arts, judo and *kendō*, and physical standards were strict. The SDF probably did not attract the same high level of personnel as other institutions in Japan. Graduates of the top universities rarely entered the armed forces, and applicants to the National Defense Academy were generally considered to be on the level of those who applied to second-rank local universities.

In 1990 general conditions of military life were not such that a career in the SDF seemed an attractive alternative to one in private industry or the bureaucracy. The conditions of service provided less dignity, prestige, and comfort than they had before World War II, and for most members of the defense establishment, military life offered less status than did a civilian occupation. Those people who entered the SDF were often unfairly perceived by the citizenry as unable to find a better job.

As special civil servants, SDF personnel were paid according to civilian pay scales that did not always distinguish rank. At times SDF salaries were greater for subordinates than for commanding officers; senior NCOs with long service could earn more than newly promoted colonels. Pay raises were not included in Defense Agency budgets and could not be established by military planners. Retirement ages for officers below flag rank ranged from fifty-three to fifty-five years, and from fifty to fifty-three for enlisted personnel. Limits were sometimes extended because of personnel shortages. In the late 1980s, the Defense Agency, concerned about the difficulty of finding appropriate postretirement employment for these early retirees, provided vocational training for enlisted personnel about to retire and transferred them to units close to the place where they intended to retire. Beginning in October 1987, the Self-Defense Forces Job Placement Association provided free job placement and reemployment support for retired SDF personnel. Retirees also received pensions immediately upon retirement, some ten years earlier than most civil service personnel. Financing the retirement system promised to be a problem of increasing scope in the 1990s, with the aging of the population.

SDF personnel benefits were not comparable to such benefits for active-duty military personnel in other major industrialized nations. Health care was provided at the SDF Central Hospital, 14 regional hospitals, and 165 clinics in military facilities and on board ship, but only covered physical examinations and the treatment of illness and injury suffered in the course of duty. There were no commissary or exchange privileges. Housing was often substandard, and military appropriations for facilities maintenance often focused on appeasing civilian communities near bases rather than on improving on-base facilities.

Uniforms, Ranks, and Insignia

In 1990 uniforms in all three SDF branches were similar in style to those worn by United States forces. GSDF uniforms were gray-blue; MSDF personnel wore traditional blue dress, white service, and khaki work uniforms; and ASDF personnel wore the lighter shade of blue worn by the United States Air Force. The arm of service to which members of the ground force were attached was indicated by piping of distinctive colors: for infantry, red; artillery, yellow; armor, orange; engineers, violet; ordnance, light green; medical, green; army aviation, light blue; signals, blue; quarter-master, brown; transportation, dark violet; airborne, white; and others, dark blue. The cap badge insignia for all displayed a dove of peace.

There were nine officer ranks in the active SDF, along with a warrant officer rank; five NCO ranks; and three enlisted ranks (see fig. 14). The highest NCO rank, first sergeant (senior chief petty officer in the MSDF and senior master sergeant in the ASDF), was established in 1980 to provide more promotion opportunities and shorter terms of service as sergeant first class, chief petty officer, or master sergeant. Under the earlier system, the average NCO was promoted only twice in approximately thirty years of service and remained at the top rank for almost ten years.

Defense Spending

According to Japanese security policy, maintaining a military establishment was only one method—and by no means the best—to achieve national security. Diplomacy, economic aid and development, and a close relationship with the United States under the terms of the 1960 security treaty were all considered more important. Even in the 1980s, defense spending was accorded a relatively

WARRANT OFFICERS AND ENLISTED PERSONNEL

GROUND SELF-DEFENSE FORCE	SANTŌ RIKUSHI	NITŌ RIKUSHI	ITTŌ RIKUSHI	RIKUSHICHŌ	SANTŌ RIKUSŌ	NITŌ RIKUSŌ	ITTŌ RIKUSŌ	RIKUSŌCHŌ	JUN RIKUI
UNITED STATES RANK TITLE	PRIVATE, E-1	PRIVATE, E-2	PRIVATE FIRST CLASS	CORPORAL	SERGEANT	STAFF SERGEANT	SERGEANT FIRST CLASS	FIRST SERGEANT	WARRANT OFFICER
MARITIME SELF-DEFENSE FORCE	SANTŌ KAISHI	NITŌ KAISHI	ITTŌ KAISHI	KAISHICHŌ	SANTŌ KAISŌ	NITŌ KAISŌ	ITTŌ KAISŌ	KAISŌCHŌ	JUN KAI
UNITED STATES RANK TITLE	SEAMAN RECRUIT	SEAMAN APPRENTICE	SEAMAN	PETTY OFFICER THIRD CLASS	PETTY OFFICER SECOND CLASS	PETTY OFFICER FIRST CLASS	CHIEF PETTY OFFICER	SENIOR CHIEF PETTY OFFICER	WARRANT OFFICER
AIR SELF-DEFENSE FORCE	SANTŌ KŪSHI	NITŌ KŪSHI	ITTŌ KŪSHI	KŪSHICHŌ	SANTŌ KŪSŌ	NITŌ KŪSŌ	ITTŌ KŪSŌ	KŪSŌCHŌ	JUN KŪI
UNITED STATES RANK TITLE	AIRMAN BASIC	AIRMAN	AIRMAN FIRST CLASS	SERGEANT	STAFF SERGEANT	TECHNICAL SERGEANT	MASTER SERGEANT	SENIOR MASTER SERGEANT	WARRANT OFFICER

OFFICERS

GROUND SELF-DEFENSE FORCE	SANTŌ RIKUI	NITŌ RIKUI	ITTŌ RIKUI	SANTŌ RIKUSA	NITŌ RIKUSA	ITTŌ RIKUSA	RIKUSHŌHO	RIKUSHŌ	RIKUJŌ BAKURYŌCHŌ
UNITED STATES RANK TITLE	2D LIEUTENANT	1ST LIEUTENANT	CAPTAIN	MAJOR	LIEUTENANT COLONEL	COLONEL	MAJOR GENERAL	LIEUTENANT GENERAL	GENERAL
MARITIME SELF-DEFENSE FORCE	SANTŌ KAII	NITŌ KAII	ITTŌ KAII	SANTŌ KAISA	NITŌ KAISA	ITTŌ KAISA	KAISHŌHO	KAISHŌ	KAIJŌ BAKURYŌCHŌ
UNITED STATES RANK TITLE	ENSIGN	LIEUTENANT JUNIOR GRADE	LIEUTENANT	LIEUTENANT COMMANDER	COMMANDER	CAPTAIN	REAR ADMIRAL	VICE ADMIRAL	ADMIRAL
AIR SELF-DEFENSE FORCE	SANTŌ KÜI	NITŌ KÜI	ITTŌ KÜI	SANTŌ KÜSA	NITŌ KÜSA	ITTŌ KÜSA	KÜSHŌHO	KÜSHŌ	KŌKÜ BAKURYŌCHŌ
UNITED STATES RANK TITLE	2D LIEUTENANT	1ST LIEUTENANT	CAPTAIN	MAJOR	LIEUTENANT COLONEL	COLONEL	MAJOR GENERAL	LIEUTENANT GENERAL	GENERAL

Figure 14. Ranks and Insignia of the Self-Defense Forces, 1990

449

low priority. For FY 1986 through FY 1990, defense's share of the general budget was around 6.5 percent, as compared to approximately 28 percent for the United States. In 1987 Japan ranked sixth in the world in total defense expenditures behind the Soviet Union, the United States, France, the Federal Republic of Germany (West Germany), and Britain. By 1989 it ranked third after the United States and the Soviet Union, mainly because of the increased value of the yen.

In addition to annual budgets, the Defense Agency prepared a series of cabinet-approved build-up plans beginning in 1957, which set goals for specific task capabilities and established procurement targets to achieve them. Under the first three plans (for 1958–60, 1962–66, and 1967–71), funding priorities were set to establish the ability to counter limited aggression. Economic difficulties following the 1973 oil crisis, however, caused major problems in achieving the Fourth Defense Buildup Plan (1972–76) and forced funding to be cut, raising questions about the basic concepts underlying defense policies (see Monetary and Fiscal Policy, ch. 4).

In 1976 the government recognized that substantial increases in spending, personnel, and bases would be virtually impossible. Instead a "standard defense concept" was suggested, one stressing qualitative improvements in the SDF, rather than quantitative ones. It was decided that defense spending would focus on achieving a basic level of defense as set forth in the 1976 National Defense Program Outline. Thereafter, the government ceased to offer buildup plans that alarmed the public by their seemingly open-ended nature and switched to reliance on single fiscal year formulas that offered explicit, attainable goals.

Defense spending increased slightly during the late 1970s, and in the 1980s only the defense and Official Development Assistance budgets were allowed to increase in real terms. In 1985 the Defense Agency developed the Mid-Term Defense Estimate objectives for FY 1986 through FY 1990, to improve SDF front-line equipment and upgrade logistic support systems. For the GSDF, these measures included the purchase of advanced weapons and equipment to improve antitank, artillery, ground-to-sea firepower, and mobile capabilities. For the MSDF, the focus was on upgrading antisubmarine capabilities, with the purchase of new destroyer escorts equipped with the Aegis system and SH–60J antisubmarine helicopters, and on improving antimine warfare and air defense systems. ASDF funds were concentrated on the purchase of fighter aircraft and rescue helicopters. The entire cost of the Mid-Term Defense Estimate for FY 1986 through FY 1990 was projected at approximately ¥18.4 trillion (approximately US$83.2 billion, at the 1985 exchange rate).

In FY 1989 the ¥3.9 trillion defense budget accounted for 6.49 percent of the total budget, 1.006 percent of the GNP. In addition to the Defense Agency itself, the defense budget supported the Defense Facilities Administration Agency and the Security Council. Defense Agency funding covered GSDF, MSDF, and ASDF, and the internal bureaus, the Joint Staff Council, the the National Defense Academy, the National Defense Medical College, the National Institute for Defense Studies, the Technical Research and Development Institute, and the Central Procurement Office.

The FY 1990 defense budget, at 0.997 percent of the forecasted GNP, dipped below the 1 percent level for the first time since it was reached in 1987. But the more than ¥4.1 trillion budget still marked a 6.1 percent increase over the FY 1989 defense budget and provided virtually all of the ¥104 billion requested for research and development, including substantial funds for guided-missile and communications technologies. Although some ¥34.6 billion was authorized over several years for joint Japan-United States research and development of the experimental FSX fighter plane, disputes over this project were believed to have convinced the Defense Agency to strengthen the capability of the domestic arms industry and increase its share of SDF contracts. After originally being cut, funds were also restored for thirty advanced model tanks and the last Aegis multiple-targeting-equipped destroyer escort needed to complete the Mid-Term Defense Estimate. The 6.1 percent defense increase was accompanied by an even larger (8.2 percent) increase in Official Development Assistance funding.

Officials resisted United States pressure to agree formally that Japan would support more of the cost of maintaining United States troops, claiming that such a move would require revision of agreements between the two nations. But in FY 1989 the Japanese government contributed US$2.4 billion—roughly 40 percent—of the total cost. The contribution slated for FY 1990 was increased to US$2.8 billion—nearly 10 percent of the total defense budget— and by the end of FY 1990 the Japanese government expected to assume all expenses for utilities and building maintenance costs for United States troops stationed in Japan.

The Defense Industry

Dismantled by occupation authorities after World War II, armaments production resumed in 1952 when the nation's manufacturers began repairing and maintaining equipment for United States forces operating in Asia. Individual producers emerged as affiliates of larger industrial conglomerates, including the former *zaibatsu* (see Glossary) of Mitsubishi and Sumitomo. After 1954 the defense industry began to arm the SDF, at first making only slight improvements on United States-designed equipment manufactured for local use. The Japanese defense industry received about US$10 billion worth of advanced technology from the United States between 1950 and 1983.

In July 1970, Defense Agency Director General Nakasone Yasuhiro established five objectives for the defense industry: to maintain Japan's industrial base for national security, to acquire equipment from Japan's domestic research and development and production efforts, to use civilian industries for domestic arms production, to set long-term goals for research and development and production, and to introduce competition into defense production. By the late 1970s, indigenous suppliers had developed and produced an almost complete range of modern equipment, including aircraft, tanks, artillery, and major surface and underwater naval combatants. Certain types of highly sophisticated weaponry, including F-15 fighters, P-3C Orion antisubmarine aircraft, and 8-inch howitzers, were produced under license. Except for the most complex and costly items, such as the E-2C airborne early-warning aircraft, little was purchased complete from foreign suppliers.

Over 25 percent of the ¥18.4 trillion Mid-Term Defense Estimate for FY 1986 through 1990 was allocated for equipment procurement, most of it domestically produced; but the most lucrative defense contract was for the FSX. Envisioned as a successor to the F-1 support fighter in the ASDF inventory, the FSX was expected to take ten years to develop at an estimated cost of ¥200 billion. In October 1985, the Defense Agency began by considering three development options for the FSX: domestic development, adoption of an existing domestic model, or adoption of a foreign model. The agency originally favored domestic development. But by late 1986, after consultation and much pressure from the United States, it decided to consider a coproduction agreement with the United States. And in October 1987, Japanese and United States defense officials meeting in Washington decided on a joint project to remodel either the F-15 or the F-16. The Defense Agency selected the F-16. Once the agreement was reached, it came under heavy criticism from members of the United States Congress concerned about loss of key United States technologies and technological leadership, risks of Japanese commercialization of technology at United States expense, and insufficient work share for American firms. As a result of the controversy, in early 1989 the United States demanded and obtained a review and revision of the

F–15J interceptor at airbase in Fukuoka Prefecture
Courtesy Asahi Shimbun

agreement, restricting technology transfer and specifying that American firms would receive 40 percent of the work. The controversy left bitterness on both sides, and Japanese industrialists, convinced that a Japanese-designed and Japanese-developed FSX would be superior to a modified F–16 codeveloped by Japan and the United States and irritated at United States pressure to renegotiate an agreement they considered already favorable to the United States, seemed in 1990 to be inclined to go it alone on future weapons research.

In the late 1980s, the defense industry, limited by the lack of research and development, inadequate testing equipment, restricted exports, and no economies of scale, accounted for only 0.5 percent of Japan's total industrial output. The Defense Production Committee of the Federation of Economic Organizations (Keizai Dantai Rengōkai—Keidanren) was an important element in defense production, negotiating with the Defense Agency and coordinating activities among defense firms. Keidanren disseminated defense information and informally limited competition by promoting agreements between companies. Nearly 60 percent of Japanese defense contracts were awarded to five large corporations: Mitsubishi Heavy Industries, Toshiba Corporation, Mitsubishi Electric Corporation, Kawasaki Heavy Industries, and Ishikawajima-Harima Heavy Industries Corporation. Competition for contracts nonetheless intensified in the 1980s, as larger portions of the defense budget were allotted to procurement. But for the Japanese defense industry to become efficient it had to depend on economies of scale that could only be achieved through export. Ishikawajima-Harima Heavy Industries indicated an interest in the arms export market when it changed its articles of incorporation to include arms in its list of products in June 1987 and later asked that weapons export restrictions be eased during the 1990s. A secret memorandum circulating among defense contractors in 1988 estimated that lifting the export ban (that existed by general interpretation of Article 9 of the Constitution) would result in Japan's capturing 45 percent of the world tank and self-propelled artillery market, 40 percent of military electronic sales, and 60 percent of naval ship construction. In 1989 a Keidanren committee headed by Kanamori Masao, chairman of Mitsubishi Heavy Industries, called for increasing defense research and development to 5 percent of the total defense budget. The FY 1990 defense budget allotted approximately 2 percent for this purpose. In the 1990s, Japanese corporations might be expected to market mainly dual-use electronics subcomponents, vehicles, and transport and communications equipment offshore or through front companies and to provide components for missiles and aircraft produced overseas, especially in the United States.

Military Relations with the United States

The 1952 Mutual Security Assistance Pact provided the initial basis for the nation's security relations with the United States (see World War II and the Occupation, 1941–52, ch. 1; Relations with the United States, ch. 7). The pact was replaced in 1960 by the Treaty of Mutual Cooperation and Security, which declares that both nations will maintain and develop their capacities to resist armed attack in common and that each recognizes that an armed attack on either one in territories administered by Japan will be considered dangerous to the safety of the other. The Agreed Minutes to the treaty specified that the Japanese government must be consulted prior to major changes in United States force deployment in Japan or to the use of Japanese bases for combat operations other than in defense of Japan itself. However, Japan was relieved by its constitutional prohibition of participating in external military operations from any obligation to defend the United States if it were attacked outside of Japanese territories. In 1990 the Japanese government expressed its intention to continue to rely on the treaty's arrangements to guarantee national security.

The Agreed Minutes under Article 6 of the 1960 treaty contain a status-of-forces agreement on the stationing of United States forces in Japan, with specifics on the provision of facilities and areas for their use and on the administration of Japanese citizens employed on the facilities. Also covered are the limits of the two countries' jurisdictions over crimes committed in Japan by United States military personnel.

The Mutual Security Assistance Pact of 1952 initially involved a military aid program that provided for Japan's acquisition of funds, matériel, and services for the nation's essential defense. Although Japan no longer received any aid from the United States by the 1960s, the agreement continued to serve as the basis for purchase and licensing agreements assuring interoperability of the two nations' weapons and for the release of classified data to Japan, including both international intelligence reports and classified technical information.

A major issue for military relations between the two nations was resolved in 1972 when the Ryūkyū Islands, including Okinawa, reverted to Japanese control, and the provisions of the 1960 security treaty were extended to cover them. The United States retained the right to station forces in these islands. In 1990, 30,000 United States troops still occupied 20 percent of Okinawa's land, a source of friction with the local population. Military relations improved after the mid-1970s. In the early 1960s, a Security Consultative Committee, with representatives from both countries, had been set up under the 1960 security treaty to discuss and coordinate security matters concerning both nations. In 1976 a subcommittee of that body prepared the Guidelines for Japan-United States Defense Cooperation that were approved by the full committee in 1978 and later approved by the National Defense Council and cabinet. The guidelines authorized unprecedented activities in joint defense planning, response to an armed attack on Japan, and for cooperation on situations in Asia and the Pacific region that could affect Japan's security.

Under the framework of the guidelines, the Japanese Joint Staff Council and the commander of United States Forces, Japan, drew up a long-range program for joint exercises to encompass all three services of both nations. Every year during the 1980s, the GSDF conducted command post and field-training exercises involving units from each of the regional armies in combined training with United States forces. Although the MSDF had participated in exercises with the United States Navy since 1955, in 1980 Japan, in an unprecedented move, permitted a task force of ships and aircraft to train in the Rim of the Pacific (RIMPAC) comprehensive naval exercise with naval forces from the United States, Australia, Canada, and New Zealand. Japan also participated in RIMPAC '88 with eight destroyers and frigates, one submarine, eight P-3C antisubmarine aircraft, and one supply ship. The ASDF also conducted numerous air defense, fighter, rescue, and command post training exercises with United States Air Force units.

In 1990 over 50,000 members of the United States armed forces were stationed in Japan, including almost 24,000 marines, 16,200 air force personnel, 8,100 members of the navy, and 2,400 army personnel, who were deployed at several locations on Honshū, Kyūshū, and Okinawa. These numbers represented a substantial increase—more than 10 percent—over 1980 figures, but the number of United States troops maintained on Japanese soil was expected to be reduced to the 1980 level by 1993.

Public Order and Internal Security

Conditions of public order in 1990 compared favorably with those in other industrialized countries. The overall crime rate was low by North American and West European standards and had shown a general decline since the mid-1960s. The incidence of violent crime was especially low, owing in part to effective enforcement of stringent firearms control laws. Problems of particular concern were those associated with a modern industralized nation, including juvenile delinquency, traffic control, and white-collar crime.

Civil disorders occurred from the early 1950s, chiefly in Tokyo, but did not seriously threaten the internal security of the state. Far less frequent after the early 1970s, they were in all cases effectively countered by efficient and well-trained police units employing the most sophisticated techniques of riot control.

In 1990 the police were an apolitical body under the general supervision of independent agencies, free of direct central government executive control. They were checked by an independent judiciary and monitored by a free and active press. The police were generally well respected and could rely on considerable public cooperation in their work.

Officials involved in the criminal justice system were usually highly trained professionals interested in preventing crime and rehabilitating offenders. They were allowed considerable discretion in dealing with legal infractions and in 1990 appeared to deserve the trust and respect accorded to them by the general public. Constitutionally guaranteed rights of habeas corpus, protection against self-incrimination, and the inadmissability of confessions obtained under duress were enforced by criminal procedures.

The prison system in 1990 was generally modern and conducted from the viewpoint of resocialization. Prisoners were treated on an individualized basis, and education was emphasized. Special attention was given to juvenile offenders who were normally housed separately from adult prisoners. A well-organized parole and probation program employed numerous citizen volunteers.

The Police System

The Japanese government established a European-style civil police system in 1874, under the centralized control of the Police

Bureau within the Home Ministry, to put down internal disturbances and maintain order during the Meiji Restoration. By the
1880s, the police had developed as a nationwide instrument of
government control, providing support for local leaders and en-
forcing public morality. They acted as general civil administrators,
implementing official policies, and thereby facilitating unification
and modernization. In rural areas especially, the police had great
authority and were accorded the same mixture of fear and respect
as the village head. Their increasing involvement in political affairs was one of the foundations of the authoritarian state in Japan
in the first half of the twentieth century.

The centralized police system steadily acquired responsibilities,
until it controlled almost all aspects of daily life, including fire
prevention and mediation of labor disputes. The system regulated
public health, business, factories, and construction, and issued permits and licenses. The Peace Preservation Law of 1925 gave police
the authority to arrest people for "wrong thoughts." Special Higher
Police were created to regulate motion pictures, political meetings,
and election campaigns. Military police operating under the army
and navy and the justice and home ministries aided the civilian
police in limiting proscribed political activity. After the Manchurian Incident of 1931, military police assumed more authority, leading to friction with their civilian counterparts (see World War II,
this ch.). After 1937 police directed business activities for the war
effort, mobilized labor, and controlled transportation.

After Japan's surrender in 1945, occupation authorities retained
the prewar police structure until a new system was implemented
and the Diet passed the 1947 Police Law. Contrary to Japanese
proposals for a strong, centralized force to deal with postwar unrest, the police system was decentralized. About 1,600 independent municipal forces were established in cities, towns, and villages
with 5,000 inhabitants or more, and a National Rural Police was
organized by prefecture. Civilian control was to be ensured by placing the police under the jurisdiction of public safety commissions
controlled by the National Public Safety Commission in the Office
of the Prime Minister. The Home Ministry was abolished and
replaced by the less powerful Ministry of Home Affairs, and the
police were stripped of their responsibility for fire protection, public
health, and other administrative duties.

When most occupation forces were transferred to Korea in
1950–51, the 75,000 strong National Police Reserve was formed
to back up the ordinary police during civil disturbances, and pressure mounted for a centralized system more compatible with
Japanese political preferences. The 1947 Police Law was amended

457

in 1951 to allow the municipal police of smaller communities to merge with the National Rural Police. Most chose this arrangement, and by 1954 only about 400 cities, towns, and villages still had their own police forces. Under the 1954 amended Police Law, a final restructuring created an even more centralized system in which local forces were organized by prefectures under a National Police Agency.

The revised Police Law of 1954, still in effect in 1990, preserved some strong points of the postwar system, particularly measures ensuring civilian control and political neutrality, while allowing for increased centralization. The National Public Safety Commission system was retained. State responsibility for maintaining public order was clarified to include coordination of national and local efforts, centralization of police information, communications, and recordkeeping facilities, and national standards for training, uniforms, pay, rank, and promotion. Rural and municipal forces were abolished and integrated into prefectural forces, which handled basic police matters. Officials and inspectors in various ministries and agencies continued to exercise special police functions assigned to them in the 1947 Police Law.

National Organization

In 1990 the mission of the National Public Safety Commission was to guarantee the neutrality of the police by insulating the force from political pressure and to ensure the maintenance of democratic methods in police administration. The commission's primary function was to supervise the National Police Agency, and it had the authority to appoint or dismiss senior police officers (see fig. 15). The commission consisted of a chairman, who held the rank of minister of state, and five members appointed by the prime minister with the consent of both houses of the Diet. The commission operated independently of the cabinet, but liaison and coordination with it were facilitated by the chairman's being a member of that body.

As the central coordinating body for the entire police system, the National Police Agency determined general standards and policies; detailed direction of operations was left to the lower echelons. In a national emergency or large-scale disaster, the agency was authorized to take command of prefectural police forces. In 1989 the agency was composed of around 1,100 national civil servants, empowered to collect information and to formulate and execute national policies. The agency was headed by a commissioner general who was appointed by the National Public Safety Commission with the approval of the prime minister. The central office included the Secretariat, with divisions for general operations, planning, information, finance, management, and procurement and distribution of police equipment, and five bureaus. The Police Administration Bureau was concerned with police personnel, education, welfare, training, and unit inspections. The Criminal Investigation Bureau was in charge of research statistics and the investigation of nationally important and international cases. This bureau's Safety Department was responsible for crime prevention, combating juvenile delinquency, and pollution control. In addition, the Criminal Investigation Bureau surveyed, formulated, and recommended legislation on firearms, explosives, food, drugs, and narcotics. The Communications Bureau supervised police communications systems.

The Traffic Bureau licensed drivers, enforced traffic safety laws, and regulated traffic. Intensive traffic safety and driver education campaigns were run at both national and prefectural levels. The bureau's Expressway Division addressed special conditions of the nation's growing system of express highways.

The Security Bureau formulated and supervised the execution of security policies. It conducted research on equipment and tactics for suppressing riots and oversaw and coordinated activities of the riot police. The Security Bureau was also responsible for security intelligence on foreigners and radical political groups, including investigation of violations of the Alien Registration Law and administration of the Entry and Exit Control Law. The bureau also implemented security policies during national emergencies and natural disasters.

In 1990 the National Police Agency maintained seven regional police bureaus, each responsible for a number of prefectures. Metropolitan Tokyo and the island of Hokkaidō were excluded from these regional jurisdictions and run more autonomously than other local forces, in the case of Tokyo, because of its special urban situation, and of Hokkaidō, because of its distinctive geography (see Geographic Regions, ch. 2). The National Police Agency maintained police communications divisions in these two areas to handle any coordination needed between national and local forces.

Local Organization

In 1987 there were 223,000 police officers nationwide, most affiliated with local police forces. Local forces included forty-three prefectural (*ken*) police forces; one metropolitan (*to*) police force, in Tokyo; two urban prefectural (*fu*) police forces, in Ōsaka and Kyōto; and one district (*dō*) police force, in Hokkaidō. These forces had limited authority to initiate police actions. Their most important activities were regulated by the National Police Agency,

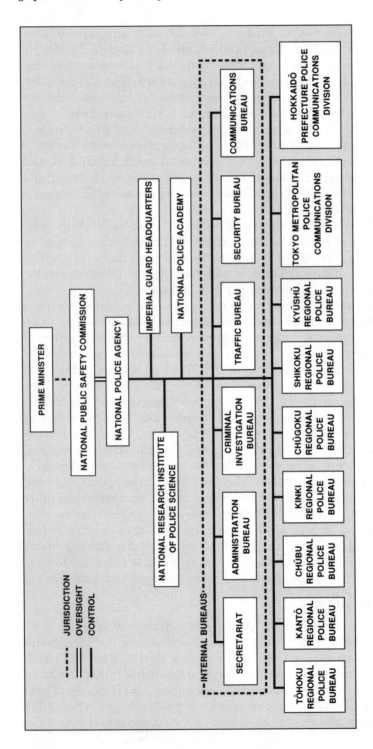

Source: Based on information from Japan, National Police Agency, *The Police of Japan, 1989*, Tokyo, 1989, 10–11.

Figure 15. Organization of the National Police Agency, 1989

which provided funds for equipment, salaries, riot, escort, and natural disaster duties, and internal security and multiple jurisdiction cases. National police statutes and regulations established the strength and rank allocations of all local personnel and the locations of local police stations. Prefectural police financed and controlled the patrol officer on the beat, traffic control, criminal investigations, and other daily operations.

Each prefectural police headquarters contained administrative divisions corresponding to those of the bureaus of the National Police Agency. Headquarters were staffed by specialists in basic police functions and administration and were commanded by an officer appointed by the local Office of the National Public Safety Commission. Most arrests and investigations were performed by prefectural police officials (and in large jurisdictions, by police assigned to substations), who were assigned to one or more central locations within the prefecture. Experienced officers were organized into functional bureaus and handled all but the most ordinary problems in their fields.

Below these stations, police boxes (*kōban*)—substations near major transportation hubs and shopping areas and in residential districts—formed the first line of police response to the public. In the late 1980s, about 20 percent of the total police force was assigned to *kōban*. Staffed by three or more officers working in eight-hour shifts, they served as a base for foot patrols and usually had both sleeping and eating facilities for officers on duty but not on watch. In rural areas, residential offices usually were staffed by one police officer who resided in adjacent family quarters. These officers endeavored to become a part of the community, and their families often aided in performing official tasks.

Officers assigned to *kōban* had intimate knowledge of their jurisdictions. One of their primary tasks was to conduct twice-yearly house-by-house residential surveys of homes in their areas, at which time the head of the household at each address filled out a residence information card detailing the names, ages, occupations, business addresses, and vehicle registration numbers of household occupants and the names of relatives living elsewhere. Police took special note of names of the aged or those living alone who might need special attention in an emergency. They conducted surveys of local businesses and recorded employee names and addresses, in addition to such data as which establishments stayed open late and which employees might be expected to work late. Participation in the survey was voluntary, and most citizens cooperated, but in the late 1980s an increasing segment of the population had come to regard the surveys as invasions of privacy.

Information elicited through the surveys was not centralized but was stored in each police box, where it was used primarily as an aid to locating people. When a crime occurred or an investigation was underway, however, these files were invaluable in establishing background data for a case. Specialists from district police stations spent considerable time culling through the usually poorly filed data maintained in the police boxes.

Riot Police

Within their security divisions, each prefectural level police department and the Tokyo police maintained special riot units. These units were formed after riots at the Imperial Palace in 1952, to respond quickly and effectively to large public disturbances. They were also used in crowd control during festival periods, at times of natural disaster, and to reinforce regular police when necessary. Full-time riot police could also be augmented by regular police trained in riot duties.

In handling demonstrations and violent disturbances, riot units were deployed en masse, military style. It was common practice for files of riot police to line streets through which demonstrations passed. If demonstrators grew disorderly or deviated from officially countenanced areas, riot police stood shoulder-to-shoulder, sometimes three and four deep, to push with their hands to control the crowds. Individual action was forbidden. Three-person units sometimes performed reconnaissance duties, but more often operations were carried out by squads of nine to eleven, platoons of twenty-seven to thirty-three, and companies of eighty to one hundred. Front ranks were trained to open to allow passage of special squads to rescue captured police or to engage in tear gas assaults. Each person wore a radio with an earpiece to hear commands given simultaneously to the formation.

The riot police were committed to using disciplined, nonlethal force and carried no firearms. They were trained to take pride in their poise under stress. Demonstrators also were usually restrained (see Civil Disturbances, this ch.). Police brutality was rarely an issue. When excesses occurred, the perpetrator was disciplined and sometimes transferred from the force if considered unable to keep his temper.

Extensive experience in quelling violent disorders led to the development of special uniforms and equipment for the riot police units. In the 1980s, riot dress consisted of a field-type jacket, which covered several pieces of body armor and included a corselet hung from the waist, an aluminum plate down the backbone, and shoulder pads. Armored gauntlets covered the hands and forearms.

Helmets had faceplates and flared padded skirts down the back to protect the neck. In case of violence, the front ranks carried 1.2-meter shields to protect against staves and rocks and held nets on high poles to catch flying objects. Specially designed equipment included water cannons, armored vans, and mobile tunnels for protected entry into seized buildings.

Because riot police duties required special group action, units were maintained in virtually self-sufficient compounds and trained to work as a coordinated force. The overwhelming majority of officers were bachelors who lived in dormitories within riot police compounds. Training was constant and focused on physical conditioning, mock battles, and tactical problems. A military atmosphere prevailed—dress codes, behavior standards, and rank differentiations were more strictly adhered to than in the regular police. Esprit de corps was inculcated with regular ceremonies and institutionalization of rituals such as applauding personnel dispatched to or returning from assignments and formally welcoming senior officers to the mess hall at all meals.

Riot duty was not popular because it entailed special sacrifices and much boredom in between irregularly spaced actions. Although many police were assigned riot duty, only a few were volunteers. For many personnel, riot duty served as a stepping stone because of its reputation and the opportunities it presented to study for the advanced police examinations necessary for promotion. Because riot duties demanded physical fitness—the armored uniform weighed 6.6 kilograms—most personnel were young, often serving in the units after an initial assignment in a *kōban*.

Special Police

In addition to regular police officers, there were several thousand officials attached to various agencies who performed special duties relating to public safety. They were responsible for such matters as railroad security, forest preservation, narcotics control, fishery inspection, and enforcement of regulations on maritime, labor, and mine safety.

In 1990, the largest and most important of these ministry-supervised public safety agencies was the Maritime Safety Agency, an external bureau of the Ministry of Transportation established to deal with crime in coastal waters and to maintain facilities for safeguarding navigation. The agency operated a fleet of patrol and rescue craft in addition to a few aircraft used primarily for anti-smuggling patrols and rescue activities. In the mid-1980s, the Maritime Safety Agency annually rescued around 500 people and arrested another 500 for violations of fishing and smuggling laws.

Other agencies with limited public safety functions included the Labor Standards Inspection Office of the Ministry of Labor, railroad police of Japan Railways Group, immigration agents of the Ministry of Justice, postal inspectors of the Ministry of Posts and Telecommunications, and revenue inspectors in the Ministry of Finance.

A small intelligence agency, the Public Security Investigation Office of the Ministry of Justice, handled national security matters both inside and outside the country. Its activities were not generally known to the public.

Police-Community Relations

Despite legal limits on police jurisdiction, many citizens retained their views of the police as authority figures to whom they could turn for aid. The public often sought police assistance to settle family quarrels, counsel juveniles, and mediate minor disputes. Citizens regularly consulted police for directions to hotels and residences—an invaluable service in cities where streets were often unnamed and buildings were numbered in the order in which they had been built rather than consecutively. Police were encouraged by their superiors to view these tasks as answering the public's demands for service and as inspiring community confidence in the police. Public attitudes toward the police were generally favorable, although a series of incidents of forced confessions in the late 1980s raised some concern about police treatment of suspects held for pretrial detention.

Conditions of Service

Education was highly stressed in police recruitment and promotion. Entrance to the force in the late 1980s was determined by examinations administered by each prefecture. Examinees were divided into two groups: upper-secondary-school graduates and university graduates. In 1985 there were ten examinees with upper-secondary diplomas and six with university degrees for every job opening. Recruits underwent rigorous training—one year for upper-secondary-school graduates and six months for university graduates—at the residential police academy attached to the prefectural headquarters. On completion of basic training, most police officers were assigned to local police boxes. Promotion was achieved by examination and required further course work. In-service training provided mandatory continuing education in more than 100 fields. Police officers with upper-secondary-school diplomas were eligible to take the examination for sergeant after three years of on-the-job experience. University graduates could take the examination after only one year. University graduates were also eligible to take the examination for

*Policewoman directing traffic
in Tokyo*
Courtesy Asahi Shimbun

assistant police inspector, police inspector, and superintendent after shorter periods than upper-secondary-school graduates. There were usually five to fifteen examinees for each opening.

About fifteen officers per year passed advanced civil service examinations and were admitted as senior officers. Officers were groomed for administrative positions and, although some rose through the ranks to become senior administrators, most such positions were held by specially recruited senior executives.

The police forces were subject to external oversight. Although officials of the National Public Safety Commission generally deferred to police decisions and rarely exercised their powers to check police actions or operations, police were liable for civil and criminal prosecution, and the media actively publicized police misdeeds. The Human Rights Bureau of the Ministry of Justice solicited and investigated complaints against public officials, including police, and prefectural legislatures could summon police chiefs for questioning. Social sanctions and peer pressure also constrained police behavior. As in other occupational groups in Japan, police officers developed an allegiance to their own group and a reluctance to offend its principles.

The Criminal Justice System

Three basic features of the nation's system of criminal justice characterized its operations in 1990. First, the institutions—police, government prosecutor's offices, courts, and correctional organs—maintained close and cooperative relations with each other, consulting frequently on how best to accomplish the shared goals of limiting and controlling crime. Second, citizens were encouraged to assist in maintaining public order and they participated extensively in crime prevention campaigns, apprehension of suspects, and offender rehabilitation programs. Finally, officials who administered criminal justice were allowed considerable discretion in dealing with offenders.

Until the Meiji Restoration in 1868, the criminal justice system was controlled mainly by *daimyō* (see Rule of Shogun and Daimyō, ch. 1). Public officials, not laws, guided and constrained people to conform to moral norms. In accordance with the Confucian ideal, officials were to serve as models of behavior; the people, who lacked rights and had only obligations, were expected to obey. Such laws as did exist were transmitted through local military officials in the form of local domain laws. Specific enforcement varied from domain to domain, and no formal penal codes existed. Justice was generally harsh, and severity depended upon one's status. Kin and neighbors could share blame for an offender's guilt: whole families and villages could be flogged or put to death for one member's transgression.

After 1868 the justice system underwent rapid transformation. The first publicly promulgated legal codes, the Penal Code of 1880 and the Code of Criminal Instruction of 1880, were based on French models. Offenses were specified, and set punishments were established for particular crimes. Both codes were innovative in that they treated all citizens as equals, provided for centralized administration of criminal justice, and prohibited punishment by ex post facto law. Guilt was held to be personal; collective guilt and guilt by association were abolished. Offenses against the emperor were spelled out for the first time.

Innovative aspects of the codes notwithstanding, certain provisions reflected traditional attitudes toward authority. The prosecutor represented the state and sat with the judge on a raised platform—his position above the defendant and the defense counsel suggesting their relative status. Under a semi-inquisitorial system, primary responsibility for questioning witnesses lay with the judge, and defense counsel could question witnesses only through the judge. Cases were referred to trial only after a judge presided over a preliminary fact-finding investigation in which the suspect was not permitted counsel. Because in all trials available evidence had already convinced the court in a preliminary procedure, the defendant's legal presumption of innocence at trial was undermined and the legal recourse open to his counsel was further weakened.

The Penal Code was substantially revised in 1907 to reflect the growing influence of German law in Japan, and the French practice of classifying offenses into three types was eliminated. More importantly, where the old code had allowed very limited judicial discretion, the new one permitted the judge to apply a wide range of subjective factors in sentencing.

After World War II, occupation authorities initiated reform of the Constitution and laws in general. Except for omitting offenses relating to war, the imperial family, and adultery, the 1947 Penal Code remains virtually identical to the 1907 version. The criminal procedure code, however, was substantially revised to incorporate rules guaranteeing the rights of the accused. The system became almost completely accusatorial, and the judge, although still able to question witnesses, decided a case on evidence presented by both sides. The preliminary investigative procedure was suppressed. The prosecutor and defense counsel sat on equal levels, below the judge. Laws on indemnification of the wrongly accused, juveniles, prisons, probation, and minor offenses were also passed in the postwar years to supplement criminal justice administration.

Crime

The National Police Agency divided crime into six main categories. Felonious offenses—the most serious and carrying the stiffest penalties—included murder and conspiracy to murder, robbery, rape, and arson. Violent offenses consisted of unlawful assembly while possessing dangerous weapons, simple and aggravated assault, extortion, and intimidation. Larceny encompassed burglary, vehicle theft, and shoplifting. Crimes classified as intellectual included fraud, embezzlement, counterfeiting, forgery, bribery, and breach of trust. Moral offenses included gambling, indecent exposure, and the distribution of obscene literature. Miscellaneous offenses frequently involved the obstruction of official duties, negligence with fire, unauthorized entry, negligent homicide or injury (often in traffic accidents), possession of stolen property, and destruction of property. Special laws defined other criminal offenses, among them prostitution, illegal possession of swords and firearms, customs violations, and possession of controlled substances including narcotics and marijuana.

In 1986 the police identified over 2.1 million Penal Code violations. Two types of violations—larceny (64.7 percent of total violations) and negligent homicide or injury as a result of accidents (25.6 percent)—accounted for over 90 percent of criminal offenses in Japan in 1986. Major crimes occurred in Japan at a very low rate. Japan experienced 1.6 robberies per 100,000 population, compared with 46.8 for West Germany, 60.1 for Britain, and 225.1 for the United States; and 1.4 murders per 100,000 population, compared with 4.5 for West Germany, 4.3 for Britain, and 8.6 for the United States. Japanese authorities also solved a high percentage of robbery cases (78.5 percent compared with 48.4 percent for West Germany, 20.4 percent for Britain, and 24.7 percent for the United States) and homicide cases (96.7 percent compared with 93.9 percent for West Germany, 76.7 percent for Britain, and 70.2 percent for the United States).

An important factor keeping crime low was the traditional emphasis on the individual as a member of groups to which he or she must not bring shame. Within these groups—family, friends, associates at work or school—a Japanese had social rights and obligations, derived valued emotional support, and met powerful expectations to conform. In 1990 these informal social sanctions continued to display remarkable potency despite competing values in a changing society. Other important factors keeping the crime rate low were the prosperous economy and a strict and effective weapons control law. Ownership of handguns was forbidden to the public, hunting rifles and ceremonial swords were registered with the police, and the manufacture and sale of firearms were regulated. The production and sale of live and blank ammunition were also controlled, as were the transportation and importation of all weapons. In the late 1980s, crimes were seldom committed with firearms.

Despite Japan's status as a modern, urban nation—a condition linked by many criminologists to growing rates of crime—the nation did not suffer from steadily rising levels of criminal activity. Although crime continued to be higher in urban areas, in the 1980s rates of crime remained relatively constant nationwide, and rates of violent crime continued to decrease.

The nation was not problem-free, however; of particular concern to the police were crimes associated with modernization. Increased wealth and technological sophistication brought new white-collar crimes, such as computer and credit card fraud, larceny involving coin dispensers, and insurance falsification. Incidence of drug abuse was minuscule compared with other industrialized nations and limited mainly to stimulants. Japanese law enforcement authorities endeavored to control this problem by extensive coordination with international investigative organizations and stringent punishment of Japanese and foreign offenders. Traffic accidents and fatalities in the late 1980s continued to consume substantial law enforcement resources.

Juvenile delinquency, although not nearly as serious as in most industrialized nations, was a great concern to authorities. In 1986 over 46 percent of persons arrested for criminal offenses (other than negligent homicide or injuries) were juveniles. Over 75 percent of the juveniles arrested were charged with larceny, mainly shoplifting and theft of motorcycles and bicycles. The failure of the Japanese education system to address the concerns of nonuniversity-bound students was cited as an important factor in the rise of juvenile crime (see Primary and Secondary Education, ch. 3).

Yakuza (underworld) groups were estimated to number more than 3,100 and together contained almost 86,000 members. Although concentrated in the largest urban prefectures, *yakuza* operated in most cities and often received protection from high-ranking officials in exchange for their assistance in keeping the crime rate low by discouraging criminals operating individually or in small groups. Following concerted police pressure in the 1960s, smaller gangs either disappeared or began to consolidate in syndicate-type organizations. In 1986 three large syndicates dominated underworld crime in the nation and controlled more than 1,000 gangs and 29,000 gangsters.

Yakuza had existed in Japan well before the 1800s and followed codes based on *bushidō*. Their early operations were usually close-knit, and the leader and gang members had father-son relationships. Although this traditional arrangement continued to exist, *yakuza* activities were increasingly replaced by modern types of gangs that depended on force and money as organizing concepts. Nonetheless, *yakuza* often pictured themselves as saviors of traditional Japanese virtues in a postwar society, sometimes forming ties with right-wing groups espousing the same views and attracting dissatisfied youths to their ranks.

Civil Disturbances

The public and government appeared to tolerate certain forms of public disorder as inherent to a properly functioning democracy. Demonstrations usually followed established forms. Groups received legal permits and kept to assigned routes and areas. Placards and bullhorns were used to express positions. Traffic was sometimes disrupted, and occasional shoving battles between police and protesters resulted. But arrests were rare and generally made only in cases involving violence.

Political extremists have not hesitated to use violence and were held responsible for bombings in connection with popular causes.

In January 1990 the mayor of Nagasaki was shot by a member of the right-wing Seikijuku (Sane Thinkers School), presumably for a statement he had made that was perceived as critical of the late Emperor Hirohito. That attack came two days after the left-wing Chūkakuha (Middle Core Faction), opposed to the imperial system, claimed responsibility for firing a rocket onto the grounds of the residence of the late emperor's brother and a day before the government announced the events leading to the enthronement of Emperor Akihito in November 1990. The enthronement ceremonies were considered likely targets for extremist groups on the left and the right who saw the mysticism surrounding the emperor as being overemphasized or excessively reduced, respectively. Although membership in these groups represented only a minute portion of the population and presented no serious threat to the government, authorities were concerned about the example set by the groups' violence, as well as by the particular violent events. Violent protest by radicals also occurred in the name of causes apparently isolated from public sentiments. Occasional clashes between leftist factions and between leftists and rightists have injured both participants and bystanders. Security in the early 1990s remained heavy at New Tokyo International Airport at Narita-Sanrizuka in Chiba Prefecture, the scene of violent protests in the 1970s by radical groups supporting local farmers opposed to expropriation of their land.

The most notorious extremists were the Japanese Red Army, a Marxist terrorist group (see Political Extremists, ch. 6). This group was responsible for an attack on Lod International Airport in Tel Aviv, Israel, in support of the Popular Front for the Liberation of Palestine in 1972. It participated in an attack on a Shell Oil refinery in Singapore in 1974 and seized the French embassy in The Hague that same year and the United States and Swedish embassies in Kuala Lumpur in 1975. In 1977 the Japanese Red Army hijacked a Japan Airlines jet over India in a successful demand for a US$6 million ransom and the release of six inmates in Japanese prisons. Following heavy criticism at home and abroad for the government's "caving in" to terrorists' demands, the authorities announced their intention to recall and reissue approximately 5.6 million valid Japanese passports to make hijacking more difficult. A special police unit was formed to keep track of the terrorist group, and tight airport security measures were instigated. Despite issuing regular threats, the Japanese Red Army was relatively inactive in the 1980s. In 1990 its members were reported to be in North Korea and Lebanon undergoing further training and available as mercenaries to promote various political causes.

Criminal Procedure

In 1990 the nation's criminal justice officials followed specified legal procedures in dealing with offenders. Once a suspect was arrested by national or prefectural police, the case was turned over to attorneys in the Supreme Public Prosecutors Office, who were the government's sole agents in prosecuting lawbreakers. Although under Ministry of Justice's administration, these officials worked under Supreme Court rules and were career civil servants who could be removed from office only for incompetence or impropriety. Prosecutors presented the government's case before judges in the Supreme Court and the four types of lower courts: high courts, district courts, summary courts, and family courts. Penal and probation officials administered programs for convicted offenders under the direction of public prosecutors (see The Judicial System, ch. 6).

After identifying a suspect, police had the authority to exercise some discretion in determining the next step. If, in cases pertaining to theft, the amount was small or already returned, the offense petty, the victim unwilling to press charges, the act accidental, or the likelihood of a repetition not great, the police could either drop the case or turn it over to a prosecutor. Reflecting the belief that appropriate remedies were sometimes best found outside the formal criminal justice mechanisms, in 1987 approximately 49 percent of criminal cases were not sent to the prosecutor.

Police also exercised wide discretion in matters concerning juveniles. Police were instructed by law to identify and counsel minors who appeared likely to commit crimes, and they could refer juvenile offenders and nonoffenders alike to child guidance centers to be treated on an outpatient basis. Police could also assign juveniles or those considered to be harming the welfare of juveniles to special family courts. These courts were established in 1949 in the belief that the adjustment of a family's situation was sometimes required to protect children and prevent juvenile delinquency. Family courts were run in closed sessions, tried juvenile offenders under special laws, and operated extensive probationary guidance programs. Young people between the ages of fourteen and twenty could, at the judgment of police, be sent to the public prosecutor for possible trial as adults before a judge under the general criminal law.

Safeguards protected the suspects' rights. Police had to secure warrants to search for or seize evidence. A warrant was also necessary for an arrest, although if the crime were very serious or the perpetrator likely to flee, it could be obtained immediately after arrest. Within forty-eight hours after placing a suspect under detention, the police had to present their case before a prosecutor, who was then required to apprise the accused of the charges and of the right to counsel. Within another twenty-four hours, the prosecutor had to go before a judge and present a case to obtain a detention order. Suspects could be held for ten days (extensions were granted in special cases), pending an investigation and a decision whether or not to prosecute. In the 1980s, some suspects were reported to have been mistreated during this detention to exact a confession.

Prosecution could be denied on the grounds of insufficient evidence or on the prosecutor's judgment. Under Article 248 of the Code of Criminal Procedures, the prosecutor, after weighing the offender's age, character, and environment, the circumstances and gravity of the crime, and the accused's rehabilitative potential, did not have to institute public action, but could deny or suspend and ultimately drop the charges after a probationary period. Because the investigation and disposition of a case could occur behind closed doors and the identity of an accused person who was not prosecuted was rarely made public, an offender could successfully reenter society and be rehabilitated under probationary status without the stigma of a criminal conviction.

Institutional safeguards checked the prosecutors' discretionary powers not to prosecute. Lay committees were established in conjunction with branch courts to hold inquests on a prosecutor's decisions. These committees met four times yearly and could order that a case be reinvestigated and prosecuted. Victims or interested parties could also appeal a decision not to prosecute.

Most offenses were tried first in district courts before one or three judges, depending on the severity of the case. Defendants were protected from self-incrimination, forced confession, and unrestricted admission of hearsay evidence. In addition, defendants had the right to counsel, public trial, and cross-examination. Trial by jury was authorized by the 1923 Jury Law but was suspended in 1943. It had not been reinstated as of 1990, chiefly owing to defendants' distrust of jurors, who were believed to be emotional and easily influenced, and the generally greater public confidence in the competence of judges.

The judge conducted the trial and was authorized to question witnesses, independently call for evidence, decide guilt, and affix a sentence. The judge could also suspend any sentence or place a convicted party on probation. Should a judgment of not guilty be rendered, the accused was entitled to compensation by the state based on the number of days spent in detention.

Criminal cases from summary courts, family courts, and district courts could be appealed to the high courts by both the prosecution and the defense. Criminal appeal to the Supreme Court was limited to constitutional questions and a conflict of precedent between the Supreme Court and high courts.

The criminal code set minimum and maximum sentences for offenses to allow for the varying circumstances of each crime and criminal. Penalties ranged from fines and short-term incarceration to compulsory labor and the death penalty. Heavier penalties were meted out to repeat offenders. Capital punishment consisted of death by hanging and could be imposed on those convicted of leading an insurrection, inducing or aiding foreign armed aggression, arson, or homicide.

The Penal System

Prisons, in existence in some feudal domains as early as the late sixteenth century, originally functioned to hold people for trial or prior to execution. Because of the costs and difficulties involved in long-term incarceration and the prevailing standards of justice that called for sentences of death or exile for serious crimes, life imprisonment was rare. Facilities were used sometimes for shorter confinement. Prisoners were treated according to their social status and housed in barracks-like quarters (see Seclusion and Social Control, ch. 1). In some cases the position of prison officer was hereditary, and staff vacancies were filled by relatives.

During the Meiji period (1868–1912), the country adopted Western-style penology along with systems of law and legal administration. In 1888 an aftercare hostel (halfway house) was opened for released prisoners. Staffed mainly by volunteers, this institution helped ex-convicts reenter society. Many ex-convicts had been ostracized by their families for the shame they had incurred and had literally nowhere to go. The Prison Law of 1908 provided basic rules and regulations for prison administration, stipulating separate facilities for those sentenced to confinement with and without labor, and for those detained for trial and short sentences.

The Juvenile Law of 1922 established administrative organs to handle offenders under the age of eighteen and recognized volunteer workers officially as the major forces in the community-based treatment of juveniles. After World War II juvenile laws were revised to extend their jurisdiction to those under the age of twenty. Volunteer workers were reorganized under a new law and in 1990 remained an indispensable part of the rehabilitation system.

The Correctional Bureau of the Ministry of Justice administered the adult prison system as well as the juvenile correctional system and three women's guidance homes (to rehabilitate prostitutes). The ministry's Rehabilitation Bureau operated the probation and parole systems. Prison personnel were trained at an institute in Tokyo and in branch training institutes in each of the eight regional correctional headquarters under the Correctional Bureau. Professional probation officers studied at the Legal Training and Research Institute of the Ministry of Justice.

In the late 1980s, Japan's prison population stood at somewhat more than 55,000 (about 44 per 100,000 general population), nearly 9,000 in short-term detention centers, the remaining 46,000 in prisons. Approximately 45 percent were repeat offenders. The United States during that period had a prison population of approximately 1 million (about 500 per 100,000 general population) with nearly 90 percent repeat offenders. While the high recidivism in the United States prison system was blamed on its failure to reform offenders, Japanese recidivism was attributed mainly to the discretionary powers of police, prosecutors, and courts, and the tendency to seek alternative sentences for first offenders.

The penal system was intended to resocialize, reform, and rehabilitate offenders. On confinement, prisoners were first classified according to sex, nationality, kind of penalty, length of sentence, degree of criminality, and state of physical and mental health. They were then placed in special programs designed to treat individual needs. Vocational and formal education were emphasized, as was instruction in social values. Most convicts engaged in labor for which a small stipend was set aside for use on release. Under a system stressing incentives, prisoners were initially assigned to community cells, then earned better quarters and additional privileges based on their good behavior.

Although a few juvenile offenders were handled under the general penal system, most were treated in separate juvenile training schools. More lenient than the penal institutions, these facilities provided correctional education and regular schooling for delinquents under the age of twenty.

According to the Ministry of Justice, the government's responsibility for social order did not end with imprisoning an offender, but also extended to aftercare treatment and to noninstitutional treatment to substitute for or supplement prison terms. A large number of those given suspended sentences were released to the supervision of volunteer officers under the guidance of professional probation officers. Adults were usually placed on probation for a fixed period and juveniles until they reached the age of twenty. Volunteers were also used in supervising parolees, though professional probation officers generally supervised offenders considered to have a high risk of recidivism. Volunteers hailed from all walks of life and handled no more than five cases at one time. They were responsible for overseeing the offenders' conduct to prevent the occurrence of further offenses. Volunteer probation officers also offered guidance and assistance to the ex-convict in assuming a law-abiding place in the community. Although volunteers were sometimes criticized for being too old compared to their charges (more than 70 percent were retired, aged fifty-five or over) and so unable to understand the problems they faced, most authorities believed that the volunteers were critically important in the nation's criminal justice system.

Public support and cooperation with law enforcement officials helped in holding down Japan's crime rate, with little or no threat to internal security. The external security threat in 1990 was also considerably reduced from previous years. The Japanese government was confident that diplomatic activity and a limited SDF, backed by United States treaty commitments, would be sufficient to deter any potential adversary.

*   *   *

The most comprehensive treatment of the SDF is available in *Jieitai nenkan* (Self-Defense Forces Yearbook), the annual white paper published by *Defense Daily*, and *Defense of Japan*, published by the Japanese Defense Agency. Other sources include James H. Buck's *The Modern Japanese Military System*, Harrison M. Holland's *Managing Defense: Japan's Dilemma*, and Malcolm McIntosh's *Japan Re-armed*. The International Institute for Strategic Studies' annual, *The Military Balance*, provides current data on the size, budget, and equipment inventory of the armed forces. Reinhard Drifte's *Arms Production in Japan* gives insight into Japan's developing defense industry.

The Police of Japan, published by the National Police Agency, gives an excellent overview of the police system and *Keisatsu hakusho* (Police White Paper), published annually by the same agency, gives updated law enforcement information and crime figures.

Journals such as *Japan Quarterly* [Tokyo], *Far Eastern Economic Review* [Hong Kong], and *Summaries of Selected Japanese Magazines* (issued monthly by the United States Embassy in Tokyo) frequently cover issues in defense and internal security and public order. (For further information and complete citations, see Bibliography.)

Appendix

Table 1. Metric Conversion Coefficients and Factors

When you know	Multiply by	To find
Millimeters	0.04	inches
Centimeters	0.39	inches
Meters	3.3	feet
Kilometers	0.62	miles
Hectares (10,000 m²)	2.47	acres
Square kilometers	0.39	square miles
Cubic meters	35.3	cubic feet
Liters	0.26	gallons
Kilograms	2.2	pounds
Metric tons	0.98	long tons
....	1.1	short tons
....	2,204	pounds
Degrees Celsius	9	degrees Fahrenheit
(Centigrade)	divide by 5 and add 32	

Table 2. Population Growth, Selected Years, 1920–2030 *
(in thousands)

Year	Total Population	Population 65 and Over	Percentage 65 and Over
1920	55,963	2,941	5.3
1930	64,450	3,064	4.8
1950	83,200	4,109	4.9
1960	93,419	5,350	5.7
1970	103,720	7,331	7.1
1980	117,060	10,647	9.1
1987	122,264	13,322	10.9
1990	124,225	14,819	11.9
2000	131,192	21,338	16.3
2010	135,823	27,104	20.0
2020	135,304	31,880	23.6
2030	134,067	31,001	23.1

* As projected by Management and Coordination Agency.

Source: Based on information from Japan, Management and Coordination Agency, Statistics Bureau, *Nihon tōkei nenkan, Shōwa 63* (Japan Statistical Yearbook, 1988), Tokyo, 1989, 25, 38.

Table 3. Adherents of Religious Traditions, 1989

Religion Branch	Adherents *
Shinto	
Shrine Shinto	86,585,845
Sect Shinto	5,146,574
Shinto-oriented new religions	3,000,344
Total Shinto	94,732,763
Buddhist	
Nichiren Shōshū	35,541,430
Jōdo	20,441,569
Shingon	15,607,203
Zen	9,523,505
Tendai	3,079,357
Nara sects	2,397,251
Other	78,370
Total Buddhist	86,668,685
Christian	
New sects	484,868
Old sects	410,692
Total Christian	895,560

* Many people observe both Shinto and Buddhist rites.

Source: Based on information from *Shūkyō nenkan, Shōwa 63* (Religion Yearbook, 1988), Tokyo, 1989, 32–135.

Table 4. Public Holidays and Festival Days

Holiday	Date
New Year's Day [1]	January 1
First Writing Day	January 2
First Business Day	January 4
Day of Mankind	Janaury 7
Adults' Day [1]	January 15
Bean-Scattering Ceremony	February 3 or 4
Risshun [2]	February 4 or 5
Needle Memorial Service	February 8
National Foundation Day [1]	February 11
Doll Festival	March 3
Spring *higan* [3]	March 17–24
Vernal Equinox Day [1]	March 21 or 22
Flower Festival	April 8
Eighty-Eighth Night [4]	May 2 or 3
Constitution Memorial Day [1]	May 3
Children's Day [1]	May 5
Summer Solstice Day	June 21 or 22
Tanabata Festival [5]	July 7
Bon Festival	July 13–15
210th Day [6]	September 1
Chrysanthemum Festival	September 9
Respect for the Aged Day [1]	September 15
Autumn *higan* [3]	September 17–20
Autumnal Equinox Day [1]	September 23 or 24
Moon-Viewing Night	Night of full moon
Sports Day [1]	October 10
Culture Day [1]	November 3
Seven-Five-Three Festival [7]	November 15
Labor Thanksgiving Day [1]	November 23
Winter Solstice Day	December 21 or 22
Emperor's Birthday [1]	December 23
New Year's Eve	December 31

[1] National holiday.
[2] Beginning of spring, based on old solar calendar.
[3] *Higan* means the other shore and is observed as a Buddhist memorial centered on the vernal equinox and the autumnal equinox.
[4] Eighty-eighth day after Old Solar New Year (February 3 or 4).
[5] Based on Chinese Weaving Maid-Cowherd legend.
[6] The 210th Day after Old Solar New Year, first day of typhoon season.
[7] Presentation at local Shinto shrines of three-year-old, five-year-old, and seven-year-old girls and boys to pray for a safe and healthy future.

Source: Based on information from *Kodansha Encyclopedia of Japan*, 2, Tokyo, 1983, 262.

Table 5. Number of Schools and Students, 1989

Type of School	Schools	Students
Preschools *	15,080	2,037,618
Elementary schools	24,851	9,606,786
Lower-secondary schools	11,264	5,619,297
Upper-secondary schools	5,511	5,644,376
Schools for the blind	70	6,006
Schools for the deaf	108	8,319
Schools for children with other disabilities	760	80,683
Technical colleges	62	51,966
Junior colleges	584	461,849
Universities	499	2,066,962
Special training schools	3,252	741,080
Other	3,572	444,381
TOTAL	65,613	26,769,323

* Does not include day-care centers operated by the Ministry of Welfare.

Source: Based on information from Japan, Ministry of Education, Science, and Culture, *Monbu jihō* (Education Review) [Tokyo], No. 1353, October 1989, 64; and Japan, Ministry of Education, Science, and Culture, *Gakkō kihon chōsa hōkokusho, 1989* (Fundamental School Survey, 1989), Tokyo, 1989, 7–11.

Table 6. Enrollment in Special Classes in Compulsory Education, 1989

Category	Elementary	Lower secondary
Number of schools	24,851	11,264
Number of classes	317,259	154,054
Number of students	9,606,627	5,619,297
Number of schools with special classes	10,288	5,260
Number of special classes	14,420	6,893
Number of students in special classes	52,701	28,352
Percentage of schools with special classes	41.4	46.7
Percentage of students in special classes	0.5	0.5

Source: Based on information from Japan, Ministry of Education, Science, and Culture, *Gakkō kihon chōsa hōkokusho, 1989* (Fundamental School Survey, 1989), 1989, 7–10, 30, 31, 63, 122, 123.

Table 7. Postsecondary Institutions and Enrollment, by Type of Institution, 1988

Type of Institution	Number of Institutions	Enrollment
Universities		
National	95	491,539
Local public	38	59,216
Private	357	1,443,861
Total universities	490	1,994,616
Junior colleges		
National	40	19,110
Local public	54	22,024
Private	477	409,302
Total junior colleges	571	450,436
Technical colleges [1]		
National	54	16,080
Local public	4	1,558
Private	4	1,257
Total technical colleges	62	18,895
Special training colleges [2]		
National	158	16,939
Local public	163	23,582
Private	2,301	481,053
Total special training colleges	2,622	521,574
Other		
National	7	19
Local public	92	5,122
Private	3,586	148,161
Total other [3]	3,685	153,302
TOTAL	7,430	3,138,853

[1] Fourth-year and fifth-year enrollments only.

[2] Includes only special training colleges offering advanced courses that had an entrance requirement of upper-secondary school completion.

[3] There were 3,685 miscellaneous schools in 1988, with an actual total enrollment of 451,988 students. The figures in the enrollment column here show only students whose entrance required at least graduation from an upper-secondary school program.

Source: Based on information from Japan, Ministry of Education, Science, and Culture, *Monbu tōkei yōran* (Statistical Abstract of Education), Tokyo, 1989, 70, 73–75, 104, 106.

Table 8. *Combined Social and Education Facilities, 1987*

Type	National	Prefectural	Municipal [1]	Private	Total
Audiovisual centers [2]	0	62	808	0	870
Children's culture centers [2] ..	0	1	44	0	45
Children's nature centers [2] ..	10	93	153	0	256
Citizens' public halls	0	0	17,422	18	17,440
Cultural facilities [2]	0	55	727	0	782
Museums	28	100	254	355	737
Public libraries	0	69	1,699	33	1,801
Sports centers [2]	0	2,266	32,143	0	34,409
Women's education centers ..	1	11	62	126	200
Youth centers [2]					
Residential	13	110	157	0	280
Nonresidential	0	10	150	0	160
Total youth centers	13	120	307	0	440
TOTAL	52	2,777	53,619	532	56,980

[1] Includes municipal syndicates.
[2] Private facilities not included.

Source: Based on information from Japan, Ministry of Education, Science, and Culture, *Monbushō, 1989,* Tokyo, 1989, 38; and Japan, Ministry of Education, Science, and Culture, *Monbu tōkei yōran* (Statistical Abstract of Education), Tokyo, 1989, 111–17.

Table 9. *Average Age and Salary for Selected Positions, 1988*

Position	Average Age	Salary *
Branch office manager	50.4	5,019
Office department manager	50.5	4,558
Office section manager	45.7	3,717
Ordinary clerk	29.7	1,800
Plant manager	51.2	4,251
Technical department manager	49.5	4,271
Technical section manager	44.9	3,503
Ordinary technical staff	31.2	2,156

* In United States dollars per month.

Source: Based on information from Japan, National Personnel Authority, Bureau of Compensation, *Nippon 1989: JETRO Business Facts and Figures,* Tokyo, 1989, 122.

Table 10. Average Monthly Earnings by Firm Size, Selected Years, 1960–87
(in thousands of yen)

Year	Number of Regular Employees		
	1 to 4	5 to 29	30 or more
1960	9	15	24
1965	20	30	39
1970	37	56	76
1975	85	133	177
1980	129	193	263
1985	153	228	317
1987	158	243	336

Source: Based on information from Japan, Management and Coordination Agency, Statistics Bureau, *Nihon tōkei nenkan, Shōwa 63* (Japan Statistical Yearbook, 1988), Tokyo, 1989, 92.

Table 11. National Budget and Fiscal Investment and Loan Program, Fiscal Year (FY) 1990
(in billions of United States dollars)

Category	Amount
Revenues	
Tax revenues	414.2
Other revenues	8.6
Receipts from NTT * stock sale	9.3
Public bonds	41.4
Total revenues	473.5
Expenditures	
Discretionary expenditures	253.0
Transfers to local governments	109.1
Social infrastructure	9.3
Debt service	102.1
Total expenditures	473.5

* Nippon Telegraph and Telephone Corporation.

Source: Based on information from Japan Economic Institute of America, *Japan Economic Survey* [Washington], October 1989, 3.

Table 12. *Personal Investment, 1989*
(in trillions of yen and billions of United States dollars)

Type of Institution	Yen	Dollars
Banks	130	929
Postal savings	126	900
Credit cooperatives	58	414
Agricultural and fishery cooperatives	48	342
Regional banks	26	185
Labor credit associations	6	43

Source: Based on information from "Japanese Utilize Postal Savings," *Japan Economic Journal* [Tokyo], February 24, 1990, 5.

Table 13. *National Government and Affiliated Agencies'*
Budgets, Selected Years, 1960–88
(in billions of yen)

Year	National Government General Accounts	National Government Special Accounts	Government-Affiliated Agencies	Total
Revenues				
1960	1,570	3,750	1,537	6,857
1965	3,658	7,215	3,237	14,110
1970	7,950	18,403	6,076	32,429
1975	21,289	39,723	12,645	3,657
1980	42,589	95,121	20,311	158,021
1985	52,500	125,744	13,235	191,479
1988	56,700	167,301	5,185	229,186
Expenditures				
1960	1,570	3,549	1,383	6,502
1965	3,658	6,708	3,090	13,456
1970	7,950	16,988	5,808	30,746
1975	21,289	36,412	12,234	69,935
1980	42,589	89,771	20,438	152,798
1985	52,500	119,531	13,307	185,338
1988	56,700	156,804	5,246	218,750

Source: Based on information from Japan, Management and Coordination Agency, Statistics Bureau, *Nihon tōkei nenkan, Shōwa 63* (Japan Statistical Yearbook, 1988), Tokyo, 1989, 438.

Table 14. Labor Productivity and Wage Cost Indexes, 1977–87 [1]
(index: 1980 = 100)

Year	Labor Productivity Index	Wage Cost Index [2]
1977	83.7	101.6
1978	90.3	99.6
1979	96.5	97.4
1980	100.0	100.0
1981	100.5	106.1
1982	100.2	110.8
1983	102.0	111.8
1984	108.2	109.1
1985	110.0	109.1
1986	109.4	109.6
1987	113.4	114.0

[1] The average annual rate of increase in the years between 1978 and 1987 was 2.6 percent for labor productivity and 1.2 percent for the wage cost index.
[2] The wage cost index is the wage index divided by the labor productivity index.

Source: Based on information from Japan, National Personnel Authority, Bureau of Compensation, *Nippon 1989: JETRO Business Facts and Figures,* Tokyo, 1989, 128.

Table 15. Work Status of the Population, 1985–88

	1985	1986	1987	1988
Population over fifteen years *				
Male	4,602	4,662	4,726	4,790
Female	4,863	4,925	4,994	5,059
Total population over fifteen years	9,465	9,587	9,720	9,849
Labor force *				
Male	3,596	3,626	3,655	3,693
Female	2,367	2,394	2,429	2,473
Total labor force	5,963	6,020	6,084	6,166
Employed people *				
Male	3,503	3,526	3,551	3,602
Female	2,304	2,327	2,360	2,409
Total employed people	5,807	5,853	5,911	6,011
Rate of unemployment (as percentage)	2.6	2.8	2.8	2.5
Labor force (as percentage of total population)	63.0	62.8	62.6	62.6

* In units of 10,000.

Source: Based on information from Japan, National Personnel Authority, Bureau of Compensation, *Nippon 1989: JETRO Business Facts and Figures,* Tokyo, 1989, 116.

Table 16. Foreign Nationals in the Technical and Skilled-Labor
Work Force, Selected Groups, Selected Years, 1970–87 [1]

Year	Technical	Skilled Labor
1970	35	182
1975	29	610
1980	59	1,035
1985		
Asian	16	1,009
European	17	170
North Americans	9	4
Others [2]	0	3
Total 1985	42	1,186
1987		
Asian	9	1,235
European	19	261
North Americans	30	1
Others [2]	0	4
Total 1987	58	1,501

[1] Based on legal entries.
[2] From Oceania and "non-nationality."

Source: Based on information from Japan, Management and Coordination Agency, Statistics
Bureau, *Nihon tōkei nenkan, Shōwa 61* (Japan Statistical Yearbook, 1986), Tokyo,
1987, 61; and *Nihon tōkei nenkan, Shōwa 63* (Japan Statistical Yearbook, 1988), Tokyo,
1989, 71.

Table 17. Labor Force over Fifty-Five Years of Age
by Sex and Age, Selected Years, 1970–87
(in tens of thousands of persons)

	1970	1975	1980	1985	1987
Males					
Age 55–64	331	344	379	478	523
Age 65 and over	158	169	184	187	190
Females					
Age 55–64	193	215	253	298	313
Age 65 and over	73	76	95	113	122
TOTAL	755	804	911	1,076	1,148

Source: Based on information from Japan, Management and Coordination Agency, Statistics
Bureau, *Nihon tōkei nenkan, Shōwa 63* (Japan Statistical Yearbook, 1988), Tokyo,
1989, 71.

Table 18. Index of Labor Productivity for Selected Economic Sectors, Selected Years, 1960–87 (1985 average = 100)

Year	Total Productivity	Public Utilities	Mining and Manufacturing	Manufacturing
1960	15.4	17.3	15.3	15.4
1965	22.6	27.0	22.4	22.2
1970	42.2	47.7	41.8	40.7
1975	55.0	62.4	54.5	54.4
1980	82.1	79.2	82.2	82.1
1985	100.0	100.0	100.0	100.0
1987	107.6	105.6	107.8	107.7

Source: Based on information from Japan, Management and Coordination Agency, Statistics Bureau, *Nihon tōkei nenkan, Shōwa 63* (Japan Statistical Yearbook, 1988), Tokyo, 1989, 113.

Table 19. Energy Consumption, Fiscal Year (FY) 1986 and FY 1995 [1]

Category	FY 1986		FY 1995	
	Amount [2]	Percentage [3]	Amount	Percentage [3]
Demand (kiloliters)	433.0	n.a.	490.0	n.a.
Supply				
Coal (in tons)	103.9	18.3	121.0	18.3
Nuclear (in kilowatts)	25.8	9.5	41.5	13.4
Natural gas (in kiloliters)	42.8	9.9	55.0	11.1
Hydroelectric				
General (in kilowatts)	20.2	n.a.	23.0	n.a.
Pumped (in kilowatts)	15.6	n.a.	19.5	n.a.
Total hydroelectric	35.8	4.2	42.5	4.5
Geothermal (in kiloliters)	0.4	0.1	2.0	0.4
New energy (in kiloliters)	5.5	1.3	12.5	2.5
Oil (in kiloliters)	246.0	56.8	245.0	49.7
Total supply (in kiloliters)	460.2	100.0	519.5	100.0

n.a.—not available.
[1] Projected.
[2] In millions.
[3] Figures may not add to totals because of rounding.

Source: Based on information from Tsuneta Yano Memorial Society, *Nippon: A Charted Survey of Japan, 1989/90,* Tokyo, 1989, 243.

Table 20. High-Technology Sector Developments, 1987

Technical Field	Kind of Product
New materials	Composite materials Amorphous alloys High-molecular separation films
Electronics	Semiconductor memory chips Charge-coupled devices
Data and communications	Computer switching boards Digital circuit Laser printers
Processing and manufacturing	Laser processors Computer Aided Design/Computer Aided Manufacturing (CAD/CAM) Hydraulic control valves
Analytical and measuring instruments	Accelerometers Spectrum analyzers
Biotechnology	Biotechnology products utilizing cellular material from animals Biotechnology products utilizing microorganisms
Aeronautical and space	Communications satellites
Large building structures	Ultra-high-rise buildings

Source: Based on information from Japan, National Personnel Authority, Bureau of Compensation, *Nippon 1987: JETRO Business Facts and Figures,* Tokyo, 1987, 27.

Table 21. Inland Freight Transportation by Sector and Volume, 1960 and 1987

	1960		1987	
	Millions of Tons	Millions of Ton-Kilometers	Millions of Tons	Millions of Ton-Kilometers
Railroads	238	54,515	83	20,561
Motor vehicles	1,156	20,801	5,046	224,053
Coastal shipping	139	63,659	463	201,386
Air transport	0	6	0.7	634
TOTAL	1,553	138,981	5,582.7	446,634

Source: Based on information from Tsuneta Yano Memorial Society, *Nippon: A Charted Survey of Japan, 1989/90,* Tokyo, 1989, 267.

Table 22. Passenger Transportation
by Sector and Volume, 1970 and 1987
(in millions)

Sector	Passengers carried		Passenger-kilometers	
	1970	1987	1970	1987
Railroads	16,445	19,972	288,816	344,729
Buses	11,812	8,470	102,894	102,895
Automobiles	12,221	28,615	181,335	437,837
Air transport	15	50	9,319	38,534
Coastal shipping	174	155	4,814	5,850
TOTAL	40,667	57,262	587,178	929,845

Source: Based on information in Tsuneta Yano Memorial Society, *Nippon: A Charted Survey of Japan, 1989/90,* Tokyo, 1989, 267.

Table 23. Self-Sufficiency Ratio for Agricultural Products,
Selected Years, 1975–87
(in percentages)

Product	1975	1980	1985	1987 *
Rice	110	87	107	100
Wheat	4	10	14	14
Fruit	84	81	77	75
Milk and dairy products	82	82	85	78
Beef	81	72	72	64
Pork	86	87	86	80
All meats	77	81	81	76
Sugar	15	27	33	34
Overall self-sufficiency for agricultural commodity foods	77	75	74	71
Self-sufficiency for cereals (foodstuffs and fodder)	40	33	31	30

* Estimated.

Source: Based on information from Japan, National Personnel Authority, Bureau of Compensation, *Nippon 1989: JETRO Business Facts and Figures,* Tokyo, 1989, 28.

*Table 24. Merchandise Exports, Imports, Trade Balance,
and Annual Rate of Export Growth, 1960–88*
(in millions of United States dollars)

Year	Exports	Imports [1]	Trade Balance [2]	Annual Rate of Export Growth (in percentage)
1960	4,055	4,491	-437	17.3
1961	4,236	5,810	-1,574	4.5
1962	4,916	5,637	-720	16.1
1963	5,452	6,736	-1,284	10.9
1964	6,673	7,938	-1,264	22.4
1965	8,452	8,169	283	26.7
1966	9,776	9,523	254	15.7
1967	10,442	11,663	-1,222	6.8
1968	12,972	12,987	-16	24.2
1969	15,990	15,024	967	23.3
1970	19,318	18,881	437	20.8
1971	24,019	19,712	4,307	24.3
1972	28,591	23,471	5,120	19.0
1973	36,930	38,314	-1,384	29.2
1974	55,536	62,110	-6,574	50.4
1975	55,753	57,863	-2,110	0.4
1976	67,226	64,799	2,427	20.6
1977	80,495	70,809	9,686	19.7
1978	97,543	79,343	18,200	21.2
1979	103,032	110,672	-7,641	5.6
1980	129,807	140,528	-10,721	26.0
1981	152,030	143,290	8,740	17.1
1982	138,831	131,931	6,900	8.7
1983	146,927	126,393	20,534	5.8
1984	170,114	136,503	33,611	15.8
1985	175,638	129,539	46,099	3.2
1986	209,151	126,408	82,743	19.1
1987	229,221	149,515	79,706	9.6
1988	264,917	187,354	77,563	15.6

[1] Customs-clearance basis.
[2] Figures may not result in balances because of rounding.

Source: Based on information from Bank of Japan, *Economic Statistics Annual, 1977,* Tokyo, 1978, 207; Bank of Japan, *Economic Statistics Annual, 1980,* Tokyo, 1981, 223; and Bank of Japan, *Economic Statistics Annual, 1988,* Tokyo, 1989, 250.

Table 25. Exports by Commodity, Selected Years, 1960–88
(in millions of United States dollars)

Commodity	1960	1970	1980	1985	1988
Foodstuffs	256	648	1,588	1,316	1,696
Textiles	1,223	2,408	6,296	6,263	6,908
Chemicals					
Plastics	14	436	1,867	2,261	4,002
Fertilizers	60	143	377	127	137
Other	107	655	4,524	5,310	9,825
Total chemicals *	181	1,234	6,767	7,698	13,964
Nonmetallic mineral					
manufactures	169	372	1,863	2,147	2,936
Metals					
Iron and steel products	388	2,844	15,454	13,566	15,321
Fabricated metal products	155	714	3,947	3,458	4,287
Nonferrous metals	26	248	1,917	1,467	2,142
Total metals *	568	3,805	21,319	18,491	21,750
Machinery and equipment					
Motor vehicles	78	1,337	23,273	34,377	48,787
Office machinery	1	329	2,280	7,785	18,406
Semiconductors and other					
electronic components	6	400	2,307	4,753	12,327
Scientific and optical					
equipment	92	498	4,526	6,831	10,835
Audio cassette recorders	10	451	3,305	8,440	7,802
Power-generating machinery ..	24	238	2,548	3,789	6,738
Videotape recorders	0	0	1,983	6,625	6,203
Vessels	288	1,410	4,682	5,929	3,947
Metalworking machinery	8	116	1,743	2,599	3,927
Electric generators and					
equipment	22	157	1,503	2,058	3,405
Watches and clocks	4	130	1,734	1,730	2,365
Radio receivers	145	695	3,009	2,654	2,212
Textile machines	48	196	871	1,007	2,161
Television receivers	3	384	1,660	2,625	1,779
Sewing machines	55	129	466	524	980
Other	251	2,471	25,591	34,453	65,091
Total machinery and					
equipment *	1,035	8,941	81,481	126,179	196,965
Other commodities					
Rubber tires and tubes	23	162	1,382	1,545	2,219
Toys	90	138	335	484	241
Other	508	1,609	8,776	11,515	18,237
Total other commodities * ..	622	1,909	10,494	13,544	20,697
TOTAL *	4,054	19,317	129,808	175,638	264,917

* Figures may not add to totals because of rounding.

Source: Based on information from Japan Tariff Association, *The Summary Report, Trade of Japan, December 1985,* Tokyo, 1986, 146–49; Japan Tariff Association, *The Summary Report, Trade of Japan, December 1988,* Tokyo, 1989, 146–49; and Bank of Japan, *Economic Statistics Annual, 1988,* Tokyo, 1989, 250–51.

Table 26. Imports by Commodity, Selected Years, 1960–88
(in millions of United States dollars)

Commodity	1960	1970	1980	1985	1988
Foodstuffs					
Fish and shellfish	0	262	3,026	4,610	10,461
Meat	0	145	1,523	1,927	4,313
Corn	78	294	1,507	1,363	1,490
Wheat	177	318	1,229	974	1,034
Sugar	111	284	1,225	210	456
Other	182	1,678	6,156	6,463	11,366
Total foodstuffs *	548	2,981	14,666	15,547	29,120
Textile materials					
Wool	265	348	689	670	1,447
Raw cotton	431	471	1,359	1,049	1,318
Other	65	144	346	436	544
Total textile materials *	762	963	2,393	2,155	3,309
Metal ores and scrap					
Nonferrous metal ores	156	1,064	3,731	2,229	4,104
Iron ore and ferrous scrap	443	1,549	3,946	3,452	3,289
Other	74	83	753	551	1,095
Total metal ores and scrap * .	673	2,696	8,430	6,232	8,488
Other raw materials					
Wood	170	1,572	6,909	3,700	7,122
Soybeans	107	366	1,310	1,206	1,426
Natural rubber	126	115	603	408	762
Other	370	964	4,115	4,343	6,933
Total other raw materials * .	774	3,017	12,937	9,657	16,243
Mineral fuels					
Petroleum and products	600	2,786	57,851	40,574	25,807
Coal	141	1,010	4,458	5,196	5,375
Other	0	110	7,682	10,020	7,174
Total mineral fuels *	741	3,906	69,991	55,790	38,356
Chemicals	265	1,000	6,202	8,073	14,830
Machinery and equipment					
Office machines	53	322	1,032	1,545	3,279
Motor vehicles	12	12	483	571	3,165
Precision instruments	27	166	1,087	1,265	2,358
Aircraft	29	294	991	1,484	2,024
Other	326	1,560	6,733	7,507	15,835
Total machinery and					
equipment *	447	2,354	10,326	12,372	26,661
Miscellaneous commodities					
Textiles	19	314	3,180	3,886	10,631
Nonferrous metals	118	945	4,480	4,041	9,312
Iron and steel products	88	276	894	1,479	4,625
Other	68	891	7,511	10,307	25,779
Total miscellaneous					
commodities *	294	2,427	16,066	19,713	50,347
TOTAL *	4,501	19,343	141,011	129,539	187,354

* Figures may not add to totals because of rounding.

Source: Based on information from Bank of Japan, *Economic Statistics Annual, 1988,* Tokyo,
1989, 253–54; Japan Tariff Association, *The Summary Report, Trade of Japan, December 1980,* Tokyo, 1981, 129; and Japan Tariff Association, *The Summary Report, Trade
of Japan, December 1988,* Tokyo, 1989, 162–65.

Table 27. Composition of Imports, Selected Years, 1960–88
(in percentages)

Commodity	1960	1970	1980	1985	1988
Foodstuffs					
Fish and shellfish	0.0	0.0	2.2	3.6	5.6
Meat	0.0	0.0	1.1	1.5	2.3
Corn	1.7	1.6	1.1	1.1	0.8
Wheat	3.9	1.7	0.9	0.8	0.6
Sugar	2.5	1.5	0.9	0.2	0.2
Other	4.1	8.9	4.3	5.0	6.0
Total foodstuffs *	12.2	13.7	10.5	12.2	15.5
Textiles materials					
Wool	5.9	1.8	0.5	0.5	0.8
Raw cotton	9.6	2.5	1.0	0.8	0.7
Other	1.4	0.8	0.2	0.3	0.3
Total textile materials *	17.0	5.1	1.7	1.6	1.8
Metal ores and scrap					
Nonferrous metal ores	3.5	5.6	2.7	1.7	2.2
Iron ore and ferrous scrap	9.9	8.2	2.8	2.7	1.8
Other	1.6	0.4	0.5	0.4	0.5
Total metal ores scrap *	15.0	14.3	6.0	4.8	4.5
Other raw materials					
Wood	3.8	8.3	4.9	2.9	3.8
Soybeans	2.4	1.9	0.9	0.9	0.8
Natural rubber	2.8	0.6	0.4	0.3	0.4
Other	8.2	5.1	2.9	3.4	3.7
Total other raw materials *	17.2	15.9	9.2	7.5	8.7
Mineral fuels					
Petroleum and products	13.4	14.8	41.2	31.3	13.8
Coal	3.1	5.3	3.2	4.0	2.9
Other	0.0	0.6	5.4	7.7	3.8
Total mineral fuels *	16.5	20.7	49.8	43.0	20.5
Chemicals	5.9	5.3	4.4	6.2	7.9
Machinery and equipment					
Office machines	1.2	1.7	0.7	1.2	1.8
Motor vehicles	0.0	0.0	0.3	0.4	1.7
Precision instruments	0.6	0.9	0.8	1.0	1.3
Aircraft	0.6	1.3	0.7	1.1	1.1
Other	7.3	8.3	4.5	5.8	8.3
Total machinery and equipment * ..	9.7	12.2	7.0	9.5	14.2
Miscellaneous commodities					
Textiles	0.4	1.7	2.3	3.0	5.7
Nonferrous metals	2.6	5.0	3.2	3.1	5.0
Iron and steel products	2.0	1.5	0.6	1.1	2.5
Other	1.5	4.7	5.3	8.0	13.7
Total miscellaneous commodities * ..	6.5	12.9	11.4	15.2	26.9
TOTAL *	100.0	100.0	100.0	100.0	100.0

* Figures may not add to totals because of rounding.

Source: Based on information from Bank of Japan, *Economic Statistics Annual, 1988*, Tokyo, 1989, 253–54; and Japan Tariff Association, *The Summary Report, Trade of Japan, December 1980*, Tokyo, 1981, 129; and Japan Tariff Association, *The Summary Report, Trade of Japan, December 1988*, Tokyo, 1989, 162–65.

Table 28. Composition of Exports, Selected Years, 1960–88
(in percentages)

Commodity	1960	1970	1980	1985	1988
Foodstuffs	6.3	3.4	1.2	0.7	0.6
Textiles	30.2	12.5	4.9	3.6	2.6
Chemicals					
Plastics	0.4	2.3	1.4	1.3	1.5
Fertilizers	1.5	0.7	0.3	0.1	0.1
Other	2.6	3.4	3.5	3.0	3.7
Total chemicals	4.5	6.4	5.2	4.4	5.3
Nonmetallic Mineral Manufactures	4.2	1.9	1.4	1.2	1.1
Metals					
Iron and steel products	9.6	14.7	11.9	7.7	5.8
Fabricated metal products	3.8	3.7	3.0	2.0	1.6
Nonferrous metals	0.6	1.3	1.5	0.8	0.8
Total metals	14.0	19.7	16.4	10.5	8.2
Machinery and equipment					
Motor vehicles	1.9	6.9	17.9	19.6	18.4
Office machinery	0.0	1.7	1.8	4.4	6.9
Semiconductors and other electronic					
components	0.1	2.1	1.8	2.7	4.7
Scientific and optical equipment	2.3	2.6	3.5	3.9	4.1
Audiotape recorders	0.2	2.3	2.5	4.8	2.9
Power-generating machinery	0.6	1.2	2.0	2.2	2.5
Videotape recorders	0.0	0.0	1.5	3.8	2.3
Vessels	7.1	7.3	3.6	3.4	1.5
Metalworking machinery	0.2	0.6	1.3	1.5	1.5
Electric generators and equipment	0.5	0.8	1.2	1.2	1.3
Watches and clocks	0.1	0.7	1.3	1.0	0.9
Radio receivers	3.6	3.6	2.3	1.5	0.8
Textile machines	1.2	1.0	0.7	0.6	0.8
Television receivers	0.1	2.0	1.3	1.5	0.7
Sewing machines	1.4	0.7	0.4	0.3	0.4
Other	6.2	12.8	19.7	19.4	24.6
Total machinery and equipment	25.5	46.3	62.8	71.8	74.3
Other commodities					
Rubber tires and tubes	0.6	0.8	1.1	0.9	0.8
Toys	2.2	0.7	0.3	0.3	0.1
Other	12.5	8.3	6.7	6.6	6.9
Total other commodities	15.3	9.8	8.1	7.8	7.8
TOTAL *	100.0	100.0	100.0	100.0	100.0

* Figures may not add to totals because of rounding.

Source: Based on information from Bank of Japan, *Economic Statistics Annual, 1988,* Tokyo, 1989, 227–30.

Table 29. *Balance of Payments, Capital Flows,*
Official Settlements, and Foreign Exchange Reserves, 1961–88
(in millions of United States dollars)

Year	Capital Flows Long-term	Capital Flows Short-term	Errors and Omissions	Overall Balance [1]	Gold and Foreign Exchange Reserves Changes	Gold and Foreign Exchange Reserves Level
1961	−11	21	20	−952	338	1,486
1962	172	107	6	237	355	1,841
1963	467	107	45	−161	37	1,878
1964	107	234	10	−129	121	1,999
1965	−415	−61	−51	405	108	2,107
1966	−808	−64	−45	337	−33	2,074
1967	−812	506	−75	−571	−69	2,005
1968	−239	209	84	1,102	886	2,891
1969	−155	178	141	2,283	605	3,496
1970	−1,591	724	271	1,374	903	4,399
1971	−1,082	2,435	527	7,677	10,836	15,235
1972	−4,487	1,966	638	4,741	3,130	18,365
1973	−9,750	2,407	−2,595	−10,074	−6,119	12,246
1974	−3,881	1,778	−43	−6,839	1,272	13,518
1975	−272	−1,138	−584	−2,676	703	12,815
1976	−984	111	117	3,024	3,789	16,604
1977	−3,184	−648	657	7,743	6,244	22,848
1978	−12,389	1,538	267	5,950	−10,171	33,019
1979	−12,618	2,377 [2]	2,333	−16,662	−12,692	20,327
1980	2,324	3,141	−3,115	−8,396	4,905	25,232
1981	−9,672	2,265	493	−2,144	3,171	28,403
1982	−14,969	1,579	4,727	−1,813	−5,141	23,262
1983	−17,700	23	2,055	5,177	1,234	24,496
1984	−49,651	−4,295	3,743	−15,200	1,817	26,313
1985	−64,542	−936	3,991	−12,318	197	26,510
1986	−131,461	−1,609	2,458	−44,767	15,729	42,239
1987	−136,532	−23,865	−3,893	−77,275	39,240	81,479
1988	−130,326	19,536	2,320	−28,982	16,183	97,662

[1] Overall balance equals the current account balance plus the balance on long- and short-term capital flows plus errors and omissions.

[2] In 1979, *gensaki* transactions (short-term capital transactions using long-term government bonds as collateral) moved from the long-term capital account to the short-term capital account.

Source: Based on information from Bank of Japan, *Economic Statistics Annual, 1988,* Tokyo, 1989, 244–58.

Table 30. *External Assets and Liabilities, Selected years, 1976–88*
(in millions of United States dollars)

	1976	1978	1980	1982	1984	1986	1988
Assets							
Long-term assets							
Private sector							
Direct investments	10,313	14,329	19,612	28,969	37,921	58,071	110,780
Trade credits	7,403	10,753	9,773	15,905	22,824	31,992	48,791
Loans	5,384	8,785	14,839	23,228	40,601	69,211	123,663
Securities	4,158	12,204	21,439	40,070	87,578	257,933	427,218
Other	528	396	841	1,853	3,022	7,497	17,716
Total private sector	27,786	46,467	66,504	110,025	191,946	424,704	728,168
Government sector	9,113	16,832	21,377	29,426	37,238	51,432	104,501
Total long-term assets	36,899	63,299	87,881	139,451	229,184	476,136	832,669
Short- and medium-term assets	31,091	55,426	71,699	88,237	112,024	251,170	636,678
Total assets	67,990	118,725	159,580	227,688	341,208	727,306	1,469,347
Liabilities							
Long-term liabilities							
Private sector							
Direct investments	2,208	2,841	3,270	3,998	4,458	6,514	10,416
Trade credits	93	66	21	24	33	23	
Loans	2,075	1,921	1,623	1,325	1,266	1,199	1,061
Securities	11,161	17,976	30,224	47,076	77,081	143,661	254,886
Other	49	88	86	698	909	835	2,045
Total private sector	15,586	22,892	35,224	53,097	83,738	152,192	268,431

Table 30.—Continued

	1976	1978	1980	1982	1984	1986	1988
Government sector	2,816	6,384	12,545	24,548	29,484	40,144	43,194
Total long-term liabilities	18,402	29,276	47,769	77,645	113,222	192,336	311,625
Short- and medium-term liabilities	40,014	53,235	100,277	125,361	153,640	354,619	865,976
Total liabilities	58,416	82,511	148,046	203,006	266,862	546,955	1,177,601
Net assets	9,574	36,214	11,534	24,682	74,346	180,351	291,746

Source: Based on information from Bank of Japan, *Balance of Payments Monthly* [Tokyo], April 1981, 69–71; and Bank of Japan, *Balance of Payments Monthly* [Tokyo], April 1988, 81–81.

Table 31. Geographical Distribution of Cumulative Direct Investment, Selected Years, 1970–88

Area and Country	Billions of United States Dollars					Shares in Total Direct Investment (in percentage)				
	1970	1975	1980	1985	1988	1970	1975	1980	1985	1988
North America										
United States	0.70	3.42	8.71	25.29	71.86	19.6	21.5	23.9	30.2	38.6
Other	0.21	0.51	1.09	1.68	3.23	5.8	3.1	3.0	2.0	1.7
Total North America	0.91	3.92	9.80	26.97	75.09	25.4	24.6	26.9	32.2	40.3
Latin America	0.57	2.88	6.17	15.64	31.62	15.9	18.1	16.9	18.7	16.9
Asia										
China	0.00	0.00	0.03	0.29	2.04	0.0	0.0	0.0	0.3	1.1
Hong Kong	0.03	0.38	1.10	2.93	6.16	0.8	2.4	3.0	3.5	3.3
Indonesia	0.25	1.78	4.42	8.42	9.80	7.0	11.2	12.1	10.1	5.3
Singapore	0.03	0.28	0.94	2.27	3.81	0.8	1.8	2.6	2.7	2.0
South Korea	0.03	0.59	1.14	1.68	3.25	0.8	3.7	3.1	2.0	1.7
Taiwan	0.09	0.20	0.37	0.76	1.79	2.5	1.3	1.0	0.9	1.0
Other	0.32	0.99	1.83	3.11	5.38	9.1	6.1	5.1	3.8	2.9
Total Asia	0.75	4.22	9.83	19.46	32.23	21.0	26.5	26.9	23.3	17.3
Middle East	0.33	0.98	2.26	2.97	3.34	9.3	6.1	6.2	3.6	1.8

Table 31.—Continued

Area and Country	Billions of United States Dollars					Shares in Total Direct Investment (in percentage)				
	1970	1975	1980	1985	1988	1970	1975	1980	1985	1988
Western Europe										
Britain	0.54	1.55	2.01	3.14	10.55	15.1	9.7	5.5	3.8	5.7
France	0.02	0.15	0.39	0.82	1.76	0.6	0.9	1.1	1.0	0.9
Luxembourg	0.01	0.07	0.11	1.22	4.73	0.3	0.4	0.3	1.5	2.5
Netherlands	0.00	0.13	0.30	1.69	5.53	0.0	0.8	0.8	2.0	3.0
West Germany	0.02	0.17	0.50	1.34	2.36	0.6	1.1	1.4	1.6	1.3
Other	0.05	0.45	1.16	2.79	5.23	1.3	2.9	3.1	3.3	2.8
Total Western Europe	0.64	2.52	4.47	11.00	30.16	17.9	15.8	12.2	13.2	16.2
Africa										
Liberia	0.01	0.13	0.79	2.45	3.66	0.3	0.8	2.2	2.9	2.0
Other	0.08	0.37	0.66	0.92	0.94	2.3	2.3	1.8	1.1	0.5
Total Africa	0.09	0.50	1.45	3.37	4.60	2.6	3.1	4.0	4.0	2.5
Pacific										
Australia	0.21	0.68	2.17	3.62	8.14	5.9	4.3	5.9	4.3	4.4
Other	0.07	0.25	0.35	0.62	1.18	2.0	1.5	1.0	0.7	0.6
Total Pacific	0.28	0.93	2.52	4.24	9.32	7.9	5.8	6.9	5.0	5.0
TOTAL	3.58	15.94	36.50	83.65	186.36	100.0	100.0	100.0	100.0	100.0

* Totals based on adding up annual investment amounts reported by the Ministry of Finance; figures may not add to totals because of rounding.

Source: Based on information from Japan, Ministry of Finance, *Koʻusai kinʼyūkyoku nempo*, Tokyo, 1982, 351–55; 1988, 519–23; 1989, 531–35.

Table 32. Exchange Rate Between Yen and United States Dollar, 1970–90 [1]

Year	Rate	Year	Rate
1970	360	1981	221
1971	351	1982	249
1972	303	1983	238
1973	271	1984	238
1974	291	1985	239
1975	292	1986	169
1976	297	1987	145
1977	269	1988	128
1978	211	1989	143
1979	219	1990	147 [2]
1980	227		

[1] Rates are the average market rate for the year.
[2] As of August 1990.

Source: Based on information from International Monetary Fund, *International Financial Statistics Yearbook, 1989,* Washington, 1989, 442–43; and "Prices and Trends," *Far Eastern Economic Review* [Hong Kong], August 30, 1990, 66.

Table 33. Trade Balance with Selected Countries,
Selected Years, 1960–88
(in millions of United States dollars)

Country	1960	1970	1980	1985	1988
Australia	−200	−28	−1,593	−2,073	−3,605
Britain	21	−449	1,828	2,906	6,439
Canada	−85	168	−2,287	−253	−1,884
China	−18	315	755	5,994	−383
Hong Kong	133	608	4,192	5,742	9,597
India	−15	−287	−99	407	278
Indonesia	40	−321	−9,709	−7,947	−6,443
Malaysia	−192	−253	−1,410	−2,162	−1,650
Philippines	−5	−79	−268	−306	−304
Singapore	73	336	2,404	2,266	5,972
South Korea	81	589	2,372	3,005	3,630
Soviet Union	−65	−140	918	1,322	364
Taiwan	38	449	2,853	1,639	5,611
Thailand	46	259	798	1,003	2,411
United States	−452	380	6,959	39,485	47,597
West Germany	−57	−958	3,255	4,010	·7,692

Source: Based on information from Bank of Japan, *Economic Statistics Annual, 1977,* Tokyo, 1978, 207–10; Bank of Japan, *Economic Statistics Annual, 1981,* 229; and Bank of Japan, *Economic Statistics Annual, 1988,* Tokyo, 1989, 247–50.

Table 34. Exports to Selected Countries,
Selected Years, 1960–88
(in millions of United States dollars)

Country	1960	1970	1980	1985	1988
Australia	144	589	3,389	5,379	6,680
Britain	120	480	3,782	4,723	10,632
Canada	119	563	2,437	4,520	6,424
China	3	569	5,078	12,477	9,476
Hong Kong	156	700	4,761	6,509	11,706
India	111	103	915	1,596	2,082
Indonesia	110	316	3,458	2,172	3,054
Malaysia	32	166	2,061	2,168	3,060
Philippines	154	454	1,683	937	1,740
Singapore	87	423	3,911	3,860	8,311
South Korea	100	818	5,368	7,097	15,441
Soviet Union	60	341	2,778	2,751	3,130
Taiwan	102	700	5,146	5,025	14,354
Thailand	118	449	1,917	2,030	5,162
United States	1,101	5,940	31,367	65,278	89,634
West Germany	66	550	5,756	6,938	15,793

Source: Based on information from Bank of Japan, *Economic Statistics Annual, 1977,* Tokyo,
1978, 207–10; Bank of Japan, *Economic Statistics Annual, 1981,* Tokyo, 1982, 229;
and Bank of Japan, *Economic Statistics Annual, 1988,* Tokyo, 1989, 247–50.

Table 35. Imports from Selected Countries,
Selected Years, 1960–88
(in millions of United States dollars)

Country	1960	1970	1980	1985	1988
Australia	344	617	6,982	7,452	10,285
Britain	99	929	1,954	1,817	4,193
Canada	204	395	4,724	4,773	8,308
China	21	254	4,323	6,483	9,859
Hong Kong	23	92	569	767	2,109
India	126	390	1,014	1,189	1,804
Indonesia	70	637	13,167	10,119	9,497
Malaysia	224	419	3,471	4,330	4,710
Philippines	159	533	1,951	1,243	2,044
Singapore	14	87	1,507	1,594	2,339
South Korea	19	229	2,996	4,092	11,811
Soviet Union	125	481	1,860	1,429	2,766
Taiwan	64	251	2,293	3,386	8,743
Thailand	72	190	1,119	1,027	2,751
United States	1,553	5,560	24,408	25,793	42,037
West Germany	123	1,508	2,501	2,928	8,101

Source: Based on information from Bank of Japan, *Economic Statistics Annual, 1977,* Tokyo,
1978, 207–10; Bank of Japan, *Economic Statistics Annual, 1981,* Tokyo, 1982, 229;
and Bank of Japan, *Economic Statistics Annual, 1988,* Tokyo, 1989, 247–50.

Table 36. Candidates Elected to House of Councillors by Party, Elections, 1956-89 [1]
(prefectural constituencies in parentheses)

Year	LDP [2]	JSP [3]	Kōmeitō	DSP [4]	JCP [5]	NLC [6]	Other	Independents	Total
1956	19 (42)	21 (28)	—	—	1 (1)	—	6 (0)	5 (4)	52 (75)
1959	22 (49)	17 (21)	—	—	1 (0)	—	5 (2)	7 (3)	52 (75)
1962	21 (48)	15 (22)	—	3 (1)	2 (1)	—	2 (0)	8 (4)	51 (76)
1965	25 (46)	12 (24)	9 (2)	2 (1)	2 (1)	—	0 (0)	2 (1)	52 (75)
1968	21 (48)	12 (16)	9 (4)	4 (3)	3 (1)	—	0 (0)	2 (3)	51 (75)
1971	21 (42)	11 (28)	8 (2)	4 (2)	5 (1)	—	0 (0)	1 (1)	50 (76)
1974	19 (43)	10 (18)	9 (5)	4 (1)	8 (5)	—	0 (1)	4 (3)	54 (76)
1977	18 (45)	10 (17)	9 (5)	4 (2)	3 (2)	1 (2)	2 (1)	3 (2)	50 (76)
1980	21 (48)	9 (13)	9 (3)	4 (2)	3 (4)	0 (0)	0 (0)	4 (6)	50 (76)
1983	19 (49)	9 (13)	8 (6)	4 (2)	5 (2)	1 (1)	4 (2)	0 (1)	50 (76)
1986	22 (50)	9 (11)	7 (3)	3 (2)	5 (4)	1 (0)	3 (0)	0 (6)	50 (76)
1989	15 (21)	20 (26)	6 (4)	2 (1)	4 (1)	0 (0)	3 (13) [7]	0 (10)	50 (76)

—Means party did not exist at time of election.
[1] Total membership of House of Councillors for a given year is sum of figures for two previous elections.
[2] Liberal Democratic Party.
[3] Japan Socialist Party.
[4] Democratic Socialist Party.
[5] Japan Communist Party.
[6] New Liberal Club.
[7] In July 1989 election, Rengō candidates won eleven prefectural seats.

Source: Based on information from Japan Foreign Press Center, *The Diet, Elections and Political Parties*, Tokyo, 1985, "Diet Election Results (1956-86)" addendum; and *Asahi nenkan, 1990* (Asahi Yearbook, 1990), Tokyo, 1990, 94.

Table 37. Candidates Elected to House of Representatives by Party, Elections, 1958-90

Year	LDP [1]	JSP [2]	Kōmeitō	DSP [3]	JCP [4]	NLC [5]	Other	Independents	Total
1958	287	166	—	—	1	—	1	12	467
1960	296	145	—	17	3	—	1	5	467
1963	283	144	—	23	5	—	0	12	467
1967	277	140	25	30	5	—	0	9	486
1969	288	90	47	31	14	—	0	16	486
1972	271	118	29	19	38	—	2	14	491
1976	249	123	55	29	17	17	0	21	511
1979	248	107	57	35	39	4	2	19	511
1980	284	107	33	32	29	12	3	11	511
1983	250	112	58	38	26	8	3	16	511
1986	300	85	56	26	26	6	4	9	512
1990	275	136	45	14	16	0	5	21	512

—Means party did not exist at time of election.
[1] Liberal Democratic Party.
[2] Japan Socialist Party.
[3] Democratic Socialist Party.
[4] Japan Communist Party.
[5] New Liberal Club.

Source: Based on information from Japan Foreign Press Center, *The Diet, Elections and Political Parties,* Tokyo, 1985; *Japan Times* [Tokyo], February 20, 1990, 1, and February 27, 1990, 1; and *Asahi nenkan, 1990* (Asahi Yearbook, 1990) Tokyo, 1990, 94.

Table 38. Order of Battle for Self-Defense Forces, 1989

Branch and Units	Personnel or Units
Ground Self-Defense Force	
Personnel	156,200
Armored division	1
Infantry divisions	12
Anti-aircraft artillery groups	8
Airborne brigades	1
Combined brigades	2
Artillery brigade	1
Artillery groups	4
Training brigade	1
Helicopter brigade	1
Helicopter squadrons	24
Antitank helicopter squadrons	2
Engineer brigades	5
Maritime Self-Defense Force Personnel	44,400
Air Self-Defense Force Personnel	46,400
Total Self-Defense Forces personnel	247,000
Total reserves	48,000

Source: Based on information from *The Military Balance, 1989-1990,* London, 1989, 162-64.

Table 39. *Major Ground Self-Defense Force Equipment, 1989*

Type and Description	Country of Origin	Estimated Number in Inventory
Armored vehicles		
T-61 medium tanks, 90mm gun, 35 tons, modeled on United States M-48 tanks ...	Japan	300
T-74 medium tanks, 105mm gun, 38 tons ..	–do–	870
T-82 and T-87 reconnaissance vehicles	–do–	230
T-60 and T-73 armored personnel carriers	–do–	700
Artillery		
105mm, 155mm, and 203mm guns and howitzers	United States Japan	500
T-74 105mm, T-75 155mm, and 203mm self-propelled howitzers	–do–	300
Mortars		
81mm and 107mm	United States	1,360
Rocket launchers		
75mm, Carl Gustav 84mm, and 106mm	Japan	2,750
T-75 130mm multiple rocket launchers	–do–	70
Air-defense guns		
35mm, 37mm, and 40mm	United States	75
Surface-to-surface missiles		
T-30	Japan	50
Antitank missiles		
T-64, T-79, and T-87	–do–	500
Surface-to-air guided missiles		
Stinger	United States	180
Improved HAWK	–do–	200
T-81 Tan	Japan	40
Aircraft		
Fixed-wing		
LR-1	Japan	17
TL-1	–do–	2
Attack helicopters		
AH-1S	United States	40
Transport helicopters		
AS-332L (VIP)	Japan	3
CH-47J	–do–	9
V-107/A	–do–	49
OH-6J/D	–do–	163
UH-1B/H	–do–	139
TH-55 (training)	–do–	20

Source: Based on information from *The Military Balance, 1989-90*, London, 1989, 162-64.

Table 40. Major Maritime Self-Defense Force Equipment, 1989

Type and Description	Country of Origin	Estimated Number in Inventory
Submarines (SS)		
Yōshio class with 533mm torpedo tubes, 7 with Harpoon surface-to-surface missiles ..	Japan	10
Uzushio class with 533mm torpedo tubes ...	–do–	4
Guided missile destroyers (DDG)		
Hatakaze class with SM–1MR Standard surface-to-air missile, Harpoon surface-to-surface missile, ASROC antisubmarine system, antisubmarine torpedo tubes, and 127mm guns	–do–	2
Tachikaze class with SM–1MR Standard surface-to-air missile, Harpoon surface-to-surface missile, ASROC antisubmarine system, antisubmarine torpedo tubes, and 127mm guns	–do–	3
Amatsukaze class with SM–1MR Standard surface-to-air missile, ASROC antisubmarine system, and antisubmarine torpedo tubes	–do–	1
Frigates with helicopters (FFH)		
Shirane class with HSS–2B Sea King antisubmarine warfare helicopters, ASROC antisubmarine system, antisubmarine torpedo tubes, and 127mm guns	–do–	2
Haruna class with HSS–2B Sea King antisubmarine warfare helicopters, ASROC antisubmarine system, antisubmarine torpedo tubes, and 127mm guns	–do–	2
Asagiri class with HSS–2B Sea King antisubmarine warfare helicopter, Harpoon surface-to-surface missiles, ASROC antisubmarine system, and antisubmarine torpedo tubes	–do–	4
Hatsuyuki class with HSS–2B Sea King antisubmarine warfare helicopter, Harpoon surface-to-surface missiles, ASROC antisubmarine system, and antisubmarine torpedo tubes	–do–	12
Frigates (FF)		
Takatsuki class with Harpoon surface-to-surface missiles, antisubmarine warfare rocket launcher, antisubmarine torpedo tubes, and 127mm guns	–do–	4
Yamagumo class with ASROC antisubmarine system, antisubmarine warfare rocket launcher, and antisubmarine torpedo tubes	–do–	6
Minegumo class with ASROC antisubmarine system, antisubmarine warfare rocket launchers, and antisubmarine torpedo tubes	–do–	3

Table 40.—Continued

Type and Description	Country of Origin	Estimated Number in Inventory
Yubari class with Harpoon surface-to-surface missiles, antisubmarine warfare rocket launchers, and antisubmarine torpedo tubes	Japan	2
Ishikari class with Harpoon surface-to-surface missiles, antisubmarine warfare rocket launcher, and antisubmarine torpedo tubes	–do–	1
Chikugo class with ASROC antisubmarine system and antisubmarine torpedo tubes ..	–do–	11
Isuzu class with antisubmarine warfare rocket launcher and antisubmarine torpedo tubes	–do–	2
Katori class with antisubmarine warfare rocket launcher and antisubmarine torpedo tubes	–do–	1
Patrol and coastal combatants	–do–	14
Mine warfare ships	–do–	47
Amphibious ships	–do–	6
Auxiliaries	–do–	12
Fixed-wing aircraft		
P-3C	United States	50
P-2J	–do–	29
EP-2J	–do–	2
UP-2J	–do–	3
U-36A	–do–	2
Queen Air 65	–do–	22
TC-90/UC-90	–do–	20
YS-11M	Japan	4
US-1/1A	–do–	9
KM-2	–do–	30
YS-11T	–do–	10
Helicopters		
HSS-2A/B	–do–	74
V-107/A	–do–	4
S-80	–do–	2
OH-6D/J	–do–	10
SH-60	United States	2
S-61	–do–	10

Source: Based on information from *The Military Balance, 1989–90,* London, 1989, 162–64.

Table 41. Major Air Self-Defense Force Equipment, 1989

Type and Description	Country of Origin	Estimated Number in Inventory
Ground-attack aircraft		
Mitsubishi F-1	Japan	74
Fighters		
F-15J/DJ	United States	120
F-4EJ	–do–	125
Reconnaissance aircraft		
RF-4EJ	–do–	15
Airborne early-warning aircraft		
E-2C	–do–	8
Transport aircraft		
C-1	Japan	27
YS-11	–do–	10
C-130H	United States	10
Surface-to-air missiles		
Nike-J (being replaced by Patriots)	–do–	180
Air-to-air missiles		
Sparrow	–do–	n.a.
Sidewinder	–do–	n.a.
Air-defense systems		
Base Air Defense Ground Environment (BADGE) control and warning units	Japan United States	28

n.a.—not available.

Source: Based on information from *The Military Balance, 1989–90,* London, 1989, 162–64.

Bibliography

Chapter 1

Arnesen, Peter Judd. *The Medieval Japanese Daimyo*. New Haven: Yale University Press, 1970.

Association of Japanese Geographers (ed.). *Geography of Japan*. Tokyo: Teikoku-Shoin, 1980.

Baerwald, Hans H., and Akira Hashimoto. "Japan in 1982: Doing Nothing Is Best?" *Asian Survey*, 23, No. 1, January 1983, 53–61.

Beasley, W.G. *Japanese Imperialism, 1874–1945*. Oxford: Clarendon Press, 1987.

_____. *The Meiji Restoration*. Stanford: Stanford University Press, 1972.

_____. *The Modern History of Japan*. New York: St. Martin's Press, 1981.

Beasley, W.G. (ed.). *Modern Japan: Aspects of History, Literature, and Society*. Berkeley: University of California Press, 1977.

Berry, Mary Elizabeth. *Hideyoshi*. Cambridge: Harvard University Press, 1982.

Bitō Masahide, and Watanabe Akio. *A Chronological Outline of Japanese History*. Tokyo: International Society for Educational Information, n.d.

Borton, Hugh. *Japan's Modern Century*. New York: Ronald Press, 1955.

Boxer, Charles R. *The Christian Century in Japan*. Berkeley: University of California Press, 1974.

Collcutt, Martin, Marius B. Jansen, and Isao Kumakura. *Cultural Atlas of Japan*. New York: Facts on File, 1988.

Connaughton, Richard M. *The War of the Rising Sun and Tumbling Bear: A Military History of the Russo-Japanese War, 1904–05*. London: Routledge, 1988.

Conroy, Hilary, Sandra T.W. Davis, and Wayne Patterson (eds.). *Japan in Transition: Thought and Action in the Meiji Era*. Rutherford, New Jersey: Fairleigh Dickinson University Press, 1984.

Cooper, Michael (ed.). *They Came to Japan: An Anthology of European Reports on Japan, 1543–1640*. (Center for Japanese and Korean Studies.) Berkeley: University of California Press, 1965.

Coox, Alvin D. *Nomonhan: Japan Against Russia, 1939*. (2 vols.) Stanford: Stanford University Press, 1985.

Craig, William. *The Fall of Japan*. New York: Dell, 1967.

Davis, Sandra T.W. *Intellectual Change and Political Development in Early Modern Japan: Ono Azusa, A Case Study.* Rutherford, New Jersey: Fairleigh Dickinson University Press, 1980.

Dower, John W. *Japanese History and Culture from Ancient to Modern Times: Seven Basic Bibliographies.* New York: Wiener, 1986.

Duus, Peter. *Feudalism in Japan.* (Studies in World Civilization Series.) New York: Knopf, 1969.

––––––. *The Rise of Modern Japan.* Boston: Houghton Mifflin, 1976.

Duus, Peter (ed.). *The Cambridge History of Japan, 6: The Twentieth Century.* New York: Cambridge University Press, 1988.

Duus, Peter, Ramon H. Meyers, and Mark R. Peattie (eds.). *The Japanese Informal Empire in China, 1895–1937.* Princeton: Princeton University Press, 1989.

Earle, Joe. *An Introduction to Japanese Prints.* London: Victoria and Albert Museum, 1980.

Elisseeff, Vadime. *Japan.* (Trans., James Hogarth.) (Ancient Civilizations Series.) London: Barrie and Jenkins, 1974.

Embree, Ainslie T. (ed.). *Encyclopedia of Asian History.* (4 vols.) New York: Scribner's in association with The Asian Society, 1988.

Etō Shinkichi, and Marius B. Jansen (trans. and eds.). *My Thirty-Three Years' Dream: The Autobiography of Miyazaki Tōten.* (Princeton Library of Asian Translations Series.) Princeton: Princeton University Press, 1982.

Farnsworth, Lee W. "Japan in 1980: The Conservative Resurgence," *Asian Survey,* 21, No. 1, January 1981, 70–83.

––––––. "Japan in 1981: Meeting the Challenges," *Asian Survey,* 22, No. 1, January 1982, 56–68.

Fletcher, William Miles, III. *The Search for a New Order: Intellectuals and Fascism in Prewar Japan.* Chapel Hill: University of North Carolina Press, 1982.

Goldsmith, Raymond W. *The Financial Development of Japan, 1868–1975.* New Haven: Yale University Press, 1983.

The Gossamer Years (Kagerō Nikki): *The Diary of a Noblewoman of Heian Japan.* (Trans., Edward G. Seidensticker.) (UNESCO Collection of Representative Works, Japanese Series.) Rutland, Vermont: Tuttle, 1964.

Grossburg, Kenneth Alan. *Japan's Renaissance: The Politics of the Muromachi Bakufu.* Cambridge: Harvard University Press, 1981.

Hall, John Whitney. *Japan: From Prehistory to Modern Times.* New York: Delacourt Press, 1970.

Hall, John Whitney, and Marius B. Jansen (eds.). *Studies in the Institutional History of Early Modern Japan.* Princeton: Princeton University Press, 1968.

Hall, John Whitney, and Jeffrey P. Maas (eds.). *Medieval Japan: Essays in Institutional History.* New Haven: Yale University Press, 1974.

Hall, John Whitney, Nagahara Keiji, and Kozo Yamamura (eds.). *Japan Before Tokugawa: Political Consolidation and Economic Growth, 1500 to 1650.* Princeton: Princeton University Press, 1981.

Hanley, Susan B., and Kozo Yamamura. *Economic and Demographic Change in Preindustrial Japan, 1600–1868.* Princeton: Princeton University Press, 1977.

Harada, Jiro. *A Glimpse of Japanese Ideals: Lectures on Japanese Art and Culture.* Tokyo: Kokusai Bunka Shinkokai (Society for International Cultural Relations), 1937.

Hsü, Immanuel C.Y. *The Rise of Modern China.* (4th ed.) New York: Oxford University Press, 1990.

Iriye, Akira. *After Imperialism: The Search for a New Order in the Far East, 1921–1931.* Cambridge: Harvard University Press, 1965.

Iriye, Akira, and Warren I. Cohen (eds.). *The United States and Japan in the Postwar World.* Lexington: University Press of Kentucky, 1989.

Irokawa Daikichi. *The Culture of the Meiji Period.* (Trans., Marius B. Jansen.) (Princeton Library of Asian Translations Series.) Princeton: Princeton University Press, 1985.

Iwao, Seiichi (ed.). *Biographical Dictionary of Japanese History.* (Trans., Burton Watson.) Tokyo: International Society for Educational Information, 1978.

Iwata, Mazakazu. *Ōkubo Toshimichi: The Bismarck of Japan.* Berkeley: University of California Press, 1964.

Jain, Rajendra Kumar. *The USSR and Japan, 1945–1980.* Atlantic Heights, New Jersey: Humanities Press, 1981.

Jansen, Marius B. "Japan." Pages 185–200 in Ainslie T. Embree (ed.), *Encyclopedia of Asian History,* 2. New York: Scribner's in association with The Asia Society, 1988.

———. *Sakamoto Ryōma and the Meiji Restoration.* Princeton: Princeton University Press, 1961.

Jansen, Marius B. (ed.). *The Cambridge History of Japan, 5: The Nineteenth Century.* New York: Cambridge University Press, 1988.

Jansen, Marius B., and Gilbert Rozman. *Japan in Transition: From Tokugawa to Meiji.* Princeton: Princeton University Press, 1986.

Jefferson, Roland M., and Alan E. Fusonie. *The Japanese Flowering Cherry Trees of Washington, D.C.: A Living Symbol of Friendship.* (National Arboretum Contribution No. 4.) Washington: Agricultural Research Service, Department of Agriculture, December 1977.

Kajima Morinosuke. *The Diplomacy of Japan, 1894–1922.* (2 vols.) Tokyo: Kajima Institute of International Peace, 1976.

Keene, Donald. *The Japanese Discovery of Europe, 1720–1830.* (Rev. ed.) Stanford: Stanford University Press, 1969.

Kidder, Edward. *Ancient Japan.* (The Making of the Past Series.) Oxford: Elsevier-Phaidon, 1977.

Kitahara, Michio. *Children of the Sun: The Japanese and the Outside World.* New York: St. Martin's Press, 1989.

Kodansha Encyclopedia of Japan. (9 vols.) Tokyo: Kodansha, 1983.

Kojiki. (Trans., Donald L. Philippi.) Princeton: Princeton University Press, 1969.

Krauss, Ellis S. "Japan in 1983: Altering the Status Quo?" *Asian Survey*, 24, No. 1, January 1984, 81–99.

Lebra, Joyce C. *Ōkuma Shigenobu: Statesman of Meiji Japan.* Canberra: Australian National Press, 1973.

Maas, Jeffrey P. *The Development of Kamakura Rule, 1180–1220: A History with Documents.* Stanford: Stanford University Press, 1979.

Maki, John M. *Government and Politics in Japan: The Road to Democracy.* New York: Praeger, 1962.

Maswood, Syed Javed. *Japan and Protection: The Growth of Protectionist Sentiment and the Japanese Response.* London: Routledge, 1989.

Morris, Ivan. *The Nobility of Failure: Tragic Heroes in the History of Japan.* London: Secker and Warburg, 1976.

————. *The World of the Shining Prince: Court Life in Ancient Japan.* Oxford: Oxford University Press, 1964.

Munro, Neil Gordon. *Prehistoric Japan.* Yokohama: 1911.

Murasaki Shikibu. *The Tale of Genji.* (Trans. and ed., Edward G. Seidensticker.) New York: Knopf, 1976.

Murdoch, James. *A History of Japan.* (3 vols., 6 pts.) New York: Ungar, 1964.

Nihongi: Chronicles of Japan from the Earliest Times to A.D. 697. (Trans., W.G. Aston.) London: Kegan Paul, Trench, Trübner, 1896.

Nish, Ian. *Japanese Foreign Policy, 1869–1942: Kasumigaseki to Miyakezaka.* London: Routledge and Kegan Paul, 1977.

Norman, E. Herbert. *Origins of the Modern Japanese State.* New York: Pantheon Books, 1975.

Oei, Lee T. "Japan's Annexation of Korea (1868–1910): An Exposition and Analysis of Japanese Perspectives," *American Asian Review*, 7, No. 3, Fall 1989, 49–98.

Oka, Yoshitake. *Konoe Fumimaro: A Political Biography.* (Trans., Shumpei Okamoto and Patricia Murray.) Tokyo: University of Tokyo Press, 1983.

Oliver, Robert T. "Meiji Japan: A Transformation Planned and Guided." Pages 26–53 in Robert T. Oliver (ed.), *Leadership in*

Asia: Persuasive Communication in the Making of Nations, 1850–1950. Newark: University of Delaware Press, 1989.

Packard, Jerrold M. *Sons of Heaven: A Portrait of the Japanese Monarchy.* New York: Scribner's, 1987.

Papinot, Edmond. *Historical and Geographical Dictionary of Japan.* Yokohama: Kelly and Walsh, 1910.

Perkins, Dorthy. *Encyclopedia of Japan: Japanese History and Culture, from Abacus to Zori.* New York: Facts on File, 1991.

The Pillow Book of Sei Shōnagon. (Trans. and ed., Ivan Morris.) (2 vols.) London: Oxford University Press, 1967.

Pittau, Joseph. *Political Thought in Early Meiji Japan, 1868–1889.* Cambridge: Harvard University Press, 1967.

Prange, Gordon W. *At Dawn We Slept: The Untold Story of Pearl Harbor.* New York: McGraw-Hill, 1981.

Reischauer, Edwin O. *Japan: The Story of a Nation.* (Rev. ed.) New York: Knopf, 1974.

_____. *The Japanese Today: Continuity and Change.* Cambridge: Belknap Press of Harvard University Press, 1988.

Reischauer, Edwin O., and Albert M. Craig. *Japan: Tradition and Transformation.* Boston: Houghton Mifflin, 1978.

Runkle, Scott F. *An Introduction to Japanese History.* Tokyo: International Society for Educational Information, 1976.

Sansom, George B. *A History of Japan to 1334.* Stanford: Stanford University Press, 1958.

_____. *A History of Japan, 1334–1615.* Stanford: Stanford University Press, 1961.

_____. *A History of Japan, 1615–1867.* Stanford: Stanford University Press, 1963.

Scalapino, Robert A. *Democracy and the Party Movement in Prewar Japan.* Berkeley: University of California Press, 1953.

Schuhmacher, Stephan, and Gert Woerner (eds.). *The Encyclopedia of Eastern Philosophy and Religion.* Boston: Shambhala, 1989.

Senda Minoru. "Territorial Possession in Ancient Japan: The Real and the Perceived." Pages 101–20 in Association of Japanese Geographers (ed.), *Geography of Japan.* Tokyo: Teikoku-Shoin, 1980.

Shillony, Ben-Ami. *Politics and Culture in Wartime Japan.* Oxford: Clarendon Press, 1981.

Shinoda, Minoru. *The Founding of the Kamakura Shogunate, 1180–1185: With Selected Translations from the Azuma Kagami.* New York: Columbia University Press, 1960.

Shulman, Frank Joseph (ed.). *Japan.* (World Bibliographical Series, No. 103.) Santa Barbara, California: ABC-Clio, 1989.

Storry, Richard. *A History of Modern Japan*. Baltimore: Penguin Books, 1960.

Suzuki, Daisetz T. *Zen and Japanese Culture*. (Bollingen Series, No. 64.) Princeton: Princeton University Press, 1959.

Takashige Susuma. "The System of Space in the Medieval Period." Pages 121–45 in Association of Japanese Geographers (ed.), *Geography of Japan*. Tokyo: Teikoku-Shoin, 1980.

Tanaka Migaku. "Prehistoric Melting Pot," *Look Japan* [Tokyo], 35, No. 402, September 1989, 32.

Tasker, Peter. *The Japanese: A Major Exploration of Modern Japan*. New York: Dutton, 1987.

Thayer, Nathaniel B. "Japan in 1984: The Nakasone Era Continues," *Asian Survey*, 25, No. 1, January 1985, 51–64.

Tiedemann, Arthur E. *Modern Japan: A Brief History*. Huntington, New York: Krieger, 1980.

Tiedemann, Arthur E. (ed.). *An Introduction to Japanese Civilization*. Lexington, Massachusetts: D.C. Heath, 1974.

Totman, Conrad. *Collapse of the Tokugawa Bakufu, 1862–1868*. Honolulu: University of Hawaii Press, 1980.

———. *Japan Before Perry: A Short History*. Berkeley: University of California Press, 1981.

Tsuda, Noritake. *Handbook of Japanese Art*. Rutland, Vermont: Tuttle, 1976.

Tsunoda, Ryusaku, Wm. Theodore de Bary, and Donald Keene (comps.). *Sources of Japanese Tradition*. (Records of Civilization, Sources, and Studies.) New York: Columbia University Press, 1958.

Umegaki, Michio. *After the Restoration: The Beginning of Japan's Modern State*. New York: New York University Press, 1988.

United States. Library of Congress. Asian Division. Japanese Section. "The Japanese Collection." (Pamphlet.) December 1989.

Varley, H. Paul. *Imperial Restoration in Medieval Japan*. (Studies of the East Asian Institute, Columbia University.) New York: Columbia University, 1971.

———. *A Syllabus of Japanese Civilization*. (2d ed.) New York: Columbia University Press, 1972.

Wakabayashi, Bob Tadashi. *Anti-Foreignism and Western Learning in Early-Modern Japan: The "New Theses" of 1825*. (Harvard East Asian Monographs, No. 126.) Cambridge: Harvard University Press, 1986.

Ward, Robert E. (ed.). *Political Development in Modern Japan*. Princeton: Princeton University Press, 1968.

Ward, Robert E., and Frank Joseph Shulman. *The Allied Occupation of Japan, 1945–1952: An Annotated Bibliography of Western*

Language Materials. Chicago: American Library Association, 1974. Reprint. Tokyo: Nihon Tosho Center, 1990.

Wray, Harry, and Hilary Conroy. *Japan Examined: Perspectives on Modern Japanese History.* Honolulu: University of Hawaii Press, 1983.

Yamamura, Kozo (ed.). *The Cambridge History of Japan, 3: Medieval Japan.* New York: Cambridge University Press, 1988.

Yoshihashi, Takehiko. *Conspiracy at Mukden: The Rise of the Japanese Military.* (Yale Studies in Political Science Series, No. 9.) New Haven: Yale University Press, 1963.

Chapter 2

Aronson, Bruce. "Compensation of Pollution-Related Health Damage in Japan," *Social Science and Medicine* [Exeter, Devon, United Kingdom], 27, No. 10, 1988, 1043–52.

Asano, Hitoshi, and Chizuru Saito. "Social Service Delivery and Social Work Practice for Japanese Elders," *Journal of Gerontological Social Work,* 12, Nos. 1–2, 1989, 131–52.

Ashihara Yoshinobu. *The Hidden Order: Tokyo Through the Twentieth Century.* (Trans. and adapt., Lynne E. Riggs.) Tokyo: Kodansha, 1988.

Association of Japanese Geographers (ed.). *Geography of Japan.* Tokyo: Teikoku-Shoin, 1980.

Austin, Lewis (ed.). *Japan: The Paradox of Progress.* New Haven: Yale University Press, 1976.

Bachnik, Jane M. "Family, Self and Society in Modern Japan." Unpublished paper, n.d.

———. "The Japanese Ie: An Organization of Self and Society." Unpublished paper, n.d.

———. "Recruitment Strategies for Household Succession: Rethinking Japanese Household Organziation," *Man* [London], 18, No. 1, 1983, 160–82.

Barshay, Andrew E. *State and Intellectual in Imperial Japan: The Public Man in Crisis.* Berkeley: University of California Press, 1988.

Befu, Harumi. *Japan: An Anthropological Introduction.* San Francisco: Chandler, 1971.

Bellah, Robert N. *Tokugawa Religion: The Values of Pre-industrial Japan.* Glencoe, Illinois: Free Press, 1957.

Benedict, Ruth. *The Chrysanthemum and the Sword.* Boston: Houghton Mifflin, 1946.

Bernstein, Gail Lee. *Haruko's World: A Japanese Farm Woman and Her Community.* Stanford: Stanford University Press, 1983.

Bestor, Theodore C. *Neighborhood Tokyo.* Stanford: Stanford University Press, 1989.

Blacker, Carmen. *The Catalpa Bow: A Study of Shamanistic Practices in Japan.* Boston: Allen and Unwin, 1986.

Buruma, Ian. *Behind the Mask: On Sexual Demons, Sacred Mothers, Transvestites, Gangsters, Drifters, and Other Japanese Cultural Heroes.* New York: Pantheon Books, 1984.

Caudill, William, and Helen Weinstein. "Maternal Care and Infant Behavior in Japan and America," *Psychiatry,* 32, No. 1, February 1969, 12–43.

Christopher, Robert C. *The Japanese Mind.* New York: Linden Press with Simon and Schuster, 1983.

Clark, Rodney. *The Japanese Company.* New Haven: Yale University Press, 1979.

Cole, Robert E. *Japanese Blue Collar: The Changing Tradition.* Berkeley: University of California Press, 1971.

Coleman, Samuel. *Family Planning in Japanese Society: Traditional Birth Control in a Modern Urban Culture.* Princeton: Princeton University Press, 1983.

Collcutt, Martin, Marius B. Jansen, and Isao Kumakura. *Cultural Atlas of Japan.* New York: Facts on File, 1988.

Cook, Alice H., and Hiroko Hayoshi. *Working Women in Japan: Discrimination, Resistence, and Reform.* Ithaca: New York State School of Industrial and Labor Relations, 1980.

Craig, Albert M., and Donald Shively (eds.). *Personality in Japanese History.* Berkeley: University of California Press, 1970.

Crome, Peter. "Japan Cleans Up," *World Press Review,* 31, No. 6, June 1984, 58.

Dalby, Liza Crihfield. *Geisha.* Berkeley: University of California Press, 1983.

Davis, Winston. *Dojo: Exorcism and Miracles in Modern Japan.* Stanford: Stanford University Press, 1980.

DeVos, George A. "Dimensions of Self in Japanese Culture." Pages 141–84 in Anthony J. Marsella, George A. DeVos, and Francis K. Hsu, (eds.), *Culture and Self: Asian and Western Perspectives.* London: Tavistock, 1985.

Dobbins, James. *Jodo Shinshu: Shin Buddhism in Medieval Japan.* Bloomington: Indiana University Press, 1989.

Doi Takeo. *The Anatomy of Dependence.* Tokyo: Kodansha, 1973.

_____. *The Anatomy of Self: The Individual in Japanese Society.* New York: Kodansha, 1986.

Dore, Ronald P. *City Life in Japan: A Study of a Tokyo Ward.* Berkeley: University of California Press, 1958.

Earhart, H. Byron. *Gedatsu-kai and Religion in Contemporary Japan: Returning to the Center.* Bloomington: Indiana University Press, 1989.

_____. "Japanese New Religions." Pages 53–73 in Richard Gid Powers and Hidetoshi Kato (eds.), *Handbook of Japanese Popular Culture.* New York: Greenwood Press, 1989.

_____. *Japanese Religion: Unity and Diversity.* (3d ed.) Belmont, California: Wadsworth, 1982.

Edwards, Walter. *Modern Japan Through Its Weddings: Gender, Person, and Society in Ritual Portrayal.* Stanford: Stanford University Press, 1989.

Fallows, Deborah. "Japanese Women," *National Geographic,* 177, No. 4, April 1990, 52–83.

Fields, George. *From Bonsai to Levi's: When West Meets East, An Insider's Surprising Account of How the Japanese Live.* New York: New American Library, 1985.

Fruin, Mark. *Kikkoman: Company, Clan, and Community.* Cambridge: Harvard University Press, 1983.

Fujie, Linda. "Popular Music." Pages 197–220 in Richard Gid Powers and Hidetoshi Kato (eds.), *Handbook of Japanese Popular Culture.* New York: Greenwood Press, 1989.

Fujii, Masao. "Maintenance and Change in Japanese Traditional Funerals and Death-Related Behavior," *Japanese Journal of Religious Studies,* 10, No. 1, March 1983, 39–64.

Gluck, Carol. *Japan's Modern Myths: Ideology in the Late Meiji Period.* Princeton: Princeton University Press, 1985.

Groth, Alexander J., and Larry L. Wade (eds.). *Public Policy Across Nations: Social Welfare in Industrial Settings.* Greenwich, Connecticut: JAI Press, 1985.

Guthrie, Stewart. *A Japanese New Religion: Rishō Kōseikai in a Mountain Hamlet.* (Michigan Monograph Series in Japan Studies, No. 1.) Ann Arbor: Center for Japanese Studies, University of Michigan, 1988.

Hamabata, Matt. *Crested Kimono: Power and Love in the Japanese Business Family.* Ithaca: Cornell University Press, 1990.

Hammel, E.A. "A Glimpse into the Demography of the Ainu," *American Anthropologist,* 90, No. 1, March 1988, 25–41.

Hane, Mikiso. *Peasants, Rebels, and Outcasts: The Underside of Modern Japan.* New York: Pantheon Books, 1982.

Hardacre, Helen. *Kurozumikyo and the New Religions of Japan.* Princeton: Princeton University Press, 1986.

_____. *Lay Buddhism in Contemporary Japan: Reiyukai.* Princeton: Princeton University Press, 1984.

_____. *Shintō and the State, 1868-1988.* (Studies in Church and State Series.) Princeton: Princeton University Press, 1989.

Hase, Toshio. "Japan's Growing Environmental Movement," *Environment*, 23, No. 2, March 1981, 14-20, 34-36.

Hendry, Joy. *Becoming Japanese: The World of the Pre-School Child* . Honolulu: University of Hawaii Press, 1986.

_____. *Marriage in Changing Japan.* London: Croom Helm, 1981.

_____. *Understanding Japanese Society.* New York: Croom Helm, 1987.

Hisako Hirota. "Japanese Women Today." (Pamphlet.) Tokyo: International Society for Educational Information, n.d.

Hori Ichirō, Ikuda Fujio, Wakimoto Tsuneya, and Yanagawa Keiichi (eds.). *Japanese Religion: A Survey by the Agency for Cultural Affairs.* (Trans., Yoshiya Abe and David Reid.) Tokyo: Kodansha, 1972.

Imamura, Anne E. *Urban Japanese Housewives: At Home and in the Community.* Honolulu: University of Hawaii Press, 1987.

International Society for Educational Information. *Facts about Japan: Religion.* Tokyo, n.d.

_____. *Facts about Japan: Sports.* Tokyo: n.d.

Irokawa Daikichi. *The Culture of the Meiji Period.* (Trans., Marius B. Jansen.) (Princeton Library of Asian Translations Series.) Princeton: Princeton University Press, 1985.

_____. "Popular Movements in Modern Japanese History." Pages 69-86 in Gavan McCormack and Yoshi Sugimoto (eds.), *The Japanese Trajectory: Modernization and Beyond.* Cambridge: Cambridge University Press, 1988.

Iwai, Noriko, and Susan O. Long. "Interpreting Differences in Japanese and American Husband-Wife Relationships." (Paper presented at the Annual Meeting of the Association for Asian Studies, Chicago, April 1990.).

Jansen, Marius B., and Gilbert Rozman. *Japan in Transition: From Tokugawa to Meiji.* Princeton: Princeton University Press, 1986.

Japan. Environment Agency. *Foreign Press Center White Paper on the Environment, 1989.* Tokyo: May 1989.

_____. Management and Coordination Agency. Statistics Bureau. *Nihon tōkei nenkan, Shōwa 63* (Japan Statistical Yearbook, 1988). Tokyo: Sōrifu, Tōkeikyoku, 1989.

_____. Ministry of Finance. *Seron Chosa Nenkan, Shōwa 63 Nenpo* (Public Opinion Survey Yearbook, 1989). Tokyo: 1989.

_____. Ministry of Health and Welfare. *Annual Report on Health and Welfare for 1983: The Trend of a New Era and Social Security.* Tokyo: October 1983.

_____. Ministry of Health and Welfare. *Foreign Press Center, Fiscal 1986: Report on Health and Welfare Administration.* Tokyo: June 1987.

_____. Ministry of Health and Welfare. *Foreign Press Center Outline of 1983: Basic Survey on Health and Welfare Administration.* Tokyo: February 1984.

_____. Ministry of Health and Welfare. *Foreign Press Center White Paper on Health and Welfare, 1987.* Tokyo: February 1988.

_____. Office of the Prime Minister. *Foreign Press Center Outline of the Results of the Third International Survey of Youth.* Tokyo: April 1984.

_____. Office of the Prime Minister. *Foreign Press Center Public Opinion Survey on Perception of Life.* Tokyo: August 1984.

_____. Office of the Prime Minister. *Foreign Press Center Public Opinion Survey on the Family and the Home.* Tokyo: January 1987.

_____. Office of the Prime Minister. *Foreign Press Center Public Opinion Survey on the Life of the Nation.* Tokyo: December 1988.

Jeremy, Michael, and M.E. Robinson. *Ceremony and Symbolism in the Japanese Home.* Honolulu: University of Hawaii Press, 1989.

Kalland, Arne. *Shingū: A Japanese Fishing Community.* (Scandanavian Institute of Asian Studies, Monograph Series, No. 44.) London: Curzon Press, 1981.

Keifer, Christie W. ''The Sanchi Zoku and the Evolution of the Metropolitan Mind.'' Pages 279–300 in Lewis Austin (ed.), *Japan: The Paradox of Progress.* New Haven: Yale University Press, 1976.

Kitagawa, Joseph. *Religion in Japanese History.* New York: Columbia University Press, 1966.

Knight, Richard V., and Gary Gappert (eds.). *Cities in a Global Society* (Urban Affairs Annual Reviews, No. 35.) Newbury Park, California: Sage, 1989.

Kodansha Encyclopedia of Japan. (9 vols.) Tokyo: Kodansha, 1983.

Kondo, Dorinne K. *Crafting Selves: Power, Gender, and Discourses of Identity in a Japanese Workplace.* Chicago: University of Chicago Press, 1990.

Krauss, Ellis S., Thomas P. Rohlen, and Patricia G. Steinhoff (eds.). *Conflict in Japan.* Honolulu: University of Hawaii Press, 1984.

Kumagai, Fumie. ''Filial Violence: A Peculiar Parent-Child Relationship in the Japanese Family Today,'' *Journal of Comparative Family Studies* [Alberta], 12, No. 3, Summer, 1981, 337–50.

Lebra, Joyce C., Joy Paulson, and Elizabeth Powers (eds.). *Women in Changing Japan.* (Westview Special Studies on China and East Asia.) Boulder, Colorado: Westview Press, 1976.

Lebra, Takie Sugiyama. *Japanese Women: Constraint and Fulfillment.* Honolulu: University of Hawaii Press, 1984.

————. "Self-Reconstruction in Japanese Religious Psychotherapy." Pages 269–83 in Anthony J. Marsella and Geoffrey M. White (eds.), *Cultural Conceptions of Mental Health and Therapy.* Dordrecht, Netherlands: Reidel, 1982.

Lebra, Takie Sugiyama, and William P. Lebra (eds.). *Japanese Culture and Behavior: Selected Readings.* (Rev. ed.) Honolulu: University of Hawaii Press, 1986.

Lent, John A. "Japanese Comics." Pages 221–42 in Richard Gid Powers and Hidetoshi Kato (eds.), *Handbook of Japanese Popular Culture.* New York: Greenwood Press, 1989.

Lock, Margaret. *East Asian Medicine in Urban Japan.* Berkeley: University of California Press, 1980.

————. "A Nation at Risk: Interpretations of School Refusal in Japan." Pages 377–414 in Margaret Lock and Deborah C. Gordon (eds.), *Biomedicine Examined.* Dordrecht, Netherlands: Kluwer Academic, 1988.

————. "Protests of a Good Wife and Wise Mother: The Medicalization of Distress in Japan." Pages 130–37 in Edward Norbeck and Margaret Lock (eds.), *Health, Illness, and Medical Care in Japan: Cultural and Social Dimensions.* Honolulu: University of Hawaii Press, 1987.

Lock, Margaret, and Deborah C. Gordon (eds.). *Biomedicine Examined.* Dordrecht, Netherlands: Kluwer Academic, 1988.

Long, Susan O. "Fame, Fortune and Friends: Constraints and Strategies in the Careers of Japanese Physicians." (Ph.D. dissertation.) Urbana: University of Illinois, 1979.

————. *Family Change and the Life Course in Japan.* (Cornell University East Asia Papers, 8756–5293, No. 44.) Ithaca: China-Japan Program, Cornell University 1987.

Long, Susan O., and Bruce D. Long. "Curable Cancers and Fatal Ulcers: Attitudes Toward Cancer in Japan." *Social Science and Medicine* [Exeter, Devon, United Kingdom], 16, No. 24, 1982, 2101–8.

Marsella, Anthony J., George A. DeVos, and Francis K. Hsu (eds.). *Culture and Self: Asian and Western Perspectives.* London: Tavistock, 1985.

Marsella, Anthony J., and Geoffrey M. White (eds.). *Cultural Conceptions of Mental Health and Theraphy.* Dordrecht, Netherlands: Reidel, 1982.

Martin, Linda G. "The Graying of Japan," *Population Bulletin,* 44, No. 12, July 1989, 1–41.

Masai, Yasuo. "Greater Tokyo as a Global City." Pages 153–63 in Richard V. Knight and Gary Gappert (eds.), *Cities in a Global Society.* (Urban Affairs Annual Reviews, No. 35.) Newbury Park, California: Sage, 1989.

Matsuzawa, Tessei. "Street Labor Markets, Day Laborers, and the Structure of Opposition." Pages 147–64 in Gavan McCormack and Yoshio Sugimoto (eds.), *The Japanese Trajectory: Modernization and Beyond.* New York: Cambridge University Press, 1988.

May, William R. "Sports." Pages 167–95 in Richard Gid Powers and Hidetoshi Kato (eds.), *Handbook of Japanese Popular Culture.* New York: Greenwood Press, 1989.

McCormack, Gavan, and Yoshio Sugimoto (eds.). *The Japanese Trajectory: Modernization and Beyond.* New York: Cambridge University Press, 1988.

McDonald, Keiko I. "Popular Film." Pages 97–116 in Richard Gid Powers and Hidetoshi Kato (eds.), *Handbook of Japanese Popular Culture.* New York: Greenwood Press, 1989.

McKean, Margaret A. *Environmental Protest and Citizen Politics in Japan.* Berkeley: University of California Press, 1981.

Metraux, Daniel A. *The History and Theology of Soka Gakkai: A Japanese New Religion.* (Studies in Asian Thought and Religion, No. 9.) Lewiston, New York: Mellen Press, 1988.

Miller, Alan S. "Three Reports on Japan and the Global Environment," *Environment,* 31, No. 6, July–August 1989, 25–29.

Moeran, Brian. "Individual, Group, and Seishin: Japan's Internal Cultural Debate," *Man* [London], 19, No. 2, 1984, 252–66. (Reprinted in Takie Sugiyama Lebra and William P. Lebra (eds.), *Japanese Culture and Behavior: Selected Readings.* (Rev. ed.) Honolulu: University of Hawaii Press, 1986.).

————. *Lost Innocence: Folk Craft and Potters of Onta, Japan.* Berkeley: University of California Press, 1984.

————. *Okubo Diary: Portrait of a Japanese Valley.* Stanford: Stanford University Press, 1985.

Moore, Richard. *Japanese Agriculture: Patterns of Rural Development.* Boulder, Colorado: Westview Press, 1990.

Morioka, Kiyomi. "Privatization of Family Life in Japan." Pages 63–74 in Harold Stevenson, Hiroshi Azuma, and Kenji Hakura (eds.), *Child Development and Education in Japan.* (Books in Psychology Series.) New York: Freeman, 1986.

————. *Religion in Changing Japanese Society.* Tokyo: University of Tokyo Press, 1975.

Nagashima, Nobuhiro, Masao Yamaguchi, Noboru Miyata, Kazuhiko Komatsu, and Teruo Sekimoto (eds.). "An Anthropological Profile of Japan," *Current Anthropology,* 28, No. 4, August–October 1987, S1–S91.

Nakane Chie. *Japanese Society*. Berkeley: University of California Press, 1970.

"Native Perspectives of Distance and the Anthropological Perspective of Culture," *Anthropological Quarterly*, 60, No. 1, 1987, 25–34.

Nikkei Biotechnology (ed.). *Biotechnology Guide to Japan, 1990–1991*. New York: Stockton Press, 1990.

Nishi, Kazuo, and Kazuo Hozumi. *What Is Japanese Architecture?* (Trans., H. Mack Horton.) Tokyo: Kondansha, 1985.

Noguchi, Paul H. *Delayed Departures, Overdue Arrivals: Industrial Familialism and the Japanese National Railways*. Honolulu: University of Hawaii Press, 1990.

Norbeck, Edward, and Margaret Lock (eds.). *Health, Illness, and Medical Care in Japan: Cultural and Social Dimensions*. Honolulu: University of Hawaii Press, 1987.

Ohnuki-Tierney, Emiko. *Illness and Culture in Contemporary Japan: An Anthropological View*. Cambridge: Cambridge University Press, 1984.

_____. *The Monkey as Mirror: Symbolistic Transformations in Japanese History and Ritual*. Princeton: Princeton University Press, 1987.

Oshima, Izumi. "Japan Draws a Line," *World Press Review*, 36, No. 11, November 1989, 18.

Ozawa, Martha N. *Women's Life Cycle and Economic Insecurity: Problems and Proposals*. New York: Greenwood Press, 1989.

Palmore, Erdman B., and Daisaku Maeda. *The Honorable Elders Revisited*. (Rev. ed.) Durham, North Carolina: Duke University Press, 1985.

Papinot, Edmond. *Historical and Geographical Dictionary of Japan*. Yokohama: Kelly and Walsh, 1910.

Park, Philip. "Japan Refuses Full Rights to Alien Residents," *Christian Century*, 107, No. 8, March 7, 1990, 236–37.

Patrick, Hugh T. (ed.). *Japanese Industrialization and Its Social Consequences*. Berkeley: University of California Press, 1976.

Pelzel, John C. "Human Nature in the Japanese Myths." Pages 29–56 in Albert M. Craig and Donald Shively (eds.), *Personality in Japanese History*. Berkeley: University of California Press, 1970.

Peterson, Michael R., and Larry L. Wade. "Environmental Pollution Policy in Japan: A Public Choice Hypothesis." Pages 71–90 in Alexander J. Groth and Larry L. Wade (eds.), *Public Policy Across Nations: Social Welfare in Industrial Settings*. Greenwich, Connecticut: JAI Press, 1985.

Plath, David W. *Long Engagements: Maturity in Modern Japan*. Stanford: Stanford University Press, 1980.

_____. "Resistance at Forty-eight: Male Pathways into Older Age in Modern Japan." (Paper presented at the Luxemborg Conference on Life Course Transitions and Aging, June 1979.)

Plath, David W. (ed.). *Work and Lifecourse in Japan*. Albany: State University of New York Press, 1983.

Plath, David W., and Jacquetta Hill. "The Reefs of Rivalry: Expertness and Competition among Japanese Shellfish Divers," *Ethnology*, 26, No. 3, July 1987, 151–63.

Population Reference Bureau. *World Population Data Sheet, 1989*. Washington: 1988.

Powers, Richard Gid, and Hidetoshi Kato (eds.). *Handbook of Japanese Popular Culture*. New York: Greenwood Press, 1989.

Reischauer, Edwin O. *The Japanese Today: Continuity and Change*. Cambridge: Belknap Press of Harvard University Press, 1988.

Robins-Mowry, Dorothy. *The Hidden Sun: Women of Modern Japan*. Boulder, Colorado: Westview Press, 1983.

Rohlen, Thomas P. *For Harmony and Strength: Japanese White Collar Organization in Anthropological Perspective*. Berkeley: University of California Press, 1974.

Sanuki, Toshio. "Changing Fortunes of Occupations in Japan," *Japanese Economic Studies* [Tokyo], 14, No. 2, Winter 1985–86, 3–29.

Schuhmacher, Stephan, and Gert Woerner (eds.). *The Encyclopedia of Eastern Philosophy and Religion*. Boston: Shambhala, 1989.

Shulman, Frank Joseph (ed.). *Japan*. (World Bibliographical Series, No. 103.) Santa Barbara, California: ABC-Clio, 1989.

Shūkyō nenkan, Shōwa 63 (Religion Yearbook, 1988). Tokyo: Kyosei, 1989.

Sievers, Sharon L. *Flowers in the Salt: The Beginnings of Feminist Consciousness in Modern Japan*. Stanford: Stanford University Press, 1983.

Smith, Charles. "Coming to Grips: Japan with Soviet Union on Disputed Islands," *Far Eastern Economic Review* [Hong Kong], 142, No. 52, December 29, 1988, 14.

———. "Four Bones of Contention: Moscow Recognizes Japan's Northern Islands Problem," *Far Eastern Economic Review* [Hong Kong], 141, No. 33, August 18, 1988, 24–25.

Smith, Robert J. *Ancestor Worship in Contemporary Japan*. Stanford: Stanford University Press, 1974.

———. *Japanese Society: Tradition, Self, and the Social Order*. Cambridge: Cambridge University Press, 1983.

———. *Kurusu: The Price of Progress in a Japanese Village, 1951–1975*. Stanford: Stanford University Press, 1978.

Smith, Robert J., and Ella Lury Wiswell. *The Women of Suye Mura*. Chicago: University of Chicago Press, 1982.

Sonoda Kyōichi. *Health and Illness in Changing Japanese Society*. Tokyo: University of Tokyo Press, 1988.

Steven, Rob. *Classes in Contemporary Japan.* Cambridge: Cambridge University Press, 1983.

Stevenson, Harold W., Hiroshi Azuma, and Kenji Hakuta (eds.). *Child Development and Education in Japan.* (A Series in Psychology, Center for Advanced Study in the Behavioral Sciences, Stanford.) New York: Freeman, 1986.

Stronach, Bruce. "Japanese Television." Pages 127–65 in Richard Gid Powers and Hidetoshi Kato (eds.), *Handbook of Japanese Popular Culture.* New York: Greenwood Press, 1989.

Sun, Margaret. "Japan Prodded on the Environment," *Science,* 241, No. 4862, July 15, 1988, 284.

Suzuki, Daisetz T. *Zen and Japanese Culture.* (Bollingen Series, No. 64.) Princeton: Princeton University Press, 1959.

Suzuki, Takao. "Language and Behavior in Japan: The Conceptualization of Personal Relations," *Japan Quarterly,* 23, No. 3, July–September 1976, 255–66. (Reprinted in Takie Sugiyama Lebra and William P. Lebra (eds.), *Japanese Culture and Behavior: Selected Readings.* (Rev. ed.) Honolulu: University of Hawaii Press, 1986.).

Tobin, Joseph J., David Y.H. Hu, and Dana H. Davidson. *Preschool in Three Cultures: Japan, China, and the United States.* New Haven: Yale University Press, 1989.

Tsuda, Hideo (ed.). *Japan 1990: An International Comparison.* (Japan Institute for Social and Economic Affairs.) Tokyo: Keizai Koho Center, 1990.

Tsunoda, Ryusaku, Wm. Theodore de Bary, and Donald Keene (comps.). *Sources of Japanese Tradition.* (Records of Civilization, Sources, and Studies.) New York: Columbia University Press, 1958.

Vogel, Ezra F. *Japan's New Middle Class.* (2d ed.) Berkeley: University of California Press, 1971.

Vogel, Suzanne H. "Professional Housewife: The Career of Urban Middle Class Japanese Women," *Japan Interpreter* [Tokyo], 12, No. 1, Winter 1978, 16–43.

Wagatsuma, Hiroshi, and George A. DeVos. *Heritage of Endurance: Family Patterns and Delinquency Formation in Urban Japan.* Berkeley: University of California Press, 1984.

White, James W. *The Sokagakkai and Mass Society.* Stanford: Stanford University Press, 1970.

White, Merry. *The Japanese Educational Challenge.* New York: Free Press, 1987.

Yoneyama, Toshinao. "Basic Notions in Japanese Social Relations." (Occasional Papers, 1, No. 3.), Richmond, Indiana: Institute for Education on Japan, Earlham College, 1989.

(Various issues of the following publications were also used in the preparation of this chapter: the Japan Insititute of Labor's *Japan Labor Bulletin* [Tokyo], 1981–89; *Japan Times* [Tokyo], 1989–90; *Mangajin,* 1990; and *New York Times,* 1987–90.)

Chapter 3

Abe, Yoshiya (ed.). *Non-University Sector Higher Education in Japan.* (Research Institute for Higher Education International Publication Series, No. 3.) Hiroshima: RIHE, Hiroshima University, 1989.

Adachi, Barbara Curtiss. "Bunraku Basics," *Japanese-American Society of Washington Bulletin,* 33, No. 8, September 1988, 1–5.

Addiss, Stephen. "The Role of Calligraphy in Japanese Society." Pages 30–37 in *Words in Motion: Modern Japanese Calligraphy: An Exhibition by the Library of Congress and the Yomiuri Shimbun, June 15, 1984–September 15, 1984.* Tokyo: Yomiuri Shimbun, 1984.

Amano, Ikuo. "Educational Crisis in Japan." Pages 23–43 in William K. Cummings, Edward R. Beauchamp, Shogo Ichikawa, Victor N. Kobayashi, and Morikazu Ushiogi (eds.). *Educational Policies in Crisis: Japanese and American Perspectives.* (Praeger Special Studies Series in Comparative Education.) New York: Praeger, 1986.

Anderson, Ronald S. *Education in Japan: A Century of Modern Development.* (United States Department of Health, Education, and Welfare, Office of Education, Publication No. 74–19110.) Washington: GPO, 1975.

_____. *Japan: Three Epochs of Modern Education.* (United States Department of Health, Education, and Welfare, Bulletin No. 11.) Washington: GPO, 1959.

Aoyama, San'u. "*Sho*: Artistic, Creative Calligraphy." Pages 26–29 in *Words in Motion: Modern Japanese Calligraphy: An Exhibition by the Library of Congress and the Yomiyuri Shimbun, June 15, 1984–September 15, 1984.* Tokyo: Yomiuri Shimbun, 1984.

Asahi Shimbun. "Bunkazai, kōkogaku, bunkashō" (Cultural Assets, Archaeology, Cultural Prizes). Pages 358–65 in *Asahi nenkan, 1989* (Asahi Yearbook, 1989). Tokyo: Asahi Shimbun, 1989.

Aso, Makoto, and Ikuo Amano. *Education and Japan's Modernization.* Tokyo: Japan Times, 1983.

August, Robert L. "Yobiko: Prep Schools for College Entrance in Japan." In Robert Leestma and Herbert Walberg (eds.),

Japanese Educational Productivity. Ann Arbor: Center for Japanese Studies, University of Michigan, forthcoming 1992.

Barrett, Gregory. *Archetypes in Japanese Films*. Selinsgrove, Pennsylvania: Susquehana University Press, 1989.

Bock, Audie. "Japanese Film Genres." Pages 53–62 in Wimal Dissanayake (ed.), *Cinema and Cultural Identity: Reflections on Film from Japan, India, and China*. Lanham, Maryland: University Press of America, 1988.

Bognar, Botond. *Contemporary Japanese Architecture: Its Development and Challenge*. New York: Van Nostrand Reinhold, 1985.

Boocock, Sarane Spence. "Controlled Diversity: An Overview of the Japanese Preschool System," *Journal of Japanese Studies*, 15, No. 1, Winter 1989, 41–65.

Bornoff, Nick. "Juzo Itami, Film Director: The Gentle Art of Savage Satire," *PHP Intersect* [Tokyo], 4, No. 7, July 1988, 28–32.

Boxer, Charles R. *The Christian Century in Japan*. Berkeley: University of California Press, 1974.

Brazell, Karen (ed.). *Twelve Plays of the Noh and Kyōgen Theaters*. (Cornell University East Asia Papers, No. 50.) Ithaca: Cornell University Press, 1988.

Brisard, Pierre. "Tange Kenzō: A Half Century of Architectural Achievements," *Japan Quarterly* [Tokyo], 31, No. 2, April–June 1984, 193.

Brown, Sidney DeVere. "Yasunari Kawabata (1899–1972)," *World Literature Today*, 62, No. 3, Summer 1988, 375–79.

Carpenter, Juliet Winters. "Tawara Machi: To Create Poetry Is to Live," *Japan Quarterly* [Tokyo], 36, No. 2, April–June 1989, 193–99.

Chambers, Gail S., and William K. Cummings. *Profiting from Education: Japan-United States Educational Ventures in the 1980s*. New York: Institute of International Education, 1990.

Copeland, Rebecca L. "Uno Chiyo: Not Just 'A Writer of Illicit Love,'" *Japan Quarterly* [Tokyo], 35, No. 2, April–June 1988, 176–82.

Cummings, Milton C., Jr., and Richard S. Katz (eds.). *The Patron States: Government and the Arts in Europe, North America, and Japan*. New York: Oxford University Press, 1987.

Cummings, William K. *The Changing Academic Marketplace and University Reform in Japan*. (Harvard Studies in Sociology.) New York: Garland, 1990.

Cummings, William K., Edward R. Beauchamp, Shogo Ichikawa, Victor N. Kobayashi, and Morikazi Ushiogi (eds.). *Educational*

Policies in Crisis: Japanese and American Perspectives. (Praeger Special Studies Series in Comparative Education.) New York: Praeger, 1986.

Cummings, William K., Ikuo Amano, and Kazuyuki Kitamura, (eds.). *Changes in the Japanese University: A Comparative Perspective*. New York: Praeger, 1979.

"Daigaku nyūshiki senta—Shiken to nyūshiki kaikaku" (Center for University Entrance Examination—Testing and Entrance Examination Reform), *Chūtō kyōiku shiryō* (Secondary Education Data) [Tokyo], No. 541, September 1988, 75–77.

DeCoker, Gary. "Japanese Preschools: Academic or Nonacademic." Pages 45–58 in James J. Shields (ed.), *Japanese Schooling: Patterns of Socialization, Equality, and Political Control*. University Park: Pennsylvania State University Press, 1989.

Desser, David. *Eros plus Massacre: An Introduction to the Japanese New Wave Cinema*. Bloomington: Indiana University Press, 1988.

DeVito, Alfred, and Masakata Ogawa, "A Japanese Education," *Science and Children*, 26, No. 7, April 1989, 21–23.

Dissanayake, Wimal (ed.). *Cinema and Cultural Identity: Reflections on Films from Japan, India, and China*. Lanham, Maryland: University Press of America, 1988.

Dore, Ronald P. *Education in Tokugawa Japan*. Ann Arbor: Center for Japanese Studies, University of Michigan, 1984.

———. "The Legacy of Tokugawa Education." Pages 99–131 in Marius B. Jansen (ed.), *Changing Japanese Attitudes toward Modernization*. Princeton: Princeton University Press, 1969.

Dower, John W. *The Elements of Japanese Design: A Handbook of Family Crests, Heraldry, and Symbolism*. New York: Walker/Weatherhill, 1971.

Duke, Benjamin. *The Japanese School: Lessons for Industrial America*. New York: Praeger, 1986.

Duus, Masayo. "Totto-chan: The Little Girl at the Window," *Journal of Japanese Studies*, 10, No. 1, Winter 1984, 236–40.

Earle, Joe. *An Introduction to Japanese Prints*. London: Victoria and Albert Museum, 1980.

Frampton, Kenneth. *New Waves of Japanese Architecture*. (Catalog No. 10.) New York: Institute for Architecture and Urban Studies, 1979.

Fujioka Hiroyasu. "The Search for Japanese Architecture in the Modern Ages," *Japan Foundation Newsletter* [Tokyo], 15, No. 3, December 1987, 1–9.

Gessel, Van C. "Echoes of Feminine Sensibility in Literature," *Japan Quarterly* [Tokyo], 35, No. 4, October–December 1988, 410–16.

————. "Fumiko Enchi as Narrator," *World Literature Today*, 62, No. 3, Summer 1988, 380–85.

Goff, Janet E. "Performing Noh at the Vatican," *Japan Quarterly* [Tokyo], 36, No. 2, April–June 1989, 201–6.

Goldberg, Marilyn. "Recent Trends in Special Education in Tokyo." Pages 176–84 in James J. Shields (ed.), *Japanese Schooling: Patterns of Socialization, Equality, and Political Control*. University Park: Pennsylvania State University Press, 1989.

Goodman, David G. *Japanese Drama and Culture in the 1960s: The Return of the Gods*. New York: Sharpe, 1988.

————. "Theater in Japan Today," *World Literature Today*, 62, No. 3, Summer 1988, 418–20.

Griffin, Jane T. "Master Ceramics/Creative Prints: Two Characteristic Aspects of Contemporary Japanese Art." (Paper presented at Columbia University Faculty Seminar, May 9, 1980.)

Harada, Jiro. *A Glimpse of Japanese Ideals: Lectures on Japanese Art and Culture*. Tokyo: Kokusai Bunka Shinkokai (Society for International Cultural Relations), 1937.

Haruna Akira. "Non-Fiction." Pages 37–41 in Isoda Kōichi (ed.), *A Survey of Japanese Literature*. (Trans., Robert N. Huey.) Tokyo: Japan P.E.N. Club, 1984.

Hata, Hiromu. "Kyōiku kaikaku itsukasei" (The Five-Day School Week in the Educational Reform). Pages 138–47 in Kanzen Shūkyū Futatsukasei Doyōbi o Shakai no Kyūjitsu ni Suru Suishin Kaigi (Congress for the Promotion of Saturdays as Holidays and Full Two-Day Weekends) (ed.), *Yutori no jidai e* (Toward an Era of Leisure). Tokyo: Nihon Hyōronsha, 1989.

Havens, Thomas R.H. *Artist and Patron in Postwar Japan: Dance, Music, Theatre, and the Visual Arts, 1955–1980*. Princeton: Princeton University Press, 1982.

————. "Government and the Arts in Contemporary Japan." Pages 333–49 in Milton C. Cummings, Jr. and Richard S. Katz (eds.), *The Patron State: Government and the Arts in Europe, North America, and Japan*. New York: Oxford University Press, 1987.

Hawkins, John. "Educational Demands and Institutional Response: Dowa Education in Japan." Pages 194–211 in James J. Shields (ed.), *Japanese Schooling: Patterns of Socialization, Equality, and Political Control*. University Park: Pennsylvania State University Press, 1989.

Hayashiya Seizō. *Japanese Ceramics Today: Masterworks from the Kikachi Collection*. Tokyo: Japan Foundation, 1983.

Hendry, Joy. *Becoming Japanese: The World of the Pre-School Child*. Honolulu: University of Hawaii Press, 1986.

Hinton-Braaten, Kathleen. "Kawai Kanjiro," *Orientations* [Hong Kong], 14, No. 11, November 1983, 28–41.

Honda, Isao. *Monsho: Family Crests for Symbolic Design.* Rutland, Vermont: Japan Publications Trading Company, 1963.

Horio Teruhisa. *Educational Thought and Ideology in Modern Japan.* (Ed. and trans., Steven Platzer.) Tokyo: University of Tokyo Press, 1988.

Hosaka Nobuto. "Gakkō itsuka-sei to doyō jiyūhi no ma ni" (Between the Five-Day School Week and Free Saturdays). Pages 126–36 in Kanzen Shūkyū Futatsukasei Doyōbi o Shakai no Kyūjitsu Ni Suru Suishin Kaigi (Congress for the Promotion of Saturdays as Holidays and Full Two-Day Weekends) (ed.), *Yutori no jidai e* (Toward an Era of Leisure). Tokyo: Nihon Hyōronsha, 1989.

Hughes, David W. "Japanese Folksong Today: Visits to the Heart's Home Town," *Japan Foundation Newsletter* [Tokyo], 17, No. 3, January 1990, 9–13.

Inoue Yasushi. "The Writer's Role in the Nuclear Age," *Japan Quarterly* [Tokyo], 31, No. 2, April–June 1984, 126–28.

Inoura Yoshinobu, and Kawatake Toshio. *The Traditional Theater of Japan.* (The Japan Foundation.) Tokyo: Weatherhill, 1981.

Inui Yoshiaki (ed.). *Gendai togei no kishu* (Standard Bearers as Modern Ceremics). (Gendai Nihon no togei Series, No. 4.) Tokyo: Kodansha, 1982.

Irokawa Daikichi. *The Culture of the Meiji Period.* (Trans., Marius B. Jansen.) (Princeton Library of Asian Translations Series.) Princeton: Princeton University Press, 1985.

Isoda Kōichi. "The Novel." Pages 7–15 in Isoda Kōichi (ed.), *Survey of Japanese Literature Today.* (Trans., Robert N. Huey.) Tokyo: Japan P.E.N. Club, 1984.

Iwamoto, Yoshio. "Yoshikichi Furui: Exemplar of the 'Introverted Generation,'" *World Literature Today,* 62, No. 3, Summer 1988, 385–90.

Iwamoto, Yoshio, and Samuel Yoshiko Yokochi. "Introduction to Japanese Writing, 1974–1984," *Literary Review,* 30, No. 2, Winter 1987, 133–40.

Iwanaga, Masaya. "Finance and Administration in the Non-University Sector." Pages 45–55 in Yoshiya Abe (ed.), *Non-University Sector Higher Education in Japan.* (Research Institute for Higher Education International Publication Series, No. 3.) Hiroshima: RIHE, Hiroshima University, 1989.

————. "Quantitative Transitions in the Post Secondary Education System." Pages 12–20 in Yoshiya Abe (ed.), *Non-University Sector Higher Education in Japan.* (Research Institute for Higher

Education International Publications Series, No. 3.) Hiroshima: RIME, Hiroshima University, 1989.

Izumi Katsuhiko. "Whither the Traditions of Local Pottery?" *Japan Quarterly* [Tokyo], 36, No. 3, July–September 1989, 287–93.

Jagusch, Sybille A. (ed.). *Japanese Children's Books and Television Today: Papers from a Symposium at the Library of Congress, November 18–19, 1987.* Washington: Library of Congress, 1990.

Jansen, Marius B. (ed.). *Changing Japanese Attitudes Toward Modernization.* Princeton: Princeton University Press, 1969.

Japan. Management and Coordination Agency. Statistics Bureau. *Nihon tōkei nenkan, Shōwa 63* (Japan Statistical Yearbook, 1988). Tokyo: Sōrifu, Tōkeikyoku, 1989.

Japan. Agency for Cultural Affairs. *Cultural Affairs and Administration in Japan, 1988.* Tokyo: 1988.

_____. Ministry of Education, Science, and Culture. *Education in Japan: A Graphic Presentation.* Tokyo: 1982.

_____. Ministry of Education, Science, and Culture. *Gakkō kihon chōsa hōkokusho, 1989* (Fundamental School Survey, 1989). Tokyo: 1989.

_____. Ministry of Education, Science, and Culture. *Monbu jihō* (Education Review) [Tokyo], No. 1353, October 1989, 64.

_____. Ministry of Education Science, and Culture. *Monbu tōkei yoran* (Statistical Abstract of Education). Tokyo: 1989.

_____. Ministry of Education, Science, and Culture. *Monbushō, 1989.* Tokyo: 1989.

_____. Ministry of Education, Science, and Culture. *Outline of Education in Japan, 1989.* Tokyo: Asian Cultural Centre for UNESCO, 1989.

_____. Ministry of Education, Science and Culture. *Shōgakkō shidōsho, dōtokuhen* (Guidebook for Teachers: Elementary School Moral Education). Tokyo: 1989.

_____. Ministry of Education, Science and Culture. *Waga kuni no shakai kyōiku* (Social Education in Japan). Tokyo: 1988.

_____. Ministry of Education, Science, and Culture. Agency for Cultural Affairs. *Cultural Affairs and Administration in Japan, 1988.* Tokyo: 1988.

_____. Ministry of Education, Science, and Culture. Agency for Cultural Affairs. *Waga kuni no bunka to bunkagyosei* (Japanese Culture and Cultural Policy). Tokyo: 1988.

_____. Ministry of Education, Science, and Culture. Higher Education Bureau. University Education Division. "Shōwa 63-nendo kokkō (shi)ritsu daigaku nyūshiki senbatsu jisshi jōkyō ni tsuite" (The Situation of College Entrance Examinations and Selection in the National, Other Public (and Private) Universities in Japan in 1988), *Chūtō kyōiku shiryō* (Secondary Education Data) [Tokyo], No. 540, August 1988, 74–77.

————. Ministry of Education, Science, and Culture. Minister's Secretariat. Research and Statistics Division. *Statistical Abstract of Education, Science and Culture.* Tokyo: 1988.

————. Ministry of Education, Science, and Culture. Minister's Secretariat. Statistics Bureau. *Shōwa 60-nen jido, seito gakkōgai gakushū katsudō* (1985 Survey of Students' Out-of-School Learning Activities). Tokyo: 1986.

————. Ministry of Education, Science, and Culture. Special Education Division. Elementary and Secondary Education Bureau. *Special Education in Japan.* Tokyo: 1988.

————. National Public Safety Commission. National Police Agency. (Untitled advertisement warning youth to stay away from drugs.) *Shūkan Asahi* [Tokyo], July 22, 1988, 54.

————. Secretariat of the Prime Minister. Public Information Department. *Shūki nyūgaku ni kansuru seron chōsa* (Public Opinion on Autumn School Entrance). Tokyo: 1988.

Japan Cultural and Trade Center. "Noh and Kyogen Lecture and Demonstration." Tokyo, April 10, 1988, 8 pp.

Jerome, Marty. "TRONs Global Net," *PC Computing,* 2, No. 12, December 1989, 178.

Kami Shōichirō. "Children's Literature." Pages 31–36 in Isoda Kōichi (ed.), *A Survey of Japanese Literature.* (Trans., Robert N. Huey.) Tokyo: Japan P.E.N. Club, 1984.

Kaneko Motohisa. *Financing Higher Education in Japan.* (Research Institute for Higher Education International Publications Series, No. 4.) Hiroshima: RIHE, Hiroshima University, 1989.

————. "The Role of Government in Japanese Higher Education: Issues and Prospects." Pages 21–38 in *The Role of Government in Asian Higher Education Systems: Issues and Prospects, Reports from the Fourth International Seminar on Higher Education in Asia.* Hiroshima: Research Insitute for Higher Education, Hiroshima University, 1988.

Kaneko Motohisa (comp.). *Kōtō kyōiku tokei dētashū* (Higher Education Statistical Data Collection). Hiroshima: Research Institute for Higher Education, Hiroshima University, 1989.

Kanzen Shūkyū Futatsukasei Doyōbi o Shakai no Kyūjitsu ni Suru Suishin Kaigi (Congress for the Promotion of Saturdays as Holidays and Full Two-Day Weekends) (ed.). *Yutori no jidai e* (Toward an Era of Leisure). Tokyo: Nihon Hyōronsha, 1989.

Kawamoto Saburō. *New Trends in Japanese Cinema.* (Orientation Seminars on Japan, No. 21.), Tokyo: Japan Foundation, 1986.

Keene, Donald. *The Pleasures of Japanese Literature.* (Companions to Asian Studies Series.) New York: Columbia University Press, 1988.

_____. *World Within Walls: Japanese Literature of the Pre-modern Era, 1600-1867.* New York: Grove Press, 1978.

Keene, Donald (ed.). *Anthology of Japanese Literature.* New York: Grove Press, 1960.

_____. *Modern Japanese Literature.* New York: Grove Press, 1960.

Kida Hiroshi. *School Lunch Programme in Japan.* (Occasional Papers, No. 2.). Tokyo: International Institute for Educational Research, 1982.

Kishibe Shigeo. *The Traditional Music of Japan.* Tokyo: Japan Foundation, 1982.

Kitamura, Kazuyuki. "Decline and Reform of Education in Japan: A Comparative Perspective." Pages 153-70 in William K. Cummings, Edward R. Beauchamp, Shogo Ichikawa, Victor N. Kobayashi, and Morikazi Ushiogi (eds.), *Educational Policies in Crisis.* (Praeger Special Studies Series in Comparative Education.) New York: Praeger, 1986.

_____. "The Structure of the Post Secondary Education System." Pages 20-25 in Yoshiya Abe (ed.), *Non-University Sector Higher Education in Japan.* (Research Institute for Higher Education International Publication Series, No. 3.) Hiroshima: RIHE, Hiroshima University, 1989.

Kitamura, Kazuyuki, and Ryōichi Kuroha. "The Present Status of Higher Education." Pages 1-11 in Yoshiya Abe (ed.), *Non-University Sector Higher Education in Japan.* (Research Institute for Higher Education International Publication Series, No. 3.) Hiroshima: RIHE, Hiroshima University, 1989.

Kobayashi, Tetsuya. "The Internationalization of Japanese Education," *Comparative Education* [Oxford], 22, No. 1, 1986, 65-71.

Kodansha Encyclopedia of Japan. (9 vols.) Tokyo: Kodansha, 1983.

Kodansha Staff (eds.). *Contemporary Japanese Prints.* Tokyo: Kodansha, 1989.

Kokuritsu Daigaku Kyōkai, et al. (eds.). *Shōwa 64 nendoban kokkōritsu daigaku gaidobukku* (1989 Guide to the National and other Public Universities in Japan). Tokyo: Dai-ichi Hōki, 1989.

Konaka, Yōtarō. "Japanese Atomic-Bomb Literature," *World Literature Today,* 62, No. 3, Summer 1988, 420-24.

Konishi Jun'ichi. "The Art of Renga," *Journal of Japanese Studies,* 2, No. 1, Autumn 1975, 33-61.

Koplos, Janet. "Mono-ha and the Power of Materials: Japan's Vital New Sculpture Bridges East and West," *New Art Examiner,* 15, June 1988, 29-32.

Kukusai Bunka Kaikan (ed.). *Modern Japanese Literature in Translation: A Bibliography.* Tokyo: Kodansha, 1979.

Kuniyoshi Kazuko. *An Overview of the Contemporary Japanese Dance Scene.* (Orientation Seminars on Japan, No. 19.), Tokyo: Japan Foundation, 1985.

Leestma, Robert, Robert August, Betty George, and Lois Peak. *Japanese Education Today.* (United States Department of Education. Office of Educational Research and Improvement.) Washington: GPO, 1987.

Lepkowski, Wil. "Japan's Science and Technology Aim Toward Globalization," *Chemical and Engineering News,* 67, No. 19, May 8, 1989, 7-14.

Lewis, Catherine C. "From Indulgence to Internalization: Social Control in the Early School Years," *Journal of Japanese Studies,* 15, No. 1, Winter 1989, 139-57.

Malm, William. "Some of Japan's Music and Musical Principles." Pages 48-62 in Elizabeth May (ed.), *Musics of Many Cultures: An Introduction.* Berkeley: University of California Press, 1980.

Matsubara, Tasuya (ed.). *Haha to ko no asobi* (Games for Mothers and Children). (2 vols.) Tokyo: Fure-beru Kan, 1985.

Matsui, Masato, Minako I. Song, Tomoyoshi Kurakawa, and Albert Ikoma. *Japanese Performing Arts: An Annotated Bibliography.* Honolulu: Center for Asian and Pacific Studies, Council for Japanese Studies, University of Hawaii, 1981.

May, Elizabeth (ed.). *Musics of Many Cultures: An Introduction.* Berkeley: University of California Press, 1980.

Mertel, Timothy. "Surinomo: Ukiyo-e Refined," *Arts of Asia* [Hong Kong], 17, No. 5, September-October 1987, 80-88.

Mikami, Tsugio. *The Art of Japanese Ceramics.* (Heibonsha Survey of Japanese Art Series, No. 29.) Tokyo: Heibansha; New York: Weatherhill, 1972.

Miki Tamon. *Masterpieces in the Museum of Modern Art of Japan since 1950: Sculpture.* Tokyo: Keishosha, 1985.

Minemura, Toshiaki. "A Blast of Nationalism in the Seventies." Pages 16-24 in *Art in Japan Today,* 2. Tokyo: Japan Foundation, 1984.

Miner, Earl, Horoko Odagiri, and Robert E. Morrell. *The Princeton Companion to Classical Japanese Literature.* Princeton: Princeton University Press, 1985.

Miyashita, Nohuo. "East Meets West in the Theatre," *Japan Quarterly* [Tokyo], 35, No. 2, April-June 1988, 184-90.

Mori Hideo. "Theatre." Pages 24-30 in Isoda Kōichi (ed.), *A Survey of Japanese Literature.* (Trans., Robert N. Huey.) Tokyo: Japan P.E.N. Club, 1984.

Munroe, Alexandra (ed.). *Contemporary Japanese Art in America.* New York: Japan Society, 1987.

_____. *Shinohara.* (Catalog of an Exhibition at Japan House.) New York: Japan Society, 1982.

Nakahara Yūsuke. "Japanese Contemporary Art and its Milieu: Focusing on the Seventies." Pages 11–15 in *Art in Japan Today,* 2. Tokyo: Japan Foundation, 1984.

Narumiya, Chie. "Opportunities for Girls and Women in Japanese Education," *Comparative Education* [Oxford], 22, No. 1, 1986, 47–52.

Nishi, Kazuo, and Kazuo Hozumi. *What is Japanese Architecture?* (Trans., H. Mack Horton.) Tokyo: Kondansha, 1985.

Oe Atsuyoshi. "The Employment of Graduates of Non-University Sector Institutions." Pages 56–65 in Yoshiya Abe (ed.), *Non-University Sector Higher Education in Japan.* (Research Institute for Higher Education International Publication Series, No. 3.) RIHE, Hiroshima: Hiroshima University, 1989.

Ōe Kenzaburō. "Japan's Dual Identity," *World Literature Today,* 62, No. 3, Summer 1988, 359–69.

_____. "Postwar Japanese Literature and the Contemporary Impasse," *Japan Foundation Newsletter* [Tokyo], 14, No. 3, October 1986, 1–6.

Ōhashi Ryōsuke. "Philosophical Reflections on Japan's Cultural Context," *Japan Echo* [Tokyo], 16, No. 1, Spring 1989, 71–78.

Ōka, Makoto. "Contemporary Japanese Poetry," *World Literature Today,* 62, No. 3, Summer 1988, 414–17.

Okada, Shinoda, and Tsutaka: Three Pioneers of Abstract Painting in 20th Century Japan. Washington: Phillips Collection, 1979.

Ōtsuka Eiji. "Comic-Book Formula for Success," *Japan Quarterly* [Tokyo], 35, No. 3, July–September 1988, 287–91.

Ozaki Hotsuki. "Popular Literature." Pages 16–23 in Isoda Kōichi (ed.), *A Survey of Japanese Literature.* (Trans., Robert N. Huey.) Tokyo: Japan P.E.N. Club, 1984.

Papadakis, Maria. *The Science and Technology Resources of Japan: A Comparison with the United States.* (Surveys of Science Resources.) Washington: Division of Science Resource Studies, National Science Foundation, 1988.

Passin, Herbert. *Society and Education in Japan.* Tokyo: Kodansha, 1982.

Peak, Lois. "Learning to Become Part of the Group: The Japanese Child's Transition to Preschool Life," *Journal of Japanese Studies,* 15, No. 1, Winter 1989, 93–123.

Powers, Richard Gid, and Hidetoshi Kato (eds.). *Handbook of Japanese Popular Culture.* New York: Greenwood Press, 1989.

Rayns, Tony. "New Mornings and Afternoon Breezes: The Rise of Young Japanese Film Makers," *Japan Foundation Newsletter* [Tokyo], 17, No. 1, August 1989, 7-8, 17.

Reischauer, Edwin O. *Japan: The Story of a Nation.* (First Tuttle Edition.) Rutland, Vermont: Tuttle, 1971.

————. *The Japanese.* Cambridge: Belknap Press of Harvard University Press, 1977.

Richie, Donald. "Japanese Cinema." Pages 19-31 in Wimal Dissanayake (ed.), *Cinema and Cultural Identity: Reflections on Films from Japan, India, and China.* Lanham, Maryland: University Press of America, 1988.

Riggs, Lynne E. "The Idioms of Contemporary Japan XVIII: Ranjuku jidai." *Japan Interpreter* [Tokyo], 11, No. 4, Spring 1977, 541-49.

Rimer, J. Thomas. *A Reader's Guide to Japanese Literature.* Tokyo: Kodansha, 1988.

Rimer, J. Thomas (ed.). *Multiple Meanings: The Written Word in Japan, Past, Present, and Future: A Selection of Papers on Japanese Language and Culture and Their Translations Presented at the Library of Congress.* Washington: Asian Division, Library of Congress, 1986.

Rimer, J. Thomas, and Keiko McDonald. *Teaching Guide for Japanese Literature on Film.* New York: Japan Society, 1989.

Rohlen, Thomas P. *Japan's High Schools.* Berkeley: University of California Press, 1983.

Rohlen, Thomas P., et al. "Symposium: Social Control and Early Socialization," *Journal of Japanese Studies,* 15, No. 1, Winter 1989, 1-157.

Ross, Michael Franklin. *Beyond Metabolism: The New Japanese Architecture.* (Architectural Record Books.) New York: McGraw-Hill, 1978.

Rubinger, Richard. *Private Academies of Tokugawa Japan.* Princeton: Princton University Press, 1982.

Saeki Shōichi. "Hidden Dimensions in Modern Japanese Literature." (Orientation Seminars on Japan, No. 18.), Tokyo: Japan Foundation, 1985.

————. "Japanese Culture in Seventeen Syllables," *Japan Echo* [Tokyo], 16, No. 1, Spring 1989, 79-84.

Sakurai, Emiko. "Japan's New Generation of Writers," *World Literature Today,* 62, No. 3, Summer 1988, 403.

Sansom, George B. *Japan: A Short Cultural History.* New York: Appleton-Century-Crofts, 1962.

Satō Tadao. "Change in the Image of Mother in Japanese Cinema and Television." Pages 63-69 in Wimal Dissanayake (ed.),

Cinema and Cultural Identity: Reflections on Film From Japan, India, and China. Lanham, Maryland: University Press of America, 1988.

_____. "The Multilayered Nature of the Tradition of Acting in Japanese Cinema." Pages 45–52 in Wimal Dissanayake (ed.), *Cinema and Cultural Identity: Reflections on Film from Japan, India, and China*. Lanham, Maryland: University Press of America, 1988.

_____. "The New Flowering of Japanese Films," *Japan Foundation Newsletter* [Tokyo], 11, No. 3, September 1983, 1–6.

Sawada Toshio. "Kokusai-teki ni mita waga kuni no kyōiku suijun" (Japan's Educational Level Seen Internationally), *Kyōiku to jōhō* (Education and Information) [Tokyo], No. 373, April 1989, 8–13.

Segraves, Julia. "The Lacquer Work of Suzuki Mustumi," *Arts of Asia* [Hong Kong], 17, No. 5, September–October 1987, 109–15.

Senda Akihiko. "Experiments in Cross-Cultural Theatre," *Japan Quarterly* [Tokyo], 36, No. 3, July–September 1989, 311–14.

_____. "Metamorphoses in Contemporary Japanese Theatre: Life-size and More-than-life-size." (Orientation Seminars on Japan, No. 22.), Tokyo: Japan Foundation, 1986.

Sengoku Tamotsu, et al. (eds.). *Nichi Bei chūgakusei hahaoya hōkokusho, 1985* (Report on Middle School Students and Their Mothers in the United States and Japan, 1985). Tokyo: Nihon Seishōnen Kenkyusho and Seimei Hoken Bunka Senta, 1985.

Shibata Minao, and Tokumaru Yoshihiko. "Cross Currents in Japanese Music: Japan's Musical Substructure," *Japan Echo* [Tokyo], 15, No. 1, Spring 1988, 71–76.

Shields, James J. (ed.). *Japanese Schooling: Patterns of Socialization, Equality, and Political Control*. University Park: Pennsylvania State University Press, 1989.

Shimahara, Nobuo. "Toward the Equality of a Japanese Minority: The Case of Burakumin," *Comparative Education* [Oxford], 20, No. 3, 1984, 339–53.

"Shōwa 63 nendō gogaku shidō nado o okonau gaikoku seinen shochi jigyō (JET puroguranu) ni tsuite" (On the 1988 JET Program to Invite Foreign Youth for such Activities as Language Teaching). *Chūtō kyōiku shiryō* (Secondary Education Data) [Tokyo], No. 9, 1988, 78–79.

Shozo Kawai (ed.). *Contemporary Japanese Prints*. Tokyo: Kodansha, 1983.

Shulman, Frank Joseph (ed.). *Japan*. (World Bibliographical Series, No. 103.) Santa Barbara, California: ABC-Clio, 1989.

Simmons, Cyril. *Growing Up and Going to School in Japan: Tradition and Trends.* Bristol, Pennsylvania: Open University Press, 1990.

Sipe, Jeffery R. "Making Films All in the Name of Making Friends," *Far Eastern Economic Review* [Hong Kong], 141, No. 34, August 25, 1988, 34–35.

Smith, Laurence. *Contemporary Japanese Prints: Symbols of a Society in Transition.* New York: Harper and Row, 1985.

Stevenson, Harold W., et al. "Learning to Read in Japan." Pages 217–35 in Harold W. Stevenson, Hiroshi Azuma, and Kenji Hakuta (eds.), *Child Development and Education in Japan.* (A Series in Psychology, Center for Advanced Study in the Behavioral Sciences, Stanford.) New York: Freeman, 1986.

Stevenson, Harold W., Hiroshi Azuma, and Kenji Hakuta (eds.). *Child Development and Education in Japan.* New York: Freeman, 1986.

Stewart, David B. *The Making of a Modern Japanese Architecture: 1868 to Present.* Tokyo: Kodansha, 1987.

Stronach, Bruce. "Japanese Television." Pages 127–65 in Richard Gid Powers and Hidetoshi Kato (eds.), *Handbook of Japanese Popular Culture.* New York: Greenwood Press, 1989.

Sugawara, Nobuo. "Takano Etsuko: Protector of Fine Cinema," *Japan Quarterly* [Tokyo], 36, No. 3, July–September 1989, 306–10.

Swartz, John, Joshua Hammer, Michael Reese, and Bill Powell. "Japan Goes Hollywood," *Newsweek,* 114, No. 15, October 9, 1989, 62–67.

Tachi, Akira. "The Content of Education in the Non-University Sector." Pages 26–34 in Yoshiya Abe (ed.), *Non-University Sector Higher Education in Japan.* (Research Institute for Higher Education International Publication Series, No. 3.) Hiroshima: RIHE, Hiroshima University, 1989.

Tada, Michitaro. "The Destiny of Samurai Films." Pages 33–43 in Wimal Dissanayake (ed.), *Cinema and Cultural Identity: Reflections on Films from Japan, India, and China.* Lanham, Maryland: University Press of America, 1988.

Takashina Shūji. "Japan and the Avant-Garde," *Japan Foundation Newsletter* [Tokyo], 14, No. 4, December 1986, 1–8.

Takashina Shūji, J. Thomas Rimer, and Gerald D. Bolas. *Paris in Japan: The Japanese Encounter with European Painting.* (Catalog of a exhibition.) Tokyo: Japan Foundation, 1987.

Takashina Shūji, Yoshiaki Tono, and Nakahara Yūsuke (eds.). *Art in Japan Toady.* Tokyo: Japan Foundation, 1974.

Takaya, Ted T. (ed. and trans.). *Modern Japanese Drama: An Anthology.* New York: Columbia University Press, 1979.

Tange Kenzō. "In Search of New Architecture," *Japan Quarterly* [Tokyo], 31, No. 4, October–December 1984, 406–9.

Tazawa Yutaka (ed.). *Biographical Dictionary of Japanese Art.* Tokyo: International Society for Educational Information, 1981.

Tobin, Joseph J., David Y.H. Hu, and Dana H. Davidson. *Preschool in Three Cultures: Japan, China, and the United States.* New Haven: Yale University Press, 1989.

Tsuda, Noritake. *Handbook of Japanese Art.* Rutland, Vermont: Tuttle, 1976.

Tsukada, Mamoru. "Institutionalized Supplementary Education in Japan: The Yobiko and Ronin Student Adaptations," *Comparative Education* [Oxford], 24, No. 3, 1988, 285–303.

Tsunoda, Ryusaku, Wm. Theodore de Bary, and Donald Keene (comps.) *Sources of Japanese Tradition.* (Records of Civilization, Sources, and Studies.) New York: Columbia University Press, 1958.

Tsurumi, Shunsuke. *A Cultural History of Postwar Japan, 1945–1980.* London and New York: KPI, 1987.

Tsuruta Kin'ya. "The Women on the other Side: Modern Japanese Literature, Search for the Prostitute Bodhisattva," *Japan Foundation Newsletter* [Tokyo], 13, No. 2, August 1985, 1–8.

Ueda, Makoto. *Modern Japanese Poets.* Stanford: Stanford University Press, 1983.

Uenami Wataru. "The Characteristics of Japanese Postwar Music." (Orientation Seminars on Japan, No. 20.) Tokyo: Japan Foundation, 1985.

United States. Library of Congress., *Words in Motion: Modern Japanese Calligraphy: An Exhibition by the Library of Congress and the Yomiuri Shimbun, June 15, 1984–September 15, 1984.* Tokyo: Yomiuri Shimbun, 1984.

University of the Air, 1989. Chiba: The University of the Air, 1989.

Uyehara, Cecil H. "The Rite of Japanese Calligraphy and the Modern Age," *Oriental Art* [Richmond, Surrey, United Kingdom]. (New Series, No. 33.) Summer 1987, 174–82.

Wada Takashi. "Dovtoyevsky's *The Idiot* in Tokyo," *Japan Quarterly* [Tokyo], 36, No. 3, July–September 1989, 315–19.

Wheeler, Donald F. "Japan's Postmodern Student Movement." Pages 194–211 in William K. Cummings, Ikuo Amano, and Kazuyuki Kitamura (eds.), *Changes in the Japanese University: A Comparative Perspective.* New York: Praeger, 1979.

Wysocki, Bernard, Jr. "Japanese Producer Sets Sights on Hollywood and Broadway," *Asian Wall Street Journal Weekly* [Hong Kong], December 25, 1989, 9.

Yanagisawa Yasumasa. "Namikawa Banri: Photographing the Silk Road," *Japan Quarterly* [Tokyo], 35, No. 4, October–December 1988, 428–31.

Yasuda Yasei. "Tokyo On and Under the Bay," *Japan Quarterly* [Tokyo], 35, No. 2, April–June 1988, 118–26.

Yawata Kazuo. "Why and Where to Relocate the Capital," *Japan Quarterly* [Tokyo], 35, No. 2, April–June 1988, 127–32.

Yoshida Kōzō. *Enamelled Porcelain of Modern Japan.* Tokyo: National Museum of Modern Art, 1979.

Yoshida, Sanraku. "An Interview with Kenzaburō Ōe," *World Literature Today,* 62, No. 3, Summer 1988, 369–74.

Zakō, Jun. "International Tenor: Ichihara Tarō," *Japan Quarterly* [Tokyo], 36, No. 1, January–March 1989, 92–94.

(Various issues of the following publications were also used in the preparation of this chapter: the Bank of Japan's *Economic Statistics Annual* [Tokyo], 1977–89; the Ministry of Education, Science, and Culture's *Monbu jihō* [Tokyo], 1989, and its *Statistical Abstract of the Ministry of Education, Science, and Culture,* 1980–89; *Japan Architect* [Tokyo], 1980–89; *Japan Times Weekly* [Tokyo], 1988–89; *Japan Times Weekly Magazine* [Tokyo], 1988–89; *Japan Update* [Tokyo], 1988–89; *Look Japan* [Tokyo], 1987–89; *New York Times,* 1980–89; and *Washington Post,* 1980–89.)

Chapter 4

Abegglen, James C., and George Stalk, Jr. *Kaisha: The Japanese Corporation.* New York: Basic Books, 1985.

Alexander, Arthur J. *Comparative Innovation in Japan and in the United States.* Santa Monica, California: Center for U.S.-Japan Relations, RAND, 1990.

Adams, Thomas Francis Merton, and Iwao Hoshii. *A Financial History of New Japan.* Tokyo: Kodansha, 1972.

Allen, G.C. *Japan's Economic Policy.* New York: Holmes and Meier, 1980.

_____. *A Short Economic History of Modern Japan.* (4th ed.) New York: St. Martin's Press, 1981.

Anchordoguy, Marie. *Computers, Inc.: Japan's Challenge to IBM.* (Harvard East Asian Monographs, No. 144.) Cambridge: Harvard University Press, 1990.

"Annual Review of Japanese Industry," *Journal of Japanese Trade and Industry* [Tokyo], 9, No. 1, January–February 1990, 2–39.

Ballon, Robert J. (ed.). *Marketing in Japan.* (Rev. ed.), Tokyo: Kodansha, 1973.

Ballon, Robert J., and Iwao Tomita. *The Financial Behavior of Japanese Corporations.* Tokyo: Kodansha, 1988.

Barnds, William J. (ed.). *Japan and the United States: Challenges and Opportunities.* (Council on Foreign Relations Books.) New York: New York University Press, 1979.

Belassa, Bela, and Marcus Noland. *Japan in the World Economy.* Washington: Institute for International Economics, 1988.

Blaker, Michael. *Japanese International Negotiating Style.* (Studies of the East Asian Institute, Columbia University.) New York: Columbia University Press, 1977.

Boltho, Andrea. *Japan: An Economic Survey, 1953–1973.* (Economies of the World Series.) London: Oxford University Press, 1974.

Brokenbrenner, Martin, and Yasukichi Yasuba. "Economic Welfare." Pages 111–24 in Kozo Yamamura and Yasukichi Yasuba (eds.), *The Political Economy of Japan, 2: The Domestic Transformation.* Stanford: Stanford University Press, 1987.

Burks, Ardath W. *Japan: A Postindustrial Power.* (3d ed., rev.) Boulder, Colorado: Westview Press, 1991.

Burstein, Daniel. "Rising Sun in Wall Street: How Japanese Money and Firms Are Moving In," *New York,* 20, No. 9, March 2, 1987, 32–38.

———. *Yen! Japan's New Financial Empire and Its Threat to America.* New York: Fawcett Columbine, 1990.

Chalmers, Norma J. *Industrial Relations in Japan: The Peripheral Workforce.* (The Nissan Institute/Routledge Japanese Studies Series.) London: Routledge, 1989.

Clark, Rodney. *The Japanese Company.* New Haven: Yale University Press, 1979.

Cusumano, Michael A. *The Japanese Automobile Industry.* (Harvard East Asian Monographs, No. 122.) Cambridge: Harvard University Press, 1985.

DeMente, Boye. *The Japanese Way of Doing Business.* (Rev. ed.) Engelwood Cliffs, New Jersey: Prentice-Hall, 1981.

Denison, Edward F., and William K. Chung. *How Japan's Economy Grew So Fast: The Sources of Postwar Expansion.* Washington: Brookings Institution, 1976.

Destler, I.M., and Hideo Sato (eds.). *Coping with U.S.-Japanese Economic Conflicts.* Lexington, Massachusetts: Lexington Books, 1982.

Deutsch, Mitchell F. *Doing Business with the Japanese.* New York: New American Library, 1984.

Dore, Ronald P. *British Factory, Japanese Factory: The Origins of National Diversity in Industrial Relations.* Berkeley: University of California Press, 1973.

Dreyfus, Joel. "Fear and Trembling in the Colossus," *Fortune International* [Tokyo], 115, No. 7, March 30, 1987, 32–36.

Drucker, Peter F. "What We Can Learn from Japanese Management." Pages 30–37 in staff of *Harvard Business Review* (eds.), *How Japan Works.* Cambridge: Harvard University Press, 1981.

"Economic Trends," *Mitsubishi Bank Review* [Tokyo], 20, No. 1, January 1987, 6.

Ellington, Lucien. "Intercultural Contact: The Japanese in Rutherford County, Tennessee." *Occasional Papers of the Virginia Consortium for Asian Studies,* 4, Spring 1987, 26–34.

Europa Year Book, 1989: A World Survey. London: Europa, 1989.

"Finance: Timid Giants: Japanese Institutional Investors," *Tokyo Business Today* [Tokyo], 6, No. 8, August 1987, 42–47.

Frank, Isaiah (ed.). *The Japanese Economy in International Perspective.* Baltimore: Johns Hopkins University Press, 1975.

Fruin, W. Mark. *Kikkoman: Company, Clan, and Community.* (Harvard Studies in Business History, No. 35.) Cambridge: Harvard University Press, 1983.

Gibney, Frank. *Miracle by Design: The Real Reasons Behind Japan's Economic Success.* New York: Times Books, 1982.

Gordon, Andrew. *The Evolution of Labor Relations in Japan: Heavy Industry, 1853–1955.* (Harvard East Asian Monographs, No. 117.) Cambridge: Harvard University Press, 1985.

Haitani, Kanji. *The Japanese System: An Institutional Overview.* Lexington, Massachusetts: Lexington Books, 1976.

Halloran, Richard. *Japan: Image and Realities.* New York: Knopf, 1969.

Hein, Laura E. *Fueling Growth: The Energy Revolution and Economic Policy in Postwar Japan.* (Harvard East Asian Monographs, No. 147.) Cambridge: Harvard University Press, 1990.

Henderson, Dan Fenno. *Foreign Enterprise in Japan: Laws and Policies.* (Studies in Foreign Investment and Economic Development.) Chapel Hill: University of North Carolina Press, 1973.

Ho, Alfred K. *Japan's Trade Liberalization in the 1960s.* White Plains, New York: International Arts and Sciences Press, 1973.

Hofheinz, Roy, and Kent Calder E. *The Eastasia Edge.* New York: Basic Books, 1982.

Ishizu Hideo. "The Missing Link: Transportation: Honshū-Shikoku Bridges," *Look Japan* [Tokyo], 34, No. 387, June 1988, 26.

Japan. Defense Agency. *Defense of Japan, 1989.* Tokyo: 1989.

————. Foreign Press Center. *Food and Agriculture in Japan*. (About Japan Series, No. 7.) Tokyo: 1988.

————. Foreign Press Center. *Labor in Japan*. Tokyo, 1988.

————. Management and Coordination Agency. Statistics Bureau. *Nihon tōkei nenkan, Shōwa 61* (Japan Statistical Yearbook, 1986). Tokyo: Sōrifu, Tōkeikyoku, 1987.

————. National Personnel Authority. Bureau of Compensation. *Nippon 1987: JETRO Business Facts and Figures*. Tokyo: 1987.

————. *Nippon 1989: JETRO Business Facts and Figures*. Tokyo, 1989.

Japan Broadcasting Corporation. "This is NHK." (Brochure.) Tokyo, Nippon Hōsō Kyōkai, 1987.

Japan Economic Institute of America. *Japan Economic Survey*. Washington: October 1989.

Japanese Center for International Exchange. *The Silent Power: Japan's Identity and World Role*. Tokyo: Simul Press, 1976.

"Japanese Utilize Postal Savings." *Japan Economic Journal* [Tokyo], 3, No. 9, February 24, 1990, 5.

Johnson, Chalmers. *MITI and the Japanese Miracle: The Growth of Industrial Policy, 1925–75*. Stanford: Stanford University Press, 1982.

Kaplan, Morton A., and Mushakōji Kinhide (eds.). *Japan, America, and the Future World Order*. New York: Free Press, 1976.

Kodansha Encyclopedia of Japan. (9 vols.) Tokyo: Kodansha, 1983.

Komatsu, Nobuyuki, Tohru Yoshikawa, and Akio Nakahara. "History of Shinkansen in 25 Years and Future Projects," *Japanese Railway Engineering* [Tokyo], 29, No. 2 (111), September 1989, 1–5.

Komiya, Ryūtarō. *The Japanese Economy: Trade, Industry, and Government*. Tokyo: University of Tokyo Press, 1990.

Komiya, Ryūtarō, Masahiro Okuno, and Kotaro Suzumura (eds.). *Industrial Policy of Japan*. Tokyo: Academic Press of Japan, 1989.

Kurian, George T. *Facts on File: Japan*. New York: Facts on File, 1989.

Latz, Gil. *Agricultural Development in Japan: The Land Improvement District in Concept and Practice*. (Geography Research Paper, No. 225.) Chicago: Committee on Geographical Studies, University of Chicago, 1989.

Lee, Chung H., and Ippei Yamazawa (eds.). *The Economic Development of Japan and Korea: A Parallel with Lessons*. New York: Praeger, 1990.

Lincoln, Edward J. *Japan: Facing Economic Maturity*. Washington: Brookings Institution, 1988.

Lockwood, William Wirt (ed.). *The State and Economic Enterprise in Japan: Essays in the Political Economy of Growth.* Princeton: Princeton University Press, 1965.

Magaziner, Ira C., and Thomas M. Hout. *Japanese Industrial Policy.* Berkeley: Institute of International Studies, University of California, 1980.

Malik, Michael (ed.). *Asia 1990 Yearbook.* Hong Kong: Far Eastern Economic Review, 1990.

Maswood, Syed Javed. *Japan and Protection: The Growth of Protectionist Sentiment and the Japanese Response.* London: Routledge, 1989.

Mead, Christopher. "Second Japanese Miracle on the Horizon." *Creative Computing,* 23, No. 8, August 1987, 1–83.

Metraux, Daniel A. *The Japanese Economy and the American Businessman.* (Mellen Studies in Business, No. 5.) Lewiston, New York: Mellen Press, 1989.

Morishima, Michio. *Why Has Japan Succeeded?: Western Technology and the Japanese Ethos.* New York: Cambridge University Press, 1982.

Morita, Akio. *Made in Japan.* New York: Dutton, 1986.

Moritani Masanori. *Japanese Technology: Getting the Best for the Least.* (Trans., Simul International.) Tokyo: Simul Press, 1982.

Morley, James W. *Dilemmas of Growth in Prewar Japan.* (Studies in the Modernization of Japan, No. 6.) Princeton: Princeton University Press, 1971.

Mushakōji Kinhide. "Nihon bunka to Nihon gaikō" (Japanese Culture and Japanese Diplomacy). Pages 31–47 in Mushakōji Kinhide (ed.), *Kokusai Seiji to Nihon* (International Politics and Japan). Tokyo: Tanryusha, 1967.

Nakamura, Takafusa. *The Postwar Japanese Economy: Its Development and Structure.* (Trans., Jacqueline Kaminski.) Tokyo: University of Tokyo Press, 1981.

Ohkawa, Kazushi, and Miyohei Shinohara (eds.), *Patterns of Japanese Economic Development: A Quantitative Appraisal.* (Economic Growth Center and Council on East Asian Studies, Yale University.) New Haven: Yale University Press, 1979.

Okimoto, Daniel I. *Between MITI and the Market: Japanese Industrial Policy for High Technology.* Stanford: Stanford University Press, 1989.

Ōkita Saburō. *The Developing Economies and Japan.* Tokyo: University of Tokyo Press, 1980.

Ouchi, William G. *Theory Z: How American Businessmen Can Meet the Japanese Challenge.* Reading, Massachusetts: Addison-Wesley, 1981.

Patrick, Hugh T., and Thomas P. Rohley. "Small-Scale Family Enterprises." Pages 331–32 in Kozo Yamamura and Yasukichi Yasuba (eds.), *The Political Economy of Japan, 2: The Domestic Transition.* Stanford: Stanford University Press, 1987.

Patrick, Hugh T., and Henry Rosovsky (eds.). *Asia's New Giant: How the Japanese Economy Works.* Washington: Brookings Institution, 1976.

Reischauer, Edwin O. *The Japanese.* Cambridge: Belknap Press of Harvard University Press, 1977.

———. *The Japanese Today: Continuity and Change.* Cambridge: Belknap Press of Harvard University Press, 1988.

Roth, Martin. *Making Money in Japanese Stocks.* Rutland, Vermont: Tuttle, 1989.

Rothacher, Albrecht. *Japan's Agro-Food Sector: The Politics and Economics of Excess Protection.* New York: St. Martin's Press, 1989.

Sanders, Sol W. *Honda: The Man and His Machines.* Tokyo: Kodansha, 1982.

Sasajima, Yoshio. *Labor in Japan.* (About Japan Series, No. 9.) Tokyo: Foreign Press Center, 1988.

Schmiegelow, Michèle, and Henrik Schmiegelow. *Strategic Pragmatism: Japanese Lessons in the Use of Economic Theory.* New York: Praeger, 1989.

Shibata, Tokue (ed.). *Public Finance in Japan.* Tokyo: University of Tokyo Press, 1986.

Shinohara Miyohei. *Industrial Growth, Trade, and Dynamic Patterns in the Japanese Economy.* Tokyo: University of Tokyo Press, 1982.

Shirai, Taishiro (ed.). *Contemporary Industrial Relations in Japan.* Madison: University of Wisconsin Press, 1983.

Shulman, Frank Joseph (ed.). *Japan.* (World Bibliographical Series, No. 103.) Santa Barbara, California: ABC-Clio, 1989.

Smith, Thomas. *Political Change and Industrial Development in Japan.* Stanford: Stanford University Press, 1955.

Stoever, William A. *Renegotiations in International Business Transactions: The Process of Dispute Resolution Between Multinational Investors and Host Societies.* Lexington, Massachusetts: Lexington Books, 1981.

Sunobe, Yoshio. *High Technology.* (Facts about Japan Series.) Tokyo: International Society for Educational Information, 1988.

Suzuki, Yoshio (ed.). *The Japanese Financial System.* (Institute for Monetary and Economic Studies of the Bank of Japan.) Oxford: Clarendon Press, 1987.

Tsuda, Hideo (ed.). *Japan 1990: An International Comparison.* (Japan Institute for Social and Economic Affairs.) Tokyo: Keizai Koho Center, 1990.

Tsuneta Yano Memorial Society. *Nippon: A Charted Survey of Japan, 1989/90.* (Annual Series.) Tokyo: Kokusei-sha, 1989.

United States. Central Intelligence Agency. *The World Factbook, 1989.* (CPAS WF 89–001.) Washington: May 1989.

―――. Central Intelligence Agency. Directorate of Intelligence. *Economic and Energy Indicators.* (DI EEI 90–011.) Washington: June 1, 1990.

Viner, Aron. *Inside Japanese Financial Markets.* Homewood, Illinois: Dow Jones-Irwin, 1988.

Vogel, Ezra F. *Japan as Number One: Lessons for America.* Cambridge: Harvard University Press, 1979.

Wray, Harry, and Hilary Conroy. *Japan Examined: Perspectives on Modern Japanese History.* Honolulu: University of Hawaii Press, 1983.

Wray, William D. (ed.), *Managing Industrial Enterprise: Cases from Japan's Prewar Experience.* (Harvard East Asian Monographs, No. 142.) Cambridge: Harvard University Press, 1989.

Yamamura, Kozo, and Yasukichi Yasuba (eds.). *The Political Economy of Japan, 2, The Domestic Transformation.* Stanford: Stanford University Press, 1987.

Yoshihara, Kunio. *Japanese Economic Development: A Short Introduction.* Tokyo: Oxford University Press, 1979.

Yoshino, Michael Y. *Japan's Managerial System: Traditional Innovation.* Cambridge: MIT Press, 1968.

Yoshino, Michael Y., and Thomas B. Lifson. *The Invisible Link: Japan's Sogo Shosha and the Organization of Trade.* Cambridge: MIT Press, 1986.

Young, Alexander K. *The Sogo Shoshu: Japan's Multinational Trading Companies.* (Westview Special Studies in International Economics and Business.) Boulder, Colorado: Westview Press, 1979.

(Various issues of the following publications also were used in the preparation of this chapter: *Asahi nenkan* (Asahi Yearbook) [Tokyo], 1986–90; *Asian Survey,* 1986–90; *Far Eastern Economic Review* [Hong Kong], 1983–90; *Japan Echo* [Tokyo], 1986–90; *Japan Economic Review* [Tokyo], 1986–90; *Japan Economic Survey,* 1987–90; *Japan Times Weekly* [Tokyo], 1986–90; *Japanese Economic Journal* [Tokyo], 1986–90; *JEI Report,* 1989–90; *Journal of Japanese Trade and Industry* [Tokyo], 1986–90; *Mitsubishi Bank Review* [Tokyo], 1986–90; *New York Times,* 1987–90; and *U.S. News and World Report,* 1987.)

Chapter 5

Abegglen, James C., and George Stalk, Jr. *Kaisha: The Japanese Corporation.* New York: Basic Books, 1985.

Advisory Committee for Trade Policy and Negotiations. "Analysis of the U.S.-Japan Trade Problem." Report submitted to the United States Trade Representative, Washington, February 1989.

Asia 1990 Yearbook. (Ed., Michael Malik.) Hong Kong: Review, 1990.

Belassa, Bela, and Marcus Noland. *Japan in the World Economy.* Washington: Institute for International Economics, 1988.

Bergsten, C. Fred, and William R. Cline. *The United States-Japan Economic Problem.* Washington: Institute for International Economics, 1985.

Boger, Karl. *Japanese Direct Foreign Investments: An Annotated Bibliography.* (Bibliographies and Indexes in Economics and Economic History, No. 8.) New York: Greenwood Press, 1989.

Castle, Emery N., and Kenzo Hemmi (eds.). *U.S.-Japanese Agricultural Trade Relations.* Baltimore: Johns Hopkins University Press, 1982.

Christopher, Robert C. *Second to None: American Companies in Japan.* New York: Ballantine Books, 1986.

Cohen, Stephen D. "United States-Japan Trade Relations." Pages 122–36 in Frank J. Macchiarola (ed.), *International Trade: The Changing Role of the United States.* (Proceedings of the Academy of Political Science, 37, No. 4.) New York: Academy of Political Science, 1990.

Destler, I.M., and Hideo Sato (eds.). *Coping with U.S.-Japanese Economic Conflicts.* Lexington, Massachusetts: Lexington Books, 1982.

Feldman, Robert Alan. *Japanese Financial Markets: Deficits, Dilemmas, and Deregulation.* Cambridge: MIT Press, 1986.

Fletcher, William Miles, III. *The Japanese Business Community and National Trade Policy, 1920–1942.* Chapel Hill: University of North Carolina Press, 1989.

Fox, John G. *The Next Wave of Japanese Investment in U.S. Real Estate.* New York: Japan Society, 1987.

Frankel, Jeffrey A. *The Yen/Dollar Agreement: Liberalizing Japanese Capital Markets.* Washington: Institute for International Economics, 1984.

Frost, Ellen. *For Richer, For Poorer: The New U.S.-Japan Relationship.* New York: Council on Foreign Relations, 1987.

Green, Gretchen. "Japan's Foreign Aid Policy: 1989 Update," *JEI Report,* No. 41A, October 27, 1989, 1–14.

―――. "Japan's Role in the Asian Development Bank," *JEI Report,* No. 23A, June 16, 1989, 1–7.

Hollerman, Leon (ed.). *Japan and the United States: Economic and Political Adversaries.* (Westview Special Studies in International Economics and Business.) Boulder, Colorado: Westview Press, 1980.

Hunsberger, Warren S. *Japan and the United States in World Trade.* New York: Harper and Row, 1964.

Inoguchi, Takeshi, and Daniel I. Okimodo (eds.). *The Political Economy of Japan, 2: The International Dimension.* Stanford: Stanford University Press, 1988.

International Financial Statistics Yearbook, 1988. Washington: International Monetary Fund, 1988.

International Financial Statistics Yearbook, 1989. Washington: International Monetary Fund, 1989.

International Monetary Fund. *International Financial Statistics, November 1989.* Washington: 1989.

Japan. Ministry of Finance. International Monetary Bureau. *Ōkurashō kokusai kin'yukyoku nenpo, Shōwa 57* (Ministry of Finance International Monetary Bureau Yearbook, 1983). Tokyo: Kin'yu Zaisei Jiho Kenkyukai, 1982.

_____. Ministry of Finance. International Monetary Bureau. *Ōkurashō kokusai kin'yukyoku nenpo, Shōwa 63 nenpan* (Ministry of Finance International Monetary Bureau Yearbook, 1988). Tokyo: Kin'yu Zaisei Jiho Kenkyukai, 1988.

_____. Ministry of Finance. Monetary Bureau. *Kokusai kin'yukyoku nenpo* (Monetary Bureau International Monetary Yearbook). Tokyo: 1982–89.

_____. Ministry of Foreign Affairs. *Japan's Official Development Assistance: 1988 Annual Report.* Tokyo: Association for Promotion of International Cooperation, 1989.

_____. Ministry of International Trade and Industry. Japan External Trade Organization. *JETRO: Promoting Trade, Creating Opportunity.* Tokyo: n.d.

Japan-United States Economic Relations Group. "Report of the Japan-United States Economic Relations Group." Washington: 1981.

Kodansha Encyclopedia of Japan. (9 vols.) Tokyo: Kodansha, 1983.

Kojima, Kiyoshi, and Terutomo Ozawa. *Japan's General Trading Companies: Merchants of Economic Development.* Paris: Organisation for Economic Co-operation and Development, 1984.

Koppel, Bruce, and Michael Plummer. "Japan's Ascendancy as a Foreign-Aid Power: Asian Perspectives," *Asian Survey,* 29, No. 11, November 1989, 1043–56.

Krause, Lawrence B., and Sueo Sekiguchi. "Japan and the World Economy." Pages 383–458 in Hugh T. Patrick and Henry

Rosovsky (eds.), *Asia's New Giant: How the Japanese Economy Works.* Washington: Brookings Institution, 1976.

Kreinin, Mordechai E. "How Closed Is Japan's Market?" *World Economy* [London], 11, No. 4, December 1988, 529–41.

Kujawa, Duane, and Daniel Bob. *American Public Opinion on Japanese Direct Investment.* New York: Japan Society, 1988.

Lawrence, Robert Z. *Imports in Japan: Closed Markets or Closed Minds?* (Brookings Papers on Economic Activity, No. 2, 1987.) Washington: Brookings Institution, 1987.

Lee, Chung H., and Ippei Yamazawa (eds.). *The Economic Development of Japan and Korea: A Parallel with Lessons.* New York: Praeger, 1990.

Lincoln, Edward J. *Japan: Facing Economic Maturity.* Washington: Brookings Institution, 1988.

———. *Japan's Economic Role in Northeast Asia.* Lanham, Maryland: University Press of America, 1987.

———. "Japan's Role in Asia-Pacific Cooperation: Dimensions, Prospects, and Problems," *Journal of Northeast Asian Studies,* 8, No. 4, Winter 1989, 3–23.

———. *Japan's Unequal Trade.* Washington: Brookings Institution, 1990.

Macchiarola, Frank J. (ed.) *International Trade: The Changing Role of the United States.* (Proceedings of the Academy of Political Science, 37, No. 4.) New York: Academy of Political Science, 1990.

MacKnight, Susan. *Japan's Expanding U.S. Manufacturing Presence, 1988 Update.* Washington: Japan Economic Institute, 1989.

Maswood, Syed Javed. *Japan and Protection: The Growth of Protectionist Sentiment and the Japanese Response.* London: Routledge, 1989.

McGuire, Sumiye O. *Soviet-Japanese Economic Relations.* (RAND Publication Series, R–3817.) Santa Monica, California: RAND Corporation, May 1990.

Moritani, Kazuo. "Impact of the EC Unification on Japan's Automobile and Electronics Industries." (JDB Research Report, No. 16.) Tokyo: Japan Development Bank, August 1989.

Motor Vehicle Statistics of Japan, 1989. Tokyo: Japan Automobile Manufacturers Association, 1989.

Murakami, Yasusuke, and Yutaka Kosai (eds.). *Japan in the Global Community: Its Role and Contribution on the Eve of the 21st Century.* Tokyo: University of Tokyo Press, 1986.

Nester, William R. *The Foundation of Japanese Power: Continuities, Changes, Challenges.* New York: Sharpe, 1990.

———. *Japan's Growing Predominance over East Asia and the World Economy.* New York: St. Martin's Press, 1990.

Okimoto, Daniel I. *Between MITI and the Market: Japanese Industrial Policy for High Technology.* Stanford: Stanford University Press, 1989.

Okimoto, Daniel I. (ed.). *Japan's Economy: Coping with Change in the International Environment.* Boulder, Colorado: Westview Press, 1982.

Ōkita Saburō. *Japan in the World Economy of the 1980s.* Tokyo: University of Tokyo Press, 1989.

_____. "Japan's Quiet Strength," *Foreign Policy,* No. 75, Summer 1989, 128–45.

Ozaki, Robert S. *The Control of Imports and Foreign Capital in Japan.* New York: Praeger, 1972.

Patrick, Hugh T., and Henry Rosovsky (eds.). *Asia's New Giant: How the Japanese Economy Works.* Washington: Brookings Institution, 1976.

Patrick, Hugh T., and Ryuichiro Tachi (eds.). *Japan and the United States Today: Exchange Rates, Macroeconomic Policies, and Financial Market Innovations.* New York: Center on Japanese Economy and Business, Columbia University, 1987.

Petri, Peter A. *Modeling Japanese-American Trade: A Study of Asymmetric Interdependence.* Cambridge: Harvard University Press, 1984.

Prestowitz, Clyde V., Jr. *Trading Places: How We Allowed Japan to Take the Lead.* New York: Basic Books, 1988.

Pugel, Thomas A., and Robert G. Hawkins (eds.). *Fragile Interdependence: Economic Issues in U.S.-Japanese Trade and Investment.* Lexington, Massachusetts: D.C. Heath, 1986.

Sato, Ryuzo, and Julianne Nelson (eds.). *Beyond Trade Friction: Japan-U.S. Economic Relations.* New York: Cambridge University Press, 1989.

Sato, Ryuzo, and John A. Rizzo (eds.). *Unkept Promises, Unclear Consequences: U.S. Economic Policy and the Japanese Response.* New York: Cambridge University Press, 1988.

Sato, Ryuzo, and Paul Wachtel (eds.). *Trade Friction and Economic Policy: Problems and Prospects for Japan and the United States.* New York: Cambridge University Press, 1987.

Saxonhouse, Gary R. "Japan's Intractable Trade Surpluses in a New Era," *World Economy* [London], 9, September 1986, 234–57.

Scalapino, Robert A. (ed.). *Economic Development in the Asia-Pacific Region: Appropriate Rules for Japan and the United States.* Berkeley: Institute of East Asian Studies, University of California, 1986.

Schlosstein, Steven B. *Trade War: Greed, Power, and Industrial Policy on Opposite Sides of the Pacific.* New York: Cougdon and Weed, 1984.

Schmiegelow, Michèle (ed.). *Japan's Response to Crisis and Change in the World Economy.* Armonk, New York: Sharpe, 1986.

Shulman, Frank Joseph (ed.). *Japan.* (World Bibliographical Series, No. 103.) Santa Barbara, California: ABC-Clio, 1989.

"Statistical Profile: Japan's Economy in 1988 and International Transactions of Japan and the United States in 1988," *JEI Report,* No. 39A, October 13, 1989, 1-44.

Stern, Robert M. (ed.). *Trade and Investment Relations among the United States, Canada, and Japan.* Chicago: University of Chicago Press, 1989.

Stokes, Bruce. *Japanese Investment in the United States: Its Causes and Consequences.* New York: Japan Society, 1988.

Takamiya, Sosumu, and Keith Thurley (eds.). *Japan's Emerging Multinationals: An International Comparison of Policies and Practices.* Tokyo: University of Tokyo Press, 1985.

Takeuchi, Kenji. *Does Japan Import Less Than It Should?* (World Bank Policy Planning and Research Working Papers, No. 63.) Washington: International Bank for Reconstruction and Development, July 1988.

Tasca, Diane (ed.). *U.S.-Japanese Economic Relations: Cooperation, Competition, and Confrontation.* New York: Pergamon Press, 1980.

Tsuda, Hideo (ed.). *Japan 1990: An International Comparison.* (Japan Institute for Social and Economic Affairs.) Tokyo: Keizai Koho Center, 1990.

U.S.-Japan Economic Relations Yearbook, 1984-1985. Washington: Japan Economic Institute of America, 1986.

United States. Congress. 99th, 1st Session. House of Representatives. Committee on Foreign Affairs. Subcommittees on Asian and Pacific Affairs and International Economic Policy. *United States-Japan Trade Relations.* (Hearings April 17-May 14, 1985.) Washington: GPO, 1985.

_____. Congress. 100th, 2d Session. House of Representatives. Committee on Foreign Affairs. Subcommittee on Asian and Pacific Affairs. *United States-Japan Relations: The Impact of Negotiated Market Openings.* (Hearings September 27-October 13, 1988.) Washington: GPO, 1989.

_____. General Accounting Office. *International Finance: Implementation of the Yen/Dollar Agreement.* (GAO/NSIAD-86-107.) Washington: GPO, 1986.

_____. General Accounting Office. *U.S.-Japan Trade: Evaluation of the Market-Oriented Sector, Selective Talks.* (GAO/NSIAP-88-205.) Washington: GPO, July 1988.

_____. General Accounting Office. *United States-Japan Trade: Issues and Problems.* (GAO ID-79-53.) Washington: GPO, 1979.

_____. International Trade Commission. *Pros and Cons of Initiating Negotiations with Japan to Explore the Possibility of a U.S-Japan Free Trade Area Agreement.* (Investigation No. TA-332-255. USITC Publication 0196-9153; 2120.) Washington: September 1988.

United States Economic Relations Group. *Report of the Japan-United States Economic Relations Group.* Washington: Japan-United States Economic Relations Group, January 1981.

United States-Japan Advisory Commission. Office of Public Communication. *Challenges and Opportunities in United States-Japan Relations: A Report Submitted to the President of the United States and the Prime Minister of Japan.* Washington: September 1984.

Yamamura, Kozo (ed.). *Japanese Investment in the United States: Should We Be Concerned?* Seattle: Society for Japanese Studies, 1989.

_____. *Policy and Trade Issues of the Japanese Economy: American and Japanese Perspectives.* Seattle: University of Washington Press, 1982.

Yearbook of U.S.-Japan Economic Relations in 1983. Washington: Japan Economic Institute of America, 1984.

Yoshida, Mamoru. *Japanese Direct Manufacturing Investment in the United States.* New York: Praeger, 1987.

Yoshihara, Kunio. *Soga Shosha: The Vanguard of the Japanese Economy.* Tokyo: Oxford University Press, 1982.

Yoshino, Michael Y., and Thomas B. Lifson. *The Invisible Link: Japan's Sogo Shosha and the Organization of Trade.* Cambridge: MIT Press, 1986.

(Various issues of the following publications were also used in the preparation of this chapter: *Asian Wall Street Journal* [Hong Kong], 1989-90; *Far Eastern Economic Review* [Hong Kong], 1980-89; *Japan Economic Journal* [Tokyo], 1980-89; *Japan Statistical Yearbook* [Tokyo], 1980-89; the Japan Tariff Association's *The Summary Report, Trade of Japan* [Tokyo], 1980-89; the Bank of Japan's *Balance of Payments Monthly* [Tokyo], 1981-88 and *Economic Statistics Annual* [Tokyo], 1977-89; the Ministry of International Trade and Industry's *Tsūshō hakusho* (Trade White Paper), 1980-89; and *Tokyo Business Today* [Tokyo], 1980-89.)

Chapter 6

Ames, Walter L. *Police and Community in Japan.* Berkeley: University of California Press, 1981.

Apter, David, and Nagayo Sawa. *Against the State: Politics and Social Protest in Japan.* Cambridge: Harvard University Press, 1984.

Asahi nenkan, 1990 (Asahi Yearbook, 1990). Tokyo: Asahi Shimbun, 1990.

Austin, Lewis. *Saints and Samurai: The Political Culture of the American and Japanese Elites.* (Yale Studies in Political Science, No. 27.) New Haven: Yale University Press, 1975.

Austin, Lewis (ed.). *Japan: The Paradox of Progress.* New Haven: Yale University Press, 1976.

Baerwald, Hans H. "Japan's House of Councillors Election: A Mini-Revolution?" *Asian Survey,* 29, No. 9, September 1989, 833–41.

_____. *Japan's Parliament: An Introduction.* London: Cambridge University Press, 1975.

_____. "Japan's 39th House of Representatives Election: A Case of Mixed Signals," *Asian Survey,* 30, No. 6, June 1990, 541–59.

Bayley, David H. *Forces of Order: Police Behavior in Japan and the United States.* Berkeley: University of California Press, 1976.

Beasley W.G. *Japanese Imperialism, 1874–1945.* Oxford: Clarendon Press, 1987.

_____. *The Modern History of Japan.* New York: St. Martin's Press, 1981.

Beer, Lawrence W. *Freedom of Expression in Japan: A Study in Comparative Law, Politics, and Society.* Tokyo: Kodansha, 1984.

_____. "Group Rights and Individual Rights in Japan," *Asian Survey,* 21, No. 4, April 1981, 437–53.

Befu, Harumi. *Ideorogii to shite no Nihon bunkaron* (Theories of Japanese Culture as Ideology). Tokyo: Shisō no Kagaku Sha, 1987.

Berger, Gordon M. "The Three-Dimensional Empire: Japanese Attitudes and the New Order in Asia, 1937–1945," *Japan Interpreter* [Tokyo], 12, Nos. 3–4, Summer 1979, 355–83.

Bernstein, Gail Lee, and Haruhiro Fukui (eds.). *Japan and the World: Essays on Japanese History and Politics in Honour of Ishida Takeshi.* Basingstoke, Hampshire, United Kingdom: Macmillan Press, 1988.

Bestor, Theodore C. *Neighborhood Tokyo.* Stanford: Stanford University Press, 1989.

Calder, Kent E. *Crisis and Compensation: Public Policy and Political Stability in Japan, 1949–1986.* Princeton: Princeton University Press, 1988.

Campbell, John Creighton. *Contemporary Japanese Budget Politics.* (Studies of the East Asian Institute.) Berkeley: University of California Press, 1977.

————. "Policy Conflict and Its Resolution with the Governmental System." Pages 244–334 in Ellis S. Krauss, Thomas P. Rohlen, and Patricia G. Steinhoff (eds.), *Conflict in Japan*. Honolulu: University of Hawaii Press, 1984.

Cary, Otis (ed.). *From a Ruined Empire: Letters, Japan, China, Korea, 1945–46*. Tokyo: Kodansha, 1984.

Cohen, Theodore. *Remaking Japan: The American Occupation as New Deal*. (Ed., Herbert Passin.) New York: Free Press, 1987.

Curtis, Gerald L. *Election Campaigning Japanese Style*. (Studies of the East Asian Institute, Columbia University.) New York: Columbia University Press, 1971.

Donnelly, Michael W. "Conflict over Government Authority and Markets: Japan's Rice Economy." Pages 335–74 in Ellis S. Krauss, Thomas P. Rohlen, and Patricia G. Steinhoff (eds.), *Conflict in Japan*. Honolulu: University of Hawaii Press, 1984.

Frager, Robert, and Thomas P. Rohlen. "The Future of a Tradition: Japanese Spirit in the 1980s." Pages 255–78 in Lewis Austin (ed.), *Japan: The Paradox of Progress*. New Haven: Yale University Press, 1976.

Fujii, Shin'ichi. *The Constitution of Japan: A Historical Survey*. Tokyo: Hokuseido Press, 1965.

Fukatsu Masumi. "Doi Takako Tackles the Obstacles of Power," *Japan Quarterly* [Tokyo], 37, No. 1, January–March 1990, 24–30.

Fukui, Haruhiro. "Electoral Laws and the Japanese Party System." Pages 119–43 in Gail Lee Bernstein and Fukui Haruhiro (eds.), *Japan and the World: Essays on Japanese History and Politics in Honour of Ishida Takeshi*. Basingstoke, Hampshire, United Kingdom: Macmillan Press, 1988.

————. "Japan in 1988: At the End of an Era," *Asian Survey*, 29, No. 1, January 1989, 1–11.

————. "The Liberal Democratic Party Revisited: Continuity and Change in the Party's Structure and Performance," *Journal of Japanese Studies*, 10, No. 2, Summer 1984, 385–436.

"*Gengō*: The Big Debate," *Japan Quarterly* [Tokyo], 26, No. 1, January–March 1979, 3–6.

Haley, John O. "Governance by Negotiation: A Reappraisal of Bureaucratic Power in Japan," *Journal of Japanese Studies*, 13, No. 2, Summer 1987, 343–58.

————. "Sheathing the Sword of Justice in Japan: An Essay on Law Without Sanctions," *Journal of Japanese Studies*, 8, No. 2, Summer 1982, 265–82.

Hane, Mikiso. *Peasants, Rebels, and Outcasts: The Underside of Modern Japan*. New York: Pantheon Books, 1982.

Harari, Ehud. "The Institutionalisation of Policy Consultation in Japan: Public Advisory Boards." Pages 144-57 in Gail Lee Bernstein and Haruhiro Fukui (eds.), *Japan and the World: Essays on Japanese History and Politics in Honour of Ishida Takeshi*. Basingstoke, Hampshire, United Kingdom: Macmillan Press, 1988.

Hardacre, Helen. *Shintō and the State, 1868-1988*. (Studies in Church and State.) Princeton: Princeton University Press, 1989.

Hata Ikuhiko. "When Ideologues Write History," *Japan Echo* [Tokyo], 13, No. 4, Winter 1986, 73-78.

Hayami Yūjirō. *Japanese Agriculture under Seige: The Political Economy of Agricultural Policies*. (Studies in the Modern Japanese Economy.) Basingstoke, Hampshire, United Kingdom: Macmillan Press, 1988.

Henderson, Dan Fenno. *The Constitution of Japan: Its First Twenty Years, 1947-1967*. Seattle: University of Washington Press, 1968.

Hoffman, Steven A. "Faction Behavior and Cultural Codes: India and Japan," *Journal of Asian Studies*, 40, No. 2, February 1981, 231-54.

Holtom, Daniel Clarence. *The Japanese Enthronement Ceremonies*. (A Monumenta Nipponica Monograph.) Tokyo: Sophia University, 1972.

_____. *The Political Philosophy of Modern Shintō: A Study of the State Religion of Japan*. (Reprint of 1922 edition.) New York: AMS Press, 1984.

Huffman, James L. "The Idioms of Contemporary Japan XI: Kinmyaku, Jinmyaku," *Japan Interpreter* [Tokyo], 9, No. 4, Spring 1975, 505-15.

Ike, Nobutaka. *The Beginning of Political Democracy in Japan*. Baltimore: Johns Hopkins University Press, 1950.

_____. *A Theory of Japanese Democracy*. (Westview Special Studies on China and East Asia.) Boulder, Colorado: Westview Press, 1978.

Inoguchi Takashi. "Explaining and Predicting Japanese General Elections, 1960-1980," *Journal of Japanese Studies*, 7, No. 2, Summer 1981, 285-318.

Iriye, Akira. *Power and Culture: The Japanese-American War, 1941-1945*. Cambridge: Harvard University Press, 1981.

Ishida, Takeshi, and Ellis S. Krauss (eds.). *Democracy in Japan*. (Pitt Series in Policy and Institutional Studies.) Pittsburgh: University of Pittsburgh Press, 1989.

Ishii Ryōsuke. *A History of Political Institutions in Japan*. Tokyo: Japan Foundation, 1980.

Japan. Foreign Press Center. *The Diet, Elections and Political Parties*. (About Japan Series, No. 13.) Tokyo: 1985.

Johnson, Chalmers. "Japan: Who Governs? An Essay on Official Bureaucracy," *Journal of Japanese Studies,* 2, No. 1, Autumn 1975, 1–28.

―――. "Omote (Explicit) and Ura (Implicit): Translating Japanese Political Terms," *Journal of Japanese Studies,* 6, No. 1, Winter 1980, 89–116.

―――. "Tanaka Kakuei, Structural Corruption, and the Advent of Machine Politics in Japan," *Journal of Japanese Studies,* 12, No. 1, Winter 1986, 1–28.

Kesavan, K.V. "Political Watershed 1989," *Japan Quarterly* [Tokyo], 37, No. 1, January–March 1990, 31–36.

Kishimoto Kōichi. *Politics in Modern Japan: Development and Organization.* Tokyo: Japan Echo, 1977.

Kodansha Encyclopedia of Japan. (9 vols.) Tokyo: Kodansha, 1983.

Koh, B.C. *Japan's Administrative Elite.* Berkeley: University of California Press, 1989.

Koppel, Bruce, and Michael Plummer. "Japan's Ascendancy as a Foreign-Aid Power: Asian Perspectives," *Asian Survey,* 29, No. 11, November 1989, 1043–56.

Koschmann, J. Victor. *Authority and the Individual in Japan: Citizen Protest in Historical Perspective.* Tokyo: University of Tokyo Press, 1978.

―――. "The Idioms of Contemporary Japan VIII: Tatemae to Honne," *Japan Interpreter* [Tokyo], 9, No. 1, Spring 1974, 98–104.

―――. "The Idioms of Contemporary Japan X: Ko to Shi," *Japan Interpreter* [Tokyo], 9, No. 3, Winter 1975, 361–67.

Krauss, Ellis S. "Conflict in the Diet: Toward Conflict Management in Parliamentary Politics." Pages 243–93 in Ellis S. Krauss, Thomas P. Rohlen, and Patricia G. Steinhoff (eds.), *Conflict in Japan.* Honolulu: University of Hawaii Press, 1984.

Kubota Akira. "The Political Influence of the Japanese Higher Civil Service," *Japan Quarterly* [Tokyo], 28, No. 2, April–June 1981, 45–55.

Kumon Shumpei. "Japan Faces Its Future: The Political-Economics of Administrative Reform," *Journal of Japanese Studies,* 10, No. 1, Winter 1984, 143–66.

Kyōgoku, Jun'ichi. *The Political Dynamics of Japan.* (Trans., Ike Nobutaka.) Tokyo: University of Tokyo Press, 1987.

Lee, T.S.Y. (ed.). "Japan." In Albert P. Blaustein and Gisbert H. Flanz (eds.), *Constitutions of the Countries of the World,* 8. Dobbs Ferry, New York: Oceana, February 1973, 15 pp.

Malik, Michael. *Asia 1990 Yearbook.* Hong Kong: Far Eastern Economic Review, 1990.

Maruyama Masao. *Thought and Behavior in Modern Japanese Politics.* (Oxford in Asia College Texts.) Tokyo: Oxford University Press, 1979.

McCormack, Gavan, and Yoshio Sugimoto. *Democracy in Contemporary Japan.* Armonk, New York: Sharpe, 1986.

McCormack, Gavan, and Yoshio Sugimoto (eds.). *The Japanese Trajectory: Modernization and Beyond.* New York: Cambridge University Press, 1988.

McIntosh, Malcolm. *Japan Re-armed.* New York: St. Martin's Press, 1986.

McKean, Margaret A. *Environmental Protest and Citizen Politics in Japan.* Berkeley: University of California Press, 1981.

McNelly, Theodore H. "'Induced Revolution': The Policy and Process of Constitutional Reform in Occupied Japan." Pages 76–106 in Robert E. Ward and Sakamoto Yoshikazu (eds.), *Democratizing Japan: The Allied Occupation.* Honolulu: University of Hawaii, 1987.

Mover, Ross, and Yoshio Sugimoto. *Images of Japanese Society: A Study in the Social Construction of Reality.* London: Kegan Paul, 1986.

Murakami, Yasusuke. "The Age of New Middle Mass Politics: The Case of Japan," *Journal of Japanese Studies,* 8, No. 1, Winter 1982, 29–72.

Muramatsu Michio. "Center-Local Political Relations in Japan: A Lateral Competition Model," *Journal of Japanese Studies,* 12, No. 2, Summer 1986, 303–28.

_____. "In Search of National Identity: The Politics and Policies of the Nakasone Administration," *Journal of Japanese Studies,* 13, No. 2, Summer 1987, 307–42.

Najita, Tetsuo. *Japan: The Intellectual Foundations of Modern Japanese Politics.* Chicago: University of Chicago Press, 1974.

Nakagawa Yatsuhiro. "Japan, the Welfare Super-Power," *Journal of Japanese Studies,* 5, No. 1, Winter 1979, 5–52.

Nakane Chie. *Japanese Society.* Berkeley: University of California Press, 1970.

Nathan, John. *Mishima: A Biography.* Boston: Little, Brown, 1974.

Odawara Atsushi. "Kaifu Toshiki: Prime Minister Betwixt and Between," *Japan Quarterly* [Tokyo], 36, No. 4, October–December 1989, 368–74.

_____. "A Vague Uneasiness Haunts Voters," *Japan Quarterly* [Tokyo], 37, No. 2, April–June 1990, 153–57.

Packard, Jerrold M. *Sons of Heaven: A Portrait of the Japanese Monarchy.* New York: Scribner's, 1987.

Pempel, T.J. *Policy and Politics in Industrial States.* Philadelphia: Temple University Press, 1982.

_____. "The Tar Baby Target: 'Reform' of the Japanese Bureaucracy." Pages 157–87 in Robert E. Ward and Sakamoto Yoshikazu (eds.), *Democratizing Japan: The Allied Occupation*. Honolulu: University of Hawaii, 1987.

_____. "The Unbundling of 'Japan Incorporated': The Changing Dynamics of Japanese Policy Formation," *Journal of Japanese Studies*, 13, No. 2, Summer 1987, 271–306.

Pempel, T.J. (ed.). *Uncommon Democracies: The One-Party Dominant Regimes*. Ithaca: Cornell University Press, 1990.

Pharr, Susan J. "The Politics of Human Rights." Pages 221–52 in Robert E. Ward and Sakamoto Yoshikazu (eds.), *Democratizing Japan: The Allied Occupation*. Honolulu: University of Hawaii, 1987.

Powles, Cyril. "*Yasukuni: Jinja Hōan*: Religion and Politics in Contemporary Japan," *Pacific Affairs* [Vancouver], 49, No. 3, Fall 1976, 491–505.

Prestowitz, Clyde V., Jr. *Trading Places: How We Allowed Japan to Take the Lead*. New York: Basic Books, 1988.

Quo, F. Quei. "The Impact of Domestic Politics on Japan's Foreign Policy." Pages 176–96 in Gail Lee Bernstein and Haruhiro Fukui (eds.), *Japan and the World: Essays on Japanese History and Politics in Honour of Ishida Takeshi*. Basingstoke, Hampshire, United Kingdom: Macmillan Press, 1988.

Reed, Steven R. "Is Japanese Government Really Centralized?" *Journal of Japanese Studies*, 8, No. 1, Winter 1982, 133–64.

Richardson, Bradley M. "Constituency Candidates Versus Parties in Japanese Voting Behavior," *American Political Science Review*, 82, No. 3, September 1988, 695–718.

_____. *The Political Culture of Japan*. Berkeley: University of California Press, 1974.

Richardson, Bradley M., and Scott C. Flanagan. *Politics: Japan*. (Little Brown Series in Comparative Politics.) Boston: Little, Brown, 1984.

Rohlen, Thomas P. "Order in Japanese Society: Attachment, Authority and Routine," *Journal of Japanese Studies*, 15, No. 1, Winter 1989, 5–40.

Sakamoto Yoshikazu. "The International Context of the Occupation of Japan." Pages 42–75 in Robert E. Ward and Sakamoto Yoshikazu (eds.), *Democratizing Japan: The Allied Occupation*. Honolulu: University of Hawaii, 1987.

Samuels, Richard J. "Japan in 1989: Changing Times," *Asian Survey*, 30, No. 1, January 1990, 42–51.

Sansom, George B. *The Western World and Japan: A Study in the Interaction of European and Asiatic Cultures*. Rutland, Vermont: Tuttle, 1977.

Sasaki Takeshi. "The LDP Teeters in the Political Balance," *Japan Quarterly* [Tokyo], 36, No. 4, October–December 1989, 375–80.

Seekins, Donald M. "Cultural Essentialism in Contemporary Japan: The Issue of Identity," *University of the Ryukyus Law Review* [Nishihara, Okinawa], No. 45, 1990, 197–232.

"Shōwa 64, Heisei 1," *Monumenta Nipponica* [Tokyo], 44, No. 1, Spring 1989, 99–101.

Shulman, Frank Joseph (ed.). *Japan*. (World Bibliographical Series, No. 103.) Santa Barbara, California: ABC-Clio, 1989.

Skinner, Kenneth. "The Idioms of Contemporary Japan XIX: Sarariman Manga," *Japan Interpreter* [Tokyo], 12, Nos. 3–4, Summer 1979, 449–57.

Smith, Charles. "Rightist Revision: The Flag-and-Anthem Furore in Schools," *Far Eastern Economic Review* [Hong Kong], 148, No. 17, April 26, 1990, 21.

Steiner, Kurt, Ellis S. Krauss, and Scott C. Flangaar (eds.). *Political Opposition and Local Politics in Japan*. Princeton: Princeton University Press, 1980.

Steinhoff, Patricia G. "Hijackers, Bombers, and Bank Robbers: Managerial Style in the Japanese Red Army," *Journal of Asian Studies*, 48, No. 4, November 1989, 724–40.

Steven, R.P.G. "Hybrid Constitutionalism in Prewar Japan," *Journal of Japanese Studies*, 3, No. 1, Winter 1977, 99–134.

Stockwin, J.A.A. *Japan: Divided Politics in a Growth Economy*. (Comparative Modern Government Series.) New York: Norton, 1975.

——. "Japanese Politics: Good or Bad?" Pages 158–75 in Gail Lee Bernstein and Haruhiro Fukui (eds.), *Japan and the World: Essays on Japanese History and Politics in Honour of Ishida Takeshi*. Basingstoke, Hampshire, United Kingdom: Macmillan Press, 1988.

Stockwin, J.A.A., et al. *Dynamic and Immobilist Politics in Japan*. Honolulu: University of Hawaii Press, 1988.

Tachibanaki, Toshiaki. "Japan's New Policy Agenda: Coping with Unequal Asset Distribution," *Journal of Japanese Studies*, 15, No. 2, Summer 1989, 345–70.

Takabatake Michitoshi. "The LDP Victory: A Clear Path for the Future?" *Japan Quarterly* [Tokyo], 37, No. 2, April–June 1990, 145–52.

——. "The Liberal Democratic Party in Crisis," *Japan Quarterly* [Tokyo], 36, No. 3, July–September 1989, 244–51.

Takagi Masayuki. "The Japanese Right Wing," *Japan Quarterly* [Tokyo], 36, No. 3, July–September 1989, 300–305.

Tanaka Hideo. "The Conflict Between Two Legal Traditions in Making the Constitution of Japan." Pages 107–32 in Robert E.

Ward and Sakamoto Yoshikazu (eds.), *Democratizing Japan: The Allied Occupation.* Honolulu: University of Hawaii, 1987.

Tanaka Hideo (ed.). *The Japanese Legal System: Introductory Cases and Materials.* Tokyo: University of Tokyo Press, 1976.

Thayer, Nathaniel B. *How the Conservatives Rule Japan.* (Studies of the East Asian Insitute, Columbia University.) Princeton: Princeton University Press, 1969.

Tsunoda, Ryusaku, Wm. Theodore de Bary, and Donald Keene (comps.). *Sources of Japanese Tradition.* (Records of Civilization, Sources and Studies.) New York: Columbia University Press, 1958.

Ueno, Chizuko. "The Japanese Women's Movement: The Countervalues to Industrialism." Pages 167–85 in Gavan McCormack and Yoshio Sugimoto (eds.), *The Japanese Trajectory: Modernization and Beyond.* New York: Cambridge University Press, 1988.

United States. Department of State. *Country Reports on Human Rights Practices for 1989.* (Report submitted to United States Congress, 101st, 2d Session, Senate, Committee on Foreign Relations, and House of Representatives, Committee on Foreign Affairs.) Washington: GPO, February 1990.

van Wolferen, Karel G. *The Enigma of Japanese Power: People and Politics in a Stateless Nation.* New York: Knopf, 1989.

_____. "The Japan Problem," *Foreign Affairs,* 65, No. 2, Winter 1986–87, 288–303.

Ward, Robert E. *Japan's Political System.* (2d ed.) Englewood Cliffs, New Jersey: Prentice-Hall, 1978.

Ward, Robert E. (ed.). *Political Development in Modern Japan.* Princeton: Princeton University Press, 1968.

Ward, Robert E., and Sakanoto Yoshikazu (eds.). *Democratizing Japan: The Allied Occupation.* Honolulu: University of Hawaii, 1987.

Who's Who in Japanese Government, 1988–89. Tokyo: International Cultural Association, 1988.

Yamamoto Taketoshi. "The Press Club of Japan," *Journal of Japanese Studies,* 15, No. 2, Summer 1989, 371–88.

Yamamura, Kozo. "Shedding the Shackles of Success: Saving Less for Japan's Future," *Journal of Japanese Studies,* 13, No. 2, Summer 1987, 429–56.

Yayama, Tarō. "The Newspapers Conduct a Mad Rhaposdy over the Textbook Issue," *Journal of Japanese Studies,* 9, No. 2, Summer 1983, 301–16.

_____. "The Recruit Scandal: Learning from the Causes of Conflict," *Journal of Japanese Studies,* 16, No. 4, Winter, 1990, 93–114.

(Various issues of the following publications were also used in the preparation of this chapter: *Asahi nenkan* (Asahi Yearbook) [Tokyo], 1987–89; *Asahi Shimbun* [Tokyo], 1989–90; *Asian Wall Street Journal* [Hong Kong], 1988–90; *Economist* [London], 1988–90; *Far Eastern Economic Review* [Hong Kong], 1988–90; *Japan Times* [Tokyo], 1988–90; and *Ryūkyū Shimpo* [Naha], 1988–90.)

Chapter 7

Abe Shintaro. *Creative Dipomacy: Japan's Initiative for Peace and Prosperity.* Tokyo: Ministry of Foreign Affairs, January 1985.

Asada, Sadai (ed.). *Japan and the World, 1853–1952: A Bibliographic Guide to Japanese Scholarship in Foreign Relations.* (Studies of the East Asian Institute, Columbia University.) New York: Columbia University Press, 1989.

Asia 1990 Yearbook. (Ed. Michael Malik.) Hong Kong: Review, 1990.

Auer, James A., et al. "Japan, 1988," *Current History,* 87, No. 528, April 1988, 115–92.

Blaker, Michael. *Japanese International Negotiating Style.* (Studies of the East Asian Institute, Columbia University.) New York: Columbia University Press, 1977.

Bloch, Julia Chang. "A U.S.-Japan Aid Alliance: Prospects for Cooperation in an Era of Conflict." (Program on U.S.-Japan Relations, Harvard University.) Cambridge, Massachusetts: 1989.

Brown, Harold. "The United States and Japan: High Tech Is Foreign Policy," *SAIS Review,* 9, No. 2, Summer–Fall 1989, 1–18.

Buzan, Barry. "Japan's Future: Old History Versus New Roles." *International Affairs* [London], 64, No. 4, October 1988, 557–73.

Clark, William, Jr. "U.S.-Japan Relations," *Department of State Bulletin,* 88, No. 2141, December 1988, 27–30.

Corning, Gregory P. "U.S.-Japan Security Cooperation in the 1990s: The Promise of High-Tech Defense," *Asian Survey,* 29, No. 3, March 1989, 268–86.

Destler, I.M., Hideo Sato, Priscilla Clapp, and Haruhiro Fukui. *Managing an Alliance: The Politics of U.S.-Japanese Relations.* Washington: Brookings Institution, 1976.

Drifte, Reinhard. *Japan's Foreign Policy.* (Chatham House Papers.) New York: Council on Foreign Relations Press, 1990.

Duus, Peter, Ramon H. Meyers, and Mark R. Peattie (eds.). *The Japanese Informal Empire in China, 1895–1937.* Princeton: Princeton University Press, 1989.

Edstrom, Bert. *Japan's Quest for a Role in the World: Roles Ascribed to Japan Nationally and Internationally, 1969–1982*. Stockholm: University of Stockholm, 1988.

Emmott, Bill. *The Sun Also Sets: The Limits to Japan's Economic Power*. New York: Times Books, 1989.

Falkenheim, Peggy L. "Evolving Regional Ties in Northeast Asia: Japan, the U.S., and the USSR," *Asian Survey*, 28, No. 12, December 1988, 1229–44.

––––––. "The Soviet Union, Japan, and East Asia: The Security Dimension," *Journal of Northeast Asian Studies*, 8, No. 4, Winter 1989, 43–59.

Fallows, James. "Containing Japan," *Atlantic Monthly*, 263, No. 5, May 1989, 51–54.

Frost, Ellen L. *For Richer, For Poorer: The New U.S.-Japan Relationship*. New York: Council on Foreign Relations, 1987.

Fukui, Haruhiro. "Japan in 1988: At the End of an Era," *Asian Survey*, 29, No. 1, January 1989, 1–11.

George, Aurelia. "Japan and the United States: Dependent Ally or Equal Partner?" Pages 237–96 in J.A.A. Stockwin, et al., *Dynamic and Immobilist Politics in Japan*. Honolulu: University of Hawaii Press, 1988.

Goble, Andrew, and James C. Carlson. "Japan's America-Bashers: America's Assertive Allies," *Orbis*, 34, No. 1, Winter 1990, 83–102.

Hasegawa, Tsuyoshi. "Japanese Perceptions and Policies Toward the Soviet Union: Changes and Prospects under the Gorbachev Era." Pages 23–37 in Pushpa Thambipillai and Daniel C. Matuszewski (eds.), *The Soviet Union and the Asia-Pacific Region: Views from the Region*. New York: Praeger, 1989.

Hellman, Donald C. *China and Japan: A New Balance of Power*. Lexington, Massachusetts: Lexington Books, 1976.

Hinton, Harold C. *Three and a Half Powers: New Balance in Asia*. Bloomington: Indiana University Press, 1975.

Horne, Mari Kuraishi. "The Northern Territories: Source or Symptom?" *Journal of Northeast Asian Studies*, 8, No. 4, Winter 1989, 60–76.

Islam, Shafiqul. "Capitalism Conflict," *Foreign Affairs*, 69, No. 1, Winter 1989–90, 172–82.

Ito, Kan. "Trans-Pacific Anger," *Foreign Policy*, No. 78, Spring 1990, 131–52.

Jain, Rajendra Kumar. *The USSR and Japan, 1945–1980*. Atlantic Heights, New Jersey: Humanities Press, 1981.

Kearns, Kevin L. "After FSX: A New Approach to U.S.-Japan Relations," *Foreign Service Journal*, 66, No. 12, December 1989, 43–48.

Kesavan, K.V. "Japan and the Tiananmen Square Incident: Aspects of the Bilateral Relationship," *Asian Survey*, 30, No. 7, July 1990, 669–81.

Kitamura, Hiroshi, Ryohei Murata, and Hisahiko Okazaki. *Between Friends: Japanese Diplomats Look at Japan-U.S. Relations.* (Trans., Daniel R. Zoll.) New York: Weatherhill, 1985.

Kodansha Encyclopedia of Japan. (9 vols.) Tokyo: Kodansha, 1983.

Kohno, Masaru. "Japanese Defense Policy Making: The FSX Selection, 1985–1987," *Asian Survey*, 29, No. 5, May 1989, 457–79.

Langdon, Frank C. *Japan's Foreign Policy.* Vancouver: University of Vancouver Press, 1973.

Lauren, Paul Gordon, and Raymond F. Wylie (eds.). *Destinies Shared: U.S.-Japanese Relations.* Boulder, Colorado: Westview Press, 1989.

Lee, Jung-Hoon. "Korean-Japanese Relations: The Past, Present and Future," *Korea Observer* [Seoul], 21, No. 2, Summer, 1990, 179–97.

L'Estrange, Michael G. *The Internationalization of Japan's Security Policy: Challenges and Dilemmas for a Reluctant Power.* (Policy Papers in International Affairs, No. 36.) Berkeley: Institute of International Studies, University of California, 1990.

Mack, Andrew, and Martin O'Hare. "Moscow-Tokyo and the Northern Territories Dispute," *Asian Survey*, 30, No. 4, April 1990, 380–94.

Makin, John H., and Donald C. Hellmann. *Sharing World Leadership?: A New Era for America and Japan.* (AEI Studies, No. 488.) Washington: American Enterprise Institute for Public Policy Research, 1989.

Mansfield, Mike. "The United States and Japan: Sharing Our Destinies," *Foreign Affairs*, 68, No. 3, Spring 1989, 3–15.

Martin, Jurek. "Trivializing the U.S.-Japan Debate," *International Economy*, 4, No. 2, April–May 1990, 26–30.

Masuzoe Yōichi. "Japan and the United States," *Japan Echo* [Tokyo], 16, No. 2, Summer 1989, 58–74.

Menon, Rajan, and Daniel Abele. "Security Dimensions of Soviet Territorial Disputes with China and Japan," *Journal of Northeast Asian Studies*, 8, No. 1, Spring 1989, 3–19.

Morley, James W. *Japan's Foreign Policy, 1868–1941: A Research Guide.* (Studies of the East Asian Institute.) New York: Columbia University Press, 1973.

Morse, Ronald A. "Japan's Drive to Pre-Eminence." *Foreign Policy*, No. 69, Winter 1987–88, 3–21.

Nakasone Yasuhiro. "Beyond the Horizon of the Pacific." (CISA Working Paper No. 63.) Los Angeles, Center for International and Strategic Affairs, University of California, 1988.

Nester, William R. *Japan's Growing Predominance Over East Asia and the World Economy*. New York: St. Martin's Press, 1990.

Niksch, Larry A., et al. "Forum: Japan-United States Relations." *CRS Review*, 10, No. 6, July 1989, 1–23.

Nish, Ian. *Japanese Foreign Policy, 1869–1942: Kasumigaseki to Miyakezaka*. London: Routledge and Kegan Paul, 1977.

Okazaki, Hisahiko. "Burden Sharing for a Military Balance," *Japan Echo* [Tokyo], 15, No. 3, Autumn 1988, 44–47.

Ōkita Saburō. *Japan in the World Economy of the 1980s*. Tokyo: University of Tokyo Press, 1989.

――――. "Japan's Quiet Strength," *Foreign Policy*, No. 75, Summer 1989, 128–45.

Orr, Robert M., Jr. "The Aid Factor in U.S.-Japan Relations," *Asian Survey*, 28, No. 7, July 1988, 740–56.

――――. "Collaboration or Conflict? Foreign Aid and U.S.-Japan Relations," *Pacific Affairs* [Vancouver], 62, No. 4, Winter 1989, 476–89.

Prestowitz, Clyde V., Jr. *Trading Places: How We Allowed Japan to Take the Lead*. New York: Basic Books, 1988.

Rubinstein, Gregg A. "U.S.-Japan Security Relations: A Maturing Partnership?" *Fletcher Forum of World Affairs*, 12, No. 1, Winter 1988, 41–54.

Saito, Shiro. *Japan at the Summit: Japan's Role in the Western Alliance and Asian Pacific Cooperation*. London: Routledge for the Royal Institute of International Affairs, 1990.

Sato, Seizaburo. "Appraising the Japan-United States Partnership," *Japan Echo* [Tokyo], 15, No. 3, Autumn 1988, 38–43.

Scalapino, Robert A. *The Foreign Policy of Modern Japan*. Berkeley: University of California Press, 1977.

Scalapino, Robert A., Seizaburo Sato, Jusuf Wanadi, and Sung-joo Han. *Asia and the Major Powers: Domestic Politics and Foreign Policy*. (Research Papers and Policy Studies, No. 13.) Berkeley: Institute of East Asian Studies, University of California, 1988.

Schlosstein, Steven B. "The New McCarthyism: Inside Washington's 'Apologist v. Revisionist' Debate," *International Economy*, 4, No. 2, April–May 1990, 32–35.

Schonberger, Howard B. *Aftermath of War: Americans and the Remaking of Japan, 1945–1952*. Kent, Ohio: Kent State University Press, 1989.

Segal, Gerald. "The USSR and Asia in 1988: Achievements and Risks," *Asian Survey*, 29, No. 1, January 1989, 101–11.

Shulman, Frank Joseph (ed.). *Japan.* (World Bibliographical Series, No. 103.) Santa Barbara, California: ABC–Clio, 1989.

Spencer, Edson W. "Japan As Competitor," *Foreign Policy,* No. 78, Spring 1990, 153–71.

Stockwin, J.A.A., et al. *Dynamic and Immobilist Politics in Japan.* Honolulu: University of Hawaii Press, 1988.

Stokes, Bruce. "Economic Report: Who's Standing Tall?" *National Journal,* 21, No. 42, October 21, 1989, 2568–73.

Swearingen, Rodger. *The Soviet Union and Postwar Japan.* Stanford: Stanford University Press, 1978.

Tanada, William, et al. "The U.S.-Japan Trade and Security Relationship," *Fletcher Forum of World Affairs,* 12, No. 1, Winter 1988, 1–80.

Thambipillae, Pushpa, and Daniel C. Makuszewski (eds.). *The Soviet Union and the Asia-Pacific Region: Views from the Region.* New York: Praeger, 1989.

Trezise, Phillip H. "Japan, the Enemy?" *Brookings Review,* 8, No. 1, Winter 1989–90, 3–13.

Tsurumi, Yoshi. "U.S.-Japanese Relations: From Brinkmanship to Statesmanship," *World Policy Journal,* 7, No. 1, Winter 1989–90, 1–33.

United States. Congress. 101st. 2d Session. House of Representatives. Committee on Foreign Affairs. Subcommittee on International Economic Policy and Trade. *U.S. Power in a Changing World: Proceedings of a Seminar Held by the Congressional Research Service—November 19-20, 1989.* Washington: GPO, May 1990.

_____. Congress. 101st. 2d Session. House of Representatives. Committee on Ways and Means. *East Asia: Challenges for U.S. Economic and Security Interests in the 1990s: A Workshop.* Washington: GPO, September 26, 1988.

_____. Congress. 101st. 2d Session. Committee on Armed Services. *U.S.-Japan Burden Sharing: Japan Has Increased Its Contributions But Could Do More.* (Report to the committee chairman, GAO/NSIAD-89-188.) August 15, 1989, Washington: August 1989.

van Wolferen, Karel G. *The Enigma of Japanese Power: People and Politics in a Stateless Nation.* New York: Knopf, 1989.

Watts, William, in collaboration with Seizaburo Sato. *America and Japan: How We See Each Other.* Washington: Commission on US-Japan Relations for the Twenty First Century, May 2, 1990.

Weinstein, Martin E. "Trade Problems and U.S.-Japanese Security Cooperation," *Washington Quarterly,* 11, No. 1, Winter 1988, 19–33.

Whiting, Allen S. *China Eyes Japan.* Berkeley: University of California Press, 1989.

Chapter 8

Akaha Tsuneo. "Japan's Response to Threats of Shipping Disruptions in Southeast Asia and the Middle East," *Pacific Affairs* [Vancouver], 59, No. 2, Summer 1986, 255-77.

Ames, Walter L. *Police and Community in Japan.* Berkeley: University of California Press, 1981.

Asia 1990 Yearbook. (Ed., Michael Malik.) Hong Kong: Review, 1990.

Barnett, Robert W. *Beyond War: Japan's Concept of Comprehensive National Security.* Washington: Pergamon-Brassey's, 1984.

Bayley, David H. *Forces of Order: Police Behavior in Japan and the United States.* Berkeley: University of California Press, 1976.

Bestor, Theodore C. *Neighborhood Tokyo.* Stanford: Stanford University Press, 1989.

Buck, James H. (ed.). *The Modern Japanese Military System.* (Sage Research Progress Series on War, Revolution, and Peacekeeping, No. 5.) Beverly Hills, California: Sage, 1975.

Capien, Brian. "An Explosion in the Making," *Asian Business* [Hong Kong], 25, No. 10, October 1989, 21-24, 26-28.

Chūma Kiyofuku. "What Price the Defense of Japan?" *Japan Quarterly* [Tokyo], 34, No. 3, July–September 1987, 251-58.

Connaughton, Richard M. *The War of the Rising Sun and Tumbling Bear: A Military History of the Russo-Japanese War, 1904-05.* London: Routledge, 1988.

Corning, Gregory P. "U.S.-Japan Security Cooperation in the 1990s: The Promise of High-Tech Defense," *Asian Survey,* 29, No. 3, March 1989, 268-86.

Drifte, Reinhard. *Arms Production in Japan: The Military Applications of Civilian Technology.* Boulder, Colorado: Westview Press, 1986.

———. *Japan's Foreign Policy.* (Chatham House Papers.) New York: Council on Foreign Relations Press, 1990.

Duus, Peter. *The Rise of Modern Japan.* Boston: Houghton Mifflin, 1976.

Endicott, John E. "U.S.-Japan Defense Cooperation in the 1990s," *Journal of Northeast Asian Studies,* 3, No. 3, Fall 1984, 48-58.

Fallows, Deborah. "Japanese Women," *National Geographic,* 177, No. 4, April 1990, 52-83.

Holland, Harrison M. *Managing Defense: Japan's Dilemma.* Lanham, Maryland: University Press of America, 1988.

Horiguchi, Robert Y. "Potential Threats and Added Tensions." *Pacific Defence Reporter* [Sydney], 12, Nos. 6–7, December 1985–January 1986, 47–48, 50–53.

Hsü, Immanuel C.Y. *The Rise of Modern China.* (4th ed.) New York: Oxford University Press, 1990.

Japan. Defense Agency. *Defense of Japan, 1988.* Tokyo: 1988.

_____. *Defense of Japan, 1989.* Tokyo: 1989.

_____. *Defense of Japan, 1990.* Tokyo: 1990.

_____. Management and Coordination Agency. Statistics Bureau. *Nihon tōkei nenkan, Shōwa 63* (Japan Statistical Yearbook, 1989). Tokyo: Sōrifu, Tōkeikyoku, 1988.

_____. Ministry of Justice. *Annual Report on Crime, 1987 (Summary).* Tokyo: 1987.

_____. National Police Agency. *Keisatsu hakusho, 1987* (Police White Paper, 1987). Tokyo: 1987.

_____. National Police Agency. *The Police of Japan, 1980.* Tokyo: 1980.

_____. National Police Agency. *The Police of Japan, 1989.* Tokyo: 1989.

_____. National Police Agency. *White Paper on Police (Summary).* Tokyo: Foreign Press Center, 1987.

_____. Office of the Prime Minister. *Public Opinion Survey on the Self-Defense Forces and Defense Problems.* Tokyo: Foreign Press Center, 1988.

Jieitai nenkan, 1989 (Self-Defense Forces Yearbook, 1989). Tokyo: Bōei Nippō, 1989.

Kamiya Fuji. "Japan's Perception of and Responses to the Threat to the Northwestern Pacific and Northeastern Asia." Pages 17–26 in *Pacific Regional Security: The 1985 Symposium.* Washington: National Defense University Press, 1988.

Kataoka Tetsuya, and Ramon H. Myers. *Defending an Economic Superpower: Reassessing the U.S.-Japan Security Alliance.* (Westview Special Studies on East Asia.) Boulder, Colorado: Westview Press, 1989.

Kodansha Encyclopedia of Japan. (9 vols.) Tokyo: Kodansha, 1983.

Kohno, Masaru. "Japanese Defense Policy Making: The FSX Selection, 1985–1987," *Asian Survey,* 29, No. 5, May 1989, 457–79.

Kosobud, Richard F. (ed.). *Northeast Asia and the United States: Defense Partnerships and Trade Rivalries.* Chicago: Chicago Council on Foreign Relations, 1983.

Kuranari, Tadashi. "The Asian Situation and Japan's Response: With an Emphasis on the Korean Peninsula," *Journal of Northeast Asian Studies,* 7, No. 4, Winter 1988, 68–75.

Langdon, Frank C. "The Security Debate in Japan," *Pacific Affairs* [Vancouver], 58, No. 3, Fall 1985, 397–410.

Masuzoe Yōichi. "Winds of Change: Reassessing Japan's Defense," *Look Japan* [Tokyo], 32, No. 368, November 10, 1986, 2–3.

McIntosh, Malcolm. *Japan Re-armed.* New York: St. Martin's Press, 1986.

Menon, Rajan, and Daniel Abele. "Security Dimensions of Soviet Territorial Disputes with China and Japan," *Journal of Northeast Asian Studies,* 8, No. 1, Spring 1989, 3–19.

The Military Balance. (Annuals 1979–1980 through 1989–1990.) London: International Institute for Strategic Studies, 1978–89.

Morison, Samuel Eliot, and Henry Steele Commager. *The Growth of the American Republic.* (7th ed.) New York: Oxford University Press, 1980.

Mushakōji Kinhide. "In Search of Formulas for Regional Peace," *Japan Quarterly* [Tokyo], 32, No. 3, July–September 1985, 234–39.

Nagashima, Atsushi. "The Accused and Society: The Administration of Criminal Justice in Japan." Pages 298–304 in Arthur Taylor von Mehren (ed.), *Law in Japan: The Legal Order in a Changing Society.* Cambridge: Harvard University Press, 1963.

Nakamura Ken'ichi. "Militarization of Post-war Japan." Pages 81–100 in Yoshikazu Sakamoto (ed.), *Asia: Militarization and Regional Conflict.* Atlantic Highlands, New Jersey: Zed Books, 1988.

Nishihara Masashi. "Nakasone's Impact and Japanese Security Policy," *Asian Defence Journal* [Kuala Lumpur], January 1989, 37–38, 40, 42–43.

Noda, Yosiyuki. *Introduction to Japanese Law.* (Trans. and ed., Anthony H. Angelo.) Tokyo: University of Tokyo Press, 1976.

O'Connell, John F. "The Role of the Self-Defense Forces in Japan's Sea Lane Defense," *Journal of Northeast Asian Studies,* 3, No. 3, Fall 1984, 59–64.

———. "Strategic Implications of the Japanese SSM-1 Cruise Missile," *Journal of Northeast Asian Studies,* 6, No. 2, Summer 1987, 53–66.

Odawara Atsushi. "No Tampering with the Brakes on Military Expansion," *Japan Quarterly* [Tokyo], 32, No. 3, July–September 1985, 248–54.

Olsen, Edward A. "Security in the Sea of Japan," *Journal of Northeast Asian Studies,* 5, No. 4, Winter 1986, 48–66.

Ōkita Saburō. "Japan's Quiet Strength," *Foreign Policy,* No. 75, Summer 1989, 128–45.

Ōtsuki Shinji. "Battle Over the FSX Fighter: Who Won?" *Japan Quarterly* [Tokyo], 35, No. 1, April–June 1988, 139–45.

Pacific Regional Security: The 1985 Symposium. Washington: National Defense University Press, 1988.

Reynolds, Gary K. *Japan's Military Buildup: Goals and Accomplishments.* Washington: Congressional Research Service, Library of Congress, 1989.

Rogers, Linda, and C. Dominique van de Stadt. "Early Warning: Military," *World Press Review,* 37, No. 1, January 1990, 6.

Sakamoto, Yoshikazu (ed.). *Asia: Militarization and Regional Conflict.* Atlantic Highlands, New Jersey: Zed Books, 1988.

Sakonjo, Naotoshi. "Security in Northeast Asia." *Journal of Northeast Asian Studies,* 2, No. 3, September 1983, 87–97.

Satō Kinko. *Why Is There Less Crime in Japan?* Tokyo: Office for the Japanese Studies Center, 1984.

Shindō Eiichi. "A Deluded Defense Policy," *Japan Quarterly* [Tokyo], 35, No. 1, January–March 1988, 71–78.

Shinnosuke Inami. "Police Boxes and Their Officers," *Japan Quarterly* [Tokyo], 34, No. 3, July–September 1987, 295–99.

Shulman, Frank Joseph (ed.). *Japan.* (World Bibliographical Series, No. 103.) Santa Barbara, California: ABC–Clio, 1989.

Simon, Sheldon W. "Is There a Japanese Regional Security Role?" *Journal of Northeast Asian Studies,* 5, No. 2, Summer 1986, 30–52.

Smith, Howard (ed.). *Inside Japan.* London: British Broadcasting Corporation, 1980.

"Strategic Significance of the Northern Island Territories," *Japan Quarterly* [Tokyo], 27, No. 1, January–March 1980, 11–14.

Takagi Yosuke. "Forcing Confessions in Japan," *World Press Review,* 36, No. 6, June 1989, 57.

Takayama Satoshi. "The Soviet Union Smiles at Japan," *Japan Quarterly* [Tokyo], 33, No. 2, April–June 1986, 129–37.

Takayanagi Kenzō. "A Century of Innovation: The Development of Japanese Law, 1868-1961." Pages 163–93 in Tanaka Hideo (ed.), *The Japanese Legal System: Introductory Cases and Materials.* Tokyo: University of Tokyo Press, 1976.

Van de Velde, James R. "Japan's Nuclear Umbrella: U.S. Extended Nuclear Deterrence for Japan," *Journal of Northeast Asian Studies,* 7, No. 4, Winter 1988, 16–39.

van Wolferen, Karel G. *The Enigma of Japanese Power: People and Politics in a Stateless Nation.* New York: Knopf, 1989.

von Mehren, Arthur Taylor (ed.). *Law in Japan: The Legal Order in a Changing Society.* Cambridge: Harvard University Press, 1963.

Wada Haruki. "Japanese-Soviet Relations and East Asian Security," *Japan Quarterly* [Tokyo], 30, No. 2, April–June 1983, 188–92.

Weinstein, Martin E. "The Evolution of the Japan Self-Defense Forces." Pages 41–63 in James H. Buck (ed.), *The Modern Japanese Military System*. Beverly Hills, California: Sage, 1975.

(Various issues of the following publications were also used in the preparation of this chapter: *Economist* [London] 1989; *Far Eastern Economic Review* [Hong Kong], 1989–90; and the Foreign Broadcast Information Service's *Daily Report: East Asia*, 1989–90.)

Glossary

Association of Southeast Asian Nations (ASEAN)—Established in 1967 to foster cooperation in food production, industry and commerce, civil aviation, shipping, tourism, communications, meteorology, science and technology, and Southeast Asian studies. The charter members were Indonesia, Malaysia, the Philippines, Singapore, and Thailand. Brunei was admitted in 1984. Papua New Guinea has observer status.

Bretton Woods System—A structure of fixed exchange rates developed at the 1944 Bretton Woods Conference, which established the International Monetary Fund (*q.v.*) and the World Bank (*q.v.*), and was in effect until 1971.

bushidō—Literally, the way of the warrior (samurai), a term applied to the principles of loyalty and honor; a code of stoic endurance, scorn of danger and death, religious worship of country and sovereign, and proper social relationships; an aesthetic life-style.

Diet—The national legislature. From 1890 to 1947, known as the Imperial Diet (in Japanese, Teikoku Gikai) with the appointed House of Peers and the elected House of Representatives; since 1947, the National Diet or Diet (in Japanese, Kokkai) with the House of Councillors and the House of Representatives, both of which are elected. The word diet comes from the Latin *dies* (day), a reference to the period of time for which a court or assembly met.

FY—Fiscal year. April 1 through March 31.

General Agreement on Tariffs and Trade (GATT)—An international instrument, under United Nations (UN) auspices, establishing rules of trade accepted by countries responsible for most of the world's trade; came into effect in 1948. Since 1968 has operated in conjunction with the UN Conference on Trade and Development (UNCTAD) to provide information and training on export markets, marketing techniques, and trade policy issues. GATT members have met in a series of "rounds" for multilateral trade negotiations since 1964.

GDP—Gross domestic product. The total value of all final (consumption and investment) goods and services produced by an economy in a given period, usually a year.

GNP—Gross national product. GDP (*q.v.*) plus income from overseas investments minus the earnings of foreign investors in the home economy.

International Monetary Fund (IMF)—Established along with the World Bank (*q.v.*) in 1945, the IMF is a specialized agency affiliated with the United Nations and is responsible for stabilizing international exchange loans to its members (including industrialized and developing countries) when they experience balance of payments difficulties. These loans frequently carry conditions that require substantial internal economic adjustments by the recipients, most of which are developing countries.

juku—Privately established schools that teach either academic or nonacademic subjects. Academic *juku* offer tutorial, enrichment, remedial, and examination preparatory classes that supplement regular school work. Most hold classes after school and/or on weekends.

Nihon (or Nippon)—The official pronunciation of the two Chinese ideographs (*riben* in pinyin romanization, literally, source of the sun) comprising the name Japan, as designated by the Ministry of Education, Culture, and Science, is Nippon (or in full, Nippon Koku—Nippon country). The common pronunciation in everyday usage, however, is Nihon (Nihon Koku). The use of Nihon antedates Prince Shōtoku's seventh-century reference to himself as the Son of Heaven of the Land of the Rising Sun and possibly dates from the establishment of the Nihon-fu (Japan Office) in the Yamato (*q.v.*) colony in southern Korea that served as a liaison office of the Yamato court to the Chinese court, probably as early as the sixth century. Marco Polo, or his scribe, referred to Zipangu (Ribenguo in pinyin romanization), which has variously appeared as Cipango, Jipangu, and Jipan, from which the current spelling of Japan undoubtedly descends.

Organisation for Economic Co-operation and Development (OECD)—Established in 1961 to promote economic and social welfare among member countries (in 1990, Australia, Austria, Belgium, Britain, Canada, Denmark, Federal Republic of Germany, Finland, France, Greece, Iceland, Ireland, Italy, Japan, Luxembourg, the Netherlands, New Zealand, Norway, Portugal, Spain, Sweden, Switzerland, Turkey, and the United States) by assisting member governments in the formulation and coordination of policy; and to encourage member-nation support of developing (Third World) nations.

rōnin—Originally, a "wave person" or a masterless samurai, who has left the service of his lord, either by choice or forced circumstances, and serves others with his bold and sometimes desperate deeds. In contemporary Japan, a student who has failed the entrance examination to the institution of choice and has chosen to spend an additional year or more in study to take the examination again.

seppuku—either voluntary (to expiate serious failure) or obligatory suicide (instead of execution) to regain one's honor in death. A privilege reserved for the samurai class. Commonly referred to as hara-kiri.

World Bank—Informal name used to designate a group of three affiliated international institutions: the International Bank for Reconstruction and Development (IBRD), the International Development Association (IDA), and the International Finance Corporation (IFC). The IBRD, established in 1945, has the primary purpose of providing loans to developing countries for productive projects. The IDA, a legally separate loan fund but administered by the staff of the IBRD, was set up in 1960 to furnish credits to the poorest developing countries on much easier terms than those of conventional IBRD loans. The IFC, founded in 1956, supplements the activities of the IBRD through loans and assistance designed specifically to encourage the growth of productive private enterprises in the less developed countries. The president and certain senior officers of the IBRD hold the same positions in the IFC. The three institutions are owned by the governments of the countries that subscribe their capital. To participate in the World Bank group, member states must first belong to the International Monetary Fund (IMF—*q.v.*).

Yamato—Refers to the country of Japan or things Japanese, such as *yamato-e* (Japanese painting) and to the ancient court from which the imperial family rose. The Yamato court was situated either in modern Nara Prefecture, from the early fourth century A.D., or in northern Kyūshū, starting perhaps in the early third century A.D.

yen (¥)—The national currency, in coins of 1, 5, 10, and 100 yen and notes of 500, 1,000, 5,000, and 10,000 yen. From 1945 to 1971, Japan maintained a fixed parity to the United States dollar of US$1 = ¥360. After a period of adjustment during the financial crises of the 1971–73 period, the value has floated according to movements in the international capital markets. The exchange rate in August 1990 was ¥147 = US$1. Fluctuations in recent years have been considerable, producing exchange rates for US$1 of ¥142 (August 1989), ¥134 (August 1988), ¥149 (August 1987), ¥155 (August 1986), and ¥239 (August 1985)

yobikō—A type of private school that specializes in preparing high-school graduates for university-entrance examinations, often through intensive full-time programs.

zaibatsu—Literally, "wealth group." *Zaibatsu* were powerful industrial or financial combines that merged during the Meiji era and were implicated in the militarist regimes of the 1930s and 1940s. They were an amalgamation of sometimes hundreds of businesses controlled by a holding company owned by a single family. The major *zaibatsu* were Mitsui, Mitsubishi, Sumimoto, and Yasuda. The *zaibatsu* were abolished in 1945 and 1946. After 1947, numerous companies formerly controlled by *zaibatsu* came together as *keiretsu* (enterprise groups)—conglomerates no longer controlled by a singe family and whose individual member companies had greater autonomy than they had had as part of a *zaibatsu*.

Index

Abe Kōbō, 190
Abe Masahiro, 34, 35; opposition to, 35
Abu Dhabi, 229
acquired immune deficiency syndrome (AIDS), 125
Administrative Management Agency, 355
administrative reform, 344, 353
aerospace industry (*see also* space program), 232, 234
Afghanistan, Soviet invasion of, 291, 377, 391, 398, 400, 404, 421
AFL–CIO. *See* American Federation of Labor-Congress of Industrial Organizations
Africa: aid to, 293–94; direct investment in, 279, 290; exports to, 290; imports from, 290
Afro-Asian Conference (Bandung), 407
Agency for Cultural Affairs, 165, 167; budget, 165; Cultural Affairs Division, 165; preservation roster, 166
age stratification, 121–23
aging: of Japanese population, 223; of labor force, 223
agriculture, 82, 199, 226, 337; labor force in, 204, 244; performance of, 231, 245; subsidies for, 204, 245
Agriculture, Ministry of, 258
agricultural cooperatives, 339
agricultural production, 33, 245; crops, 79, 81, 82; livestock, 246; self-sufficiency in, 246
agricultural products: import restrictions on, 266, 339; imported from United States, 283
AIDS. *See* acquired immune deficiency syndrome
Aikokusha (Society of Patriots), 42
Ainu, 13, 93, 329, 335; handicrafts of, 178; population of, 77
Air Defense Command, 443–44
Air Developing and Proving Command, 443
airlines, 236, 240
Air Matériel Command, 443
airports, 240
Air Self-Defense Force, 429, 451, 452, 455; matériel, 444; missions, 435, 444;

number of, 443; training, 444; units of, 443
Air Support Command, 443
Akahata (Red Flag), 361–62
Akihito (Heisei emperor), 310, 332; accession of, 310, 312, 470
Akira (Otomoto), 192
Akutagawa Prize, 167
Alien Registration Law, 459
Allied Expeditionary Force, 51
All Nippon Airways, 240, 345
amakudari, 213, 354
Amami Islands, 72, 387
Amaterasu Ōmikami (Sun Goddess), 4, 11
American Federation of Labor-Congress of Industrial Organizations (AFL–CIO), 340
Andō Tadao, 169–70
Ansei Reform, 35
Anti-Comintern Pact, 58
archaeology, 4, 166
architecture, 168–70; in Meiji period, 168; in Muromachi culture, 23; New Wave, 169; origins of Japanese style of, 4; skyscraper design, 168; synthesis of Western and traditional, 169; traditional styles, 168
armed forces. *See* military
art (*see also under art forms*): Chinese influence on, 162; facilities for, 167–68; imitative, 164; individuality in, 98; international, 164; miniature forms, 162; patronage for, 167; schools, 165; structural devices, 163; suggestion in, 163; synthesized Western and traditional, 164; Zen Buddhist influence on, 164
art, traditional, xxxii; endangered, on preservation roster, 166; as *mukei bunkazai*, 166–67; in Muromachi culture, 22–23; in popular culture, 117; taught to children, 132; technical virtuosity as hallmark of, 165; training in, 165; under Tokugawa, 32
art, Western, xxxii; in Meiji period, 164
Article 9 ("no war" clause), 312, 375, 421, 428
artisans, 30

books, 342
Boxer Uprising, 47
Brady Plan (1989), 262, 290
Brazil, 289
Bretton Woods System, 256, 271, 272, 280
Brezhnev, Leonid I., 405
Britain, 223; agreements with, 50; deterioration of relations with, 58; exports, 282, 286; exports as percentage of GNP, 267; imports from, 286; investment by, in United States, 285; Japan as ally of, 54, 374; political relations with, 47
British Trades Union Congress, 340
Broadcasting Law (1950), 193, 243
Brunei, xxxv, 228, 408
Buddha, Amida, 20
Buddha Dainichi, 11
Buddhism, xxvii, 31, 32, 100, 101–4; adoption of, 8, 11; ancestral and funerary rites, 104, 107–8; and art, 131; clergy, 104; festivals, 108; in Kamakura period, 19–20; influence of, xxxii, 101, 131; introduction of, xxvii, 7, 133; music in, 180; origin of, 101; "poignancy of things," 131, 190–91; prohibitions against killing, 91; resistance to, 8; resurgence of, 37–38; spread of, 12; syncreted with Shinto, 11; temples, 104; three treasures of, 11; values, 104; world view, 101
Buddhism, Heian, 18–20
Buddhism, Jōdō (Pure Land), 19–20, 101–4
Buddhism, Nara, 11
Buddhism, Nichiren Shōshū, 64, 101–4, 106, 336, 360
Buddhism, Shingon (True Word), 12, 23
Buddhism, Tendai (Heavenly Terrace), 12
Buddhism, Zen, 18–20, 106; appeal of, for samurai, 104; artistic forms in, 131, 176; importance of education in, 133; influences of, 22; influence of, on art, 163–64, 174; in poetry, 189; priests, 22
Buddhist commentary, 187
budget process, 356
bugaku, 180
bullying, 145, 147, 150
Bungei Shunjū (Literary Annals), 342
bunraku (puppet) theater, xxxii, 32, 180, 182–83; elements of, 182; women in, 183

burakumin, 90, 91–93, 329, 334; discrimination against, 91; identification of, 92; isolation of, 92; liberation of, 92–93
Burakumin Liberation League, 92, 335
bureaucracy. *See* civil service
Bureau for Investigation of Constitutional Systems, 43
burial chambers, 6
Burma, 407
buses, 239
Bush, George, 391
bushi. See samurai
bushidō. See also under samurai, 422–23; development of, 31, 423; legacy of, xxvii, 422, 423
butoh dance, 185–86

cabinet, 317–18, 458; responsibilities of, for foreign affairs, 378
Cabinet Law, 436
Cabinet Legislative Bureau, 318
Calder, Kent, 336, 337, 338
calligraphy, xxxii, 174; Bokusho abstract school of, 174; incorporated into painting, 173, 174; styles of, 174; Zen Buddhist influence on, 174
Cambodia, xxxv, 398, 411–12
Canada, 455; balance of trade with Japan, 285; cooperation of, in space program, 244; exports as percentage of GNP, 267; imports from, 282; investment by, in United States, 285; limits by, on Japanese imports, 295; nuclear technology imported from, 229
capital flows, 275–80, 281; controls on, 278; decontrol of, 278; direct investment, 279; effect of government policy on, 277–78; foreign-exchange reserves, 277; gold reserves, 277; growth of, 276; long-term, 276; short-term, 277
capital markets: liberalization of, 278; participation in, 276
capital movements, 276
Caroline Islands, 50, 424
castles, 25
Central Association of Korean Residents in Japan, 335
Central Council on Education, 138
Central Japan Railway Company, 236
Central Procurement Office, 451
Central Union of Agricultural Cooperatives, 339

electronics, consumer, xxxi, 232, 296–98; export of, 296; foreign investment in, 296–98; growth of, 201

Emishi. *See* Ainu

emperor, xxviii, 166, 422, 470; divinity repudiated, 60, 101, 110, 308; revering, 36, 55; role of, 110, 307, 308–12; as symbol of unity, 36, 307; succession, 10, 310; Tokugawa power over, 28–29

Emperor's Private Office, 13, 14

empire, twentieth century, xxviii–xxix, 199

Employee Pension Insurance Plan, 125

employees, permanent, 217; bonuses, 220; changing attitudes, 222–23; compensation for, 217, 223; evaluation of, 217; fringe benefits, 220; job switching by, 222–23; of large corporations, 216; layoffs of, 218; loyalty, 222; promotion of, 217, 218; qualifications, 217; retirement, 218, 223–24; training of, 217; working conditions, 220; working hours, 220

employment, 116, 197; in agriculture, 244; bosses, 116; lifetime model, 116, 117, 330; mandatory retirement, 116, 122; permanent, 217; small business as provider of, 215; team effort, 116; and university background, 152, 216

Endō Shusaku, 190

energy, 228–29; coal, 228, 270; consumption, 228, 229; electric, 200, 228, 229; geothermal, 229; hydroelectric, 74, 81, 228; importation of, 271; natural gas, 79, 227, 228–29; nuclear, 207, 227, 228, 229; oil, 79, 228, 270; price increase in, 257

Ensemble Nipponica, 183

entertainment, 118; bar hopping as, 94; in late twentieth century, 71; under Tokugawa, 33

Enthronement Ceremony, 310

entrance examinations, 152, 154; debate over, 154–55; kinds of, 154; preparation for, 154

Entry and Exit Control Law, 459

Environmental Agency, 85, 341

environmental disasters, 84, 341

environmental issues, 204; citizens' movements regarding, 84–85, 229; public perception of, 85–86

Equal Employment Opportunity Law, 120

Equipment, Bureau of, 436

Ethnological Museum, 167

Etorofu (*see also* Kuril Islands), xxxv, 72, 400–3

Etō Shimpei, 41

Europe: "learning mission" to, 40; students in, 198

European Commission, xxxv

European Community, xxxv; cooperation with, xxxv; trade with Japan after EC92, 287, 295, 414

Europe, Eastern: aid to, 413–14; collapse of communism in, 349, 369, 381, 385; support for, 391; trade with, 290

Europe, Western: cooperation of, in space program, 244; direct investment in, 287; exports to, 286; imports from, 286; involvement in Japanese product development, 233; relations with, 414; restrictions by, on Japanese imports, 287, 295; trade deficits with Japan, 287

exchange rate: determining import levels, 271; fixed, 257, 281; in 1971, 281; in 1973, 281

Exim Bank. *See* Japan Export-Import Bank

Expo '70. *See* Ōsaka International Exposition

export policy, xxi, 264–65; incentives, 264; restraining, 264–65

export products, 269; demand for, 268; price competitiveness of, 268; quality of, 268

exports, xxx, 267–69; aggressive backing of, 268–69; destinations of, 282; growth of, 257, 267, 268; importance of, 207; limits on, 295; nature of, 255; to pay for imports, 255; as percentage of GNP, xxxi, 267; promotion of, 264; to the United States, 265, 282, 384; value of, during 1960s, 256; and value of yen, 277

Ezoe Hiromasa, 321

face, 114

factions in Liberal Democratic Party, 345; in election campaigns, 346; funding by, 345; leaders, 345; number of, 345; services, 345

Fair Trade Commission, 214, 258, 379

family, 111–14; beyond life of current members, 112, 113; business, 117;

Jimmu, 4
Jinnō shōtō ki (Chronicle of the Direct Descent of the Divine Sovereigns) (Kitabatake), 3, 23
Jiyūtō (Liberal Party), 42, 44
Jōdō sect. *See* Buddhism, Jōdō
Jōei Code, 18
Johnson, Chalmers, 351
Joint First Stage Achievement Test, 154; content of, 154–55; schedule of, 154–55
Joint Staff Council, 436, 451; members of, 436–37; reorganization of, 437
Jōkyū Incident, 18
Jōmon culture, 4–5; era, 4; musical instruments of, 180; pottery of, 4
Jordan, 392
judges: appointment and removal of, 324
judicial system, 324–29; courts in, 324–25; judges in, 324; structure of, 325
juku, 143, 151–52; academic, 151; attendance, 151; educational functions of, 151; expense, 152; nonacademic, 151; self-study materials published by, 152; social role of, 151
Justice, Ministry of, 92, 326, 353, 465, 471; Correctional Bureau, 473–74; Legal Training and Research Institute, 326; Public Security Investigation Office, 464; Rehabilitation Bureau, 474
Juvenile Law (1922), 473

Kabuki Society, 168
Kabuki theater, xxxii, 180, 18, 1882; conventions, 182, 186; dance in, 183; themes in, 182, 186; women barred from performing in, 165, 182
Kades, Charles, 312
Kagerō nikki (The Gossamer Years) ("Mother of Michitsuna"), 15
Kagoshima, 24
Kaifūsō (Fond Recollections of Poetry), 11
Kaifu Toshiki, xxxiv, xxxvi, 317, 349, 381, 391, 409
Kaishintō (Constitutional Study Party), 44
Kamakura, 17
Kamakura period, 17, 188
kami, 7, 32, 100, 332; defined, 4
kamikaze, 20, 23
Kammon Bridge, 81
Kammu (emperor), 12; avoidance of reform, 12; military offensives, 13; succession to, 13

kana, 14, 174; *hiragana*, 14; *katakana*, 14
Kanamori Masao, 454
Kanazawa, 79
Kanematsu-Gosho, 260
Kaneshiro Jirō, 178
kanji, 14, 174, 176
Kanō ink painting, 173
kanpaku, 14, 26
Kansai International Airport, 74, 240
Kantō, 78; industry, 78; population density, 78
Kantō Plain, 74
Karafuto (*see also* Sakhalin), 34
Kara Jōrō, 186
karaoke, 184
KARAS Company, 185
Katayama Tetsu, 356
Katsura Shijaku, 183
Katsura Taro, 49, 50
Kawabata Yasunari, 190
Kawai Kanjirō, 177
Kawasaki Heavy Industries, 453
Kazan Rettō. *See* Volcano Islands
Kaze no matasaburō (Children of the Wind) (Miyazawa), 192
Keidanren. *See* Federation of Economic Organizations
keiretsu, 202
Keizai Dōyū Kai. *See* Japan Committee for Economic Development
kejime, 349
Kellogg-Briand Pact, 54, 312
Kemmu Restoration, 21
Kenseikai (Constitutional Government Association), 52
Kenseitō (Constitutional Party), 49
Khubilai Khan, 20; demand for tribute, 20
Kido Kōin, 38, 40, 42
"Kimigayo," 311
Kimmei (emperor), 8
King Lear (Shakespeare), 186
Kinki, 80
Kinki Plain, 74
Kishi Nobusuke, 388
Kitabatake Chikafusa, 23
Kitadake mountain, 74
Kitakyūshū, 81, 82
Kitaro, 184
Kiyomizu Kyūbei, 172
koan, 164, 174
Kobayashi Issa, 188
Kobayashi Masaki, 192

Published Country Studies

(Area Handbook Series)

550–65	Afghanistan	550–87	Greece
550–98	Albania	550–78	Guatemala
550–44	Algeria	550–174	Guinea
550–59	Angola	550–82	Guyana and Belize
550–73	Argentina	550–151	Honduras
550–169	Australia	550–165	Hungary
550–176	Austria	550–21	India
550–175	Bangladesh	550–154	Indian Ocean
550–170	Belgium	550–39	Indonesia
550–66	Bolivia	550–68	Iran
550–20	Brazil	550–31	Iraq
550–168	Bulgaria	550–25	Israel
550–61	Burma	550–182	Italy
550–50	Cambodia	550–30	Japan
550–166	Cameroon	550–34	Jordan
550–159	Chad	550–56	Kenya
550–77	Chile	550–81	Korea, North
550–60	China	550–41	Korea, South
550–26	Colombia	550–58	Laos
550–33	Commonwealth Caribbean, Islands of the	550–24	Lebanon
550–91	Congo	550–38	Liberia
550–90	Costa Rica	550–85	Libya
550–69	Côte d'Ivoire (Ivory Coast)	550–172	Malawi
550–152	Cuba	550–45	Malaysia
550–22	Cyprus	550–161	Mauritania
550–158	Czechoslovakia	550–79	Mexico
550–36	Dominican Republic and Haiti	550–76	Mongolia
550–52	Ecuador	550–49	Morocco
550–43	Egypt	550–64	Mozambique
550–150	El Salvador	550–35	Nepal and Bhutan
550–28	Ethiopia	550–88	Nicaragua
550–167	Finland	550–157	Nigeria
550–155	Germany, East	550–94	Oceania
550–173	Germany, Fed. Rep. of	550–48	Pakistan
550–153	Ghana	550–46	Panama